Why Do You Need this New Edition?

1. New chapter titled, Race and Cranial Measurements
2. Bone Biology chapter now includes a section on joint morphology
3. More information with new illustrations on the bones of the face
4. Additional illustrations of carpal and tarsal bones to aid identification
5. Additional illustrations of the pelvis to further clarify sex differences
6. Updated information on research and methods
7. Updated bibliography
8. Updated and more comprehensive glossary

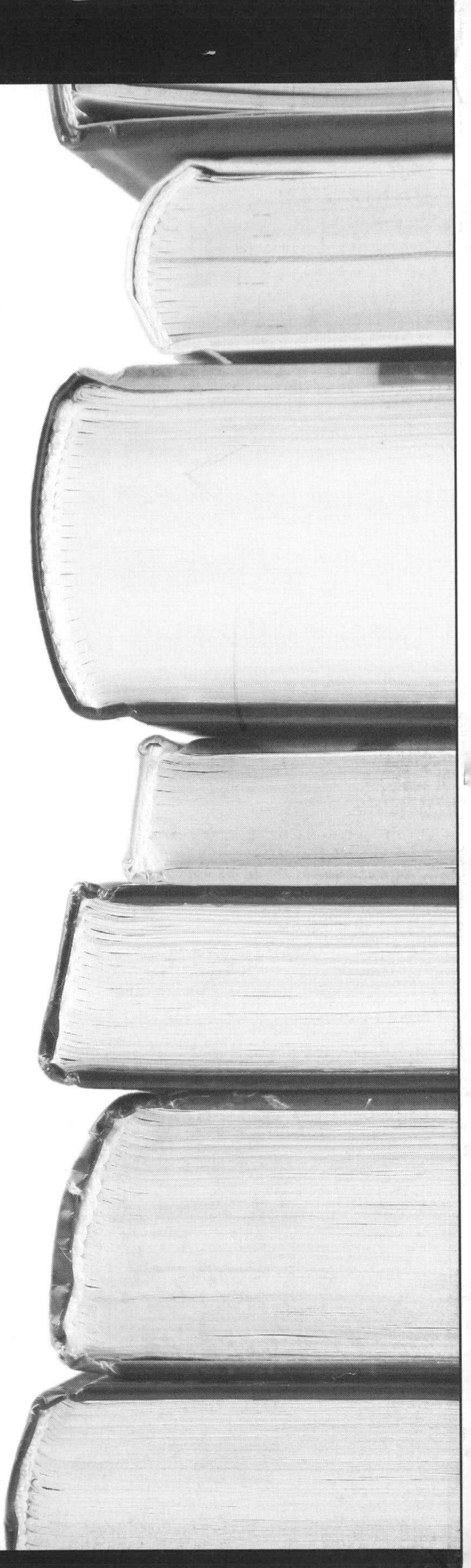

PEARSON

Forensic Anthropology Training Manual

Forensic Anthropology Training Manual

Third Edition

Karen Ramey Burns

Illustrations by Joanna Wallington

PEARSON

Boston Columbus Indianapolis New York San Francisco Upper Saddle River
Amsterdam Cape Town Dubai London Madrid Milan Munich Paris Montréal Toronto
Delhi Mexico City São Paulo Sydney Hong Kong Seoul Singapore Taipei Tokyo

Editorial Director: Craig Campanella
Editor-in-Chief: Dickson Musslewhite
Publisher: Nancy Roberts
Editorial Project Manager: Nicole Comforti
Editorial Assistant: Nart Varoqua
Director of Marketing: Brandy Dawson
Senior Marketing Manager: Laura Lee Manley
Senior Managing Editor: Ann Marie McCarthy
Project Manager: Cheryl Keenan
Manufacturing Manager: Mary Fischer
Operations Specialist: Alan Fischer
Creative Director, Cover: Jayne Conte
Cover Design: Suzanne Behnke
Cover Art: Lipowski/Fotolia.com
Digital Imaging Specialist: Corrin Skidds
Director, Digital Media: Brian Hyland
Digital Media Editor: Rachel Comerford
Composition and Full-Service Project Management: GEX Publishing Services
Printer / Binder: Courier/Kendallville
Cover Printer: Lehigh-Phoenix Color Corp
Text Font: 10/12 New Century Schoolbook

Credits and acknowledgments borrowed from other sources and reproduced, with permission, in this textbook appear on appropriate page within text.

Copyright © 2013, 2007, and 1999 by Pearson Education, Inc. All rights reserved. Printed in the United States of America. This publication is protected by Copyright and permission should be obtained from the publisher prior to any prohibited reproduction, storage in a retrieval system, or transmission in any form or by any means, electronic, mechanical, photocopying, recording, or likewise. To obtain permission(s) to use material from this work, please submit a written request to Pearson Education, Inc., Permissions Department, One Lake Street, Upper Saddle River, New Jersey 07458 or you may fax your request to 201-236-3290.

Library of Congress Cataloging-in-Publication Data

Burns, Karen Ramey.
Forensic anthropology training manual / Karen Ramey Burns; illustrations by Joanna Wallington. -- 3rd ed.
p. cm.
Includes bibliographical references and index.
ISBN 978-0-205-02259-5 (pbk.)
1. Forensic anthropology--Handbooks, manuals, etc. I. Title.
GN69.8.B87B87 2013
614'.17--dc23

2011050425

10 9 8 7 6 5 4 3 2 1

ISBN-10: 0-205-02259-6
ISBN-13: 978-0-205-02259-5

To Lawrence Anthony Burns

Brief Contents

Contents

Chapter 4 The Shoulder Girdle and Thorax: Clavicle, Scapula, Ribs, and Sternum 56

Chapter 5 The Vertebral Column 73

Chapter 6 The Arm: Humerus, Radius, and Ulna 85

Chapter 7 The Hand: Carpals, Metacarpals, and Phalanges 98

Chapter 8 The Pelvic Girdle: Illium, Ischium, and Pubis 108

Chapter 9 The Leg: Femur, Tibia, Fibula, and Patella 122

Preface

The *Forensic Anthropology Training Manual,* third edition, is designed to serve as an introduction to the discipline of forensic anthropology, a framework for training, and a practical reference tool. The first chapter informs judges, attorneys, law enforcement personnel, and international workers of the range of information and services available from a professional forensic anthropologist. The first section (Chapters 2–11) is a training guide to assist in the study of human skeletal anatomy. The second section (Chapters 12–17) focuses on the specific work of the forensic anthropologist, beginning with an introduction to the forensic sciences. Tables and formulae are provided for general use and reference throughout the book. A variety of forms are available in the appendix for use in the field or laboratory.

The chapters of the manual are presented in a sequence designed for effective teaching. Basic human osteology precedes laboratory analysis, and all of the information on the skeleton is completed before the chapters on field work and specific applications are presented. The reason for the learning sequence is simple: people *learn* to see. We fail to notice many of the things that are not already part of our life experience. Beginning students, for example, fail to recognize 80 percent of the human skeleton and confuse bones of other animals with human bones. The most effective workers go into the field equipped with knowledge obtained from previous experience in the classroom and laboratory.

The organization of the third edition differs from the second edition in two ways. The section dedicated to joints is now in the chapter on bone biology, and methods for the determination of race are in a separate chapter. Instructors may wish to continue to discuss joints using the arm as an example of types of movement, but hopefully, they will be able to locate the joint section easier with the other aspects of skeletal biology.

Racial analysis is placed after the end of the osteology section of the book because it requires a working knowledge of cranial anatomy and experience with osteometrics. Race can be an overwhelming topic if it is introduced to students when basic anatomy is still a challenge. I believe the educational experience is improved if students return to the skull to consider race near the end of the academic term.

This is *not* a self-instruction manual. The manual contains the basic information necessary to successfully collect, process, analyze, and describe skeletonized human remains. However, effective education requires professional guidance and plenty of hands-on experience. Anyone seeking proficiency should use this manual as one of many steps to knowledge. Be persistent in the pursuit of information, supplement class work with additional reading, and use every opportunity available for practical self-testing.

The *Forensic Anthropology Training Manual,* third edition, can serve as a primary text for courses in human osteology and in forensic anthropology and archaeology, and as a supplementary text for courses in anthropology and human rights, as described here:

1. *Human Osteology:* A complete course in human skeletal biology and anatomy, including recognition of fragmentary material, the range of normal skeletal variation, sexual and genetic differences, and the basics of age determination
2. *Forensic Anthropology and Archaeology:* A course in location and exhumation of burials, human identification from skeletal remains, proper handling of physical evidence for legal purposes, professional report writing, and expert witness testimony
3. *Anthropology and Human Rights:* Application of the methods of forensic anthropology to international human rights missions and the special problems of mass graves, cultural differences, and lack of antemortem records

Each of these courses can be taught as intensive short courses or as term-length college courses. Both formats have about the same amount of student-teacher contact time, but there are advantages and disadvantages to each. The intensive course is excellent for laboratory and field work, but has little time for reading, research, and writing. The standard college course has the valuable out-of-class time, but loses considerable lab and field time to starting and stopping.

What's New in this Edition

- A new chapter titled Race and Cranial Measurements
- A section on joint morphology in the Bone Biology chapter
- More information with new illustrations on the bones of the face
- Additional illustrations of carpal and tarsal bones to aid identification
- Additional illustrations of the pelvis to further clarify sex differences
- Updated information on research and methods
- Updated bibliography
- Updated and more comprehensive glossary

Acknowledgments

The genesis of this work can be traced to Dr. Audrey Chapman, Director of the Science and Human Rights Program of the American Association for the Advancement of Science (AAAS). Dr. Chapman encouraged me to put information into a format that can be used in the field and translated for areas of the world trying to recover from war and the ultimate of human rights violations. The AAAS supplied the initial funding. (This book is now available in a Spanish edition, *Manual de Antropolog¡a Forense* [2008], published by Edicions Bellaterra in Barcelona, Spain.)

My professor and mentor, the late Dr. William R. Maples, contributed to this work through his no-nonsense attitude and profound knowledge of the discipline. Dr. Clyde C. Snow shared his unique perspective on the world and the work of an anthropologist. I'm indebted to them both.

I appreciate the many thoughtful comments and questions from my colleagues and students in Guatemala, North Carolina, Georgia, Colombia, and Utah. I would like to acknowledge the reviewers who provided suggestions for the new edition: Christina Brooks–Winthrop University; Midori Albert–University of North Carolina, Wilmington; Monica Faraldo–University of Miami; Margaret Judd–University of Pittsburgh. I'm also very grateful to Nicole Conforti, Pearson Project Manager, for her superior organizational abilities and her cheerful perseverance. This book would not have been possible without the talent, hard work, and friendship of Joanna Wallington, the illustrator. And, as always, I'm grateful to my family for their love, support, and good humor.

About the Author

Karen Ramey Burns is a practicing forensic anthropologist, teacher, writer, and human rights worker. She received her graduate education in forensic anthropology under the direction of the late Dr. William R. Maples at the University of Florida and developed experience in major crime laboratory procedures while working for the Georgia Bureau of Investigation, Division of Forensic Sciences. She has testified as an expert witness in local, state, and international cases.

Dr. Burns has devoted much of her professional career to international work, providing educational and technical assistance in the excavation and identification of human remains in Latin America, Haiti, the Middle East, and Africa. She documented war crimes in Iraq after the Gulf War (1991) and provided testimony in the Raboteau Trial in Gonaïve, Haiti (2000). She is the author of the "Protocol for Disinterment and Analysis of Skeletal Remains," in the *Manual for the Effective Prevention and Investigation of Extra-Legal, Arbitrary, and Summary Executions* (1991), a United Nations publication.

Dr. Burns was a 2007 Fulbright Scholar at the University of the Andes in Bogotá, Colombia. She is also a founding member of EQUITAS (est. 2005), the Colombian Interdisciplinary Team for Forensic Work and Psychosocial Assistance, where she now serves on the board of directors.

In times of national emergency, she works for the Disaster Mortuary Operational Response Team (DMORT), a part of the National Disaster Medical System, U.S. Department of Health and Human Services. She was deployed for the Katrina/Rita hurricane disasters in 2005; Tri-State Crematory incident in 2002; the World Trade Center terrorist attack in 2001; the Tarboro, North Carolina, flood in 1999; and the Flint River flood of 1994.

Dr. Burns has contributed to several historic research projects, including a study of the Phoenician genocide in North Africa (Carthage), the identification of the revolutionary war hero Casimir Pulaski, and the search for Amelia Earhart. Dr. Burns is a coauthor of the award-winning book, *Amelia Earhart's Shoes, Is the Mystery Solved?* (2001), a discourse on the continuing archaeological investigations on the island of Nikumaroro in the Republic of Kiribati.

Her research interests include microstructure of mineralized tissues, effects of burning and cremation, and decomposition. She has taught at the Universities of Georgia, North Carolina at Charlotte, and Utah. She also teaches short courses for the U.S. Department of Justice's International Criminal Investigative Training Assistance Program (ICITAP), as well as for law enforcement agencies, judges, continuing education programs, and human rights organizations. Dr. Burns is presently teaching human osteology, forensic anthropology methods, and an introduction to the forensic sciences at the University of Utah.

About the Illustrator

Joanna Wallington, B.F.A., is a freelance professional illustrator and designer living in Atlanta, Georgia. She is proficient in a wide range of artistic media from pen and pencil to computer graphics and photography. Ms. Wallington is a graduate of the University of Georgia's College of Fine Arts. Her major educational emphasis was scientific illustration with a minor in anthropology. She completed a senior thesis in comparative primate anatomy.

Ms. Wallington, a native of Great Britain, has lived in the United States since 1977. She served in the United States Marine Corps as a firefighter emergency medical technician.

CHAPTER 1

Introduction to Forensic Anthropology

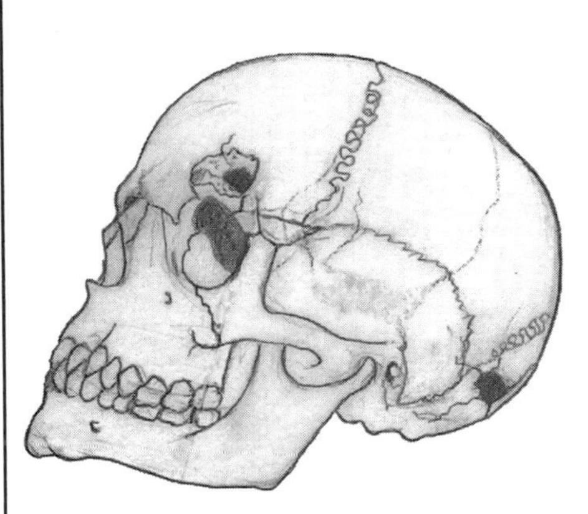

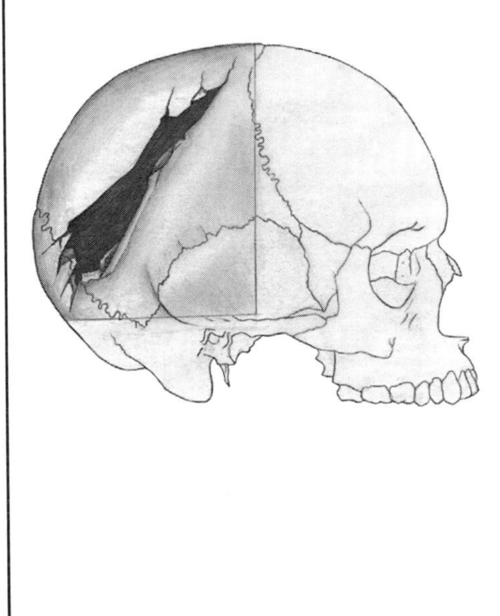

CHAPTER OUTLINE

Introduction: The Problem of the Unidentified

The body of knowledge known as forensic anthropology offers a unique humanitarian service to a world troubled by violence. Clandestine deaths cast a shadow on everyone. Missing persons and unidentified dead—the "disappeared" of this world—are too often the result of the worst criminal and political behavior of humankind. Peace and humanity begin with the effort to identify the dead and understand their fate.

Who Are the "Missing, Unidentified, and Disappeared"?

Some unidentified bodies are those of derelicts who simply wandered off and died. Some are suicides who didn't want to be found. But many are unresolved homicides, hidden long enough to assure impunity for the perpetrators. The unidentified may be teenagers executed by gang members, women raped by soldiers, or children abused by caretakers. They are sometimes the evidence of serial killers who walk the streets without fear. In many countries, the missing and unidentified are known as "the disappeared." They are the result of genocide and extreme misuse of authority.

The odd thing about an unidentified body is its *silence*. It may seem that all dead bodies are silent, but an unidentified body is even more silent. No one calls and complains when it is forgotten. No one exerts pressure or wields political or financial power on behalf of an unidentified person. If shipped off to a morgue and buried as a "John Doe," it doesn't even take up space at a responsible agency.

It appears that no one cares, but this is not true. Those who care suffer in silence with nowhere to turn for relief. They suffer the agony of not knowing the fate of their loved ones. They put their lives on hold. They become victims who are afraid to move to a new location, to remarry, or to rebuild their lives. They feel that they might show a lack of love by giving up hope and assuming the person to be dead. After all, what if the person does return and finds his or her home gone?

Parents of soldiers missing in action say that not knowing is far worse than being able to grieve. Instead of feeling buoyed by hope, they are paralyzed by the fear that their child is suffering somewhere.

Families of missing persons say that they experience a sense of relief when the bodies of loved ones are finally identified. They find a sense of closure and even empowerment through the process of funeral rituals.

Why Is Identification So Difficult?

The general attitude of law enforcement personnel toward unidentified bodies tends to be defeatist. Standard comments are, "If it is not identified within two weeks, it won't be identified," or "If it is not a local person with a well-publicized missing person record, forget it." These are self-fulfilling prophecies. While the law of diminishing returns is no doubt applicable, the door *can* be left open for success. However, leaving the door open is not easy. It requires a thorough analysis of the remains and maintaining a record of *correct* information.

Unfortunately, correct information is as useless as incorrect information if it is not communicated. This may be the Information Age, but the world is still struggling with the practical and responsible use of information. The technology is available, but intelligent use of technology is a challenge. Within the United States, the National Crime Information Center is a good place to store and search for information, especially when used in combination with NamUs, a recent web-based system of missing and unidentified persons databases. In developing countries, similar databases are also being established. This is being accomplished with slow determination by local activists and numerous international agencies as well as nongovernmental organizations such as the

American Association for the Advancement of Science, Physicians for Human Rights, and the Carter Center of Emory University.

When the doors are left open for identification, and an identification is finally made, the remains must be relocated. Storing human remains (especially decomposing remains) is not as easy as storing most other types of evidence, but it can be done. However, the ethics of the situation are controversial. Is it more important to identify a deceased person, inform the family, and possibly apprehend a murderer, or is it more important to "honor" the dead with an anonymous burial?

The Discipline of Forensic Anthropology

Forensic anthropology is best known as the discipline that applies the scientific knowledge of physical anthropology (and often archaeology) to the collection and analysis of legal evidence. More broadly speaking, it is anthropological knowledge applied to legal issues. Forensic anthropology began as a subfield of physical anthropology but has grown into a distinct body of knowledge, overlapping other fields of anthropology, biology, and the physical sciences.

Recovery, description, and identification of human skeletal remains are the standard work of forensic anthropologists. The condition of the evidence varies greatly, including decomposing, burned, cremated, fragmented, or disarticulated remains. Typical cases range from recent homicides to illegal destruction of ancient Native American burials. Forensic anthropologists work individual cases, mass disasters, historic cases, and international human rights cases.

Forensic anthropologists are also called to work on cases of living persons where identity or age is in question. Comparisons of video tapes, photographs, and radiographs are within the capability and experience of most forensic anthropologists.

History of Forensic Anthropology

The public views forensic anthropology as a young discipline, and it is. However, it has a long developmental history in the works of physical anthropologists fascinated by the anatomical collections of museums and universities. Anthropologists were making observations about skeletal differences and writing papers for professional societies decades before any legal application for their knowledge was ever considered. The earliest beginnings of what we call forensic anthropology can be attributed to a few bright attorneys mired in complicated legal battles. They searched out the knowledge they needed to win and made use of it in court. Little by little, over the last 150 years, anthropologists have responded with goal-driven research. Along the way, they learned about the work of law enforcement investigators, the capabilities of other forensic scientists, and the requirements of a courtroom environment.

There is no date for the beginning of the study of human skeletons, but there is a firm date for the first use of skeletal information in a court of law—the 1850 **Webster/Parkman trial**. Oliver Wendell Holmes and Jeffries Wyman, two Harvard anatomists, were called to examine human remains thought to be those of a missing physician, Dr. George Parkman. A Harvard chemistry professor, John W. Webster, was accused of the crime of murder. The evidence was substantial even before the anatomists became involved. Webster owed Parkman money; a head had been burned in Webster's furnace; body parts were found in his lab and privy; and a dentist had identified Parkman's dentures found in the furnace. (Forensic dentistry was getting a start, too.) Holmes and Wyman testified that the remains fit the description of Parkman, and Webster was hanged.

My favorite case took place a few years later (1897) in Chicago. This time, the expert witness was actually an anthropologist—George A. Dorsey, a curator at the Field Museum of Natural History. Dorsey was called to examine a few bits and pieces of bone from the sludge at the bottom of a sausage-rendering vat. Louisa Luetgert, wife of a sausage factory owner, was missing, and her husband, Adolph, was accused of murder. Again, the evidence was substantial even before the anthropologist became involved. Adolph was seeing another woman; the Luetgert marriage was on the rocks; Adolph had closed down his plant for several weeks; he had ordered extra potash before closing the plant; he had given the watchman time off on the night of the disappearance; and, most incriminating of all, Louisa's rings were found in the vat. Dorsey had only to prove that the bones were human, not pig, and he did. Adolph Luetgert was imprisoned for life. By the way, this is a good case to support the importance of learning to recognize fragments and all the other tiny "insignificant" bones.

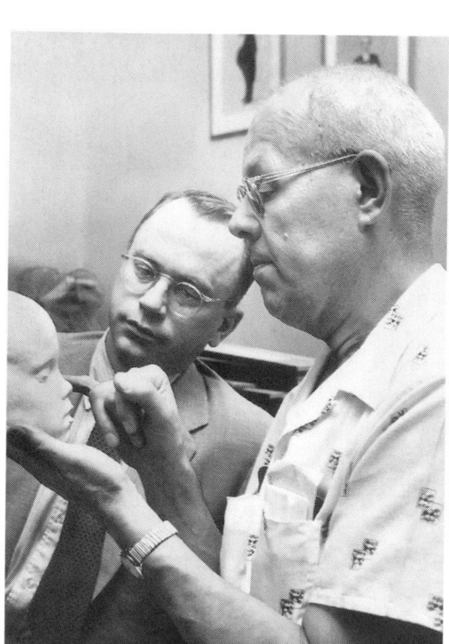

Figure 1.1

Wilton Marion Krogman (right) examining the death mask of a murder victim, 1957. From University of Pennsylvania Archives.

T. Dale Stewart (1901–1997) designated **Thomas Dwight** (1843–1911) of Harvard University as the "Father of Forensic Anthropology in the United States." This is partially based on the fact that Dwight wrote a prize-winning essay on the subject of identification from the human skeleton in 1878. Dwight may not have been the very first actor in what we now call forensic anthropology, but he was the first to publish.

Early in the twentieth century, many anthropologists contributed to the developing discipline, but **Wilton Marion Krogman** (1902–1987) was the first to speak directly to law enforcement with his "Guide to the Identification of Human Skeletal Material," published by the *FBI Law Enforcement Bulletin* in 1939. He followed it with "The Role of the Physical Anthropologist in the Identification of Human Skeletal Remains" (1943). These publications were significant, but not widely read. Most investigators still took any human remains straight to the medical doctor. I remember **J. Lawrence (Larry) Angel** (1915–1986), Curator of Physical Anthropology at the Smithsonian Museum (1962–1977) telling me that it had been a big day when the FBI discovered the physical anthropologists at the Smithsonian. He said, "If they wanted answers, all they had to do was to walk across the street with a box of bones!"

Figure 1.2

T. Dale Stewart. From Human Studies Film Archives, National Anthropological Archives, Smithsonian Institution.

Forensic anthropology may have dawned early in Washington, D.C., but not much was happening in the rest of the country. In the late 1960s, my mentor, **William R. Maples**, chose *The Human Skeleton in Forensic Medicine* by Wilton Krogman (1962) as a textbook for a human osteology class. At that time, Maples was still studying baboons and Krogman's references to "medicolegal cases" were a curiosity rather than a reality. Krogman didn't even use the term *forensic anthropology,* but he did write that his purpose was "to acquaint the law enforcement agencies of the world with what the bones tell and how they tell it." He kept pushing the ball along, but it still wasn't rolling on its own.

Forensic anthropology finally began to evolve as a recognizable discipline during the 1970s. **T. Dale Stewart** edited a Smithsonian publication, *Personal Identification in Mass Disasters* (1970). Next, **William M. Bass** published the first practical textbook, *Human Osteology: A Laboratory and Field Manual* (1971). By that time, a few physical anthropologists had begun to attend meetings of the American Academy of Forensic Sciences. They realized they could probably pull together enough colleagues to form a section of physical anthropologists within the Academy, so they met in a hotel room with a phone and did just that. Fourteen people formed the Physical Anthropology Section in 1972. Soon after, a few adventurous persons started calling themselves "forensic" anthropologists rather than "physical" anthropologists. By the end of the 1970s, T. Dale Stewart published *Essentials of Forensic Anthropology* (1979)—the first textbook to actually carry the name "forensic anthropology" in its title.

Even in the 1970s forensic anthropology was not an undergraduate subject—or even a graduate degree. Future forensic anthropologists focused on physical anthropology in graduate school and wrote theses with forensic applications. "Forensic Anthropology" degree titles are a phenomenon of the late 1980s and 1990s. And the job title "Forensic Anthropologist" is even newer.

It has been interesting to watch the evolution of forensic anthropology in the nonacademic work force. It began as a few anthropology departments sending trained forensic anthropologists out into the world without jobs. The graduates could choose to settle in a university or a museum like their mentors, but that's not what they wanted. Only a very few landed jobs that matched their training. One by one, most accepted jobs where they would at least be available, if not paid, to handle skeletal cases. Then slowly, they were hired by other agencies because of their experience, leaving a void at the original place. The abandoned agency then had to recognize the contribution of the lost anthropologist and start paying someone for the work. It has been slow in coming, but today, forensic anthropologists are employed by state, national, and international agencies around the world.

There is much more information available about the history of forensic anthropology in the writings of Stewart (1979), Snow (1982), Joyce and Stover (1991), Ubelaker and Scammell (1992), and Maples and Browning (1994).

Figure 1.3
William R. Maples. Photo by Gene Bednarek, University of Florida News Bureau.

Educational Requirements

Forensic anthropologists usually specialize first in anthropology or biology and then obtain graduate or postgraduate training in forensic anthropology. Most are competent in human biology, anatomy, and osteology, and are experienced in archaeological field techniques. Many have additional training in medical fields, such as emergency medicine, nursing, anatomy, pathology, and dentistry.

Most forensic anthropologists learn the basics of medical-legal death investigation through on-the-job training. The education itself is a never-ending process. It is renewed by reading scientific periodicals, participating in short courses, and being an active member in professional organizations such as the American Academy of Forensic Sciences, the International Association for Identification, and the American Association of Physical Anthropologists. The American Board of Forensic Examiners also offers continuing educational opportunities.

A Ph.D. is desirable because it requires competence in research methods, writing, and teaching. All of these skills are useful to the professional forensic anthropologist and are important to the role of expert witness. There are, however, many competent forensic anthropologists with master's degrees working in government laboratories and nongovernmental agencies around the world.

How Is the Work of an Anthropologist Different from the Work of a Pathologist or Medical Examiner?

Typically, a medical doctor is called on to examine a fleshed body, and an anthropologist is called on to examine a skeleton. The medical doctor focuses on information from soft tissues, and the anthropologist focuses on information from hard tissues. However, since decomposition is a continuous process, the work of these specialists tends to overlap. A medical doctor may be useful when mummified tissues are present on the skeleton, and an anthropologist is useful when decomposition is advanced or when bone trauma is a major element in the death. Simple visual identification is usually impossible in an anthropological investigation. Therefore, more time and attention are devoted to a thorough analysis and description of physical traits.

Legal authority also differs. The medical examiner has the authority to conduct an autopsy and to state cause and manner of death. The forensic anthropologist carries out a skeletal analysis and contributes an opinion, but not a legal statement, regarding cause and manner of death.

Objectives of an Anthropological Investigation

The objectives of anthropological investigation are the same as those of a medical-legal investigation of a recently deceased person. That is, the anthropologist is seeking to provide a thorough description, achieve a personal identification, and estimate the time of death or postmortem interval. The anthropologist is also expected to collect and document all associated physical evidence and see that it is transferred to the appropriate analyst.

Anthropologists are often asked to give opinion regarding the circumstances of death, but the legal responsibility for determination of cause and manner of death is in the hands of the medical examiner, forensic pathologist, or coroner, not the anthropologist. (See the section on cause and manner of death.)

In effect, the work of the anthropologist overlaps the work of both the crime scene investigator and the medical examiner. The specific anthropologist for the case is dictated by the circumstances of the case and the material to be examined.

- An anthropologist with osteological training (usually a physical anthropologist) can maximize the information gained from skeletonized human remains.
- An anthropologist with archaeological training can optimize the recovery of buried evidence from a crime scene.
- An anthropologist with socio-cultural training may interface more effectively with families and facilitate interviews, particularly in multi-cultural circumstances. (Socio-cultural anthropologists are more frequently part of the investigatory team in countries other than the United States.)

Questions Basic to Personal Identification

- Are the remains human? (Frequently they are not.)
- Do the remains represent a single individual or several individuals?
- What did the person look like? (The description should include sex, age, race, height, physique, and handedness.)
- Who is it? Are there unique skeletal traits or anomalies that could serve to provide a tentative or positive identification?

Forensic anthropologists also collect physical evidence that aids in solving questions about the circumstances of death. This is another area in which broad-spectrum anthropological training is very useful, particularly in cross-cultural circumstances.

Questions Regarding the Circumstances of Death

- When did death occur?
- Did the person die at the place of burial, or was he or she transported after death?

- Was the grave disturbed, or was the person buried more than once?
- What was the cause of death (e.g., gunshot wound, stabbing, asphyxiation)?
- What was the manner of death (i.e., homicide, suicide, accident, or natural)?
- What is the identity of the perpetrator(s)?

Cause and Manner of Death

The phrase, "cause and manner of death," is used so often that it's easy to think of "cause" and "manner" as the same thing. However, they are not. The phrase is a combination of independent medical and legal determinations. Both are important to the legal consequences of the death.

Cause of death is a *medical* determination. It includes any condition that leads to or contributes to death. Typically, cause is listed in simple terms, such as cancer, heart attack, stroke, gunshot wound, drowning, and so on. However, cause of death can become complicated when numerous factors are considered over a period of time. There can be an underlying cause such as a long-term disease (e.g., lymphoma), an intermediate cause (e.g., chemotherapy), and an immediate cause (e.g., pneumonia). The choice of terms and wording is up to the medical doctor in charge of the postmortem.

Manner of death is a *legal* determination based on evidence and opinion. It is decided by government-appointed or elected medical examiners and/or coroners. There are five standard categories of manner of death:

1. *Natural:* A consequence of natural disease or "old age."
2. *Accidental:* Unintended, but unavoidable death; not natural, suicidal, or homicidal.
3. *Suicidal:* Self-caused and intentional. (Society does not include self-caused deaths due to ignorance or general self-destructive behavior.)
4. *Homicidal:* Death caused by another human.
5. *Undetermined:* There is not enough evidence on which to make a decision.

Stages of an Investigation

There are three major stages of investigation in a typical case: (1) collection of verbal evidence, (2) collection of physical evidence, and (3) analysis of the evidence. Within the United States, the collection of verbal evidence is usually carried out by police investigators. There are countries, however, in which the anthropologist is expected to take the initiative in obtaining verbal evidence as well as physical evidence. Under such circumstances, forensic anthropologists become involved in the entire process of interviewing, searching records, and gathering physical evidence. This is when socio-cultural training becomes essential. International forensic anthropology teams frequently hire social and cultural anthropologists to deal with interviews and other verbal evidence. This practice is helping to expand the definition of "forensic anthropologist" to include *all* anthropologists who apply their training to legal issues, not just the physical anthropologists.

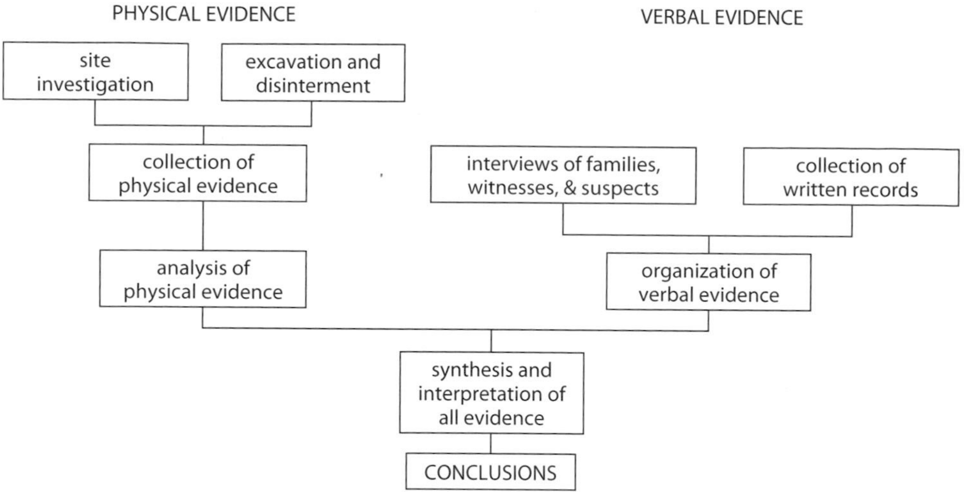

Figure 1.4
Flowchart of a Forensic Investigation

The accompanying flowchart shows the stages of investigation leading to a synthesis and interpretation of information. Each box within the flowchart is a subject unto itself. The flowchart is introduced here to give an overall view of a forensic investigation. This book will focus on the left side of the chart, but, in the final analysis, both channels of investigation are essential.

CHAPTER 2

The Biology of Bone and Joints

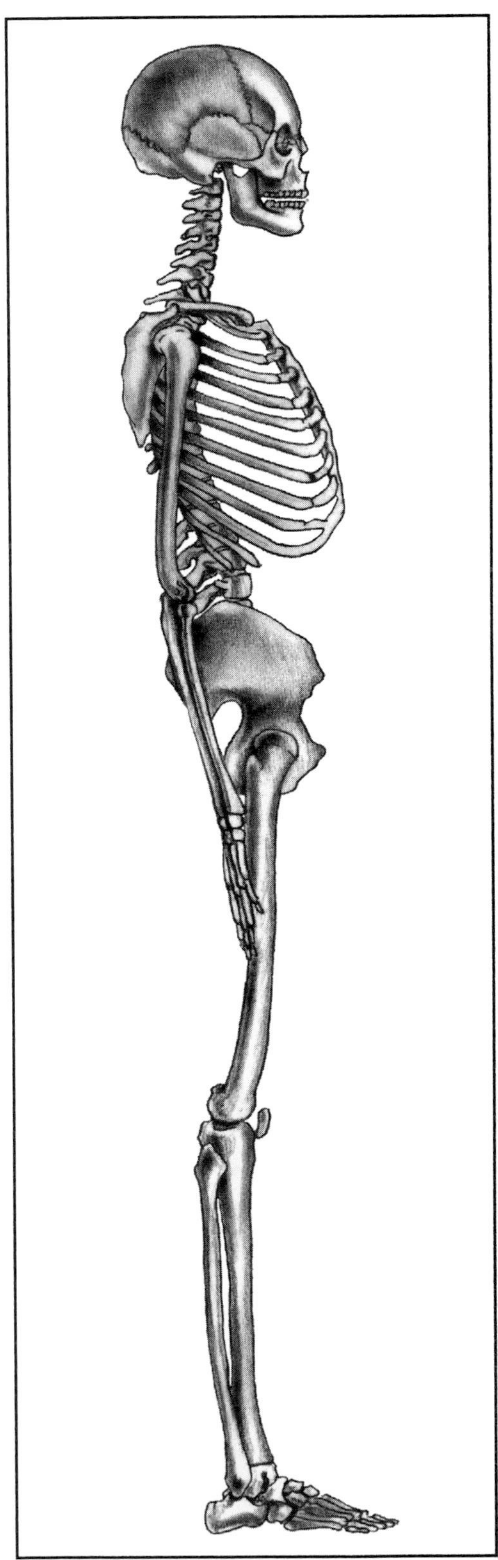

CHAPTER OUTLINE

Introduction

Osteology is the study of bones. It is the science that explores the development, structure, function, and variation of bones. Research in human osteology includes the effects of genetic origin, age, sex, diet, trauma, disease, and decomposition.

Why study human osteology?

The skeleton is more durable than the rest of the human body. It is often the only surviving record of a life on this earth. A knowledge of human osteology is prerequisite to reading the physical record of humankind.

Imagine receiving a book written in an obscure language. If you have no knowledge of the language, you could describe the color and texture of the pages, but you would not be able to read the information that the writer intended to communicate.

It is the same with bones. You may describe them, but you will not understand their meaning until you learn their language. And just as you find that a dictionary is still useful in your own language, you will find it necessary to continue learning the language of bones as long as you work with them.

What are the practical applications?

Depending on the condition of the remains and the availability of antemortem information, a competent osteologist may be able to provide much of the following information from skeletal remains:

- Description of the living person
- Evaluation of the health of the person
- Recognition of habitual activities
- Identification of the deceased person
- Recognition of the cause and manner of death
- Determination of the approximate time since death
- Information about postmortem events

Structure and Function of the Skeletal System

Tissues: Communities of Cells with a Common Purpose

A **tissue** is a group of closely associated cells, similar in structure and performing related functions. The cells are bound together in matrices of nonliving extracellular material that varies greatly from one tissue to another. The body's organs are built from tissues, and most organs contain the four basic tissue types. See Table 2.1 for a comparison of tissue types, functions, and examples of each.

Table 2.1 Basic Tissues Types

Basic Tissue Types	Tissue Functions	Examples
EPITHELIAL TISSUE	covering	skin, hair, nails
CONNECTIVE TISSUE	support, protection, hydration	bone, cartilage, fat, ligaments, fascia, blood
MUSCLE TISSUE	movement	muscle
NERVOUS TISSUE	control	nerves

Connective Tissue: The Most Durable Tissue of the Body

There are many forms of **connective tissue**, but all connective tissues consist of more or less numerous cells surrounded by an extracellular matrix of fibrous and ground substance.

Classes and Subclasses of Connective Tissue

Connective tissue includes connective tissue proper, cartilage, bone, and blood. Connective tissue proper forms the supporting framework of many large organs of the body and is classified as either "loose" or "dense." Collagen fibers make all the difference. **Loose connective tissue** contains very little collagen. Adipose tissue (fat) is one of several types of loose connective tissue. **Dense connective tissue** has much more collagen and contributes more directly to the skeletal system. The dense connective tissues, cartilage, and bone are each discussed in separate sections.

General Functions of Connective Tissues

(Acronym: "SHAPE")

- *Support* in areas that require durable flexibility
- *Hydration* and maintenance of body fluids
- *Attachment* of the various body parts to one another
- *Protection* for bones and joints during activity
- *Encasement* of organs and groups of structures

Basic Connective Tissue Cell

The basic connective tissue cell is a **mesenchymal cell**. It is a primitive cell with the capability to differentiate into other types of cells, including the cells that actually produce and maintain the connective tissues. Specific cell types are discussed in their appropriate sections.

Dense Connective Tissue: Holding Everything Together

Dense connective tissue is capable of providing enormous tensile strength. Bundles of white fibers are sandwiched between rows of connective tissue cells. The fibers all run in the same direction, parallel to the direction of pull.

Dense connective tissue is subdivided into irregular, regular, and elastic connective tissues. **Irregular dense connective tissue** forms the fibrous capsules surrounding kidneys, nerves, bones, and muscles. **Regular dense connective tissue** forms ligaments, tendons, aponeuroses, and fascia. **Elastic dense connective tissue** combines greater elasticity with strength. It makes up vocal cords and some of the ligaments connecting adjacent vertebrae.

Types and Functions of Dense Connective Tissue

- **Ligaments** connect *bone* to bone, to cartilage, and to other structures. They are bands or sheets of fibrous tissue.
- **Tendons** attach *muscle* to bone. They tend to be narrower and more cord-like than ligaments.
- **Periosteum** encases (covers) the *outer* surfaces of compact bone. It is a fibrous sheath that is cellular and vascularized.
- **Endosteum** covers the *inner* surfaces of compact bone. It is a thinner fibrous sheath than the periosteum.
- **Fascia** encases muscles, groups of muscles, and large vessels and nerves. It is the "plastic wrap" of the body, binding structures together and providing stability.

DENSE CONNECTIVE TISSUE CELLS

Fibroblasts are the cells that produce collagen fibers, the basic organic fibers of dense connective tissues. Inactive fibroblasts are called **fibrocytes**.

CARTILAGE: A STRONG BUT FLEXIBLE CONNECTIVE TISSUE

Cartilage consists primarily of water (60 to 80 percent by weight). Because of its high water content, cartilage is very *resilient.* It is capable of springing back when compressed, so it makes a good cushion and shock absorber for movable joints.

It is also resistant to *tension* because of a strong network of collagen fibrils. It is not, however, resistant to shear forces (twisting and bending). This weakness is the reason for the large number of torn cartilages in sports injuries.

Cartilage contains no blood vessels. Nutrients are passed from the surrounding perichondrium by diffusion, an adequate method because of the high water content. Cartilage is capable of fast growth because there is no need for slow vascular formation. However, unlike bone, cartilage has very little capacity for regeneration in adults.

TYPES OF CARTILAGE

- **Hyaline cartilage** caps the ends of bones, shapes the nose, completes the rib cage, forms the fetal skeleton, and provides a model for growing bone.
- **Elastic cartilage** is hyaline cartilage with elastic fibers added. It forms the epiglottis, the tip of the nose, and the external ear.
- **Fibrocartilage** is embedded in dense collagenous tissue. It forms the vertebral discs, the pubic symphysis, and articular discs in joint capsules.

CARTILAGE CELLS

Cartilage Function

- support
- flexibility
- friction reduction
- model for growing bone

In the growing cartilage, **chondroblasts** build cartilage. They are capable of rapid multiplication when necessary. **Chondroclasts** break down cartilage and absorb it. **Chondrocytes** are adult cartilage cells. Unlike cells of most other tissues, chondrocytes cannot divide. The little healing that does take place in cartilage is due to the ability of the surviving chondrocytes to secrete more extracellular matrix.

Cartilage cells live in an extracellular matrix—a jelly-like ground substance with collagen fibers and watery tissue fluid. The extracellular matrix is important for transport of cells and maintenance of the cartilage. (Remember, there are no blood vessels.)

BONE: THE STRONGEST, LEAST FLEXIBLE CONNECTIVE TISSUE

TYPES AND FUNCTIONS OF BONE

Definition Note

Bone is a tissue as well as a unit of the skeleton.

Two basic types of bone exist in the adult skeleton—dense bone and spongy bone. Unfortunately, several descriptive terms are used for each type of bone. **Dense bone** is also known as *compact, lamellar,* or *cortical* bone. It consists mainly of concentric lamellar osteons and interstitial lamellae that provide strength and resistance to torsion. Dense bone forms the bone cortex, the main portion of the shaft surrounding the medullary cavity.

Spongy bone is also called *cancellous* or *trabecular* bone. It is characterized by thin bony spicules, or trabeculae, creating a latticework filled with bone marrow or embryonal connective tissue.

Woven bone is a third type of bone. It is not found in the healthy adult skeleton but is normal in the embryonic skeleton or healing bone. The matrix is irregular, and there is no osteonal structure.

Support is the primary function of bone, but bone also provides for protection, movement, blood cell formation, and mineral storage. The armor-like bones of the skull and the pelvis and the flexible bones of the rib cage surround and protect vulnerable organs. Opposing muscle groups use the lever action of one bone on another to make movement possible. The marrow cavities of bone produce blood cells, and the bone itself stores minerals when there is an abundance in the diet, then provides needed minerals when a dietary shortage occurs.

Consider the functions of bone and cartilage as you use Table 2.2 to compare the characteristics and the structure of each.

Bone Function

- support
- protection
- movement/attachment
- blood cell formation
- mineral storage

CHEMICAL COMPOSITION OF BONE

Bone has both organic and inorganic components. The organic component is approximately 35 percent of the bone mass. It is composed of cells, collagen fibers, and ground substance. Ground substance is amorphous material in which structural elements occur. It is composed of protein polysaccharides, tissue fluids, and metabolites.

The inorganic component is approximately 65 percent of the bone mass. It is composed of mineral salts, primarily calcium phosphate, which form tiny crystals and pack tightly into the extracellular matrix of collagen fibers. The crystalline material is called **hydroxyapatite**.

Definition Note

Hydroxyapatite
$Ca_{10}(PO_4)_6(OH)_2$

The natural mineral structure that the crystal lattice of bones and teeth most closely resembles.

BONE CELLS

Three basic types of cells build and maintain healthy bone tissue. **Osteoblasts** build the bone matrix. They are found at sites of bone growth, repair, and remodeling. **Osteoclasts** are large, multinucleated cells capable of breaking down bone. They are found at sites of repair and remodeling. **Osteocytes** are long-term maintenance cells. They are transformed from osteoblasts that become lodged in their own bony matrix. Osteocytes occupy the lacunae of lamellar bone. They extend cellular processes into the canaliculi of the bone. (See Figure 2.3 for illustration of lacunae and canaliculi.)

MACROSTRUCTURE (GROSS ANATOMY)

The basic **macrostructure** of a long bone is defined by its growth and development. The primary center of ossification forms the **diaphysis**. It appears first and becomes the shaft of the adult bone.

Secondary centers of ossification become **epiphyses**. They form the ends of the bone as well as tuberosities, trochanters, epicondyles, and other additions to the final form of the bone. Some epiphyses are substantial in size; others are no more than bony flakes. **Pressure epiphyses** form the ends of bones and provide a dense, smooth surface for articular cartilage. **Traction epiphyses** form attachment areas and provide dense, irregular, pitted surfaces for muscle

Table 2.2 A Comparison of Bone and Cartilage

	BONE	CARTILAGE
CHARACTERISTICS	solid	solid
	inflexible	flexible
	vascular	avascular
CELLULAR COMPONENT	osteocytes	chondrocytes
	osteoblasts	chondroblasts
	osteoclasts	chondroclasts
EXTRACELLULAR MATRIX	collagen fibers, ground substance, and crystalline lattice of hydroxyapatite	collagen and/or elastic fibers, ground substance, and no inorganic component

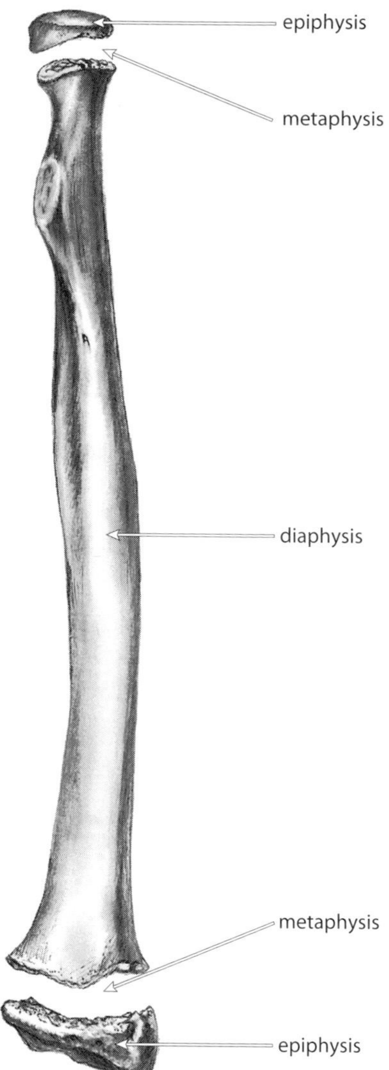

Figure 2.1
Juvenile Long Bone Structure (Radius)

attachment. **Atavistic epiphyses** are all the others. They are small and irregular with no specific function in humans— e.g., costal notch flakes in the sternum (Scheuer, 2000).

A **metaphysis** (or "growth plate") is an area of active growth. The metaphysis is not calcified. It is, therefore, represented by a gap between the bones in the illustration. In life, the metaphysis is growing cartilage, calcifying at each bony surface. The bone ceases to lengthen when the cartilage ceases to grow. The metaphysis then becomes the site of epiphysis-diaphysis fusion

Some sources will refer to the ends of mature bones as epiphyses and the shafts as diaphyses. Technically, these terms are are used for parts of growing bone. The adult form should be referred to as the distal or proximal end, or by the name of the completed structure, such as the head of the humerus.

The medullary cavity lies within the shaft of the long bone. It is an open or less calcified area, sheltering the body's blood cell factory.

The layers of the long bone shaft can be seen in a cross section. The **periosteum** is the outermost layer. It is the fibrous membrane that encompasses the bone somewhat like plastic shrink wrap. **Sharpey's fibers** hold the periosteum tightly in place. **Nutrient foramina** pierce the periosteum and the bone, providing access for **nutrient vessels**. The vessels pass through both compact bone and trabecular bone to reach the center of the **medullary cavity** (marrow cavity).

The periosteum, Sharpey's fibers, and nutrient vessels decompose after death. Therefore, they are not visible on clean, dry bone, but evidence of their presence remains in the texture of the bone surface.

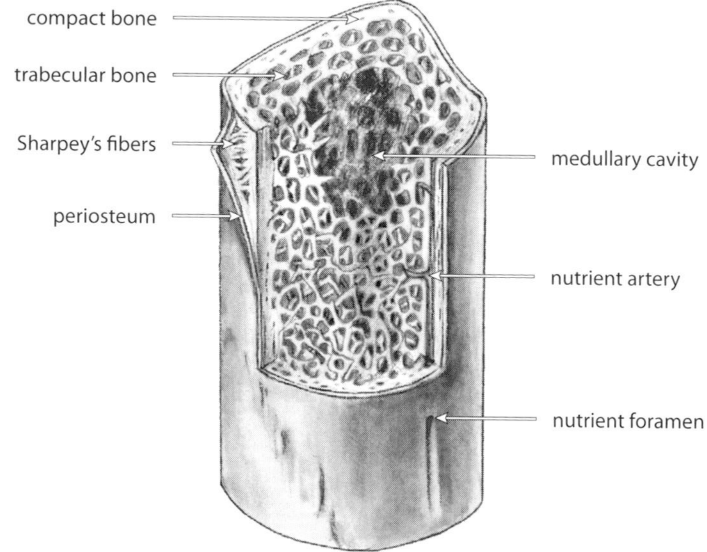

Figure 2.2
Layers of a Long Bone Shaft

MICROSTRUCTURE (MICROSCOPIC ANATOMY OR HISTOLOGY)

Bone is built by cells called osteoblasts, maintained by osteocytes, broken down by osteoclasts, and built again. In adult bone, all stages of remodeling can be viewed in a single thin section of compact bone. It is estimated that 5 percent of compact (dense) bone and 25 percent of trabecular (spongy) bone is renewed each year (Martin et al., 1998).

Dense bone is lamellar in structure. **Circumferential lamellae** encase the entire bone, and **concentric lamellae** are wound tightly into structures called **osteons** or **Haversian systems**. Each lamella of bone is a single layer of bone matrix in which all of the collagen fibers run in one direction. Fibers of adjacent lamellae run in opposite directions, and the result is much like well-made plywood. Together, many layers of lamellae can resist torsion.

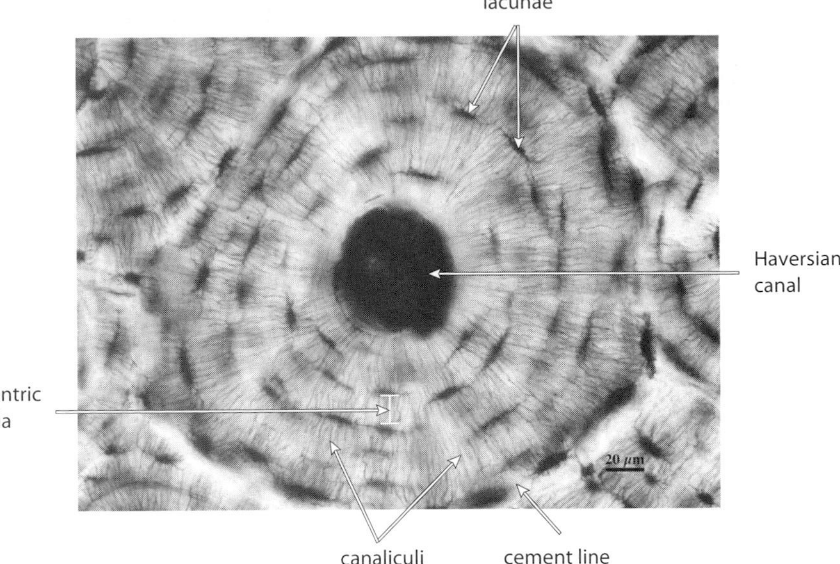

Figure 2.3
Microstructure of Compact Bone, One Osteon (300 Micron Diameter).
Robert V. Blystone, Ph.D, Trinity University.

Osteons are the basic structural component of dense bone. They are cylindrically shaped structures oriented parallel to the long axis of the bone. Each osteon is made of a vascular **Haversian canal** surrounded by calcified concentric lamellae. Osteons are dynamic structures, filled with living cells and are continuously changing or remodeling. They are nourished by self-contained blood vessels that travel within the central Haversian canals of the osteons and interconnect by **Volkmann's canals**. Osteocytes, the long-term bone maintenance cells, occupy tiny spaces called **lacunae**, which are interconnected by minute canals called **canaliculi**.

Spongy bone is much less complex in organization than dense bone. Spongy bone is made up of **trabeculae**, each of which has a few layers of lamellae, but lacks osteons and self-contained blood vessels. It is nourished by diffusion from capillaries in the surrounding **endosteum**.

OSTEOGENESIS (BONE FORMATION AND GROWTH)

All bone develops by replacing a pre-existing connective tissue—either a connective tissue membrane or a cartilaginous model. Bone growth that takes place within a membrane is called **intramembranous ossification**. It begins early in fetal development and continues throughout life as bone heals and remodels beneath the periosteal membrane. The flat bones of the cranial vault and bones of the face and mandible are all formed by intramembranous ossification. Some, such as the clavicle and scapula are partially formed by intramembranous ossification.

Bone growth that takes place within a cartilaginous model is called **endochondral ossification**. It takes place after a template for the bone is formed in cartilage and vascularized. It begins later in fetal development than intramembranous ossification and, unlike intramembranous ossification, continues only until the bone reaches its mature size. Endochondral ossification does not take place in adults. Even though the ends of long bones are the primary examples of endochondral ossification, much of the compact bone in the diaphysis of the long bone forms within the periosteal membrane. Short bones, vertebral bodies, and other bones with significant amounts of trabecular bone also grow by endochondral ossification.

More complete information about bone formation can be found in textbooks entirely devoted to the subject. Developmental Juvenile Osteology by Scheuer and Black (2000) is an excellent source. It provides well-illustrated descriptions for the origin and growth of each individual bone, from first embryological appearance to final adult form.

BONE ARCHITECTURE AND STRENGTH

In bone, just as in cathedral construction, stress is the key to form. The shape of each bone is a result of the stresses most commonly placed on it. Bones are subjected to **compression** as weight bears down on them and **tension** as muscles pull on them. Healthy bone is half as strong as steel in resisting compression and is fully as strong as steel in resisting tension. Because of the inequality in resistance, bone tends to bend under unequal loading. Bending compresses one side and stretches the other. Compression and tension are greatest at the outer parts of the bones and least at the inner parts. Therefore, strong, compact bone tissue is necessary at the periphery of bones and spongy bone is sufficient in the internal regions.

The internal regions of bones appear weak because of the porous, spongy nature. In fact, the trabeculae of spongy bone align along stress lines and provide lightweight struts that buttress and further strengthen the bone. At the same time, they provide a well-protected space for essential bone marrow.

Form Follows Function

"Every change in the form and the function of a bone or in its function alone, is followed by certain definite changes in its internal architecture and secondary alterations in its external conformation" (*PDR Medical Dictionary*, 1995).

WOLFF'S LAW (FORM FOLLOWS FUNCTION)

A nineteenth-century German anatomist, Julius Wolff (1836–1902), observed that the form of bone changes when its use changes. **Wolff's Law** is based on the fact that bone grows and thrives under tension whereas it fails and reabsorbs under long-term compression. Bone is normally under tension because of the balance of muscle groups—flexors and extensors, adductors and abductors. However, tension can be altered by changes in activity—both type and amount. It can also be altered by damage to muscles or the nerves that innervate them. The result is bone remodeling or bone loss causing change in form.

CLASSIFICATION AND DESCRIPTION OF BONES

The skeletal system can be described and classified by several different systems, depending on the aspect of the skeleton that is the focus of attention. Bones are categorized by location, by size and shape, by origin, and by structure.

BY LOCATION

The **axial skeleton** is the foundation or base to which the appendicular skeleton is attached. With the exception of the ribs, the bones of the axial skeleton are singular (not paired). The axial skeleton is composed of the skull, hyoid, backbone, sternum, and ribs.

The **appendicular skeleton** is attached to the axial skeleton. All of the appendicular bones are paired (i.e., a right and a left version). The appendicular skeleton is composed of the pectoral girdle, arms, hands, pelvic girdle, legs, and feet.

BY SIZE AND SHAPE

Most bones are classified as either long bones or flat bones, but some are classified as short or irregular. Long and flat bones are easier to recognize and agree on. Short and irregular classifications can be inconsistent.

Long bones are much longer than wide. Bones of the arms, legs, fingers, and toes are long bones. (Bones of the fingers and toes may *seem* short, but they are longer than they are wide. Therefore, they are long bones.) **Flat bones** are, as you might expect, flat. Bones of the skull, pelvis, and shoulder blade are flat bones.

Short bones are small rounded bones. The carpal bones of the wrist and the tarsal bones of the ankle are short bones. Sesamoid bones are also considered to be short bones.

Irregular bones include the bones of the spine and the hyoid. Many other bones may seem irregular, but few are *called* irregular.

By Origin

Bones form by intramembranous or endochondral ossification. See "Osteogenesis" on page 15.

By Structure

Normal adult bone is either dense or spongy. See "Types and Functions of Bone" on page 12 and "Microstructure (Microscopic Anatomy or Histology)" on page 14.

Figure 2.4
Description of a Single Bone
How many ways can you describe this bone? Think about name, condition, location, shape, origin, and structure.

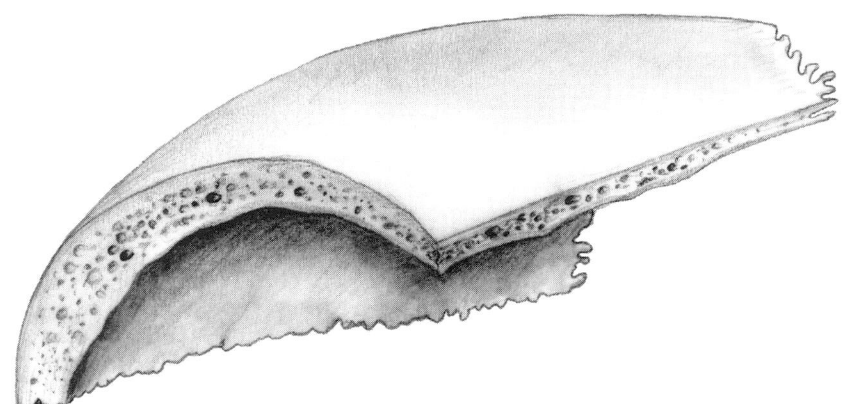

Answer: This is a *parietal bone* with two *sawed edges*. It is one of the *paired bones* of the skull. It is a *flat bone*, and it is part of the *axial skeleton*. It is *intramembranous* in origin. The outer and inner tables of the parietal are *compact bone*. The internal (sandwiched) layer is *spongy bone*.

Directional and Sectional Terms for the Human Body

Correct terminology is essential. The terms shown in Table 2.3 must be understood and employed to find your way around the human body and communicate with others who are trying to do the same. Begin by talking with your laboratory partners. Communicate using the terms and names rather than simply pointing at structures. Directional terms are consistent for most of the body. The only areas requiring unique terms are the hands, feet, and mouth. The terms for the mouth will be covered in Chapter 11. Note that the hands have a palmar (or volar) surface, and the feet have a plantar (or volar) surface.

Table 2.3 Directional Terms for the Human Body

TERM	DEFINITION	OPPOSITE
ANTERIOR	toward the front of the body	posterior
AXILLARY	in the armpit area	
CAUDAL	in the area of the tail (the coccyx in human)	cranial
CRANIAL	in the area of the head or toward the head	caudal
DISTAL	away from the body (used with limbs)	proximal
DORSAL	toward the back of the body, the back of the hand, or the top of the foot	ventral, palmar, plantar, or volar
EXTERNAL	outside the body	internal
FRONTAL	toward the front	dorsal, occipital
INFERIOR	below	superior
INTERNAL	inside the body	external
LATERAL	toward the side	medial
MEDIAL	toward the midline	lateral
POSTERIOR	toward the back	anterior
PALMAR	toward the palm of the hand	dorsal
PLANTAR	toward the sole of the foot	dorsal
PROFUNDUS	deep inside the body	superficial
PROXIMAL	toward the body (used with limbs)	distal
RADIAL	toward the radius; the lateral side of the arm	ulnar
SUPERFICIAL	toward the surface of the body	profundus
SUPERIOR	above	inferior
ULNAR	toward the ulna; the medial side of the arm	radial
VENTRAL	toward the abdomen	dorsal
VOLAR	palm of the hand, sole of the foot	dorsal

JOINTS

Knowledge of joints is extremely important to forensic anthropologists or anyone trying to learn about the life of a person from the condition of their bones. Joints provide information about how the individual used his or her body. This goes beyond simple age, sex, and stature. Evidence of age shows up throughout the skeleton, but information about the life of the individual appears in specific areas—usually in the joints of the back, knees, shoulders, and elbows. The likelihood of trauma in specific areas is associated with types of activities. For instance, the dominant side of the body can be recognized in an active person by comparing the joints of the arms. Certain types of athletes may be recognized by the trauma to the joints of the knees or elbows. Manual laborers may be distinguished from office workers by changes in the joints of the shoulder, back, and wrist.

A joint is defined as an articulation or a place of union between two or more bones. It is normally more or less moveable. The word, **arthrosis**, is a less-used synonym for joint. It is worth remembering because it appears in many compound words referring to joints, for example, pseudarthrosis (false joint), or diarthrosis (synovial joint).

As with the rest of the body, it is important to recognize what is normal before trying to distinguish the unusual. Begin by analyzing each

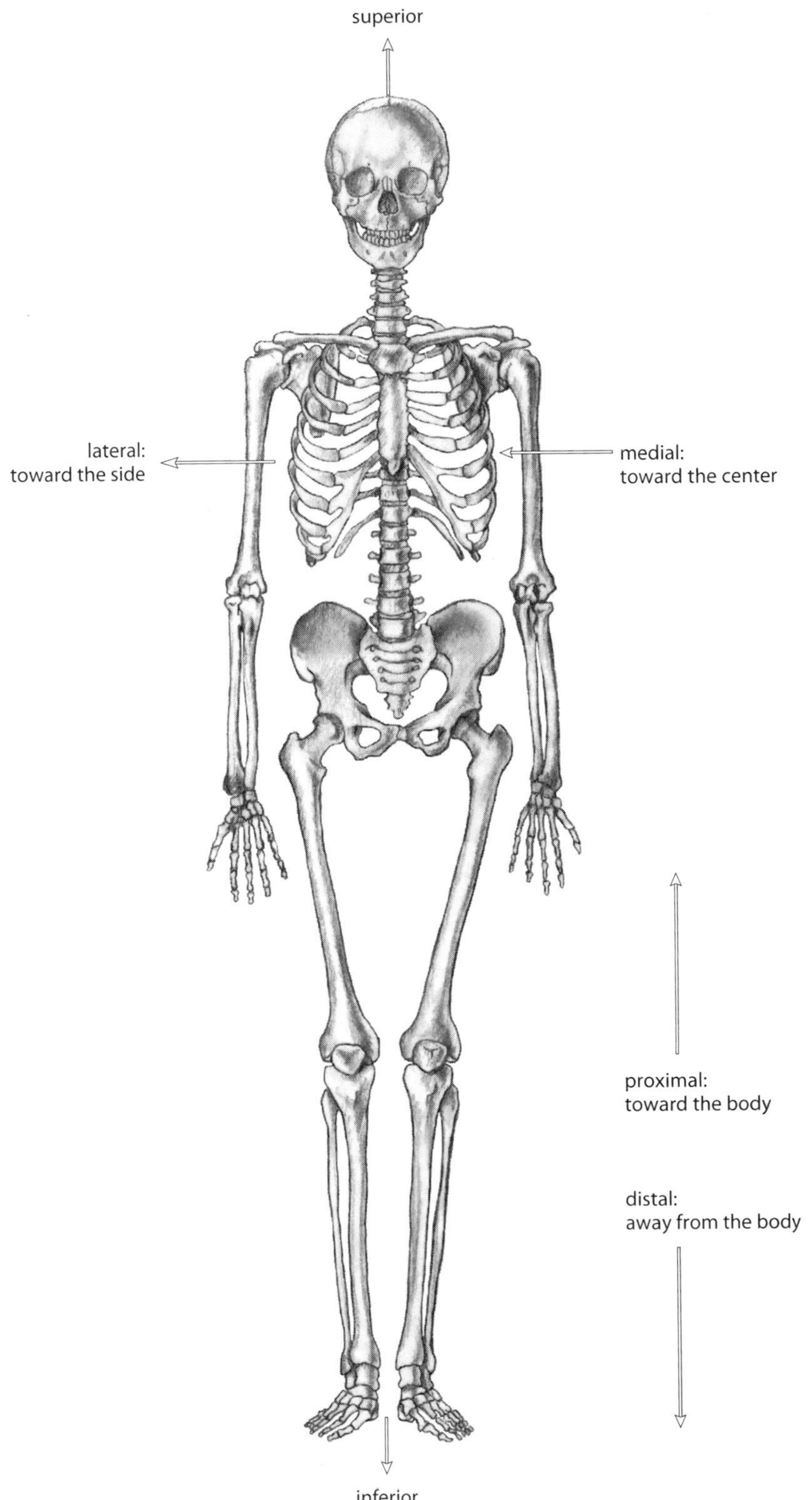

Figure 2.5a
Directional Terms, Frontal View

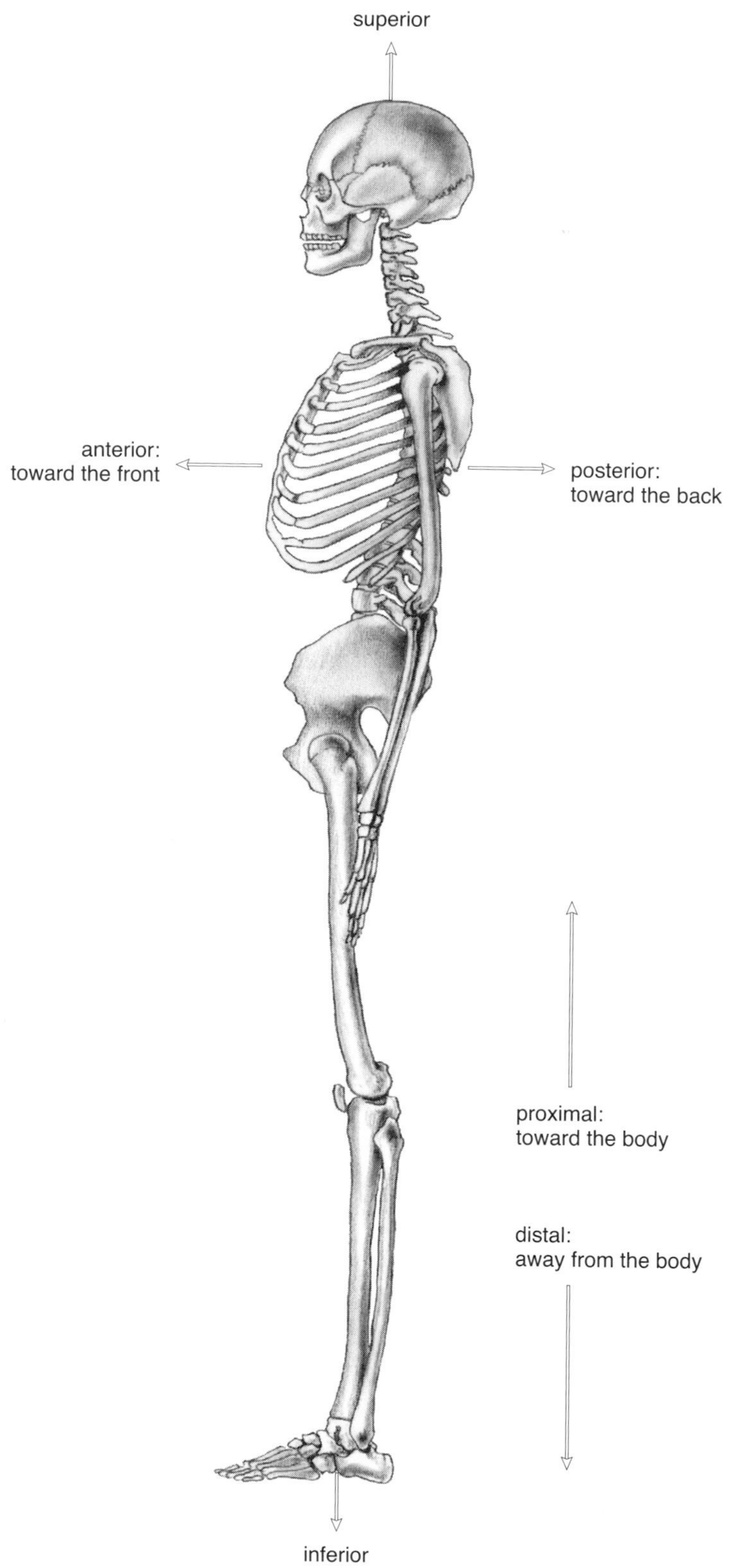

Figure 2.5b
Directional Terms, Lateral View

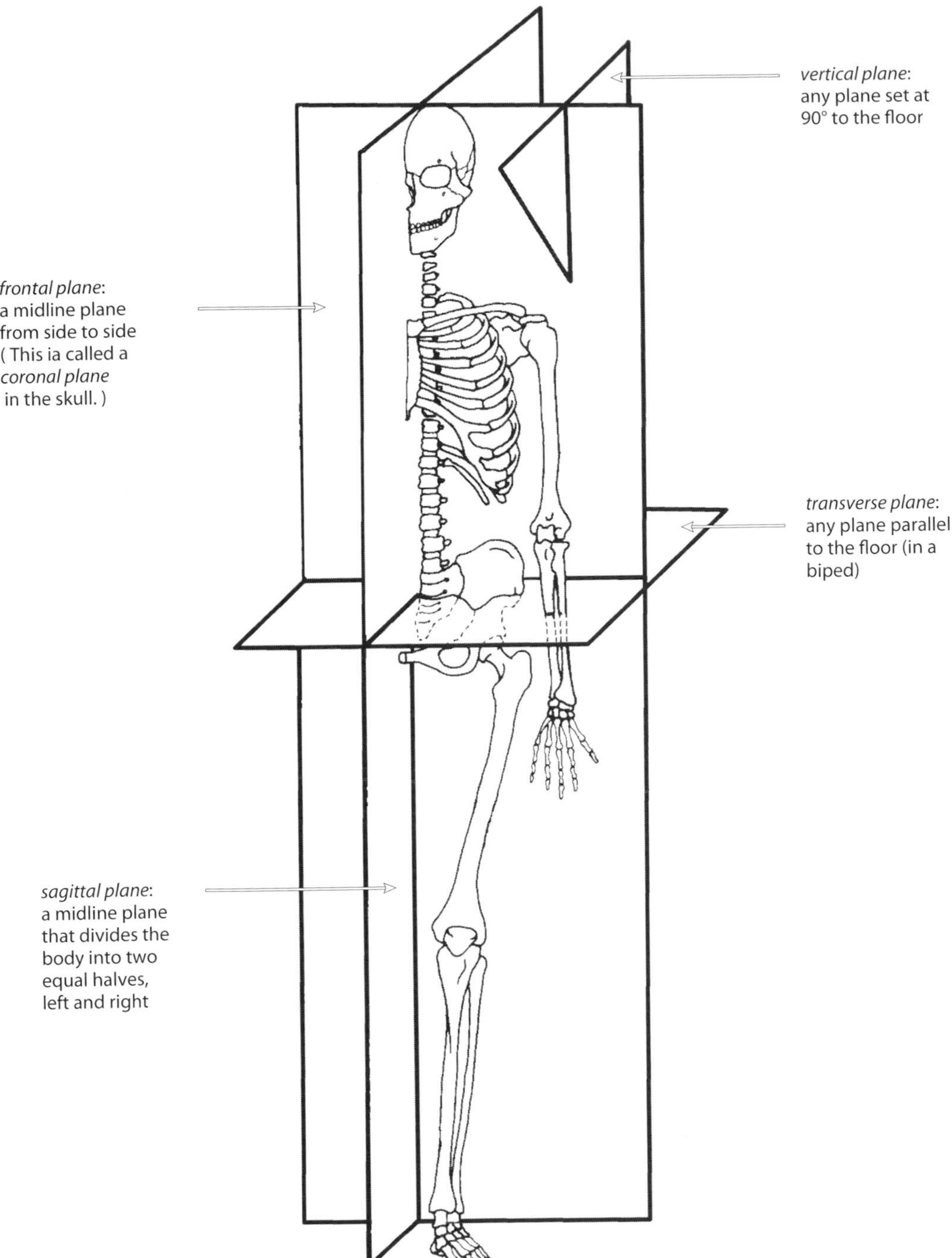
vertical plane:
any plane set at
90° to the floor
frontal plane:
a midline plane
from side to side
(This ia called a
coronal plane
in the skull.)
transverse plane:
any plane parallel
to the floor (in a
biped)
sagittal plane:
a midline plane
that divides the
body into two
equal halves,
left and right

Figure 2.5c
Planes or Sections of the Body

joint according to the requirements for both movement and stability at that particular area of the body. Consider the normal direction of movement and the perils of slipping into the wrong direction.

Structure, Function, and Movement of Joints

Joints are classified by structure, function, and direction of movement. The structural classification depends on the type of connective tissue holding the joint together and the presence or absence of an articular capsule and a fluid-filled (synovial) cavity. **Fibrous joints (synarthroses)** have no articular capsule and no synovial cavity. They are held tightly together by fibrous connective tissue and hence, have no significant movement. **Cartilaginous joints (amphiarthroses)** also have no articular capsule or synovial cavity. They are held together by fibrocartilage or hyaline cartilage and have very restricted movement. The majority of joints in the body are **synovial joints (diarthroses)**. They have a layered articular capsule with a synovial cavity and a wide range of movement.

FIBROUS JOINTS

Fibrous joints are virtually immovable. They allow for growth and some shock absorption, but in adulthood, some fibrous joints fuse without functional consequence.

Examples of fibrous joints, based on structure, are as follows:

1. **Sutures**—The union of two bones formed in membrane. The fibrous connective material is continuous with the periosteal membrane and is called a sutural ligament. These joints are tightly bound and the fibrous tissue is minimal (example: the cranium).
2. **Syndesmoses**—(Desmosis means "ligament" in Greek.) The opposing surfaces are united by fibrous connective tissue creating a strong, ligamentous union. The amount of movement depends on the length of the ligaments (examples: parts of the wrist and ankle, the tibia and fibula).
3. **Gomphoses**—A peg-in-socket articulation. Teeth are the only example of this type of articulation. The connection is formed by the fine fibers of the periodontal ligament. (See Chapter 11 for more about the periodontal ligament.)

CARTILAGINOUS JOINTS

Cartilaginous joints show very minimal movement. They allow for growth and shock absorption. Most cartilaginous joints occur at the growth plates (metaphyses) in juveniles. The cartilage holds the diaphysis and epiphysis together and allows for the proliferation of bone cells. A few cartilaginous joints remain into adulthood in areas of significant stress.

Examples of cartilaginous joints, based on structure, as as follows:

1. **Synchondroses**—Hyaline cartilage unites two adult bones or two centers of ossification in a juvenile bone (examples: ribs to sternum and epiphyseal plates).
2. **Symphyses**—Fibrocartilage unites the bones resulting in strength with a small amount of flexibility. Symphyses are useful for shock absorption (examples: intervertebral disks and pubic symphysis).

SYNOVIAL JOINTS

Synovial joints are the most common joints in the body. They are freely movable and are classified according to type of movement.

Synovial joints are much more structurally complex than other types of joints. The adjacent surfaces of the bones are covered with **articular cartilage (hyaline cartilage)**, and a **joint cavity** separates the bones. The joint cavity is a narrow space filled with lubricating **synovial fluid**. An articular capsule encloses the entire joint. It is built of two layers—an outer **fibrous layer** and an inner **synovial membrane** of loose connective tissue. (See Figure 2.6.) Some joint cavities also contain an **articular disc** or meniscus—a pad of fibrocartilage dividing the joint cavity into compartments and stabilizing the joint. (Articular discs are found in the jaw, knee, sternoclavicular, and radioulnar joints.)

Examples of synovial joints, based on movement, are as follows:

Synovial joints are distinguished by types of movement, and they are affected and modified by amount of use, specific activities, and trauma during the life of the individual.

1. **Uniaxial joints** allow angular movement (flexion and extension) or rotation around a long axis.
   - hinge—the elbow, ankle, and phalanges
   - pivot—the proximal radioulnar joint (the head of the radius pivots on the ulna) and the dens of the axis

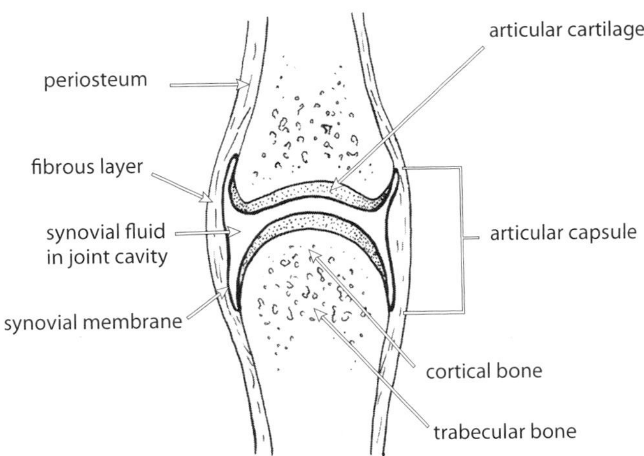

Figure 2.6
Structure of a Synovial Joint (metacarpophalangeal joint)

2. **Biaxial joints** allow limited rotation around a point. They allow abduction and adduction as well as flexion and extension, but not smooth, complete circular rotation.
   - saddle shaped—the first carpometacarpal joint (the thumb)
   - condyloid (egg shaped)—the occipital, distal radius, and proximal ends of proximal phalanges
3. **Multiaxial joints** allow complete rotation around a point.
   - ball and socket (universal joint)—the shoulder and hip
4. **Nonaxial joints** allow limited slipping in all directions.
   - plane or gliding (flat surfaces)—the intertarsal joints, intercarpal joints, claviculoscapular joints, and intervertebral joints.

Common Osteological Terms

Table 2.4 Terms for General Communication about Bone

Function	Name	Definition
ARTICULATION WITH OTHER BONES	articular surface	any joint surface normally covered by articular cartilage
	articular facet	a small, smooth area; a small joint surface normally covered by articular cartilage
ATTACHMENTS	attachment area	any area of tendon or ligament attachment (enthesis)
	attachment site	a circumscribed area of attachment
PROTECTION	fossa	any depression
PASSAGE	aperture	any hole

Table 2.5 Terms to Describe Form and Function of Bony Structures

Form	Function	Name	Definition	Example
PROJECTION	articulation with other bones	capitulum	a small, ball-shaped surface	capitulum of humerus (for articulation with the head of the radius)
		condyle	a rounded, hinge-like projection	mandibular condyle
		head	a rounded, smooth, articular eminence on long bone	femoral head
		process	any kind of projection, including articular	superior articular process of vertebrae
		trochlea	a pulley-like structure	trochlea of the distal humerus
	attachment or support	ala	wing-like structure	ala of sacrum
		apophysis	a process formed from a separate center of ossification	temporal apophysis (mastoid)
		conoid	cone-shaped process	conoid tubercle of clavicle
		coronoid	shaped like a crow's beak	coronoid process of ulna
		crest	sharp border or ridge	interosseous crest
		epicondyle	above a condyle	medial epiphysis
		line	narrow ridge, less prominent than a crest	temporal line
		promontory	a projecting part	sacral promontory
		ridge	an elongated, rough, narrow elevation	supraorbital ridge
		spine	a long, sharp prominence	scapular spine
		styloid	resembling a stylus; a long, thin, pointed projection	styloid process of the radius
		tubercle	small tuberosity	rib tubercle
		tuberosity	rounded eminence—larger than a tubercle	deltoid tuberosity
		trochanter	large prominence for rotator m. attachment	greater trochanter of the femur
DEPRESSION OR HOLE	articulation with another bone	cavity	hollow space or sinus	glenoid cavity
		fossa	an indentation in a structure	mandibular fossa
		notch	an indentation at the edge of a structure	ulnar notch
		pit	a small hole or pocket	costal pit on vertebral body
	passage for vessels, nerves and tendons; also enclosures	canal	a narrow passage or channel	auditory canal of the temporal bone
		fissure	a narrow slit-like opening	superior orbital fissure
		foramen	a hole	occipital foramen
		fovea	a pit or cup-like depression	fovea capitus in the head of the femur
		groove	a narrow depression extending for some distance	intertubercular groove of the humerus
		incisure	a notch or indentation at the edge of a structure	incisure mastoidea of the temporal bone
		meatus	a canal-like passageway	external auditory meatus
		sinus	hollow space or cavity	frontal sinus
		sulcus	a groove	preauricular sulcus

Chapter 3

The Skull and Hyoid

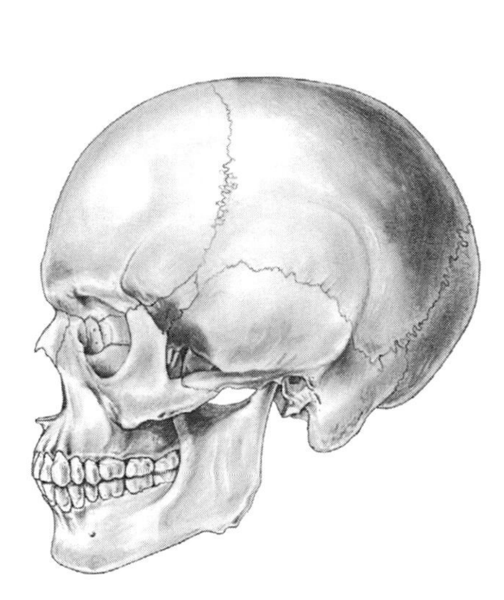

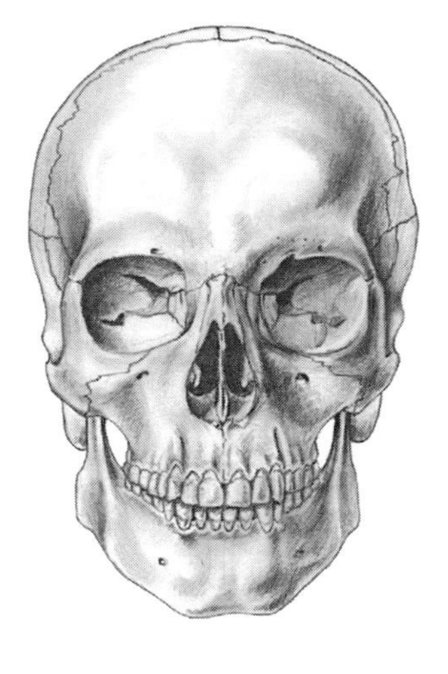

CHAPTER OUTLINE

INTRODUCTION

The skull is made up of twenty-two separate bones, not including the six ear ossicles and miscellaneous sutural bones. Eight of the skull bones are paired and six are unpaired. The skull as a whole is subdivided into regions. The **cranium** is the skull without the mandible; the **neurocranium** is the cranium without the face (the cranial vault); the **viscerocranium** is the bones of the face including the mandible. The neurocranium can be further divided into a **calvaria** (skull cap or calotte) and a **cranial base** (floor of the cranial vault).

The skull can be further divided into functional units such as, orbital bones, nasal bones, ear bones, basilar structures, and so on. As you examine each bone of the skull, think about its contribution to the overall architecture of the skull. Mentally place each bone in its proper location and consider its function. In order to better visualize relationships between individual skull bones, study disarticulated skulls or casts of natural bone. To gain familiarity with details of bone structure, study bone fragments out of context.

In spite of the number of bones contributing to the skull, mobile synovial joints are present only at the occipital condyles and the mandibular condyles. Most of the bones of the skull are connected by relatively immobile fibrous joints (sutures). Some of these joints become wholly immobile as sutures fuse with advancing age.

LEFT/RIGHT SIDING

All of the bones of the skull can be oriented according to anatomical position. The paired bones of the skull can be distinguished by side, and all of the bones, including the unpaired bones, can be oriented according to anterior/posterior, superior/inferior, and medial/lateral surfaces. Even the smallest bones such as nasal and lacrimal bones have sufficient distinguishing characteristics to separate left from right. The orientation of each skull bone is discussed separately, where necessary, in the following sections.

INDIVIDUALIZATION

The skull is so complex that there is tremendous opportunity for discovery of identifiable individual characters, such as unusual suture patterns, extra sutures, extra bones, unique sinus shapes, and extra foramina. Specific examples are found with the discussions of each cranial bone.

Definition Note

Key characters identify the bone.

Individual characters help to identify the person. Learn to recognize the difference by comparing as many individuals as possible.

ORIGIN AND GROWTH

Skull formation begins very early in fetal development (seven to eight weeks). Each skull bone grows from its own center(s) of ossification. The process begins in the base of the skull during the second fetal month and proceeds anteriorly. In general, the facial bones are the last to ossify. Details are included in the sections that discuss specific bones.

Sutural details are developmentally determined, not genetic. If antemortem radiographs are available, sutural detail may provide positive identification.

In the following pages, the skull is presented from six standard perspectives (Figures 3.1 to 3.6). Refer to these illustrations as you study the individual bones separately. Also compare the skull in the illustrations with as many sample skulls as possible. Look for patterns of similarity between skulls and details of difference.

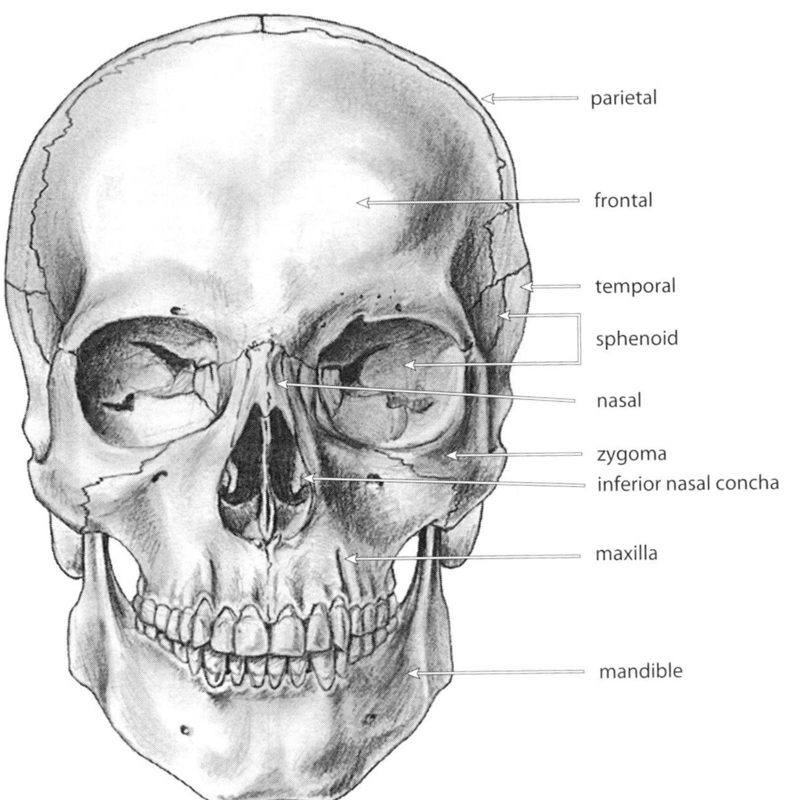

Figure 3.1
Skull, Frontal View, Major Bones and Sutures

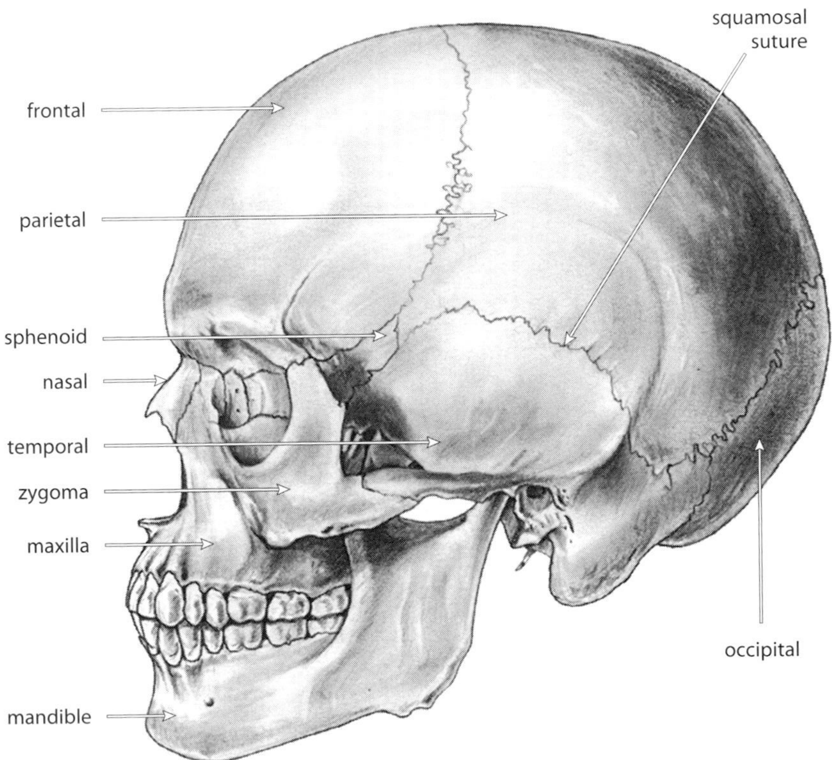

Figure 3.2
Skull, Lateral View, Major Bones and Sutures

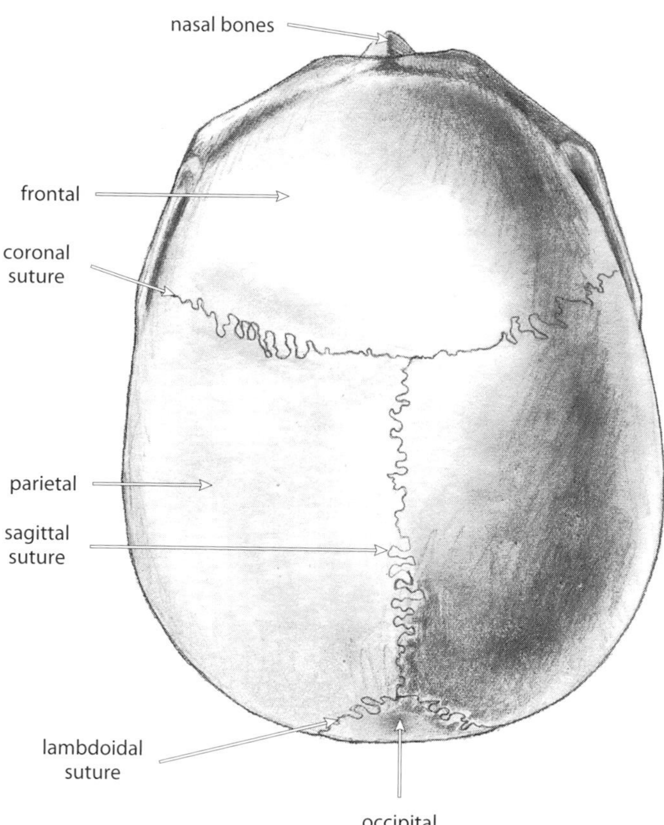

Figure 3.3
Cranium, Coronal View, Major Bones and Sutures

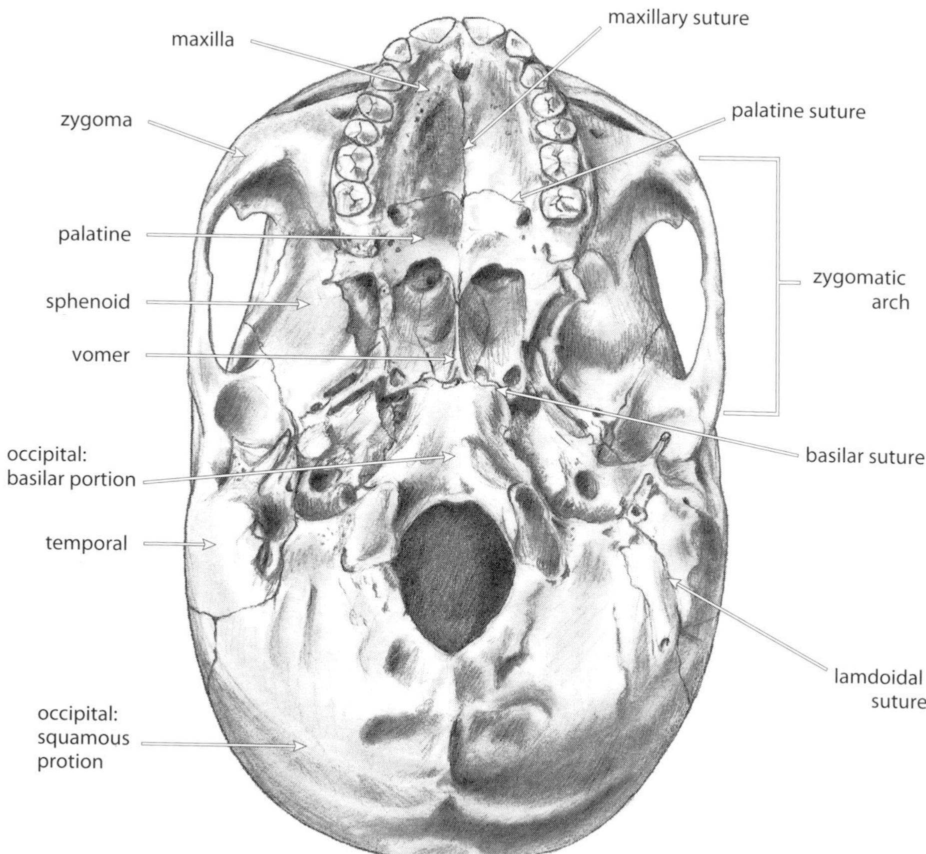

Figure 3.4
Cranium, Basilar View, Major Bones and Sutures

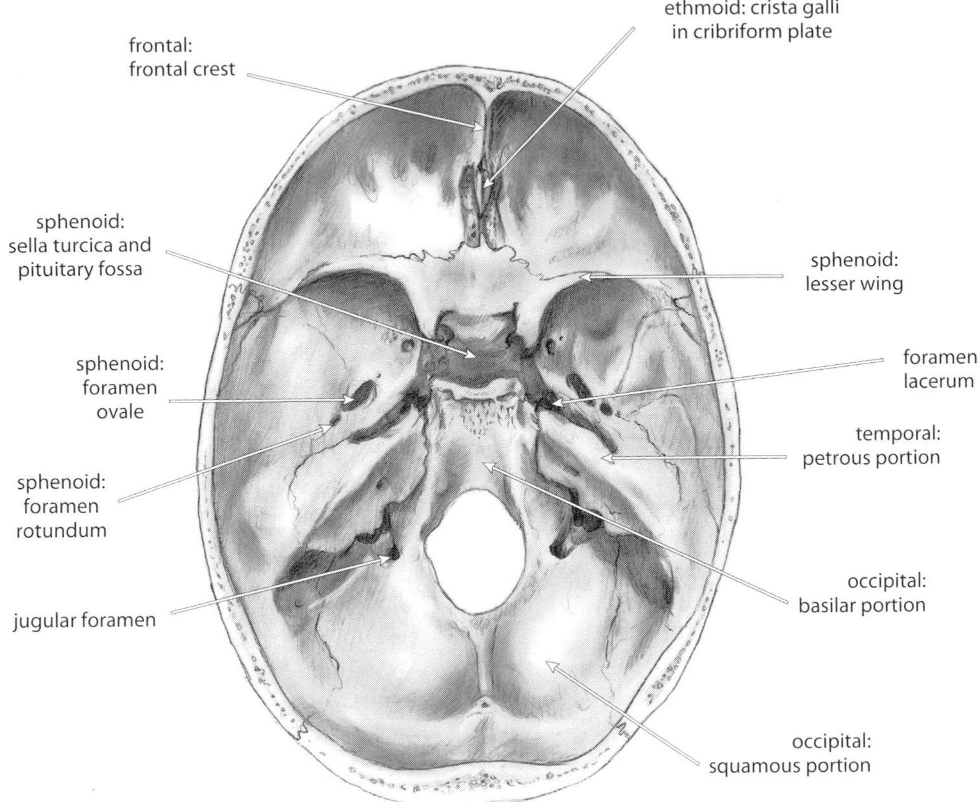

Figure 3.5
Cranial Base, Cerebral View

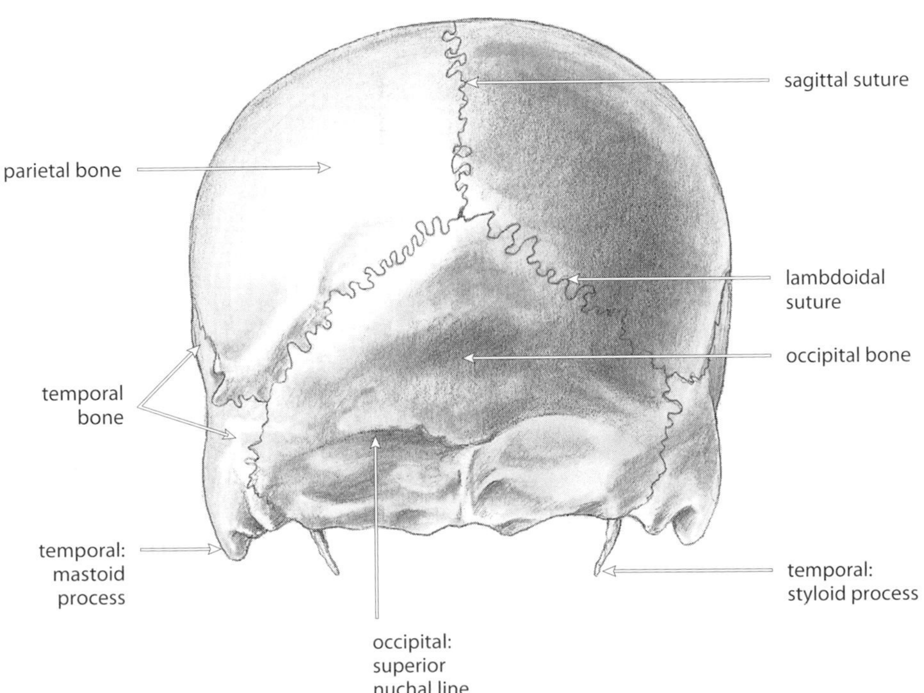

Figure 3.6
Cranium, Posterior View, Major Bones and Sutures

Frontal Bone

Description, Location, Articulation

The adult frontal bone is usually unpaired, forming the broad curvature of the forehead and the anterior wall of the neurocranium (brain case or cranial vault). It shapes the brow, the roof of the orbits, and the insertion for the bridge of the nose. Sinuses exist within the central portion of the supraorbital region.

The frontal articulates with the parietals, the greater wings of the sphenoid, the zygomas, the frontal processes of the maxillae, the nasals, lacrimals, and the cribriform plate of the ethmoid.

Individualization

Occasionally, the halves of the frontal bone fail to fuse, resulting in a retained midline suture and paired frontal bones in the adult. The midline frontal suture is called a **metopic suture**.

The **frontal sinuses** are located within the anterior portion of the frontal bone (the lower part of the forehead). Configuration of the frontal sinuses is developmentally determined and therefore highly individual, even between family members (Cameriere et al., 2008). Anteroposterior (A-P) skull radiographs provide good visualization of the frontal sinuses and an excellent method for positive identification. Unfortunately, an effective numerical method has not been devised; therefore frontal sinus patterns cannot be searched like fingerprints. Only superimposition pattern matching is effective (Besana & Tracy 2010).

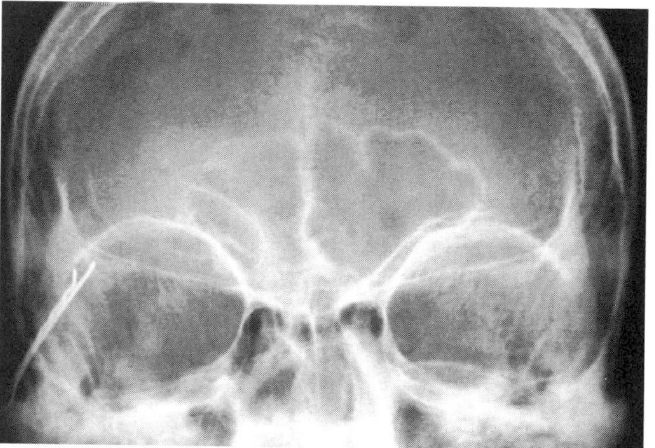

Figure 3.7
Frontal Sinus Radiograph

Origin and Growth

The frontal bone ossifies from two centers—right and left. At birth, the frontal bone is in two halves, separated by the metopic suture. The two halves of the frontal and the two parietal bones come together around the **anterior fontanelle**, the large "soft spot" at the top of the baby's head. The anterior fontanelle usually closes at one to two years of age. The two halves of the frontal usually fuse at 2 to 4 years of age.

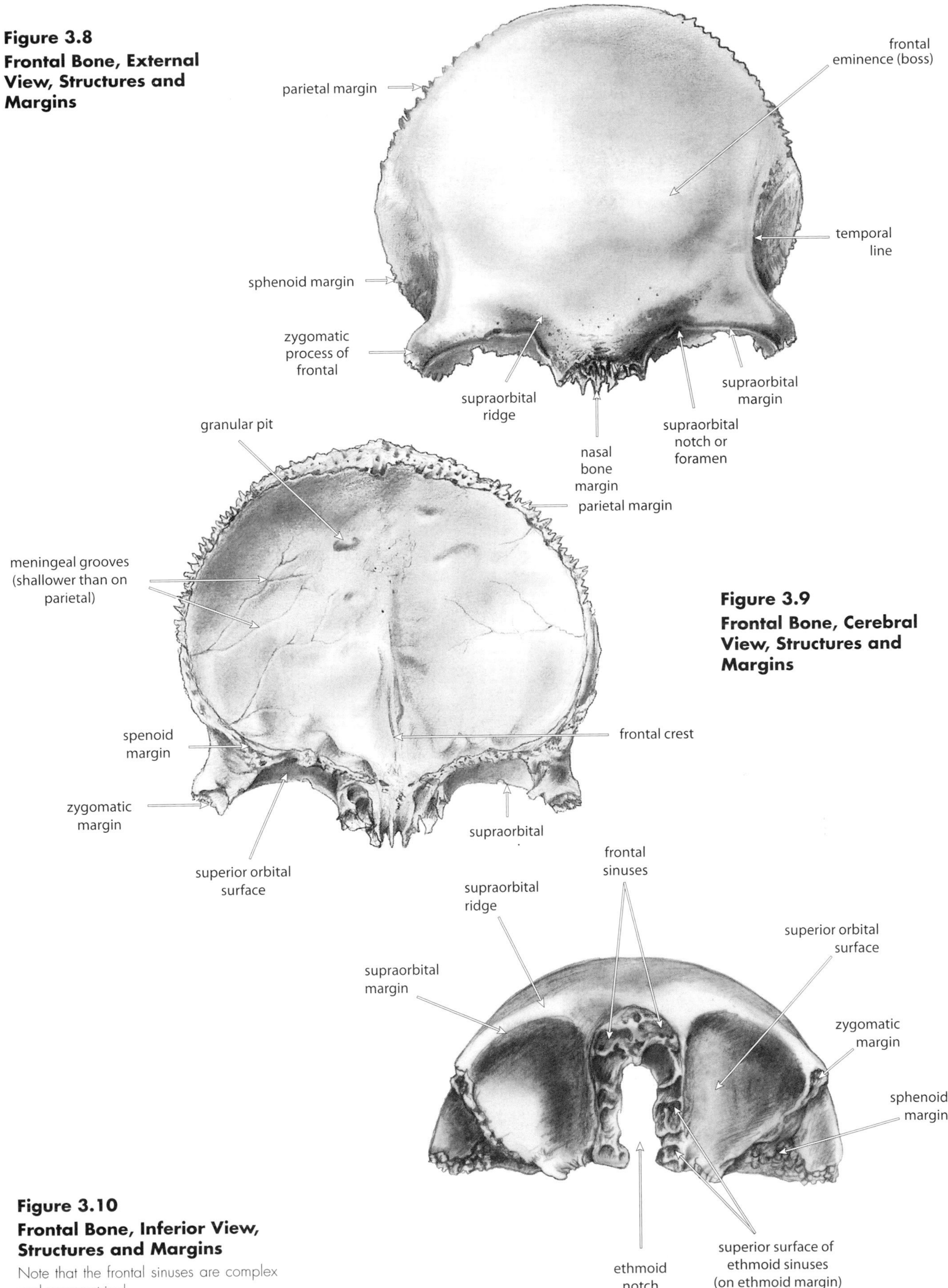

Figure 3.8
Frontal Bone, External View, Structures and Margins

Figure 3.9
Frontal Bone, Cerebral View, Structures and Margins

Figure 3.10
Frontal Bone, Inferior View, Structures and Margins
Note that the frontal sinuses are complex and asymmetrical.

PARIETAL BONES

DESCRIPTION, LOCATION, ARTICULATION

The parietal bones are paired bones forming the superolateral walls of the neurocranium. They are fairly rectangular in outline and are the least complicated of the cranial bones. The major distinguishing characteristics are the **parietal foramina** on either side of the sagittal suture, the **temporal lines** curving anteroposteriorly, and the strong vascular (meningeal) grooves on the inner surface. The **meningeal grooves** tend to spread outward from the anterior inferior margin.

Each parietal articulates with the other parietal medially (sagittal suture), the frontal anteriorly (coronal suture), and the occipital posteriorly (lambdoid suture). These three sutures are serrated and interdigitated. The lambdoid suture (occipital margin) is the most deeply serrated. The parietal articulates with the temporal at the lateral (temporal) margin, but the suture is different from the other three. The margin is sharp when compared to the others and it is plainly beveled externally. The squamous portion of the temporal bone overlays the parietal. The narrow articulation with the sphenoid varies in form and is mentioned in the section on individualization.

LEFT/RIGHT SIDING

The left parietal can be distinguished from the right by first locating the sharp, beveled, lateral margin for the temporal bone articulation. Then place the thinner end of the temporal margin anterior and the thicker end posterior. The near-90 degree angle (where the parietal meets the frontal) should be anterior and the more obtuse angle (where the parietal meets the occipital) should be posterior.

INDIVIDUALIZATION

Usually, the anterolateral angle of the parietal reaches out and articulates with the greater wing of the sphenoid, but occasionally the lateral area is reconfigured so that the frontal meets the temporal and the parietal is separated from the sphenoid. Another anomaly is the formation of a separate bone at the junction of the parietal, frontal, sphenoid, and temporal (the pterion region of the skull). It is called a **pterion ossicle**. Both anomalies aid identification from cranial radiographs.

ORIGIN AND GROWTH

At the time of birth, the parietal is quadrangular and recognized by the **parietal eminence**, a prominent thickening at the center of the thin, convex bone. In childhood, the parietal eminence slowly disappears as the bone takes on the relatively uniform thickness of the adult form. The parietal does not fuse with any other bones during development. Most fusion of cranial sutures results from the aging process rather than growth and development. Even in advanced age, the parietal does not normally fuse with the temporal bone.

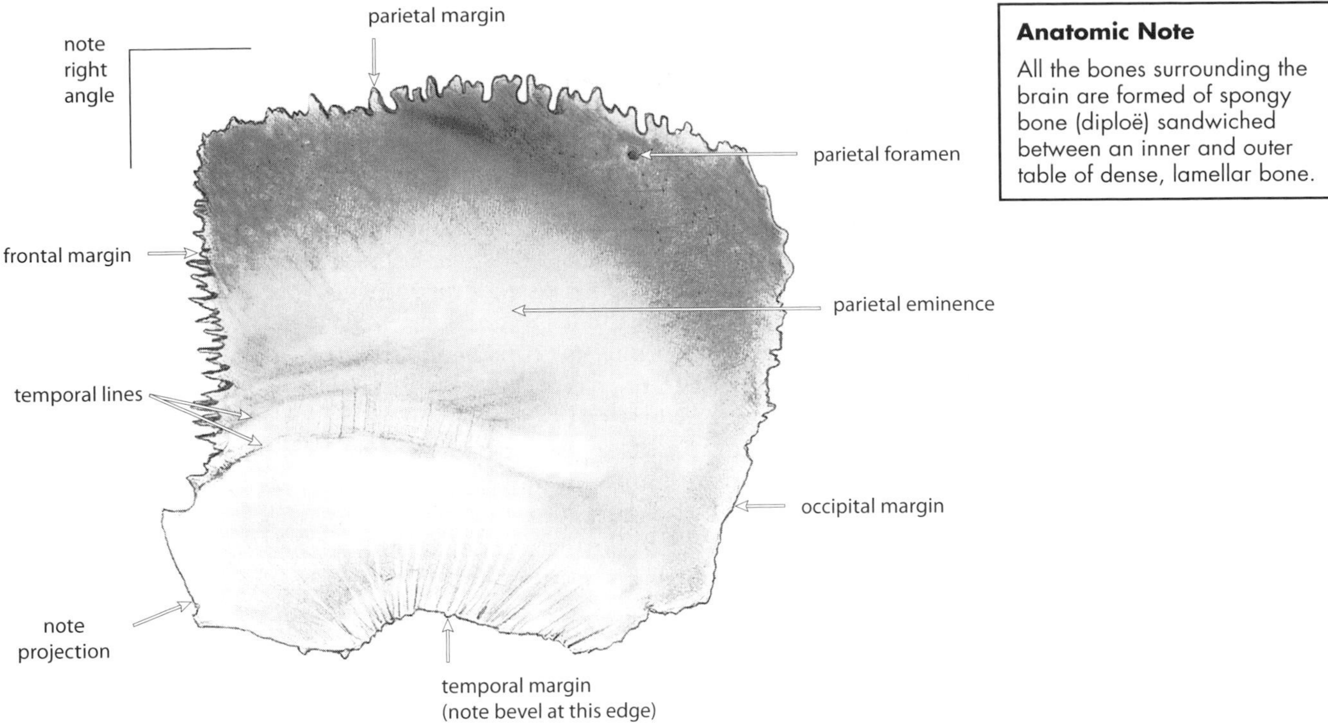

Figure 3.11
Left Parietal, External View, Structures and Margins

Anatomic Note

All the bones surrounding the brain are formed of spongy bone (diploë) sandwiched between an inner and outer table of dense, lamellar bone.

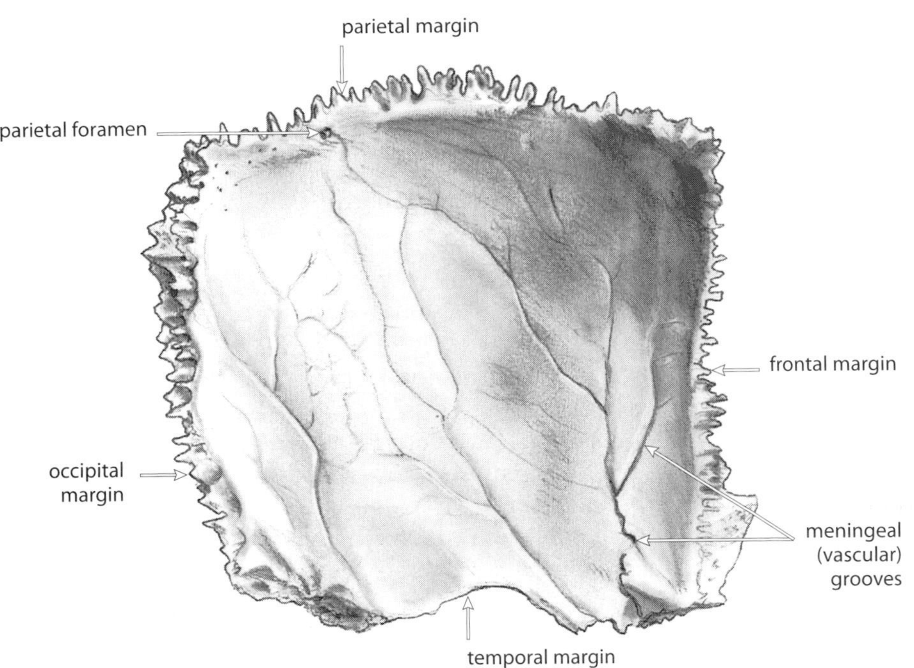

Figure 3.12
Left Parietal, Cerebral View, Structures and Margins

Occipital Bone

Description, Location, Articulation

The occipital bone is an unpaired bone forming the posterior-most wall and part of the base of the neurocranium. It is fairly ovoid in outline and is more concave and thicker than the other walls of the neurocranium. The adult bone is easily recognized by the **foramen magnum**, the opening through which the spinal cord reaches the brain.

The occipital consists of four parts: a **squamous portion**, two lateral portions, and a basilar portion (the **basioccipital**). The inner surface of the squamous portion is recognized by a cruciform buttress with a thick center, the **internal occipital protuberance**. The outer surface is ridged horizontally with a thick center, the **external occipital protuberance**.

The occipital articulates with the parietals superolaterally, the petrous portions of the temporals inferolaterally, and the sphenoid anteriorly (at the base of the brain). It essentially tucks under the brain and completes the bony encasement by attaching to posterior, lateral, and anterior cranial bones. The occipital also articulates with the atlas of the vertebral column at the moveable (synovial) joints of the occipital condyles.

Left/Right Siding

The occipital bone can be oriented by placing the foramen magnum inferior with the basilar portion anterior and the squamous portion extending posteriorly and superiorly.

Forensic Note
The unfused basilar portion of the occipital and the petrous portion of the temporal often persist in a grave when the rest of the immature skeleton has decomposed. It is important to be able to recognize the immature form.

Individualization

The squamous part of occipital is sometimes divided horizontally, isolating a larger-than-usual sutural bone, called an **Inca bone**. It is either triangular or quadrangular, as illustrated in Chapter 14, Figure 14.7, and is more common among Native Americans than any other group.

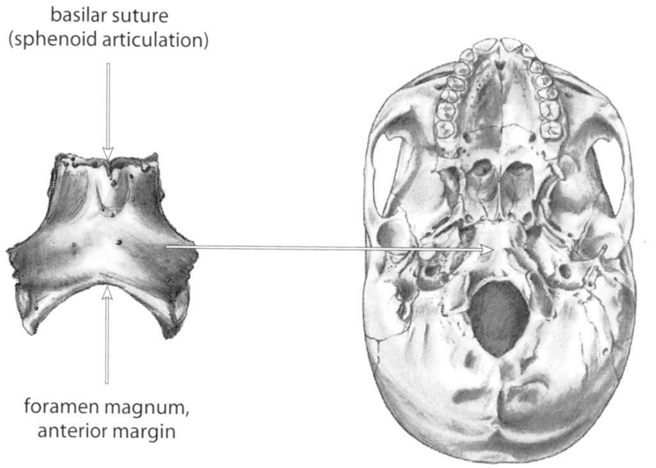

Origin and Growth

At the time of birth, the occipital is composed of four separate components—a **squamous portion**, two **lateral portions** (*pars lateralis*), and a basilar portion (the basioccipital or *pars basilaris*). The squamous portion is the large, flat, concave part that stretches up to meet the temporals and parietals. The lateral portions form the sides of the foramen magnum and bear the occipital condyles. The basilar portion, or basioccipital, forms the anterior-most margin of the foramen magnum. The lateral portions fuse with the squamous portion at one to three years. The basioccipital fuses to the larger part of the occipital at five to seven years. It does not fuse with the sphenoid until ages eleven to sixteen in females and thirteen to eighteen in males.

basilar suture (sphenoid articulation)

foramen magnum, anterior margin

Figure 3.13
Basioccipital, External View, Juvenile (3 years old) with Adult Comparison

The juvenile basioccipital is illustrated in Figure 3.15 because it tends to survive burial conditions and it is easy to recognize in the remains of an immature skeleton.

Sex Note

The external occipital protuberance is usually more pronounced in male skulls. The superior and inferior nuchal lines are also clearer. Both of these characteristics are consistent with larger neck and back musculature.

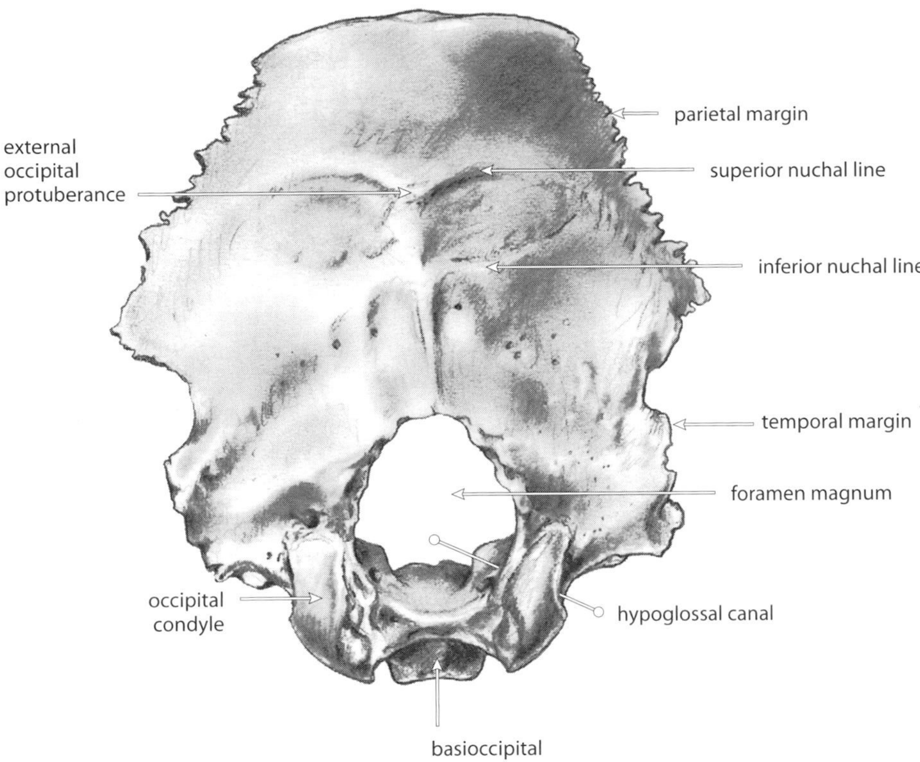

Figure 3.14
Occipital External View, Structures and Margins

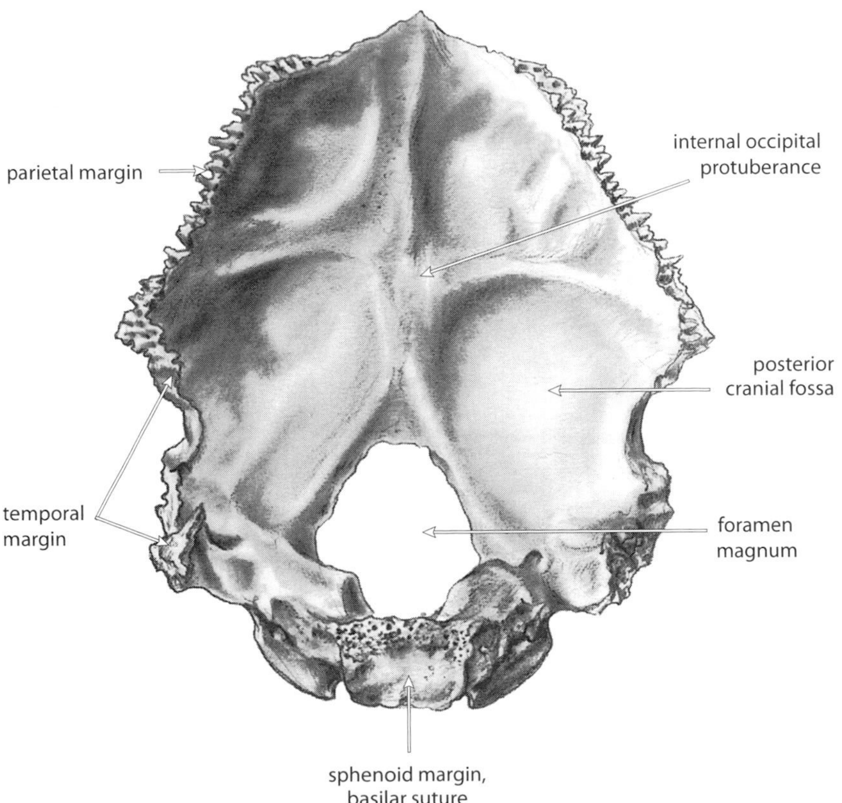

Figure 3.15
Occipital, Cerebral View, Structures and Margins

Temporal Bones

Description, Location, Articulation

The temporal bones are paired bones forming the lateral-most walls and part of the base of the neurocranium. The temporal bone is more complicated than the frontal, parietal, or occipital bone(s) because it houses the **auditory ossicles** (ear bones) and the **auditory canal**. Each temporal bone articulates with the occipital, parietal, zygoma, and sphenoid. It also articulates with the mandible at the **temporomandibular joint**.

Each temporal bone is composed of several major parts—the squamous portion, the mastoid process, the petrous portion, the styloid process, and the zygomatic process. These parts can all be described in relation to the **external auditory meatus**, the outer opening of the ear canal.

- The **squamous portion** is the thin wall that extends upward and outward from the ear. It articulates with the parietal, the greater wing of the sphenoid, and the squamous part of the occipital.
- The **mastoid process** is the large conical projection directly posterior to the ear. It is between the external auditory meatus and the occipital.
- The **styloid process** is the thin process that extends downward from the inferior margin of the external auditory meatus. It points slightly anteriorly and medially. The styloid process is fragile and unprotected in skeletal remains, so it frequently breaks off.
- The **petrous portion** extends anteriorly and medially between the lateral portions of the occipital and the sphenoid. It houses the **auditory canal**. (See Figures 3.4 and 3.5.)
- The **zygomatic process** of the temporal extends anteriorly from the external auditory meatus. It articulates with the temporal process of the zygoma and forms the **zygomatic arch**. The temporomandibular joint lies inferior to the base of the zygomatic process, immediately anterior to the external auditory meatus.

Left/Right Siding

Left and right temporal bones can be separated and recognized by pointing the petrous portion medially and the zygomatic process anteriorly and by remembering that the mastoid process is posterior to the external auditory meatus.

Individualization

The temporal is usually separated from the frontal bone by the juncture of the greater wing of the sphenoid and the parietal. Occasionally, the sutural pattern is altered and the temporal shares a suture with the frontal. This configuration may be useful in the identification process if radiographs are available.

The mastoid process tends to be larger in males than females. The mastoid provides the attachment site for one of the major muscles of the neck (the sternocleidomastoid). The sexual difference in mastoid process size is consistent with the enlarged neck musculature of a mature male. It can also be an indication of the overall robustness of the person.

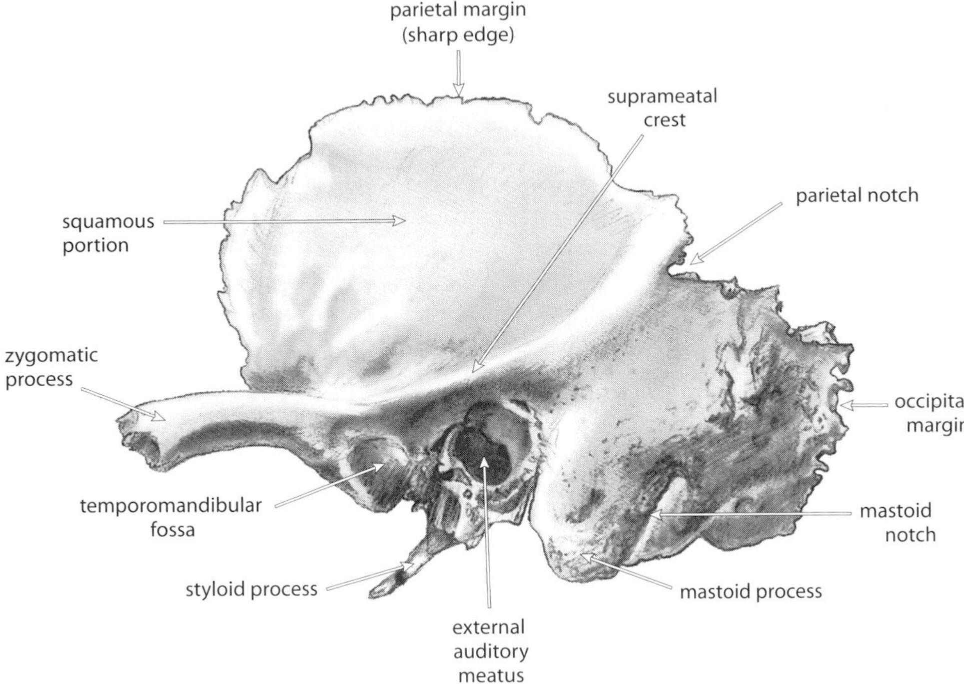

Figure 3.16
Left Temporal, External View, Structures and Margins

> **Sex Note**
> A bony ridge, the **suprameatal crest**, forms at the root of the zygomatic process. Usually, the crest ends at the external auditory meatus in females but extends beyond the external auditory meatus in males.

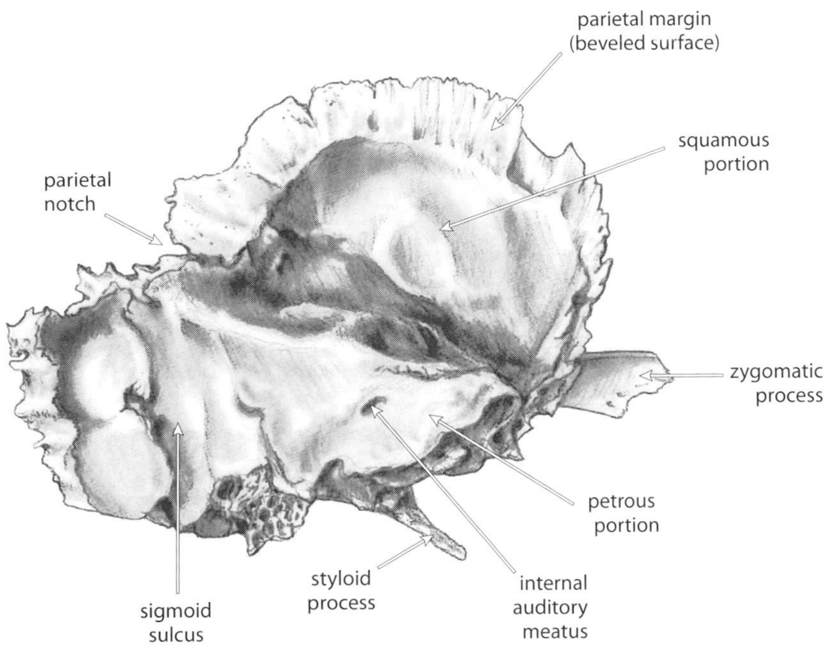

Figure 3.17
Left Temporal, Cerebral View, Structures and Margins

Origin and Growth

The temporal is formed from three parts—the petrous portion, the squamosal portion, and the tympanic ring (the fetal bone that provides the structural framework for the external auditory meatus). By the time of birth, the tympanic ring has fused with the squamous portion and two major parts are present—the petromastoid and the squamotympanic. During the first year, the two parts fuse, and by age five, the architecture of the ear is complete. The mastoid process continues to enlarge through childhood, and the male mastoid is not fully developed until adulthood.

Zygomatic Bones (Zygomas or Malars)

> **Anatomic Note**
>
> The **temporal process** of the zygoma meets the **zygomatic process** of the temporal to form the **zygomatic arch**. In other words, the zygomatic arch is formed from parts of *two* different bones.

Description, Location, Articulation

The zygomatic bones are paired facial bones. They complete the lateral margin and wall of the orbit and support the curvature of the cheek. Each zygomatic bone is characterized by three processes—the **maxillary process**, **frontal process**, and **temporal process**. The processes are named for the connecting bone, just as roads leaving a city are often named for the city they head toward. For example, the frontal process of the zygoma extends toward the frontal bone and connects with the zygomatic process of the frontal.

The zygoma articulates with the maxilla, the greater wing of the sphenoid, and the zygomatic processes of both the temporal bone and the frontal bone.

Left/Right Siding

The zygomatic bone can be sided by recognizing the smoothly curved orbital margin and placing it anteromedially. On the correct side, the frontal process (with orbital margin) points superiorly and the temporal process (without orbital margin) points posteriorly.

Individualization

The zygomaxillary suture pattern is loosely characteristic of the racial group. It may also provide an individual characteristic if antemortem radiographs are available. Occasionally a zygoma is divided into two or three separate bones. This is called bipartite or tripartite zygoma or an *os japonicum* and is more common in Asian populations. There may also be multiple zygomaticofacial foramina.

Origin and Growth

The zygomatic bone develops from a single center of ossification. At the time of birth, the bone is a thin, Y-shaped bone with a notched inferior border and tapered processes. By two to three years of age, the adult proportions are recognizable and the ends of the processes develop a serrated sutural form.

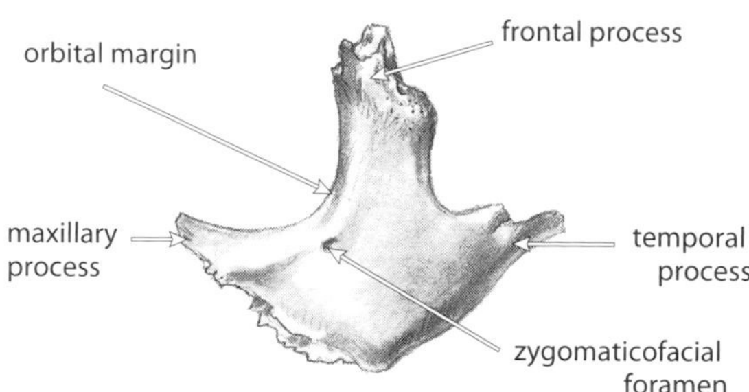

Figure 3.18
Left Zygoma, External View, Structures and Margins
Note that each process extends toward the bone that it is named for.

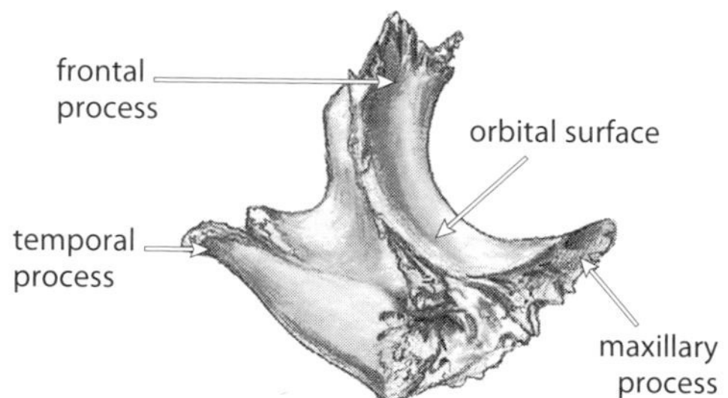

Figure 3.19
Left Zygoma, Internal View, Structures and Margins

Sphenoid

Description, Location, Articulation

The sphenoid is an unpaired, butterfly-shaped bone. It lies between the brain and the bones of the face and forms the anterior wall of the neurocranium and the posterior wall of the orbits. In this central position, the sphenoid articulates with most of the bones of the skull—the occipital, temporal (both petrous and squamous portions), parietals, frontal, zygomatics, ethmoid, palatines, and vomer.

> **Anatomic Note**
>
> Visualize the sphenoid by mentally breaking off the face—the whole front of the sphenoid is exposed.

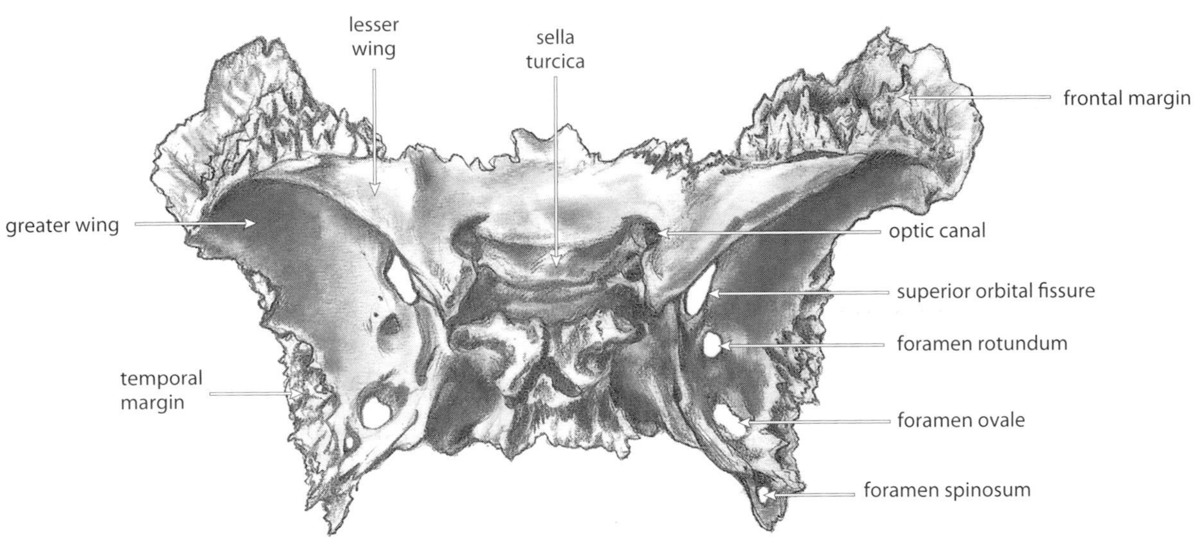

Figure 3.20
Sphenoid, Superior View, Structures and Margins

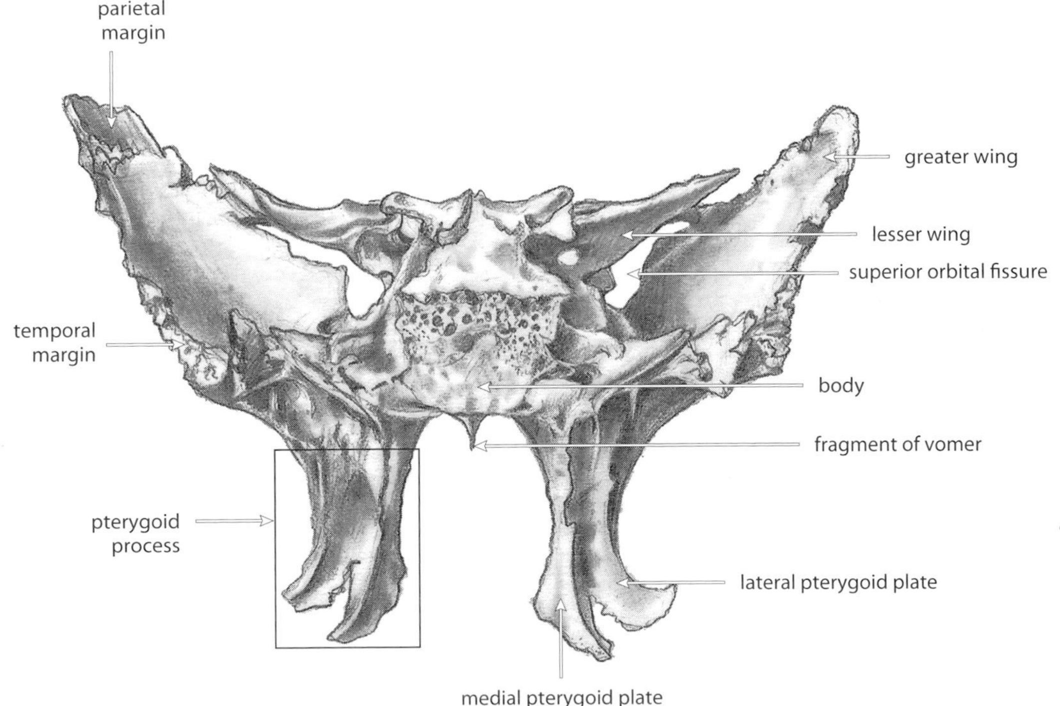

Figure 3.21
Sphenoid, Posterior View, Structures and Margins

The sphenoid is composed of several major parts—the body, lesser wings, greater wings, medial pterygoid plates, and lateral pterygoid plates. (The wings are also called "ala.")

- The **body** is a central core-like structure that articulates with the basilar part of the occipital posteriorly and the ethmoid anteriorly.
- The **lesser wings** extend out horizontally from the superior surface of the body.
- The **greater wings** extend out laterally and superiorly from the body. They can be seen on the outer and inner lateral walls of the skull, between the squamous temporal and the frontal.
- The **pterygoid plates** (both lateral and medial) extend inferiorly from the lateral surfaces of body.

Left/Right Siding

The sphenoid can be oriented by placing the greater wings superior and the pterygoid process inferior. The body of the sphenoid should be posterior and the face of the sphenooccipital synchondrosis should be visible.

Origin and Growth

The sphenoid ossifies from a large number of centers. At the time of birth, the centers have fused into three parts—the body fuses with the lesser wings, and the two separate greater wings with attached pterygoid plates. During the first year, the greater wings fuse with the body.

Maxillae

Description, Location, Articulation

The maxillae are paired facial bones. They make up a large part of the middle/lower face and contribute to the lateral surfaces of the nose, the nasal cavity, the roof of the oral cavity, the orbital floors, and the inferior orbital margins. Two major processes extend from the body of each maxilla—the **frontal process** articulates with the frontal bone and the **zygomatic process** articulates with the zygoma. All of the upper teeth are supported by the **alveolar ridges** of the maxillae. (Also called alveolar processes.) Much of the lateral portion of each maxilla encloses the large **nasal sinus**.

The maxillae articulate with the zygomatic bones, frontal, nasals, lacrimals, nasal conchae, ethmoid, and palatine bones.

Left/Right Siding

The left maxilla can be distinguished from the right by orienting the nasal cavity medial, the alveolar process anterolateral, and the palate inferior. The frontal process should be superior.

Individualization

The maxillae are essential to the overall appearance of the face. Both racial identification and individual identification may be based on maxillary shape. The maxillae determine the shape of the dental arch, the width of the nasal aperture, the projection of the nose, and the prominence of the mouth. See Chapter 14 for information on racial differences in the skull.

Origin and Growth

At the time of birth, the maxilla is very small in relation to the overall size of the skull, but all of the major parts are present. The most prominent part is the alveolar ridge, filled by **dental crypts** for the development of the deciduous teeth and the first permanent molar. The crowns of the deciduous teeth are present and the first adult molar (M_1) has begun to calcify. The maxillary bone is so fragile that usually only the tooth buds are recovered from the facial area of an infant burial.

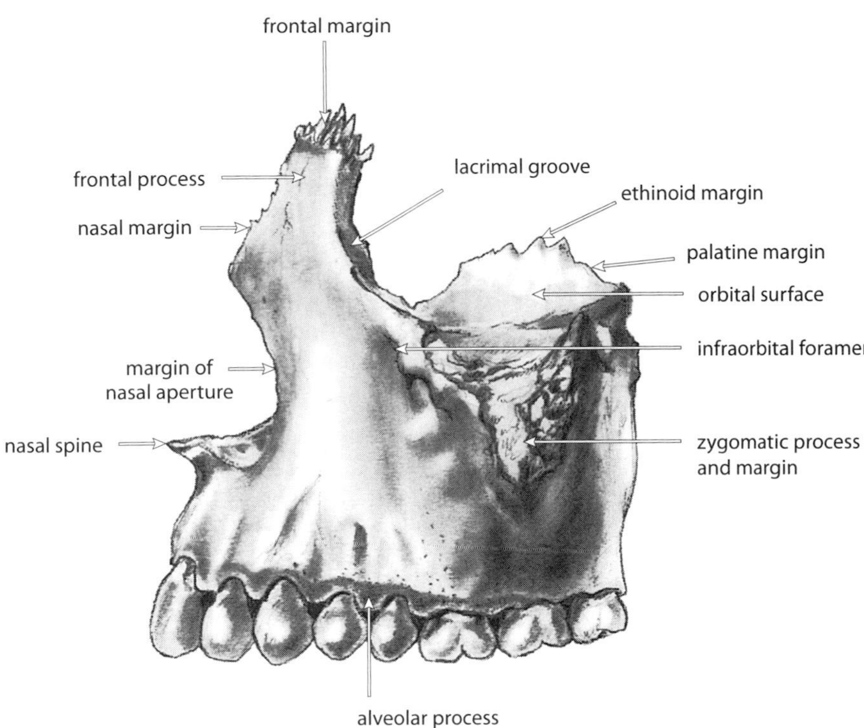

Figure 3.22
Left Maxilla, Lateral View, Structures and Margins

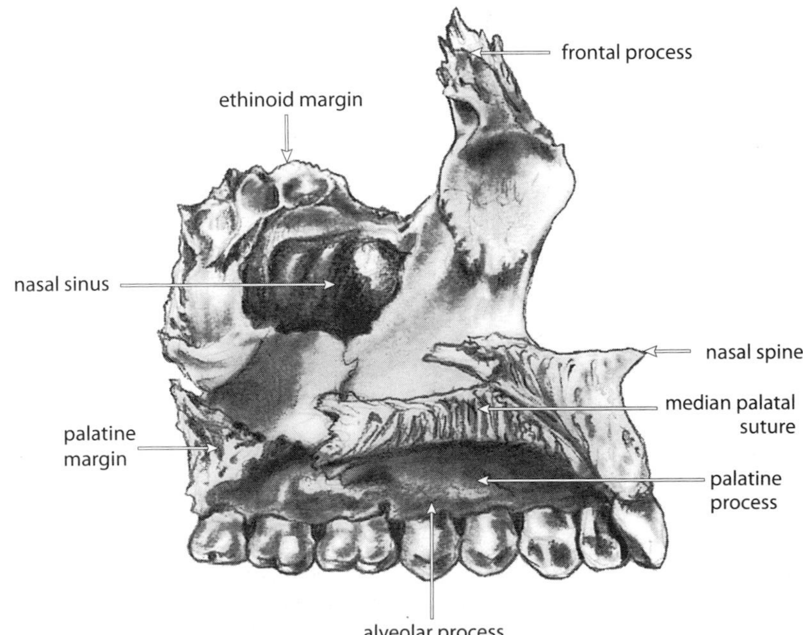

Figure 3.23
Left Maxilla, Medial View, Structures and Margins

Palatine Bones

Description, Location, Articulation

The palatine bones are paired facial bones. They are small, thin L-shaped bones located immediately posterior to the maxilla and anterior to the pterygoid process of the sphenoid. The palatine is easy to overlook, but it contributes to many internal facial structures, including the oral cavity, the nasal passage and the eye orbit.

The **horizontal plate** of the palatine bone articulates with the palatine process of the maxillae, forming the posterior part of the hard palate (the roof of the mouth). The **perpendicular plate** is posterior and slightly lateral to the inferior nasal concha and forms part of the lateral wall of the nose. The perpendicular plate ends in two processes. The lateral **orbital process** forms a small part of the floor of the orbit and the inferior orbital fissure. The medial **sphenoidal process** articulates with the medial pterygoid plate of the sphenoid and the vomer. Another short process, the **pyramidal process** extends posteriolaterally from the angle of the two palatine plates and sits between the inferior tips of the two pterygoid plates.

Left/Right Siding

The left palatine can be distinguished from the right by orienting the longer perpendicular plate superolateral and the short horizontal plate inferomedial. In the correct orientation, the pyramidal process extends posteriolaterally.

Individualization

The palatine bones contribute to the shape of the **transverse palatine suture** which is considered to be useful in racial identification. See Chapter 14, Figures 14.4, 14.5, and 14.6. The most common anomaly is lack of fusion of the two horizontal plates, resulting in a cleft palate.

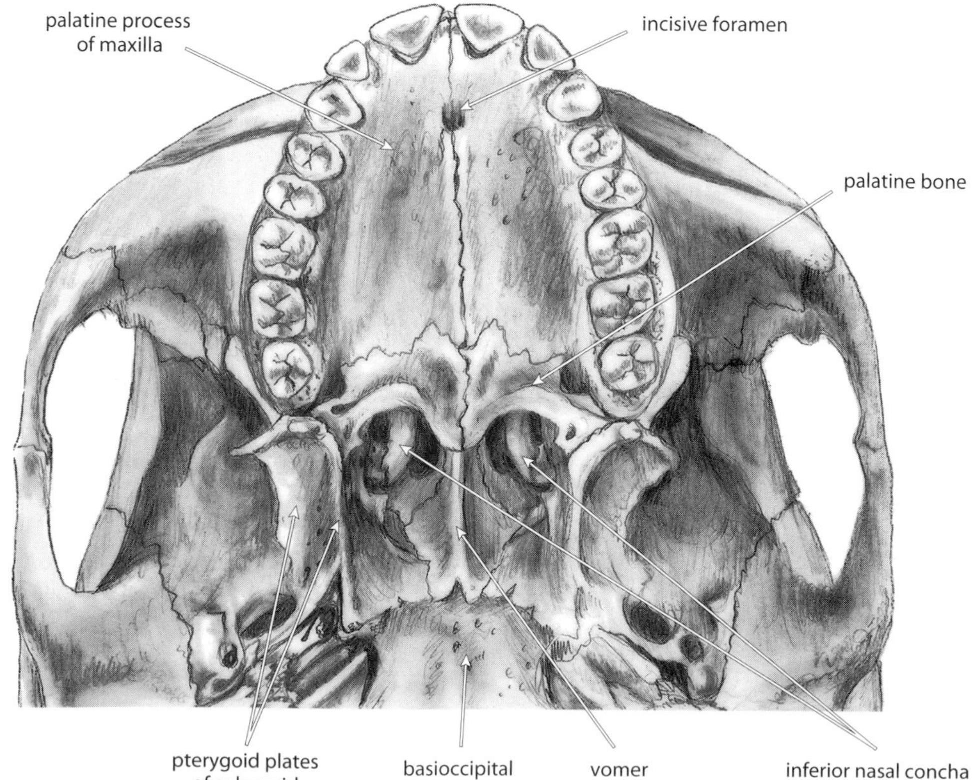

Figure 3.24
Maxilla, Palatal View (with Associated Bones)

Origin and Growth

Each palatine grows from two membranous centers of ossification. The palatine bone is recognizable in isolation at the time of birth.

Vomer

Description, Location, Articulation

The vomer is a singular (unpaired) facial bone located in the midline of the nasal cavity. It is thin and plow-shaped. (The word *vomer* means "plowshare" in Latin.) It forms the posterior part of the nasal septum together with the perpendicular plate of the ethmoid. (See Figure 3.25.)

The vomer attaches firmly to the body of the sphenoid between the pterygoid plates. (See Figure 3.24.) Other, more delicate, articulations are with the perpendicular plate of the ethmoid, the palatine bones, and the maxilla. (See Figure 3.27.)

Left/Right Siding

The vomer can be oriented by placing the flat, thicker end superior and posterior, and the thin pointed end anterior and inferior.

Individualization

Variations in the vomer can contribute to a deviated septum. A perforated septum may be the result of incomplete ossification, trauma or chronic inflammation in the vomer.

Origin and Growth

The vomer develops primarily in membrane from two centers of ossification, but also has a cartilaginous component to its growth. It is ossified by the time of birth.

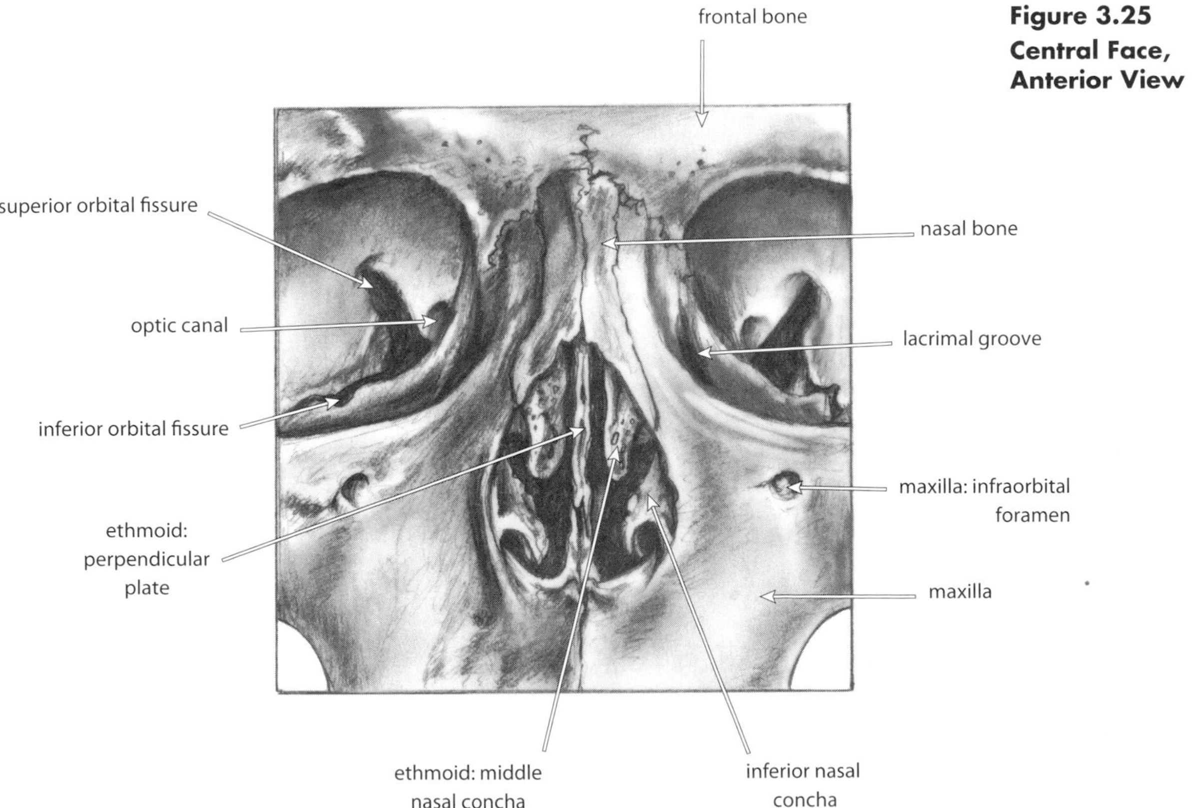

Figure 3.25 Central Face, Anterior View

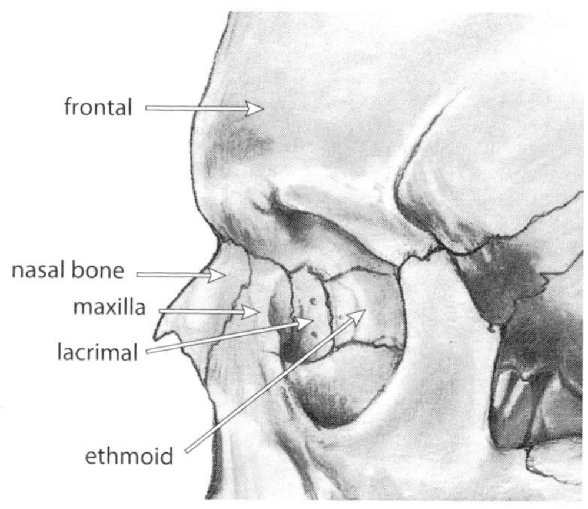

Figure 3.26
Medial Orbital Wall, Lateral View
Note the cribriform plate and crista galli are best seen from a superior (cerebral) view such as in Figure 3.5.

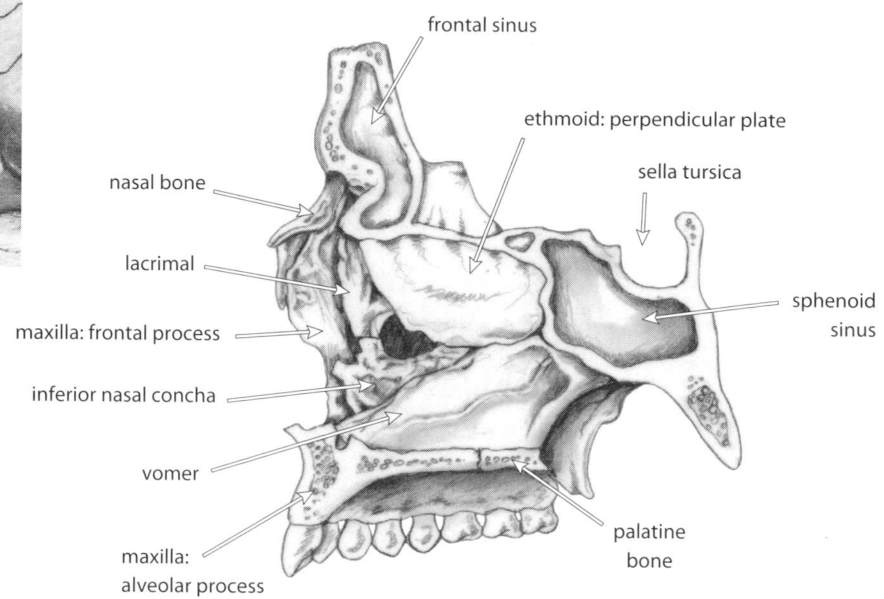

Figure 3.27
Nasal Septum (Ethmoid and Vomer), Sagittal View

Caution Note

Never pick up a cranium by the orbits.

All of the bones of the medial orbital wall are thin and fragile. They are easily broken by careless handling.

Ethmoid

Description, Location, Articulation

The ethmoid is a singular (unpaired) facial bone located between the orbits of the eyes and within the ethmoid notch of the frontal bone. When removed intact, it is has the (loose) appearance of a rectangular box with dangling and curling pieces of paper attached inside. The top is full of tiny holes and the bottom is not there. In reality, the ethmoid is composed of a horizontal cribriform plate, a midline perpendicular plate, and two lateral labyrinths.

The **cribriform plate** is pierced with foramina through which pass the vessels and nerves associated with the sense of smell.

The superior portion of the **perpendicular plate** forms the **crista galli** which emerges from the *anterior portion* of the cribriform plate into the neurocranium. The inferior portion of the perpendicular plate articulates with the vomer to form the bony part of the **nasal septum**.

The **labyrinths** are composed of the **medial orbital plates**, the **superior nasal conchae**, and the **middle nasal concha**. The labyrinths also contain the **ethmoidal cells**.

The ethmoid articulates anteriorly with the lacrimals, superiorly with the frontal, and inferiorly with the maxilla and palatine. The perpendicular plate articulates medially with the vomer.

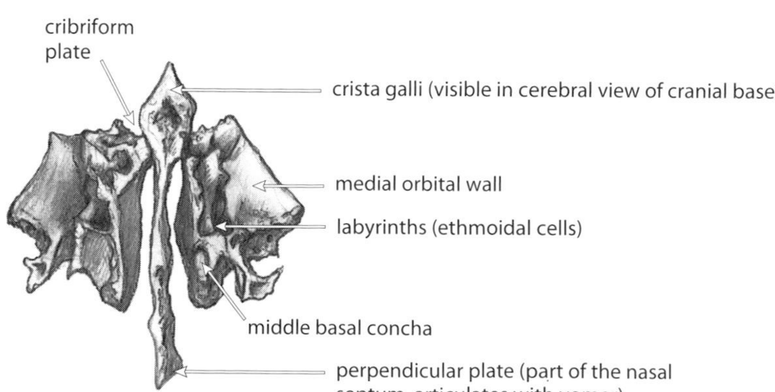

Figure 3.28
Ethmoid, Frontal View

Left/Right Siding

The ethmoid can be oriented by locating the flat, smooth medial orbital plates and orienting them laterally. Then orient the perpendicular plate so that the crista galli are superior and anterior. (The crista galli is named for a cock's comb and, like the comb, it juts upward from above the "beak.")

Individualization

The cribriform plate of the ethmoid has been shown to change with age (Kalmey et al., 1998). The foramina decrease in size and may contribute to the lessening of olfactory function in older persons.

Anomalies in the position of the perpendicular plate may contribute to a deviated septum. The septum may also become perforated as a result of chronic infection and various forms of trauma including cocaine abuse.

Origin and Growth

The ethmoid forms in membrane from several centers of ossification. At the time of birth, only the labyrinths are ossified. The cribriform and perpendicular plates are cartilaginous.

Inferior Nasal Conchae

Description, Location, Articulation

The inferior nasal conchae are paired facial bones inferior to the ethmoid labyrinth and attached to the lateral walls of the nasal cavity. They can be viewed from both the anterior or posterior openings to the nasal cavity.

The inferior nasal conchae are larger but similar in appearance to the superior and middle nasal conchae which are part of the labyrinth of the ethmoid bone. The bone is thin, slightly curled, and wrinkled-looking. (The conchae are covered with mucous membrane in life.)

Anteriorly, the inferior nasal concha articulates with the maxilla and a short inferior process of the lacrimal. Laterally, it attaches to the maxilla, and posteriorly, it attaches to the perpendicular plate of the palatine. It articulates slightly with part of the ethmoidal labyrinth also.

Left/Right Siding

The left inferior nasal concha can be distinguished from the right by first noting that the bone curls lengthwise and the concave surface is lateral. Also, note that the sheet of bone on one side of the curvature is longer than the other and has a thickened inferior border. The longer sheet of bone is medial. A short, hook-like process is on the anterior end and a longer, tapered point is posterior.

Individualization

Anomalies occur, but little is known that can be used for individualization or personal identification.

Origin and Growth

Unlike most of the face, the inferior nasal conchae develop endochondrally. At the time of birth, the nasal conchae are recognizable but extremely fragile. They often fuse to the maxilla in midlife, which explains why they are often seen within the nasal cavity of well-preserved crania.

Nasal Bones

Description, Location, Articulation

The nasal bones are small, thin, paired facial bones. They are located between the eye orbits where they form the bridge of the nose and the superior margin of the nasal aperture. Each bone is perforated near the mid-center by a nutrient foramen. The medial and lateral margins of the individual nasal bone are somewhat parallel. The superior margin is thicker and jagged where it joins the frontonasal suture. The inferior margin is sharp where it forms part of the border of the nasal aperture. The inferolateral angle is longer than the inferomedial angle and a notch usually exists between the angles.

The nasal bones articulate superiorly with the frontal bone and laterally with the frontal processes of the maxillae.

Left/Right Siding

The left nasal bone can be distinguished from the right by orienting the short, thick edge superior and the short, thin edge inferior. The longer long edge is the lateral edge, and the smoother surface is anterior.

Individualization

The nasal bones contribute to the appearance of the face, and particularly, the shape of the nose. Irregularities due to trauma (such as a broken nose) can sometimes be seen in photographs as well as radiographs.

Origin and Growth

Each nasal bone grows from a single membranous ossification center and is present and recognizable by the time of birth. The newborn nasal bone is more triangular-shaped than the adult form. Like the other small bones of the face, it is unlikely that it would be found in skeletonized remains of infants because of its size and fragility.

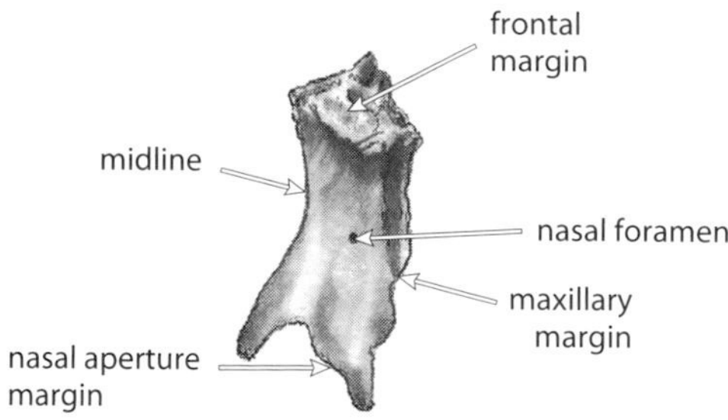

Figure 3.29
Left Nasal Bone, Lateral (External) View

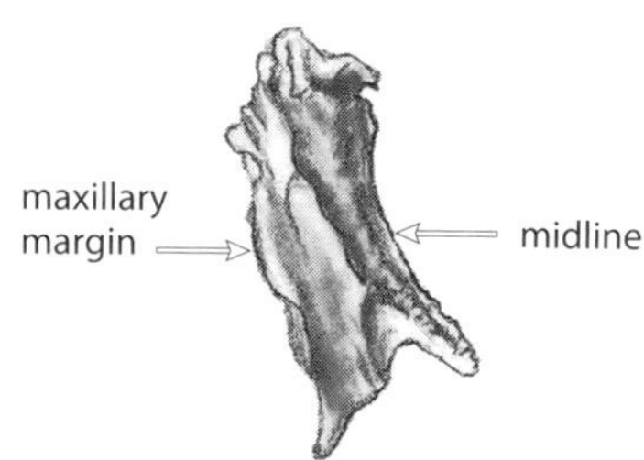

Figure 3.30
Left Nasal Bone, Medial (Internal) View

LACRIMAL BONES

DESCRIPTION, LOCATION, ARTICULATION

The lacrimal bones are small, very thin, paired facial bones. The shape is somewhat rectangular and characterized by the **lacrimal groove** (nasolacrimal canal) which occupies most of the anterior margin of the bone and extends over the margin into the posterior margin of the frontal process of the maxilla. (See Figure 3.25.)

The lacrimal bone is located in the anterior medial orbital wall and articulates anteriorly and inferiorly with the maxilla, superiorly with the frontal, and posteriorly with the ethmoid. (See Figure 3.26.) A small part of the medial surface articulates with the inferior nasal conchae. (See Figure 3.27.)

LEFT/RIGHT SIDING

The left lacrimal can be distinguished from the right by orienting the edge with the lacrimal groove anterior and lateral. The groove is narrow at the superior edge and widens as it progresses inferiorly.

INDIVIDUALIZATION

The lacrimal bones vary in shape and are susceptible to several anomalies. They may even be absent, but the adjacent bones fill in the space and function. According to Post (1969), restricted lacrimal canal openings and longer canals are associated with dacrocystitis (inflammation of the nasolacrimal canal).

ORIGIN AND GROWTH

Each lacrimal grows from a single membranous ossification center. At the time of birth, the lacrimals are recognizable but extremely fragile.

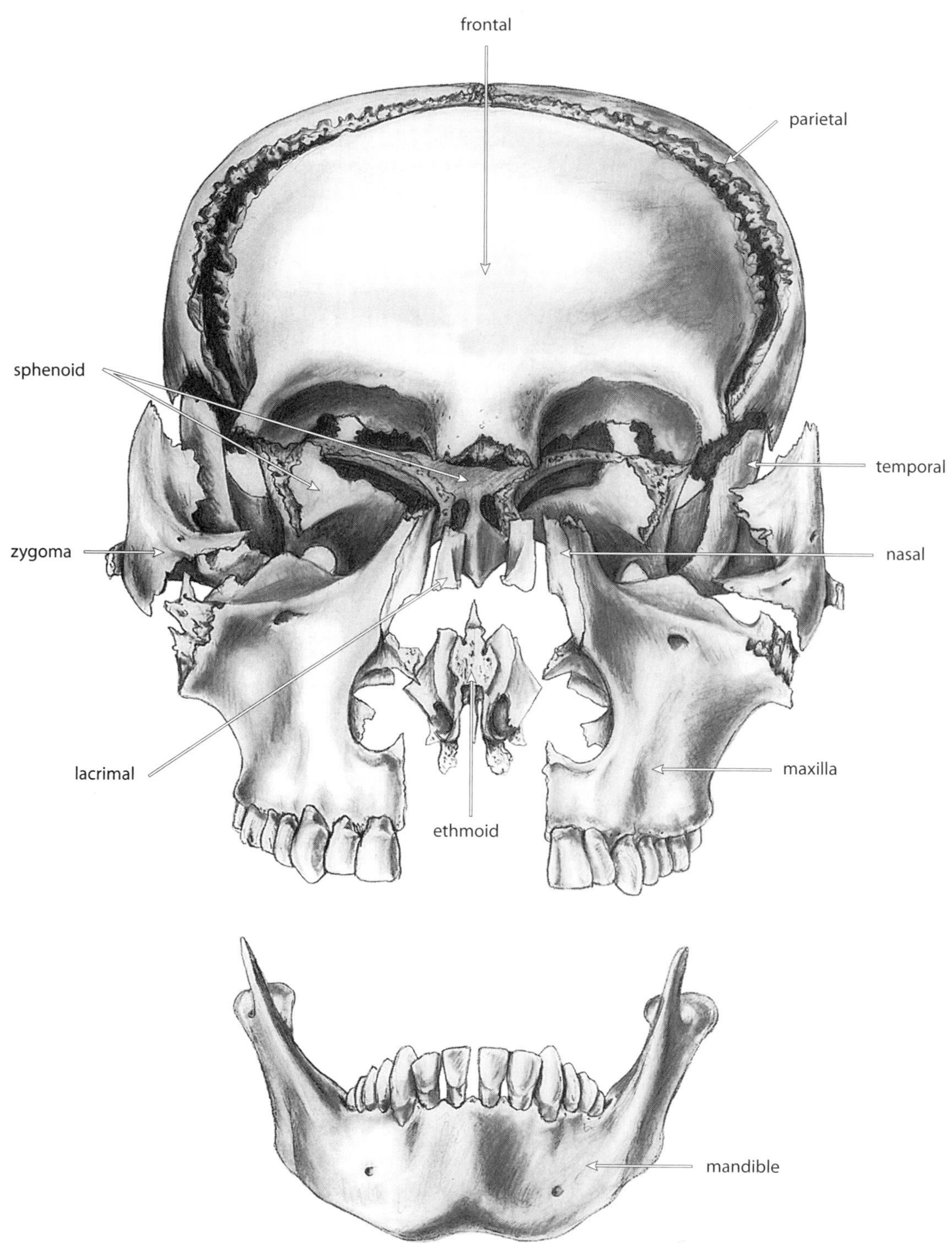

Figure 3.31
Disarticulated Skull

This is also known as a Beauchene Exploded Skull after the French anatomist who first constructed the type of presentation. The individual bones have been disarticulated and mounted so each bone is in correct position relative to the others. (Wires are omitted from this illustration.) Note that the lacrimal bones appear medial to the nasal bones in this view. They are actually posterior—deeper into the orbit. See Figure 3.26.

Mandible

Description, Location, Articulation

The mandible is a singular U-shaped bone, forming the lower part of the face, the chin, and the angle of the jaw. The mandible is much more massive than the maxilla. It provides attachment for the muscles of mastication, the tongue, and the floor of the mouth. All of the lower teeth are supported by the mandibular **alveolar ridge**. The mandible is more likely to endure than is the maxilla.

The mandible articulates only with the temporal bone. The moveable articulation (synovial joint) is between the **mandibular condyles** and

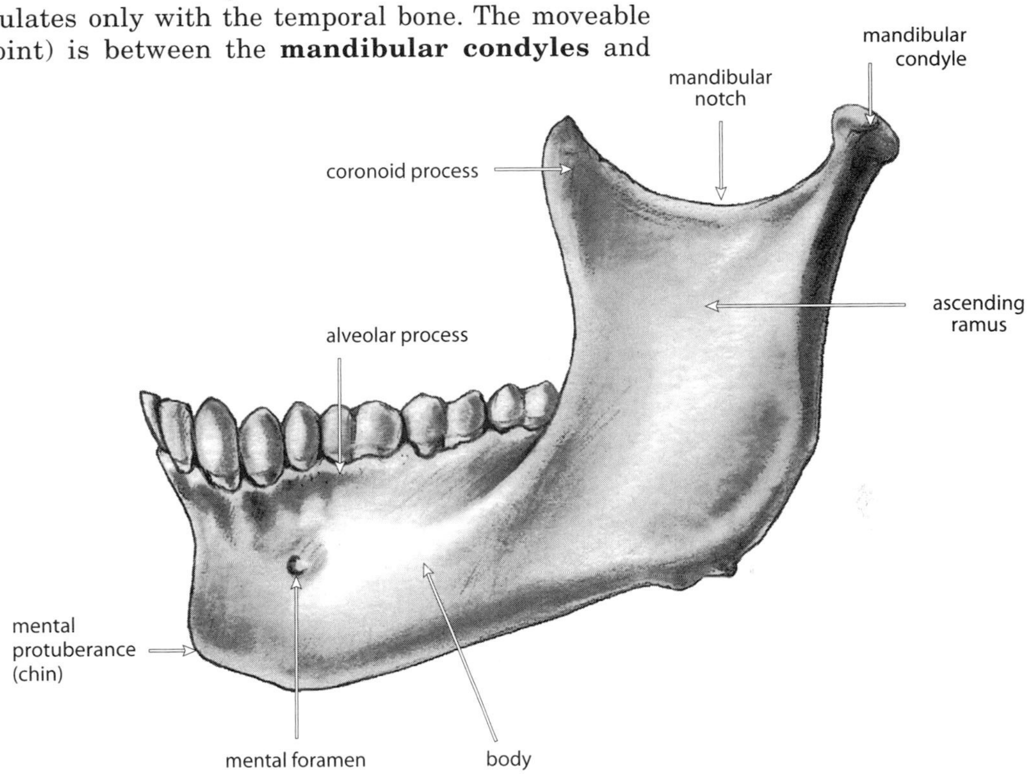

Figure 3.32
Left Mandible, Lateral View

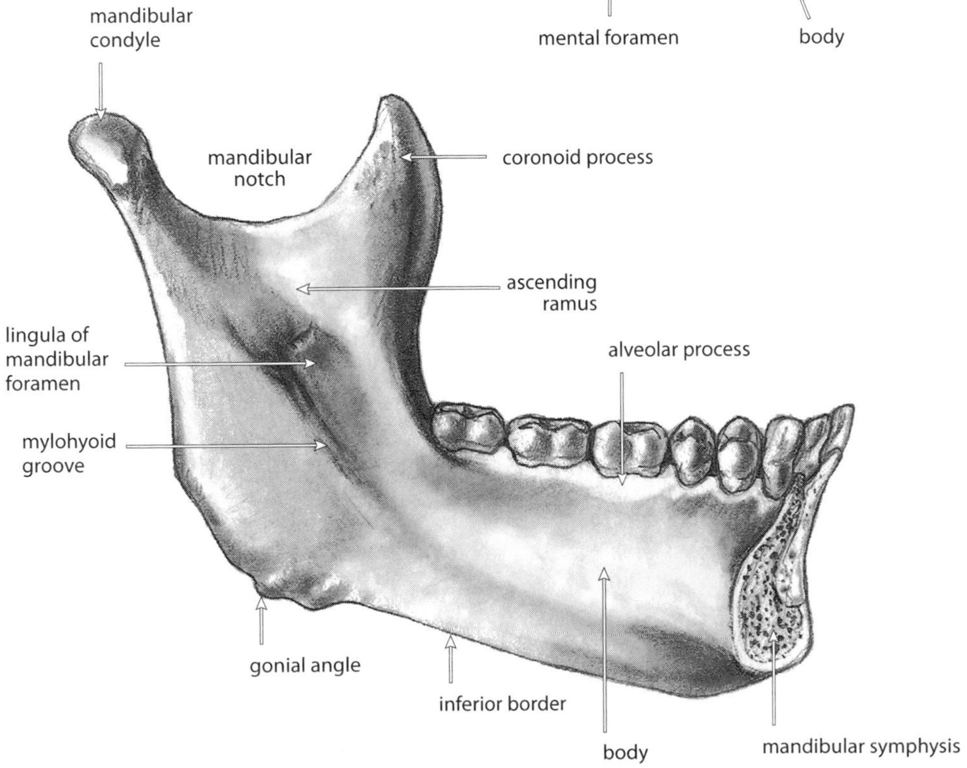

Figure 3.33
Left Mandible, Medial View

the **mandibular fossae** of the temporal bones. This joint is called the **temporomandibular joint** or TMJ.

Individualization

Because the mandible is the major bone of the lower face, it is useful in individual facial identification. Take note of the shape and projection of the chin as well as the overall outline and angle of the jaw (**gonial angle**).

Origin and Growth

The mandible grows from two centers of ossification—one for each half. At the time of birth, each half is well defined and the dental crypts (rounded compartments) are formed for all the deciduous teeth as well as the first permanent molar (M_1). The crowns of the deciduous teeth are present and M_1 has begun to calcify.

The mandibular halves fuse at the midline **mandibular symphysis** during the first year of life. Fusion is usually complete by six to eight months of age.

The Hyoid

Forensic Note

Strangulation may or may not cause fracture of the hyoid, depending on the area of constriction. In skeletal cases, the hyoid is so fragile that it is necessary to clearly demonstrate a "greenstick fracture" before considering strangulation.

Description, Location, Articulation

The **hyoid** is a small U-shaped bone in the upper part of the neck, tucked between the mandible and the larynx. It is the only bone in the body that does not articulate with another bone

The hyoid is composed of a central body, two greater horns, and two lesser horns. The body is slightly cup-shaped, with a curvature that fits the tip of a digit. The greater horns are spatulate at the medial end and taper into small tubercles at the lateral end. The lesser horns are small conical projections pointing superiorly and attaching at the intersection of the body and greater horns.

The hyoid serves as an important attachment site for several muscles and ligaments of the head and neck. Delicate stylohyoid ligaments attach the lesser horns of the hyoid to the styloid processes of the temporal bone. Other ligaments attach the hyoid to the larynx (voice box) and raise and lower the larynx during swallowing. Muscles of the floor of the mouth also attach to the hyoid, providing a movable base for the tongue.

Origin and Growth

The hyoid grows from three centers of ossification. The center for the body appears in the first few months after birth and the centers for the greater horns appear in the medial ends after 6 months. Ossification is completed by puberty in the body and greater horns of the hyoid, but the lesser horns may remain cartilaginous throughout life (Scheuer & Black, 2000).

The horns frequently fuse to the body of the hyoid, but sometimes on only one side. The timing of fusion is highly irregular and seems to occur more frequently in men than women (O'Halloran & Lundy, 1987).

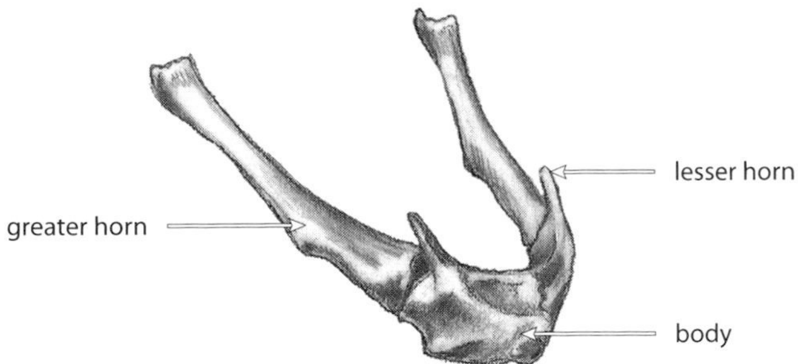

Figure 3.34
Hyoid, Body Fused with Greater and Lesser Horns, 3/4 View

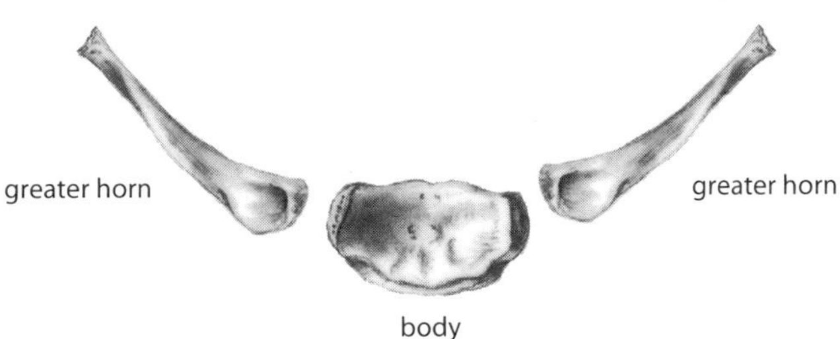

Figure 3.35
Hyoid, Unfused Body and Greater Horns, Juvenile, Posterior View

Age Changes in the Skull

During the aging process, the bones of the skull, particularly the brain case, tend to fuse with one another. Fusion begins at the posterior extreme of the sagittal suture and progresses anteriorly. The coronal suture usually fuses next and the lambdoidal suture last. The squamous suture seldom fuses. Many attempts have been made to quantify the rate of cranial suture closure for use in age estimation. Buikstra and Ubelaker (1994: 32–38) synthesize and describe the methods, but most anthropologists agree that suture closure provides a rough estimate, at best (Hershkovitz et al., 1997).

Even when sutures do not fuse, they *do* change, and cranial sutures still can be examined as part of the total age assessment. With age, the bone along the edges of sutures tends to round and bulge. Todd and Lyon (1924) called this condition "lapsed union" and classified lapsed union as if the suture was closed.

Another characteristic of an aging cranium is an increasing number of **granular pits**, also called **pacchionian depressions**. They occur on the inner surface of the skull, mainly along the midline. During life, the pits contain arachnoid granulations, which tend to calcify with advanced age. (See Figure 3.8).

Sex Note

The terms *sex* and *gender* are commonly confused. Sex is biologically defined; gender is culturally defined. The two may be inconsistent due to a number of factors, including ambiguous genitalia, psychological orientation, or surgery. The "simple" task of separating males from females is not always so simple.

Sex Differences in the Skull

When learning to distinguish male and female skulls, begin with one skull of each sex. Compare them for each of the characteristics listed in this section and Table 3.1. Then test yourself with as large a sample as possible. Remember that these are nonmetric traits and the expression of each trait is continuous, not discrete. There is substantial overlap between male and female forms.

1. First note the differences in overall size, shape, and rugosity.
2. Then compare the foreheads. Run your fingertips over the frontal bones.
   - How large is the supraorbital ridge?
   - How sharp is the orbital rim?
   - Are there bumps on the frontal? One, two, or maybe three?
3. Now, turn the skull and compare the facial profiles.
   - What is the shape and contour of the forehead?
   - Does the brow ridge protrude?
4. Next, look at the area of the skull where the ear once was.
   - How large is the mastoid process?
   - Where does the zygomatic arch end in relation to the ear opening?
5. Compare the cranial bases.
   - Are the nuchal ridges rough or smooth? Is there a line along the ridge?
   - Is there a bony projection in the middle of the occipital?
6. Finally, compare the mandibles.
   - Is the chin squared or oval?
   - How sharp is the angle of the mandible? Is it flared?

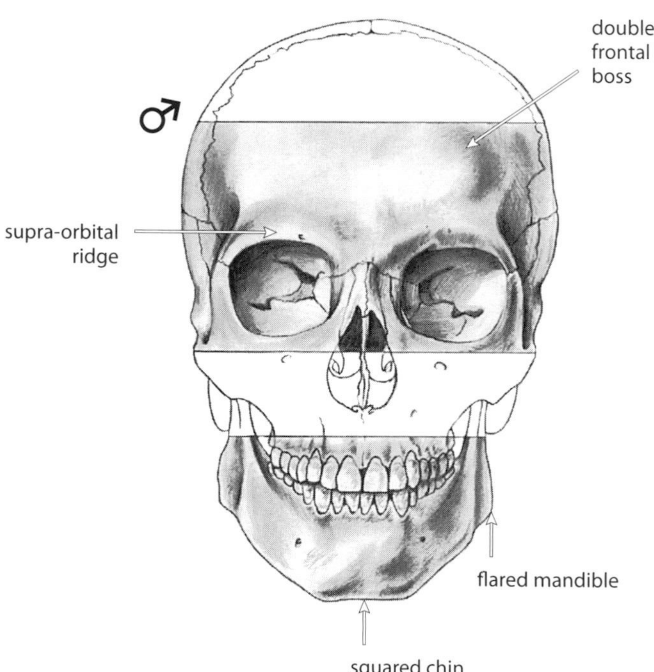

Figure 3.36a
Comparison of Male and Female Skulls, Frontal View

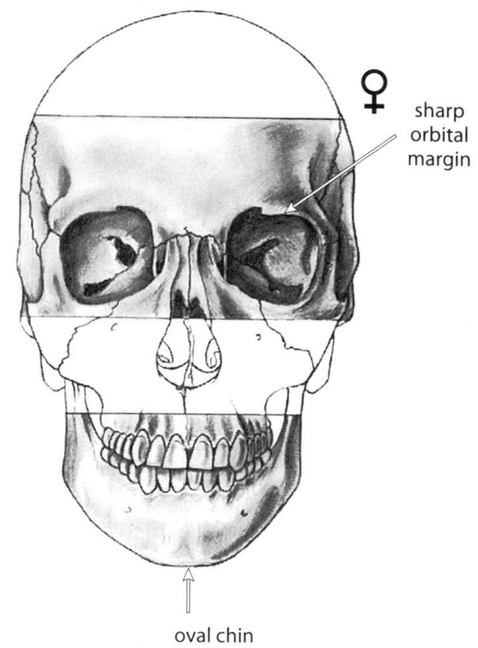

Figure 3.36b

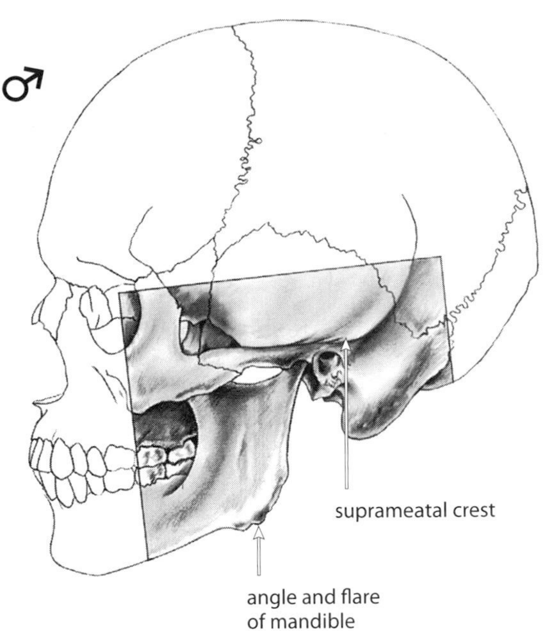

Figure 3.37a
Comparison of Male and Female Skulls, Lateral View

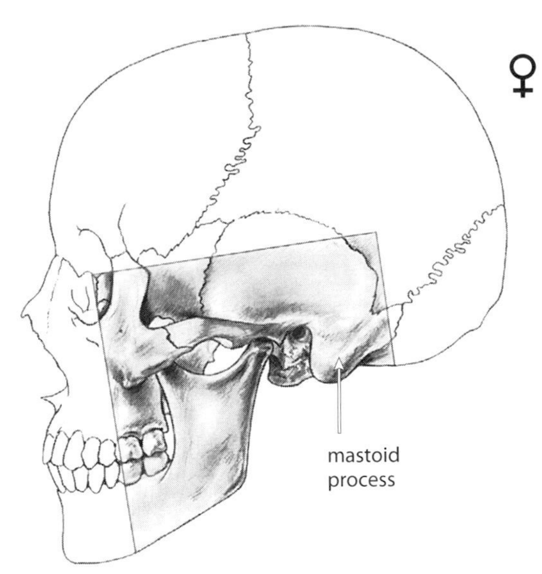

Figure 3.37b

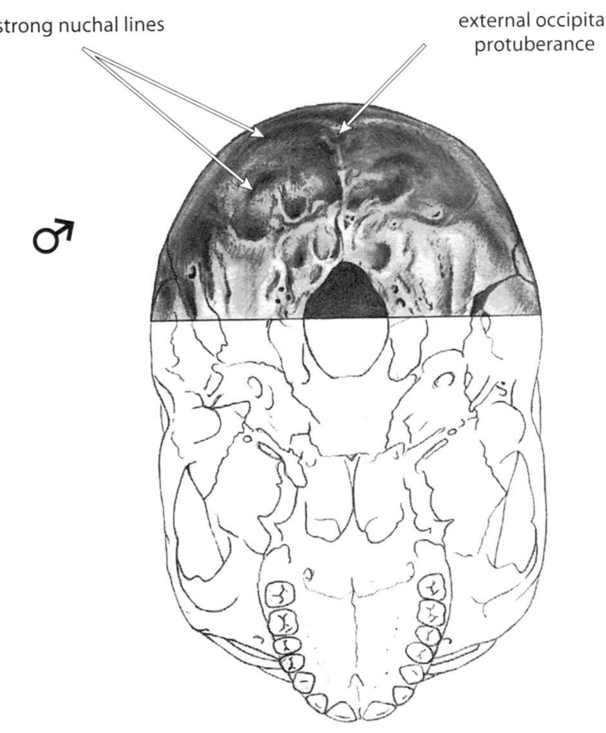

Figure 3.38a
Comparison of Male and Female Skulls, Basilar View

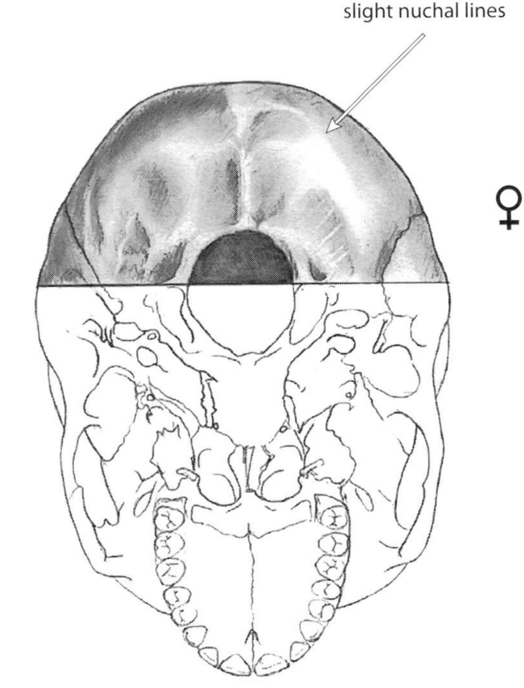

Figure 3.38b

Table 3.1 Nonmetric Sexual Cranial Traits and Trends

Bone	Elements of Difference	Male	Female
FRONTAL	**supraorbital ridge**	prominent	absent
	upper orbital margin	rounded	sharp
	frontal bossing	double boss	single central boss
TEMPORAL	**mastoid process**	large	small
	zygomatic process length	extends beyond the external auditory meatus	ends by the external auditory meatus
OCCIPITAL	**nuchal lines**	strong muscle attachment sites	slight muscle attachment sites
	external occipital protuberance	heavier and more prominent	less prominent or absent
MANDIBLE	**ramus**	wide, sharply angled, flared	narrow, less angled
	chin shape	square, protuberant	rounded or pointed

Table 3.2 Skull Vocabulary

Term	Definition	Example
ALA	a wing-like structure	ala of sphenoid
ARCH	any vaulted or arch-like structure	zygomatic a.; dental a.
BONE	1. A unit of osseous tissue of definite shape and size, forming a part of the adult skeleton. Distinguish the bone itself from a structure or component of the bone.	The temporal is a bone. The mastoid process is a structure located on the temporal bone.
	2. A hard tissue consisting of cells in a matrix of ground substance and collagen fibers.The fibers are impregnated with mineral substance, chiefly calcium phosphate and calcium carbonate. Adult bone is about 35 percent organic matter by weight.	
BOSS	a rounded eminence	frontal boss
CALVARIA	skullcap, the upper dome-like portion of the skull	the calvaria is superior to the brain
CRANIUM	The bones of the head without the jaw	The skull is composed of a cranium and a mandible.
FORAMEN	any aperture or perforation through bone or membranous structure	occipital foramen
LINE	a thin mark distinguished by texture or elevation—often the outer edge of a muscle or ligament attachment	temporal line on the parietal bones
MARGIN	an edge, a border	orbital m., parietal margin
PROCESS	any bony projection	styloid p. of temporal bone
RIDGE	a crest, a long narrow elevation	alveolar ridge
SKULL	the bones of the head as a unit, including the jaw	
SUTURE	a fibrous joint between bones of the skull	coronal suture

Auditory Ossicles: Malleus, Incus, and Stapes

Description, Location, and Articulation

The auditory ossicles (also called middle ear bones or ear ossicles) are the smallest bones in the human body and seldom recovered from skeletonized remains. They are located within the tympanic cavity (middle ear) of the auditory canal of the temporal bone. During life, the three ossicles are held in place by surrounding soft tissues, but after death and decay, they tend to fall out unnoticed. Occasionally they are found when well-packed burial dirt is removed carefully from the external auditory meatus and sifted with a fine mesh screen.

The largest of the three ossicles is the **malleus**, commonly characterized as a hammer. The malleus is comprised of a long tapered process (the handle or manubrium) with a prominent ball-shaped head set at a slight angle from the manubrium. A small spur-like process juts out at the junction between the manubrium and the neck-like area of the head. In life, the full extent of the manubrium is attached to the tympanic membrane. The head articulates with a depression in the body of the incus. The greatest length of the malleus is approximately 7–8 mm.

The **incus** is V-shaped and characterized as an anvil. It lies between the malleus and the stapes. One side (crura) of the V is a shorter and thicker. The other side is longer, more slender, and slightly hooked at the tip. This longer process articulates at the tip with the third and smallest ossicle, the stapes. The greatest length of the incus is approximately 5–6 mm.

The **stapes** looks like a tiny stirrup. A tiny process at the top of the stirrup articulates with the incus and the flat base of the stirrup attaches to the membrane of the oval window (fenestra ovalis), leading to the vestibule of the inner ear. The greatest length of the stapes is approximately 3–4 mm.

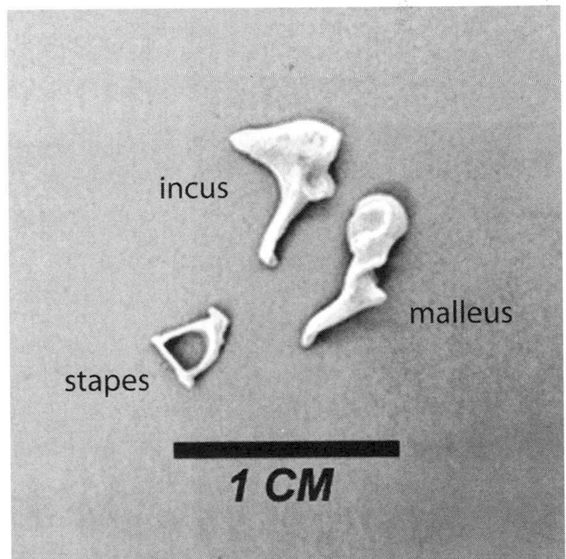

Figure 3.39
Auditory Ossicles, Right Side
These tiny bones are located in the auditory canal of the temporal bone. They are shown at approximately 300% natural size. The photo is courtesy of Bone Clones Inc.

Individualization

Individual variation exists in auditory ossicles, but the extent of variation is infrequently studied except for clinical purposes. Occasionally the ossicles fuse, creating the condition called otosclerosis and causing hearing loss. If greater effort were devoted to recovering the auditory ossicles, evidence related to hearing may occasionally be discovered.

Left/Right Recognition

It is possible to separate right from left auditory ossicles, but magnification and comparative bones may be necessary.

Origin and Growth

The structures of the ear develop early. By the second half of prenatal life, the auditory ossicles have achieved adult morphology and size.

Chapter 4

The Shoulder Girdle and Thorax: Clavicle, Scapula, Ribs, and Sternum

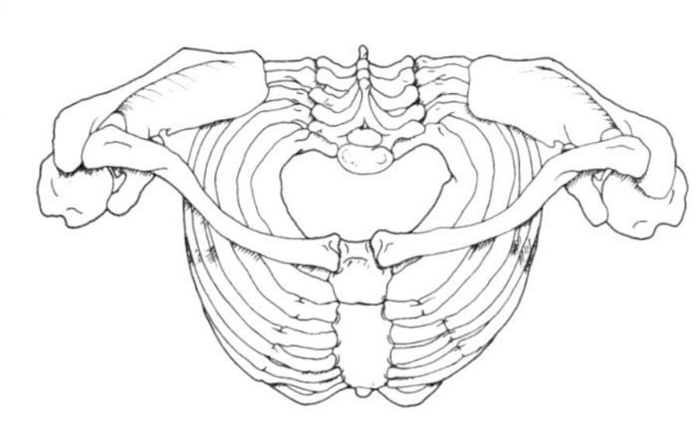

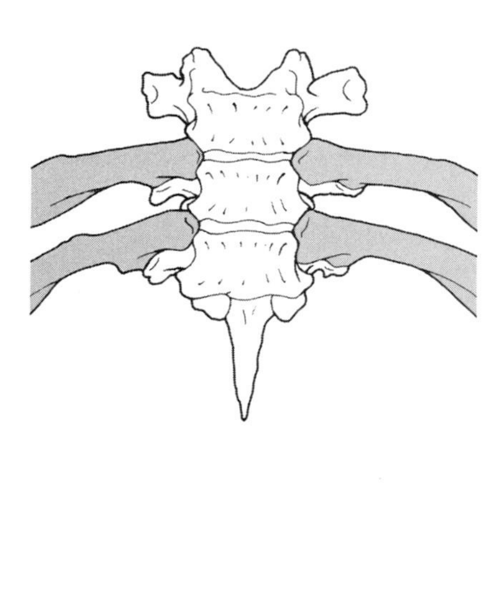

CHAPTER OUTLINE

Introduction

The shoulder girdle and the thorax, together with the thoracic vertebrae, comprise the upper part of the trunk. They are packaged together, but the shoulder girdle is part of the appendicular skeleton, and the thorax is part of the axial skeleton. The shoulder girdle consists of clavicles and scapulae, and the thorax consists of the ribs and sternum.

The bones of the shoulder girdle almost encircle the top of the barrel-shaped thorax and articulate with the sternum anteriorly. The shoulder girdle does not connect with any bone posteriorly. This arrangement allows far greater flexibility in the shoulder girdle than exists in the pelvic girdle.

The articulation between the arm and the shoulder girdle is at the glenoid fossa of the scapula—a very slightly concave articular surface. When compared with the deep acetabulum of the hip joint, the shoulder is obviously less stable. The benefit is greater mobility. The shoulder joint cannot withstand the degree of stress that the hip joint can, but it provides a far greater range of motion.

The ribs and the sternum of the thorax make up the rib cage. All of the ribs articulate with the thoracic vertebrae posteriorly, and the upper ten ribs connect with the sternum via costal cartilage anteriorly. The structure of the thorax provides resilient protection for the internal organs of the chest.

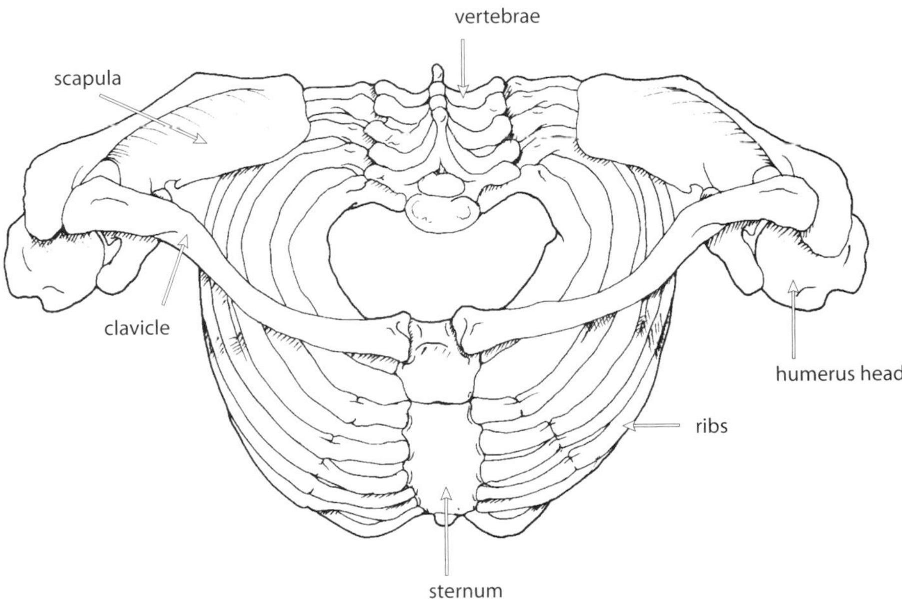

Figure 4.1
Superior View of the Articulated Shoulder Girdle
Note the barrel shape of the rib cage and the placement of the shoulder girdle. It articulates only at the sternal manubrium and is open at the vertebral column.

Clavicle: The Collar Bone

Description, Location, Articulation

The clavicle is commonly known as the "collar bone." It is an S-shaped long bone, and is the one horizontal long bone in the human body. The medial end is circular in cross section and articulates with the manubrium of the sternum. The lateral end is compressed and spatulate in shape. It articulates with the acromion process of the scapula, forming a small oval facet. Beginning at the medial end, the clavicle curves anteriorly before it curves posteriorly. The roughened surface is internal and the smoother surface is external.

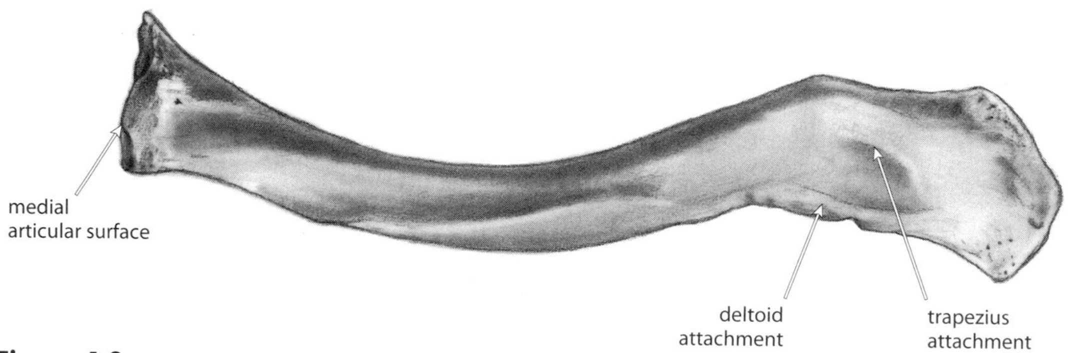

Figure 4.2
Superior View of the Left Clavicle (90% Natural Size)
Note the superior side of the clavicle is without pits or tubercles.

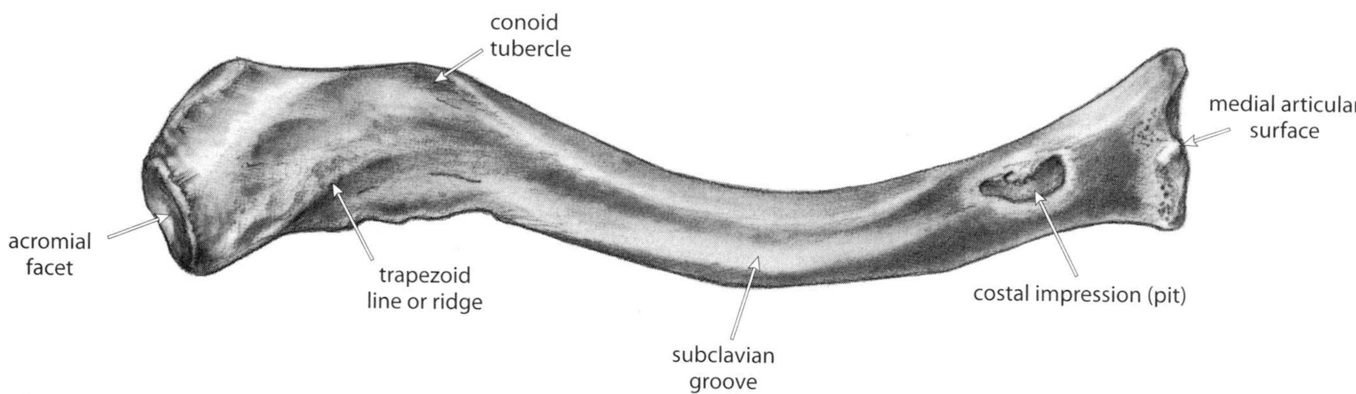

Figure 4.3
Inferior View of the Left Clavicle (90% Natural Size)
Note the inferior side of the clavicle has a long groove and a prominent pit.

Left/Right Recognition

The S-shape of the clavicle causes some confusion in side determination. This can be resolved by locating the **costal pit** on the inferior side of the medial end and the **conoid tubercle** on the inferior side of the flattened lateral end. The superior surface of the clavicle is smoother than the inferior surface.

Origin And Growth

The clavicle is the first bone to begin ossifying in the fetus and the last bone to finish ossifying in the young adult. It begins formation through intramembranous ossification at the lateral end. It then develops two centers of endochondral ossification. The two centers fuse into one shaft by the time of birth.

A secondary center of ossification forms **the medial clavicular epiphysis**. There is no lateral epiphysis and most of the growth in length takes place at the sternal (medial) end. The medial clavicular epiphysis is usually the last to fuse in the human body. Fusion usually takes place in the mid-twenties. The widest reported age range is 15 to 32, but extremes outside of the twenties are unusual. Figure 4.4 shows a medial view of the epiphyseal surface of a clavicle before, during, and after fusion. The epiphysis appears as an irregular "flake" in the center of the undulating metaphyseal surface of the diaphysis. (This is an example of an atavistic epiphysis.) The epiphysis slowly expands to cover the entire surface. The last evidence of the epiphysis is a line of fusion around the circumference of the smooth articular surface. In older adults, the articular surface becomes porous and sometimes develops pits. Do not confuse the porous, pitted surface of the elder adult with the dense, undulating surface of the young adult. Neither is smooth.

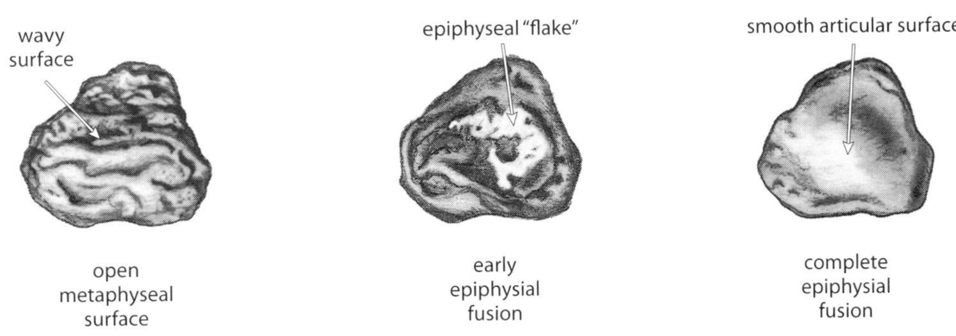

Figure 4.4
Medial Clavicular Surface in Three Stages of Development (Natural Size)
Note the epiphysis begins as an irregular flake near the center of the medial surface.

Table 4.1 Clavicle Vocabulary

Term	Definition	Articulations and Attachments
ACROMIAL FACET	the small oval articular surface on the anterolateral surface	articulates with the acromial process of the scapula
CONOID TUBERCLE	the small rounded elevation on the posterior surface of the lateral end	attachment for the conoid ligament
COSTAL PIT OR IMPRESSION	the fossa on the inferior surface of the medial end	attachment for the costoclavicular ligament
MEDIAL EPIPHYSIS	the epiphysis on the sternal end (the clavicle has no lateral epiphysis)	articulates with the clavicular notch on the manubrium

Scapula: The Shoulder Blade

Description, Location, Articulation

The scapulae are flat bones that cover the upper part of the back. In common language, they are "shoulder blades." The major part of the scapula is the **body**, the large triangular part. The flat side of the body is anterior, adjacent to the ribs. The **spine** of the scapula traverses the posterior surface and terminates in the acromion process. The **glenoid fossa** is the large, ovoid articular surface. The **coracoid process** curls out at the superior edge of the glenoid fossa. It is close to the anterosuperior part of the upper arm and serves as attachment for a number of muscles, ligaments, and fascial sheets necessary for the functioning of the shoulder joint. The **acromion process** is recognized in a living person as the "shoulder bone." It curves higher and wider than the coracoid and serves as attachment for both the trapezius and the deltoideus muscles.

Much of the scapula is described by borders and angles—the **axillary border**, the **inferior angle**, the **vertebral border**, the **superior angle**, and the **superior border**.

The scapula articulates with the humerus at the glenoid fossa and with the clavicle at the anterior edge of the acromion process.

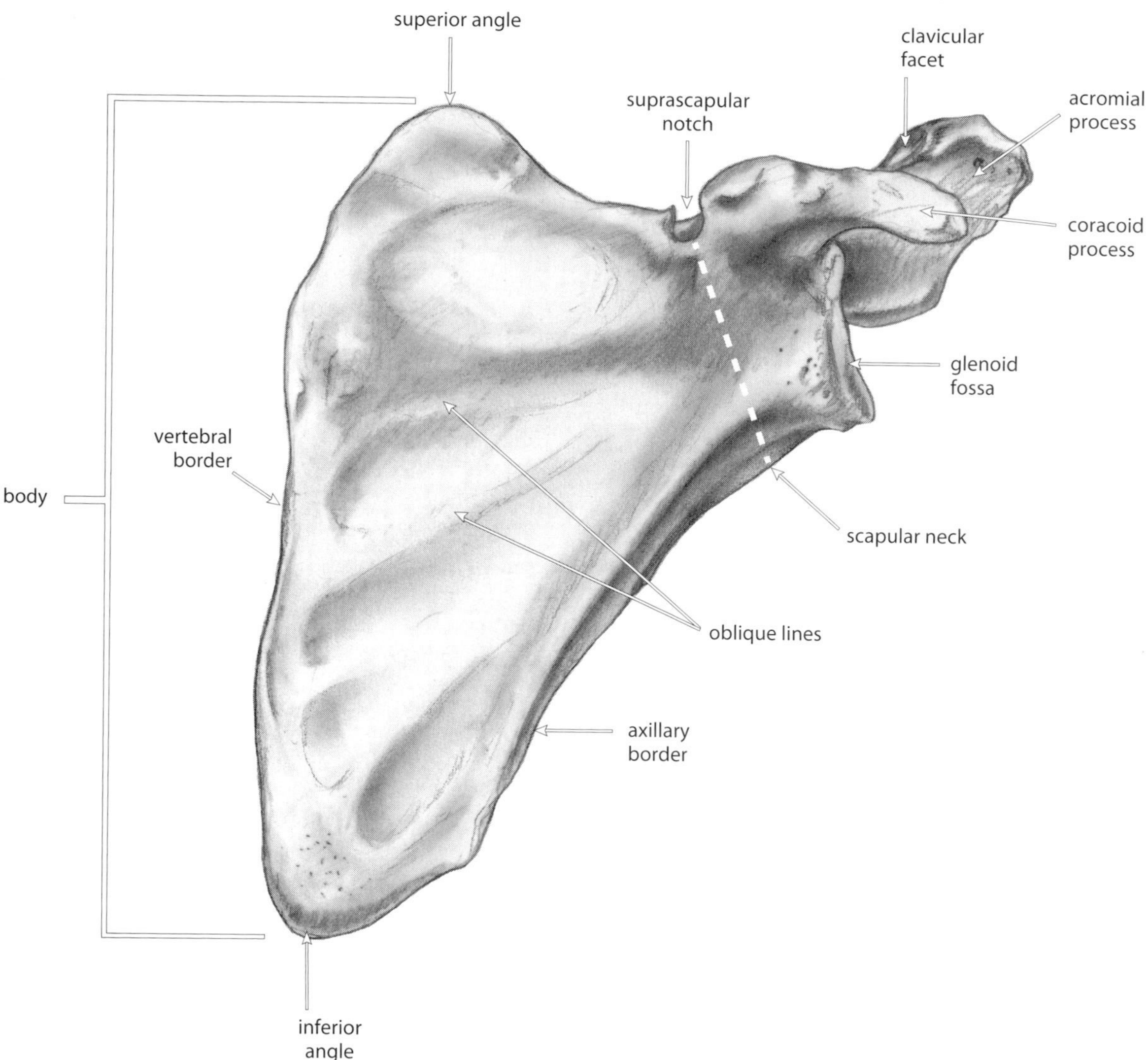

Figure 4.5
Left Scapula, Costal (Anterior) View (70% Natural Size)
Note the thickness of the axillary border compared with the other borders.

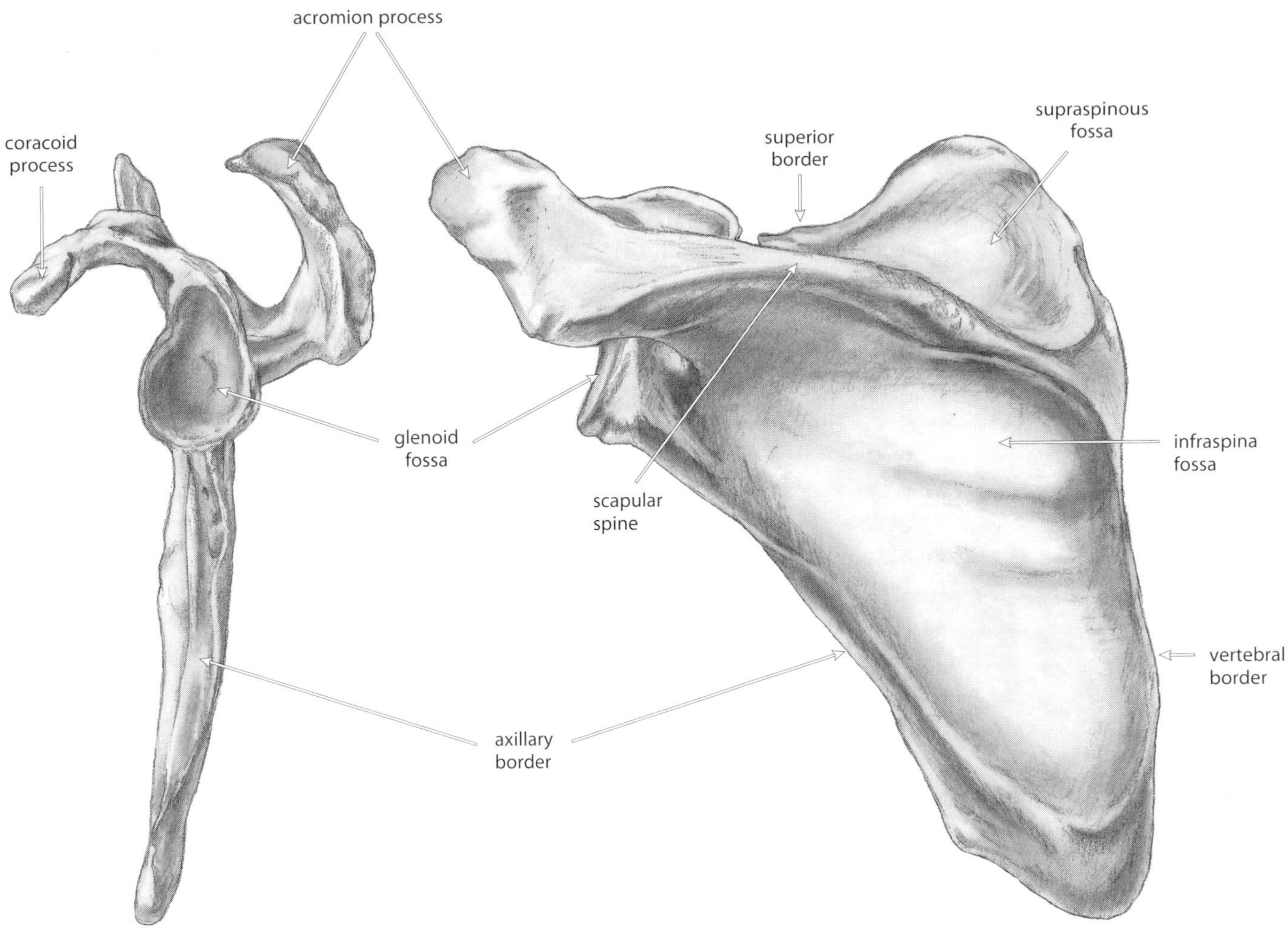

Figure 4.6
Left Scapula, Lateral View (70% Natural Size)
Note the anterior curvature of the processes. They appear to rotate up and over the shoulder.

Figure 4.7
Left Scapula, Posterior View (70% Natural Size)
Note the spatulate shape of the acromion process.

Left/Right Recognition

The scapula is easy to orient because superior and inferior are obvious. It is only necessary to be sure that the spine is dorsal (posterior) and the glenoid fossa is lateral for articulation with the humerus. The two scapular processes—the smaller coracoid and larger acromion—rotate upward and forward over the shoulder.

Individualization: Handedness, Left/Right Dominance

The scapula can be useful for determination of left/right dominance, or "handedness." Most people use their dominant arm more frequently, and over a wider range of motion. Use is apparent in the size and rugosity of muscle attachment areas on the arm and development of degenerative changes in the joints. Range of motion is demonstrated in the form of the glenoid fossa.

In an adult, the area immediately posterior to the dorsal rim is more likely to be beveled on the dominant side. The sharp rim is the result of simple osteoarthritic changes (osteoarthritic lipping). The beveled rim may be a result of repeated extension and hyperextension of the arm. Both beveling and lipping are progressive age changes; therefore, handedness is more apparent on the scapulae of older adults and physical laborers.

T. Dale Stewart recommends a simple method for evaluating the glenoid bevel in his textbook, *Essentials of Forensic Anthropology* (1979: 239–244). Begin by making the rim of the glenoid fossa more clearly visible by drawing the side of a long piece of chalk across the surface. (A piece of lead from a mechanical pencil works well also.) The chalk will leave a line of color on the protruding parts of the glenoid fossa. Next, hold the right scapula in your right hand and the left scapula in your left hand while looking at the two glenoid fossae. Compare the dorsal rims of the left and right glenoid fossa, and evaluate the amount of bone posterior to the glenoid fossa. If one rim is beveled and the other is not, the person probably used the arm on the beveled side more. The arm showing more use is usually the dominant arm and, by inference, the dominant hand. (See Chapter 13 for more on handedness.)

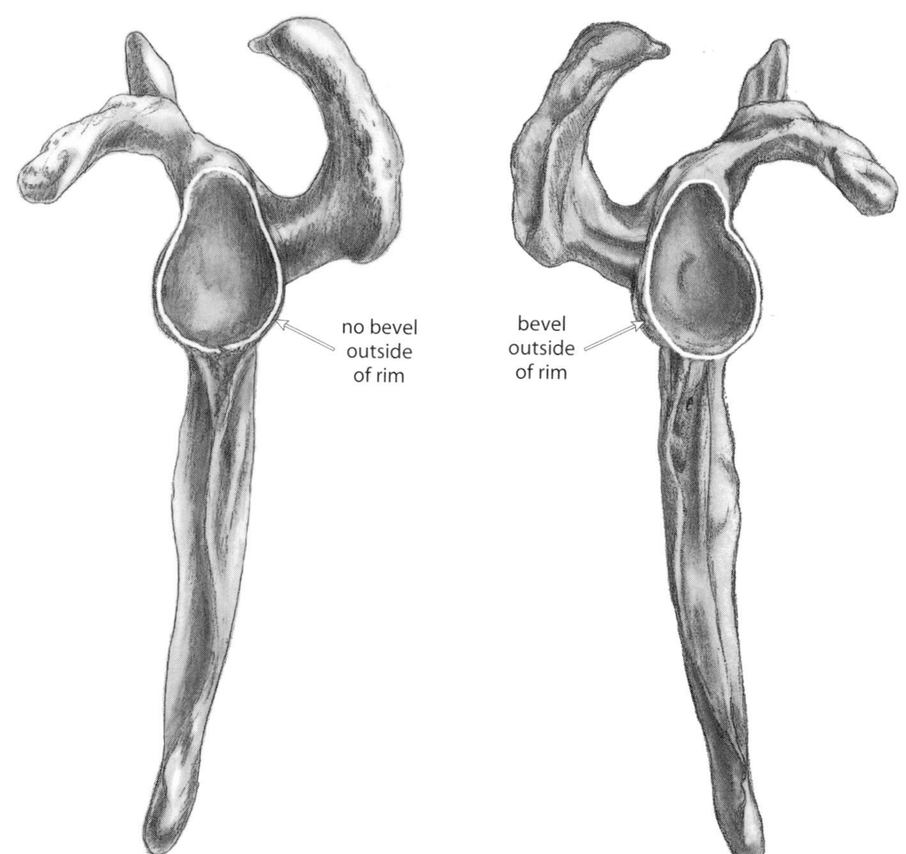

Figure 4.8
Scapulae of Right-Handed Adult, Rim of Glenoid Fossa Highlighted
Note a small amount of bone visible *posterior* to the rim of the right glenoid fossa. The rim is sometimes beveled or more rounded on the dominant side of older adults and physical laborers.

Origin And Growth

The scapula grows by a combination of endochondral and intramembranous ossification. The primary center of ossification is located near the upper center of the scapula. Endochondral growth takes place laterally to include the glenoid fossa and medially to the vertebral border. Intramembranous growth fills in most of the "blade" of the scapula.

The coracoid process is formed from a separate center of ossification. It appears during the first year of life and fuses in the mid-teens (15 to 17 years).

A number of secondary centers of ossification develop around the edges of the scapula. They are not major articular epiphyses, so they take on the appearance of flakes and fill-ins. In all, secondary centers occur at the vertebral border, the inferior angle, the acromion process, the coracoid process, and the glenoid fossa. The scapula is complete by the early twenties.

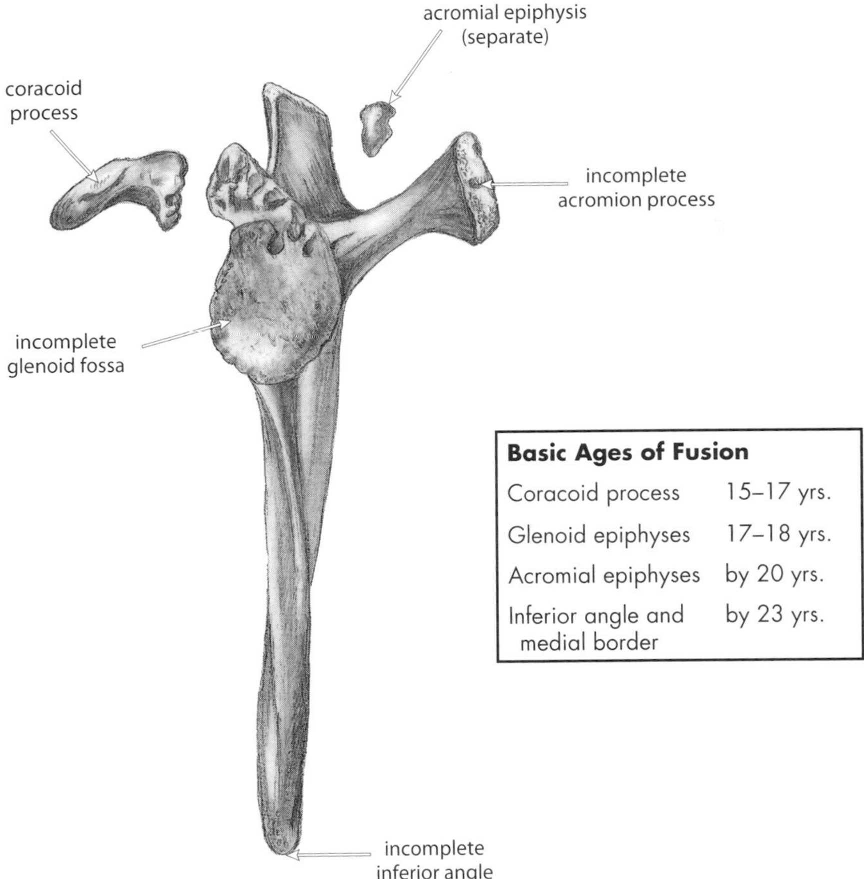

Basic Ages of Fusion	
Coracoid process	15–17 yrs.
Glenoid epiphyses	17–18 yrs.
Acromial epiphyses	by 20 yrs.
Inferior angle and medial border	by 23 yrs.

Figure 4.9
Juvenile Scapula (Age 12), Left Side, Lateral View
Note the coracoid process is a significant and identifiable epiphysis whereas the acromion epiphysis is flake-like and variable in form.

Table 4.2 Scapula Vocabulary

Term	Definition	Articulations and Attachments
ACROMION PROCESS	the larger, more posterior and superior of the two scapular processes	articulates with the lateral end of the clavicle and attachment for the trapezius and the deltoid
BODY OF SCAPULA	the main part of the shoulder blade; a large, thin triangular plate of bone	
CORACOID PROCESS	the smaller, more anterior of the two scapular processes	attachment for the short head of the biceps brachii, coracobrachialis, and pector alis minor
BORDER, AXILLARY	the lateral border of the scapula	attachment for the teres major
BORDER, SUPERIOR	the uppermost border of the scapula	
BORDER, VERTEBRAL	the medial border of the scapula	attachment for the levator scapulae and the rhomboids
COSTAL SURFACE	the anterior (rib) surface	covered by the subscapularis
DORSAL SURFACE	the posterior (back) surface	covered by the supraspinatus, the infraspinatus, and the teres minor
GLENOID FOSSA	the large ovoid articular surface on the superior-lateral corner of the scapula	articulates with the head of the humerus
NECK	the slight constriction separating the glenoid fossa and coracoid process from the remainder of the scapula	
SUPRA-GLENOID TUBERCLE	the small projection at the superior edge of the glenoid fossa	attachment for the long head of the biceps brachii
SUPRASCAPULAR NOTCH	the notch on the superior border of the scapula	
SPINE	the long, thin elevation on the dorsal surface of the scapula that ends laterally as the acromion process	attachment for the trapezius (superior edge) and the deltoid (inferior edge)

Ribs

Ribs are sometimes disregarded simply because they are fragile, broken, and hard to sort. However, ribs are important in skeletal analysis because they house the organs essential to life. A careful examination of the ribs may provide evidence for cause or manner of death. Evidence of gunshot wounds, knife wounds, and perimortem fractures can be used to draw inferences about events leading to death and the condition of underlying organs at the time of death. Of course, the value of the evidence is lost if the ribs are not on the correct side or in the correct order.

Description, Location, Articulation

The adult skeleton usually has twelve pairs of ribs. They articulate with the thoracic vertebrae on the back, circle the chest cavity, and terminate in extensions of hyaline cartilage (costal cartilage) in the front.

The upper six ribs attach directly to the sternum, and the costal margins are wider than the margins of the lower ribs. Rib #7 is variable. Ribs #8 through #10 articulate with the sternum via a common cartilaginous connection and the sternal ends are somewhat tapered. The last two pairs do not articulate with the sternum and the sternal ends are flat and completely tapered.

The typical rib consists of a **head** with a single or double articular facet, a slightly more slender **neck**, a **tubercle** with a single articular facet, and a **shaft** or body. The shaft extends outward from the tubercle and turns forward, forming the **angle** of the rib.

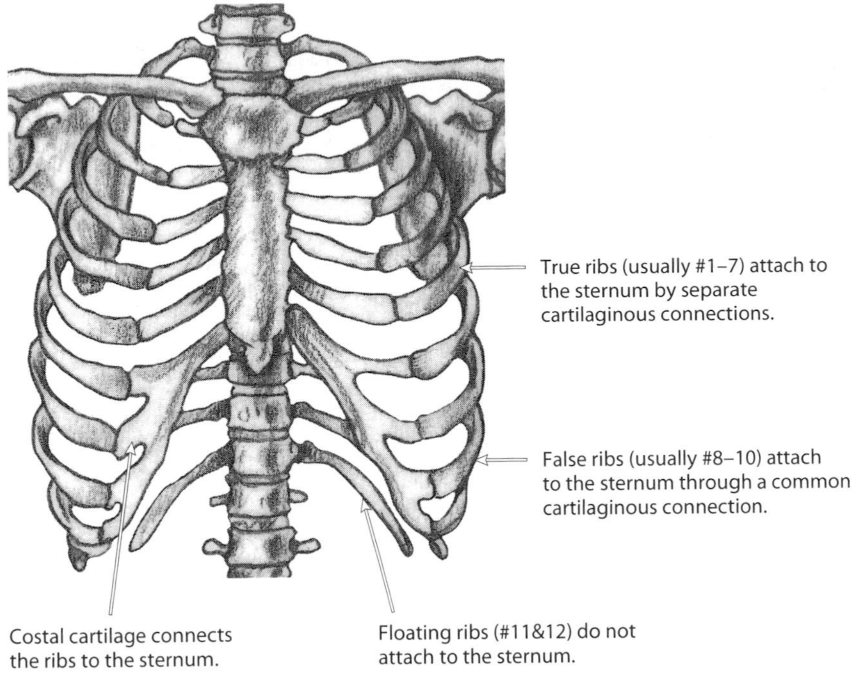
True ribs (usually #1–7) attach to the sternum by separate cartilaginous connections.
False ribs (usually #8–10) attach to the sternum through a common cartilaginous connection.
Costal cartilage connects the ribs to the sternum.
Floating ribs (#11&12) do not attach to the sternum.

Figure 4.10
Thorax, Frontal View
Note how each set of ribs articulates (or not) with the sternum.

> **Forensic Note**
> Perimortem damage to underlying organs may be revealed through careful analysis of rib trauma.

The rib head articulates with the lateral surface of the vertebral body, near the base of the vertebral arch. A second articulation occurs between the rib tubercle and the transverse process of the vertebra. The second articulation is present only on the upper nine or ten ribs. The lower ribs articulate only with the bodies of the vertebrae.

Rib Sorting: Left/Right and Superior/Inferior Recognition

With practice, it is possible to sort all of the ribs correctly and determine which may be missing or damaged. Start with the following guidelines:

1. Before beginning to sort the ribs, look at the curvature of an intact rib cage. It is shaped like a barrel, not a pyramid. The inner surfaces of the uppermost ribs face downward; the inner surfaces of the central ribs face medially; and the inner surfaces of the lowest ribs, the floating ribs, face slightly upward. You will see this change in orientation as you lay out the ribs from top to bottom on a flat surface. Almost everyone confuses the right and left twelfth ribs until they can visualize the top-to-bottom change in orientation.
2. Now, locate the first ribs. They are short, tightly curved, and almost flat. They also have relatively long necks. (The neck is the extension of bone between the two vertebral facets.) Place the first ribs on a flat surface. If the head is angled downward and touching the surface, the dorsal (superior) surface is up.
3. Next, find the floating ribs (#11 and #12) and separate them out. They have fan-shaped heads, no neck, and well-tapered sternal ends. (The sternal end is not cup shaped.) **The inner surface is superior, not inferior as is the case with the first rib.**
4. Sort the other nine pairs of ribs into groups of right ribs and left ribs. The head is posterior, the sternal end is anterior, and the sharp edge is inferior.

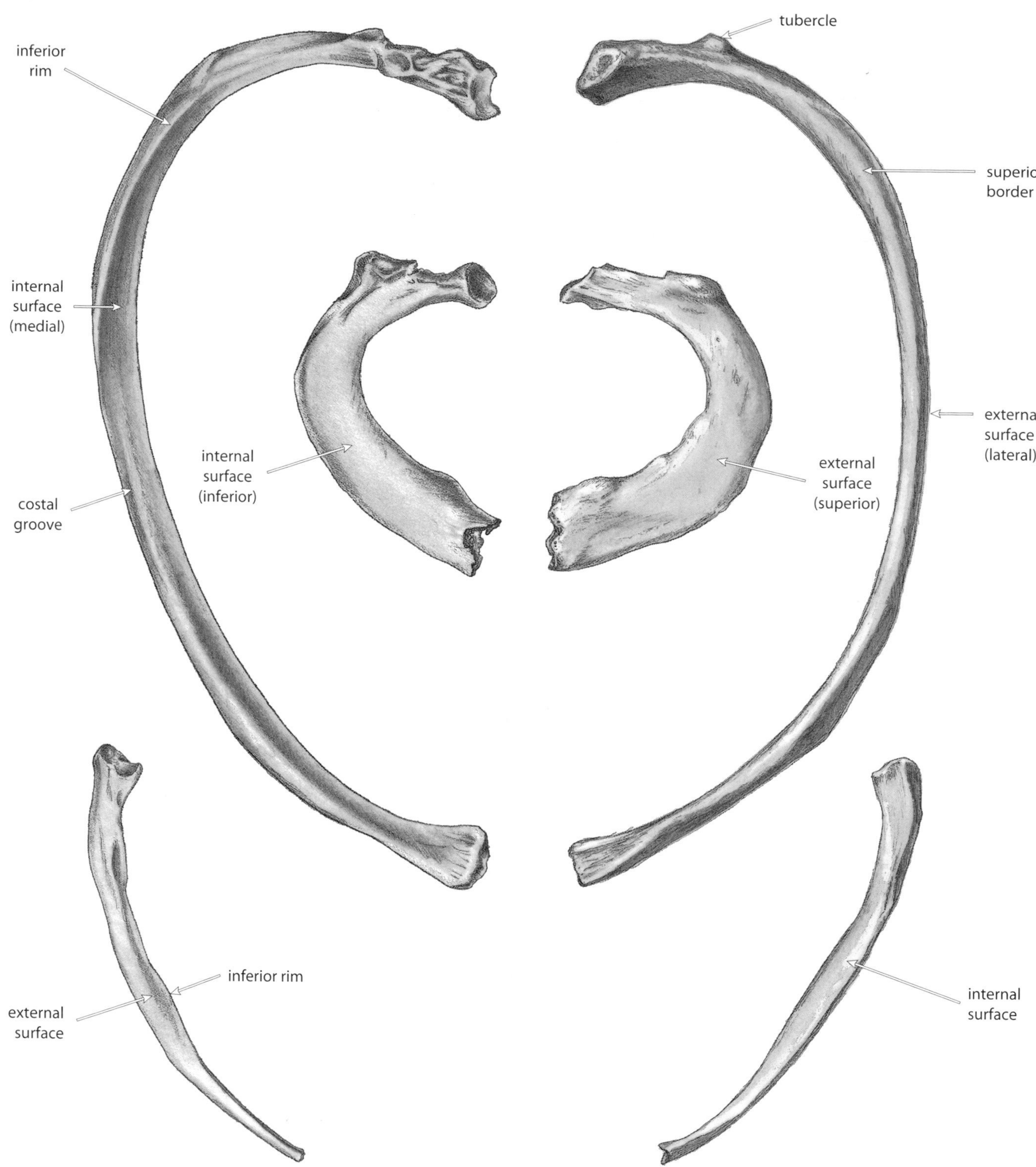

Figure 4.11
Left Ribs #1, #7 and #12, Inferior and Superior Views (70% Natural Size)
Note the inferior view of the first rib faces downward, but the inferior view of the last rib faces somewhat upward.

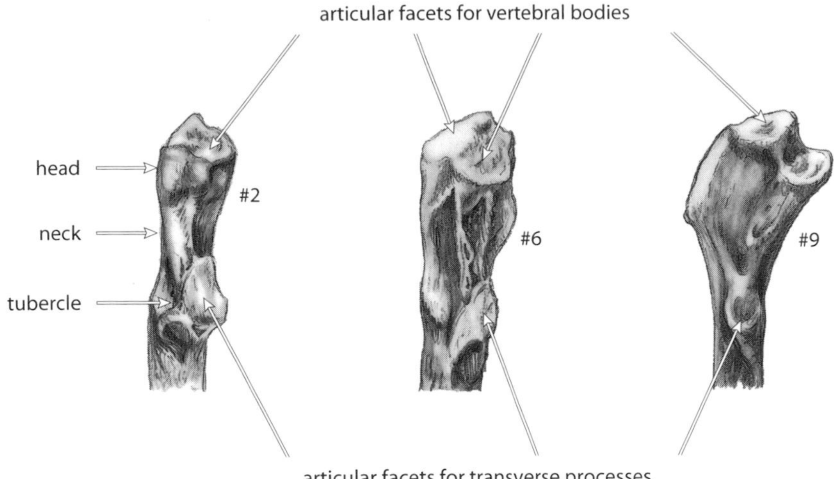

Figure 4.12
Rib Heads #2, #6, and #9
Note the changes in the shape of the head and the length of the neck from the upper ribs to the lower ribs.

5. With rib #1 as a starting point, sort one side from top to bottom, then the other. The shape of the heads change gradually from long and narrow to fan-shaped (see Figure 4.12). The length of the necks gradually shortens. The curvature of the ribs changes as the ribs conform to the outer surface of the barrel-shaped chest. The inner surface of the upper ribs faces toward the table surface**; the inner surface of the lower ribs faces away from the table surface.**
6. Check the arrangement of ribs from first to last. The head of rib #7 or #8 is usually the highest from the surface of the table. **Each rib conforms to the curvature of the adjacent ribs**. If the curvature is not consistent with the curvature of the adjacent ribs it is in the wrong place. Recheck the shape of the head and the length of the neck.
7. End by comparing each rib with the rib from the opposite side for consistency in overall shape and length.

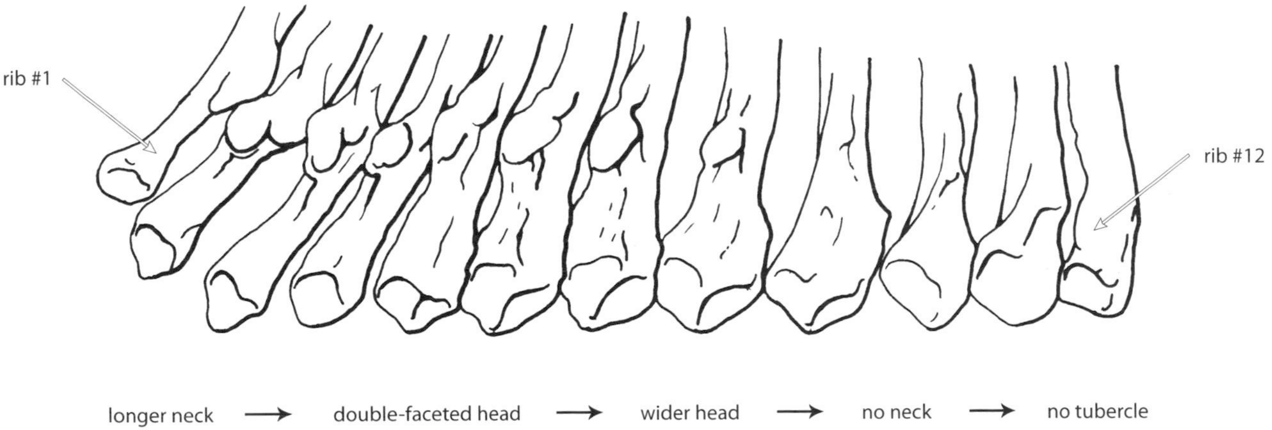

Figure 4.13
Comparison of Rib Heads, from #1 to #12
Note the progression of head size, neck length, and tubercles from upper to lower ribs.

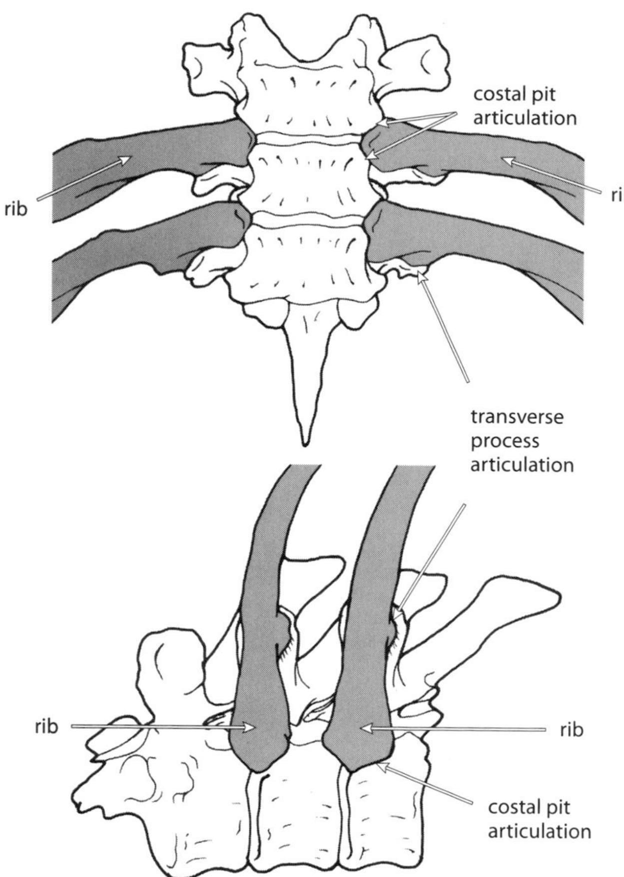

Figure 4.14
Rib Articulations, Anterior View and Lateral View
Ribs #2 through #10 usually articulate with two adjacent vertebral bodies as well as the intervertebral disk. Look for double facets on the rib heads, one facet for each half-pit on the superior and inferior edges of the vertebral bodies.

Individualization: Costo-Vertebral Articulations and Abnormalities

Rib abnormalities are not unusual. There can be more or less than twelve pairs. Sometimes the last pair of ribs is extremely reduced or missing. Ribs also fuse, flare, bridge, or bifurcate. It is easy to distinguish congenital anomalies from irregularities due to trauma by the presence or absence of callus formation. Rib abnormalities are usually asymptomatic, so they are useful for individual identification only if comparative radiographs are available.

Considerable individual variation exists in costo-vertebral articulations. The configuration described here is standard, but in some individuals, the whole rib cage is shifted cerebrally (toward the head). In others, the rib cage is shifted caudally (toward the lower back). This results in rib facets on lower cervical vertebrae or on upper lumbar vertebrae without the presence of actual cervical or lumbar ribs.

Origin and Growth

The primary centers of ossification are all present at birth. Three epiphyses develop at the vertebral end of the rib and none at the sternal end. The flake-like epiphyses are located at the head and both the articular and non-articular regions of the tubercle. The epiphyses of the tubercle fuse in the mid-teens and the epiphysis of the head fuses at 17 to 25 years of age.

Table 4.3 Rib Vocabulary

Term	Definition and Examples
GROOVE, COSTAL	the groove on the inferior edge of the inner surface of the rib
BODY OF RIB	the main part of the rib
RIB HEAD	the vertebral end of the rib
RIB NECK	the constricted part below the rib head on upper ribs (not obvious on lower ribs)
RIB TUBERCLE	the center of ossification between the neck and the body; part of the tubercle articulates with the vertebral transverse process
RIB, STERNAL END	the end of the rib that connects to the sternal cartilage; useful for aging purposes. Floating ribs have tapered sternal end, also called a floating end.
TRUE RIB	#1–#7, attach directly to the sternum via cartilage
FALSE RIB	#8–#10, join the sternum via the seventh rib cartilage
FLOATING RIB	#11–#12, do not attach to the sternum
STERNAL-END OSSIFICATION	osteophytic growth from the rib end into the sternal cartilage; cartilaginous calcification increases with age and varies with sex

STERNUM: THE BREAST BONE

DESCRIPTION, LOCATION, ARTICULATION

The adult **sternum** is commonly called a "breastbone." It is comprised of three elements: the **manubrium**, **the body of the sternum**, and the **xiphoid process**. The manubrium is superior. It forms the **jugular notch** at the base of the throat, between the two clavicles, and is clearly visible on the living person.

The body of the sternum articulates superiorly with the manubrium at a cartilaginous joint. The two bones are not in the same plane; therefore, the joint is palpable at the sternal angle, a couple of inches below the jugular notch. The angle of the joint provides for the outward curvature of the upper chest. The body sometimes fuses with the manubrium, particularly in older individuals. (This fusion is too variable to aid in age estimation.)

The body of the sternum articulates inferiorly with the xiphoid process. The joint is also cartilaginous and usually ossifies, fusing the body of the sternum with the xiphoid process by middle age.

The xiphoid is flat dorsoventrally but highly irregular in other dimensions. It can be narrow, wide, pointed, bifid, and/or perforated. The xiphoid process may appear insignificant, but it serves as the attachment point for much of the musculature of the abdomen.

The upper ten ribs attach to the sternum by cartilaginous extensions called "costal cartilage." The costal cartilage of the first rib attaches to the manubrium. The cartilage of the second rib attaches at the junction of the manubrium and the sternal body. Ribs #3 to #7 attach only to the body. Ribs #8 to #10 form a single cartilaginous connection and join with #7 at the inferior border of the sternal body.

INDIVIDUALIZATION

Rib attachments vary in number, the body varies in width, and the xiphoid process varies in shape. The body may be solid or perforated by a sternal foramen. The sternum is one more location to examine for possible radiographic identification.

> **Forensic Note**
>
> A perforated sternum may look like a gunshot wound. Beware of confusion.

ORIGIN AND GROWTH

The sternum is comprised of six primary centers of ossification. The manubrium and the upper three segments of the body are present at birth. The fourth segment of the body appears in the first year and the xiphoid begins to form after age 3. The sternal segments then fuse with each other in sequence from bottom to top.

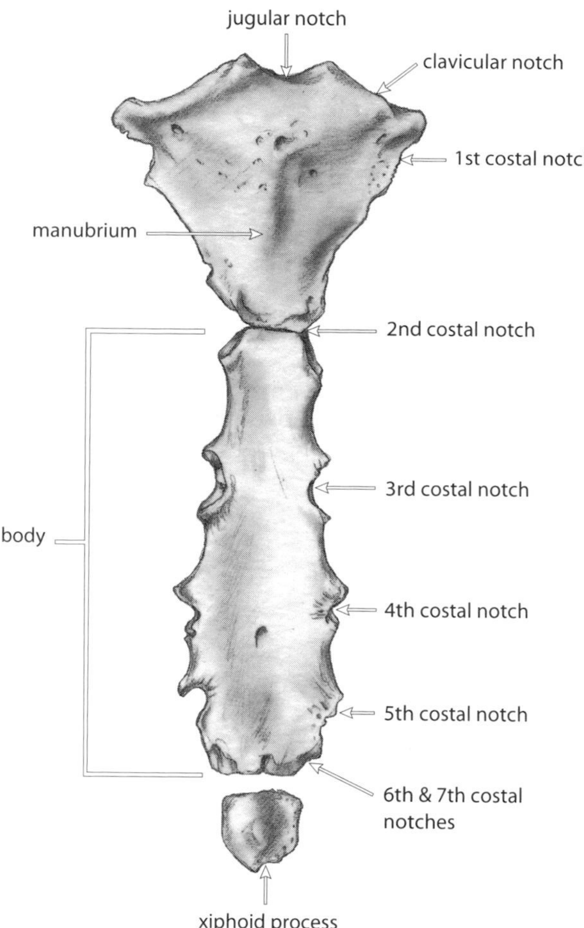

Figure 4.15
Adult Sternum, Anterior View (60% Natural Size)
Note the three basic parts of the adult sternum—manubrium, body, and xiphoid process. Further fusion is highly variable.

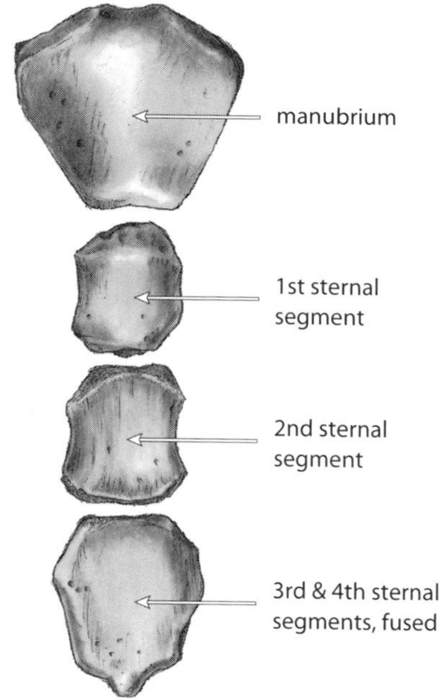

Figure 4.16
Juvenile Sternum (age 4), Anterior View (Natural Size)
Note the 3rd and 4th segments have fused and the xiphoid is not present. The age of appearance of the xiphoid is between 3–6 years.

Anatomic Note

The xiphoid can exhibit a variety of shapes—wide, narrow, rounded, pointed, bifid, perforated, and so on. It commonly fuses with the sternal body in adults.

Basic Ages of Fusion

segments 3 and 4	4–10 years
segment 2 with 3–4	11–16 years
segment 1 with 2–3–4	15–20 years
xiphoid to body	40+ years

Table 4.4 Sternum Vocabulary

Definition	Articulations and Attachments
BODY OF STERNUM	the main part of the sternum, the corpus sterni, fused from the four central centers of ossification
CLAVICULAR NOTCH	the articular facets for the clavicles, located on either side of the jugular notch of the manubrium
COSTAL NOTCH	the seven pairs of notches for joining of the costal cartilage with the sternum
JUGULAR NOTCH	the medial, superior notch on the manubrium
MANUBRIUM	the superior-most section of the sternum
STERNAL FORAMEN	an anomalous foramen in the sternal body
XIPHOID PROCESS	the inferior projection or tip of the sternum

The Aging Rib Cage

Age Changes in Sternal Rib Ends of Males

Ribs, like the rest of the skeleton, change with advancing age. The sternal end of the rib is connected to the sternum by cartilage. As the bone–cartilage interface is subjected to the normal stresses of life, the bone responds by steadily remodeling and gradually ossifying the cartilage.

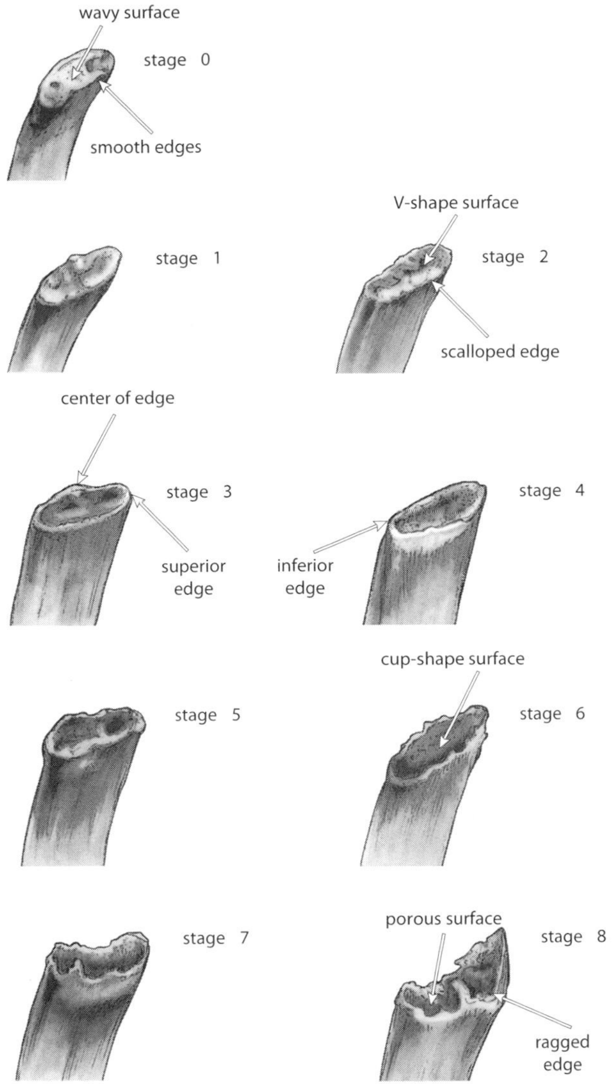

Stage 0: Child (Less than Midteens)

- A fairly flat rib end (no concavity)
- Smoothly rounded edges
- A slightly wavy or undulating surface

Stages 1–2: Teenager+ (Midteens to Early 20s)

- Beginnings of a V-shaped concavity
- Slightly sharper, scalloped edges
- A less wavy surface

Stages 3–4: Young Adult (Mid-20s to Early 30s)

- Deepening V-shaped concavity
- Less regular edges
- Centers of the flat edges project more than the superior and inferior rib edges
- Total loss of wavy surface

Stages 5–6: Older Adult (Mid-30s to Mid-50s)

- V-shaped concavity expands into a cup-shaped concavity
- Sharper edges
- Superior and inferior edges project as far as centers of edges

Stages 7–8: Elderly Adult (Older than Mid-50s)

- A deep, porous and irregular concavity
- Sharp, thin edges, increasingly ragged-looking
- Superior and inferior edges project more than the centers of the flat edges
- Development of "crab-claw" appearance

Figure 4.17
Sternal Rib End Aging, Stages 0–8, with Abbreviated Descriptions
Işcan and colleagues (1985) describe rib age changes by nine stages (beginning with Stage 0). The series of ribs illustrated here is simplified from the Işcan examples. It provides an overview of the basic changes in rib ends of males. For more detail, refer to the original publication and practice with casts of the original material available through France Casting. See page 300 for further information.

Sex Differences in Aging Ribs

Before applying the basic Işcan model to all ribs, note that the pattern of change in rib ends tends to differ between the sexes. Males are more likely to ossify along the margins of the rib cartilage, and females are more likely to ossify outward from the rib end and through the center of the rib cartilage. The crab-claw appearance is more characteristic of elderly males than females (McCormick & Stewart, 1988).

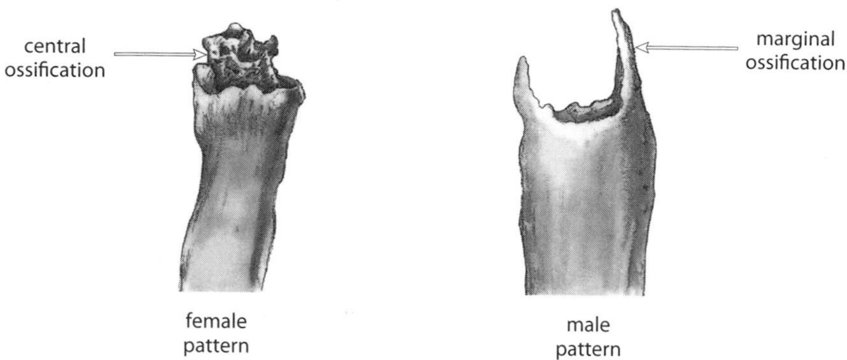

Figure 4.18
Sex Differences in Aging Sternal Rib Ends
Note that costal cartilage ossifies differently in male and female rib ends.

CHAPTER 5

The Vertebral Column

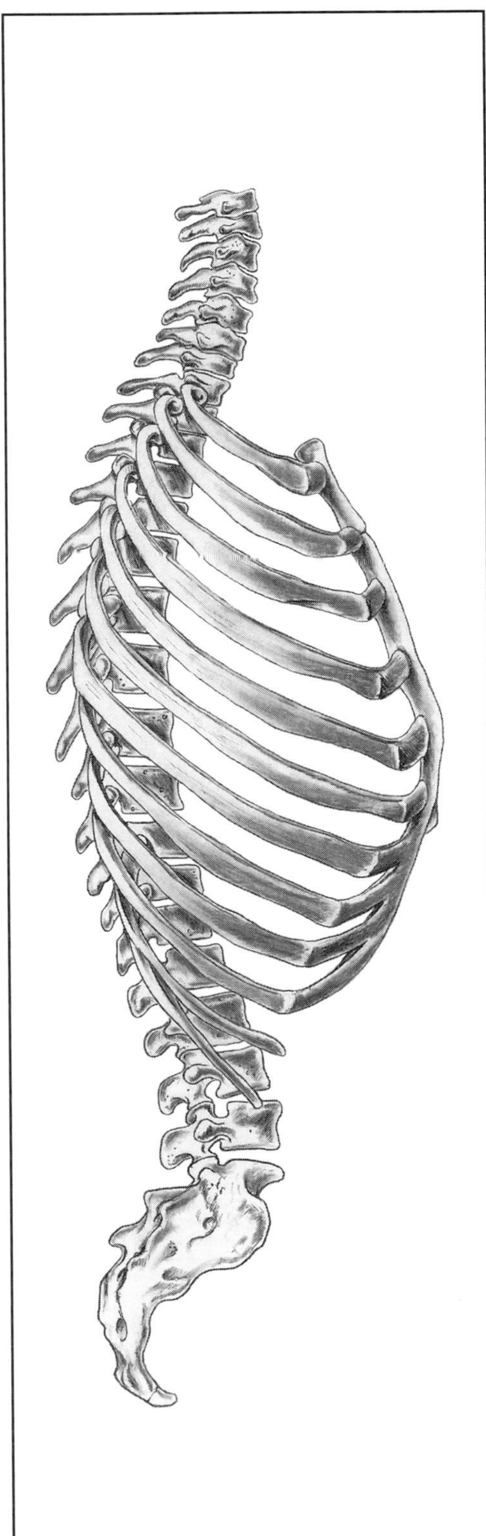

CHAPTER OUTLINE

INTRODUCTION

The vertebral column, or backbone, is composed of a sequence of irregular bones providing support and flexibility to the trunk of the body. The vertebral column defines the midline of the back from the base of the skull to the coccyx, a rudimentary internal tail. The number of vertebrae vary, but normally there are thirty-three, divided into five sections—seven **cervical**, twelve **thoracic**, five **lumbar**, five **sacral**, and four **coccygeal**.

DESCRIPTION, LOCATION, ARTICULATION

The vertebrae of the adult backbone are characterized by an anterior **vertebral body**, a posterior **vertebral arch**, and numerous processes for ligament attachment and bony articulation. The body and the arch encircle the **vertebral foramen**. Each vertebra forms a segment of the **vertebral canal**, which provides protection for the spinal nerve cord.

The arch has several distinct areas (See Figure 5.2):

- Two **pedicles** attach the arch to the body. They are pillar-like in form.
- Two **transverse processes** stretch out laterally. They articulate with the tubercles of the ribs in the thoracic vertebrae.
- Four **articular processes** (two superior and two inferior) reach out to articulate with adjacent vertebrae. C1 also articulates with the occipital bone, and the alae (wings) of the sacrum articulate with the ilium.
- Two **lamina** (flat surfaces) form the posterior surface of the arch. They are the walls of the arch, connecting the transverse processes with the spinous process.
- One **spinous process** projects posteriorly and inferiorly. (You can see and feel the tips of the spinous processes up and down the middle of the back.)

SUPERIOR/INFERIOR RECOGNITION

Begin by placing the spinous process toward you and the vertebral body away. Then look at the articular facets to determine the anatomical position of the vertebra. The superior facets face posteriorly and the inferior facets face anteriorly. In other words, the superior facets face the spinous process side and the inferior facets face the spinal canal and vertebral body.

INDIVIDUALIZATION

Vertebral columns carry a wide variety of unusual features which are characteristic of the individual, easy to visualize in antemortem radiographs, and serve to identify persons. The most obvious is the vertebral degeneration which advances with age and trauma. Vertebral bodies compress, osteophytes develop, Schmorl's nodes form.

Some developmental differences are less obvious. These include shifts in articulations between vertebrae and ribs. The rib cage may be shifted superiorly or inferiorly, resulting in articular facets on the seventh cervical or the first lumbar vertebra. Borders between sections of vertebra may shift also. The fifth lumbar vertebra may fuse with the first sacral vertebra and become integrated into the sacrum, or the first sacral vertebra may remain separate from the sacrum and appear to be a lumbar vertebra.

Other anomalies include spina bifida occulta, supernumary vertebrae, fused (block) vertebral bodies, and butterfly vertebrae. See paleopathology textbooks for plenty of examples (Aulderheide, 1998; Barnes, 1994; Waldron, 2009).

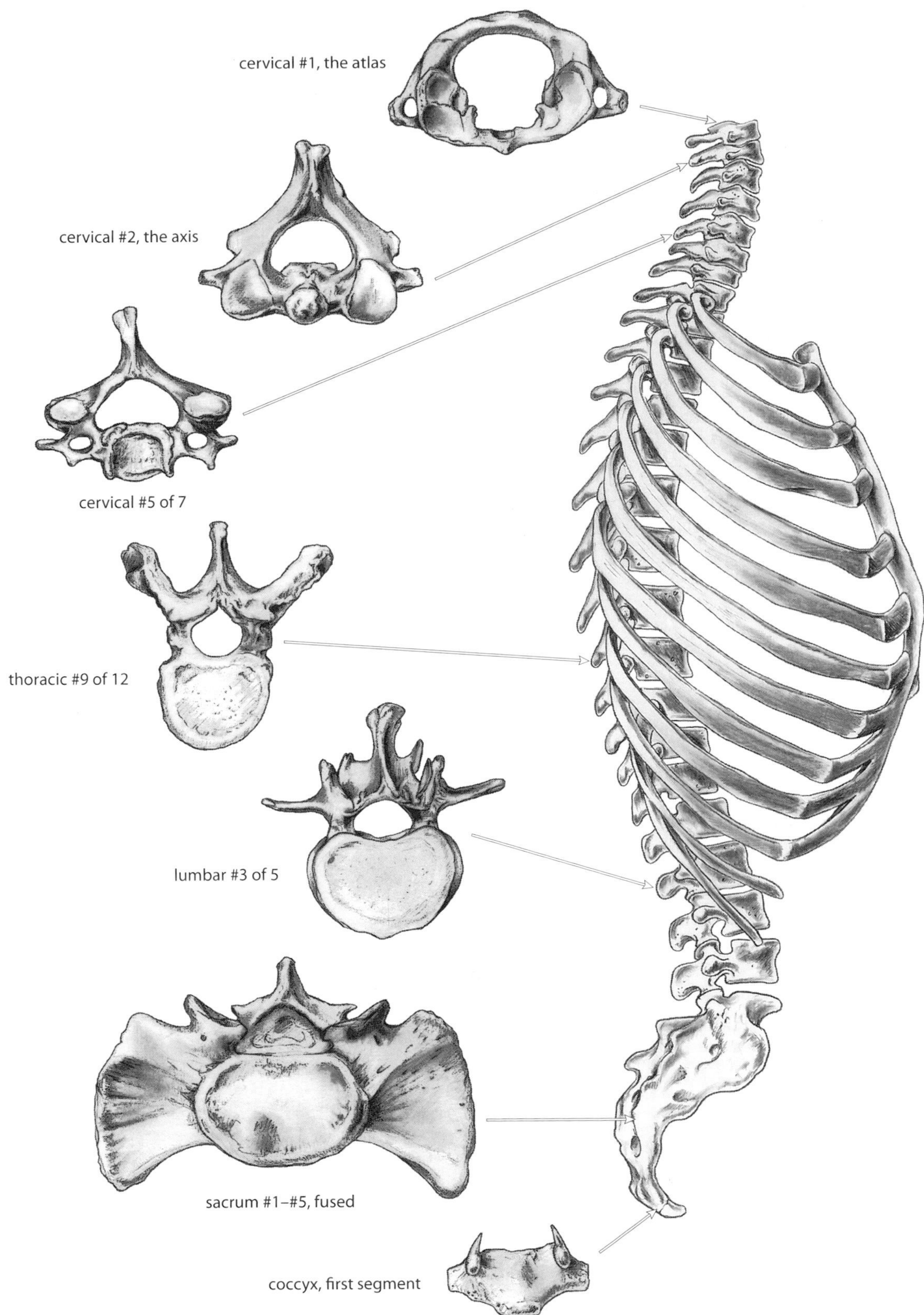

Figure 5.1

Vertebral Column, Lateral View with Examples: Superior Views of C1, C2, C5, T9, L3, and Sacrum, Dorsal View of Coccyx

Note each example is either unique, as C1 and C2 or characteristic of a specific section of the column, that is cervical, thoracic, lumbar, sacral, and coccygeal.

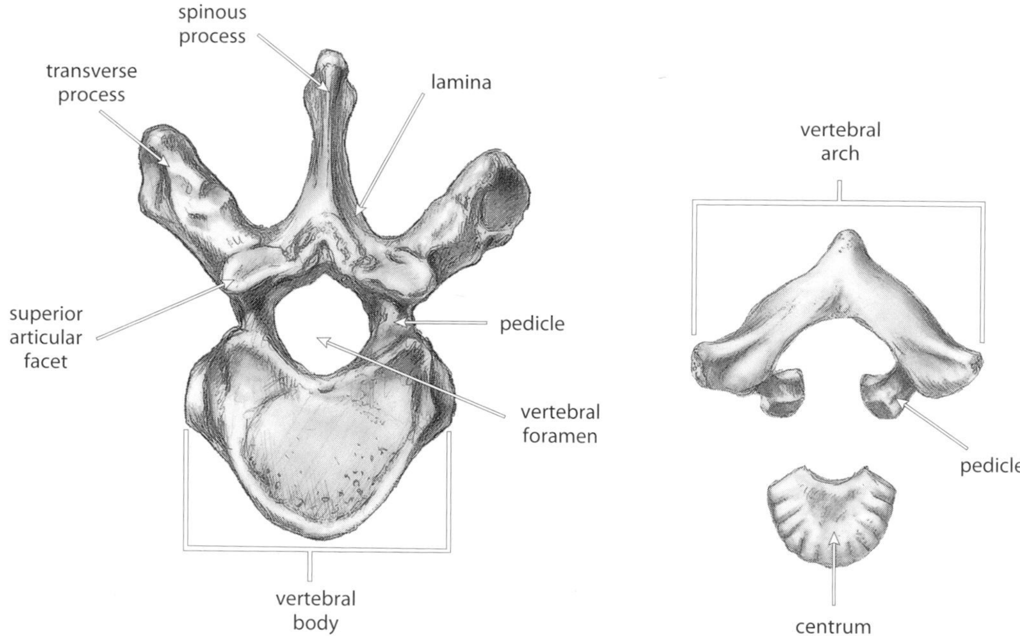

Figure 5.2
Typical Adult Vertebra (T6), Superior View (Natural Size)

Figure 5.3
Typical Immature Vertebra (2–5 years old), Superior View (Natural Size)
Note the absence of secondary centers of ossification.

Origin and Growth

A typical vertebra develops from three primary centers of ossification—a **centrum** and two halves of the **vertebral arch**. The thoracic vertebral arches begin fusing in the second half of the first postnatal year. The arches of the cervical vertebrae may still be open at the beginning of the second year and the lower lumbar arches may be open as late as the fifth year.

The pedicles of the vertebral arch fuse to the centrum of the body between 2 and 5 years of age. The ends of the pedicles actually become part of the adult vertebral body, making the overall shape of the body more oval.

The mature vertebra is distinguished from the immature form by the addition of five epiphyses, or secondary centers of ossification: the tips of the transverse processes, the tip of the spinous process, and the superior and inferior edges of the vertebral bodies (known as **epiphyseal rings**).

The secondary centers appear at the beginning of puberty (12 to 16 years of age) and fuse by the end of puberty (18 to 24 years of age). See Figure 5.10, Age Changes in Vertebral Bodies.

Development of the sacrum is more complex than other vertebrae. It grows from approximately twenty-one primary centers of ossification. Each sacral segment begins with the same three centers as the other vertebrae, but, in addition, there are separate centers of ossification lateral to the upper sacral bodies. The extra centers fuse with the bodies and pedicles to form the alae (wings) of the sacrum.

Cervical Vertebrae (Atlas, Axis, and C3–C7)

Seven cervical vertebrae make up the neck. All cervical vertebrae are characterized by **transverse foramina**, one on each side of the vertebral body, in the base of the transverse process. Occasionally, C7 has a half rib facet at the inferior edge, but it can still be recognized by the transverse foramina.

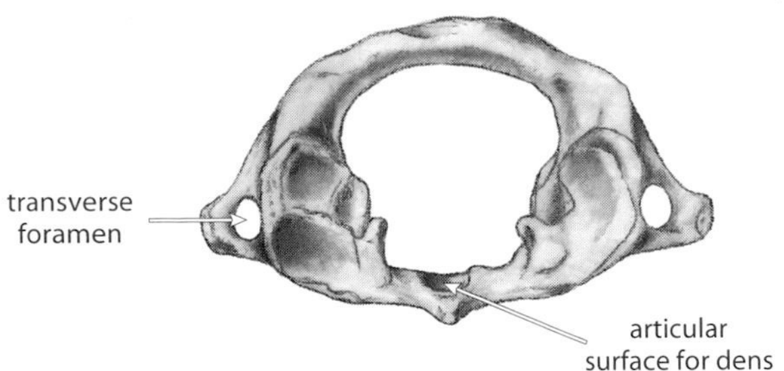

Figure 5.4a
Atlas, Superior View (80% Natural Size)
Note the absence of a vertebral body.

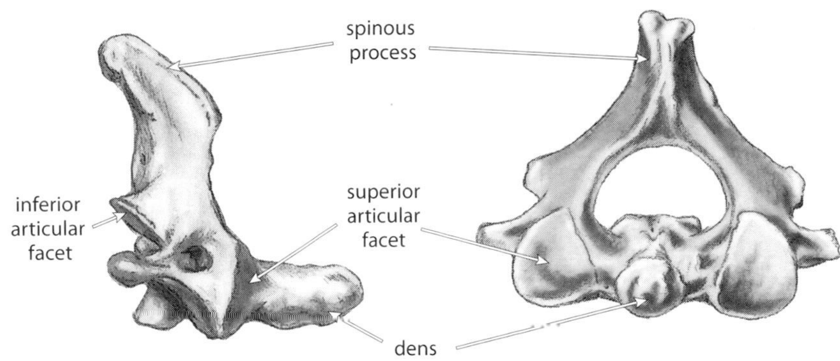

Figure 5.4b
Axis, Lateral View (80% Natural Size)
Note the presence of the dens.

Figure 5.4c
Axis, Superior View (80% Natural Size)
Note the slightly bifid spinous process.

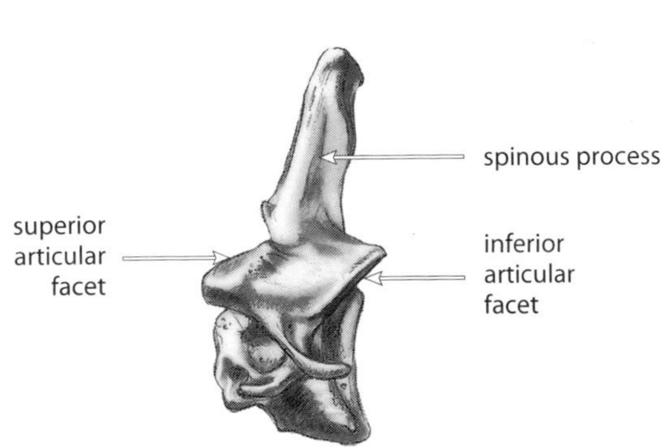

Figure 5.4d
C5, Lateral View (80% Natural Size)

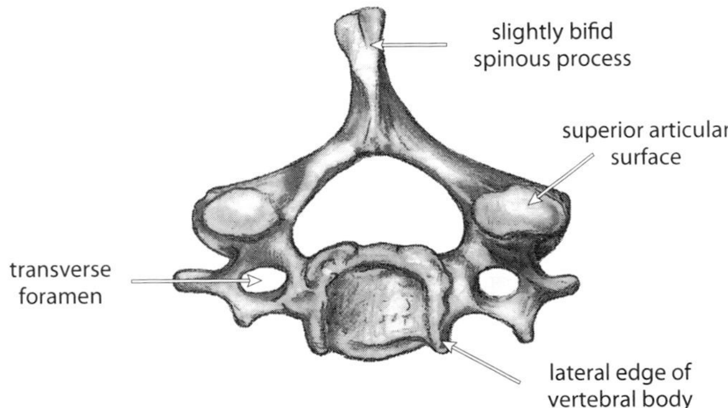

Figure 5.4e
C5, Superior View (80% Natural Size)
Note the key characteristic of all cervical vertebrae: transverse foramina.

The occipital condyles of the cranium articulate with the first cervical vertebra, which is appropriately called the **atlas**. The atlas is a ring-like bone with no vertebral body. It rotates on the **dens** of the second cervical vertebra, the **axis**. (The dens is sometimes called an **odontoid process** because of its tooth-like appearance.) The dens extends upward from the body of the axis, and it is, in fact, the "misplaced" centrum of the atlas. During fetal development, the center of ossification that appears in the position of the first centrum proceeds to fuse with the second centrum, becoming part of the axis instead of the atlas. The atlas and the axis, by their curious arrangement of parts, aid in providing both stability and mobility for the head.

The subsequent five cervical vertebrae (C3–C7) are less distinctive in appearance and do not have individual names. The spinous processes are frequently bifid and the vertebral bodies are laterally elongated or squared in shape. It is not unusual for the lateral edges of the vertebral body to lip upward.

Thoracic Vertebrae (T1–T12)

The thoracic vertebrae connect with the rib cage; therefore, each thoracic vertebra is characterized by the presence of **rib facets**, also known as **costal pits**. (See Figure 4.14, Rib Articulations.) T1 through T10 have rib facets on each side of the vertebral bodies and on the anterior surface of the transverse processes. T11 and T12 have facets only on the vertebral bodies, not on the transverse processes.

There is variation in the way that ribs articulate with vertebrae, but the following is a typical pattern, as viewed from the side (lateral view):

- T1 has one complete facet, a half facet, and a facet for the rib tubercle on the transverse process.
- T2 through T9 have two half facets—at the superior and inferior edges of the centrum—and a facet on the transverse process.
- T10 has one complete facet and a facet on the transverse process.
- T11 has one complete facet and no facet on the transverse process.
- T12 has one complete facet, no facet on the transverse process, and a widened inferior surface of the body, matching the lumbar pattern.

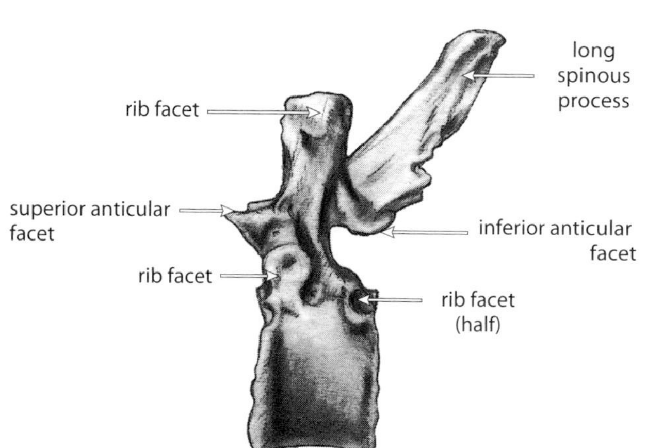

Figure 5.5a
T9, Lateral View (80% Natural Size)
Note the key characteristic of all thoracic vertebrae: rib facets.

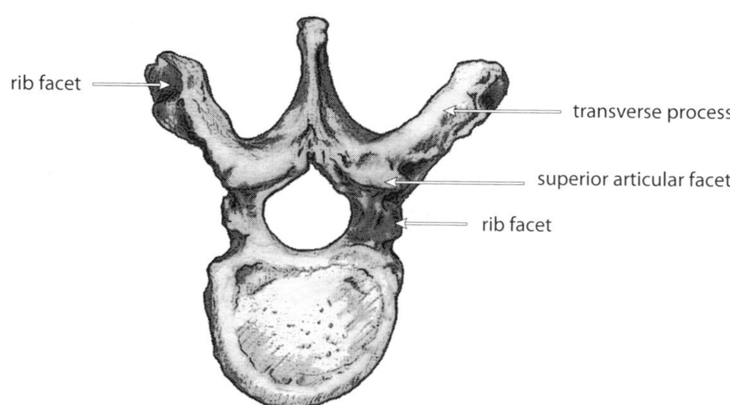

Figure 5.5b
T9, Superior View (80% Natural Size)
Note the angle of the transverse processes and the flat articular facets.

Lumbar Vertebrae (L1–L5)

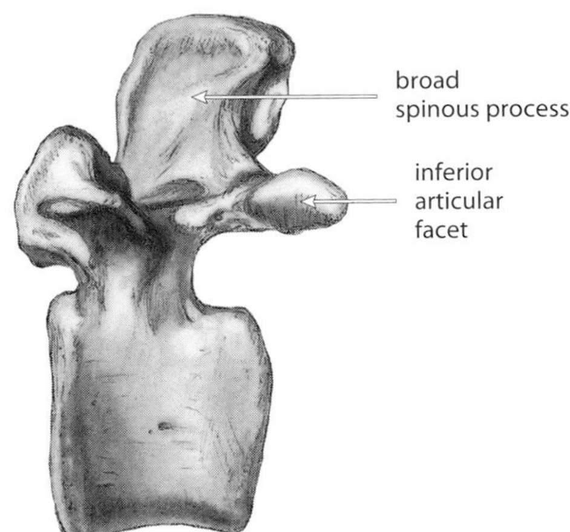

Figure 5.6a
L3, Lateral View (80% Natural Size)
Note the key characteristic of lumbar vertebrae: no rib facets.

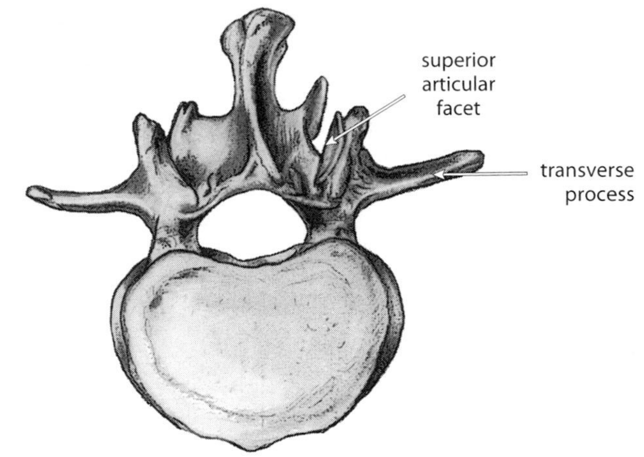

Figure 5.6b
L3, Superior View (80% Natural Size)
Note the horizontal transverse processes and the curved articular facets.

The lumbar vertebrae are the bones of the lower back. The key characteristic of lumbar vertebrae is not what you see, but rather what you don't see. Lumbar vertebrae have neither transverse foramina nor rib facets. They are large vertebrae with short, wide spinous processes and flattened transverse processes. L1 is easily confused with T12, but T12 usually has a clear costal facet whereas L1 normally has none, although there are occasional exceptions in which L1 has a half facet at the superior margin.

The superior and inferior articular facets gradually change in both curvature and angle from the cervical to the lumbar vertebrae. The facets of the upper vertebrae are flat; those of the lumbar vertebrae are U-shaped. The lumbar region is most likely to sustain damage from strenuous activity, but the articular facets help counter this tendency by limiting the range of movement and providing some stability in the lower back.

The lumbar spinous processes tend to be flat and rather squared instead of pointed as in thoracic vertebrae.

Anatomic Note
L5 is sometimes incorporated into the sacrum.

Sacral Vertebrae (S1–S5 or Sacrum)

The **sacrum** is the large, wedge-shaped bone that makes up the curved posterior wall of the pelvic girdle. It is formed from fusion of the five sacral vertebrae and their lateral extensions, the **alae** (wings). The sacral bodies are large and the spinous processes are greatly reduced. The sacrum connects laterally, at the **auricular surfaces** with the innominates. (The word, auricular, refers to the ear-like shape of the surface.) The most anterior point of the sacrum is the **promontory**, located at the center of the superior border of the first sacral body.

Sex Note

The sacrum tends to be more curved in males and flatter in females; however, this is difficult to assess except in extreme cases.

Age Note

The transverse line between S1 and S2 fuses in the midtwenties or later.

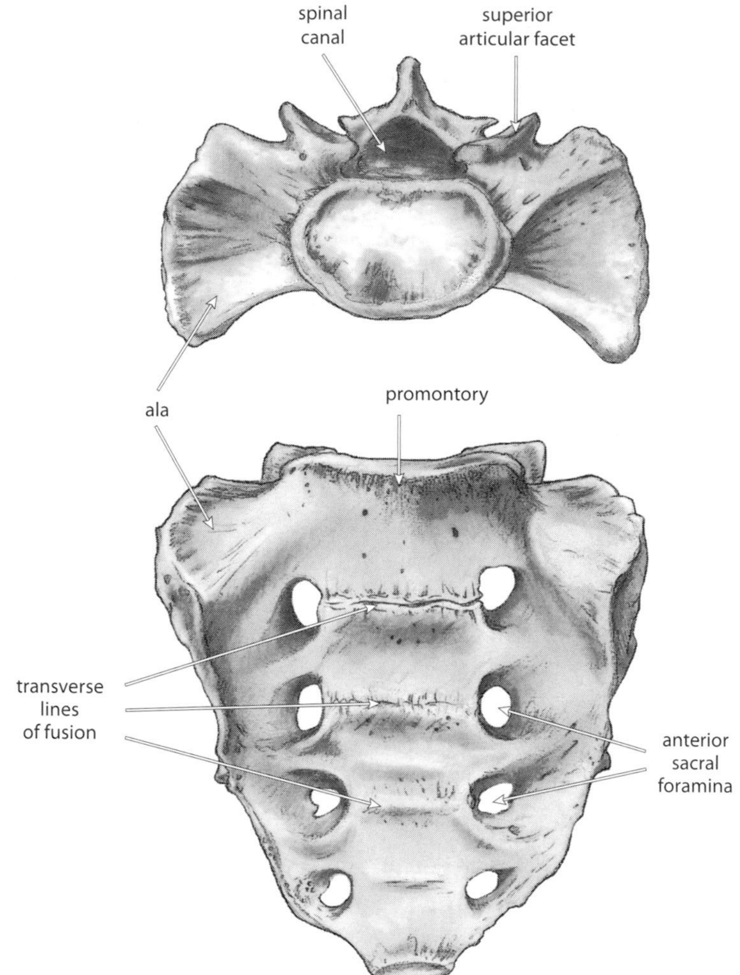

Figure 5.7
Sacrum, Superior and Anterior Views (70% Natural Size)

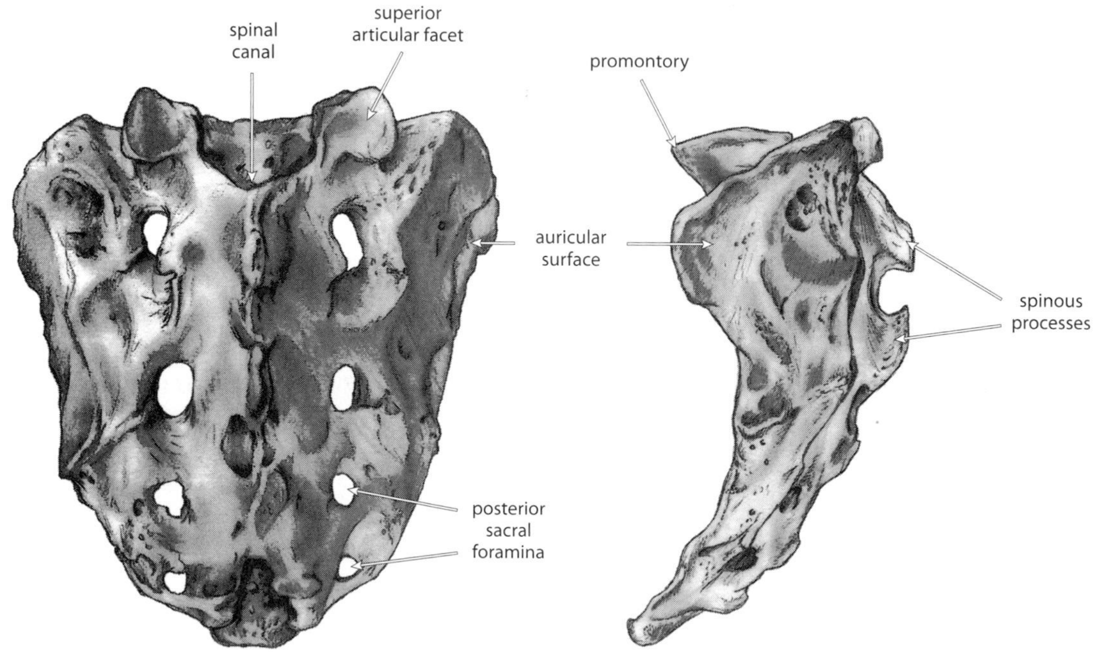

Figure 5.8
Sacrum, Posterior and Lateral Views (70% Natural Size)

Coccygeal Vertebrae (Coccyx)

The **coccygeal vertebrae** make up the "tail bone." As a group they are called the **coccyx**. The number of segments varies from three to five (usually four). The first section, the **cornua** (horns), is distinctive in that it has rudimentary transverse processes and superior articular processes without articular surfaces. The other coccygeal segments are very small and variable in shape. They can be mistaken for medial and distal toe phalanges.

It is not unusual for all of the coccygeal bones to fuse with each other or for the coccyx to fuse with the sacrum. If not fused, these tiny bones are frequently lost or go completely unnoticed.

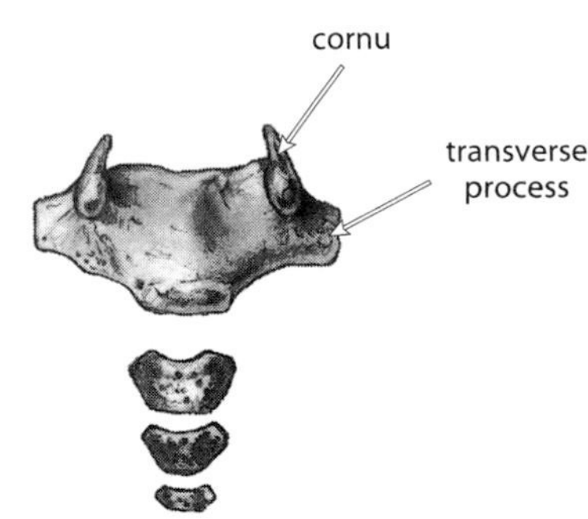

Figure 5.9
Coccyx, Posterior View (Natural Size)
Note the shape of the smaller segments. They are sometimes confused with medial and distal toe phalanges.

Reassembling the Vertebral Column, Step by Step

The process of reassembling a vertebral column in correct order need not be difficult. Approach it methodically and the bones will usually go together quickly and easily. Remember to sort first. Then begin at the top and work downward using the steps described here.

The assembled column is easier to examine and photograph if it is placed on a towel or paper that is rolled from two sides to make a long central groove. Rubber bands work well to secure the ends of the towel and keep the apparatus from unrolling. The vertebrae can be placed on the groove with the dorsal spines down, the transverse processes down, or the vertebral bodies down.

Sort First

1. Sort the vertebrae by section in three rows—cervical, thoracic, and lumbar.
2. Place each vertebra on the table with the dorsal spine pointed away.
3. Turn each vertebra so that the superior surface is up and the inferior surface is on the table.

Begin at the Top

4. Fit the atlas and axis together.
5. Look at the inferior surface of the axis—then look for the cervical with a superior surface that closely resembles the inferior surface of the axis.
6. When you find C3 and fit it to the axis, look at the inferior surface of C3 and search the remaining cervicals for a matching superior surface.
7. Continue matching the surfaces of adjacent vertebral bodies one by one from top to bottom.

Stop and View the Results

Look at the completed assemblage from all sides. Compare each element of each vertebra—vertebral bodies, spinous processes, transverse processes, articular surfaces. There should be consistency in the flow from one vertebra to another with no sudden changes in size or shape. All of the articular surfaces should approximate neatly.

Table 5.1 Vertebral Vocabulary

TERM	DEFINITION
ARCH, VERTEBRAL	the neural arch—formed from two halves which fuse between the ages of 1 and 3 years
ARTICULAR FACET	any bony surface that articulates with another bony surface (superior articular facet of the vertebra)
AURICULAR SURFACE	the lateral ear-shaped surface of the sacrum that articulates with the innominate; the surface of the sacroiliac joint
CENTRUM	the body of the vertebra, especially the body without epiphyseal rings
COCCYX	the tailbone, the inferior segment of the vertebral column, composed of 3–5 separate vertebrae, often fused together and sometime fused to the sacrum
COSTAL PIT	articular surface for rib on the thoracic vertebral body and transverse processes (rib facet)
DENS	a tooth-like projection; odontoid process of atlas (*dens epistropheus*)
EPIPHYSEAL RING	the secondary centers of ossification that fuse to the superior and inferior surfaces of the vertebral centrum
FORAMEN, TRANSVERSE	the aperture in the transverse process of the cervical vertebrae
FORAMEN, VERTEBRAL	the aperture between the vertebral arch and the vertebral body encircling the spinal cord
PROCESS, TRANSVERSE	lateral vertebral processes, some of which articulate with ribs
PROCESS, SUPERIOR ARTICULAR	vertebral processes that articulate with the inferior articular processes of the next higher vertebra
PROCESS, INFERIOR ARTICULAR	vertebral processes that articulate with the superior articular processes of the next lower vertebra
PROCESS, SPINOUS	the process that projects toward the dorsal surface of the back
PROCESS, ARTICULAR	any projection that serves to articulate
PROMONTORY; PROMONTORIUM	a raised place; the most ventral prominent median point of the lumbosacral symphysis; the most anterosuperior point on the sacrum
VERTEBRA (PL. VERTEBRAE)	a single segment of the spinal column. There are seven cervical vertebrae, twelve thoracic vertebra, five lumbar, five sacral (fused to form the sacrum), and four coccygeal (often fused together and sometimes fused to the sacrum)
VERTEBRAL CANAL	the channel formed by the vertebrae and encircling the spinal cord
VERTEBRAL BODY	the centrum and its epiphyseal rings; the arch and the body fuse between the ages of 3 and 7 years

THE AGING VERTEBRAL BODY

The vertebral body changes with advancing age, just as the rest of the skeleton. Albert and Maples (1995) showed that the advancement of epiphyseal ring fusion can be used to age persons between 16 and 30 years of age. Further analysis can be accomplished by assessing the development of osteoarthritic lipping at the edges of vertebral bodies, but after age 30, vertebral age assessment is less accurate.

AGE CHANGES IN VERTEBRAL BODIES, SUPERIOR AND LATERAL VIEWS

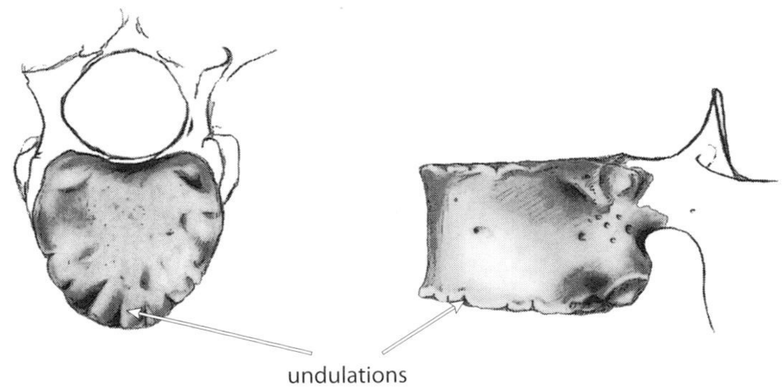

STAGE 1: CHILD (LESS THAN 16 YEARS)

- The epiphyseal ring is absent.
- Regular undulations are present on edges of vertebral body.

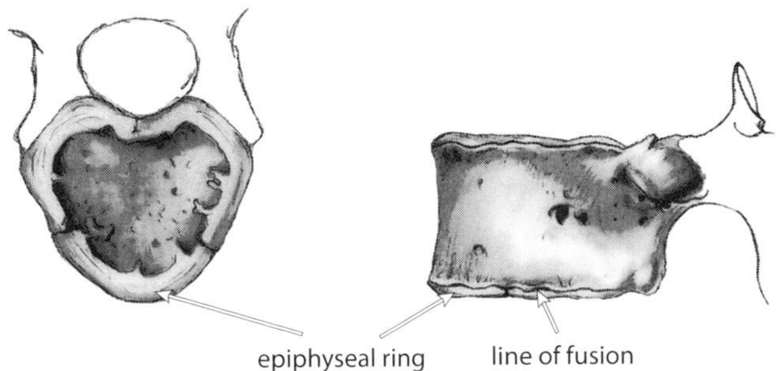

STAGE 2: LATE TEENAGER (16–20 YEARS)

- The epiphyseal ring is in the process of fusing.
- The line of fusion is clear.
- The epiphyseal ring chips off easily.

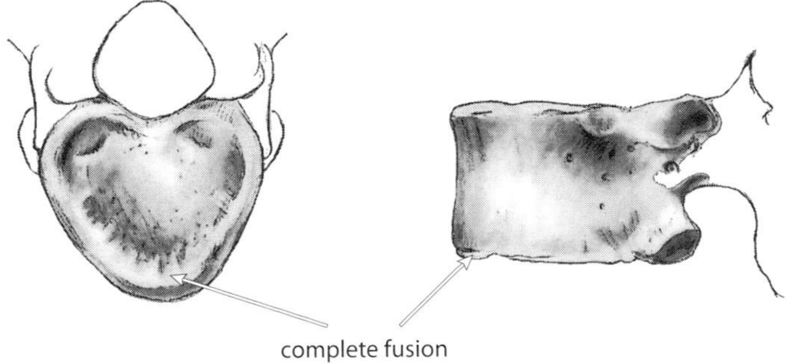

STAGE 3: YOUNG ADULT (20–29 YEARS)

- The epiphyseal ring is completely fused.
- The line of fusion is not visible.
- No osteoarthritis is visible.
- The bone is smooth and solid.

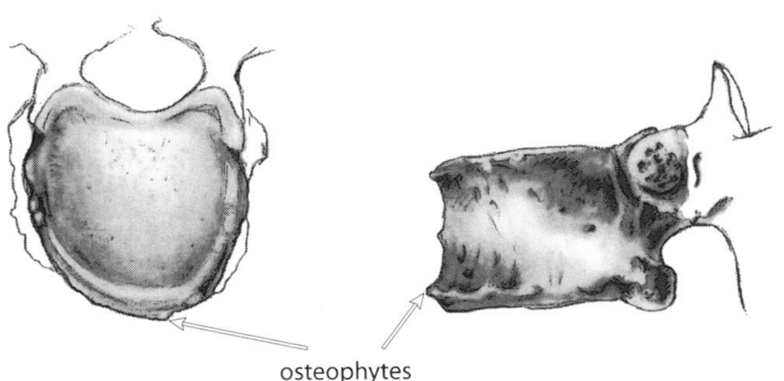

STAGE 4: OLDER ADULT (OVER 30 YEARS)

- The epiphyseal ring is obliterated.
- Osteophytic growth is progressing on the edges of the vertebral bodies.
- The bone (particularly the intervertebral surface) is increasingly porous.

Figure 5.10
Vertebral Aging in Four Stages with Abbreviated Descriptions
These illustrations are adapted from the Albert and Maples (1995) examples. They provide an overview of the basic age-related changes in vertebral bodies. For more detail, refer to the original publication and practice with casts of the original material available through Bone Clones. See page 300 in the section, "Sources for Casts, Instruments, and Tools" for more information.

Age Changes in Older Vertebral Bodies: Osteophytic Growth

Vertebral osteoarthritis has been used for age estimation by an elaborate method of scoring osteophytes in both the thoracic and lumbar vertebrae (Snodgrass, 2004; Stewart, 1958). There is no question about the progression of osteophytic growth with age, but it is greatly affected by level and type of activity. I'm not going to present the full method here, but it is available in the literature. Right now, the important thing is to recognize osteophytes and notice the difference between individual trauma-induced osteophytes in a young back and generalized osteophytic growth in an older back.

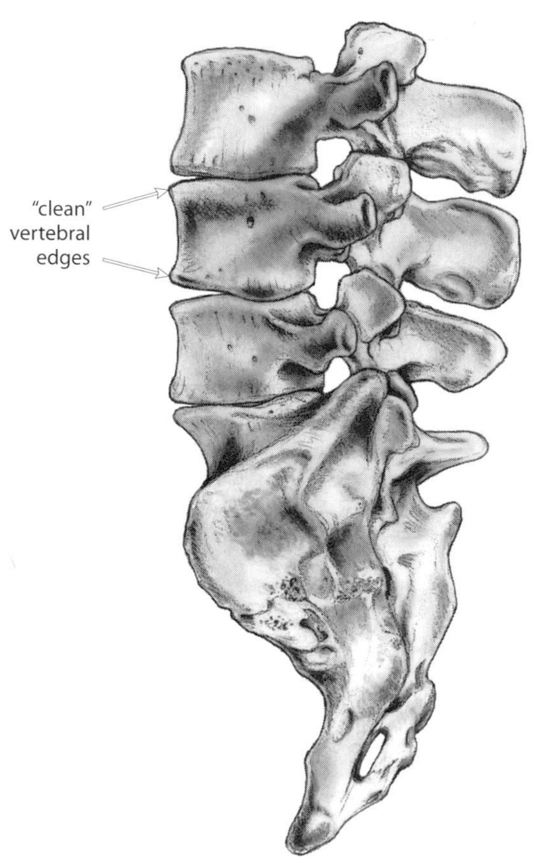

Figure 5.11a
A Young-Looking Back
The lumbar vertebrae shown here are typical of a young person who has experienced no unusual back trauma. The edges of the vertebral bodies are smooth and regular in shape. The auricular surface of the sacrum is smooth and dense, but not sharply lipped.

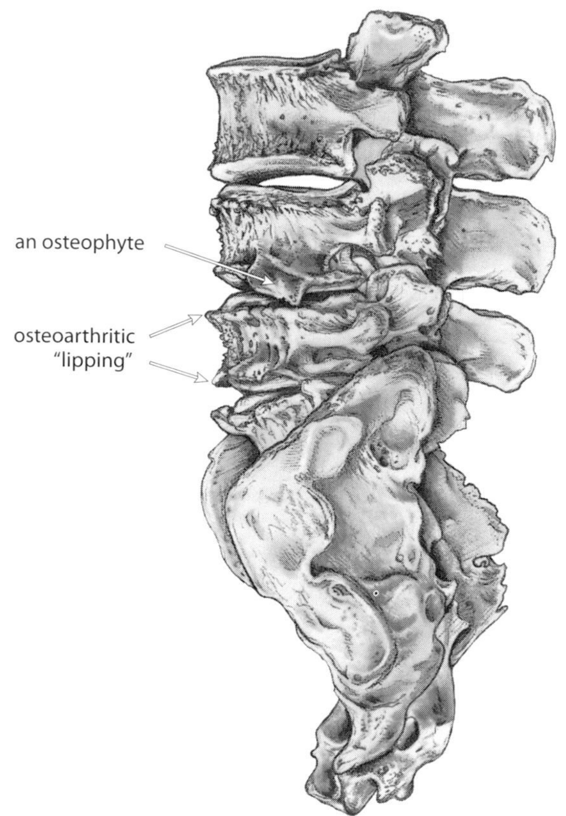

Figure 5.11b
An Elderly or a "Hard-Working" Back
The lumbar vertebrae shown here are typical of either an elderly person or a person with a history of heavy labor (or both). The edges of the vertebral bodies are sharp and irregular. Bony outgrowths (osteophytes) are present. The auricular surface of the sacrum is rough and porous with sharply defined edges.

CHAPTER 6

The Arm: Humerus, Radius, and Ulna

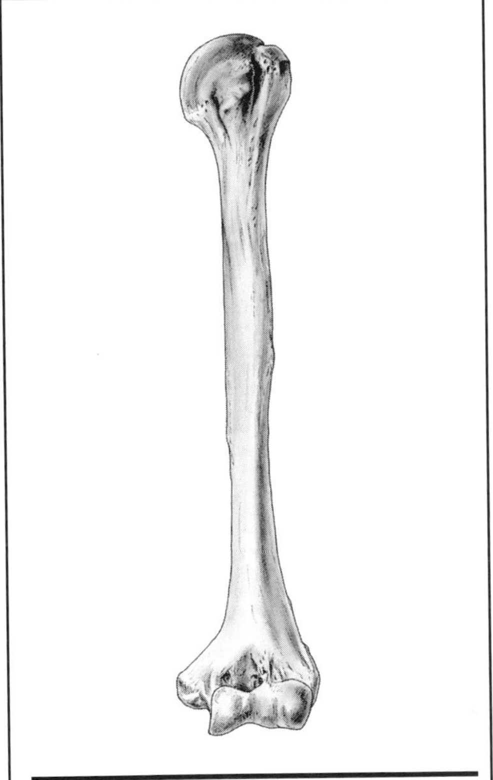

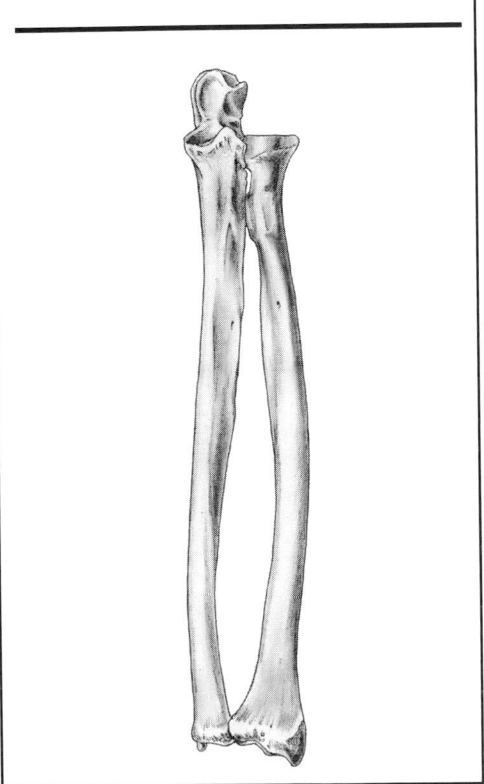

CHAPTER OUTLINE

Introduction

Three bones are present between the shoulder and the wrist—one in the upper arm, two in the forearm. The upper arm bone is the humerus; the forearm bones are the radius and the ulna. Together, they form a versatile mechanical system capable of flexion, extension, and rotation—three major types of joint movement.

Humerus—The Upper Arm

Description, Location, Articulation

The **humerus** is one of the major long bones of the skeleton. It can be quickly recognized by the **head**, a half-ball-shaped structure at the proximal end. The head articulates with the scapula at the shoulder. The entire head is an articular surface that moves on the small, ovoid articular surface of the scapula, the glenoid fossa. The range of movement is enormous in this type of joint. (The probability of dislocation is also significant.)

Two tubercles are present on the anterior surface of the proximal humerus. The **greater tubercle** is larger and protrudes anterolaterally. The **lesser tubercle** protrudes anteriorly.

The mid-shaft is fairly circular in cross section. It is differentiated from the other long bone shafts by the lack of full-length ridges. (The radius, ulna, tibia, and fibula display interosseous crests, and the posterior femur has a long muscular insertion site, the linea aspera.)

The distal humerus articulates with the radius and ulna at the elbow. The distal articular surface of the humerus is irregular, but it can be divided into two distinct parts. The **trochlea** is the larger, spool-like surface that serves as a bidirectional surface for the olecranon process of the ulna. The **capitulum** is a smaller, rounded surface lateral to the trochlea on the anterior side. It serves as a rotational surface for the head of the radius. Two distinct types of movement are possible at this one joint—flexion and extension at the trochlea, rotation at the capitulum.

Fossae (depressions) are present on both the anterior and posterior surfaces of the distal humerus. On the posterior surface, the **olecranon fossa** receives the olecranon process of the ulna during extension. On the anterior surface, the smaller **coronoid fossa** receives the coronoid process of the ulna during maximum flexion.

Left/Right Recognition

Epicondyles bulge laterally and medially above the condyles of the distal humerus. The **medial epicondyle** is larger than the **lateral epicondyle** and serves as a good clue for distinguishing right from left. If the olecranon fossa is posterior and distal, the medial epicondyle points toward the body.

If only the shaft is available, locate the spiral groove and move your thumb along the groove and away from your body. The shaft twists away from the side of origin. It doesn't matter which end of the bone is up.

Handedness

The **deltoid tuberosity** (the attachment area for the deltoideus muscle) tends to be slightly larger and sometimes more rugged on the dominant side. Compare the two humeri for differences.

Sexual Differences

The humerus is particularly useful for physical description because the deltoid tuberosity provides one of the more obvious indicators of the degree of upper-body muscular development. The *deltoideus,* one of the major abductor muscles of the arm, attaches at the deltoid tuberosity. As muscle size increases, the attachment area enlarges by increasing in rugosity and bulging outward. It is typical for attachment areas to change in contour more than diameter. (*Suggestion:* Gain experience by lining up a series of adult humeri and comparing the size, shape, and rugosity of the deltoid tuberosities.)

It is not uncommon for an **olecranon foramen** or septal aperture (a small hole) to appear within the thin bony plate of the olecranon fossa. This is more common in gracile individuals, and females are more likely to have an olecranon foramen than males. Females are also more likely to be capable of hyperextension at the elbow joint.

According to Stewart (1979), sex can be estimated by the vertical diameter of the humeral head. As with all other methods, consider the population and only make decisions after considering multiple variables.

Table 6.1 Sex Estimation from the Vertical Diameter of the Humeral Head

Females	Indeterminant	Males
<43 mm	43–47 mm	>47 mm

Origin and Growth

The humerus develops from no less than eight centers of ossification—the shaft, head, greater tubercle, lesser tubercle, capitulum, trochlea, lateral epicondyle, and medial epicondyle. The major centers, most likely to be found with skeletonized juvenile remains, are actually composite epiphyses. The proximal epiphysis is composed of the ossification centers for the head and both tubercles. The three centers are evident in the Y-shaped groove on the metaphyseal surface of the proximal epiphysis. The distal epiphysis is composed of the ossification centers for the trochlea and capitulum.

The Forearm

Two bones, the radius and ulna, make up the **forearm**. They lie parallel to each other between the elbow and the wrist. The unique design of the elbow joint makes **pronation** of the hand possible without a change in upper arm position.

Think of each articular surface in terms of function. In the forearm, the radius takes care of **rotation**, and the ulna controls **flexion** and **extension**. The cylinder of the radial head rotates in the radial notch of the ulna and on the capitulum of the humerus. In the same joint, the semilunar notch of the olecranon process moves bidirectionally on the trochlea of the humerus. The result is joint stability together with a wide range of motion.

Note that the head of the radius is proximal and the head of the ulna is distal. Also examine the **nutrient foramina** of the radius and ulna. Both foramina enter the shafts toward the elbow, just as the foramen of the humerus enters toward the elbow.

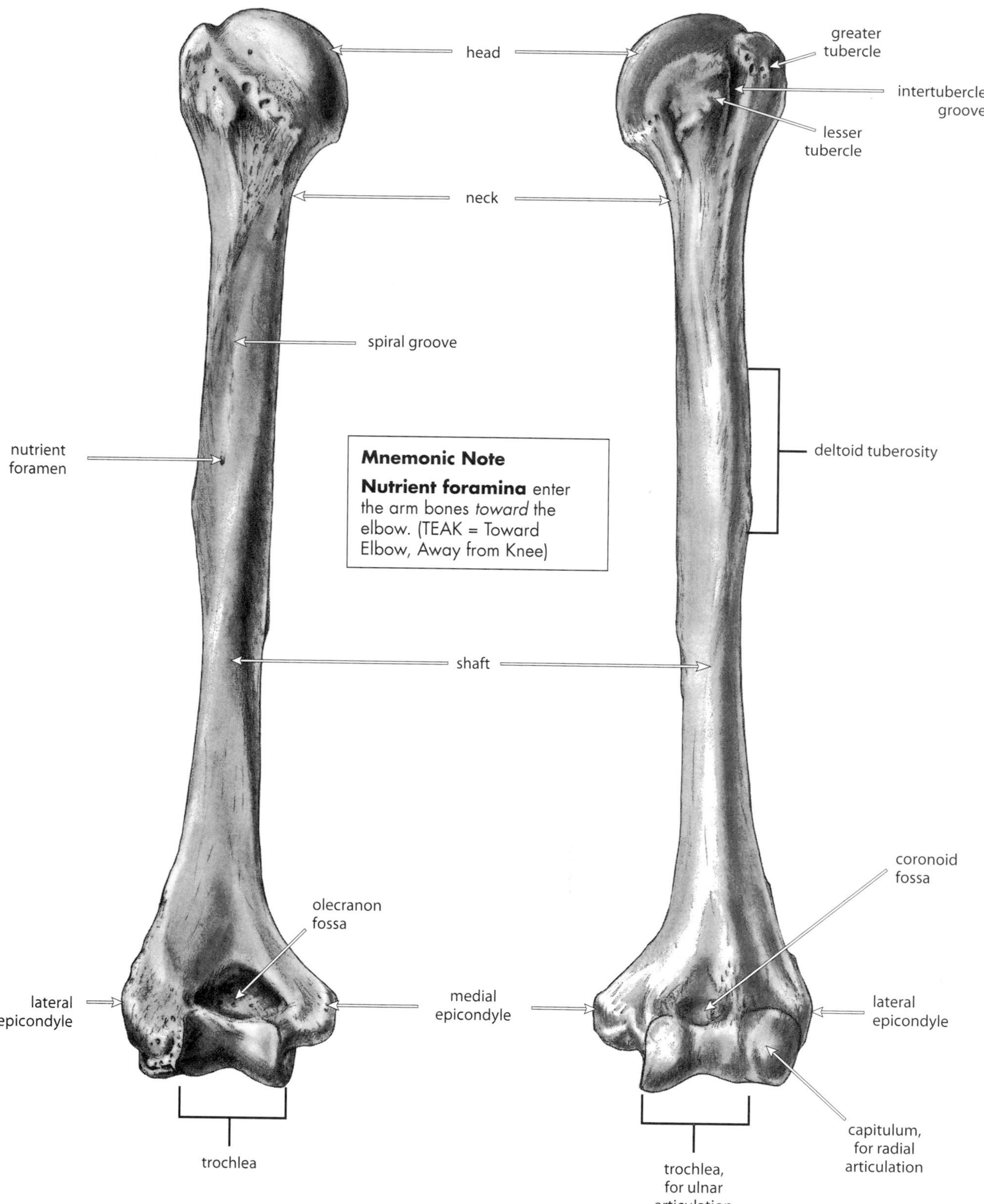

Mnemonic Note

Nutrient foramina enter the arm bones *toward* the elbow. (TEAK = Toward Elbow, Away from Knee)

Figure 6.1
Left Humerus, Posterior View and Anterior View (60% Natural Size)
Note that the tubercles are anterior and the olecranon fossa is posterior.

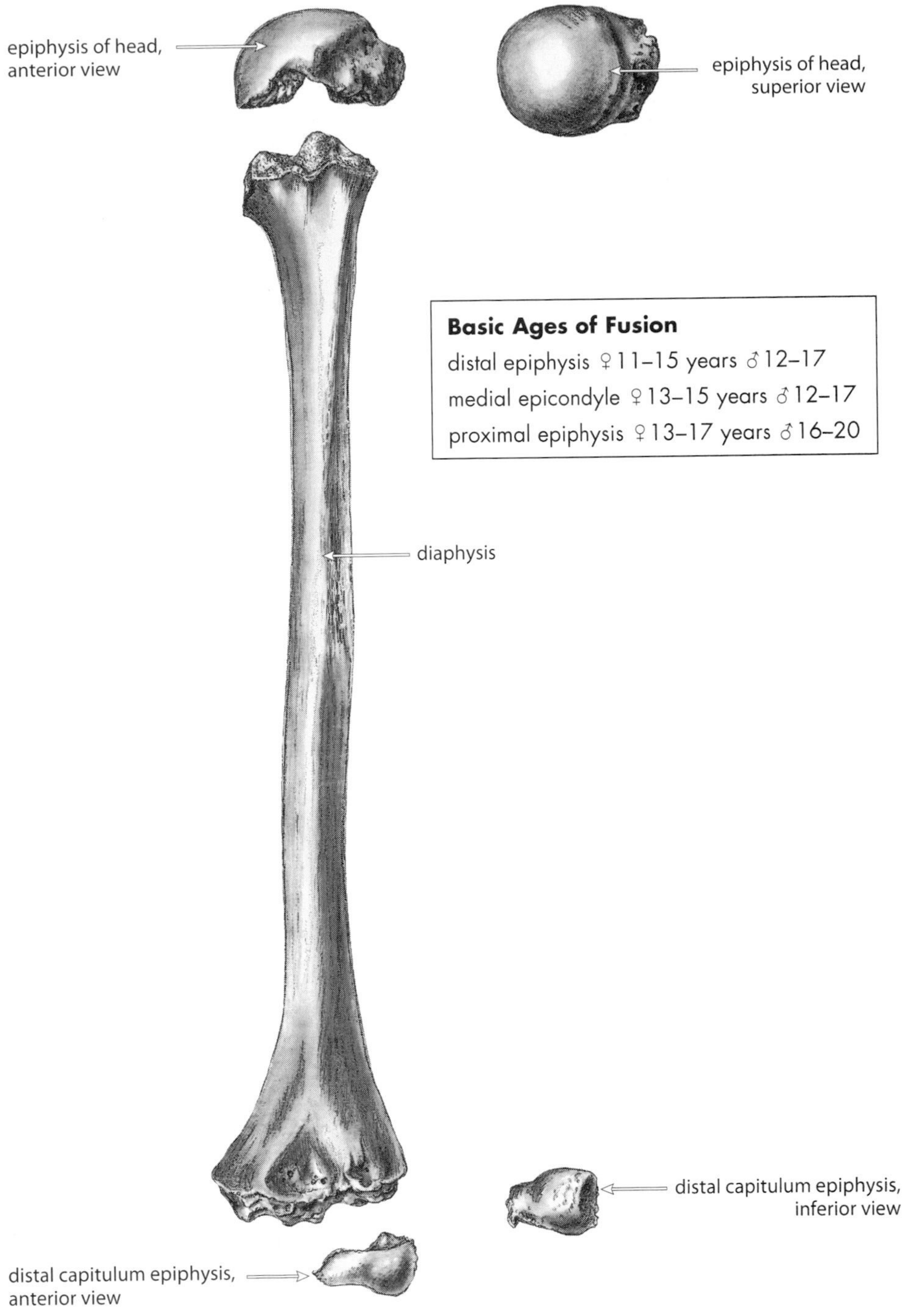

Figure 6.2

Juvenile Left Humerus with Proximal Epiphysis and Distal Capitulum Epiphysis, Anterior View; Proximal Epiphysis, Proximal View; Distal Capitulum Epiphysis, Distal View

Note three additional distal epiphyses are not pictured here.

Take time to look at the the cross-sectional shape of the radius and ulna. They are both teardrop-shaped. The ridges point toward each other, providing attachment for the single **interosseus membrane** holding the two bones together. The only bones of similar diameter are the clavicle and the fibula, but the clavicle is round in cross section and the fibula is triangular in cross section.

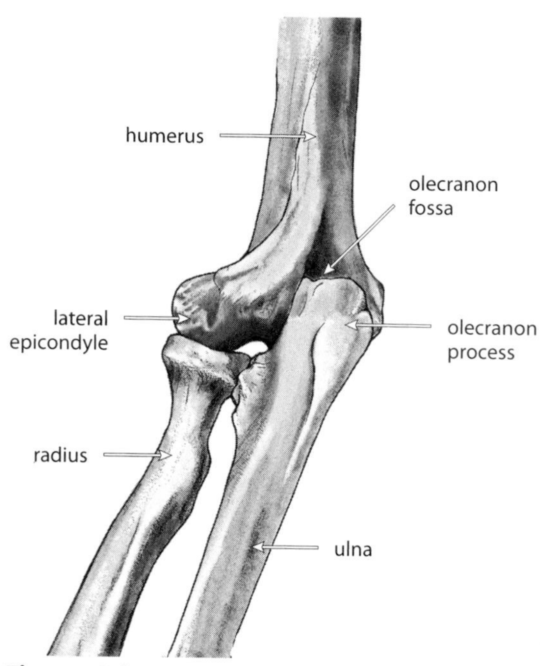

Figure 6.3
Elbow Joint

Note the ulna moves in only two directions. It is the radius that rotates.

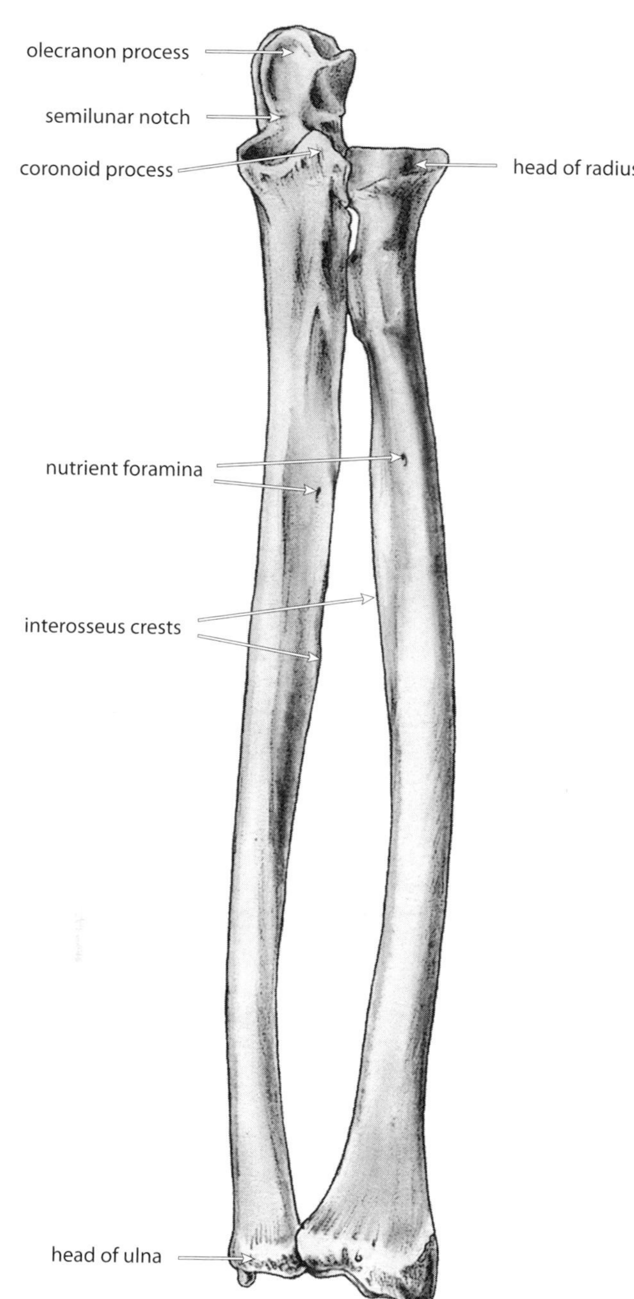

Figure 6.4
Left Radius and Ulna Articulated, Anterior View (60% Natural Size)

Note the interosseus crests point toward each other.

Radius

Description, Location, Articulation

The **radius** is the long bone lateral to the ulna, on the same side of the forearm as the thumb. It is easily recognized by the round, button-like head. The head of the radius is at the proximal end of the shaft and articulates with the **capitulum** of the humerus and the **radial notch** of the ulna.

The flared part of the radius is distal. The lateral side of the distal end articulates with the head of the ulna, and the distal surface articulates with the scaphoid and lunate carpal bones. The distal surface of the radius is double-faceted.

Left/Right Recognition

With the radius, distinguishing left from right seems to be more difficult than it should be. The problem is usually anatomical orientation of the forearm, not the radius itself. If the anterior surface of the radius is presented, the distal portion is smooth (no tubercles) and the **radial tuberosity** is visible on the proximal shaft. The **styloid process** at the distal end of the radius is lateral and indicates the direction of the thumb and, therefore, the side of origin.

Handedness

The radial tuberosity (attachment area for the biceps muscle) may be slightly larger on the dominant side.

Sexual Differences

The head of the radius shows sexual dimorphism, just as the rest of the body. Berrizbeitia (1989) measured the radii of the Terry Collection at the Smithsonian Institution and found that sex could be predicted for both blacks and whites using the sectioning criteria shown in Table 6.2. As with all other methods, consider the population and only make decisions with multiple variables.

Table 6.2 Sex Estimation from Maximum Diameter of the Radial Head

Females	Indeterminant	Males
≤21 mm	22–23 mm	≥24 mm

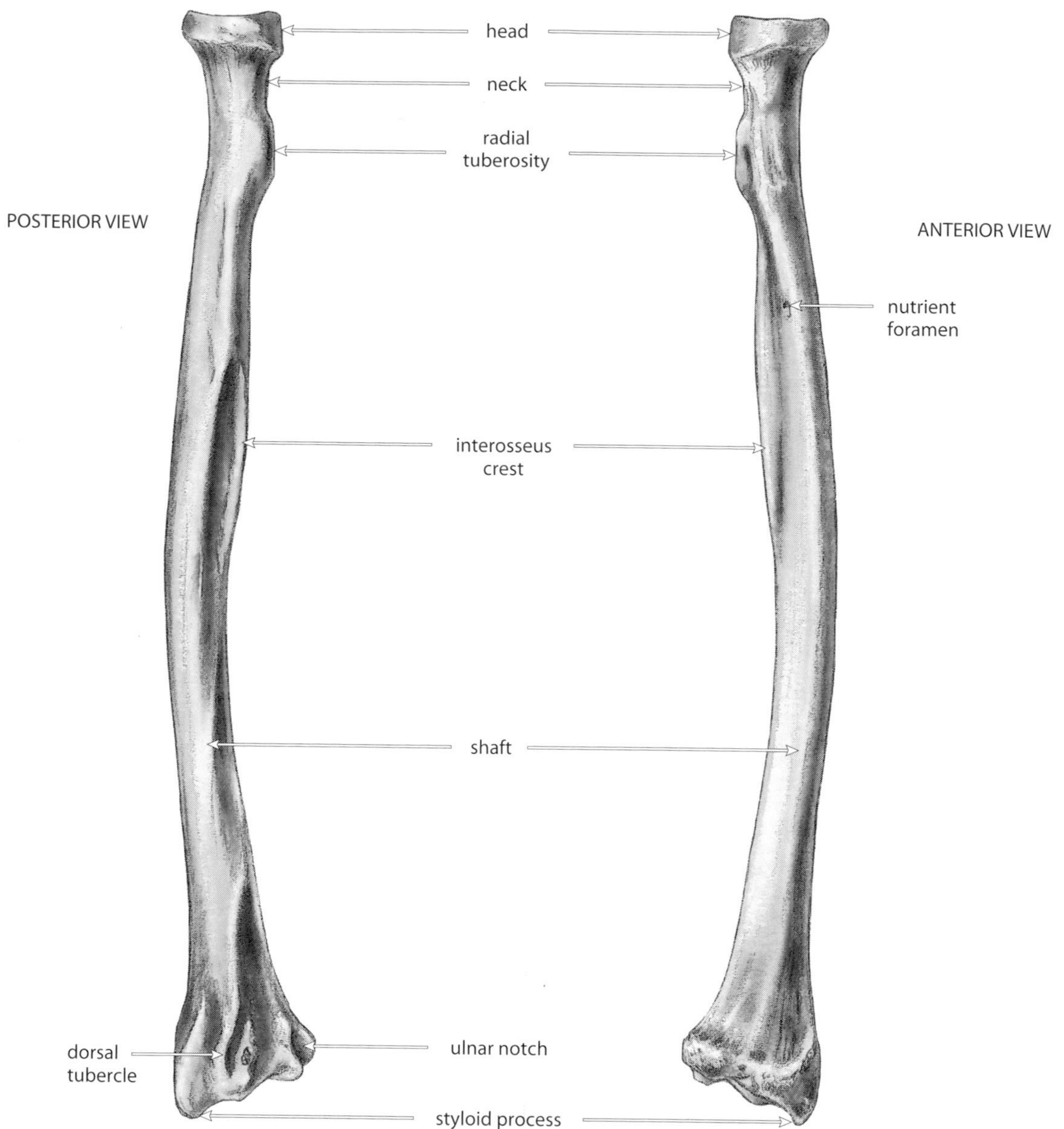

Figure 6.5
Left Radius, Posterior View and Anterior View (60% Natural Size)
Note the distal end: the tubercles are posterior and the smooth surface is anterior.

Origin and Growth

The radius develops from three centers of ossification—the shaft, the head, and the distal end. The superior surface of the proximal epiphysis (the head) is a smooth disk with a slightly convex surface. (The proximal epiphysis is occasionally found in archaeological work and puzzled over as a "button without holes.")

The inferior surface of the distal epiphysis is somewhat D-shaped, with a notch for the articulation of the ulna on part of the curve.

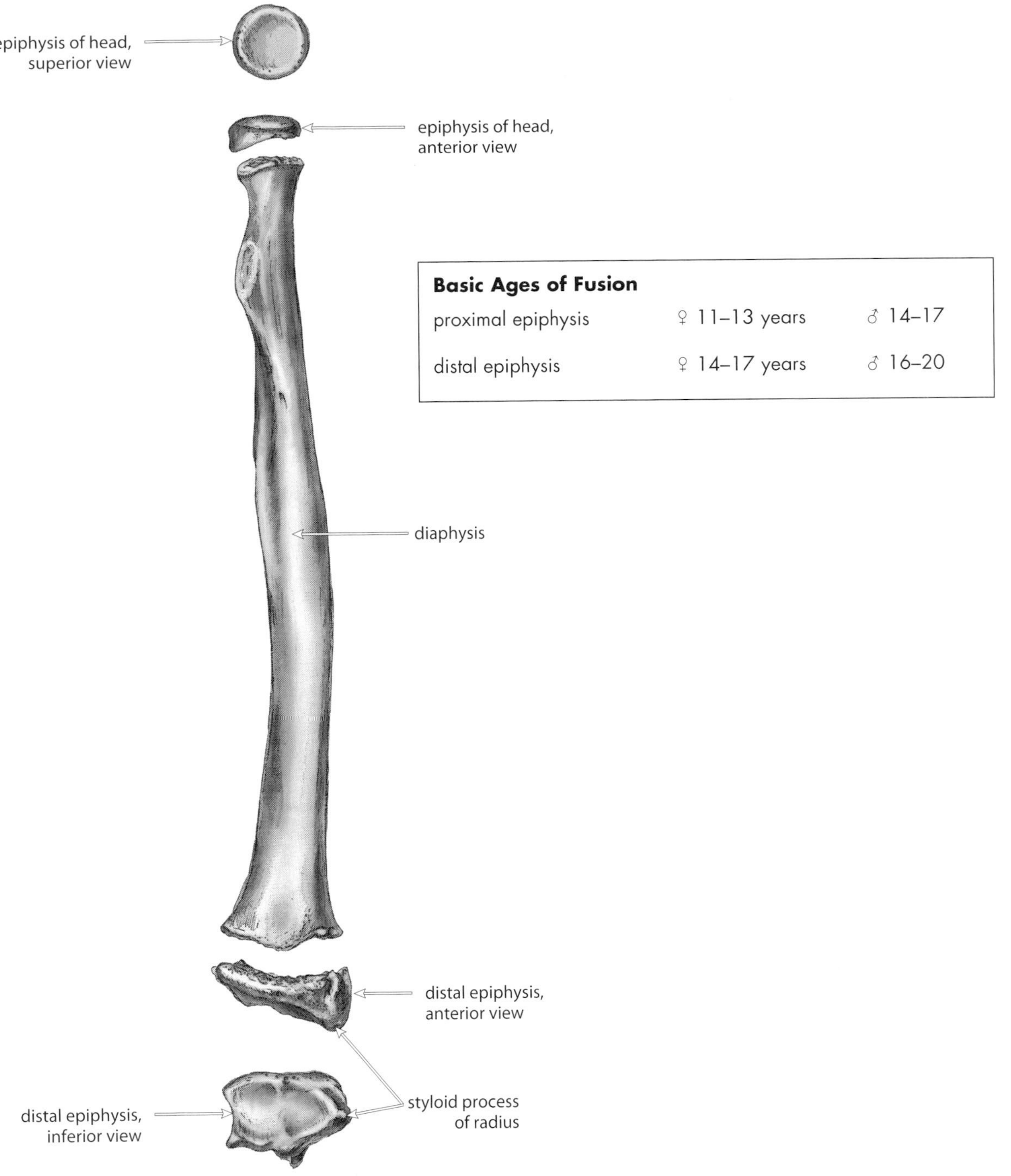

Basic Ages of Fusion

proximal epiphysis	♀ 11–13 years	♂ 14–17
distal epiphysis	♀ 14–17 years	♂ 16–20

Figure 6.6
Left Juvenile Radius with Proximal and Distal Epiphyses, Anterior View; Proximal Epiphysis, Proximal View; Distal Epiphysis, Distal View

Note the double facet on the distal surface of the distal epiphysis. Both the scaphoid and the lunate carpal bones articulate here.

ULNA

DESCRIPTION, LOCATION, ARTICULATION

The **ulna** is the long bone medial to the radius. It is easily recognized by the hook-shaped **olecranon process** at the proximal end. The bulb-like part of the olecranon process is commonly referred to as the "elbow bone." Unlike the humerus and the radius, the small **head** of the ulna is distal, not proximal. The diminutive **styloid process** on the head extends toward the fifth finger on the posterior surface of the ulna and the **extensor carpi ulnaris groove** is lateral and slightly anterior to the styloid process.

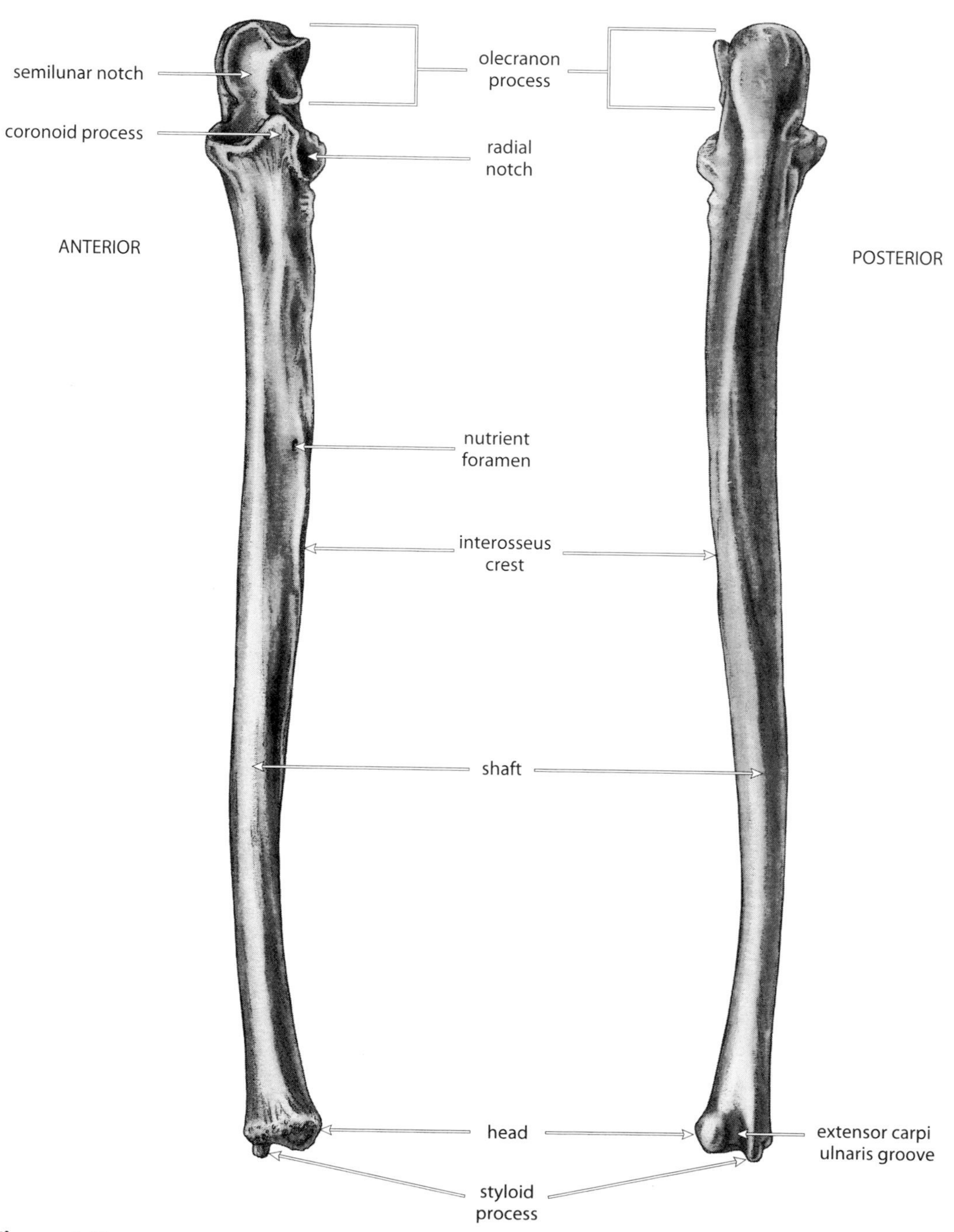

Figure 6.7
Left Ulna, Posterior View and Anterior View (60% Natural Size)

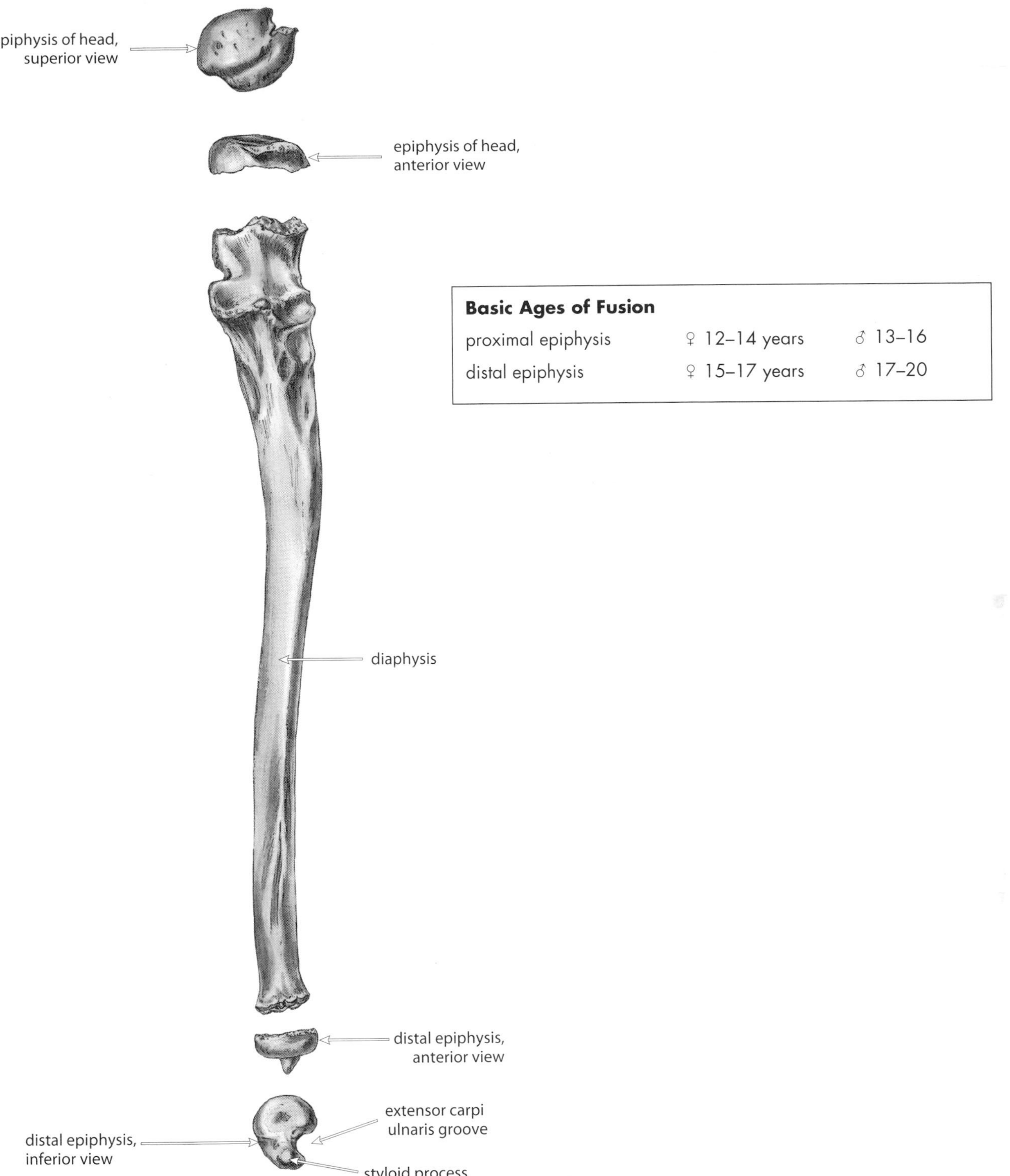

Basic Ages of Fusion		
proximal epiphysis	♀ 12–14 years	♂ 13–16
distal epiphysis	♀ 15–17 years	♂ 17–20

Figure 6.8
Juvenile Left Ulna with Proximal and Distal Epiphyses, Anterior View; Proximal Epiphysis, Proximal View; Distal Epiphysis, Distal View
Note the positions of the extensor carpi ulnaris groove and the styloid process on the inferior view of the distal epiphysis. They are useful for siding the distal ulna.

Proximally, the ulna articulates with the trochanter of the humerus and the head of the radius. Distally, the ulna articulates at the ulnar notch of the radius. The head of the ulna appears to also articulate with the lunate, but it is separated from the carpals by an articular disc.

Left/Right Recognition

The ulna can be sided by looking at the anterior side (with the olecranon process proximal) and locating the radial notch on the lateral margin of the coronoid process. The radius is lateral to the ulna so its articular surface (the radial notch) is on the side of origin.

If only the distal end of the ulna is available, locate the styloid process and the adjacent extensor carpi ulnaris groove. Looking at the distal surface with the styloid process upward, the groove is on the side of origin.

Origin and Growth

The ulna develops from three centers of ossification—the shaft, the proximal olecranon process, and the distal head. The proximal epiphysis includes only the beak-like tip of the full process and its features are somewhat indistinct. The distal epiphysis is comma shaped with a clear nub forming the styloid process.

Table 6.3 Arm Vocabulary

Bone	Term	Definition
HUMERUS	capitulum	the articular surface for the head of the radius at the distal end of the humerus
	coronoid fossa	the depression on the anterior surface of the distal humerus for the coronoid process of the ulna in flexion
	deltoid tuberosity	the attachment area for the deltoid on the lateral part of the anterior surface of the humeral shaft; a roughened, somewhat bulging surface
	greater tubercle	the larger of the two tubercles on the anterior side of the proximal end—lateral to the lesser tubercle
	head	the proximal articular surface—hemispherical in shape (a half ball)
	intertubercular groove	the deep groove between greater and lesser tubercles—for the tendon of the long head of the biceps muscle
	lateral epicondyle	the bulbous area on the lateral side above the distal condyle; the origin of the extensor muscles of the hand
	lesser tubercle	the smaller of the two tubercles on the anterior side of the proximal end—medial to the greater tubercle
	medial epicondyle	the bulbous area on the medial side above the distal condyle; the origin of the flexor muscles of the hand
	neck	the area immediately distal to the head of the humerus; a common fracture site (the surgical neck)
	nutrient foramen	the major vascular opening on the shaft of the humerus; it enters the shaft pointing toward the distal end
	olecranon foramen	a hole in the olecranon fossa—infrequent appearance, more common in females; also called septal aperture
	olecranon fossa	the large depression on the posterior surface of the distal humerus for the olecranon process of the ulna in extension
	radial nerve groove	the diagonal groove on the posterior and lateral surface of the shaft—more a spiraling surface than a groove
	shaft	the diaphysis of the humerus
	trochlea	the spool-shaped articular surface for the ulna on the distal end of the humerus

BONE	TERM	DEFINITION
RADIUS	distal articular surface	the broad triangular end that articulates with both the scaphoid and lunate carpal bones
	dorsal tubercles	the bumps on the dorsal surface of the distal end, providing slots for tendons of the hand
	head	the proximal end of the radius; it articulates with the capitulum of the humerus and the radial notch of the ulna
	interosseous crest	the somewhat sharp edge on the shaft directed toward the ulna for attachment of the interosseus ligament
	neck	the area of the shaft immediately distal to the head of the radius
	nutrient foramen	the major vascular opening on the shaft of the radius; enters the shaft pointing toward the proximal end
	radial tuberosity	the large bump distal to the neck of the radius, one insertion of the biceps muscle; also called bicipital tuberosity
	shaft	the diaphysis of the radius
	styloid process	the point on the lateral edge of the distal end of the radius; the brachio-radialis muscle inserts on the styloid
	ulnar notch	the facet for the ulna on the medial side of the distal end of the radius
ULNA	coronoid process	the smaller of the two processes at the proximal end of the ulna forming the semilunar notch
	head	the distal end of the ulna, articulating laterally with the ulnar notch of the radius
	interosseous crest	the somewhat sharp edge on the shaft directed toward the radius for attachment of the interosseous ligament
	nutrient foramen	the major vascular opening on the shaft of the ulna. It enters the shaft pointing toward the proximal end
	olecranon process	the larger process at the proximal end of the ulna; forming the semilunar notch and the elbow
	radial notch	the concavity for the radius on the lateral side of the proximal end of the ulna
	semilunar notch	the articular surface for the trochlea of the humerus; formed by the olecranon and coronoid processes
	shaft	the diaphysis of the ulna
	styloid process	the small process extending from the head of the ulna and pointing toward the fifth finger

CHAPTER 7

The Hand: Carpals, Metacarpals, and Phalanges

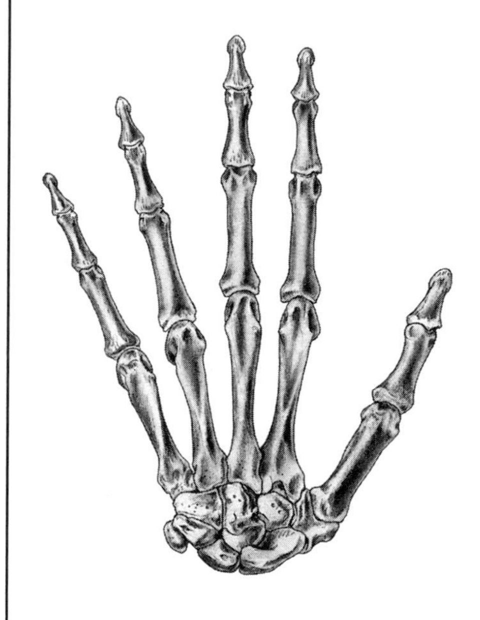

CHAPTER OUTLINE

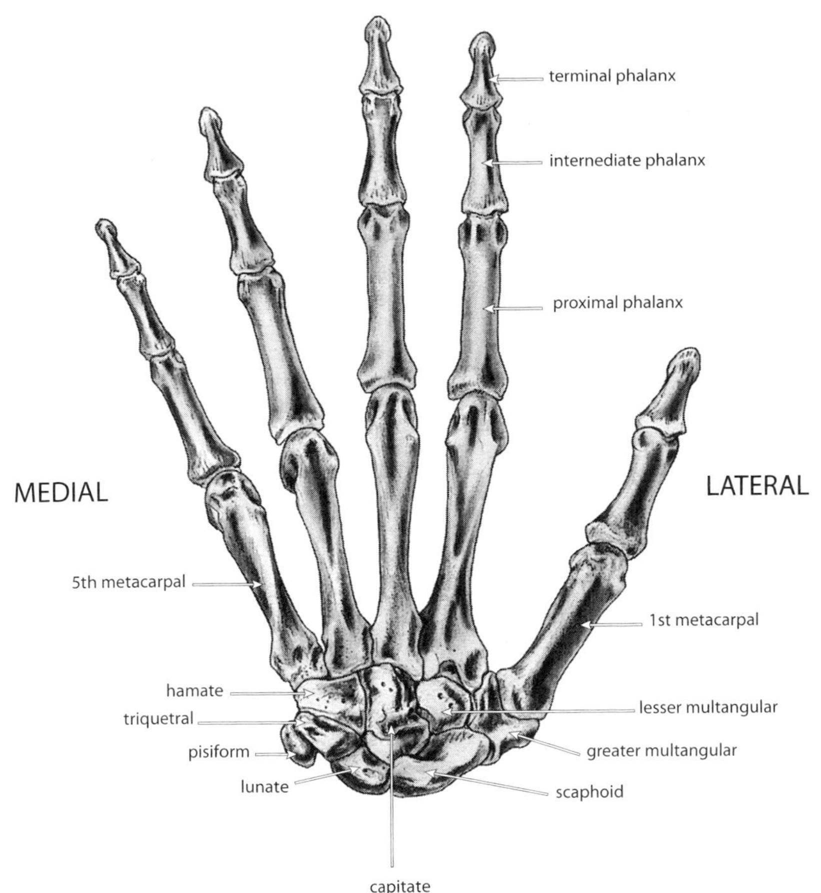

Anatomic Note

The thumb is *radial* (the lateral part of the hand); the little finger is *ulnar* (the medial part of the hand).

Figure 7.1a
Left Hand and Wrist, Dorsal View (65% Natural Size)

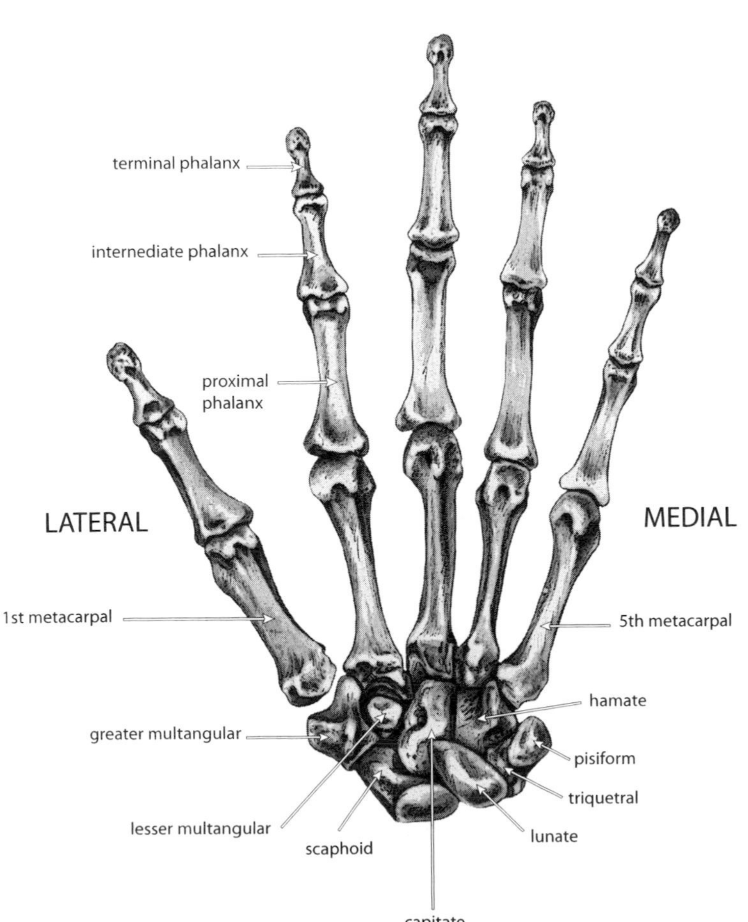

Figure 7.1b
Left Hand and Wrist, Palmar View (65% Natural Size)

Introduction

Approximately half of the bones in the adult human body are found in the hands and feet—a total of 106 bones! Each hand contains twenty-seven bones. There are eight carpal bones (wrist bones), five metacarpal bones (the bones of the palm), and fourteen phalanges (finger bones).

Orientation is the first challenge in working with the hand. Standard anatomical position is used just as with any other part of the body. In anatomical position, the thumb points away from the body. The back of the hand is posterior and the surface is called *dorsal;* the palm of the hand is anterior and the surface is called *palmar.* The thumb is lateral (radial); the little finger is medial (ulnar).

Each carpal and metacarpal can be recognized, and the right can be distinguished from the left. The phalanges are more difficult. Proximal, intermediate, and terminal phalanges can be distinguished, but right and left cannot be separated with certainty. Therefore, it is very important to bag the hands separately during collection or disinterment. Any finger that may contribute to identification because of trauma or anomaly should be separated and labeled by digit number (i.e., "fourth finger, left hand").

Carpal Bones: Wrist Bones

Description, Location, Articulation

The carpal bones are eight pebble-like bones between the bones of the forearm and the bones of the palm. They serve to increase the overall flexibility of the hand. These little bones are frequently lost or ignored, but they are not unimportant.

Left Greater Multangular (Trapezium) (Natural Size)

The greater multangular has a prominent saddle-shaped facet for articulation with the base of the first metacarpal. A ridge extends down from one side of the major facet and points toward the side of origin.

Figure 7.2a Dorsomedial View, Lesser Multangular and Scaphoid Facets

Figure 7.2b Palmar View, First Metacarpal Facet

a.

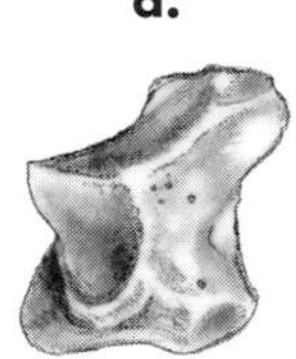

b.

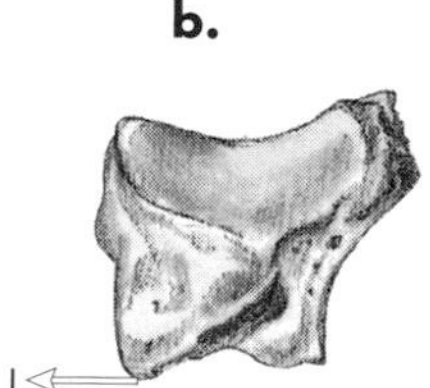

Left Lesser Multangular (Trapezoid) (Natural Size)

The lesser multangular fits within the V-shaped indentation at the base of the second metacarpal. It is shaped like a tiny boot. One side of the "boot" has a Y-shaped ridge. From this side, the toe of the boot points toward the side of origin.

Figure 7.3a Medial View, Second Metacarpal and Capitate Facets

Figure 7.3b Lateral View, Gr. Multangular and Second Metacarpal Facets

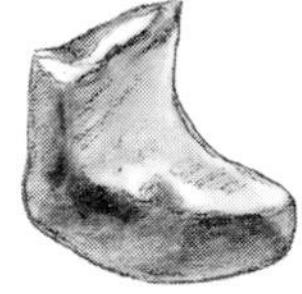

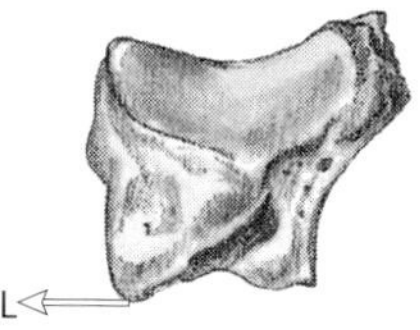

Left Capitate (Natural Size)

The capitate is the largest carpal bone. It has a knob-like head that articulates in the center of the wrist with the scaphoid and lunate. The base articulates with the third metacarpal. One side has a long, curved facet that points toward the side of origin.

Figure 7.4a Lateral View, Hamate Facet

Figure 7.4b Medial View, Lesser Multangular Facet

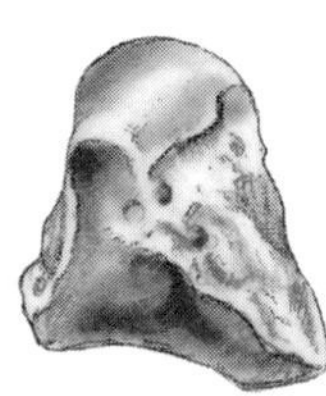

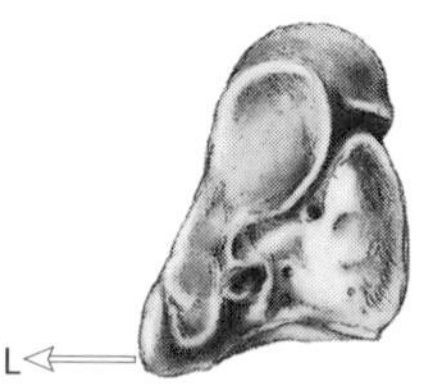

Left Hamate (Natural Size)

The hamate is the only carpal with a long curved non-articular process, the hamulus (an attachment point for the flexor retinaculum). If the hamulus is pointed up and curving toward you, it is on the side of origin. (Both the fourth and fifth metacarpals articulate with the hamate.)

Figure 7.5a Medial View, Triquetral Facet
Figure 7.5b Lateral View, Capitate Facet

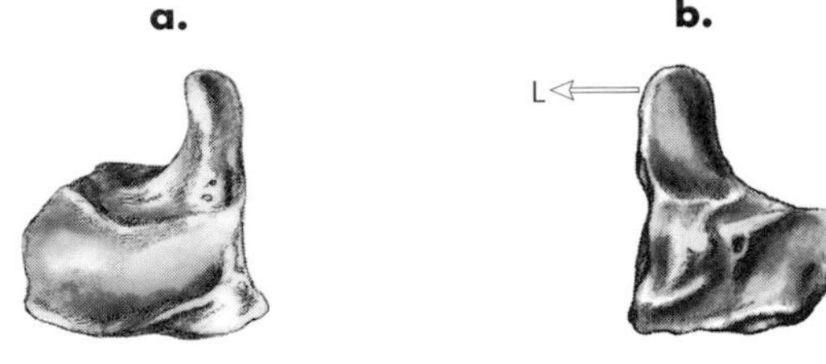

Left Scaphoid (Natural Size)

The scaphoid is sometimes described as "S-shaped." It also looks like a flattened oval, pinched at each end and twisted 90 degrees. Look at the concave surface of the flatter end. If it is oriented so the other end curves downward, it points toward the side of origin.

Figure 7.6a Proximal View, Radial Facet
Figure 7.6b Distal View with Capitate Facet

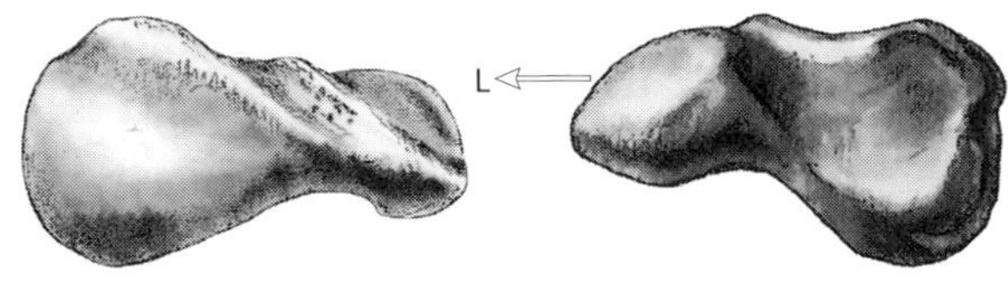

Left Lunate (Natural Size)

The lunate is shaped like the crescent of a new moon. If the crescent is downward and the large rounded facet is away, a single facet is visible, leaning toward the side of origin.

Figure 7.7a Proximal View, Radial Facet
Figure 7.7b Mediodistal View, Triquetral Facet

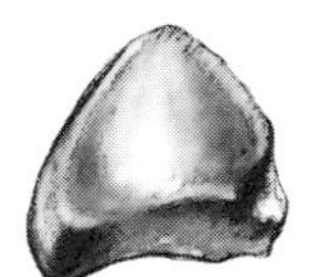
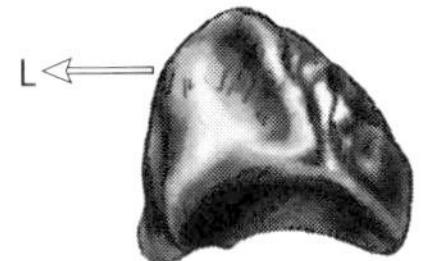

Left Triquetral (Natural Size)

The triquetral is somewhat triangular. It has a round facet for the pisiform and two facets adjoining at a right angle for the lunate and the hamate. With the point upward, the largest facet curves toward the side of origin.

Figure 7.8a Dorsal View
Figure 7.8b Lateral View, Hamate Facet

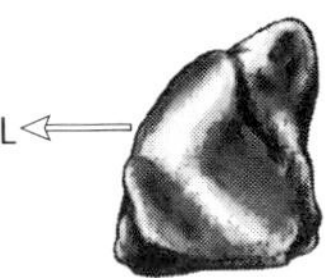

Left Pisiform (Natural Size)

The pisiform is a little pea-shaped sesamoid bone that forms within the tendon of the flexor carpi ulnaris muscle. It can be felt at the base of the medial palmar surface (the hypothenar eminence).The pisiform has one round facet for the triquetral. One side of the pisiform bulges out slightly more than the other. Turn the bulging side away with the facet downward. The "toe" points toward the side of origin, as in the illustration.

Figure 7.9a Dorsal View, Triquetral Facet
Figure 7.9b Palmar View

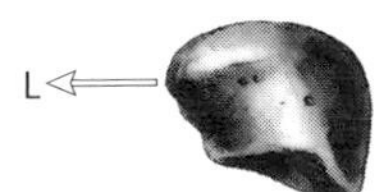

The carpals can be divided into two rows. The distal carpals (lateral to medial) are the **greater multangular** and **lesser multangular**, **capitate**, and **hamate**. All of the distal carpals articulate with metacarpals. The proximal carpals (lateral to medial) are the **scaphoid**, **lunate**, **triquetral**, and **pisiform**. Of the proximal carpals, the scaphoid and the lunate articulate directly with the radius. The lunate and the triquetral come close to the ulna, but a thick, fibrocartilaginous articular disk inhibits direct articulation.

Left/Right Recognition

It takes time and practice to be able to recognize each carpal bone and tell right from left, but it *is* possible. The words in the illustrations are clues from other students to help you get started. Use your own imagination to carry you further.

Origin and Growth

Each carpal grows from a single center of ossification. The capitate is the first to appear (2 to 4 months postnatal) and the pisiform is last (8 to 10 years). The sequence has been studied by several investigators, and a summary was published by Scheuer and Black (2000). Carpals (and the hand as a whole) are a good guide for age determination in infants and children.

Table 7.1 Carpal Articulations

Carpals	Alternate Terms	Articulations
SCAPHOID	navicular	radius, lunate, capitate, greater and lesser multangulars
LUNATE	semilunar	scaphoid, capitate, triquetral
TRIQUETRAL	triquetrium	lunate, hamate, pisiform
PISIFORM		triquetral
GREATER MULTANGULAR	trapezium	metacarpal #1, scaphoid, lesser multangular
LESSER MULTANGULAR	trapezoid	metacarpal #2, greater multangular, scaphoid, capitate
CAPITATE		metacarpal #3, lesser multangular, scaphoid, lunate, hamate
HAMATE		metacarpals #4 & #5, triquetral, capitate

Metacarpal Bones: The Palm of the Hand

Description, Location, Articulation

Metacarpal bones are the long bones that support the palm of the hand. There are five metacarpals in each hand. They articulate proximally with the carpal bones and distally with the phalanges. Students often confuse metacarpals with finger bones (phalanges). This may be the result of studying articulated skeletal hands without using a fleshed hand for comparison. The solution is your own hand. Identify the knuckles on both the fleshed hand and the skeletal hand. Remember that the metacarpal *heads* are the large rounded knuckles at the *bases* of the fingers.

Left/Right Recognition

The entire proximal end of each metacarpal is the key to determining both side and metacarpal number. In the illustrations, each metacarpal is pictured in three views—lateral, medial, and proximal. The lateral view is on the left and the medial view is on the right so that the palmar surfaces face each other. Examine the length, width, and curvature of the shaft of each metacarpal; then compare the characteristics of each base. Look for the articular facets on each side of the base and compare adjacent facets.

Forensic Note

Hands are often the site of defense wounds.

Origin and Growth

Each metacarpal develops from two (not three) centers of ossification. The primary center is the shaft. The secondary centers form distal epiphyses (the knuckles) in metacarpals #2–#5. In metacarpal #1, the secondary center is proximal.

Sex

Several investigators have developed methods for determining sex from metacarpals. (Scheuer & Elkington, 1993; Falsetti, 1995; Stojanowski, 1999). Burrows and colleagues (2003) compared the three methods and were most successful with Stojanowski's method. They concluded that "the potential utility of metacarpals in determining sex of human skeletal remains may be limited, especially if used as a sole determinant" (p. 20). In other words, to the extent possible, evaluate age with the whole body. If you want to use the hand, refer to the original publications for complete lists of discriminant functions.

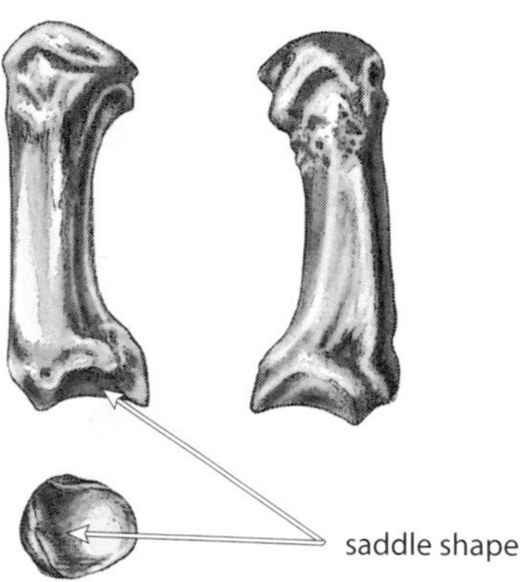

Figure 7.10
Metacarpal #1, Lateral, Medial, and Proximal Views (80% Natural Size)
Metacarpal #1 is short and wide in comparison to the other metacarpals. It has no articular surfaces on the lateral or medial sides. From the dorsal side, the base points toward #2. From the proximal articular surface, the base points toward the palmar surface. A view of the proximal surface shows a saddle-shaped facet that articulates with the saddle of greater multangular.

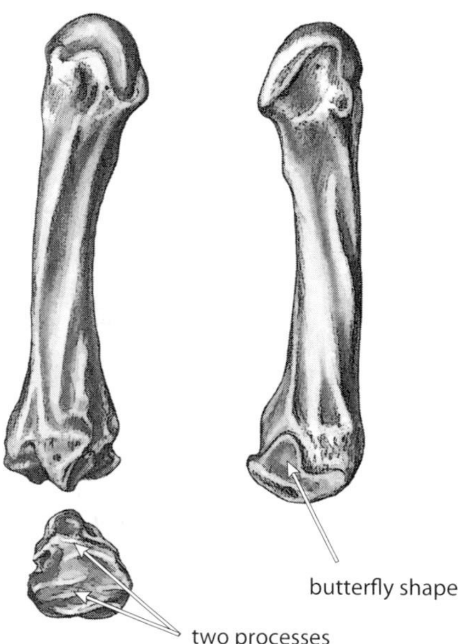

Figure 7.11
Metacarpal #2, Lateral, Medial, and Proximal Views (80% Natural Size)
Metacarpal #2 is one of the two larger metacarpals. It is the only metacarpal with two processes at the base—one broad and the other pointed. The processes are easiest to see in the full-hand illustration (Figure 7.1). From the dorsal side, the longer, larger process points toward and articulates with #3. The medial facet (for #3) is wide and "butterfly shaped." Compare it with the lateral facet on #3. On the proximal surface, the two processes create a groove for the lesser multangular.

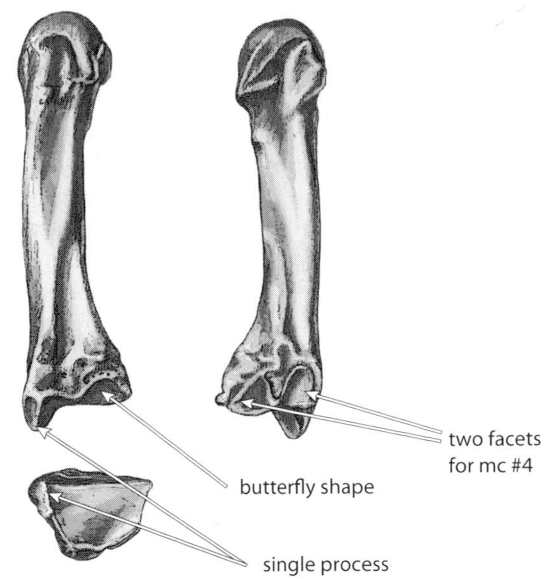

Figure 7.12
Metacarpal #3, Lateral, Medial, and Proximal Views (80% Natural Size)

Metacarpal #3 is about the same size as #2, but it has only one major process at the base. From the dorsal side, the single process points toward #2. The lateral facet is wide and "butterfly shaped." Compare it with the medial facet on #2. The proximal surface is slanted and somewhat triangular in outline. It articulates with the distal capitate.

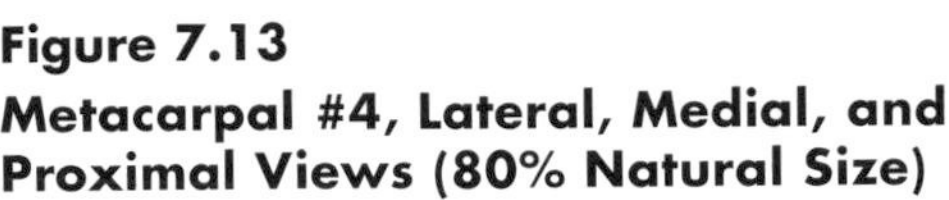

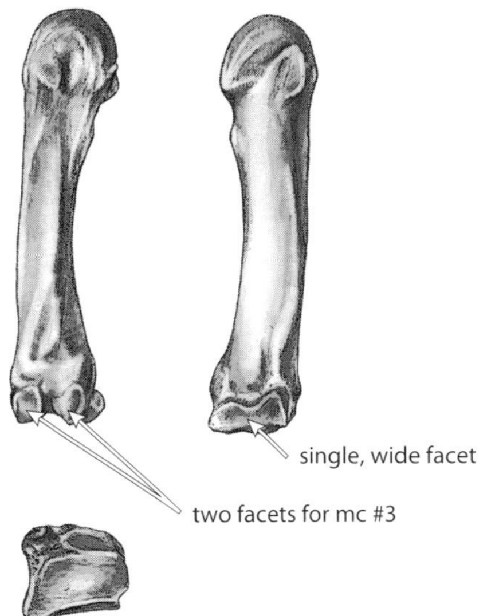

Figure 7.13
Metacarpal #4, Lateral, Medial, and Proximal Views (80% Natural Size)

Metacarpal #4 is one of the two smaller metacarpals. The base is narrower than the other metacarpals, and no processes protrude from the proximal surface. Metacarpal #4 has articular facets on both sides of the base. The medial facet (for #5) is single, wide, and "butterfly shaped." The lateral facet is double (two small facets for #3). The two lateral facets for #3 are prominent and visible from the proximal view. The proximal facet articulates with the lateral part of the of the distal hamate surface.

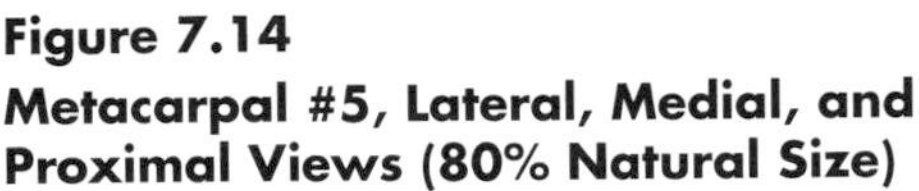

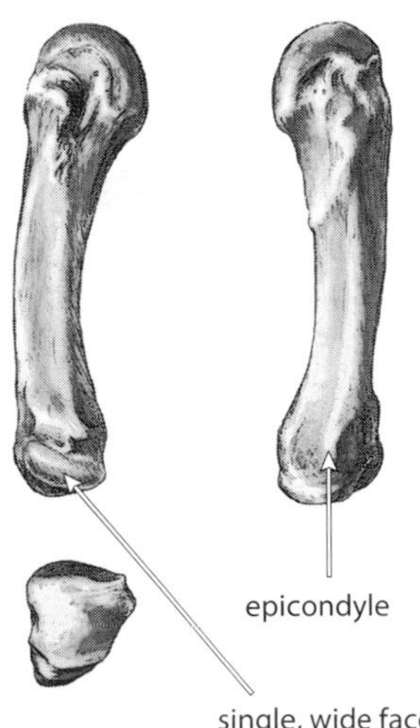

Figure 7.14
Metacarpal #5, Lateral, Medial, and Proximal Views (80% Natural Size)

Metacarpal #5 is the other of the two smaller metacarpals. The base is wider than #4 because an epicondyle bulges from the medial surface. Metacarpal #5 has no processes on the base, and only a single, wide, sometimes "butterfly-shaped" lateral facet (for #4). The proximal surface is rather round and the facet articulates at the distal hamate.

Table 7.2 Metacarpal and Phalanx Articulations

Bone	Articular Facet	Adjacent Bone
METACARPAL #1	base	greater multangular
	medial surface	no bone—not even #2
	lateral surface	no bone
	head	proximal phalanx
METACARPAL #2	mid-base	lesser multangular
	medial base	metacarpal #3
	lateral surface	greater multangular
	head	proximal phalanx
METACARPAL #3	base	capitate
	medial surface	metacarpal #4
	lateral surface	metacarpal #2
	head	proximal phalanx
METACARPAL #4	base	hamate
	medial surface	metacarpal #5
	lateral surface	metacarpal #3
	head	proximal phalanx
METACARPAL #5	base	hamate
	medial surface	no bone—only a tubercle
	lateral surface	metacarpal #4
	head	proximal phalanx
PROXIMAL PHALANX	base	metacarpal head
	head	intermediate phalanx
INTERMEDIATE (MEDIAL) PHALANX	base	proximal phalanx
	head	distal phalanx
DISTAL (TERMINAL) PHALANX	base	intermediate phalanx
	head	no bone—only fingernail

Phalanges of the Hand: Finger Bones

Description, Location, Articulation

A **phalanx** is one of the fourteen bones in the fingers (or toes) of a hand (or foot). The thumb has two phalanges, the proximal and distal. Each of the other four digits has three phalanges—**proximal**, **intermediate**, and **distal**. The distal phalanx is also called a terminal phalanx.

The intermediate phalanx is also called a medial or middle phalanx. However, the word *intermediate* is probably the most explicit because the word *medial* is used to mean toward the midline of the body, and the word *middle* is used for the middle finger (the third digit).

Proximal phalanges articulate with the heads of the metacarpals. The intermediate and distal phalanges articulate only with phalanges.

Left/Right Recognition

Siding is usually not possible with phalanges. Even within the same hand, there can be confusion between the second and fourth fingers. Use extreme caution in recovering, documenting, and storing individual fingers, depending on the needs of the case.

Forensic Note

Always bag hands and feet separately!

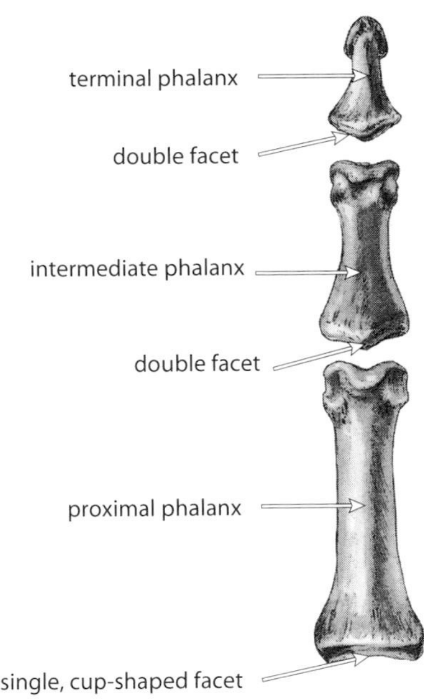

Figure 7.15
Finger Phalanges, Terminal, Intermediate, Proximal (Natural Size)
Note that the proximal surface of the proximal phalanx has a single facet whereas the proximal surface of the intermediate phalanx has a double facet.

Origin and Growth

Each phalanx forms from two centers of ossification—the primary diaphyseal shaft, and one proximal epiphysis (no distal epiphysis). The epiphysis of the phalanx is flat and oval-shaped.

A Method for Sorting Phalanges

1. First, identify all of the terminal phalanges and set them aside.
   - **a.** The distal end has no facet for articulating with another bone. Instead, it is shaped to hold a fingernail and provide support for the fingertip.
   - **b.** The palmar side is flat and roughened for attachment of tendons.
2. Next, examine the *proximal* ends of the other phalanges and separate them into two groups: double facets and single facets.
   - **a.** The intermediate phalanx has a double-faceted proximal end. It has a scalloped appearance. The double-facet fits the indented surface of the distal end of the proximal phalanx.
   - **b.** The proximal phalanx has a single, cup-shaped proximal end that fits against the rounded head of the metacarpal.

Note: For a comparison of finger and toe phalanges, refer to Chapter 10, "The Foot."

Chapter 8

The Pelvic Girdle: Illium, Ischium, and Pubis

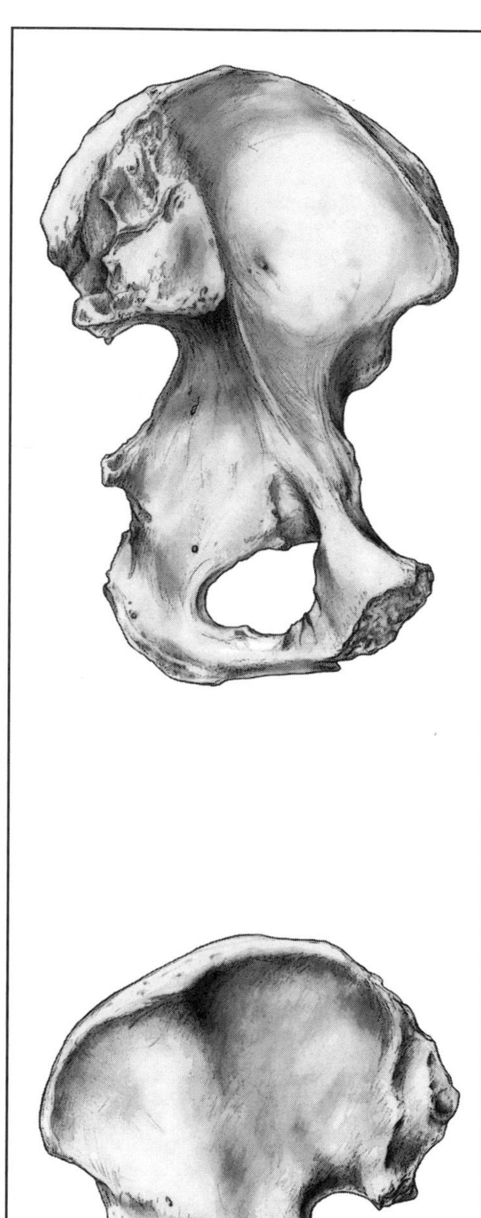

CHAPTER OUTLINE

INTRODUCTION

In adulthood, the completed pelvis is formed from two **innominate** bones and a sacrum. Together, they create a bowl-shaped support for the organs of the lower trunk—the intestines, bladder, uterus, and so forth. The human pelvis also provides the bony structure that makes bipedal locomotion—upright walking—possible. This chapter focuses on the innominate; the sacrum is covered with the rest of the vertebral column in Chapter 5.

Innominate is a strange word for a bone. It is derived from Latin and means nameless. Os coxae is another Latin name for the bone. It is the plural form of os coxa and means hip bones, however, it is frequently used as a synonym for innominate which is a singular form. Coxal bone is probably the best name because coxal is an adjective for hip and there is no singular/plural confusion. Unfortunately, coxal bone is rarely used in recent literature. So, as with many anatomical terms, use the easiest or most familiar term and remember all the others for whenever they may be needed.

INNOMINATE: ILIUM, ISCHIUM, AND PUBIS

Just as the skull is formed of many individual bones, the innominate results from the fusion of three individual bones—the **ilium,** the **ischium,** and the **pubis.** The three bones are referred to by their distinct names except when a composite name is more accurate, e.g., "The right innominate was found intact, but only the left ischium was recovered."

DESCRIPTION, LOCATION, ARTICULATION

The ilium is the most superior bone of the innominate. It is the large, flaring portion that forms the structure commonly recognized as a "hip bone." The waist is immediately above the **iliac crest** of the ilium.

The ischium is the most inferior bone of the innominate. The **ischial tuberosity** is the dense, rounded part of the ischium that carries the weight of a sitting person.

The pubis is the most anterior bone of the innominate. Left and right pubic bones approximate each other at the **pubic symphysis**, the lower midline of the trunk. The symphyseal faces do not fuse under normal conditions. They are separated throughout life by a dense fibrocartilaginous disc.

The innominate articulates with the sacrum and the femur. The sacrum articulates only with the ilium at the auricular (ear-shaped) surface. The femur articulates at the acetabulum. Since the ilium, ischium, and pubis come together and fuse to create the acetabulum, the femur actually articulates with all three bones of the innominate.

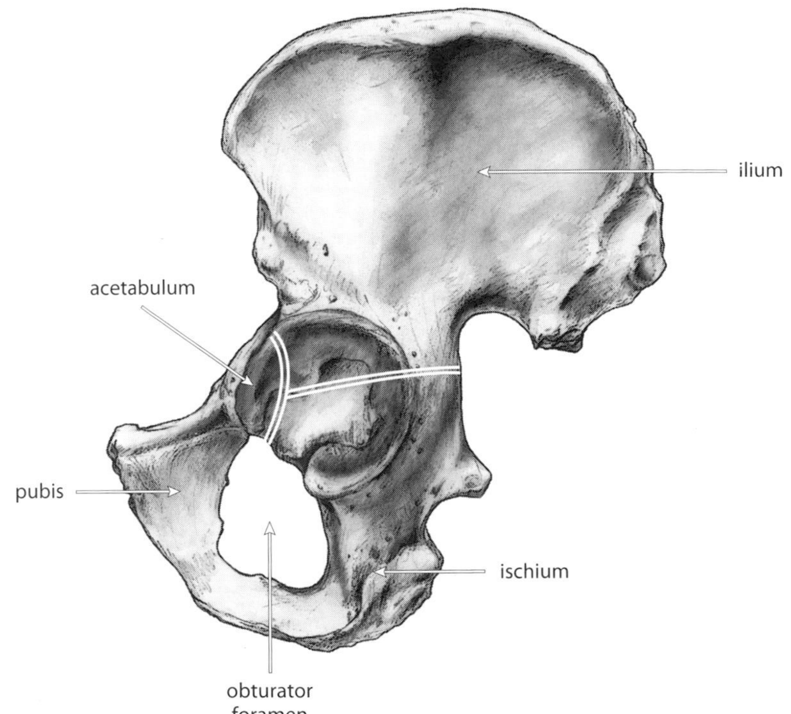

Figure 8.1
Innominate with Ilium, Ischium, and Pubis Delineated
This Illustration is provided to demonstrate the limits of individual bones.

Anatomy Notes

- The sacrum articulates on the *inner* (anteromedial) surface of the ilium at the **auricular surface.**
- The femur articulates on the *lateral* surface of the innominate at the **acetabulum.**
- The pubis curves outward like the lip of a bowl, not inward like the greater part of a bowl.
- The thickest part of the innominate is the **ischial tuberosity,** the bone in closest association with the chair.
- The **iliopubic ramus** is thicker and twisted; the **ischiopubic ramus** is flatter and narrower.

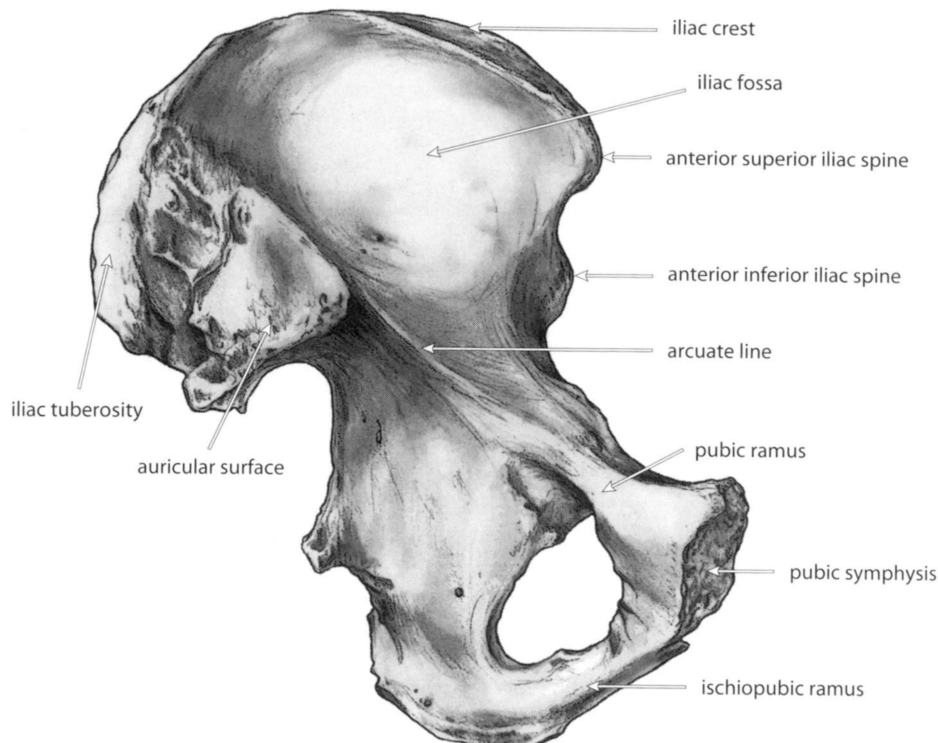

Figure 8.2
Left Innominate, Internal View

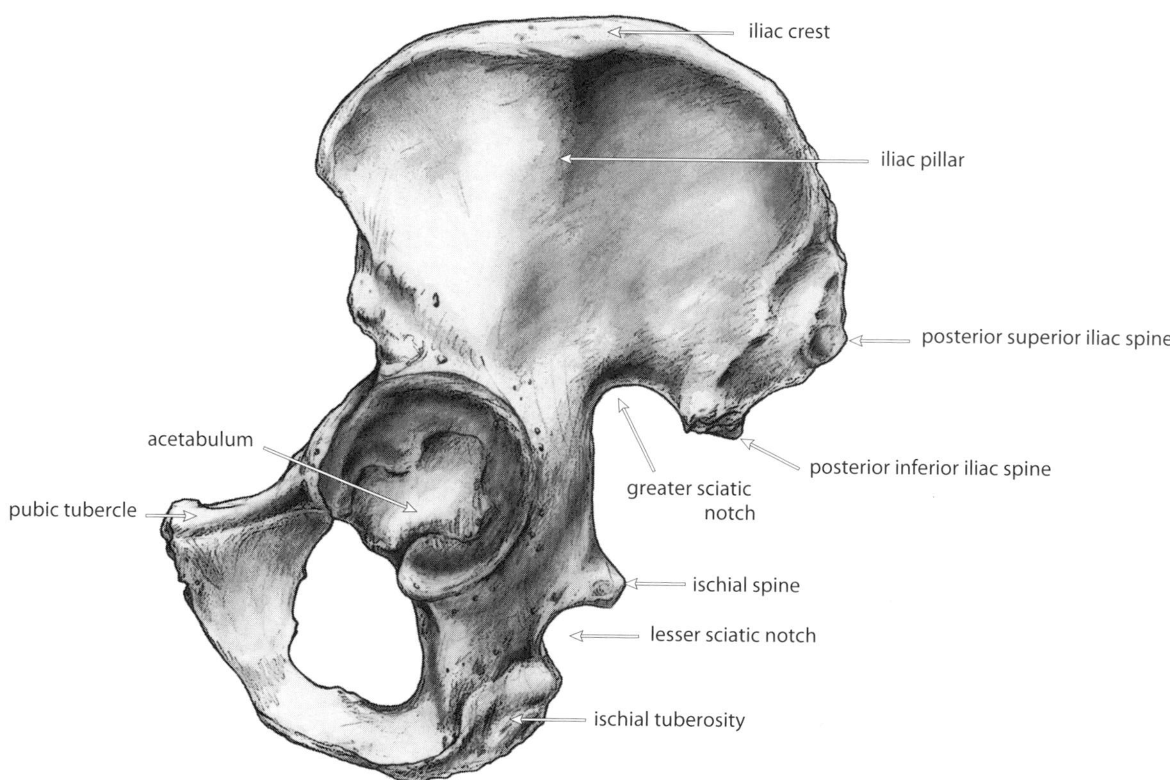

Figure 8.3
Left Innominate, External (Lateral) View

Left/Right Recognition

There is little problem orienting the complete innominate. When the iliac crest is superior and the ischial tuberosity is inferior, the pubis is anterior. In this position, the acetabulum is lateral. Hold the innominate in your right hand with the pubis in front and the ilium up. If the acetabulum is lateral (toward your palm), the bone is from the right; if not, the bone is from the left.

Fragments are a little more difficult, but the bowl shape of the pelvis helps define the inner surface of the ilium and ischium. Look at the concavity and orient the iliac crest superior or the ischial tuberosity inferior; then check the location of the rim of the acetabulum. It must be lateral.

An unattached pubis is often misidentified because the inner curvature is convex rather than concave. Keeping the opposite curvature in mind, put the symphyseal face medial and orient by the ramus shape. The *superior* **pubic ramus** is thicker and twisted. The *inferior* **ischiopubic ramus** is more slender and flat.

Origin and Growth

The innominate forms from the union of three bones, the ilium, ischium, and pubis. Each one has one primary center of ossification. The ilium has two secondary centers that meet and form the iliac crest, and the ischium has one secondary center that forms the ischial tuberosity. Three major secondary centers grow within the cartilage of the triradiate area of the acetabulum. Several minor centers complete the acetabulum and form the tips of the iliac spines. Only the iliac crest epiphysis and ischial epiphysis are easily identifiable. The iliac crest epiphysis fuses in the late teens to early twenties, but it can sometimes appear to have an open line of fusion in older individuals (Burns, 2009). This may possibly be an artifact of osteoporosis and postmortem erosion.

Forensic Note

The epiphyses of the iliac crest do not fully fuse until the late teens or early twenties; therefore, the crest may be useful in establishing that the individual is legally an adult.

Basic Ages of Fusion

ischiopubic ramus 5–8 years
acetabulum 11–17 years
ischial tuberosity 16–20 years

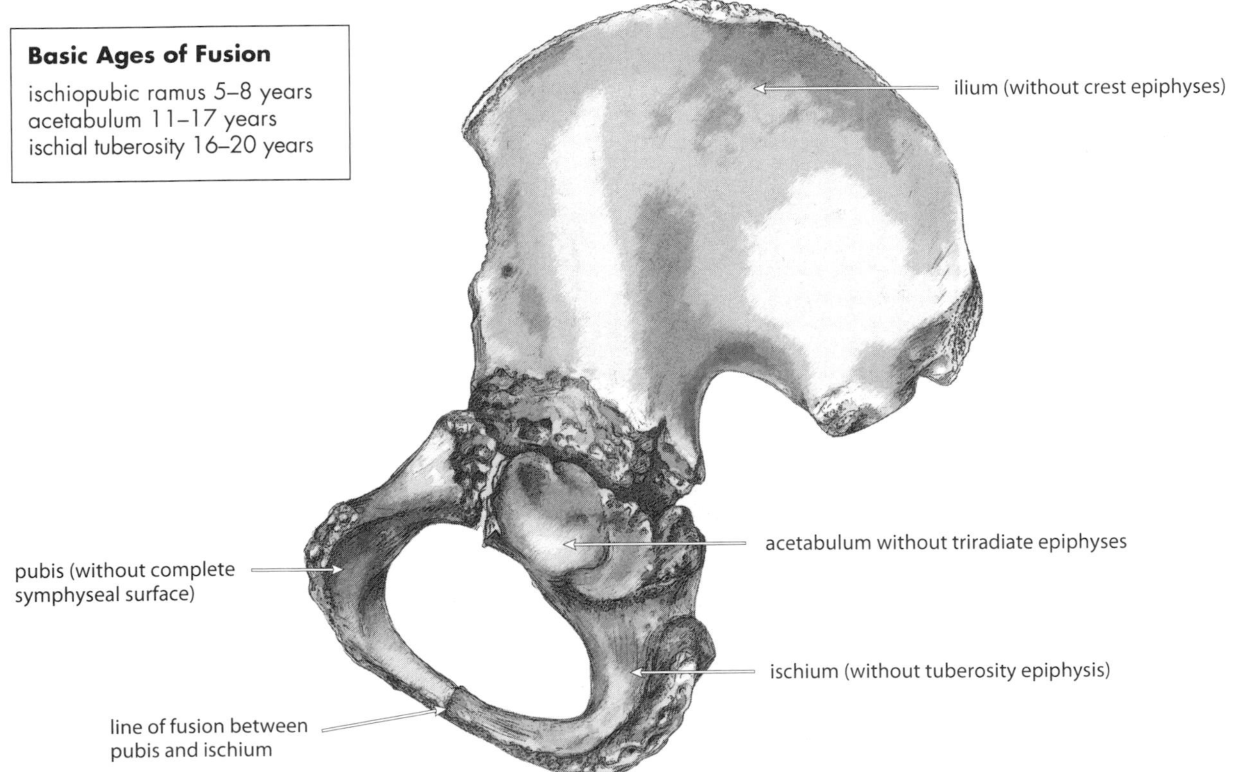

Figure 8.4
Left Ilium, Ischium, and Pubis, Juvenile, 3 Years Old, Lateral (External) View
The epiphyses are not included here, but are described in the text.

Sexual Differences

The adult pelvis is the single most reliable structure for sex determination. During puberty, the male pelvis grows larger and more robust, but the female pelvis actually changes in shape, resulting in wider female hips and a larger pelvic inlet, which accommodates childbirth.

Numerous sexing techniques and methods are published. They include visual assessment of traits (Phenice, 1969; Iscan & Derrick, 1984; Bruzek, 2002), metric techniques (Schulter-Ellis, et al., 1983 & 1985; Steyna & Iscan, 2008; Klales et al., 2009), and the latest in virtual determination of sex using both metric and non-metric techniques (Decker et al., 2011). Most of the earlier methods have been tested repeatedly on various populations, either to improve the methods and/or to obtain statistical information on reliability and validity, e.g. Kelley (1978) and Sutherland and Suchey (1991).

The goal here is not to teach sexing methods for the pelvis, but rather to introduce the *anatomical basis* for the methods. With an understanding of pelvic bone morphology and knowledge of the specific areas that are known to be sexually dimorphic, it is possible to test a variety of methods and select the most effective for the purpose, considering the condition of the material and the population of origin. For example, if the pubic bones are damaged, select methods based on the ilium or sacrum (Iscan & Derrick, 1984; MacLaughlin & Bruce, 1986). If the population is from South Africa, use African-based research (Patriquin et al., 2005), etc.

Sexual Differences in the Pubis

When compared to the male pubis, the female pubis appears to have been stretched out toward the midline. The result is a female **pubic body** that is rather square in shape compared to the narrow, vertically-oriented male pubic body. As the female pubic body widens, several other changes appear in the subpubic area (immediately inferior to the pubic symphysis). The **subpubic angle** widens, a **subpubic concavity** develops, and the medial aspect of the ischiopubic ramus becomes sharper. On the body of the pubis, a diagonal ridge—the **ventral arc**—develops.

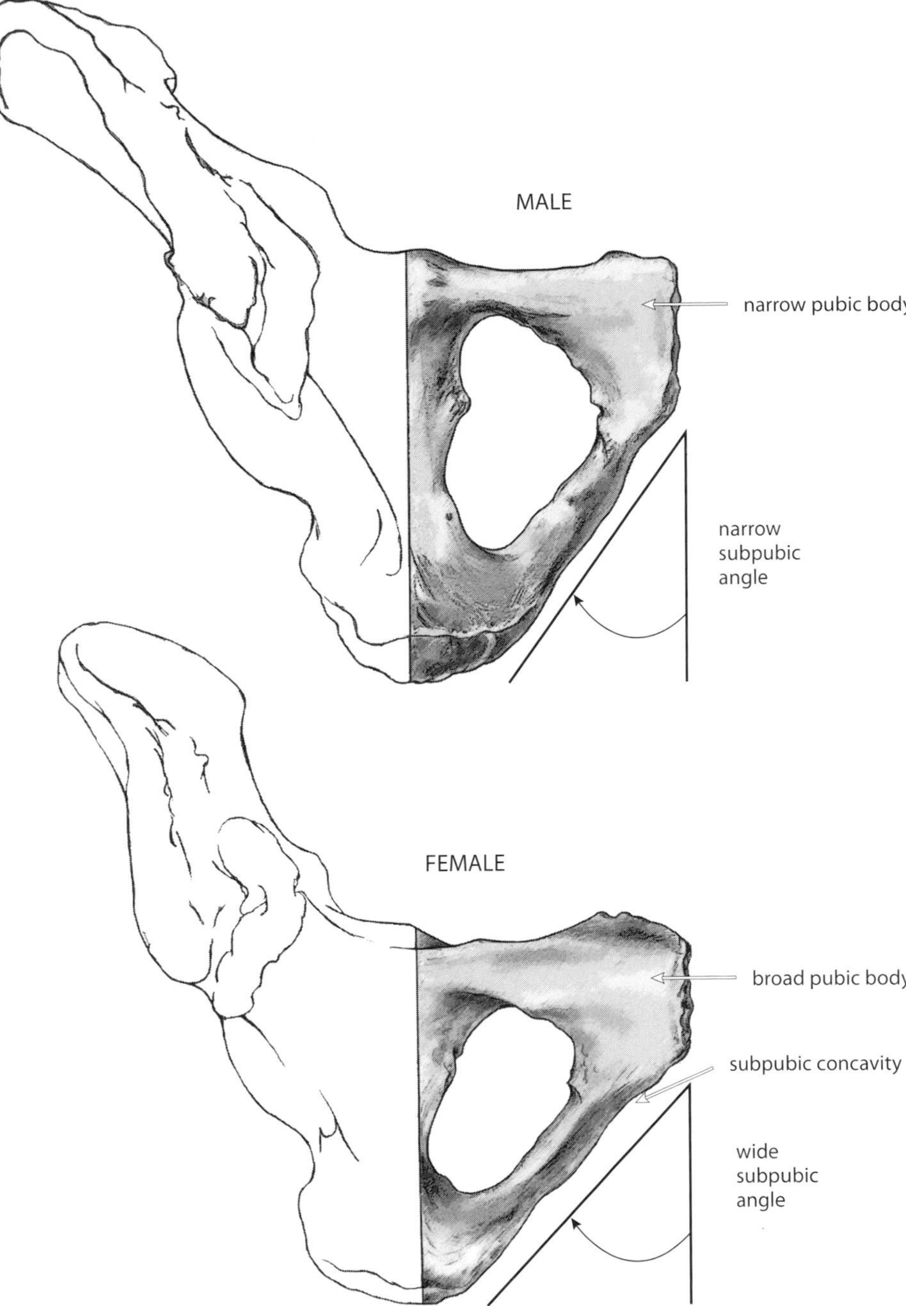

Figure 8.5
Male and Female Innominates, Internal Surface of Pubis and Ischiopubic Ramus

Compare each of the following characteristics:

- pubic bone width (female is wider)
- subpubic angle (female is wider)
- ventral arc (female is more pronounced)
- parturition pits (more common in females)

Circular depressions sometimes form on the otherwise smooth dorsal surface of the pubis. These irregularities are known as **parturition pits** (or scars) because they are found more often on female pubes and were originally attributed to the trauma of childbirth. It is known that the correlation with childbirth is not consistant (Holt, 1978). Parturition pits can be found in females who have not born children as well as in males. I suggest that the pits may result from a wide range of trauma to the posterior pubic ligament, including both childbirth and sporting activities.

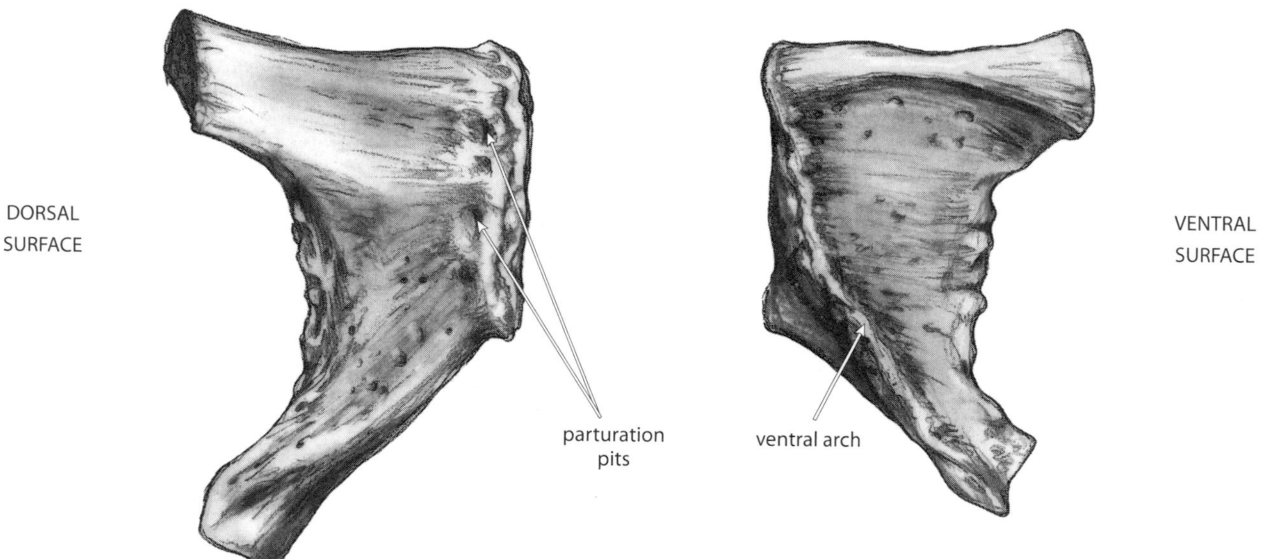

Figure 8.6
Adult Female Pubic Bone, Dorsal and Ventral Surfaces (Natural Size)
This is the same bone viewed from both sides. It was originally removed at autopsy and cleaned for age estimation analysis. Note the parturation pits on the dorsal surface and the ventral arc on the ventral surface. Both are common female traits.

Compare each of the following characteristics:

- sciatic notch width (female is wider)
- sciatic notch depth (female is shallower)
- existence of preauricular sulcus (more common in females)

Sexual Differences in the Ilium

When compared to the male ilium, the female form appears more flared at the widest point and narrower toward the base of the iliopubic ramus. This is partially the result of a wider, shallower **greater sciatic notch**. Studies by MacLaughlin and Bruce (1986) and Steyna and İscan (2008) have shown the sciatic notch to be a particularly poor discriminator of sex, but it may still be useful when taken into consideration with all other evidence.

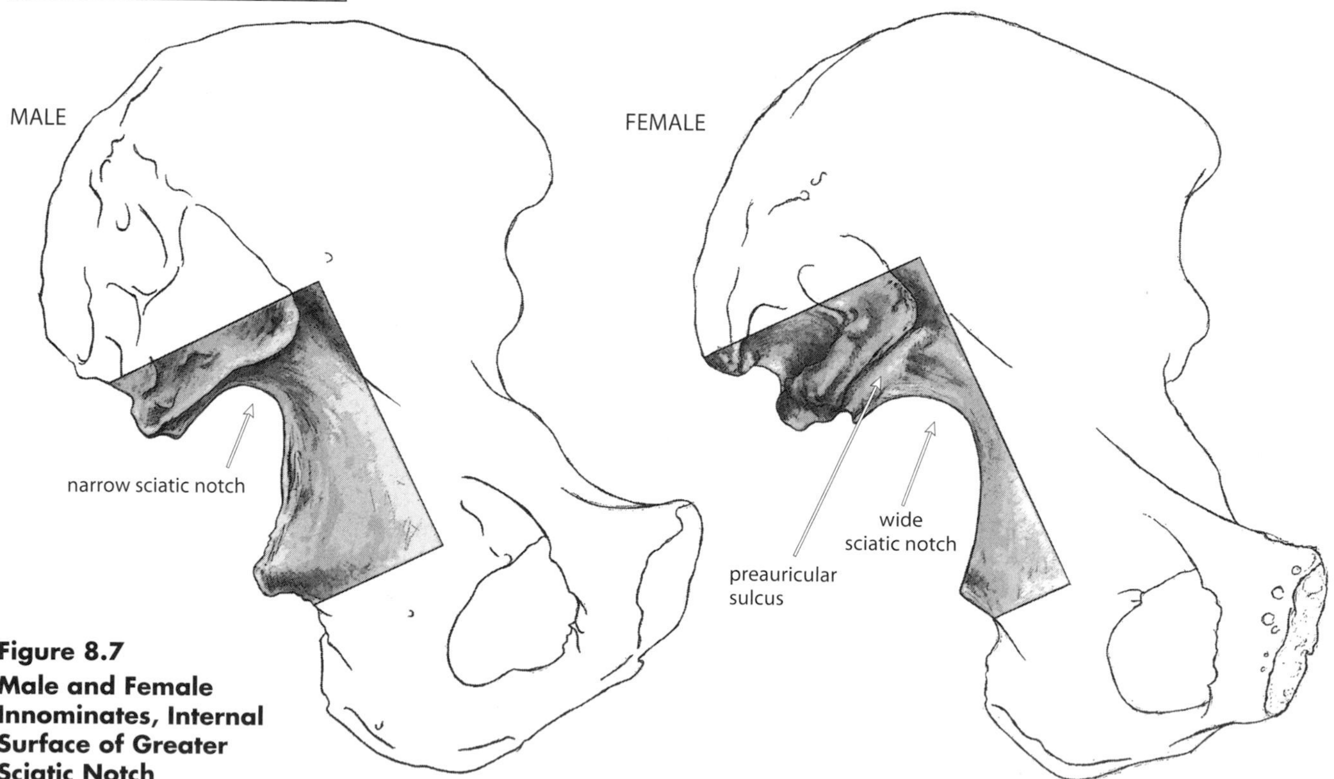

Figure 8.7
Male and Female Innominates, Internal Surface of Greater Sciatic Notch

Females tend to develop a groove at the anterior inferior edge of the auricular surface more frequently than males. Because of its location, it is called a **preauricular sulcus**. Like parturition pits, the preauricular sulcus probably results from stress to ligaments which may or may not be related to childbirth. As with other sexual characteristics, there are many intermediate and inconclusive forms.

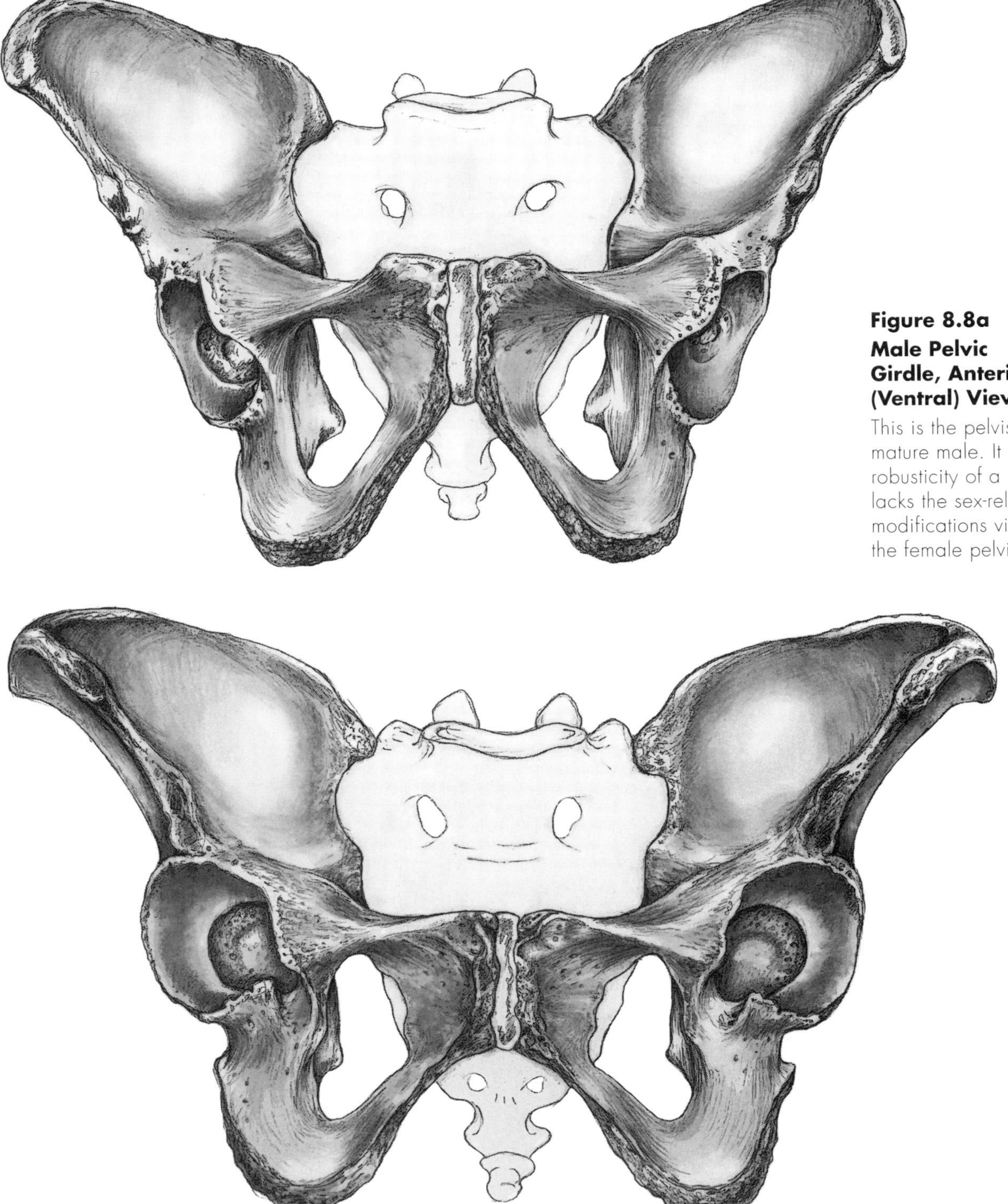

Figure 8.8a
Male Pelvic Girdle, Anterior (Ventral) View
This is the pelvis of a mature male. It has the robusticity of a male and lacks the sex-related modifications visible in the female pelvis.

Figure 8.8b
Female Pelvic Girdle, Anterior (Ventral) View
This is the pelvis of a mature female. It has all the characteristics of a female pelvis, and age-related osteophytes are visible at the rims of the acetabula.

Age Changes

The innominate is one of several postcranial bones systematically studied for adult (degenerational) age changes. Tested and revised methods exist for both the pubic symphysis and the auricular surface of the ilium. The pubic symphysis tends to be more reliable and easier to utilize, but there are cases in which the auricular surface is the only available source of age estimation.

Age Changes in the Pubic Symphysis

Component analysis of pubic symphyses was first suggested by Todd in 1920. He published a readable description of the ten phases of the pubic symphysis with illustrations of each phase. Todd's sample is entirely male orientated and not an adequate representation of the wide variation encountered throughout the world, but Todd's work was instrumental in establishing the pubic symphysis as a source of aging information and encouraging further research and it is quite helpful as an aid to understanding the sequence of aging events. It is included here for general use.

- **I.** *First post-adolescent phase (age 18–19).* Symphysial surface rugged, traversed by horizontal ridges separated by well-marked grooves; no ossific (epiphyseal) nodules fusing with the surface; no definite delimiting margin; no definition of extremities (Todd, 1920, p. 301).
- **II.** *Second post-adolescent phase (age 20–21).* Symphysial surface still rugged, traversed by horizontal ridges, the grooves between which are, however, becoming filled near the dorsal limit with a new formation of finely textured bone. This formation begins to obscure the hinder extremities of the horizontal ridges. Ossific (epiphyseal) nodules fusing with the upper symphysial face may occur; dorsal limiting margin begins to develop; no delimitation of extremities; foreshadowing of ventral bevel (Todd, 1920, pp. 302–303).
- **III.** *Third post-adolescent phase (age 22–24).* Symphysial face shows progressive obliteration of ridge and furrow system; commencing formation of the dorsal plateau; presence of fusing ossific (epiphyseal) nodules; dorsal margin gradually becoming more defined; beveling as a result of ventral rarefaction becoming rapidly more pronounced; no delimitation of extremities (Todd, 1920, p. 304).
- **IV.** *Fourth phase (age 25–26).* Great increase of ventral beveled area; corresponding diminution of ridge and furrow formation; complete definition of dorsal margin through the formation of the dorsal plateau; commencing delimitation of lower extremity (Todd, 1920, p. 305).
- **V.** *Fifth phase (age 27–30).* Little or no change in symphysial face and dorsal plateau except that sporadic and premature attempts at the formation of a ventral rampart occur; lower extremity, like the dorsal margin, is increasing in clearness of definition; commencing formation of upper extremity with or without the intervention of a bony (epiphyseal) nodule (Todd, 1920, p. 306).
- **VI.** *Sixth phase (age 30–35).* Increasing definition of extremities; development and practical completion of ventral rampart; retention of granular appearance of symphysial face and ventral aspect of pubis; absence of lipping of symphysial margin (Todd, 1920, p. 308).

VII. *Seventh phase (age 35–39).* Changes in symphysial face and ventral aspect of pubis consequent upon diminishing activity; commencing bony outgrowth into attachments of tendons and ligaments, especially the gracilis tendon and sacrotuberous ligament (Todd, 1920, p. 310).

VIII. *Eighth phase (age 39–44).* Symphysial face generally smooth and inactive; ventral surface of pubis also inactive; oval outline complete or approximately complete; extremities clearly defined; no distinct "rim" to symphysial face; no marked lipping of either dorsal or ventral margin (Todd, 1920, p. 311).

IX. *Ninth phase (age 45–50).* Symphysial face presents a more or less marked rim; dorsal margin uniformly lipped; ventral margin irregularly lipped (Todd, 1920, p. 312).

X. *Tenth phase (age 50 and upward).* Symphysial face eroded and showing erratic ossification; ventral border more or less broken down; disfigurement increases with age (Todd, 1920, p. 313).

Todd's work was tested and modified by Brooks (1955), Brooks and Suchey (1990), McKern and Stewart (1957), Hanihara and Suzuki (1978), Snow (1983), Katz and Suchey (1986), Suchey, Wiseley, and Katz (1986), and others. Each investigator set out to find out if the method really worked and, if so, how to improve or simplify it. Many became proficient in analyzing the hills and valleys of the pubic symphysis, but no one actually made the method easy to use. Katz and Suchey (1986) cut the number of stages from ten to six, and the whole group of researchers proved that intense study of large quantities of information leads to increasingly better observation of detail.

It was long thought that pubic symphysis aging could be used only for males because the trauma of childbirth was bound to have a destructive and false aging effect on female pubes. However, determined researchers developed separate standards for female pubic symphyses and proved them to be useful (Gilbert & McKern, 1973; Suchey, 1979; Suchey et al., 1986). A study by Klepinger and colleagues (1992) validated the methods for both males and females. Formulae and illustrations for female pubic symphyses are not included here, but the casts and instructions can be obtained from France Casting. Casts are preferred over illustrations whenever possible.

As with all things biological, there are many variables and many responses by the body. The result is expressed as trends rather than as clearly delineated steps. Study the trends, use the methods, compare your samples to casts from people of known ages, but do not rely wholly on the pubic symphysis or any other single method alone for age determination. In a mass grave of people from the same population group, it is at least possible to derive a fairly good age sequence.

Analysis of the Pubic Symphysis

Before attempting age analysis of a pubic symphysis, study the anatomy and learn to recognize each of the significant characteristics listed here:

1. Identify the ventral and dorsal surfaces of the pubis. The ventral surface is concave; the dorsal surface, convex.
2. Identify the symphysial face. It is the same as the symphysial surface. The two faces "face" each other in life, separated only by fibrocartilage.
3. Recognize a ridged surface and distinguish it from smooth and porous surfaces. A ridged surface can also be described as undulating, rippled, wavy, or billowing.
4. Locate the ossified nodules. They are bony bumps, elevated from the plane of the symphysial surface.
5. Locate the oval outline. It is the outer margin of the symphysial surface.
6. Feel the symphysial rim. It is an extension of the oval outline, slightly elevated from the plane of the symphysial surface.

Table 8.1 Correlation and Comparison of the Katz and Suchey Six-Phase System and the Todd Ten-Phase System

Note that the number of years within the age range increases by over 15 percent between phase 1 and phase 6. In other words, the higher the phase number, the less it tells you.

Todd	Katz and Suchey	Age Range	Years
I, II, III	1	15–23	8
IV, V	2	19–35	16
VI	3	22–43	21
VII, VIII	4	23–59	36
IX	5	28–78	50
X	6	36–87	51

Age Changes in the Auricular Surface of the Ilium

The auricular surface of the ilium also changes with age. Lovejoy and colleagues (1985a) developed a method for age determination based on changes in five areas of the auricular surface. Just as Todd's work (1920) revealed the sequence of aging events in the pubic symphysis, Lovejoy's work defined age changes in the auricular surface. Lovejoy described eight phases covering five-year intervals from ages 20 to >60. The Lovejoy method is not as easy to use as the pubic symphysis method, but the ilium often survives conditions that destroy the more fragile pubis. In other words, the auricular surface may be the only available age determination information.

Lovejoy's method has been tested and revised several times (Meindl & Lovejoy, 1989; Murray & Murray, 1991; Bedford et al., 1993; Buckberry & Chamberlain, 2002; Osborne et al., 2004), but it continues to be difficult for many users. Insufficient comparative materials may be one reason for the difficulty. Photographs have been published several places, including Ubelaker and Buikstra (1994) and Lovejoy and colleagues (1995), but, at the time of this writing, no comparative casts are available.

Murray and Murray (1991) found that the amount of degenerative change in the auricular surface is not dependent upon race or sex in any given age category. They also stated that the rate of degenerative change is too variable to be used alone for age estimation. The work of Osborne and colleagues (2004) seems to confirm Murray's statement, but as stated earlier, the ilium may be the only source of information. In such a case, the method should be used to the limits of its predictability.

AGE CHANGES IN PUBIC SYMPHYSES OF MALES

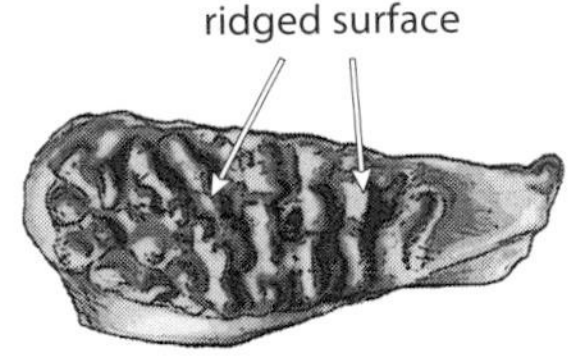

PHASE 1: 15 TO 23 YEARS—COMPLETELY RIDGED SURFACE

- Early: *completely ridged surface,* no nodules, no beveling, no symphysial rim, no lipping
- Late: ossified nodules begin to form as ridges slowly disappear

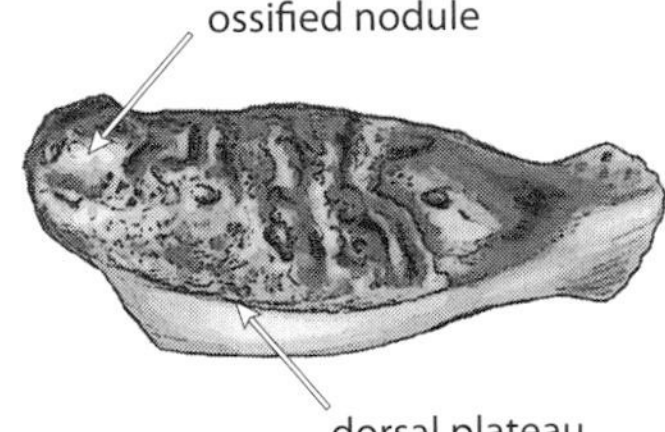

PHASE 2: 19 TO 35 YEARS—OSSIFIED NODULES

- Ossified nodules obvious
- Dorsal plateau formed
- Ventral beveling begins

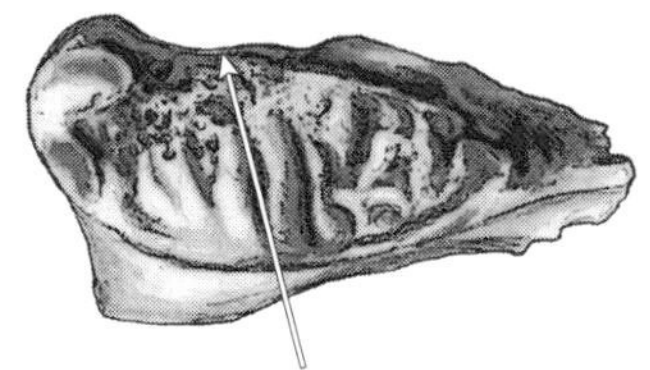

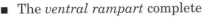

PHASE 3: 22 TO 43 YEARS—VENTRAL RAMPART

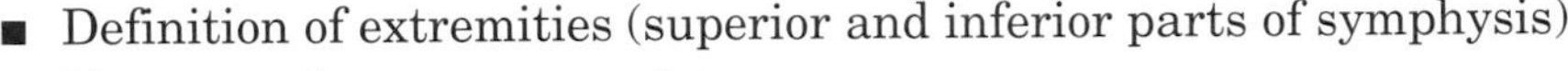

- Definition of extremities (superior and inferior parts of symphysis)
- The *ventral rampart* complete
- No symphysial rim, no lipping

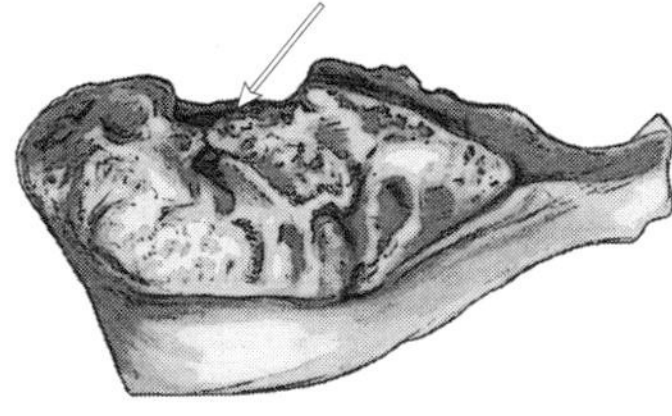

PHASE 4: 23 TO 59 YEARS—OVAL OUTLINE

- Smoother symphysial face
- The *oval outline* almost complete
- No symphysial rim, no lipping

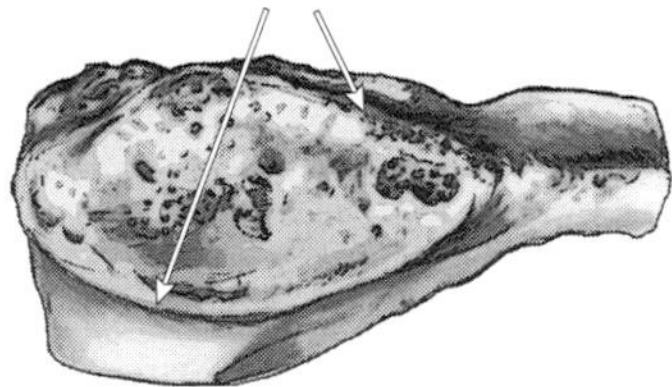

PHASE 5: 28 TO 78 YEARS—SYMPHYSIAL RIM

- Marked *symphysial rim*
- Dorsal margin lipped
- Ventral margin irregularly lipped

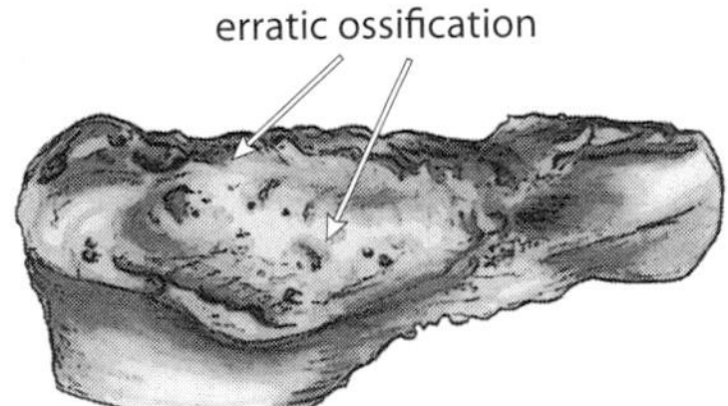

PHASE 6: 36 TO 87 YEARS—ERRATIC OSSIFICATION

- Eroded *erratic ossification*
- Irregular lipping
- Broken down ventral border

Figure 8.9
Male Pubic Aging in Six Phases with Abbreviated Descriptions
These illustrations and descriptions are provided only as an overview of the sequence of normal age changes in the pubic symphysis. The illustrations are adapted from male pubic bone casts produced by France Casting for use with the six-phase Suchey–Brooks Method of pubic symphysis aging. To use the Suchey–Brooks method, consult the literature directly and use the descriptions and photographs provided by the researchers (Katz & Suchey, 1986; Brooks & Suchey, 1990; Suchey & Katz, 1998) as your guide.

Areas

- Auricular surface: the articular surface for the sacrum (It looks ear-shaped.)
- Apex: the anterior angle of the auricular surface, located at the termination of the arculate line
- Superior demiface: the area of the auricular surface above the apex
- Inferior demiface: the area of the auricular surface below the apex
- Retroauricular area: the entire area posterior to the auricular surface

Characteristics

- Billowing: transverse ridges, undulations
- Striations: thin lines, scrapes
- Porosity: tiny perforations, holes
- Granularity: small bumps, like sandpaper
- Apical activity: rim formation at the auricular apex

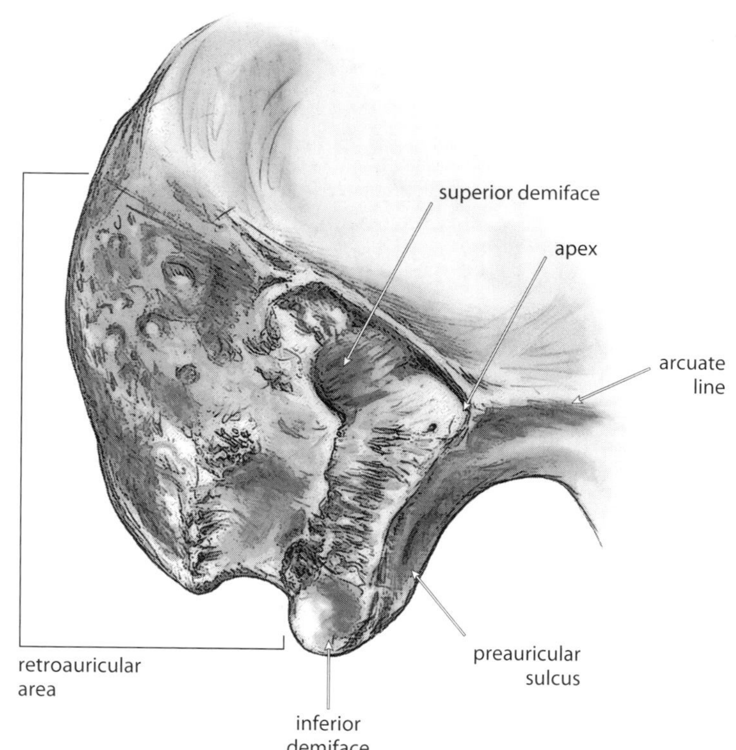

Figure 8.10
Auricular Surface, Anatomical Areas for Age Determination

Table 8.2 Osborne's Six-Phase Modification of the Lovejoy Eight-Phase Method with Prediction Intervals

Phase	Morphological Features	Mean Age	Suggested Age Range
1	billowing with possible striae; mostly fine granularity with some coarse granularity possible	21.1	≤27
2	striae; coarse granularity with residual fine granularity; retroauricular activity may be present	29.5	≤46
3	decreased striae with transverse organization; coarse granularity; retroauricular activity present; beginnings of apical change	42	≤69
4	remnants of transverse organization; coarse granularity becoming replaced by densification; retroauricular activity present; apical change; macroporosity is present	47.8	20–75
5	surface becomes irregular; surface texture is largely dense; moderate retroauricular activity; moderate apical change; macroporosity	53.1	24–82
6	irregular surface; densification accompanied by subchondral destruction; severe retroauricular activity; severe apical change; macroporosity	58.9	29–89

Modified from Osborne et al., 2004: 202, Tables 8, 9.

Table 8.3 Pelvis Vocabulary

Bone	Term	Definition
INNOMINATE	acetabulum	the articular surface for the rotation of the head of the femur
	acetabular fossa	the non-articular central surface deep within the acetabulum
	obturator foramen	large opening bordered by the pubis, the ischium, and the ischio-pubic ramus
ILIUM	auricular surface	ear-shaped surface for the articulation of the sacrum
	arcuate line	the slight ridge on the medial (inner) surface of the ilium, beginning at the pubis and ending at the edge ("apex") of the auricular surface
	preauricular sulcus	groove anterior/inferior to the auricular surface, thought to be related to the trauma of bearing children
	iliac crest	superior edge of the ilium
	iliac fossa	smooth, concave inner surface of the ilium
	iliac tuberosity	the posterior, inner thickening of the ilium, superior to the auricular surface
	anterior superior iliac spine	the upper of the two projections on the ventral edge of the ilium
	anterior inferior iliac spine	the lower of the two projections on the ventral edge of the ilium
	posterior superior iliac spine	the upper of the two projections on the dorsal edge of the ilium
	posterior inferior iliac spine	the lower of the two projections on the dorsal edge of the ilium; the projection that forms the superior boundary of the greater sciatic notch
	greater sciatic notch	the large notch on the posterior edge of the ilium and extending down onto the ischium; an area of distinct sexual dimorphism (♂ narrow, ♀ wide)
ISCHIUM	ischial tuberosity	the largest, thickest portion of the ischium; human sits on the two ischial tuberosities
	ischial spine	the projection of bone that forms the inferior boundary of the greater sciatic notch
	lesser sciatic notch	the smaller notch inferior to the greater sciatic notch
PUBIS	dorsal plateau	the elevated ridge that appears on the dorsal surface (the convex innermost surface of the pubis) in the early phases of pubic symphysis aging
	ischiopubic ramus	the bridge of bone formed from processes of both ischium and pubis
	pubic ramus	the superior bridge of the pubis extending toward the ilium
	pubic symphysis	the cartilaginous joint between the two pubic bones; the symphysial bone surfaces change progressively with age
	pubic tubercle	the small bony bump on the superior anterior surface of the pubic bone
	subpubic angle	the angle formed beneath the pubic symphysis when the two pubic bones are anatomically aligned
	subpubic concavity	the lateral curvature inferior to the female pubic symphysis
	symphysial rim	the lip that circumscribes the face of the pubic symphysis in later phases of pubic symphysis aging
	ventral rampart	the bevel that appears on the ventral surface (the concave, outer surface) in middle phases of pubic symphysis aging
	ventral arc	the slightly elevated ridge of bone on the ventral aspect of the female pubis
	parturition pits	indentations or circular depressions on the inner surface of the pubis adjacent to the pubic symphysis

CHAPTER 9

The Leg: Femur, Tibia, Fibula, and Patella

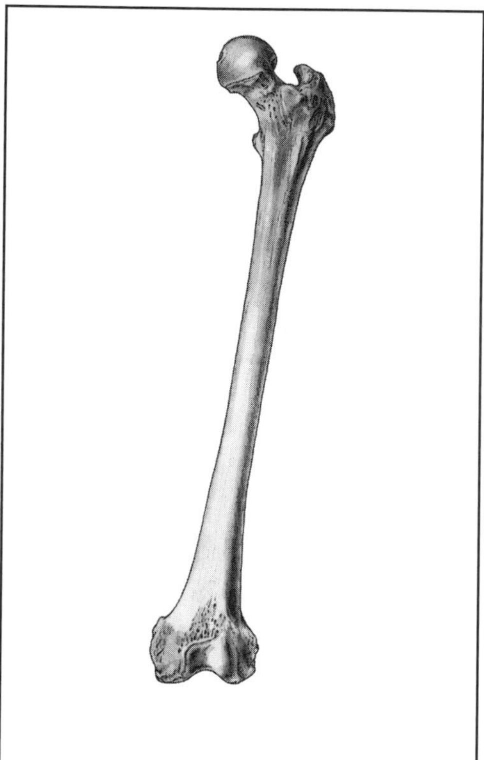

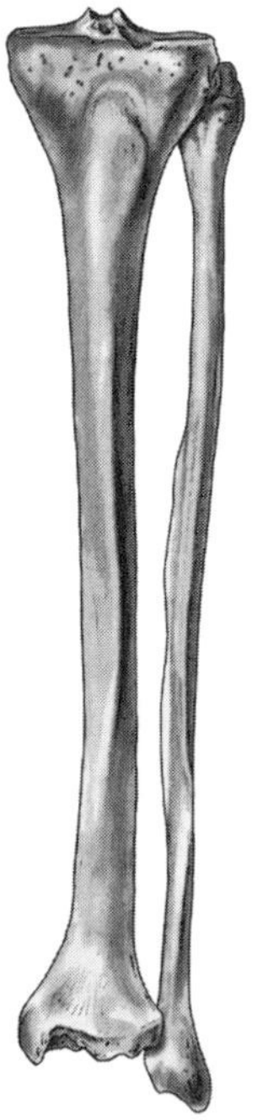

CHAPTER OUTLINE

Introduction

The long bones of the leg are similar to those of the arm in that there is one proximal long bone and two distal long bones. Unlike the arm, however, a large sesamoid bone (the patella) exists in the joint, and the distal two long bones (the tibia and fibula) are unequal in size and strength.

Femur: Upper Leg, Thigh Bone

Description, Location, Articulation

The femur is commonly called the "thigh bone" and is usually the heaviest and strongest bone of the body. It is important in forensic settings because it endures longer than most other bones, and it is useful for stature estimates and genetic analysis. The femur is easily recognized by the ball-shaped **head** projecting at an angle from the proximal end and the two large condyles at the distal end. The shaft is slightly bowed and recognized by the **linea aspera**, a thick elevated ridge that runs most of the length of the distal surface. The linea aspera serves as the insertion site for major muscles of the hip and knee. The femur articulates proximally with the acetabulum of the innominate and distally with the tibia and the patella.

The femur angles medially (inward) from the acetabulum of the pelvis toward the knee. It does not form a straight line with the tibia. The **medial condyle** is longer than the **lateral condyle** in order to reach and articulate with the horizontal platform of the tibia. The relative orientation of the femur and the tibia in the human leg contributes to a smoothly balanced stride. (See the subsection on sexual differences.)

Left/Right Recognition

In anatomical position, the head is medial, and the **greater trochanter** is lateral. The greater and **lesser trochanters** are connected by the **intertrochanteric crest** across the posterior surface. The medial condyle is longer and the lateral condyle is broader. The surface for articulation of the patella is anterior.

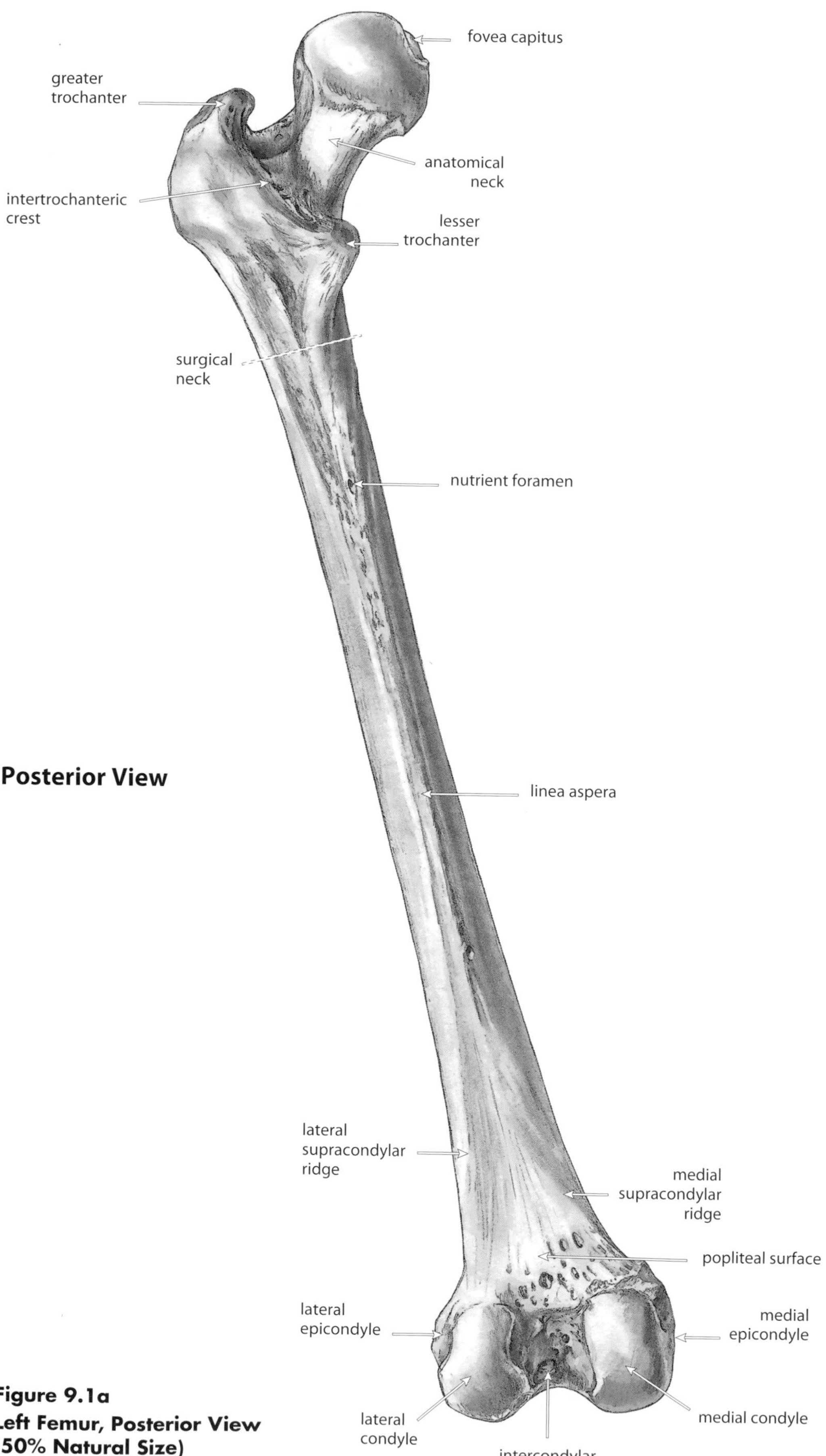

Figure 9.1a
Left Femur, Posterior View (50% Natural Size)

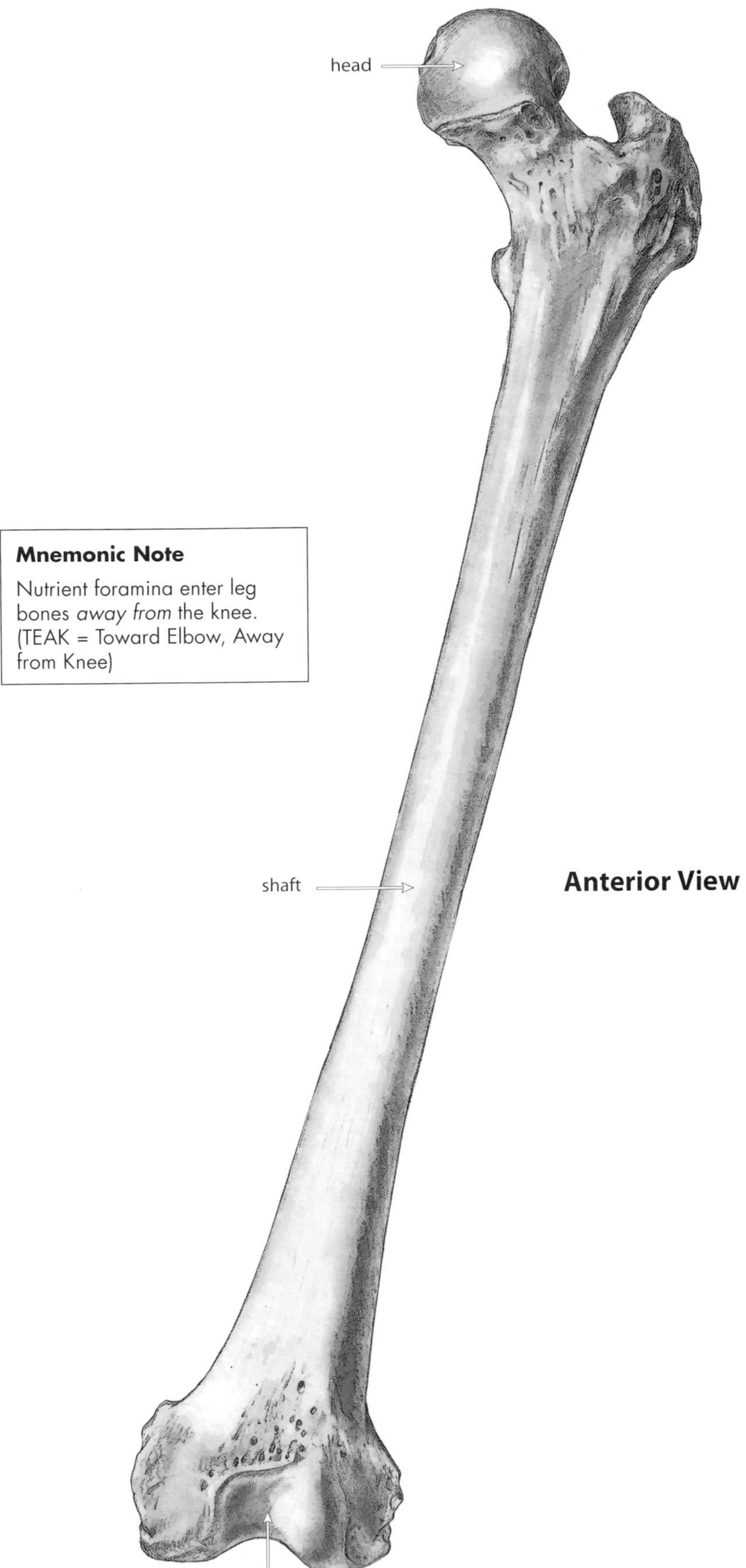

Mnemonic Note

Nutrient foramina enter leg bones *away from* the knee. (TEAK = Toward Elbow, Away from Knee)

Anterior View

Figure 9.1b
Left Femur, Anterior View (50% Natural Size)

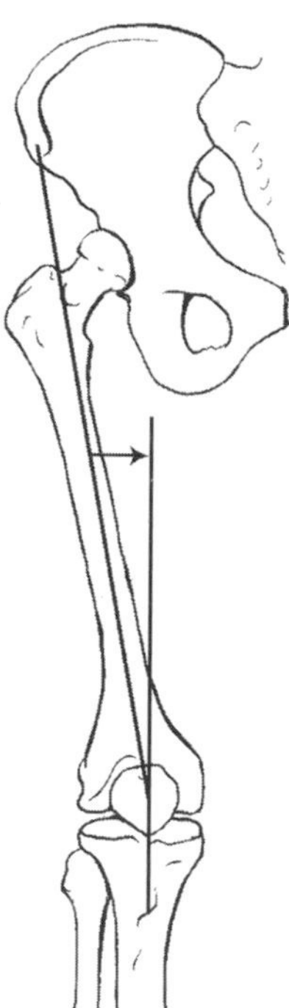

Figure 9.1c
The Femoral-Tibia Angle ("Q-angle")
Females have greater Q-angles than males. The difference reflects the wider pelvis and affects differences in the ways that men and women run and walk.

Sexual Differences in the Femur

The condyles of the femur meet the platform of the tibia at a slight angle. This angle is known as a **Q-angle** or quadriceps angle because it follows the path of the quadriceps femoris muscle. In the living person, the angle is measured by drawing a line from the anterior superior iliac spine to the center of the patella. A second line is then drawn vertically, using the center of the patella and the center of the anterior tibial tuberosity as guide points. (See Figure 9.1c.)

A range of Q-angles are reported for males and females of different populations, but there is general agreement that the female Q-angle is larger (Livingston, 1998). In a North Carolina population, Horton (1989) reported a mean value of 15.8 ± 4.5 degrees for females and 11.2 ± 3 degrees for males. In an East Indian population, Raveenfranath (2009) reported a mean value of 14.48 ± 2.02 degrees for females and 10.98 ± 1.75 degrees for males. For general purposes, the female Q-angle is about 15 degrees, and the male angle is about 11 degrees.

In skeletal material, evidence of the Q-angle is apparent in the angle of the femoral neck to the shaft and the relative lengths of the two femoral condyles. Compare angles by holding male and female femora upright, with both condyles resting on the surface of a table.

Sex can also be estimated with femoral head measurements. This is based on basic sexual dimorphism, anticipating that males are larger than females. The method is useful if there is no pelvis or skull and if the unidentified individual is from a well-documented population. An unknown corpse from a heterogeneous population such as found in major U.S. cities may not be a good candidate for this type of analysis.

Stewart (1979: 120) offers the set of numbers shown in Table 9.1 based on his tests of the earlier work of Pearson (1917–1919) for use in sexing dry bones of American whites. Šlaus et al., (2003) tested the method on a Croatian population with positive results. To use the method, measure the greatest diameter of the femur with standard sliding calipers and compare femoral head measurements with the measurements in Table 9.1 .

Table 9.1 Estimation of Sex from the Femoral Head Diameter

Female	Female?	Indeterminate	Male?	Male
42.5 mm	42.5–43.5 mm	43.5–46.5 mm	46.5–47.5 mm	47.5 mm

Another, more elaborate, method of femoral head measurement proved to be effective in the work of Purkait (2003). It is based on an East Indian population and may be useful when a similar population is suspected. If possible, always consider the population of origin before using a method with confidence.

Racial Differences in the Femur

Anterior curvature of the femur varies with individuals and populations. Stewart (1962) suggested that individuals of African origin have less anterior curvature and thus straighter femora. Gilbert (1976) tested Stewart's observations and concluded that "the assumed genetic basis for expression of anterior femoral curvature . . . seems to be a feature of human plastic response to body weight rather than to temporal, clinal, postural or equestrian influences." Nevertheless, Ballard (1999) completely refined the method for measuring femoral curvature and verified the tendency of femora of European origin to have more anterior curvature, and African origin less. It is recommended that the articles be read thoroughly before drawing conclusions.

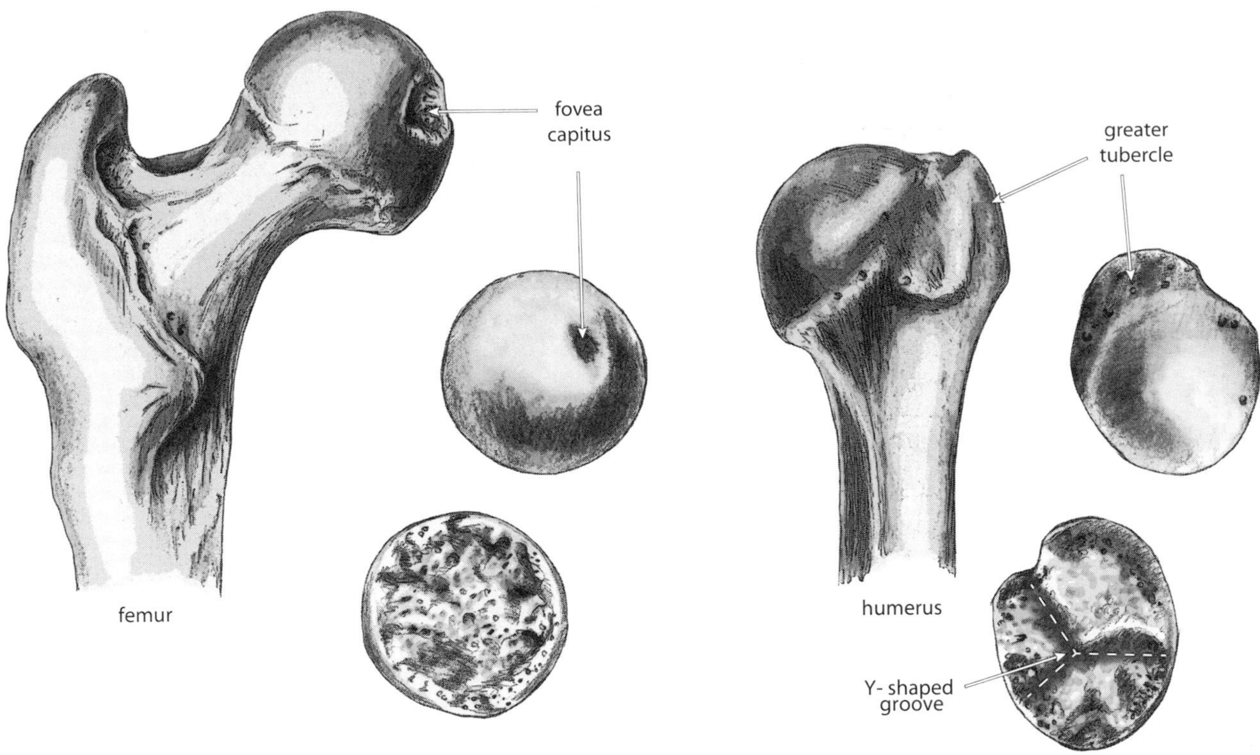

Figure 9.2
Comparison of Heads of Femur and Humerus (Left Sides, Posterior View of Femur, Anterior View of Humerus, External and Metaphyseal Views of Epiphyses)
The fovea capitus (on the external surface) is the key characteristic of the femoral head. The Y-shaped groove (on the metaphyseal surface) and the proximal portions of the tubercles and are the key characteristics of the humeral head.

Bones of Confusion

Fragments of femur are sometimes confused with the tibia or the humerus, but they are all different in cross section. The tibia is triangular, and the humerus and femur are more rounded. The circumference of the humerus is fairly smooth, whereas the circumference of the femur is interrupted by the protrusion of the linea aspera.

The heads of the femur and humerus are sometimes confused when the neck is not present, but there are several identifiable characteristics. The head of the humerus is a smooth, unblemished hemisphere, whereas the head of the femur is a more complete ball, attached to an extended neck and dimpled by the **fovea capitus**, the insertion site of the ligamentum teres femoris.

The proximal epiphyses are further distinguishable in that the femoral epiphysis ossifies from a single center and the humeral epiphysis ossifies from three centers—the head and the greater and lesser tubercles. Identify the femoral proximal epiphysis by the presence of the fovea capitus. Identify the humeral proximal epiphysis by the greater tubercle protruding beyond the margin of the articular surface and the Y-shaped groove delineating the three centers of ossification on the metaphyseal surface. (See Figure 9.2.)

Origin and Growth

The femur is formed from one primary center and four secondary centers of ossification. The primary center is the diaphysis of the shaft. The secondary centers, in order of appearance, include the epiphyses of the condyles, the head,

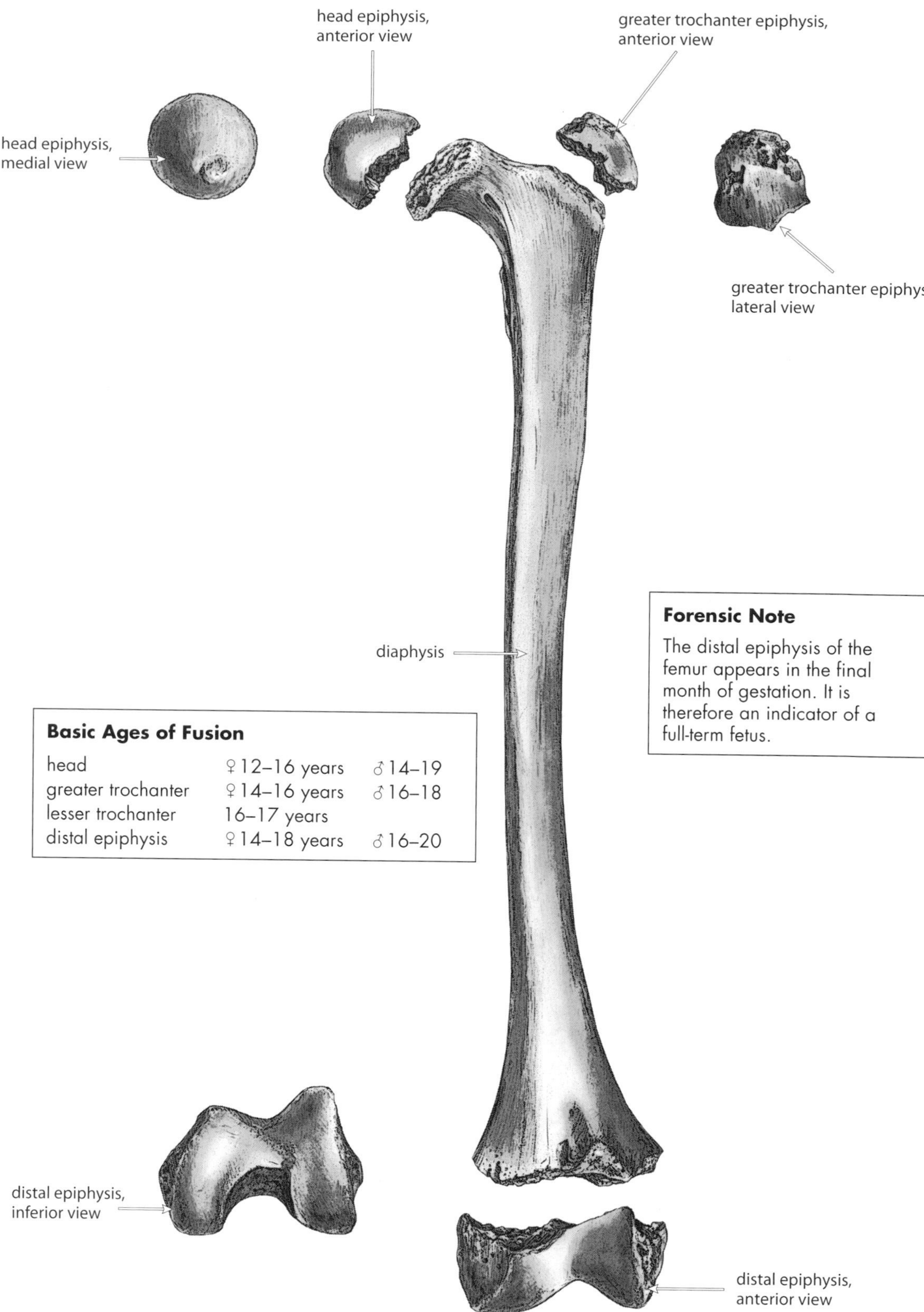

Forensic Note

The distal epiphysis of the femur appears in the final month of gestation. It is therefore an indicator of a full-term fetus.

Basic Ages of Fusion

head	♀12–16 years	♂14–19
greater trochanter	♀14–16 years	♂16–18
lesser trochanter	16–17 years	
distal epiphysis	♀14–18 years	♂16–20

Figure 9.3
Juvenile Left Femur, Anterior View
The femur ossifies from one primary center (the diaphysis) and four secondary centers (the condyles, the head and the greater and lesser trochanters). The epiphysis of the lesser trochanter is not illustrated here.

and the greater and lesser trochanters. The order is important for estimating the age of an infant because the distal epiphysis appears in the final month of gestation (36–40 weeks) and the head appears after birth (6–12 months).

Patella: Kneecap

Description, Location, Articulation

The patella is commonly known as a "kneecap." It is the largest **sesamoid bone** in the body. The shape is roughly heart-shaped with a thicker, slightly beveled, proximal portion and a distal point (the **apex**). The anterior surface is roughened with longitudinal lines, and the posterior surface is smooth and rimmed. The posterior surface is divided into medial and lateral surfaces for articulation with the trochlear surface of the distal femur. The lateral articular surface is usually the larger of the two.

The patella is located on the anterior surface of the knee in the tendon of the quadriceps femoris muscle. The inferior aspect of the patella is held in place by the patellar ligament, which originates on the apex of the patella and inserts on the tibial tuberosity.

The patella appears simply to shield the knee joint, but its main function is to increase the biomechanical efficiency of the knee in extension. It holds the patellar tendon away from the axis of movement and increases the pull of the quadriceps muscle.

Left/Right Recognition

Place the patella on a flat surface with the anterior surface up and the apex pointed away. The patella will fall toward the larger facet—the lateral one. This is the side of origin (i.e., the right patella falls to the right and the left patella falls to the left).

Origin and Growth

Ossification is irregular in the patella. Typically, several centers of ossification appear between 1.5 and 3.5 years and coalesce soon afterward. (There are no epiphyses.) The patella becomes biconvex in shape at 4 to 5 years and assumes an adult appearance during puberty (Scheuer & Black, 2004).

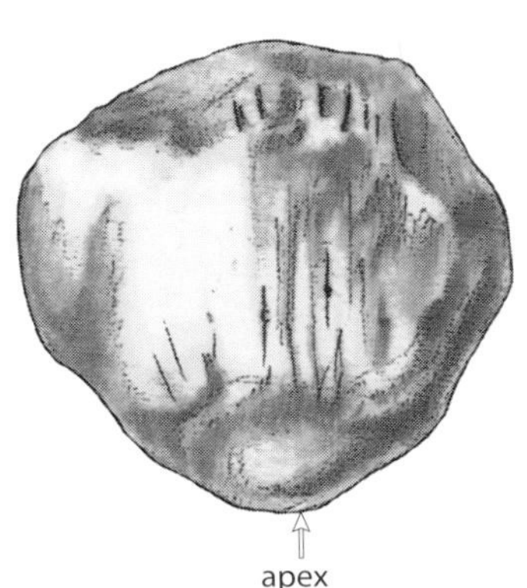

Figure 9.4a
Left Patella, Anterior View (Natural Size)
Note the anterior vertical striations and the slightly beveled superior shelf.

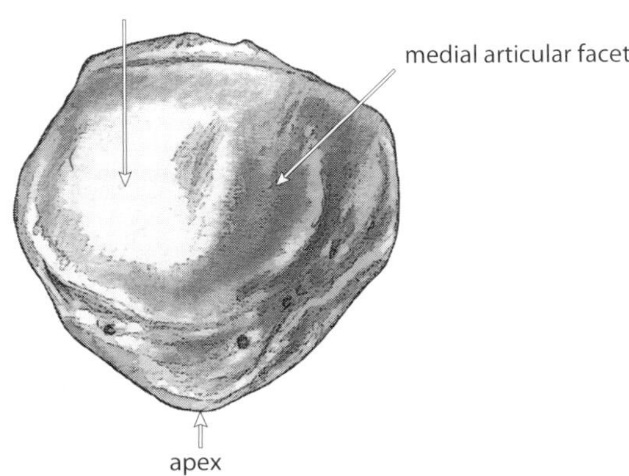

Figure 9.4b
Left Patella, Posterior View (Natural Size)
Note the lateral articular facet is larger than the medial facet.

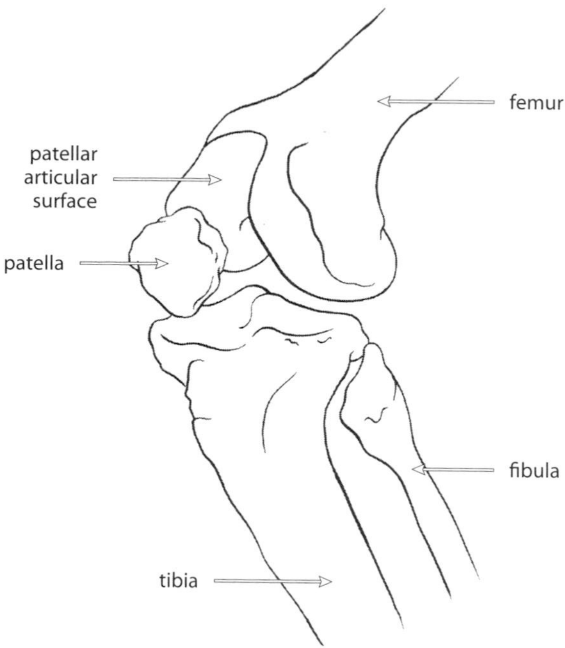

Figure 9.5
Knee Joint and Vertical Location of Patella
The patella glides on the trochlear surface of the femur.

Lower Leg: Tibia and Fibula

The tibia and fibula comprise the bones of the lower leg, but unlike the bones of the forearm, the tibia and fibula are completely unequal in size. The tibia is the major weight-bearing bone, and the fibula is a slender companion, providing long ridges for muscle attachment.

Note the manner in which the fibula fits against the outside of the tibia.

- The **head** of the fibula is inferior to the lateral platform of the proximal tibia.
- The **lateral malleolus** of the distal end of the fibula mirrors the **medial malleolus** of the distal end of the tibia. (Each malleolus is commonly called an "ankle bone.")
- The lateral malleolus (of the fibula) extends below the base of the fibular notch of the tibia and articulates with the lateral surface of the body of the talus.

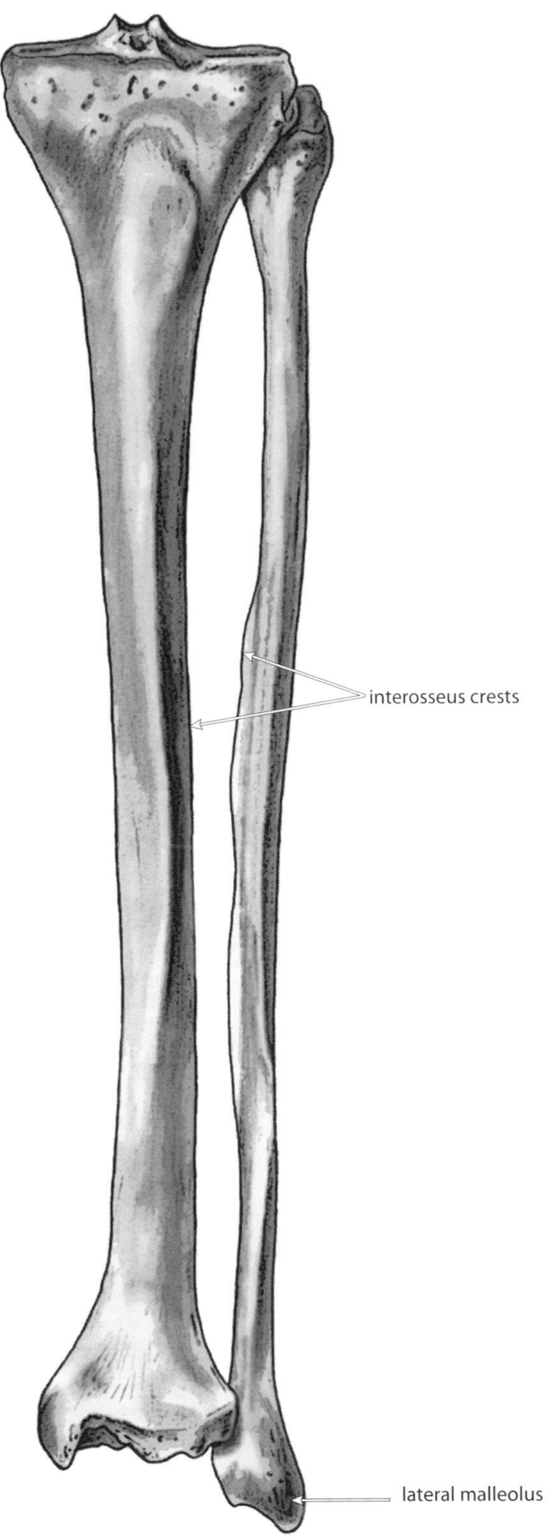

Figure 9.6
Left Tibia and Fibula Together, Anterior View (50% Natural Size)

Note that the interosseus crests face each other and the lateral malleolus extends below the tibia to articulate with the talus in the ankle.

Tibia: Lower Leg, Shin Bone, Medial Ankle Bone

Description, Location, Articulation

The **tibia** is the second largest long bone and is commonly called the "shin bone." It is straighter than the femur and positioned vertically. The tibia is somewhat triangular in cross section with the sharpest angle anterior. It is the **anterior crest** of the tibia that frequently sustains bumps and bruises in the course of an active life.

The proximal end of the tibia forms a horizontal platform, the **tibial plateau**, for articulation with the distal femur. The platform is divided into a **medial articular surface** and **lateral articular surface**. Each surface is only slightly depressed. Stability of the knee joint is highly dependent on soft tissue support and binding. Fibrocartilaginous, semilunar menisci raise the outer rim of each condyle to fit the femoral condyles. Numerous ligaments bind the joint together.

The thin ridge on the lateral side of the tibia is the **interosseous crest**. It provides an attachment line for the interosseous membrane between the tibia and fibula. The interosseous crest serves the same function as the interosseous crests on the radius and ulna. The distal end of the tibia is identified by the projection of the medial malleolus, commonly known as an "ankle bone." The tibia contributes *only* the inner ankle bone. (The distal fibula provides the outer ankle bone.)

The tibia articulates proximally with the femur (but not the patella), and it articulates distally with the talus (the most superior of the tarsal bones). It also articulates laterally with the fibula, at both proximal and distal ends.

Sexual Differences in the Tibia

The width of the knee tends to be larger in males than females and sex can be estimated by discriminant function analysis of tibia measurements (Işcan & Miller-Shaivitz, 1984). Işcan and Miller-Shaivitz also demonstrate that sexual prediction can be race-dependent. In other words, there is more sexual dimorphism in some racial groups than others. Thus, in estimation of sex, the genetic (racial) nature of the population is important as well as the standard sexual differences, size, and activity level. (This should be a general assumption.)

Left/Right Recognition

Study the tibia and fibula together to recognize left/right characteristics. Note each of the following characteristics:

- The interosseous crest of the tibia points laterally, toward the fibula.
- The medial malleolus of the tibia points *anteriorly* when viewed from the medial surface.
- The lateral malleolus of the fibula points *posteriorly* when viewed from the lateral surface.

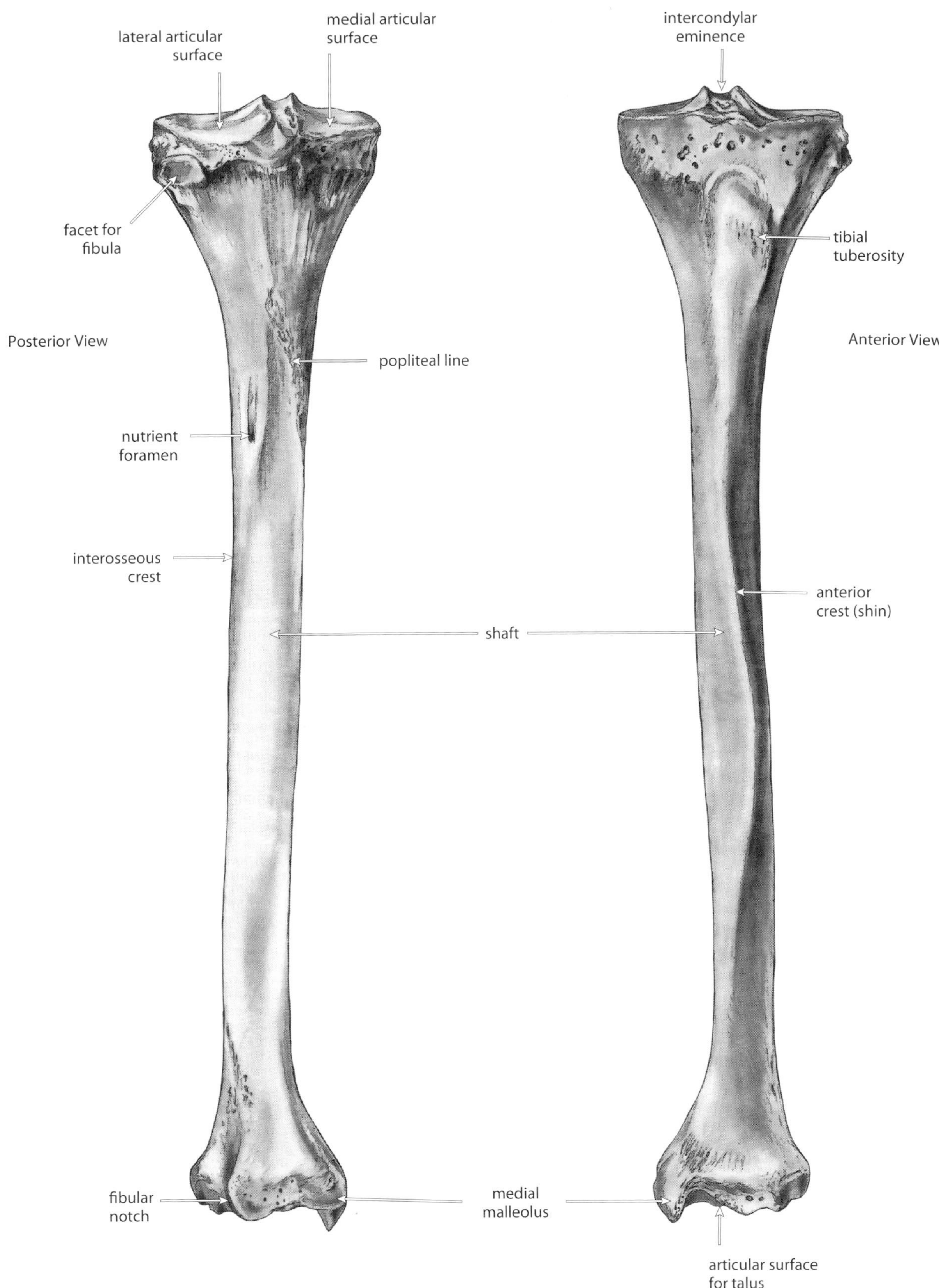

Figure 9.7
Left Tibia, Posterior and Anterior Views (50% Natural Size)

Origin and Growth

The tibia is formed from one primary center of ossification (the diaphysis of the shaft) and two secondary centers of ossification, the proximal and distal epiphyses. The proximal epiphysis appears first (36–40 weeks fetal).

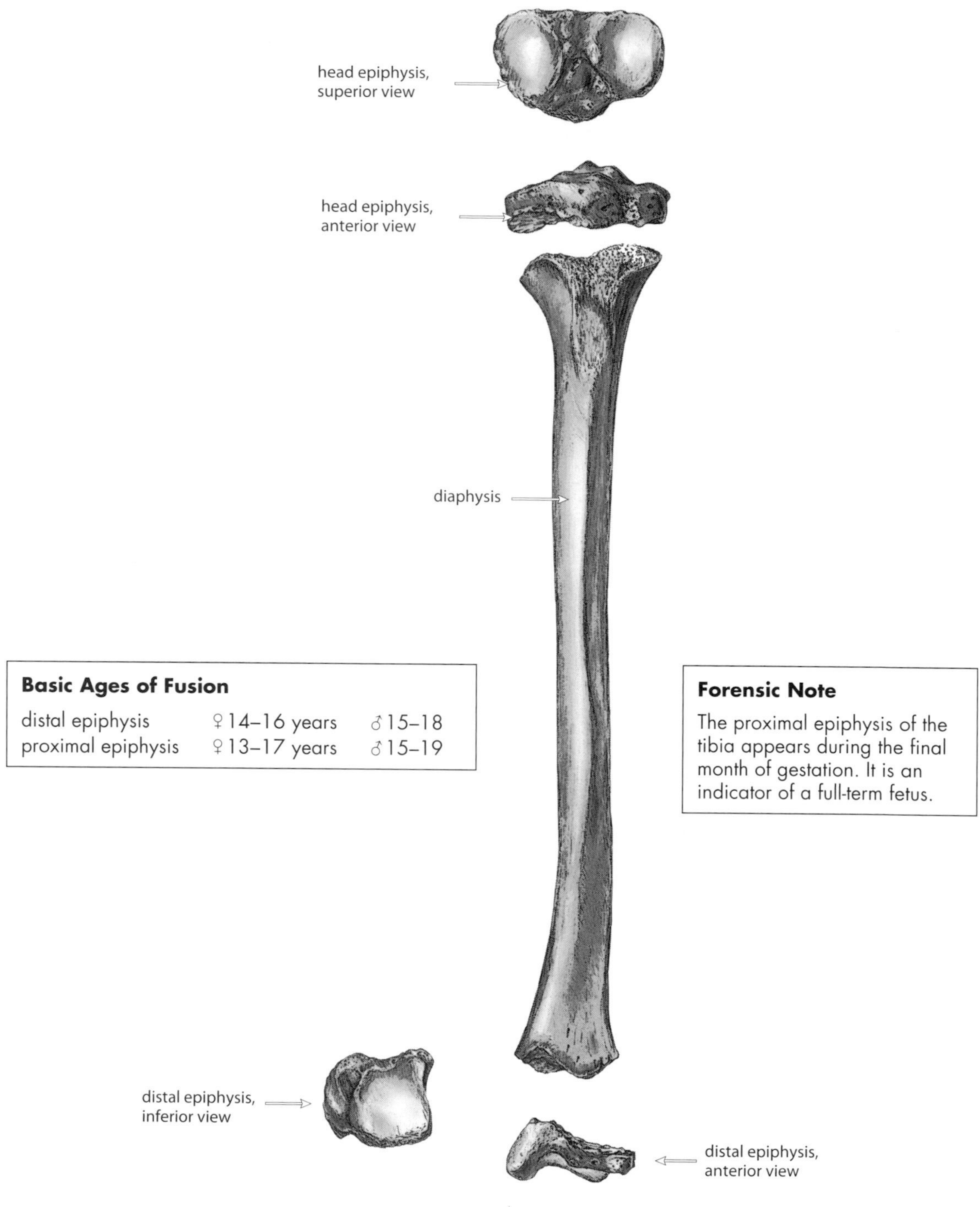

Basic Ages of Fusion

distal epiphysis	♀14–16 years	♂15–18
proximal epiphysis	♀13–17 years	♂15–19

Forensic Note

The proximal epiphysis of the tibia appears during the final month of gestation. It is an indicator of a full-term fetus.

Figure 9.8
Juvenile Left Tibia, Anterior View

Fibula: Lower Leg, Lateral Ankle Bone

Description, Location, Articulation

The **fibula** is the long, thin bone on the lateral side of the lower leg. It is so thoroughly embedded in soft tissue that, in most living persons, the only palpable part of the fibula is the lateral "ankle bone" and a short portion of shaft extending upward from the ankle.

The fibula is firmly connected to the tibia by an interosseus membrane attaching at the interosseus crest. The proximal end is a knob-like head. It has an articular facet on the medial aspect of the superior surface, and one small rounded projection, the **styloid process**. The distal end is the lateral malleolus. It is more pointed than the proximal end and slightly mediolaterally flattened. The lateral surface bulges and the medial surface has a flat, triangular-shaped facet.

The proximal fibula articulates with the proximal tibia at a small oval facet inferior to the lateral extension of the condylar platform of the tibia. The distal end of the fibula does not articulate with the tibia. It passes through the **fibular notch** of the tibia and articulates with the lateral side of the talus.

Left/Right Recognition

The easiest way to side the fibula is with the distal end. When looking at the lateral malleolus from the lateral side, the tip points posteriorly. (The medial malleolus of the tibia points anteriorly.)

The fibula can also be sided with the shaft alone by noting the direction of the spiral curvature. The curvature is right-handed on a right fibula and left-handed on a left fibula. A right-handed spiral advances clockwise, and a left-handed spiral, counterclockwise. Begin by examining the longitudinal surfaces of the fibula. Choose the flat surface that is the most uniform in width and flow from one end to the other. Starting at the posterior surface of the distal end, place the right thumb on the flat surface and slide the thumb outward along the same surface toward the other end. If the right thumb advances toward the right index finger, the fibula is right. (The direction of the spiral is a property of the bone, so it will be the same from proximal to distal as from distal to proximal.)

Bones of Confusion

Fragments of fibula are sometimes confused with the radius or the ulna, but they differ in cross section. The fibula is triangular, and the radius and ulna are tear-drop shaped.

Origin and Growth

The fibula is formed from one primary center of ossification (the diaphysis of the shaft) and two secondary centers of ossification, the proximal and distal epiphyses. The distal appears first (9–22 months).

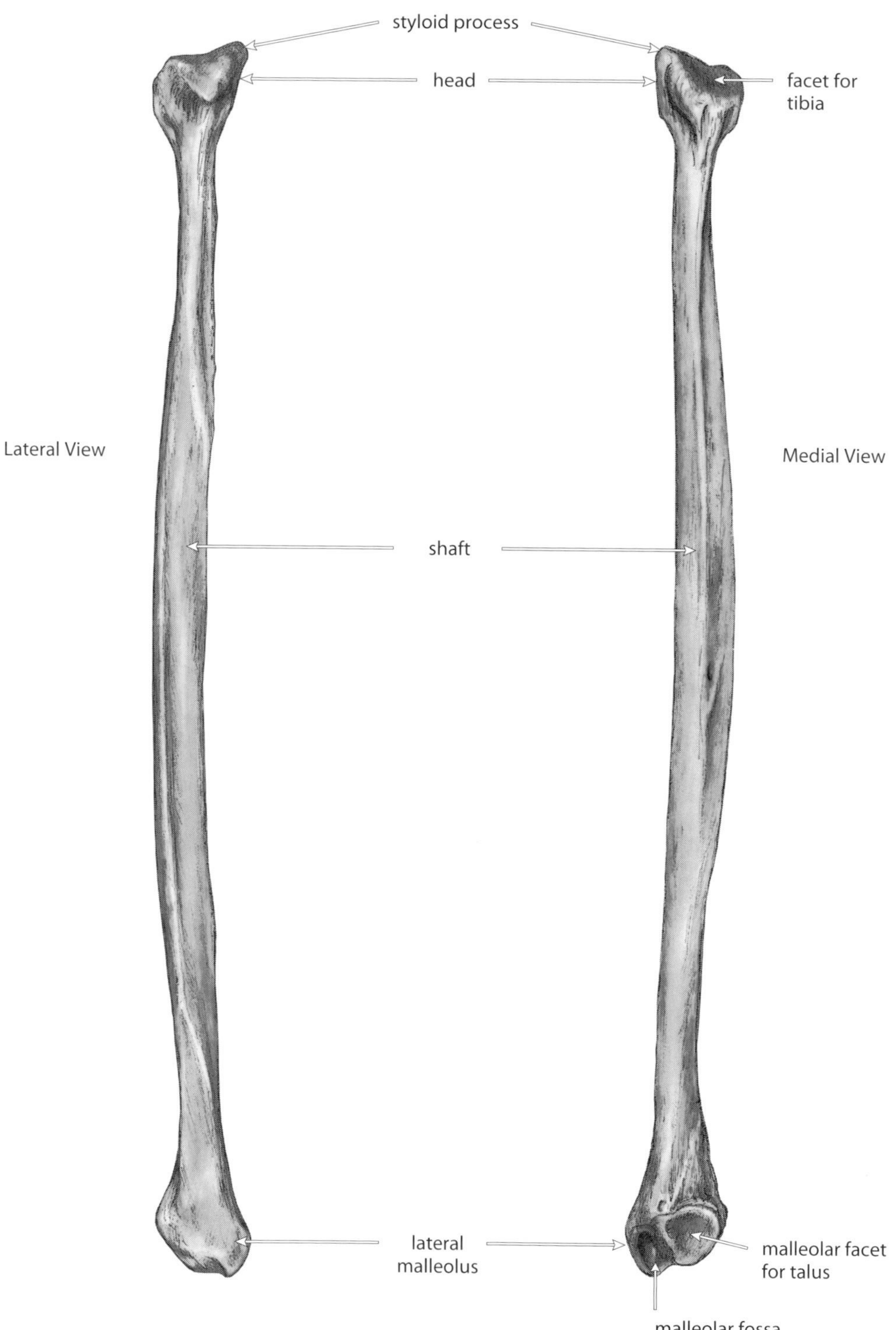

Figure 9.9
Left Fibula, Lateral and Medial Views (50% Natural Size)
Note the main smooth surface on the lateral view. It curves laterally and is useful for siding when only a shaft is available. Run a thumb along it to feel the lateral twist.

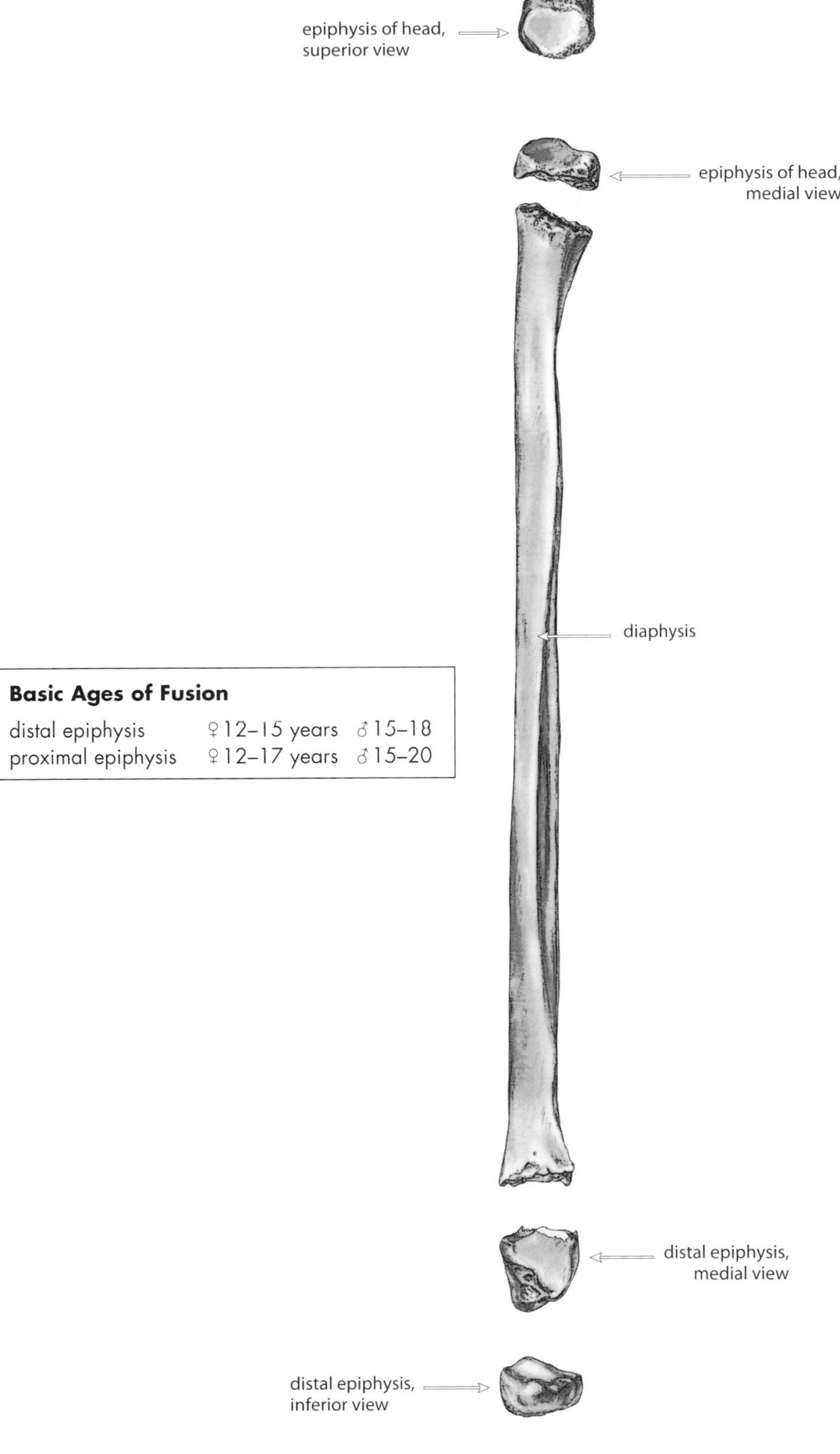

Figure 9.10
Juvenile Left Fibula, Medial View

Table 9.2 Leg Vocabulary

Bone	Term	Definition
FEMUR	head	the ball-shaped upper extremity of the femur; the femoral head articulates within the acetabulum of the innominate; the proximal epiphysis
	fovea capitis	the pit in the femoral head providing attachment for the ligamentum teres
	neck	the constricted portion just below the head of the femur—the anatomical neck is proximal to the two trochanters; the surgical neck is distal to the trochanters
	greater trochanter	the larger and more superior of the two protuberances between the neck and the shaft; a separate center of ossification
	lesser trochanter	the smaller and more inferior of the two protuberances between the neck and the shaft; a separate center of ossification
	shaft	the major portion of the femur formed from the diaphysis
	linea aspera	the muscle attachment line on the posterior surface of the femoral shaft
	nutrient foramen	the aperture through which vessels pass between the inner and outer surfaces of the femoral shaft; the vessels pass inward as they progress away from the knee
	trochlear articular surface	the anterior-most articular surface on the distal end of the femur; the patellar articular surface
	medial epicondyle	the protuberance proximal and medial to the medial condyle
	medial condyle	the medial articular surface for the tibia
	lateral epicondyle	the protuberance proximal and lateral to the lateral condyle
	lateral condyle	the lateral articular surface for the tibia
	intercondylar fossa	the depression between the two condyles on the posterior surface of the femur
PATELLA	medial articular facet	the articular surface that articulates with the anterior of the medial condyle of the femur
	lateral articular facet	the articular surface that articulates with the anterior of the lateral condyle of the femur
TIBIA	medial condyle	the proximal articular surface that articulates with the medial condyle of the femur
	lateral condyle	the proximal articular surface that articulates with the lateral condyle of the femur
	intercondylar eminence	the bony projection between the two condylar platforms of the tibia; also called intercondyloid eminence
	fibular articular surface	the flat oval facet on the inferior surface of the lateral condylar platform; it articulates with the head of the fibula
	fibular notch	the indentation on the lateral surface of the distal end of the tibia; the distal shaft of the fibula is bound into the notch by the tibiofibular ligament
	shaft	the major part of the tibia, formed from the diaphysis
	anterior crest	the sharp ridge on the anterior shaft of the tibia, the shin
	interosseous crest	the low sharp border the length of the lateral side, the attachment site for the interosseous membrane between tibia and fibula
	medial malleolus	the projection on the disto-medial end of the tibia; the inner "ankle bone"
	popliteal line	on the superior and posterior surface of the tibia, a curved roughened attachment surface
	nutrient foramen	the aperture through which vessels pass between the inner and outer surfaces of the femoral shaft; the vessels pass inward as they progress away from the knee
	tibial plateau	the horizontal surface at the proximal end of the tibia; provides the articular surfaces for the femoral condyles
FIBULA	styloid process	the slightly sharp projection of bone pointing upward from the proximal end (the head) of the fibula
	head	the knob-like proximal end
	shaft	the major part of the fibula, formed from the diaphysis
	lateral malleolus	the distal end of the fibula, the lateral "ankle bone"
	interosseous crest	the sharp border on the length of the medial side; the attachment site for the interosseous membrane between tibia and fibula
	malleolar fossa	the indentation or groove posterior to the distal articular surface

CHAPTER 10

The Foot: Tarsals, Metatarsals, and Phalanges

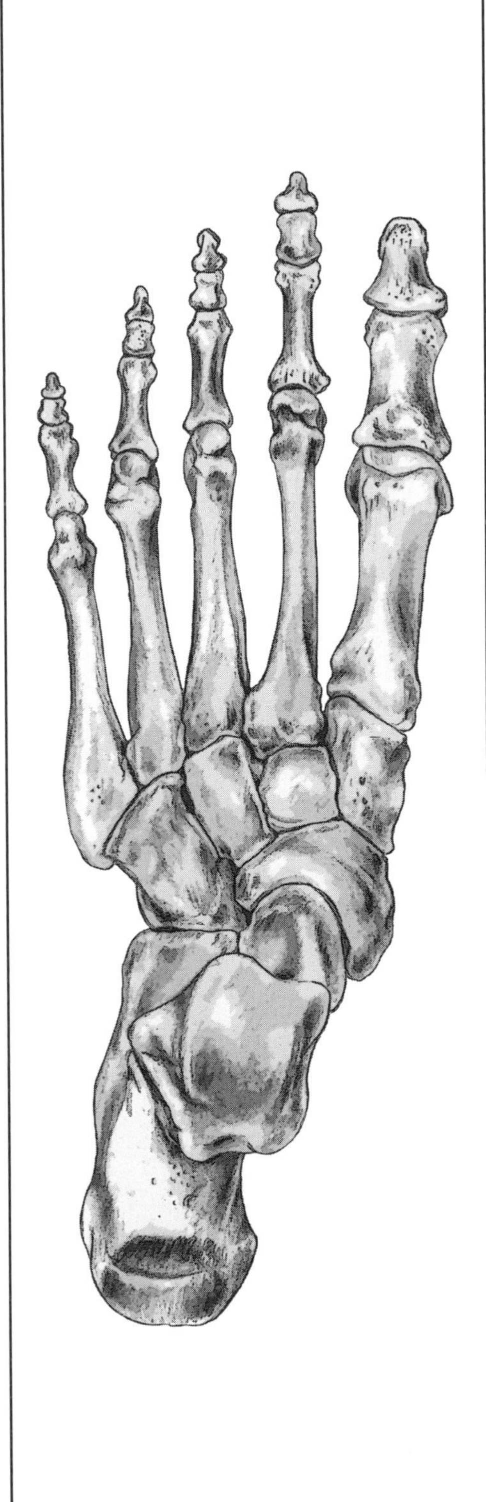

CHAPTER OUTLINE

Introduction

The human foot is built of twenty-six bones. There are seven tarsal bones, five metatarsal bones, and fourteen phalanges. The tarsals articulate with the leg and form the heel and the major arch of the foot, the metatarsals extend from the arch to the toes, and the phalanges form the toes.

Forensic Note

Always bag hands and feet separately.

Anatomy Note

The base of the second metatarsal articulates with all three cuneiforms.

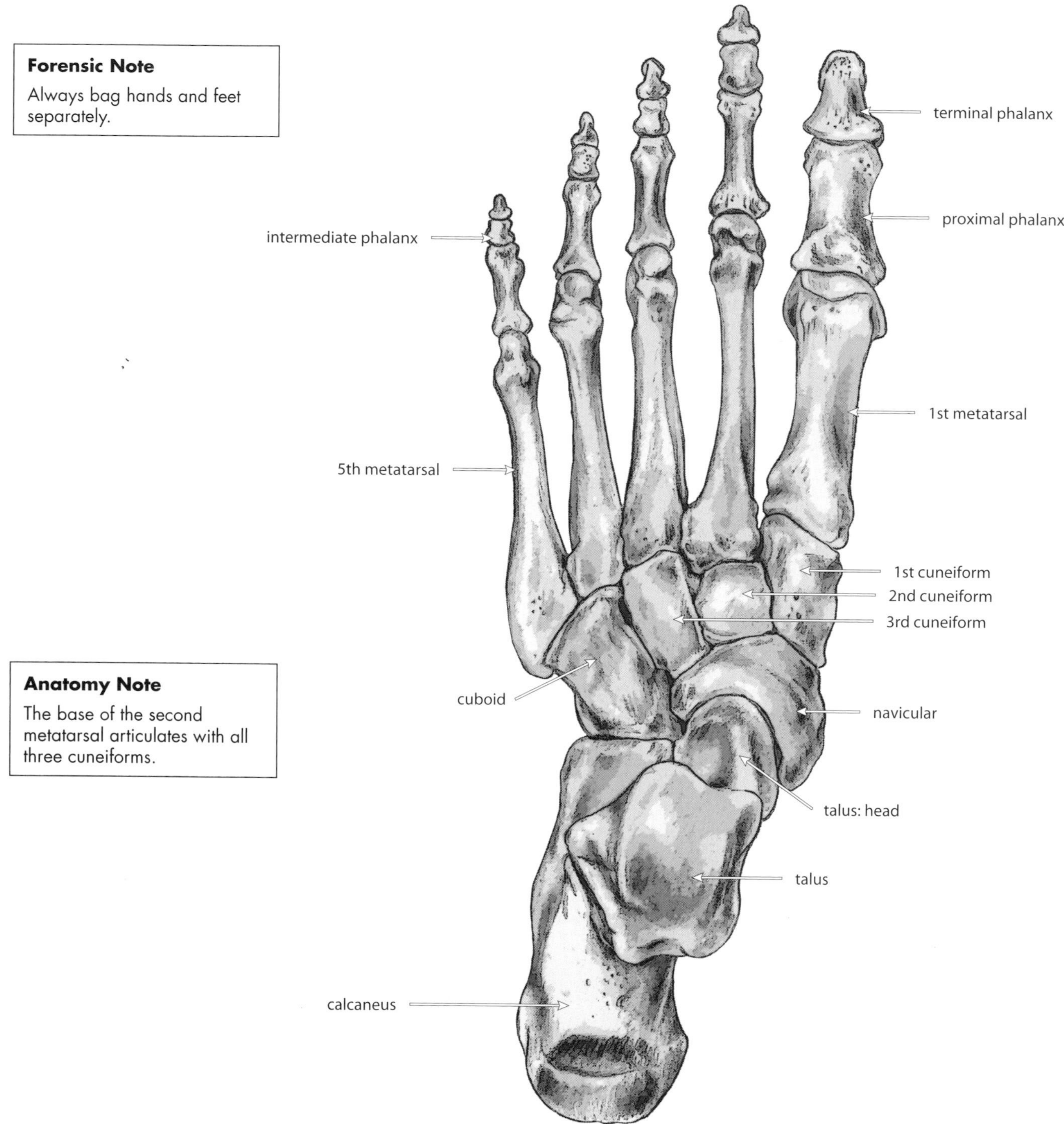

Figure 10.1a
Left Foot, Dorsal (Superior) View (80% Natural Size)
Note that the base of the second metatarsal is inset between the three cuneiforms. However, it does not articulate with the first metatarsal.

As with the hand, the terms used for orientation of the foot are specific to the structure. The top of the foot is superior and the surface is called *dorsal.* The sole of the foot is inferior and the surface is called *plantar*. Each tarsal and metatarsal can be recognized, and right can be distinguished from left. The phalanges are more difficult. Proximal, intermediate, and terminal phalanges can be distinguished, but right and left cannot be separated with certainty, except usually, the first toe.

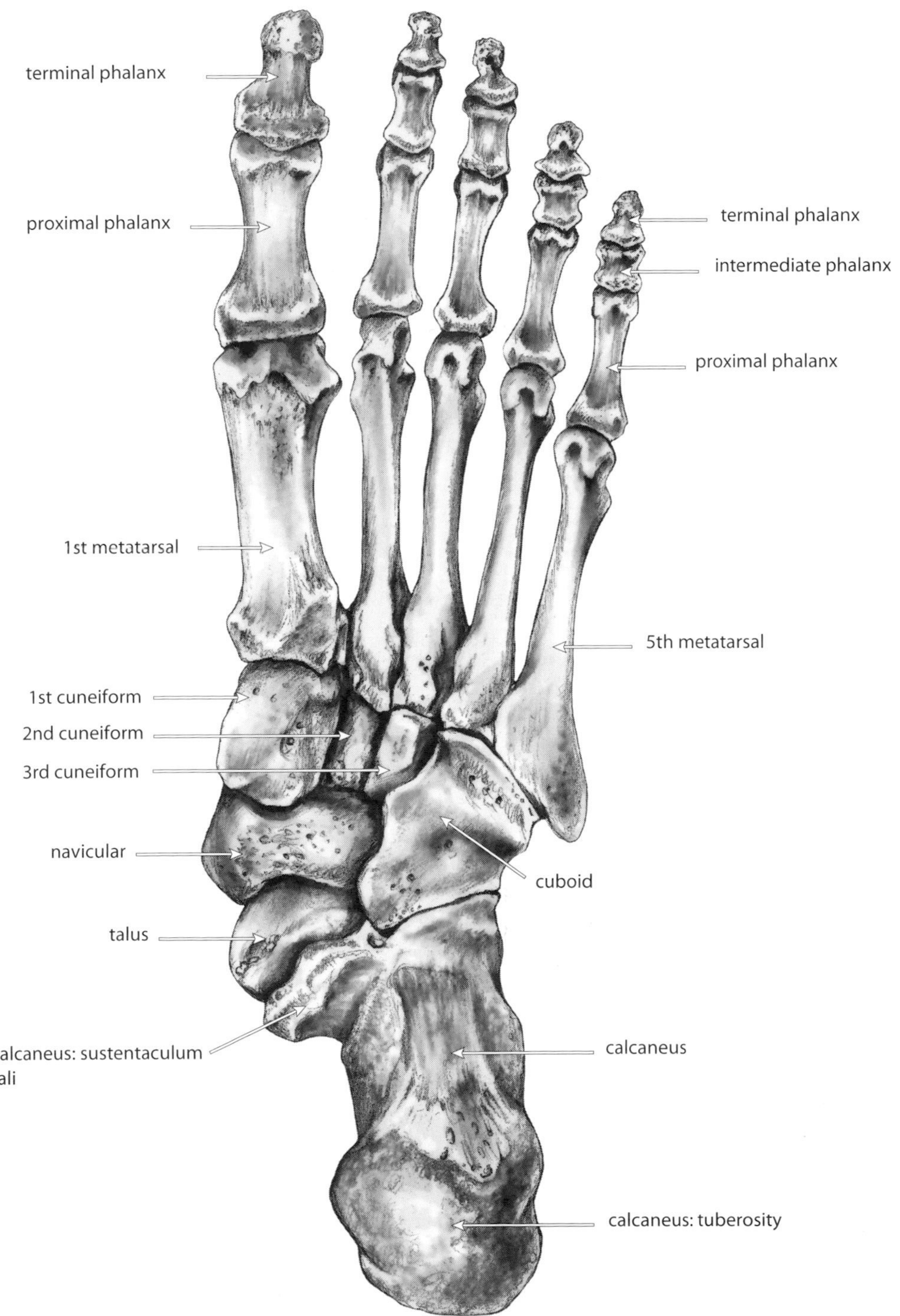

Figure 10.1b
Left Foot, Plantar (Inferior) View (80% Natural Size)

Tarsal Bones: Ankle and Arch of the Foot

Description, Location, Articulation

> **Definition Note**
>
> The words *tarsal* and *metatarsal* are adjectives to use with a noun (e.g., tarsal bone, metatarsal joint). In common usage, however, they are nominalized to "tarsals" and "metatarsals" for convenience and brevity.

The **tarsal bones** are seven irregular bones between the leg and the anterior half of the foot. Only one of the tarsals, the talus, is considered to be part of the ankle. It provides for the hinge-type movement with the tibia. The other six tarsals are foot bones.

Together, the tarsals form the posterior half of the foot, including the heel and the major part of what is commonly called the "arch" of the foot. The foot actually has two arches, the major, longitudinal (proximal/distal) arch, and a less noticed, transverse (medial/lateral) arch. The longitudinal arch is sometimes subdivided into the larger, medial arch and the smaller, lateral arch. Keep the arches in mind while examining the architecture of the foot.

The tarsal bones can be divided into two groups. Moving from proximal to distal, the superior/medial group includes the **talus**, **navicular**, and three **cuneiforms**. The inferior/lateral group includes the proximal **calcaneus** and distal **cuboid**. The cuboid also articulates with the third cuneiform on the distal row of tarsals.

First Cuneiform

The first cuneiform is the largest cuneiform. It articulates with the navicular proximally and the first metatarsal distally. Look at the lateral facet (the second cuneiform articulation) with the point up. The tip points toward the correct side.

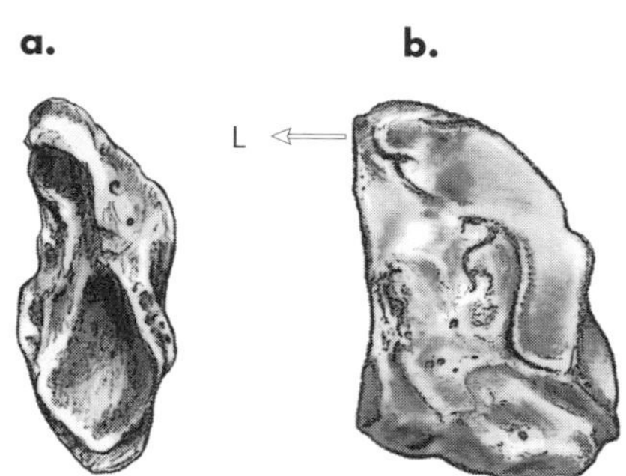

Figure 10.2a Left First Cuneiform, Proximal View (Natural Size)

Figure 10.2b Left First Cuneiform, Lateral View (Natural Size)

Second Cuneiform

The second cuneiform is the smallest cuneiform. It articulates proximally with the navicular and distally with the second metatarsal. Look at the medial facet (the first cuneiform articulation). It is pistol shaped. The "barrel" points toward the correct side.

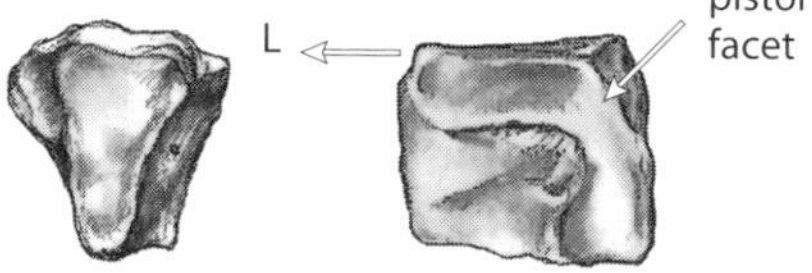

Figure 10.3a Left Second Cuneiform, Distal View (Natural Size)

Figure 10.3b Left Second Cuneiform, Medial View (Natural Size)

Third Cuneiform

The third cuneiform is longer than the second. It articulates proximally with the navicular and distally with the third metatarsal. When the "butterfly" facet (the double facet for the second cuneiform) faces you, the narrow plantar end points toward the correct side.

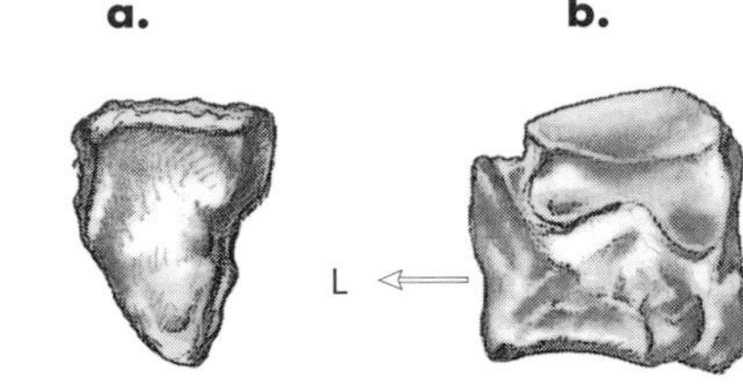

Figure 10.4a Left Third Cuneiform, Distal View (Natural Size)

Figure 10.4b Left Third Cuneiform, Medial View (Natural Size)

Navicular

The navicular is bowl-shaped. It has a large concave facet on the proximal surface for articulation with the head of the talus. The distal surface is a three-part facet for articulation with the three cuneiforms. A tail-like process extends from the medial surface. Facing the three-part facet with the curved dorsal side up, the "tail" points toward the correct side.

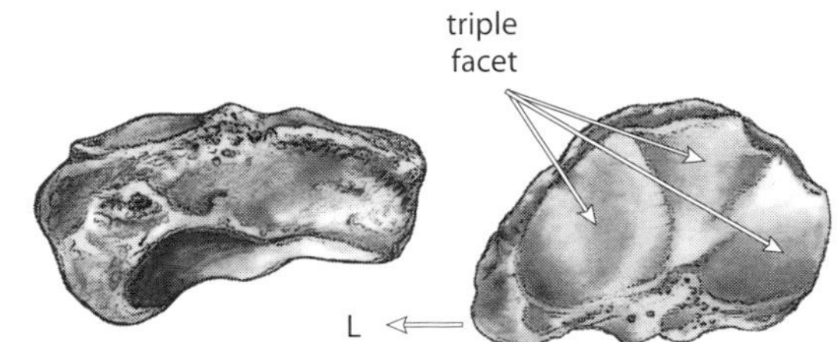

Figure 10.5a Left Navicular, Plantar View (Natural Size)

Figure 10.5b Left Navicular, Distal View (Natural Size)

Cuboid

The cuboid is bulkier than any of the other cuneiforms. It articulates proximally with the calcaneus and distally with the fourth and fifth metatarsals. Facing the dorsolateral side and pointing the large curved facet down, the narrow margin points toward the correct side.

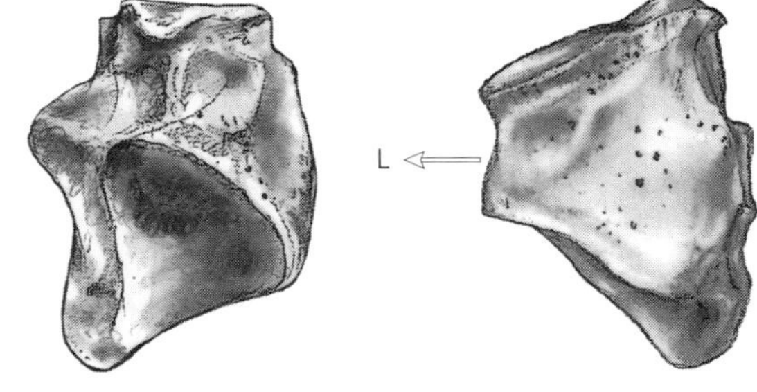

Figure 10.6a Left Cuboid, Lateral View (Natural Size)

Figure 10.6b Left Cuboid, Dorsolateral View (Natural Size)

Talus

The talus is one of the two large tarsals. It is the only tarsal with a headlike structure. The smooth, partial hemisphere articulates with the navicular. The saddle-shaped dorsal surface articulates with the distal tibia. The plantar surface articulates with the calcaneus at two surfaces. Face the saddle facet with the head pointed away. The lateral process points toward the correct side.

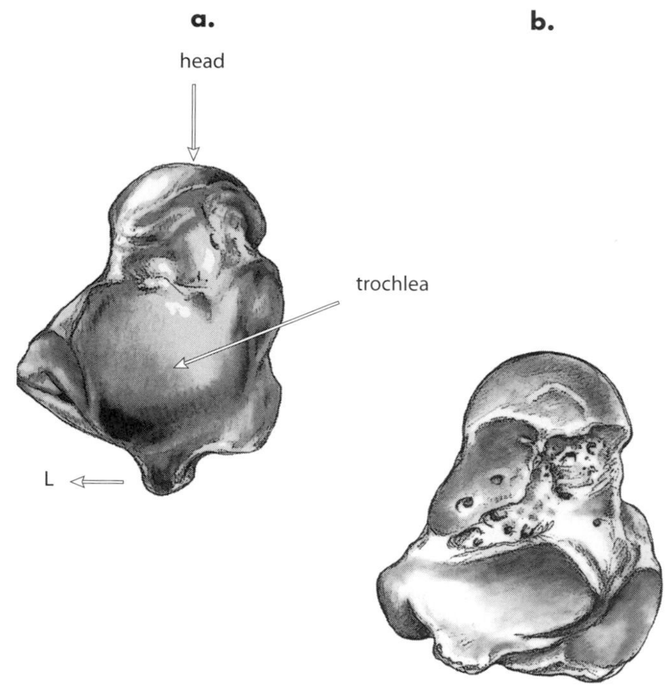

Figure 10.7a Left Talus, Superior View 85% Natural Size)

Figure 10.7b Left Talus, Plantar View (85% Natural Size)

Calcaneus

The calcaneus is the largest tarsal bone. It forms the heel of the foot. Face the talar facets with the heel pointing toward you. The sustentaculum tali is medial. It helps to remember that the sustentaculum tali is the most proximal bony support for the major arch of the foot.

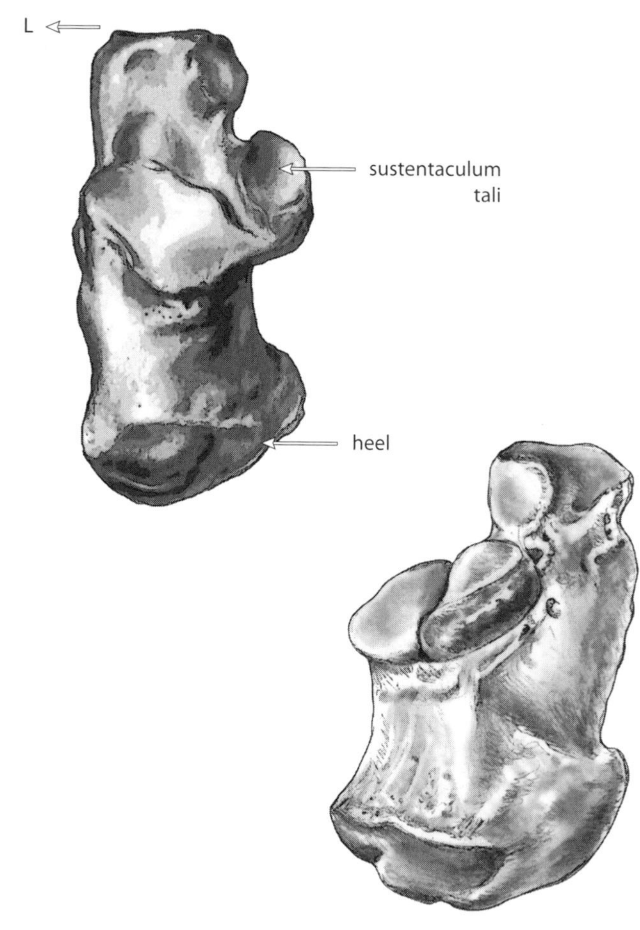

Figure 10.8a Left Calcaneus, Superior View (85% Natural Size)

Figure 10.8b Left Calcaneus, Medial (85% Natural Size)

Left/Right Recognition

It takes time and practice to be able to recognize each tarsal bone and tell right from left, but it *is* possible. The positions in Figures 10.2–10.8 are clues from other students. Examine all surfaces, compare articular surfaces for adjacent bones, and use your own imagination.

Origin and Growth

The calcaneus is the first tarsal bone to begin ossification (fourth to fifth fetal month). At the time of birth, only the calcaneus and talus are present. The other tarsal bones appear one by one over the next five years with the navicular last (2–6 years). The sequence has been studied by many investigators, and a summary has been published by Scheuer and Black (2000 and 2004). Tarsals (and the foot as a whole) are a good guide for age determination in infants and children.

Table 10.1 Tarsal Articulations

Bone	Articular Facet	Adjacent Bone
TALUS	trochlea	tibia
	head	navicular
	planar facets	calcaneus
	lateral facet	fibula
CALCANEUS	dorsal facet	talus
	sustentaculum tali facet	talus
	distal facet	cuboid
NAVICULAR	proximal surface	talus
	distal surfaces	all three cuneiforms
FIRST CUNEIFORM	proximal surface	navicular
	medial surface	no bone
	lateral surface	second cuneiform and metatarsal #2
	distal surface	metatarsal #1
SECOND CUNEIFORM	proximal surface	navicular
	medial surface	first cuneiform
	lateral surface	third cuneiform
	distal surface	metatarsal #2
THIRD CUNEIFORM	proximal surface	navicular
	medial surface	second cuneiform and metatarsal #2
	lateral surface	cuboid
	distal surface	metatarsal #3
CUBOID	proximal surface	calcaneus
	medial surface	third cuneiform
	distal surface	metatarsals #4 and #5

Metatarsal Bones: Foot Bones

Description, Location, Articulation

Metatarsals are similar to metacarpals, but they are longer and thinner than metacarpals. They are also slightly more curved. The specific descriptions and articulations are given in the captions for each metatarsal illustration. Also see Table 10.2 for a summary of articulations. Note that the descriptions are guidelines for metatarsal recognition. Individual variation abounds in well-used feet, particularly in the shape and extent of facets.

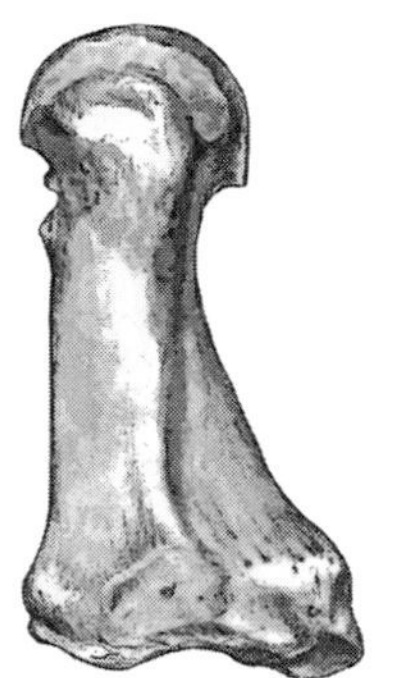
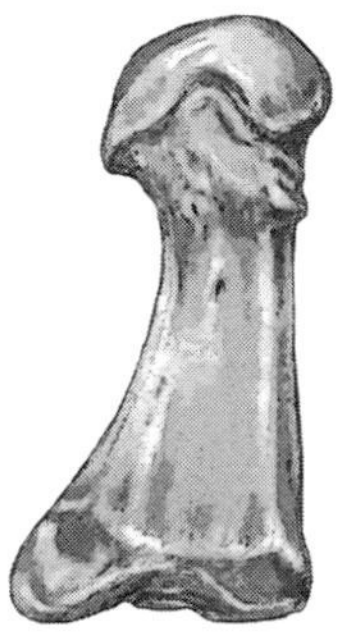
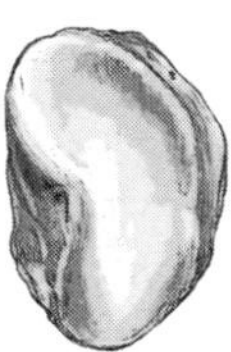

Figure 10.9
Metatarsal #1, Medial, Lateral, and Proximal Views (80% Natural size)

Metatarsal #1 is the thickest metatarsal. It has a D-shaped base that articulates directly with the first cuneiform. The curved side of the "D" is medial, following the curvature of the foot. The flat side is lateral.

Like the first metacarpal, metatarsal #1 usually has no lateral facet. The base only articulates with the first cuneiform.

Determine side by looking at the proximal end with the head pointed away and the dorsal surface up. The flat side is on the correct (lateral) side.

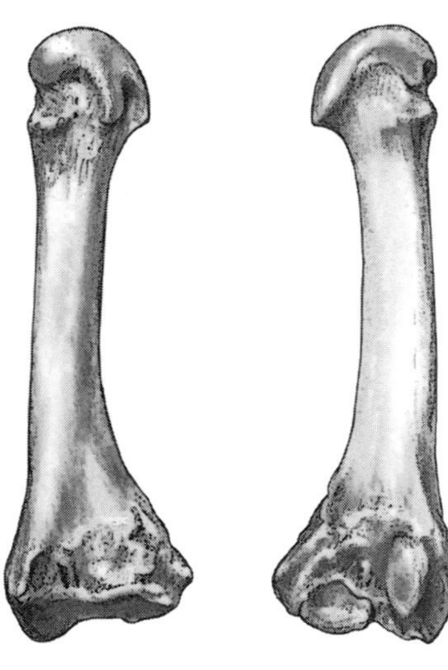

Figure 10.10
Metatarsal #2, Medial, Lateral, and Proximal Views (80% Natural Size)

Metatarsal #2 is the longest metatarsal. The base is triangular, conforming to the distal surface of the second cuneiform. The base of metatarsal #2 is inset between the distal ends of the first and third cuneiforms and articulates with all three cuneiforms as well as metatarsal #3. The result is a small medial facet for the first cuneiform and a double facet on the lateral side for both the third cuneiform and the next metatarsal. This double facet bevels the proximal lateral corner and provides a key characteristic.

Determine side by looking at the proximal end from the dorsal surface with the head pointed away. The sharper corner points toward the correct side. Refer to the whole foot illustration for a dorsal view.

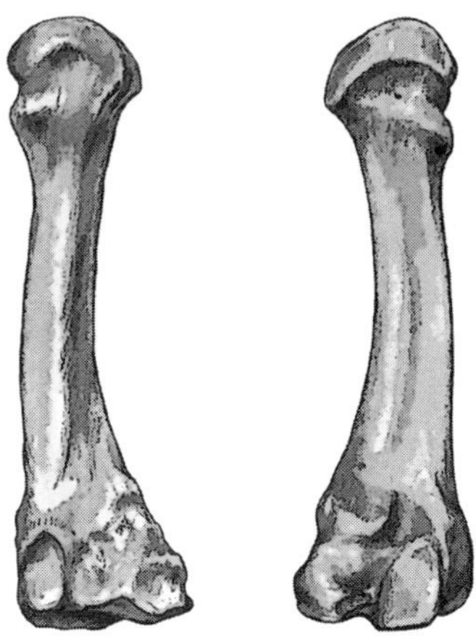

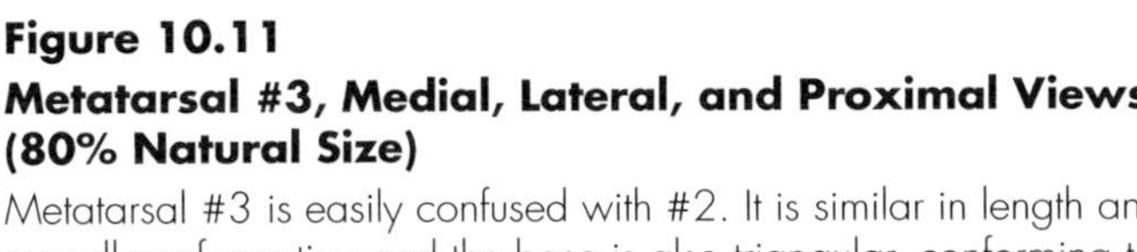

Figure 10.11
Metatarsal #3, Medial, Lateral, and Proximal Views (80% Natural Size)

Metatarsal #3 is easily confused with #2. It is similar in length and overall conformation and the base is also triangular, conforming to the shape of the third cuneiform. But the facet on the lateral side of the base of #3 is large, flat, and adjacent to the base. The proximal lateral corner is pointed, not beveled.

Determine side by looking at the proximal end from the dorsal surface with the head pointed away. The sharper corner points toward the correct side. Refer to the whole foot illustration for a dorsal view.

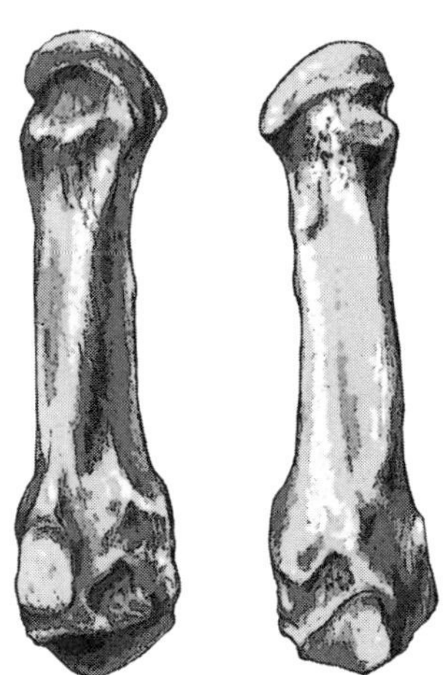

Figure 10.12
Metatarsal #4, Medial, Lateral, and Proximal Views (80% Natural Size)

Metatarsal #4 is somewhat inset, but only on the medial side. The lateral facet is large and adjacent to the base. The base is rectangular, not triangular like #2 and #3. It articulates with the cuboid.

Determine side by looking at the proximal end from the dorsal surface with the head pointed away. The sharper corner points toward the side.

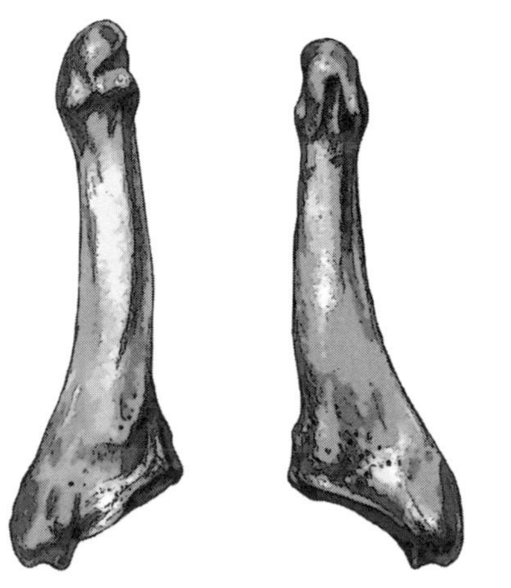

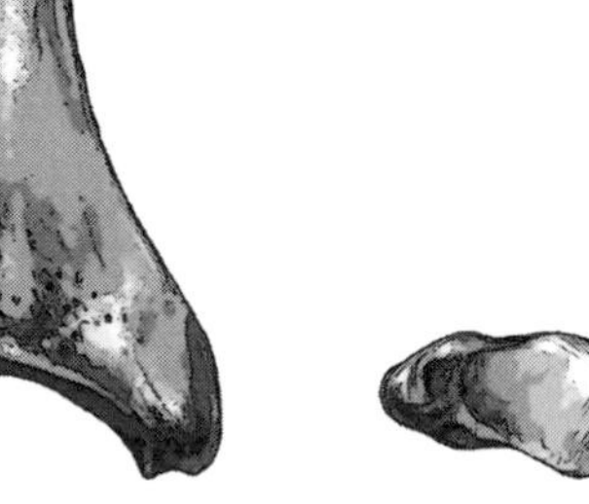

Figure 10.13
Metatarsal #5, Medial, Lateral, and Proximal Views (80% Natural Size)

Metatarsal #5 is the only metatarsal with a long tail-like process on the proximallateral aspect. The medial facet is a large simple surface for articulation with metatarsal #4. The proximal facet articulates with the cuboid.

Determine side by looking at the proximal end from the dorsal surface with the head pointed away. The dorsal side is smooth; the plantar side is grooved. The "tail" (a styloid process) points toward the correct side.

Left/Right Recognition

It is easier to distinguish sides in metatarsals than metacarpals. The proximal surfaces (bases) of the second through the fifth all slant so that the lateral edge is an acute angle which points toward the correct side. (See the full foot illustration, Figure 10.1.) The plantar surfaces of metatarsals #2–#4 are pointed (see illustrations of bases in Figures 10.10 to 10.12). The first metatarsal can be sided by the curvature of the comma-shaped base. The curvature of the tail points toward the correct side.

Origin and Growth

Just as in the hand, each metatarsal develops from two (not three) centers of ossification. The primary center is the shaft. The secondary centers form distal epiphyses (the heads) in metatarsals #2–#5. In metatarsal #1, as in metacarpal #1, the secondary center is proximal.

Table 10.2 Metatarsal and Phalanx Articulations

Bone	Articular Facet	Adjacent Bone
METATARSAL #1	base	first cuneiform
	medial surface	no bone
	lateral surface	no bone—not even metatarsal #2
	head	proximal phalanx
METATARSAL #2	base	second cuneiform
	medial surface	first cuneiform
	lateral surface	third cuneiform and metatarsal #3
	head	proximal phalanx
METATARSAL #3	base	third cuneiform
	medial surface	metatarsal #2
	lateral surface	metatarsal #4
	head	proximal phalanx
METATARSAL #4	base	cuboid
	medial surface	metatarsal #3
	lateral surface	metatarsal #5
	head	proximal phalanx
METATARSAL #5	base	cuboid
	medial surface	metatarsal #4
	lateral surface	no bone
	head	proximal phalanx
PROXIMAL PHALANX	base	metatarsal head
	head	intermediate phalanx
INTERMEDIATE PHALANX	base	proximal phalanx
	head	distal phalanx
DISTAL OR TERMINAL PHALANX	base	intermediate phalanx
	head	no bone—only a toenail

PHALANGES: TOE BONES

DESCRIPTION, LOCATION, ARTICULATION

A **phalanx** is one of the fourteen bones in the toes. (The word, phalanx, is also used for the finger bones.) The big toe has two phalanges, proximal and distal. Each of the other four digits has three phalanges—proximal, intermediate, and distal. The intermediate phalanx is sometimes called a medial phalanx, but the term, intermediate is less ambiguous. The distal phalanx is also called a terminal phalanx. In the foot, the intermediate phalanx is very short. Often the length is no more than the width, forming a tiny square of bone.

Proximal phalanges articulate with the heads of the metacarpals. The intermediate and distal phalanges articulate only with phalanges.

LEFT/RIGHT RECOGNITION

Whereas each tarsal and metatarsal can be separated from all the others, and right can be distinguished from left, the phalanges are more difficult. Proximal, intermediate, and terminal phalanges can be distinguished, but right and left cannot be separated with certainty in any but the first toe, which usually deviates laterally, toward the rest of the foot, particularly in shoe-wearing people. Just as with the hands, it is important to bag feet separately during collection or disinterment. Any toe that may contribute to identification because of trauma or anomaly should be separated and labeled by number.

INDIVIDUALIZATION

The big toe may display clues about a person's life—particularly habitual posture, athletic activities, shoe use, and shoe type. The critical joint is the metatarsophalangeal joint—the articulation of the first metatarsal and the proximal phalanx. Three primary conditions that are common among different groups are as follows:

- Hyperextension or extreme **dorsiflexion** of the big toe occurs when kneeling is a habitual posture and the toes are hyperextended for balance. It is best known from Native American populations, particularly women, who spent long hours grinding corn while kneeling. The bony evidence is elongation of the articular surface onto the dorsal aspect of the first metatarsal. It is usually accompanied by osteoarthritis of the joint.
- **Hallux valgus** is the inward or lateral deviation of the big toe. It is common in modern shoe-wearing populations and is more common in women, particularly when pointed-toe shoes are worn. A large bump (bunion) often forms on the medial surface of the foot at the distal end of the first metatarsal. This condition can be seen in the angle of metatarsophalangeal articulation and the enlargement of the medial epicondyle of the first metatarsal.
- **Hallux varus** is the outward or medial deviation of the big toe. It is more common in archaic populations or other non-shoe-wearing people. Hallux varus may also suggest use of sandals relying on a strap between the first and second toe.

Origin and Growth

Each phalanx forms from two centers of ossification—the primary diaphyseal shaft, and one epiphysis at the proximal surface (not the distal surface as in metatarsals #2–#4). The fourth and fifth toes are irregular in development. Toes are seldom recovered in skeletonized individuals, and epiphyses of phalanges are even rarer.

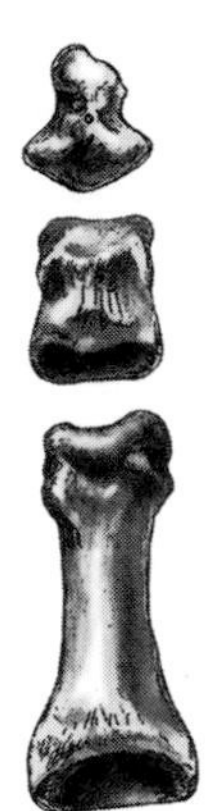

Figure 10.14
Toe Phalanges, Dorsal View (Natural Size)
Note the squarelike shape of the intermediate phalanx. The intermediate and terminal toe phalanges frequently fuse, probably because of trauma (a lifetime of toe stubbing).

A Finger–Toe Comparison

The proximal phalanges of the finger and toe look very much alike, but notice that the *finger* phalanx is dorso-palmarly compressed. It is flatter and more oval in cross section than the toe phalanx. The shaft of the toe phalanx is medio-laterally compressed. It is narrower and waist-like.

The intermediate *finger* phalanx is much longer than the intermediate *toe* phalanx. Whereas the proximal and intermediate finger phalanges can be confused if the observer does not look closely at the proximal articular surfaces, the proximal and intermediate *toe* phalanges are not likely to be confused because of the great difference in size.

Frequently, the tiny distal toe phalanx fuses to the intermediate phalanx. This is particularly common with the fourth and fifth toes. Fusion is unusual in fingers.

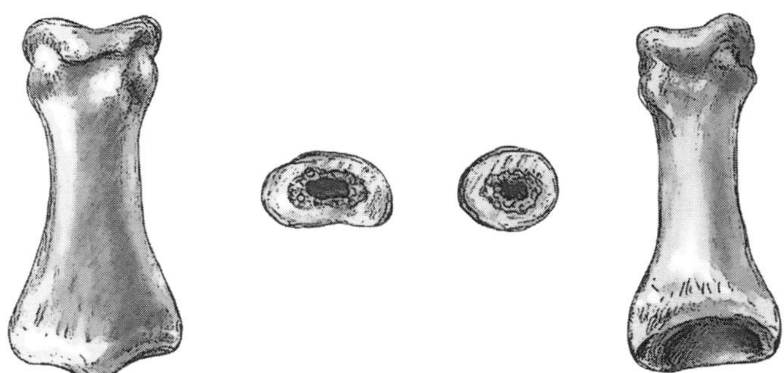

Figure 10.15
Cross Section Comparison of Finger and Toe Phalanges
Note that the finger phalanx is oval in cross section, and the toe phalanx is round in cross section. Roll the bones between your fingers to feel the difference.

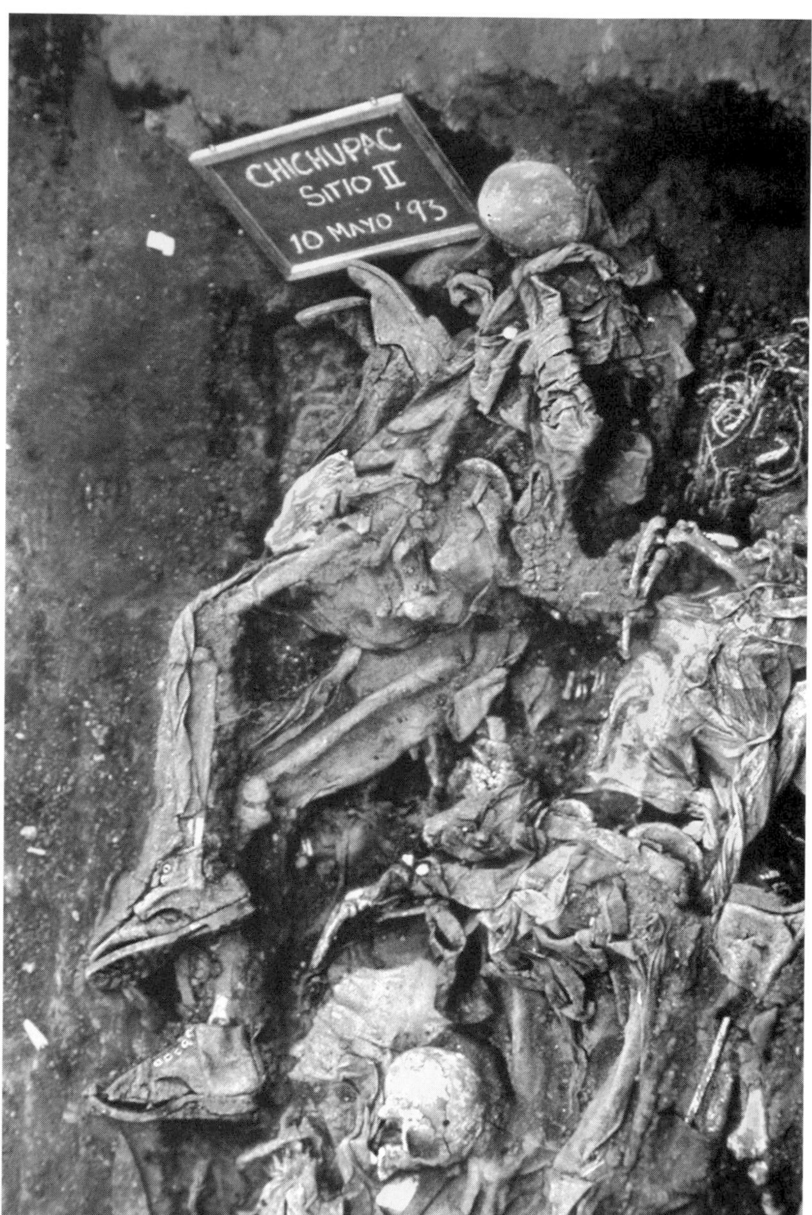

Figure 10.16
The Value of Shoes

Shoes are often found on the feet of the dead in both clandestine graves and surface burials. Whereas the bones of the hands are often scattered, the bones of the feet may be intact and well preserved, thanks to shoes. They serve to slow decomposition and protect the feet from scavengers. In some cases, the only remaining information about age, sex, and health may be from the foot bones. Photo courtesy of Lancerio López

Chapter 11

Odontology (Teeth)

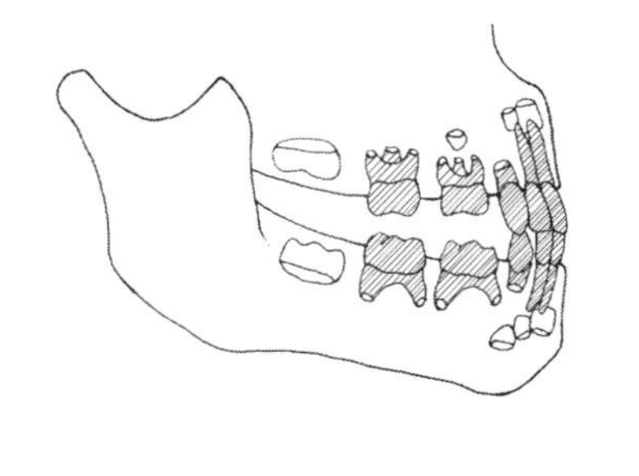

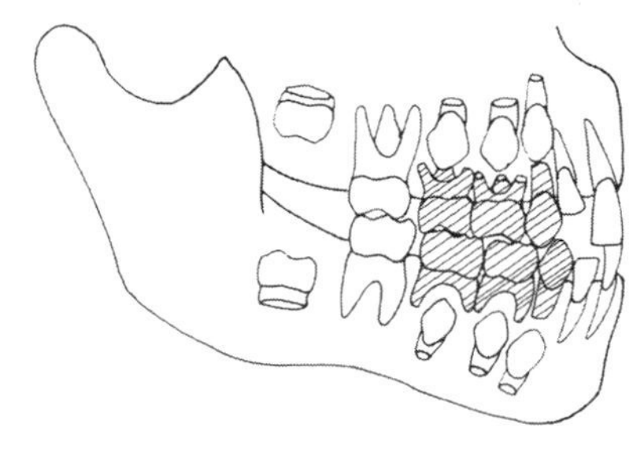

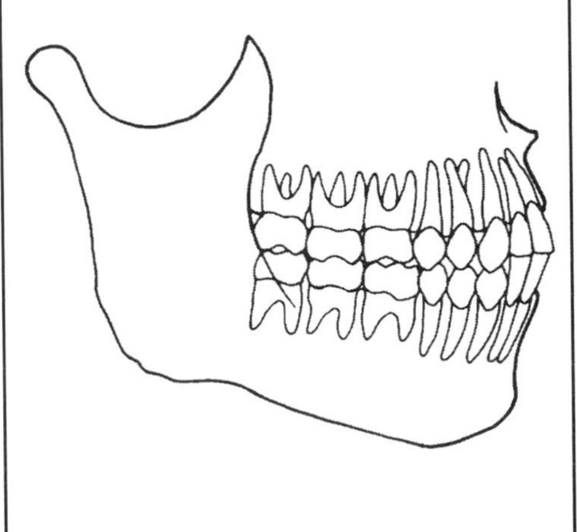

CHAPTER OUTLINE

Introduction

Teeth may be just another part of the skull, but they are fascinating. A single tooth contains enough information to make it a subject unto itself. There is information about genetic heritage, age, diet, health, medical care, personal hygiene, personal habits, cultural status, economic condition, and more.

Odontology is the study of teeth—their development, structure, function, and degeneration. Odontology is the science behind the practice of dentistry.

Use this chapter to learn to identify teeth and find your way around the oral cavity using the correct terminology. As in the rest of the body, learn what is normal so that you can recognize the variations that serve to identify the individual. The long-term objective is better communication between the forensic anthropologist and the dentist (or any professional odontologist).

As with any scientific discipline, the most reliable work is accomplished by the best-trained person. The odontologist—a dentist, orthodontist, periodontist, oral surgeon, or oral pathologist—has years of study and experience with the structures of the oral cavity. A forensic dentist has additional training in human identification and related subjects such as bitemark evidence. The anthropologist may be the first one to see the teeth, chart them, and report on them, but the final analysis is usually in the hands of the dentist. If the mouth contains restored (filled or crowned) teeth, a practicing dentist from the same region as the victim is usually the best person to provide the analysis. If dental prostheses are present, a local dentist can often date the work and sometimes even identify the workmanship.

Why not just skip this chapter and call a forensic dentist? It won't work. After extolling the virtues of dental professionals, I still insist that forensic anthropologists need to learn about teeth, and there are at least three good reasons as to why:

1. There may be no dentist to call. Under such conditions, the anthropologist who knows more about teeth is going to find more, see more, and understand more.
2. The anthropologist who can use dental and oral terminology can communicate with dental professionals, make accurate use of dental records, and incorporate the information into a larger picture of the unidentified person.
3. Not all dental information is included in the dental school curriculum because it is of no practical interest to the dentist. The anthropologist is more likely to have knowledge about genetic variation due to geographic and ethnic isolation, cultural differences in hygiene and nutrition, ritual dental practices, and decompositional changes due to burial conditions.

Structure and Function of Teeth and Supporting Tissues

Both hard and soft tissues are essential to healthy teeth, and teeth contain both.

Enamel overlays the dentin and covers the tooth crown. Enamel is not only hard, but crystalline in structure. It has no living cells or blood supply, and, therefore, is not capable of self-repair.

Dentin is the main component of the tooth. It has both organic and inorganic components. The original dentin to be formed is called **primary dentin**. It is tubular in structure. The tubules lead from the **dentinoenamel junction** (DEJ) to the pulp.

Two other types of dentin appear after the tooth is fully formed. (Usually the tooth is functional at this point.) They are the cellular response to chronic and acute stress, and are, therefore, age-related changes. **Secondary dentin** is laid down within the pulp chamber. It is first seen at the incisal tip and progresses slowly toward the root apex. The pulp tissue recedes as the secondary dentin forms. Secondary dentin is non-tubular and, therefore, denser than primary dentin. The third type of dentin is **reparative dentin** or tertiary dentin. It is formed within the dentinal tubules and creates areas of relative transparency in the primary dentin.

Cementum is a hard, porous substance covering the dentin of the root. It provides a surface for attachment of the fibers of the periodontal ligament. In young teeth, the cementum and the enamel meet at the **cementoenamel junction** (CEJ). In older teeth, dentin is often exposed in the area of the CEJ.

The **periodontal ligament** surrounds the tooth root. Collagen fibers attach the periodontal ligament to the periosteum of the **alveolus** (tooth socket) and anchor the tooth in place. The periodontal ligament connects tightly to the tooth at or near the CEJ, forming a **periodontal attachment line** on the root.

The **gingiva** is commonly called "gums" or "gum tissue." It is connective tissue covered by mucous membrane. Gingiva surrounds the teeth and envelops the **alveolar bone** of the maxilla and mandible. The gingiva is continuous with the periodontal ligament at the CEJ.

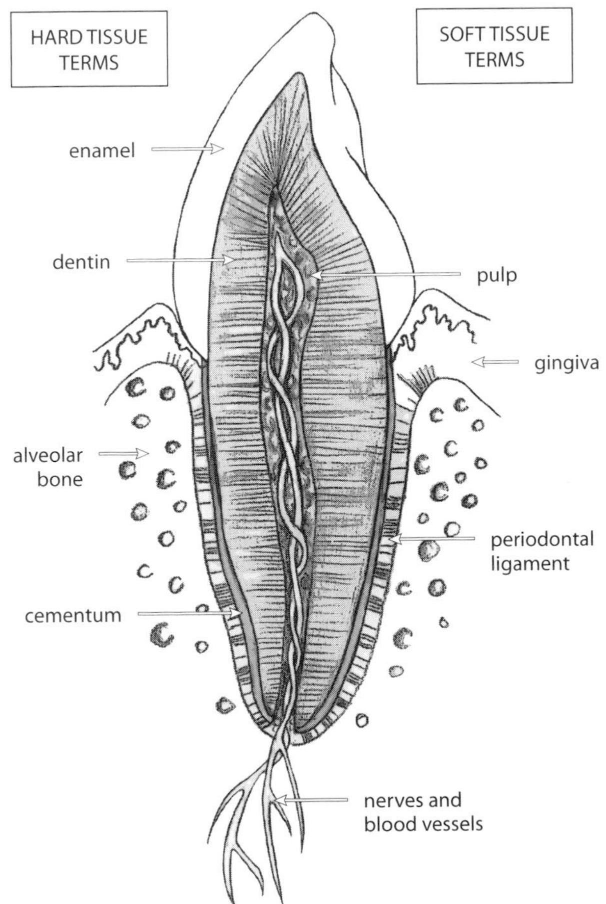

Figure 11.1
Cross Sectional Diagram of a Tooth and Surrounding Tissues
Note the hard tissue terms are on the left and the soft tissue terms are on the right.

Notes

1. Enamel is a dense, nonorganic tissue with a crystalline structure.
2. Dentin is a dense organic tissue with a tubular structure.
3. Alveolar bone is mostly cancellous bone.
4. Cementum is hard and porous.
5. Pulp is soft connective tissue filled with blood vessels and nerves.
6. The periodontal ligament is fibrous connective tissue.
7. Gingiva is a fibrous connective tissue covered with mucous membrane.

Directions, Surfaces, and Anatomy

Directional terms in the mouth are different from the rest of the body. They are defined by the oral structures rather than the whole body. Start at the midline and move along the dental row in either direction. Anything toward the back of the dental row is **distal**. Anything toward the midline of the dental row is **mesial** (not medial). Other directions are defined by the tongue (**lingual**), the cheek (**buccal**), and the lips (**labial**).

The surfaces of the teeth are named with directional terms. The principles are the same as for the rest of the body, but the terms are different, so it helps to spend time thinking them through, tooth by tooth. Refer to the illustrations and note that there is a different name for each surface. The human body has two lateral sides, but the tooth has a mesial and distal side as defined by the dental row and not by the body. The second incisor may be lateral to the first incisor, but it is distal to the first incisor.

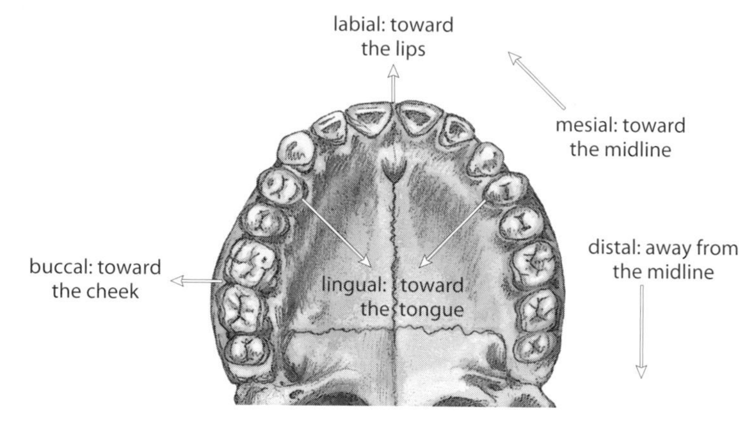

Figure 11.2
Directional Terms for the Mouth
This is a palatal view of the maxilla with arrows indicating directions and tooth surfaces within the oral cavity. Note that the oral terms are different than the ones used for the rest of the body. **Mesial surfaces** are on the same side as the midline. **Distal surfaces** are away from the midline. **Buccal surfaces** face the cheek. **Labial surfaces** face the lips. **Lingual surfaces** face the tongue.

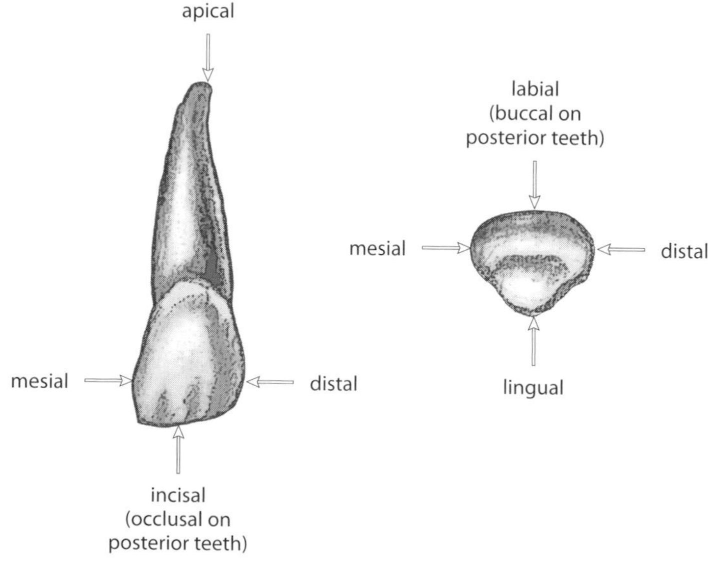

Figure 11.3
Directional Terms for the Surfaces of a Single Tooth
This is tooth #10, the upper left lateral incisor. Each surface is named according to its position in the mouth. The surface nearest the central incisor is mesial; the surface against the canine is distal (not lateral); the cutting surface is incisal (not inferior); and the root tip is apical (not superior). Note that the anterior teeth have incisal edges and posterior teeth have occlusal surfaces.

Table 11.1 Directional Terms for Teeth and Mouth

TERM	DEFINITION	OPPOSITE
APICAL	toward the root tip	incisal or occlusal
BUCCAL	surface toward the cheek (posterior teeth only)	lingual
CERVICAL	around the base of the crown, the neck of the tooth, or the CEJ	none
DISTAL	away from the midline of the dental row	mesial
FACIAL	toward the lips or cheek (i.e., both labial and buccal surfaces) (used for multiple teeth)	lingual
INCISAL	toward the cutting edge of the anterior teeth	apical
INTERPROXIMAL	between adjacent teeth	none
LABIAL	surface toward the lips (anterior teeth only)	lingual
LINGUAL	surface toward the tongue (all teeth)	labial or buccal
MESIAL	toward the midline of the dental row	distal
OCCLUSAL	toward the grinding surface of the posterior teeth	apical

Source: Adapted from Gustafson, 1966.

The anatomical terms refer to tooth structures, not tissues. Each structure is formed of more than one dental tissue (enamel, dentin, cementum, and/or pulp).

- The **crown** is the part covered with enamel. It is the first tooth structure to appear as the tooth develops.
- **Cusps** are the conical elevations on the tooth surface. All but the incisors have at least one cusp. The cusps are named according to their position (e.g., mesiolingual cusp, distobuccal cusp).
- The **root** is the part of the tooth covered with cementum and anchored to the alveolus by the periodontal ligament. It grows and develops as the tooth erupts into the oral cavity.
- The **neck** or **cervix** is the area where the crown and root meet—the CEJ—and the gingiva attaches. It is a dynamic area, vulnerable to age and health changes.
- The root **apex** is the tip of the root through which vessels and nerves enter the pulp chamber. It is the last structure to be completed in the growing tooth. Normally, the apex forms when the crown reaches the **occlusal plane** (the plane at which the upper and lower teeth meet).

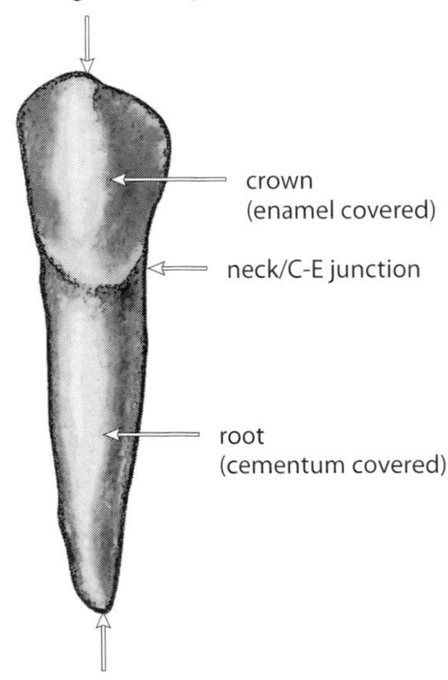

Figure 11.4
Anatomical Terms
This is tooth #22, the lower left canine, labial view. Use this example to clarify the difference between tissues and structures. For example, the crown is a tooth *structure* covered by enamel *tissue*. The root is a tooth *structure* covered by the *tissue*, cementum. Enamel and cementum (two *tissues*) meet at the neck (a tooth *structure*).

Tooth Numbering Systems

Many parts of the skeleton can be seen or felt by the observer within his or her own body. In other words, bones from the left side are easily pictured within the left side of the observer's body. The mouth is different. Most people look at their own mouth in a mirror where left and right can be easily confused. Therefore, to study the mouth and teeth, use the methods of a dental professional—visualize the mouth and teeth of another person. In this way, the observer's right is always left, and the observer's left is always right.

There are several different numbering systems. Some require symbols that do not reproduce well on a keyboard. Others are simple abbreviations such as "ULM3" (Upper Left Molar #3). Others are based on quadrants such as "28." The "2" refers to the second quadrant (the maxillary left quadrant), and the "8" refers to the eighth tooth from the center (M3).

The standard in the United States is the Universal Numbering System. It is easy to understand, but it requires a little time and concentration before each tooth can be visualized by number. The teeth are numbered sequentially from 1 to 32 beginning with the upper right third molar. One way to remember the system is to look at the open mouth as if it were a clock. Begin the count at 9:00 and always move clockwise.

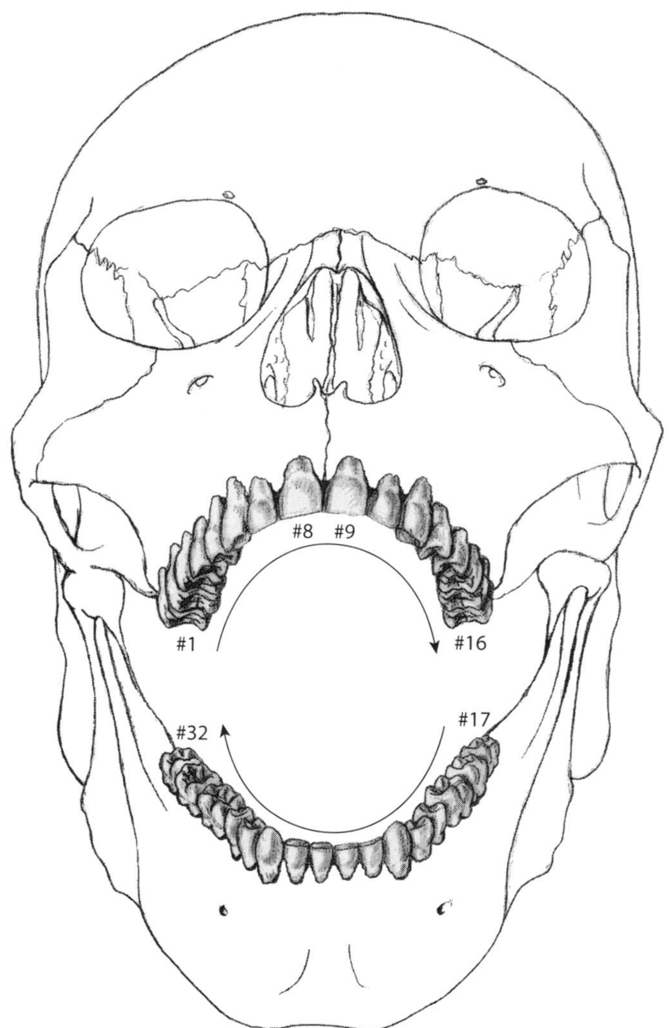

Figure 11.5
Universal Numbering System

Teeth are numbered sequentially, beginning with the upper right third molar, progressing clockwise around the open mouth, and ending with the lower right third molar.

Tooth Recognition

There are four categories of teeth: incisors, canines, premolars, and molars. A child has twenty **deciduous teeth** (baby teeth), five in each quadrant (two incisors, one canine, and two molars). There are no premolars in the deciduous dentition.

The normal adult has thirty-two **permanent teeth**, eight in each quadrant (two incisors, one canine, two premolars, and three molars). The premolars form and erupt beneath the deciduous molars. The permanent molars erupt distal to the deciduous molars.

There are many variations on the ideal dental model. This is due to both genetic heritage and the dynamic nature of the oral cavity. It is best to begin by studying what is considered to be normal. It will then be easier to recognize individual anomalies and population variation in more advanced studies.

In the following section, each type of permanent tooth is described briefly. For a more complete description, I recommend *Concise Dental Anatomy and Morphology,* 4th ed., by Fuller and Denehy (2001).

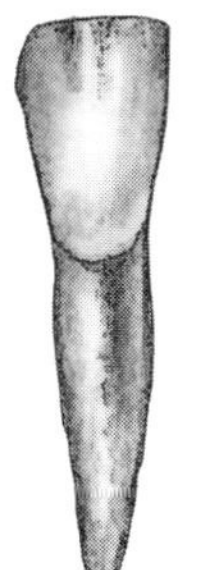

Figure 11.6
Incisor

Incisors are the biting teeth in the anterior part of the mouth. They have a single, relatively straight **incisal edge**, no cusps, and a single root. The upper central has the greatest length and breadth of all the incisors; the four lower incisors are the shortest and narrowest incisors.

When incisors first erupt into the oral cavity, the incisal edge tends to be scalloped. The scallops or "bumps" are called **mamelons**.

Dentists often refer to incisors as "centrals" and "laterals." Centrals are medial; laterals are distal. The central incisors can be abbreviated, I1, and the lateral incisors, I2.

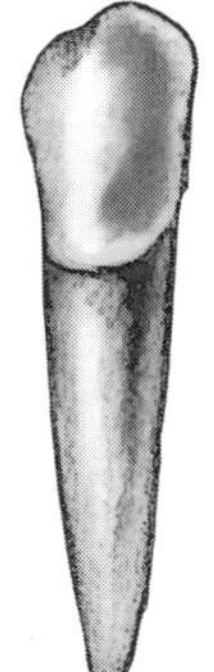

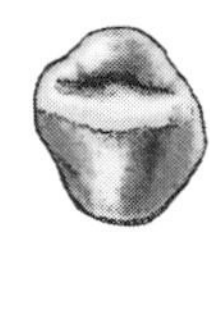

Figure 11.7
Canine

Canines are the pointed teeth on either side of the incisors. They are the longest teeth in the mouth. Canines have one cusp and a single root.

Dentists may refer to canines as "cuspids," but a common name in English is "eye tooth." The canine can be abbreviated with the letter, C.

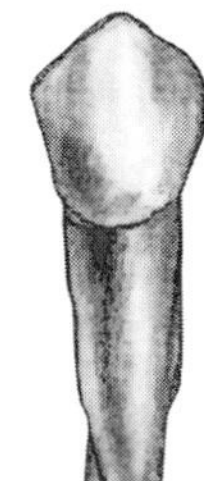

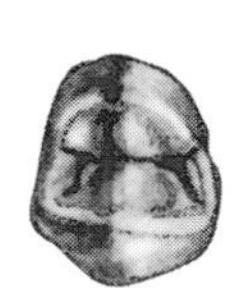

Figure 11.8
Premolar

Premolars are the two teeth distal to the canine. They have two cusps and one or two roots. Lower premolars are rounded in cross section whereas upper premolars tend to be mesiodistally compressed.

The buccal cusp is larger on both upper and lower premolars, but the cusp size difference is greater on the lower premolars. The difference is so pronounced on the lower premolar that it is commonly mistaken by students for a canine. The main cusp of the lower premolar occludes between the two cusps of the upper premolar.

Dentists may call premolars "bicuspids." Premolars are abbreviated P1 and P2.

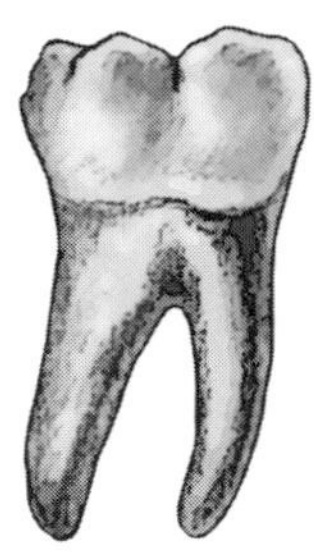

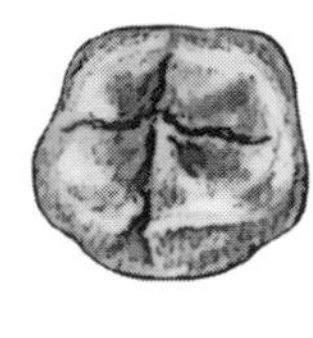

Figure 11.9
Molar

Molars are the three teeth distal to the premolars. They are the chewing or grinding teeth. Molars have multiple cusps and multiple roots. They vary more than any of the other teeth in size and shape.

Upper molars usually have three roots; lower molars usually have two roots. The cusp patterns are distinctive. The first molars usually have the largest **occlusal surface,** whereas the third molars tend to be reduced in size, usually with fewer roots or fused roots.

The third molars are more variable in form than the first and second molars, therefore they can be more difficult to recognize. Learn the first and second molars first.

Dentists may call molars the "first molar, second molar, and third molar." In common language, the molars are often referred to by the general time of eruption—the 6-year molar, the 12-year molar, and the 18-year molar. The third molar is more commonly called the "wisdom tooth" because it erupts after puberty.

Molars are abbreviated M1, M2, and M3.

Tips for Distinguishing Similar Teeth

It is relatively easy to sort teeth into incisors, canines, premolars, and molars. But the next step is to sort maxillary from mandibular teeth, left from right, and first from second in series (e.g., first and second maxillary right premolars). All of this can be accomplished with normal dentition, but it takes practice. The only real problem may be the lower incisors. Sometimes the only way to be sure is to see which fits into which socket of the mandible.

The illustrations help with the preliminary sorting of maxillary from mandibular incisors, premolars, and canines.

Distinguishing Maxillary Incisors From Mandibular Incisors (200% Natural Size)

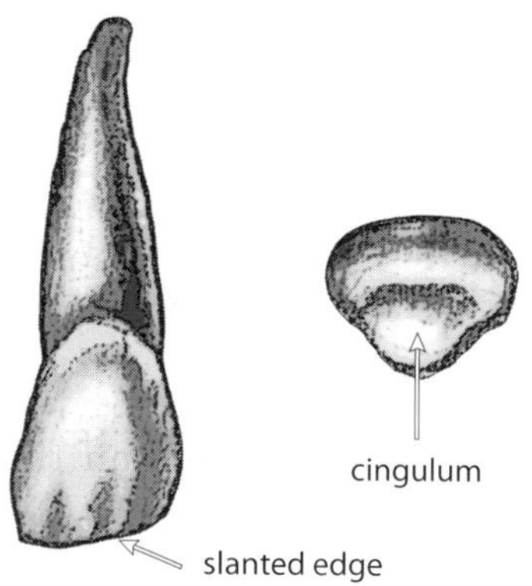

Figure 11.10a
Maxillary Lateral—#10, Labial and Incisal Surfaces

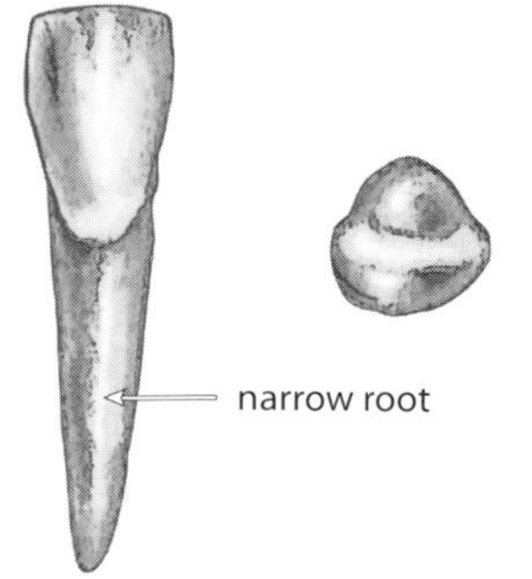

Figure 11.10b
Mandibular Lateral—#23, Labial and Incisal Surfaces

Study the two incisors. The primary difference is the shape of the root. The maxillary incisor root is rounded in cross section, and the mandibular incisor root is mesiodistally flattened.

The incisal edge of the lateral maxillary incisor is more likely to be slanted with the mesial edge longer, whereas the incisal edge of the mandibular incisor is more likely to be horizontal. In other words, the incisal corners of the mandibular incisor are nearer to 90-degree angles, whereas the incisal corners of the lateral maxillary incisor are mesially acute and distally obtuse.

The **cingulum** of the maxillary incisor is a well-defined shelf on the lingual surface. The lingual surface of the mandibular incisor is curved, but not quite so shelflike.

Distinguishing Maxillary Premolars From Mandibular Premolars (200% Natural Size)

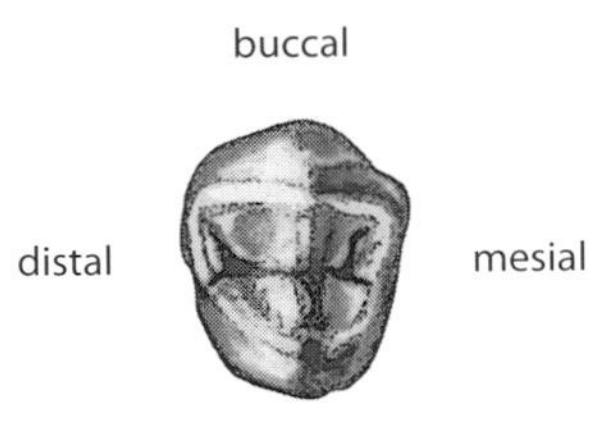

Figure 11.11a
Maxillary Premolar (#5), Occlusal Surface

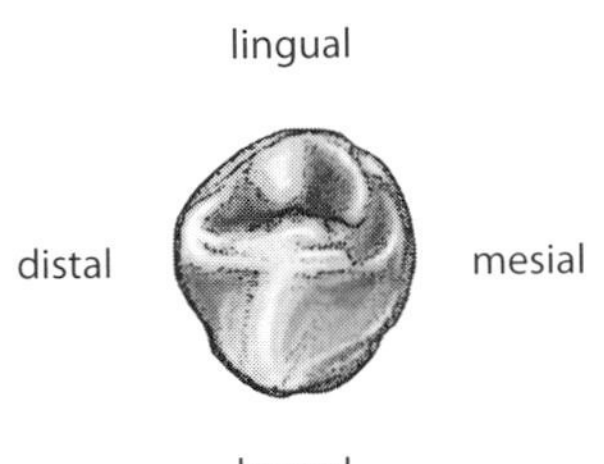

Figure 11.11b
Mandibular Premolar (#28), Occlusal Surface

Examine the two premolars. On both premolars, the buccal cusps are larger than the lingual cusps. The difference, however, is much greater between the size of the two cusps on the mandibular premolar than on the maxillary premolar.

The cross-sectional shape is also different. The maxillary premolar is mesiodistally compressed, whereas the mandibular premolar is rounded.

The maxillary first premolar usually has two well-defined roots, whereas the maxillary second and the mandibular premolars usually have a single root.

The first maxillary premolar is the same size or slightly larger than the second maxillary premolar. The first mandibular premolar is almost always smaller than the second mandibular premolar.

Distinguishing Maxillary Molars From Mandibular Molars (200% Natural Size)

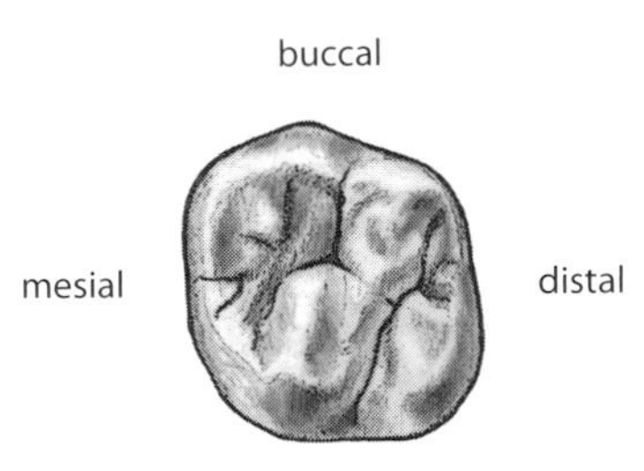

Figure 11.12a
Maxillary First Molar (#14), Occlusal Surface

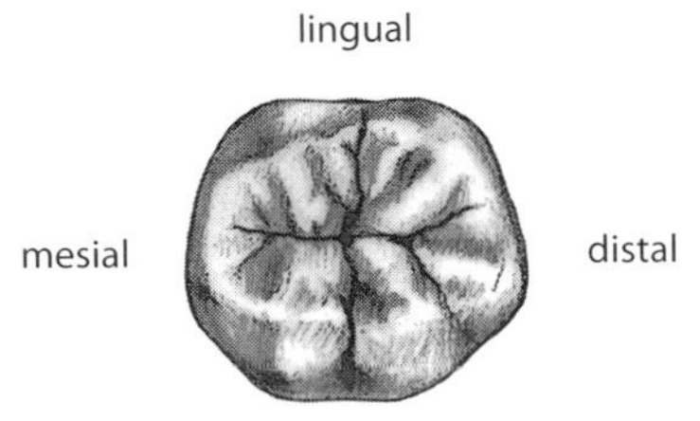

Figure 11.12b
Mandibular First Molar (#19), Occlusal Surface

Take a good look at the two first molars. Notice that the cusps and grooves form a completely different pattern. The cusps of the maxillary molar are not in a symmetrical relationship, whereas the cusps of the mandibular molar are symmetrical. The mesiolingual cusp predominates on the maxillary molar, whereas no single cusp predominates on the mandibular molar. The distolingual cusp of the maxillary molars is separated from the other three by the diagonal **distolingual groove**. The mandibular molar cusp pattern is square and the grooves tend to form a plus sign.

Complete Permanent Dentition

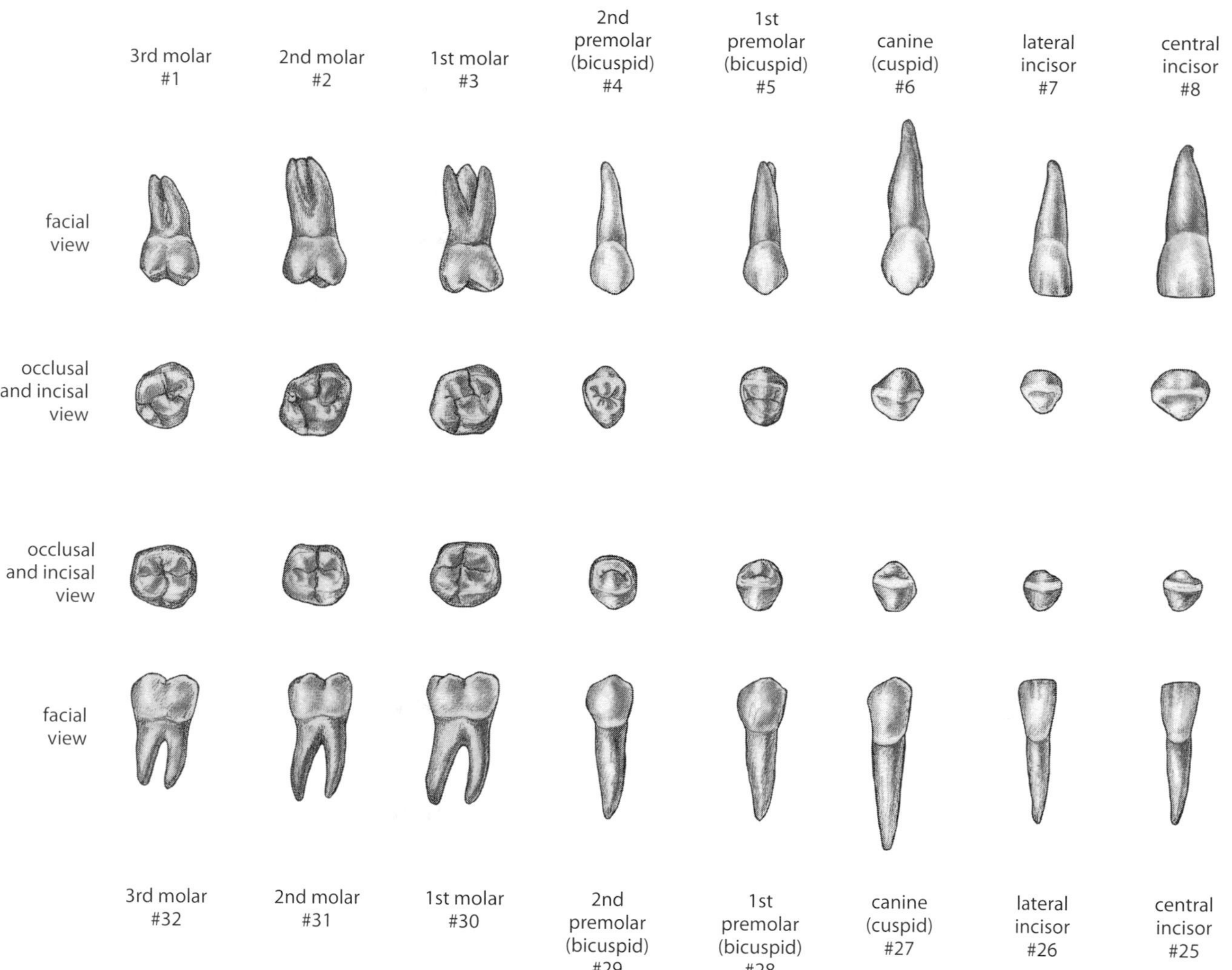

Figure 11.13
Permanent Dentition, Facial View and Occlusal/Incisal View

> **Anatomy Note**
> Root tips tend to curve distally.

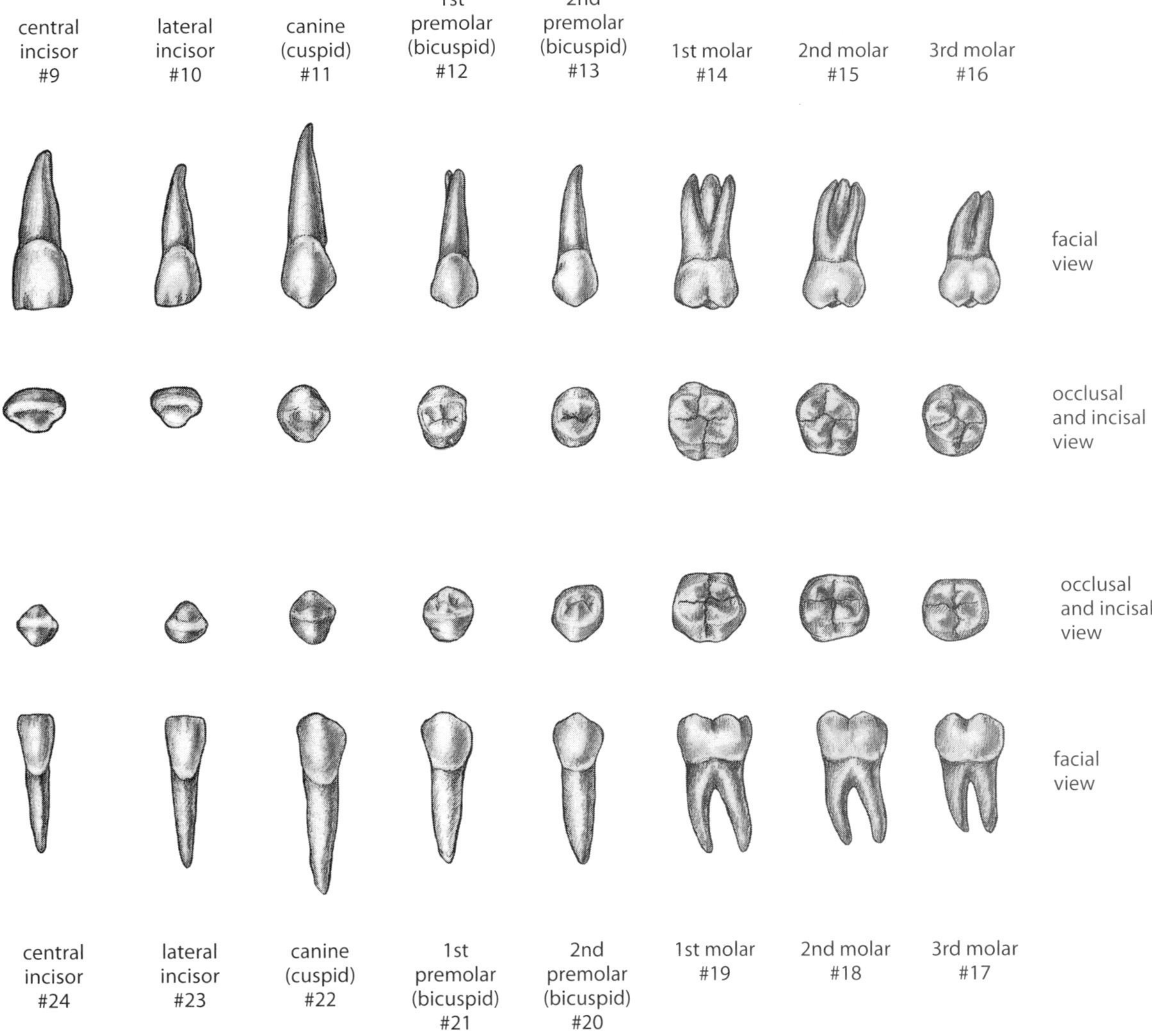
central
incisor
#9
lateral
incisor
#10
canine
(cuspid)
#11
1st
premolar
(bicuspid)
#12
2nd
premolar
(bicuspid)
#13
1st molar
#14
2nd molar
#15
3rd molar
#16
facial
view
occlusal
and incisal
view
occlusal
and incisal
view
facial
view
central
incisor
#24
lateral
incisor
#23
canine
(cuspid)
#22
1st
premolar
(bicuspid)
#21
2nd
premolar
(bicuspid)
#20
1st molar
#19
2nd molar
#18
3rd molar
#17

Recognizing Racial Traits

There are many variants of the "standard" dentition, but only two dental traits stand out as easy-to-recognize characteristics of major racial groups. As with all other racial indicators, dental traits cannot stand alone in racial identification.

Shovel-Shaped Incisors

Maxillary incisors tend to be **shovel-shaped** among groups with Asian ancestry. This includes Native Americans. The lateral edges of the incisor fold lingually to form a rough version of a coal shovel, or, in extreme cases, a rolled cone. Shovel-shaped incisors are found in close to 100 percent of some Native American groups, but they are also found (in low frequency) in other parts of the world (Scott & Turner, 2000).

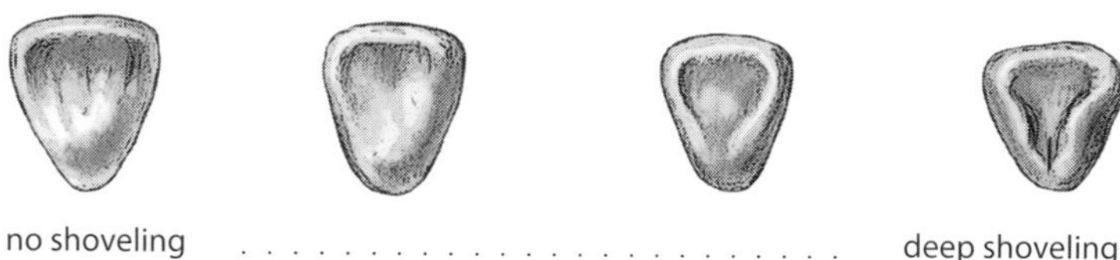

Figure 11.14
Shovel-Shaped Incisor, An Asian Origin/Native American Indicator

Carabelli's Cusp

Among people of European ancestry, the first maxillary molar sometimes displays an accessory cusp on the mesiolingual surface. The cusp can be found in a range of sizes from a small "leaflet" to a size equivalent to the other four cusps. The frequency of **Carabelli's cusp** is low (< 20 percent) in most of the world, but higher (20 to 30 percent) in Western Eurasia (Scott & Turner, 1997). (It is also called Carabelli's trait or Carabelli's tubercle.)

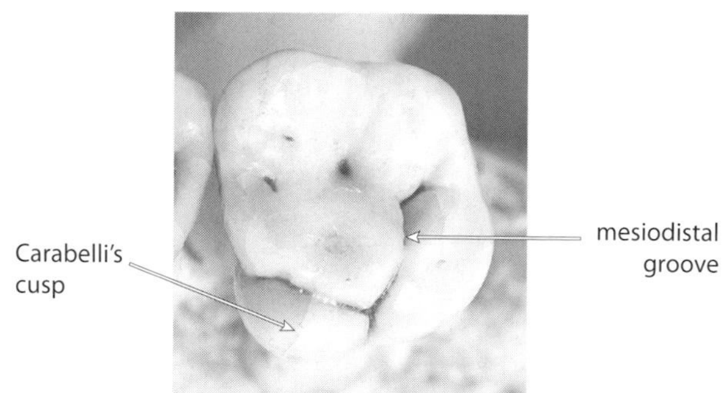

Figure 11.15
Carabelli's Cusp on Maxillary Molar, a European Indicator
Photo Courtesy of Bone Clones, Inc., www.boneclones.com.

Dental Aging

Age estimation from teeth has been employed by numerous researchers seeking better and more convenient ways to determine age from human remains. Just as with bone, the formative years provide better age estimates than the degenerative years. The sequence of tooth formation and eruption is well documented. Formation is influenced by nutrition and health care, as well as by inheritance, but dental formation is less dependent on behavioral factors than are dental aging and degeneration.

Formative Changes in Teeth

Tooth formation and eruption are very useful for determining the age of infants, children, and young adults. The rate of tooth growth and the details of tooth morphology vary from population to population, and anomalies appear in individuals, but the stages of development are the same. Study how teeth form and develop. Learn to recognize the definable stages of growth in both exfoliated teeth and radiographs. Then apply the knowledge to understanding methods for age determination.

Each of the following steps occurs, in sequence, in the formation of teeth. All can be seen on dental radiographs.

- *Commencement of crown development:* The cusps form first.
- *Completion of crown development:* The enamel is complete.
- *Commencement of root development:* The CEJ is visible.
- *Bifurcation of the root in multirooted teeth:* The floor of the pulp chamber is visible in molar teeth.
- *Eruption into the oral cavity:* The crown is no longer completely enclosed in alveolar bone.
- *Attainment of occlusion:* The cusps are level with the occlusal plane.
- *Closure of the root tip:* The outer walls of the tooth root curve toward each other and the sharp terminal edges thicken.

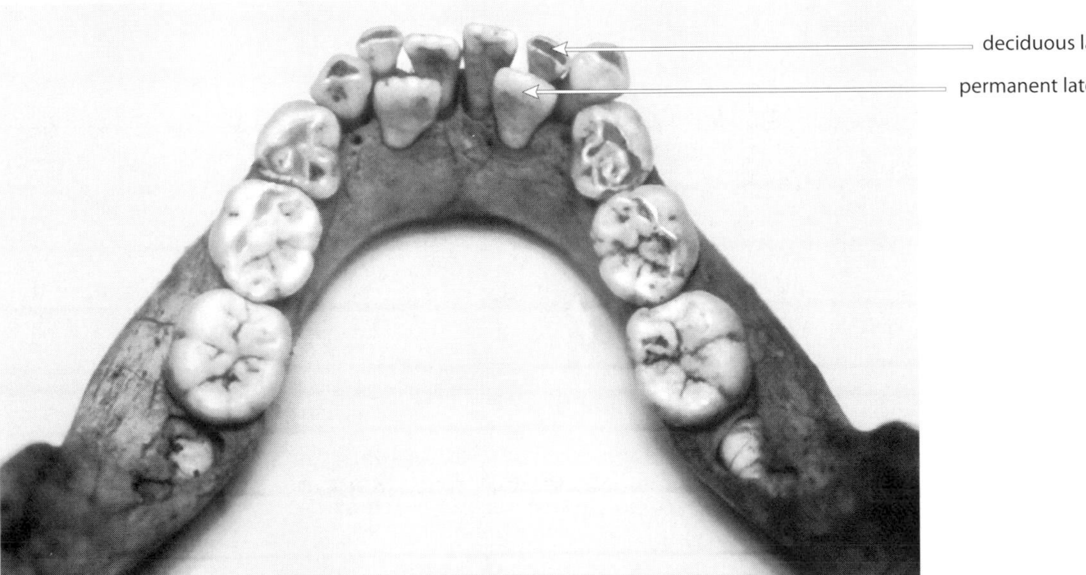

Figure 11.16
Mixed Dentition Mandible
The full deciduous dentition is present with the exception of the deciduous central incisors. The permanent first molars and the permanent central incisors are in occlusion. The permanent lateral incisors have erupted lingual to the deciduous lateral incisors. (Mamelons are visible on incisal surfaces of the permanent teeth, and exposed dentin can be seen on the incisal surfaces of the deciduous teeth.) The permanent second molars can be seen within the alveolar bone. Use the charts on the following pages to estimate the age of this child.

Infant and Toddler: Deciduous Dentition

The illustrations on pages 166 to 168 are adapted from Ubelaker's 1989 Dental Aging Chart from *Human Skeletal Remains (Fig. 71)* and provide an overview of dental development in relation to age. Note the increasing range of variation for each stage of development. Deciduous teeth are cross-hatched; adult teeth are white.

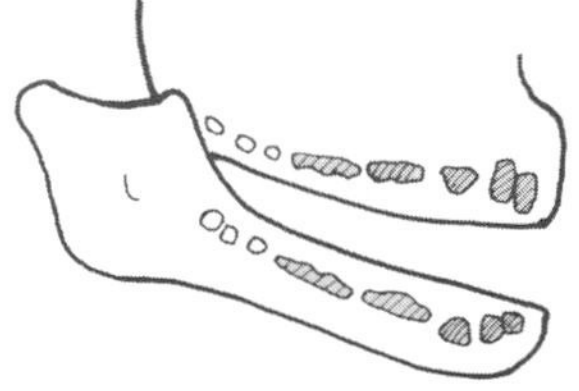

Figure 11.17a
Birth ±2 months

No teeth have erupted, but the maxilla and mandible are packed with growing teeth.

- Crowns of the deciduous incisors are near completion.
- All other deciduous teeth are present.
- The crown of the first permanent molar is beginning to develop.

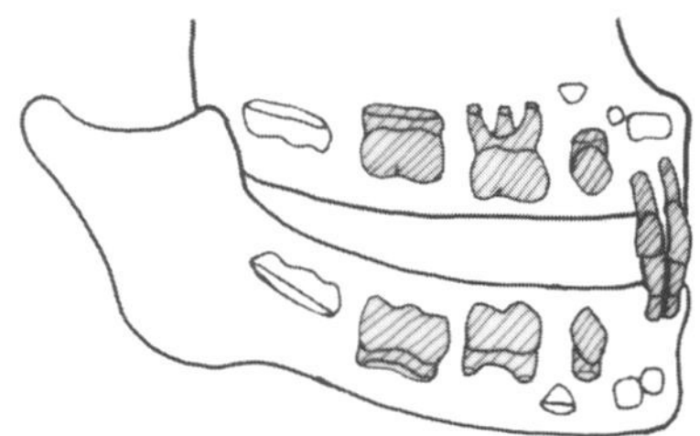

Figure 11.17b
1 Year ±4 months

The deciduous incisors have erupted.

- The first deciduous molar is ready to erupt.
- Crowns of the first permanent molar, incisors, and canine are beginning to develop.

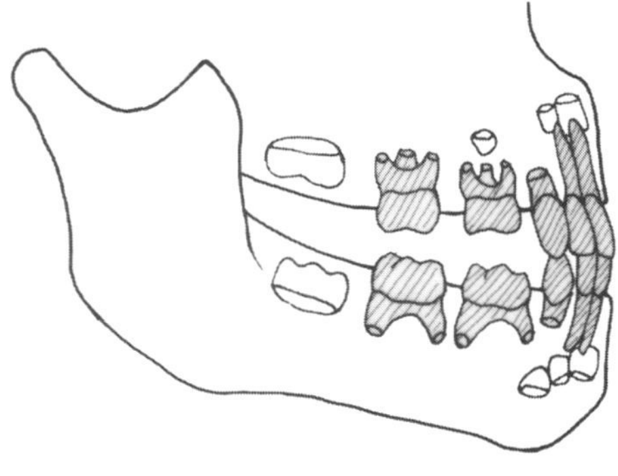

Figure 11.17c
2 Years ±8 months

The deciduous dentition is completely erupted, but the roots are incomplete.

- The crown of the first permanent molar is near completion.
- The crown of the upper first permanent premolar has begun to develop.

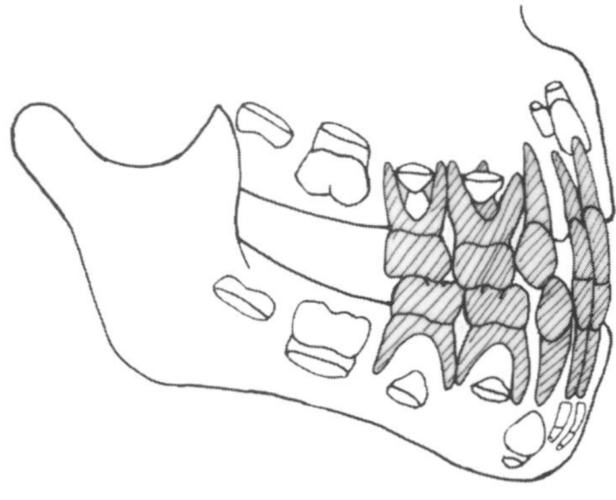

Figure 11.17d
4 Years ±12 Months

The deciduous dentition is complete, including root tips.

- The crown of the second permanent molar is beginning to develop.
- All of the permanent teeth except the third molar are now growing in the developing mandible.

Child: Mixed Dentition

The deciduous dentition is cross-hatched. The adult dentition is white.

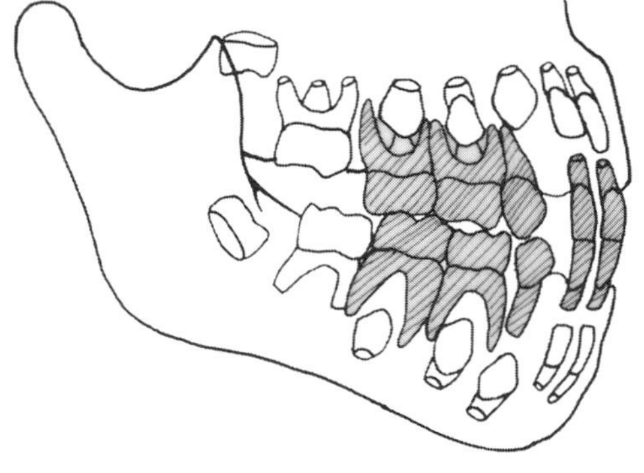

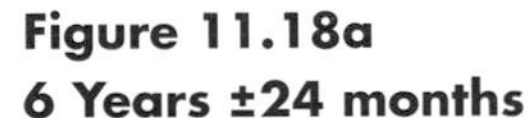

Figure 11.18a
6 Years ±24 months

- The first permanent molar is erupting.
- The permanent incisors are ready to erupt.
- The second permanent molar is beginning to develop.

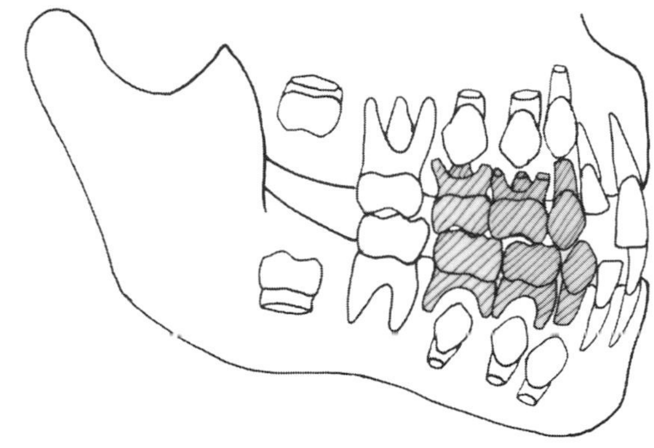

Figure 11.18b
8 Years ±24 months

- Exfoliation of deciduous teeth has begun.
- Permanent incisors have erupted.
- The root tips of the first permanent molar are complete.
- The root of the second permanent molar is developing.
- The roots of the canine and premolars are developing.

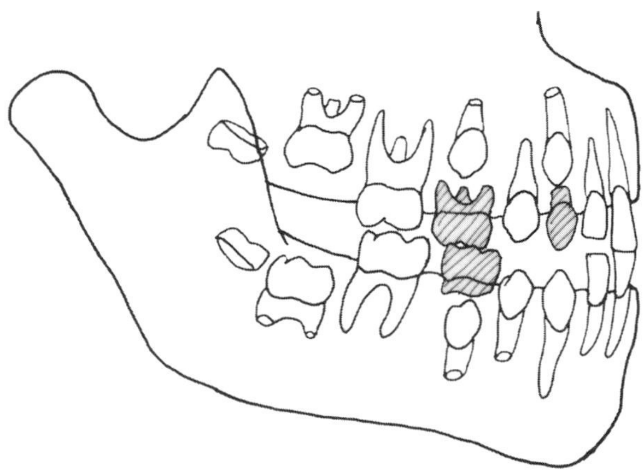

Figure 11.18c
10 Years ±30 months

- Exfoliation and replacement is near completion. Only the upper canine and second deciduous molars remain.
- The root bifurcation of the second permanent molar is complete.
- The third permanent molar is beginning to develop.

Teenager And Adult: Permanent Dentition

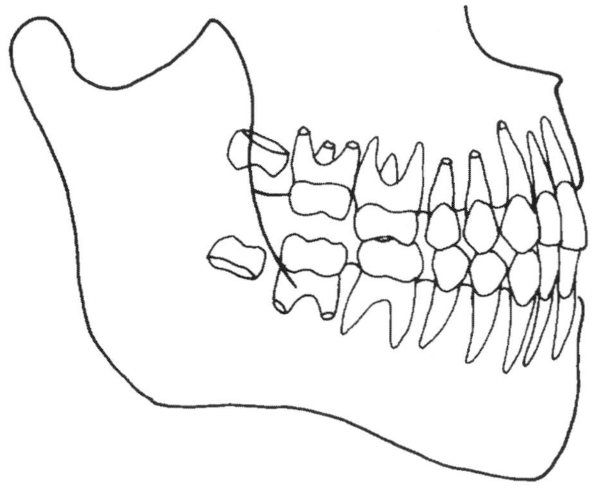

Figure 11.19a
12 Years ±30 months

- No deciduous teeth remain.
- The second permanent molar has erupted.
- Many of the root tips are incomplete.
- The crown of the third molar is developing.

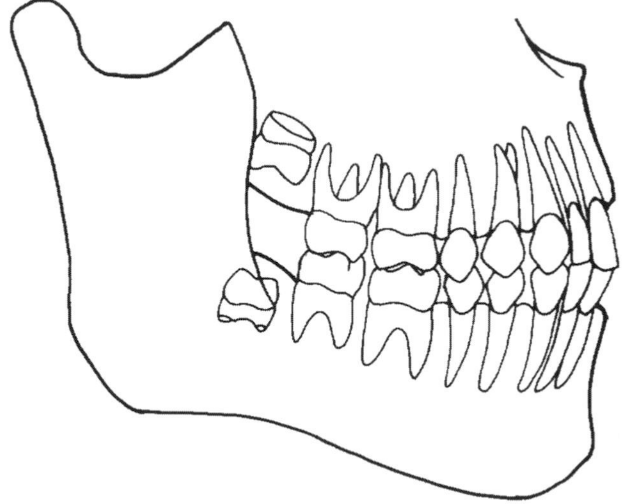

Figure 11.19b
15 Years ±30 months

- The root tips of the erupted teeth are all complete.
- The root of the third molar is developing.

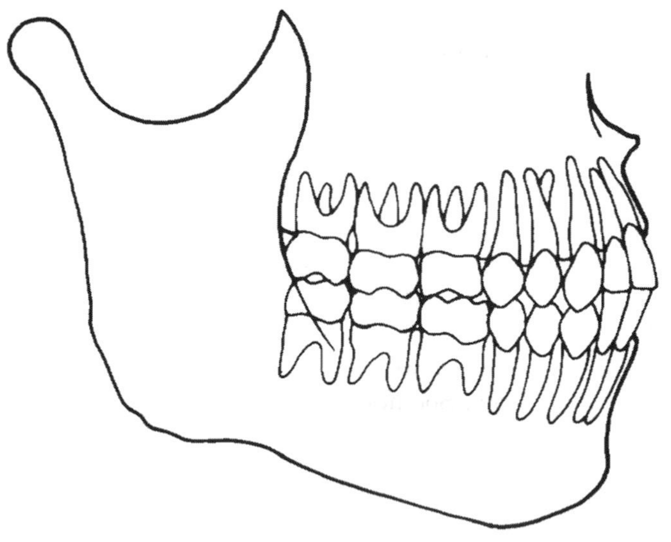

Figure 11.19c
21 Years or More—Complete Permanent Dentition

- All thirty-two teeth have erupted.
- All have reached occlusion.
- All root tips are fully formed.

Age Changes in Adult Teeth

Teeth are an ideal source of age-related information. They survive longer than any other part of the body and are still available when the rest of the body is mutilated or decomposed. In ancient and primitive populations, dental attrition (wear) is directly correlated with age. It is possible to look at the teeth of a young adult, compare the wear on the first molar (erupted at 6 years) with the second molar (erupted at 12 years), and know about how much attrition to expect in six years of the local diet. But modern populations are not so simple. Processed foods and professional dental care can make the teeth of a 60-year-old look like those of a 20-year-old at first glance. The teeth are still aging, but in less visible ways. Modern tooth aging methods are designed to use the obscure changes along with the obvious ones.

Before discussing methods, it is important to understand what is actually happening as a tooth ages. Teeth, just like bone, are adaptive. They change throughout life. The enamel is nonliving and incapable of regeneration, so it just wears away through the process of abrasion. But as the tooth enamel disappears, the underlying dentin grows stronger. Minerals are deposited in the pulp chamber (secondary dentin) and the dentinal tubules sclerose and become translucent or transparent (this is also called reparative or tertiary dentin).

If the timing is right, the dentin is ready to serve as a chewing surface by the time the occlusal enamel is worn down. Then the pulp chamber is ready to do the same by the time the occlusal dentin is worn off. With good oral health, teeth can be chewed to the original gum line and slightly below.

Gingival tissues (gums) also recede. In the newly erupted tooth, the gums are attached to the tooth root at the cervix, but with time and stress, the attachment moves toward the root apex. The older adult is called "long in the tooth" for a reason. As the attachment moves, the underlying alveolar bone resorbs, and more and more of the root surface is exposed.

The only tissue that grows (minimally) is the cementum at the apical end of the tooth. As less and less of the tooth root is held within the bony socket, the cementum, vital to periodontal attachment, grows thicker.

Loss of crown height and change in periodontal attachment level are the only two age changes that can be evaluated on direct examination in the mouth. Root transparency can be seen in intact teeth with strong transmitted light, and root transparency and secondary dentin can be seen fairly well on radiographs. All age changes can be seen and measured on thin sagittal sections of intact (not decalcified) teeth.

Aging Methods for Adult Teeth

Over the last few decades, several dental aging techniques have advanced. The first was a scoring method published by Gösta Gustafson, a Swedish odontologist, in 1947 (English version in 1950). He used ground sections of teeth to view the six major age changes described in the last section—attrition, secondary dentin, periodontal attachment level, root transparency, and cementum deposition. He also included root resorption, a change that is more difficult to recognize and assess.

The goal of subsequent methods was to improve on Gustafson's method by determining age with greater precision and making it applicable to more diverse populations. There have been improvements in sectioning methods, more elaborate statistics, and increases in population size and diversity. Some methods used fewer criteria, others used more. The more recent goal has been to obtain reasonably reliable results with the very simplest methods possible. Soomer and colleagues (2003) tested eight of the methods, including Kvaal and Solheim (1994) for in situ and extracted teeth, Solheim (1993) for in situ and sectioned teeth, Lamendin and colleagues (1992) for extracted teeth, Johanson (1971) for sectioned teeth, and Bang and Ramm (1970) for extracted and sectioned teeth.

It was found that methods for sectioned teeth gave more reliable results when compared to methods for intact teeth. This is no surprise—sections reveal more information.

The two best-known aging methods are included here—one for sectioned teeth (Gustafson, 1950) and one for whole teeth (Lamendin et al., 1992). Both of these have been tested and improved upon. In other words, there are better formulae available, but these are the simplest techniques and they provide a starting point for all the others. I recommend a thorough study of all the methods to anyone considering using a dental aging method. The choice of method depends on several factors:

1. *Which teeth are available?* Most of the methods can only be used on anterior teeth. A few methods include posterior teeth (Burns & Maples, 1976; Maples, 1978).
2. *Can the remains be removed, altered, or destroyed to obtain information?* If not, methods for in situ or intact teeth are required (Bang & Ramm, 1970; Kvaal & Solheim, 1994; Lamendin et al., 1992; Prince & Ubelaker, 2002).
3. *What equipment is available?* A thin sectioning saw or something similar is necessary for histological methods and dental radiographic equipment for x-ray methods. A light table is also useful.
4. *What information is already known about the individual?* Prince and Ubelaker's (2002) modifications to the Lamendin method require knowledge of sex and ancestry.
5. *What is the level of training of the observers?* Sectioned teeth require more training.
6. *What are the requirements for precision and accuracy?* Sectioned teeth provide more information..

GUSTAFSON'S METHOD

Gustafson's method (1950, 1966) requires thin sections of single-rooted teeth. Gustafson used hand ground sections. The same or better results can be obtained with a Buehler Isomet low-speed saw.

Steps for Age Estimation from Tooth Sections, based on Gustafson (1950, 1966)

1. Cut a section from the center of the tooth. The sections should be thin enough to allow transmitted light (100 to 300 microns). It should be possible to locate and examine microstructural features.
2. Mount the section on a glass slide for stability and maintenance and number the slide.
3. Score each of the age-related factors according to Table 11.2.
4. Apply the scores to the Gustafson formula and compare results with any and all other age-related information available from the remains.

Gustafson Formula

Age = 11 + 4.56 $(A + P + S + C + R + T)$ +/– 10.9 (standard error of the estimate)

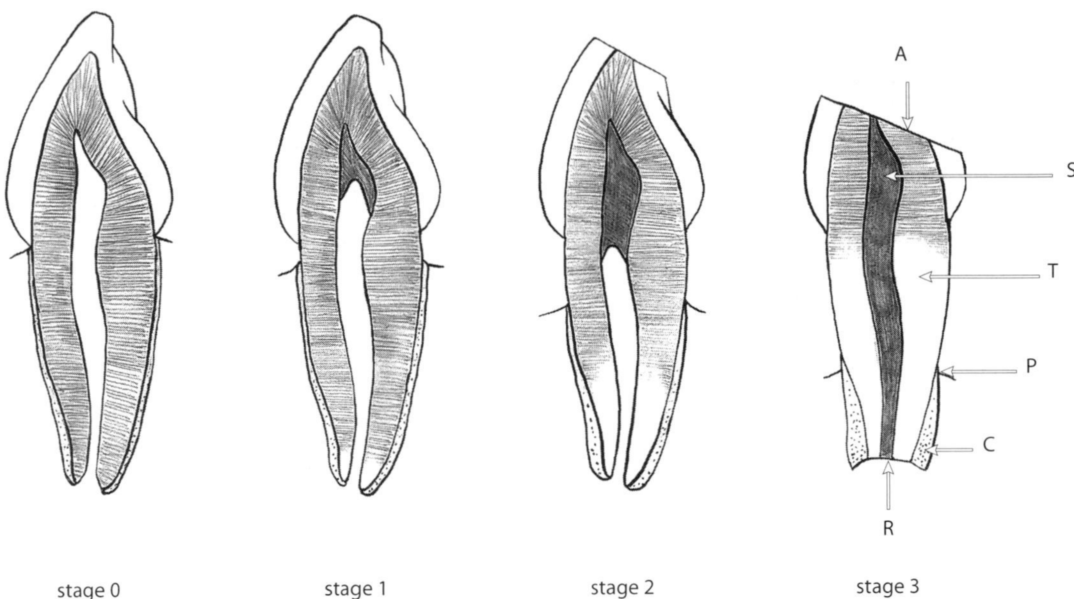

Figure 11.20
Age Changes in Adult Teeth
These illustrations depict the four stages of the six age changes defined by Gustafson (1950). The crown is wearing down (A); secondary dentin is filling the pulp chamber (S); the periodontal attachment level is moving toward the root apex (P); the root is becoming transparent (T); the cementum is thickening near the apex (C); and the apex of the root is resorbing (R). Each of these changes is defined in Table 11.2.

Table 11.2 Scoring Information for Age-Related Data from Teeth

Score	Stage 0	Stage 1	Stage 2	Stage 3
A CROWN ATTRITION	no attrition	attrition into enamel only	attrition into dentin	attrition into original pulp chamber
S SECONDARY DENTIN	no secondary dentin	secondary dentin visible	secondary dentin filling 1/3 of the pulp chamber	secondary dentin filling most of the pulp chamber
P PERIODONTOSIS	periodontal attachment at CE junction	reduced periodontal attachment	periodontal attachment at the upper 1/3 of root	periodontal attachment at the lower 2/3 of the root
T ROOT TRANSPARENCY	no transparency	beginning transparency	transparency of the apical 1/3 of root	transparency of the apical 2/3 or more of the root
C CEMENTUM	thin, even cementum	increasing cementum	thick layer of cementum	heavy layer of cementum
R ROOT RESORPTION	no resorption and open apex	beginning resorption and closed apex	flattening of root apex, affecting only cementum	flattening of root apex, affecting both cementum and dentin

LAMENDIN'S METHOD

The Lamendin method (1992) is embraced by many because of its simplicity. Prince and Ubelaker (2002) tested the Lamendin method with a larger, more variable sample. They claimed that the mean errors could be reduced when ancestry and sex are considered. The International Commission on Missing Persons in Sarajevo, Bosnia and Herzegovina uses the Lamendin method regularly. The Commission reports no difference in overall results between Lamendin and Prince, but it recommends separate formulae for individual teeth (Sarajlić et al., 2005).

Lamendin's method is not used for anyone less than 25 years old, but other methods are available for the younger age group.

Steps for Age Estimation from Intact Teeth, based on Lamendin (1992)

1. Extract tooth carefully, do not scrub or alter the periodontal line of attachment.
2. Measure **periodontosis height** on the labial surface of the root from the cementoenamel junction to the periodontal attachment line. If no soft tissue remains, the line appears as a smooth yellowish area below the enamel. Stain and calculus deposits are common along the line.
3. Measure **transparency height** from the apex of the root to the maximum height of transparency on the labial surface. (View with transmitted light.)
4. Measure **root height** from the apex of the root to the cementoenamel junction.
5. Apply Lamendin formula:

$$\text{Age} = (0.18 \times P) + (0.42 \times T) + 25.53$$

$$P = (\text{periodontosis height} \times 100)/\text{root height}$$

$$T = (\text{transparency height} \times 100)/\text{root height}$$

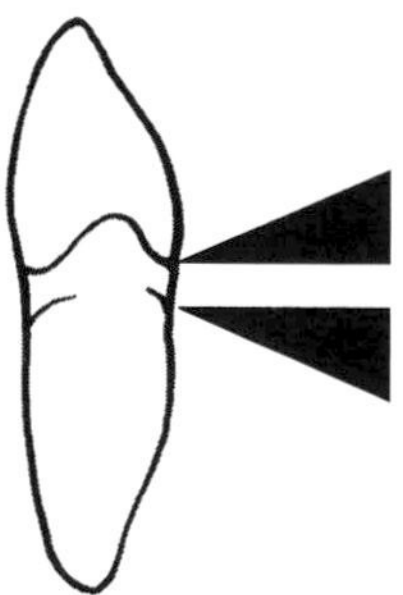

Figure 11.21 Periodontosis Height

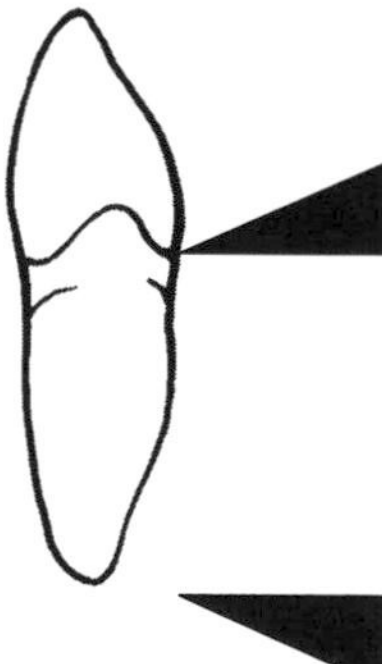

Figure 11.22 Root Height

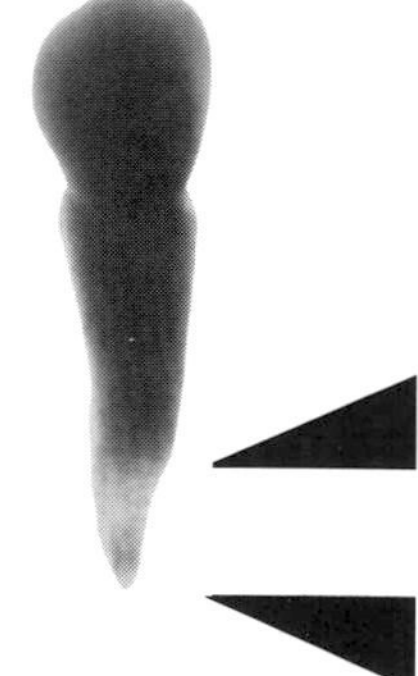

Figure 11.23 Transparency Height (on Light Board)

Dental Anomalies

There are many minor variations in secondary cusps, fissure patterns, marginal ridges, supernumerary roots, and so forth. Any unusual trait may be useful for identification by dental records, and dental anomalies can be helpful for matching traits of family members in mass graves. There are several dental anomalies common enough to be named and a few examples are listed here.

1. Gemination. Adjacent teeth are sometimes fused, or "twinned," and two teeth form from one tooth bud. This usually affects central and lateral incisors.
2. Fusion. Two teeth fuse during development and erupt as one, unusually large tooth. This also affects incisors more than other teeth.
3. Supernumerary teeth. Extra teeth (hyperodontia), adding to the usual 2-1-2-3 dental formula. The extra tooth may be either normal or anomalous in form. It may appear either as a separate structure or be fused to other teeth.
4. Missing teeth. It is slightly more common to have missing teeth (agenesis or hypodontia) than extra teeth. The third molar is missing more often than any other tooth. It may be difficult to tell if a tooth is congenitally missing or extracted, especially if the tooth is a third molar or a bicuspid. Bicuspids are frequently extracted as part of orthodontic treatment.
5. Abnormal crown forms. There are many variants on the normal crown form, but only a few that are common enough to have names.
   a. Conical lateral incisor (microdontia, peg-shaped incisors). A simple, primitive-looking tooth.
   b. Hutchinson's incisors. Screwdriver-shaped incisors. Usually associated with congenital syphilis.
   c. Tricuspid premolar. A maxillary premolar with three cusps—two buccal and one lingual.
   d. Mulberry molar. A molar covered with many small cusps or bumps. Usually associated with congenital syphilis.
6. Amelogenesis imperfecta. The enamel fails to form normally. The mild form looks like cloudy enamel; the more severe form results in very thin enamel and yellow or brown teeth.
7. Dentinogenesis imperfecta. The dentin fails to form normally, and the teeth may appear as mere stubs.
8. Enamel hypoplasia. The enamel fails to mineralize normally, leaving ridges on the surface of the tooth.

Dentistry and Oral Disease

As the major entrance to the interior of the body, the mouth admits many uninvited guests, otherwise known as pathogens. Even the healthiest person usually shows some evidence of oral or dental disease. Oral diseases are extensive enough to fill entire books and require years of study. Here, however, the focus is only on the most common diseases that leave their mark in the oral tissues most likely to be found in skeletonized remains. Each of the following conditions should be reported. They all provide clues about the life history of the individual.

Dental Caries

The most common chronic disease in the modern world is **dental caries** or "cavities." It is caused by microbial invasion of the teeth. The organisms first demineralize the inorganic substance of the teeth, and then destroy the organic substance. If not arrested, the sensitive nerve tissue at the center of the tooth is exposed and the entire tooth is consumed. The pulp chamber and the root provide free and easy access to the alveolar bone that supports the tooth, and the bone itself can also be invaded and destroyed. Once inside the bone, the infection can proceed to the sinus cavities and even the brain. The pain is so great, however, that few people allow the disease to advance so far before finding a way to extract the tooth.

Dental caries is most common among modern populations with high-carbohydrate diets (e.g., corn agriculturalists). The occurrence of caries is greatest in groups that have both high-carbohydrate diets and drinking water with low mineral content. Modern societies counter this problem by adding stannous fluoride (or stannous hexafluoroziconate) to drinking water and toothpaste. Fluorine reduces the incidence of caries by making the tooth enamel harder and less penetrable.

Periodontal Disease

Periodontal tissues support and anchor the tooth. Any disease in the periodontal tissues endangers the tooth also. Usually periodontal disease begins with simple plaque, followed by calculus formation. Calculus is rough and porous. It easily harbors bacteria. The result is irritation and inflammation of the surrounding gingival tissues.

Underlying alveolar bone is affected by the inflamation in the gingiva, and the bone resorbs and remodels. The result is pocket formation around the teeth, more bacteria, more plaque, more calculus, more inflammation, and more bony resorption.

Eventually, the tooth root is exposed to the oral cavity and the tooth becomes unstable. Finally, the tooth has insufficient bone for support and it simply falls out. By this time, the alveolar bone is highly irregular in appearance and very little tooth socket is visible. (See Figure 11.24.)

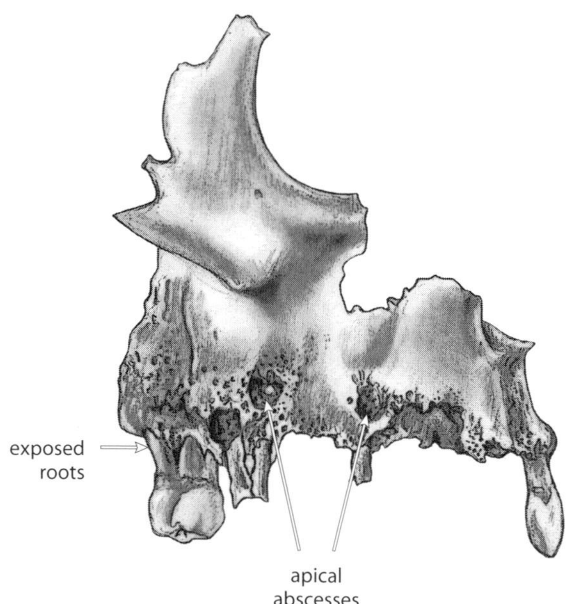

Figure 11.24a

Evidence of Advanced Periodontal Disease in the Maxilla, Lateral View

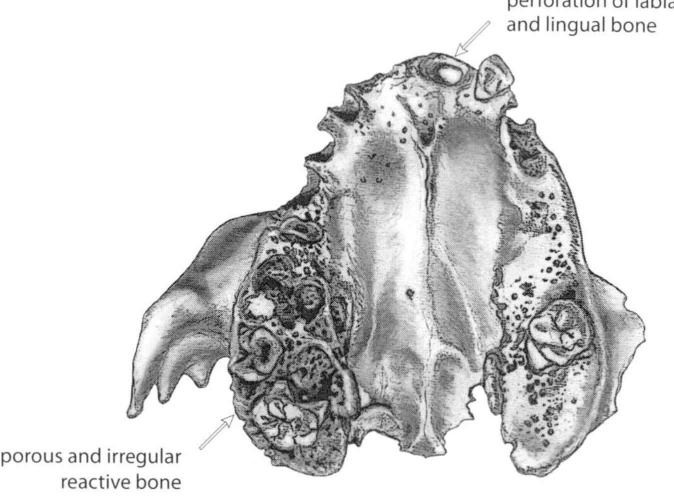

Figure 11.24b

Evidence of Advanced Periodontal Disease in the Maxilla, Palatal View

Note the extreme alveolar bone loss. The existing bone is porous and irregular. The tooth roots are exposed. During life, the remaining teeth were loose and near exfoliation. Apical abscesses had perforated both the labial and palatal bone. This is good evidence that the deceased individual was experiencing pain and halitosis (bad breath).

Apical Abscess

An **apical abscess** is the result of microbial invasion of the tooth root. The abscess forms at the apex of the root and a cavity develops in the bone. The shape of the cavity is rounded and smooth walled. This is a result of the body's efforts to wall off the infection. The abscess will often drain by perforating the labial or buccal bony plate. (See Figure 11.24.)

Calculus Accumulation

Calculus or "dental tartar" is the hard substance that forms around the neck of the tooth—in the area of the CEJ. It is **dental plaque** that has undergone mineralization. In some individuals, dental calculus accumulates to the extent that it forms a "bridge" between teeth. In extreme cases, a tooth may be held in place only because it is attached to adjacent teeth by the calculus bridge. Occasionally, a calculus "collar" will grow into a calculus "crown," literally covering the entire tooth. Calculus on the occlusal surface is an indication that the tooth is not used for chewing.

Occlusion and Malocclusion

Maxillary and mandibular teeth fit together in a variety of ways. The exact occlusion is dependent on genetics, use or behavior, and disease or trauma. Dentists, and particularly orthodontists, classify occlusion into three general classes. Each can be considered normal or abnormal according to oral health and function. Personal expectations and societal norms tend to influence what is considered normal also.

1. *Class I occlusion:* All of the top teeth line up with the bottom teeth, including the anterior teeth. This is also called an "edge-to-edge" bite and is normal in many groups of people.
2. *Class II occlusion:* The upper teeth stick out past the lower teeth when the molars are occluded. This is also called an "overbite" and is a normal condition in people of European and African origin. The lower incisors occlude with the cingulum instead of the incisal edge of the upper incisors. (Class II Malocclusion is a more extreme condition, also called "buck teeth.")
3. *Class III occlusion:* A type of bite where the lower teeth stick out past the upper teeth. This is also called an "underbite."

Dental Staining

Stained teeth are exposed to the world throughout life, so they make good identification tools. But before considering all the lifetime possibilities, rule out postmortem effects. If the stains are the result of burial conditions, the teeth should be consistent in color with the rest of the skull and any adhering soil.

Antemortem tooth discoloration can be related to external staining agents, dental restorations, trauma, or systemic disease. The normal color of teeth is determined by the white of the enamel (with tints of blue and pink) and the underlying yellow of dentin. A clean, "unstained" tooth may appear yellowish simply because of thin enamel.

Most of us know the causes of generalized external staining—lack of dental hygiene, coffee, tea, tobacco, red wine, and so on. Most of these are generalized yellowish brown stains, except for wine, which tends to leave a purplish gray stain. Tobacco produces a recognizable pattern of staining. Smokers show an overall brownish stain that intensifies on the lingual surfaces. A person who uses chewing tobacco will have more stain (and more periodontal disease) in the area where the "wad" is habitually placed—typically the buccal surface of one side of the mouth.

Other yellowish-brown stains can be caused by tetracycline, an antibiotic that deposits in hard tissues during development. It affects developing teeth until about 12 years of age. It crosses the placental barrier and is secreted in breast milk. Tetracycline was first used in the mid-1950s and the effect on developing teeth was recognized within a few years. It is unlikely that such staining would be seen on younger persons today.

Congenital diseases such as amelogenesis imperfecta and dentinogenesis imperfecta also cause yellow teeth, but the teeth are malformed. There is little reason to confuse these diseases with simple staining.

Metallic stains produce brownish or grayish coloration, depending on the metal. Iron oxide, a common drinking water contaminant, stains brown. Amalgam dental restorations and silver endodontic treatments stain gray. In dental restorations, the metal either shows through the enamel directly or it slowly infiltrates open dentinal tubules to reach the dentinoenamel junction with the same gray result.

White or "cloudy" spots can be caused by fluorosis—excessive fluoride intake. Fluorosis may be due to naturally occurring water supplies or an excess of fluoride treatment.

Pink, purple, and blue teeth can be caused by trauma to individual teeth resulting in hemorrhage within the pulp. Red blood cells are too big to travel up dentinal tubules, but when the red blood cell membrane ruptures, the contents are released. Iron oxides can travel up the dentinal tubules, where they may release oxygen and change color from red to purple to blue, just like the blood cells in a bruise. Pinkish teeth can also result from postmortem changes through the same mechanism. There are reports of pink teeth in carbon monoxide poisoning and drowning, and some medical investigators say that the position of the body contributes to the pattern of coloration.

If possible, find out what is normal for the locality. If a specific type of staining is common to all people living in the area, the condition may place the unidentified person within the population, but it won't identify him or her. In some groups, staining is so common that unstained teeth are more interesting than stained teeth. Unusually white teeth may be the result of unusual dietary habits, or, in recent years, the popular "teeth whitening" agents. Either way, a bit of social information can be gained from unstained teeth. (See Watts & Addy, 2001, for a more thorough review of staining.)

"Meth Mouth": Effects of Methamphetamine Use

The effects of methamphetamine use have been reported only recently (see Davey, 2005), but dentists who work in prisons or drug clinics recognize it instantly. They call it "meth mouth." The teeth are grayish brown, or blackened stumps. The most characteristic effect is erosion of the enamel, beginning at the gum line and moving toward the crown. The teeth twist and break off near the gum line, leaving decaying roots in the alveoli. One dentist said it looked like someone had taken a hammer to the teeth and shattered them.

The damage is evidently caused by several associated factors. The caustic ingredients in the methamphetamine lead to enamel damage and cause dry mouth. Without saliva, bacteria multiply rapidly. Without intact enamel, decay is rampant. Users are constantly thirsty and crave carbonated high-sugar drinks, which increases the progress of decay. Jaw clenching and tooth grinding, effects of a methamphetamine high, weaken, twist, and break the teeth.

At this writing, the dental effects of methamphetamine are not well researched, but the phenomenon is well enough known to be useful for anthropologists faced with identification of possible drug addicts.

The Edentulous Condition: Effects of Long-Term Tooth Loss

Compare the two skulls below. They are approximately the same size and of the same sex and race. But the lower halves of the faces are very different. When teeth are extracted, the alveolar bone that supports the teeth is no longer under tension. The only force becomes compression as a person "gums" food. Therefore, the alveolar ridge resorbs, the maxilla and mandible are shortened, and the facial appearance changes drastically. Dentures can increase the distance between the maxilla and mandible, but no prosthesis can replace the critical tension supplied by the periodontal ligament.

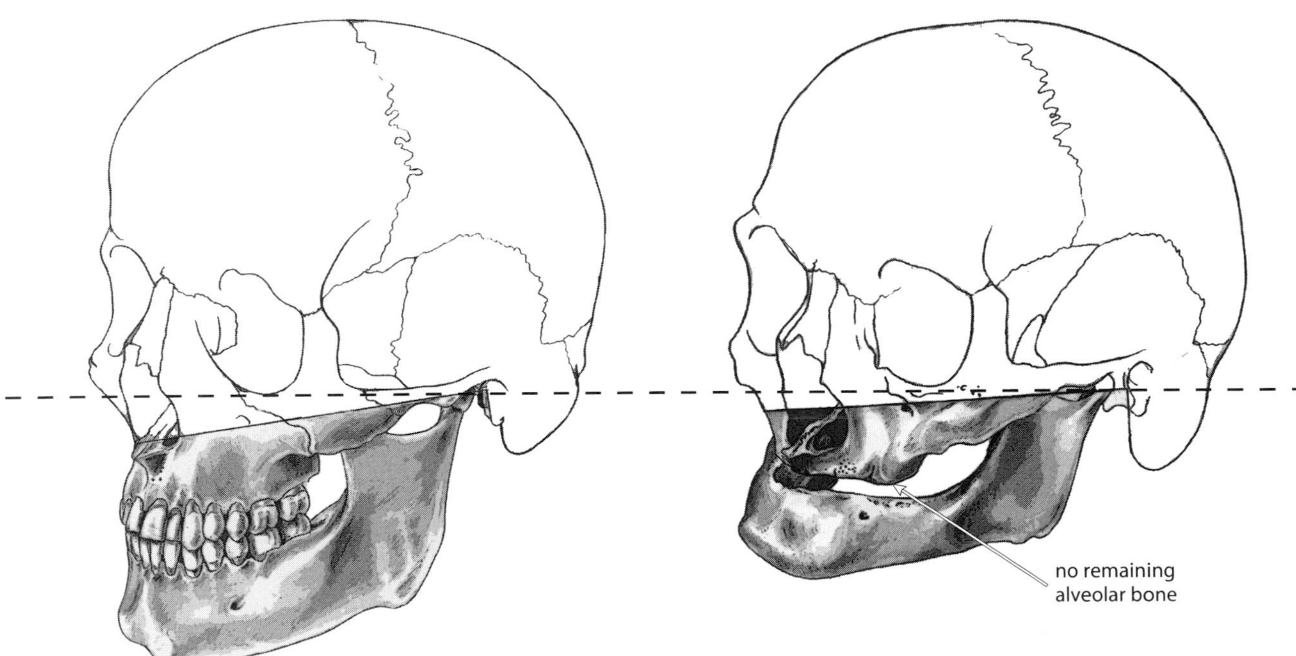

Figure 11.25
Normal Dentition and Edentulous Mouth

The skull on the left is of a European male with only the third molars missing. The alveolar ridge fully supports the teeth and the facial profile is normal. The skull on the right is of a European male without teeth. The teeth were lost years before death and all of the tooth sockets have healed and resorbed. The maxilla and mandible have remodeled to exclude the alveolar ridge. The result is forward projection of the chin, shortening of the lower face, and a change in overall facial proportions.

Table 11.3 A Few of the More Common Terms Used in Dentistry

These terms may help the anthropologist communicate more effectively with the odontologist.

Term	Definition
AMALGAM	a restoration made of a metal in mercury solution (usually 67% Ag, 27% Sn, 5% Cu, and 1% Zn); one part alloy and two parts mercury are mixed and packed into the cleaned and sealed dental cavity; the amalgam hardens in about 24 hours
BRIDGE	a fixed or removable replacement for missing teeth, attached to natural teeth by wires or crowns
COMPOSITE	a plastic resin restoration that mimics the appearance of enamel
CROWN	a permanent replacement for a natural crown, made of porcelain on metal, or metal alone (gold or other stable metal)
DENTAL PROSTHESIS	fixed or removable replacement of one or more teeth and/or associated oral structures; denture, bridgework, or oral appliance
DENTURE	a complete or full denture replaces all of the natural dentition of the maxilla or mandible; a partial denture replaces one or more teeth and is retained by natural teeth at one or both ends
EDENTULOUS	toothless; a mouth without teeth
INLAY	a prefabricated restoration (usually gold or porcelain) sealed in the cavity with cement
PULPECTOMY	removal of the entire pulp, including the root; commonly known as a "root canal"; the tooth is no longer living
RADIOGRAPH, BITE-WING	a film of posterior teeth produced by exposure of laterally oriented intraoral film; the x-ray beam is angled between the teeth; the crowns are the main focus of the films
RADIOGRAPH, APICAL	a film produced by exposure of vertically oriented intraoral film; the x-ray beam is angled from above maxillary teeth or below mandibular teeth to capture the complete tooth, including the apex
RADIOGRAPH, PANORAMIC	a film of the entire oral cavity produced by immobilizing the head and moving the x-ray beam behind the head while film moves in synchronization in front of the face
RESTORATION	any inlay, crown, bridge, partial denture, or complete denture that restores or replaces lost tooth structure, teeth, or oral tissues

Table 11.4 Dental Vocabulary

Term	Definition
ALVEOLAR PROCESS	the ridge of the maxilla or mandible that supports the teeth
ALVEOLUS DENTALIS	the tooth socket in which teeth are attached by a periodontal membrane
ATTRITION	the wearing down of a tooth surface due to abrasion and age
CARIES, DENTAL	a localized, progressively destructive disease beginning at the external surface with dissolution of inorganic components by organic acids produced by microorganisms
CEMENTUM	a porous layer of calcification covering the tooth root; the cementum provides a site for periodontal fibers to anchor
CERVIX (NECK)	the slightly constricted part of the tooth between the crown and the root
CINGULUM	the lingual ridge or shelf at the base of upper incisors and canines; in normal occlusion, the lower anterior teeth touch the cingulum of the upper anterior teeth
CROWN	the enamel-capped portion of the tooth that normally projects beyond the gum line
CROWN, CLINICAL	the portion of the tooth visible in the oral cavity
CROWN, ANATOMIC	the portion of a natural tooth that extends from the cementoenamel junction to the occlusal surface or incisal edge
CUSP	a conical elevation arising on the surface of a tooth from an independent calcification center; cusps are named according to their position (e.g., mesiolingual cusp, distobuccal cusp)
CUSP, CARABELLI'S	an extra cuspid on the mesiolingual surface of upper molars; more common within the Caucasian race

TERM	DEFINITION
CUSP PATTERN	the recognizable alignment of cusps on a particular tooth type
DENTIN, PRIMARY	forms until the root is completed; tubular dentin
DENTIN	the main mass of the tooth; 20% is organic matrix, mostly collagen with some elastin and a small amount of mucopolysaccharide; 80% is inorganic, mainly hydroxyapatite with some carbonate, magnesium, and fluoride; structured as parallel tubules
DENTIN, SECONDARY	forms after the tooth has erupted, due to irritation from caries, abrasion, injury, or age
DENTIN, SCLEROTIC	generalized calcification of dentinal tubules as a result of aging
DENTIN, REPARATIVE	calcification of dentinal tubules immediately beneath a carious lesion, abrasion, or injury
DENTINAL TUBULE	the tubules extending from the pulp to the dentinoenamel junction; odontoblastic processes extend into the tubules from the pulp surface
ENAMEL	the dense mineralized outer covering of the tooth crown; 99.5% inorganic hydroxyapatite with small amounts of carbonate, magnesium, and fluoride, and 0.5% organic matrix of glycoprotein and keratin-like protein; structured of oriented rods consisting of rodlets encased in an organic prism sheath
GINGIVA	the gums, gum tissue; the dense fibrous tissue covered by mucous membrane that envelops the alveolar processes of the upper and lower jaws and surrounds the necks of the teeth
JUNCTION, CEMENTOENAMEL (CEJ)	the line around the neck of the tooth at which the cementum and enamel meet
JUNCTION, CEMENTODENTINAL	the surface at which the cementum and dentin meet
JUNCTION, DENTINOENAMEL (DEJ)	the surface at which the dentin and enamel meet
MAMELONS	small, regular bumps on the incisal edges of recently erupted incisors; indication of youth or (occasionally) lack of occlusion
PERIAPICAL	around the tip of the root
PERIODONTAL DISEASE	inflammation of the tissues surrounding the teeth resulting in resorption of supporting structures and tooth loss
PERIODONTAL LIGAMENT	the fibrous tissue anchoring the tooth by surrounding the root and attaching to the alveolus
PERIODONTOSIS	lowering of the attachment level of the periodontal ligament
PITS AND FISSURES	the depressed points and lines between cusps
PULP	the soft tissue in the central chamber of the tooth, consisting of connective tissue containing nerves, blood vessels, lymphatics, and at the periphery, odontoblasts capable of dentinal repair
PULP CHAMBER	the central cavity of the tooth surrounded by dentin and extending from the crown to the root apex
ROOT	the cementum-covered part of the tooth, usually below gum line
ROOT, ANATOMICAL	the portion of the root extending from the cementoenamel junction to the apex or root tip
ROOT, CLINICAL	the imbedded portion of the root; the part not visible in the oral cavity
SHOVEL-SHAPED INCISORS	central incisors formed with lateral margins bent lingually, resembling the form of a flat shovel or a coal shovel; common in people of Asian origin (e.g., Native Americans)

CHAPTER 12

Introduction to the Forensic Sciences

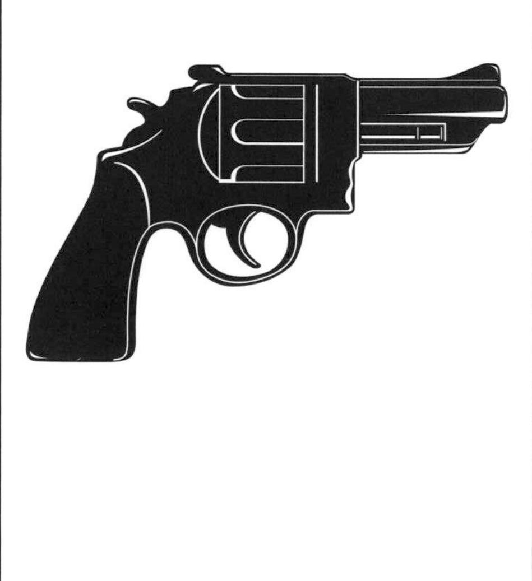

CHAPTER OUTLINE

INTRODUCTION

Forensic science is knowledge based on scientific method used to investigate and establish facts in criminal and civil courts of law. It is a multidisciplinary field, and any systematic form of knowledge applied to legal issues can be called a forensic science.

Prior to the twentieth century, the courts relied primarily on evidence contained in verbal testimony. Much of the world still does. However, modern courts have been persistent in the search for more reliable ways to obtain facts, and the scientific community has responded. Increasingly, scientists are finding ways to expand on the specific aspects of their disciplines which are most useful to legal issues. Forensic questions are being explored, and an ever-increasing number of research reports are published in scientific literature. New forensic subdisciplines have grown out of the effort and training programs and advanced degrees are now available.

Scientific disciplines actively contributing to the growth of the forensic sciences are medicine, dentistry, chemistry, biology, anthropology, and engineering. The technical specialties include fingerprint identification, questioned documents examination, blood spatter analysis, accident reconstruction, and photography. This wide assortment of forensic sciences has one thing in common—evidence.

Etymology of Forensic (Adjective) and Forensics (Noun)

Forensic is an adjective used for anything relating to, used in, or appropriate for courts of law, public discussion, argumentation, or debate. **Science** is a noun which encompasses the wide range of systematic methodologies used to increase understanding of the physical world. Forensic science is any scientific methodology applied to legal issues and courts of law. Recent popular usage shortened forensic sciences to **forensics**, a noun used to encompass all forensic sciences and technology.

EVIDENCE

Evidence is any object or testimony offered as a basis for belief. It can take any form, and its key element is the power to convince. Evidence makes something apparent to others whether or not they were present at the critical time or place. It is also the term used for the statement itself, as presented before a court of law.

The two main categories of evidence are verbal (testimonial) evidence and physical evidence. A third category of evidence is called demonstrative evidence. It did not originate with the event or the crime and is important only for teaching or explaining. It will be discussed separately in Chapter 16.

Verbal evidence is oral or written testimony from a witness about his or her own observations or knowledge. The person who gives verbal evidence may be an eyewitness or a character witness. The words within a document are verbal evidence, but the document itself is physical evidence.

Physical evidence is tangible. It may be substantial, or it may be delicate (as in "trace" evidence). It is material that can be collected, analyzed, and interpreted by scientific method. The person who presents physical evidence in a court of law is called an expert witness.

In the early 1900s, an innovative French scientist, **Edmond Locard** (1877–1966), introduced a concept that would change crime scene investigation forever. Locard was trained in both medicine and law, and he used his broad training to explore the nature of evidence. His work led to the discovery of minute physical evidence that no one else had noticed. He is best known today for his assertion that information is exchanged whenever two objects come into contact. This information is in dust, hair, dyes, pollen, etc. that constantly transfer from surface to surface (Locard, 1930). Today, it is called trace evidence, and crime scene technicians search for it because they have no doubt whatsoever that it exists. Prior to Locard, trace evidence was not mentioned. It was not found because no one considered its presence or usefulness and, therefore, no one was looking for it. Locard's assertion came to be known as **Locard's Exchange Principle** and is considered to be the guiding theory of modern forensic science.

In the United States, high-profile trials of the last two decades have demonstrated to the public that physical evidence is critical. The trials of O. J. Simpson and Timothy McVeigh are prime examples. People can forget, lie, and distort the truth, but, in and of itself, physical evidence is incapable of deception. The challenge is in finding a way for the evidence to speak. It must be collected without contamination, analyzed correctly, interpreted accurately, and recorded honestly. To accomplish all this, the forensic scientist requires specialized education, training, experience, and a strong sense of ethics.

Direct and Indirect Evidence

Physical evidence can be further classified as direct or indirect evidence. **Direct evidence** is capable of proving something on its own. It is obvious to the observer and needs no further interpretation. It is sometimes called real evidence, but the word *real* is not recommended because it is overused and imprecise.

Indirect evidence is also called **circumstantial evidence**. It proves something by inference or deduction. Its significance may not be generally recognized or understood, therefore, explanation is important. The expert witness is critical when indirect evidence is used in a court of law.

Managing and Processing Physical Evidence

It may seem that physical evidence can simply be found and collected, but this is far from the truth. Evidence can be difficult to recognize and it is useless if it is not handled properly from first sighting to final presentation. If evidence is to be convincing and acceptable to the courts, it requires complete documentation, careful collection, proper handling, effective preservation, appropriate analysis, correct interpretation, and accurate reporting. Haste is the worst enemy of good evidence collection. It is better to step back from the scene and plan carefully than to rush in and touch something without appropriate planning. All too often an enthusiastic but inadequately prepared person—official or not—has become the inadvertent enemy of the judicial process. The following sections are a general introduction to methods of handling physical evidence. A more thorough discussion for anthropologists is found in the chapter on field methods (Chapter 15).

Documentation

Documentation of evidence begins at the moment of discovery. The evidence should be recorded in photographic and written form (including maps) before it is disturbed. (If the evidence is first discovered by someone from the general public, the person should be located and interviewed.) Documentation continues

Table 12.1 Examples of Physical Evidence from a Recent Crime Scene and a Burial

Note the similarities and differences in types of physical evidence recovered in each venue. Different experts may be necessary to recognize, collect, and process the specific evidence.

RECENT CRIME SCENE	BURIAL
fleshed body	decomposing or skeletonized body
latent fingerprints	mummified fingers
hair	hair
fibers	fibers
clothing	decomposing clothing
footprints	footprint impressions
projectiles & cartridges	projectiles & cartridges
blood spatter	coffin parts
other body fluids	plant residues
documents	insect pupae
weapons	shovel marks

at each stage of recovery, each time that any procedure is performed, and each time that the evidence changes hands (chain of custody).

Chain of Custody

It is necessary to account for the integrity of each piece of evidence by tracking all handling and storage from the time the evidence is collected to final disposition. A custody form is a standard means of tracking. The form accompanies the evidence and is signed (together with date and time) by each and every person who handles the evidence. Each person checks to see that the evidence is as described in the record before signing. The unbroken record makes it possible to trace any unauthorized alterations and locate opportunities for substitutions. The chain of custody maintains the value of the physical evidence for legal purposes.

Collection

After a record is made of each item in situ (photos, map, and written description), the evidence can be collected. The goal is to collect evidence without alteration or contamination. It is important to think before touching. Keep in mind that Locard's Exchange Principle applies as much to the crime scene technician as to the victim and perpetrator. Modern conditions usually require the use of rubber gloves and other protective clothing.

Packaging must be marked so that it can be located, identified, and matched easily with records. This means labeling or tagging with indelible ink. If the evidence is packaged properly, tampering should be obvious. This can be accomplished by securing the package with one-use tamper-evident tape or by adding a signature or initials across the tape, beginning on the tape and ending on the package itself. Keep in mind that some types of evidence require airtight packaging and other items require porous packaging such as paper bags.

Preservation and Storage

It is important to maintain the evidence for future analysis by other scientists or with improved methods. Good preservation requires that the evidence be maintained as stable as possible. Every type of sample has its own requirements but "cool, dry, and away from sunlight" are almost always good guidelines. Antimicrobial agents may be useful in some cases, and avoidance of over-drying is important in others. It is important to use common sense and check with experts on specific substances.

The evidence should be packaged in such a way that it is well protected and easily retrieved. The boxes should be as uniform as possible and the labels should be in standardized easy-to-find locations.

Analysis

Methods of analysis change over time, but it is important that the analysis be appropriate for the material and the resources. It is also important that the methods be consistent with generally accepted practices within the specific scientific discipline. In addition, the methods must be shown to be valid, reliable, and repeatable (replicable). **Validity** can be shown by the use of controls. Known samples should produce the expected result. **Reliability** can be demonstrated by consistency in results. (Note that a method may be reliable but not valid.) The method should produce the same result over and over again. To demonstrate **repeatability**, different analysts at different times should be able to produce the same results. (Note that a method may be reliable for one analyst but not another.) See the chapter on laboratory analysis (Chapter 13) for methods of analysis in forensic anthropology.

Interpretation

Interpretation of the evidence must first take into account the limits (validity, reliability, and repeatability) of the analytical method(s) being used. In addition, the size of the sample, origin of the sample, and the composition of the sample population must be taken into account. The analyst is continually challenged to avoid overstating the results and produce a balanced and accurate interpretation of evidence.

Reporting

Documentation must be thorough and detailed, but the final reporting of results should be as simple and direct as possible. The report must be clear and understandable to nonscientists. Refer to the chapter on professional results (Chapter 16) for a discussion of forensic reports.

Forensic Scientists Typically Employed by Crime Laboratories

Forensic science is a multidisciplinary field. No specialist can ignore the work of the others any more than a plumber, electrician, and carpenter can avoid one another on a building project without causing costly mistakes. The success of an investigation may depend on the fact that one person knows when to call in another.

Crime lab scientists and technicians usually have backgrounds in law enforcement, chemistry, biology, or medicine. Some of the specialists work directly with the body; others focus on evidence from the scene. Some specialists spend more time in the field; others in the laboratory. Some spend a lot of time testifying in court; others submit their reports and are rarely called to court.

The following is a short list, in alphabetical order, of typical crime lab scientists and a brief description of the work each one does.

Ballistic specialists or firearm examiners are experts capable of recognizing and analyzing weapons and projectiles. Many come from a police or military background and training. They can determine if a weapon has been fired and match a projectile to the specific weapon that fired it. Computer capabilities are also important. Most major labs use the **Integrated Ballistics Identification System** (IBIS) for collecting, storing, and correlating digital images of ballistics evidence.

Crime scene investigators are usually police officers who specialize in processing crime scenes and gathering forensic evidence. Ideally, scene investigators arrive on the scene soon after the initial responders. They are trained to recognize, photograph, map, organize, and collect evidence. The evidence is then sent to a forensic laboratory for secure storage and a more thorough analysis with equipment not available at the crime scene. Scene investigators are typically knowledgeable about fingerprints, footprints, hair, fibers, blood spatter dynamics, and weapons of all types. Most crime scene investigators call on death investigation specialists to deal with human remains.

Shutterstock.com

Criminalists are a broadly-trained group of scientists and technicians within the forensic sciences. Many are chemists, and most have extensive on-the-job training. The work of the criminalist focuses on the physical evidence from the crime scene, but not the body itself. Much of the physical evidence is trace evidence such as glass fragments, fibers, hair, paint, tool marks, soil, and anything else that may reveal information. Criminalists rely on a wide range of advanced technical equipment for microscopy, chromatography, spectrophotometry, mass spectrometry, and so on.

Death investigators are similar to crime scene investigators and, in some jurisdictions, the jobs are carried out by the same people. In jurisdictions with a medical examiner's office separate from the crime laboratory, the death investigator is the medical examiner's representative in the field. This person focuses on evidence from the body rather than the scene. The death investigator reports to the medical examiner or forensic pathologist in charge of the case.

Drug analysts are chemists who analyze and identify the wide variety of drugs and poisons available to man. They are usually excellent chemists with knowledge of pharmaceutical products as well. Drug analysts are different from toxicologists in that they analyze different forms of evidence. For example, they may both be looking for cocaine, but the drug analyst receives a packet of powder, and the toxicologist receives a tube of blood.

Fingerprint specialists collect latent fingerprints from a wide variety of surfaces and materials. They enhance the prints for identification, classify fingerprints, and compare them for identification. This work used to be based largely on ink and powder, but chemical enhancement and computer imaging and analysis are now essential to the work. In the United States, most fingerprint experts use the **Automated Fingerprint Identification System** (AFIS) for matching unidentified and known fingerprint patterns.

Forensic pathologists are medical doctors who have completed a residency in pathology and an *additional* residency in forensic pathology—usually in a medical examiner's office. They use their knowledge of disease and death for legal purposes. They conduct autopsies on fleshed bodies to determine cause and manner of death. Many are employed as medical examiners by government agencies. It is often the medical examiner who requests additional analysis by forensic dentists and anthropologists. (Note that *most* pathologists are not trained in forensic work. They are medical doctors who specialize in the recognition and diagnosis of diseases. They work in hospitals and private laboratories.)

Questioned document examiners are best known for their expertise in handwriting analysis, but they also perform a wide range of analyses that include just about any type of surface and mark—from subway graffiti to computer printouts. In the profession of document examination, the word *document* is broadly defined. It can mean any sign or symbol that is written, printed, or inscribed on a surface to convey a message from one person to another. Questioned document examiners may also be experts in the analysis of ink, paper, writing tools, typewriters, printers, and copy machines.

Serologists and geneticists are part of a larger group of forensic biologists. Serologists work specifically with body fluids. They identify blood, sperm, saliva, and other biological fluids. They also determine blood types. Often they are called to analyze residues of fluids recovered from clothing or discarded items at crime scenes.

During the 1980s, advances in the field of genetics made DNA analysis practical. By the 1990s many crime laboratories were sending samples to private laboratories or installing their own dedicated laboratories. Today, forensic geneticists are fully incorporated into many crime labs. For identification purposes, they utilize the **FBI Laboratory's Combined DNA Index System** (CODIS). This system allows laboratories to exchange profiles and seek out DNA matches with the same ease as fingerprint matches.

At first, it appeared that the move to DNA analysis would negate the need for serologists. However, human identification is not the only question in a crime. Serologists are needed to identify the source of the DNA. It is still important to know from which body fluid the DNA is extracted. The presence of saliva has very different implications from the presence of semen. Also, serological tests work well for rapid preliminary testing. They are inexpensive and help to separate out specific evidence for further testing thereby reducing the burden of carrying out expensive tests on items of no evidentiary value.

Toxicologists are chemists who specialize in extracting drugs and poisons from body tissues and fluids. Typically, blood and/or urine samples are sent to the toxicologist if there is a question of alcohol or drug overdose or impairment, carbon monoxide poisoning, or lead or arsenic poisoning. The toxicologist may also extract and identify a wide range of other foreign substances from tissue samples.

Scientists Typically Consulted by Crime Laboratories in Death Investigation Cases

The following is a short list, in alphabetical order, of forensic scientists typically consulted by crime laboratories and/or medical examiner's offices for death investigation cases. These specialists are seldom employed full-time by the average crime lab unless they are working in other capacities as well. (Many other consultants serve the forensic sciences in capacities not related to death investigation.)

Forensic anthropologists are typically physical or biological anthropologists with a strong background in human osteology. They apply their knowledge of anthropology to legal issues such as recovery, analysis, description, and identification of human remains. Other anthropologists, particularly archaeologists, are included by many within this title or given the more specific title, forensic archaeologist. More information is contained in Chapter 1.

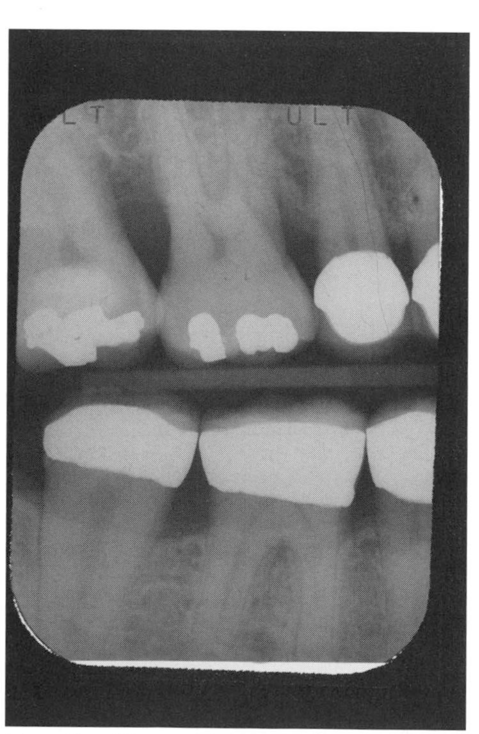

Julian Chen/Shutterstock.com

Forensic odontologists (also called forensic dentists) are dentists with additional training in the use of dental evidence for human identification. Some also specialize in bitemark analysis. They have knowledge of oral anatomy and pathology, radiography, dental materials, and restoration methods. They also have a familiarity with the wide variety of methods for charting and annotating used by dentists.

There are at least three computerized dental identification systems utilized by forensic odontologists. Probably the most popular is the **WinID Dental Identification System**.

Forensic entomologists are specialists in the life cycles of the insects that are attracted to decomposing bodies (necrophagous or carrion-feeding insects). They are not involved in human identification as are the anthropologist and odontologist. Instead, they contribute to the determination of time since death and sometimes, the analysis of perimortem trauma when it is not known if damage to the body can be attributed to insect or human action.

Forensic entomologists also study the arthropod pests that contribute to disease and death through food contamination. In addition, they testify on cases of abuse and neglect where insect evidence is present.

Forensic botanists bring their knowledge of plants, plant life cycles and ecology to legal cases. They identify plants, seeds, and trace evidence such as pollen. They are capable of calculating the season of burial based on the succession of plants on disturbed ground and plant reside found in fill dirt. They can also determine the origin of plant residue based on knowledge of plant ecology.

Choosing the Correct Forensic Specialist in Death Investigation Cases

When human remains are involved, law enforcement officers have to decide who to involve in the recovery and documentation. The medical examiner or death investigator is called first, but who else is required to adequately process the remains?

As time passes, physical evidence changes. If a scene is preserved, it is probably because it is covered—usually with dirt. If anything remains of the body, it is most commonly the hard tissues of the skeleton and the teeth. With sufficient time, the focus of an investigation changes from crime scene and autopsy to excavation and skeletal analysis. The forensic specialists also change. In historic and ancient cases, the archaeologist replaces the crime scene investigator, and the physical anthropologist replaces the forensic pathologist.

The person in charge of an investigation should be able to recognize when one specialist might be more effective than another. For the dead body, this question can be answered by taking a careful look at the processes at work on the time line of death and decay. There are two critical points—loss of visual identification of the remains and change in legal consequence regarding the death. Neither point can be pinpointed precisely, because they are both subject to environmental and legal factors.

When No Visual Identification is Possible

The first critical point on the time line occurs when simple visual identification of the body is no longer possible. This may be the result of decomposition, burning, or disarticulation. Beyond this point, the remains can no longer be recognized by relatives or friends.

When There is No Immediate Legal Consequence

The second critical point on the time line is the loss of immediate legal consequence with regard to identification or death investigation. Beyond this point, it is unlikely (although not impossible) that identification or knowledge of manner of death will result in legal action on issues such as homicide, inheritance, or life insurance claims. Most statutes of limitations are exceeded, the concerned relatives or friends are dead, and the person who may be responsible for the death is dead. Discoveries of remains beyond this point are classified as historical or ancient deaths.

There are, of course, legal consequences to disturbing graves of any time period, but the laws vary by jurisdiction with the exception of Native American graves. They are federally protected by the Native American Graves Protection and Repatriation Act (NAGPRA), Pub. L. No. 101-601, 104 Stat. 3048 (1990).

In Table 12.2, note which specialists are most appropriate for investigation of the scene and the analysis of the body in each section of the time line. The involvement of forensically-trained anthropologists is most important in the years between loss of visual identification and loss of immediate legal consequence.

Table 12.2 Choice of Specialist

The most appropriate specialist for the job is determined by (1) the condition of the body and (2) the legal consequences of the investigation.

	RECENT DEATH	THE YEARS IN BETWEEN	ANCIENT DEATH
VISUAL IDENTIFICATION	possible	not possible	not possible
LEGAL CONSEQUENCES	immediate	immediate or uncertain	limited
INVESTIGATION OF THE SCENE	office of medical examiner or coroner	office of medical examiner or coroner with forensic anthropologists and archaeologists	archaeologist
ANALYSIS OF THE REMAINS	forensic pathologist forensic odontologist	forensic anthropologist forensic odontologist	physical anthropologist

CASE EXAMPLES: INTERDISCIPLINARY INVESTIGATIONS

Critical Evidence from the Document Examiner

A box of bones, ragged clothing, and assorted garbage had gathered dust in the back of a government morgue for many months. There had been little hope of identifying the incomplete remains found in an empty city lot, so other cases were given priority.

When I took custody of the box, I sorted the contents and found three plastic hospital identification bracelets. They were badly weathered and no ink was visible, but I knew that questioned document examiners often use alternative light sources to reveal hidden ink. Within the hour, the questioned document examiner had a tentative identification, and before the week was over, a positive identification was established by multiple radiographic comparisons.

Critical Evidence from the Fingerprint Examiner

A police officer had been working on an unidentified person case. A pathologist had told him to look for a missing woman in her mid-twenties, but no matches had surfaced in six long months of searching. Finally, the officer decided to ask for help through another jurisdiction. After examining the skeleton, I explained that the officer would have to look for a teenaged male, not an older female. More important, I also noted that the remains included mummified fingers that could be printed. The 18-year-old male was positively identified by fingerprint comparison. His remains were returned to his family in a foreign country for burial.

CHAPTER 13

Laboratory Analysis

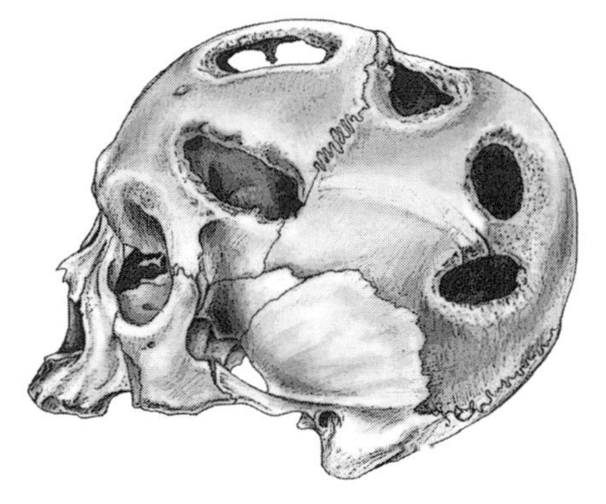

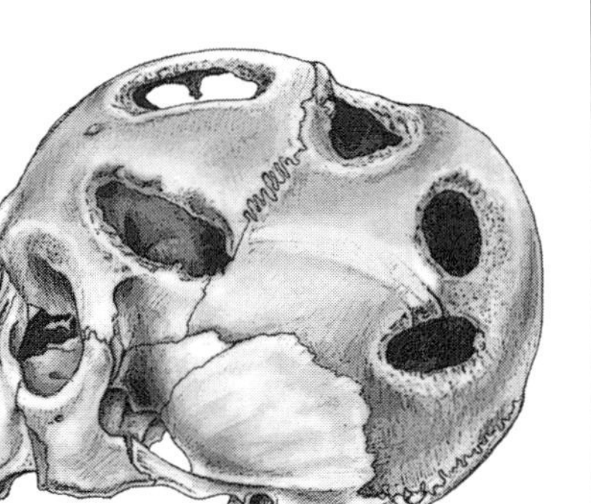

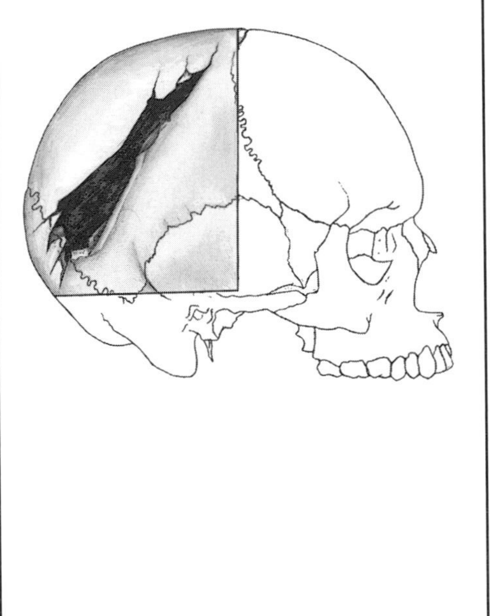

CHAPTER OUTLINE

Introduction

Analysis is the examination and study of a whole item through the study of its component parts. An analysis can be descriptive (qualitative) or numerical (quantitative). The objective of skeletal analysis is information—the maximum amount possible. It is usually both qualitative and quantitative. Description and identification of the deceased are only parts of the desired result. The full skeletal analysis should also provide insight into the activities of the deceased, the circumstances surrounding death, the postmortem interval (time since death), and the fate of the remains during that interval. This information can be powerful if handled correctly.

The investigator has a responsibility to the evidence throughout the process of analysis and beyond. For this reason, a good skeletal analysis should be approached like the crime scene itself. Stop, look, and record at every step. Avoid the tendency to rush through the mundane in search of something "interesting." Keep track of everything, even changes of opinion. Organize the process from the beginning to the end—from the laboratory design to the final testimony. Maintain a careful sequence of analysis throughout. The sequence is presented in the following list, and the details of each step are provided in the following sections.

Basic Sequence of Analysis

1. Prepare the laboratory.
2. Manage the evidence through numbers, files and forms.
3. Inventory the evidence.
4. Transfer nonskeletal evidence to the appropriate specialists.
5. Clean and stabilize the evidence.
6. Analyze the evidence.
7. Preserve samples for further analysis.
8. Return the evidence or store in a secure place.
9. Report all findings.

Preparation for Analysis

Physical Facility

There are three basic requirements for a good physical facility—security, space, and utilities. Security is most important. Without security for the evidence, nothing else matters. Space is second. There must be sufficient space for at least three separate areas with lockable doors between each—receiving, analysis, and storage. Each area has a different level of access/security.

> **Note**
>
> Many different structures can be used as temporary laboratories—barns, garages, and even tents will work. Tables can be created from sawhorses and plywood. Lights can be battery operated. Running water may be difficult to obtain, but buckets can suffice. The hardest thing to arrange is security.

The **receiving area** is the least secure because it is the point where evidence changes hands and enters the system. The receiving area can also be the office area as long as no evidence or reports are stored there.

The **analysis area** is accessible only to the employees. It needs to be large enough to allow for separate work areas, including wet and dry areas, and large tables. The analysis area must have adequate lighting and be cleanable. It is helpful to have dividers between individual work areas.

The **storage area** is the area of highest security. It is locked at all times, and only designated persons have access. It should not have windows, but it needs to be cool and dry. Good organization is essential and adequate shelving is important.

Equipment, Supplies, and Reference Materials

Basic Equipment

- Sliding calipers or dial calipers
- Spreading calipers
- Osteometric board or tree calipers
- Brushes, picks, and other small instruments
- Large tables or plywood and sawhorses
- Chairs or benches
- Camera with macro capability and supplies
- Extra lights and extension cords
- Background cloth for photos
- Gauge or ruler to include in photographs
- Colanders, trays, buckets, tubs
- Computer and printer
- Software: spreadsheet, word processor, and osteological analysis
- Chalkboard or whiteboard
- Hot plate
- Hot wax glue gun
- Dust pan and brush

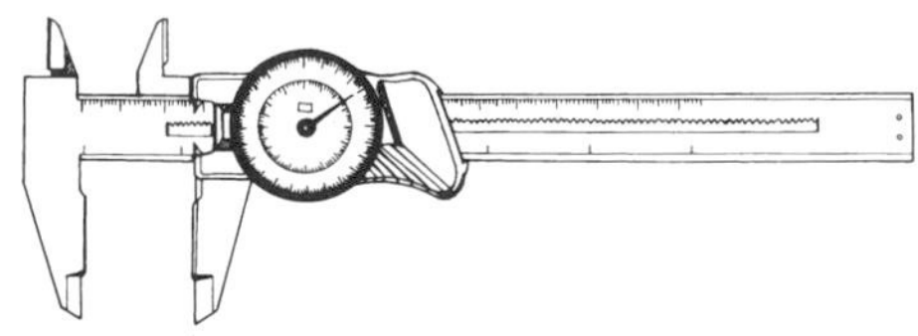

Figure 13.1a
Dial Calipers

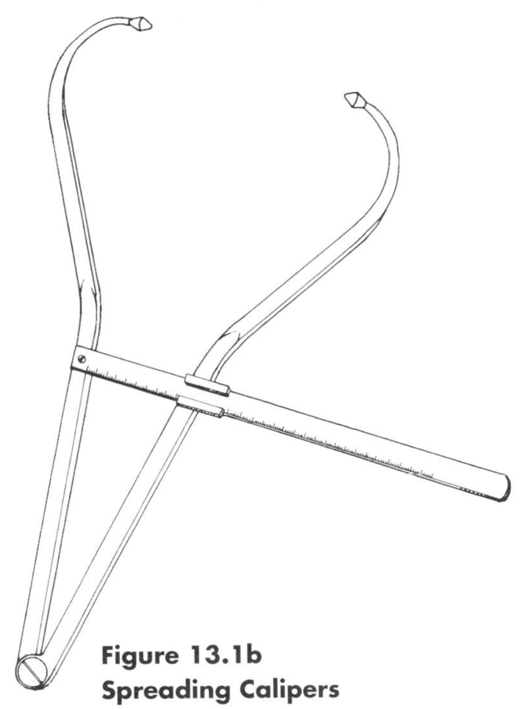

Figure 13.1b
Spreading Calipers

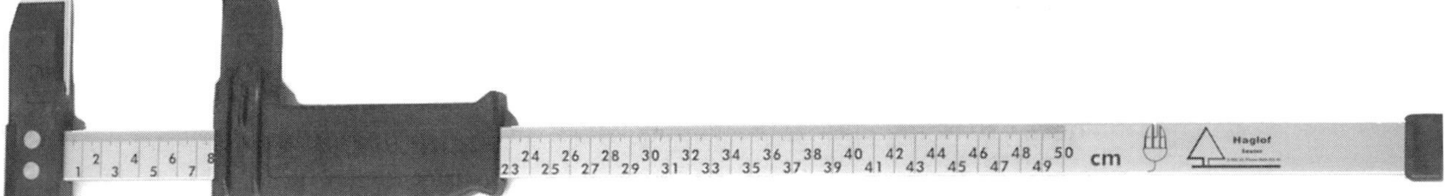

Figure 13.1c
Tree Calipers
Modified for measuring long bones (www.haglofsweden.com)

Basic Supplies

- Cards for labels
- Pens—indelible ink and others
- Osteometric forms, notebooks
- Soap and other cleaning supplies
- Brown paper or plastic table covers (the paper cover is good for quick notes)
- Glue, tape
- Chalk (for handedness determination)
- Rubber gloves and surgical gloves
- Bags, boxes, and packing material

REFERENCE MATERIALS

Reference materials are essential to good skeletal analysis. Begin with the following casts, charts, and reference books and add others whenever possible.

Instructional Skeletons or Casts

- Disarticulated human skull
- Juvenile skull
- Postcranial skeleton
- Suchey–Brooks pubic symphysis plastic cast sets for males and females
- Işcan–Loth sternal rib end plastic cast sets for females and males

Charts and Photographs

- Anatomical charts for the adult skeleton and juvenile epiphyseal union
- Dental charts for adult dentition and juvenile calcification and eruption sequence

Books

- *Juvenile Osteology, A Laboratory and Field Manual*, 2009, by M. Schaefer, S. Black, and L. Scheuer.
- *Identification of Pathological Conditions in Human Skeletal Remains*, 2003, by D. J. Ortner
- *Data Collection Procedures for Forensic Skeletal Material*, 1994, by P. M. Moore-Jansen, S. D. Ousley, and R. L. Jantz
- *Standards for Data Collection from Human Skeletal Remains*, 1994, edited by J. E. Buikstra and D. H. Ubelaker
- *Classification of Musculoskeletal Trauma*, 1999, P. B. Pynsent, J. C. T. Fairbank, and A. J. Carr (if you are dealing regularly with trauma cases)
- A general anatomy textbook

OPTIONAL EQUIPMENT (DEPENDING ON TYPE AND EXTENT OF ANALYSIS)

- Refrigerator
- Power bone saw
- Radiographic equipment
- Thin sectioning saw
- Microscope
- 3-D digitizer
- Scale

EVIDENCE MANAGEMENT

ASSIGN CASE NUMBER

The case number is issued and entered into a database when custody is initiated and the material "enters the system." This should happen first at the time of recovery. If the same agency remains in control, the original number may be sufficient, but if another agency is in charge of the laboratory, a new number is issued as the evidence enters the new system. The old number is noted in the records. A single piece of evidence can accumulate a list of case numbers over time.

If you are initiating a numbering system, think it through carefully. Begin by defining *case* for your use. Is it a single individual, an excavation, a site location, a specific job, or a single piece of evidence? The case number should provide a sufficient amount of information to be easy to use and maintain continuity over time. The information should include some reference to the agency or consultant, date, location, and specific unit. It should be ordered from the most general to the most specific so that it is sortable and searchable. For example, consider the number, HBI-06-BW-132: HBI is the agency abbreviation or the consultant's initials; 06 is the year; BW is an abbreviation for the site or location; and 132 is the unit number at the BW site. Each part of the alphanumeric system is a subset of the previous part.

If additional subsets are found (such as fragments of an unexpected second individual) letters can be appended to case numbers (e.g., HBI-06-BW-132a and HBI-06-BW-132b).

Organize Database

The database can be computerized or based on a simple logbook, but it must be backed up and kept secure. The database should include the following information:

- Case number
- Any other numbers associated with the evidence
- All dates and times (receipt, change in custody, release)
- Names of persons in the chain of custody
- Description of packaging (e.g., plain brown cardboard box, 13 × 14 × 9 inches, taped with duct tape and initialed over the tape border)
- Basic description of the evidence (e.g., clay-covered bones, miscellaneous clothing, hair)
- Procedures requested and performed
- Reports submitted
- Disposition of the evidence (To whom was custody released? Provide date, name, and address.)

Prepare Case File

Every agency has standard procedures for creating and maintaining case files. This section provides an overview for students and independent consultants who are creating a case file for the first time.

A case file can be contained in a notebook or file folder. It can also be completely digital. The file should contain the chain of custody form, a checklist of procedures, a photographic log, and all forms pertinent to the case. Each form should include the case number, date, and name of investigator. The case file stays with the case during analysis, even if more than one person examines the case. There should be no stray notes or separate records.

The photographic log provides a record of all photos for the case. It is impossible to go back for missed photos, so plan ahead. There should be photos of the original condition, the inventory as a whole, and specific areas of interest, both in context and close-up. If the final state of the evidence is different from the initial state, a photo should be taken before storage.

A series of forms are included in the Appendix. Use them as they are or use them as a starting point from which to develop new forms to fit specific needs. The major categories of laboratory forms include a skeletal inventory form, measurement forms, and diagrams of skeletons, skulls, and teeth.

> **Note**
>
> Except in government laboratories, most lab notes are not read by anyone but the analyst/investigator. But occasionally, highly sensitive cases will require that all notes be turned over to the court along with the report. Be complete, but avoid writing anything you cannot explain in court.

Inventory and Record Initial Observations

Begin recording information from the time the container is opened. This is an opportunity to note gut reactions, strange smells, and other oddities before you begin to get used to them.

Lay out the bones in anatomical order or a practical modification thereof, and fill out an inventory form. The Bone Inventory Form in the Appendix is provided for this purpose. Use the diagrams of the full skeleton, skull, thorax,

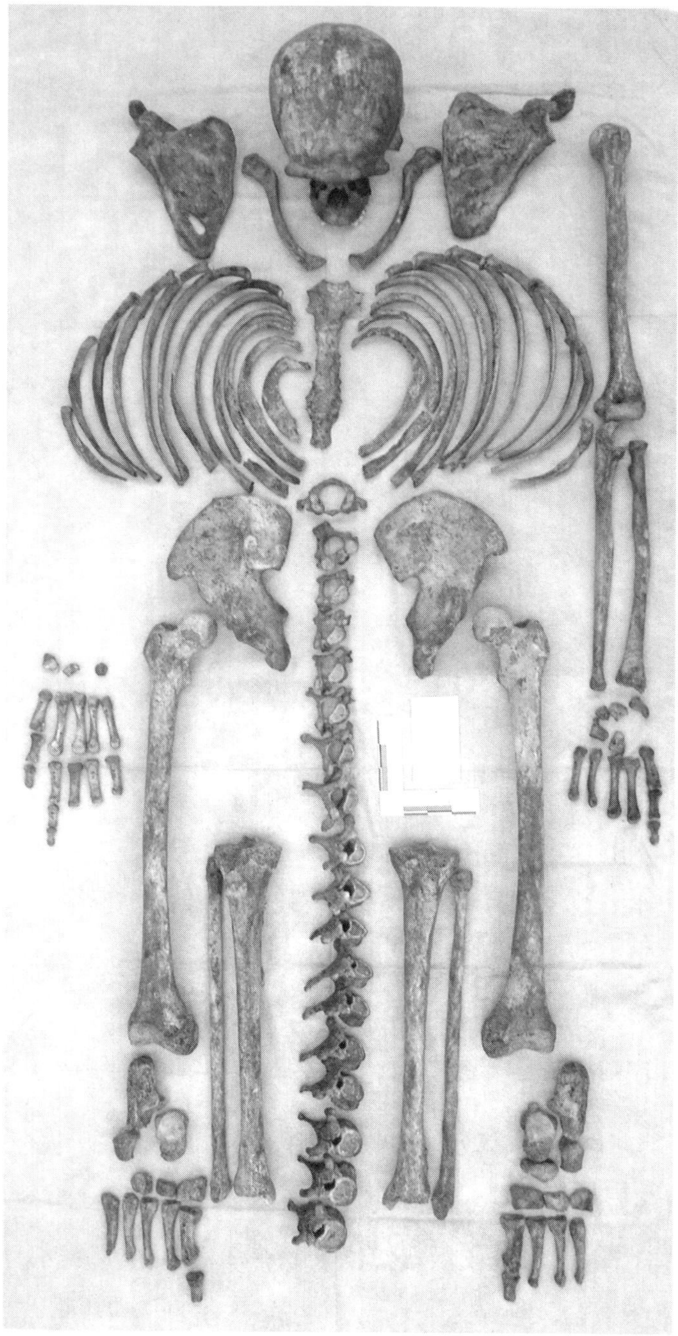

Figure 13.2
Inventory Photo
The skeleton is laid out in an unconventional pattern, but the right and left elements are on the correct sides and it is easy to ascertain what is missing from the assemblage. The objective is to try to photograph everything in one frame. Close-up pictures can then be referenced to the inventory photo.

pelvis, hands, and feet to supplement the inventory forms. It is important to have both written and graphic records.

Use this time to examine each element in detail. Note anomalies for future examination. It may be necessary to find comparative material, refer to textbooks, or discuss the case with colleagues before reaching conclusions.

Record all observations at this time, for example:

- Stains of any type (blood, metal oxides, insects, leaves, etc.)
- Sun bleaching or erosion
- Tool marks
- Tooth marks (carnivore, rodent, etc.)
- Anything that may seem out of place such as sand in the ear canal of remains recovered in nonsandy soil

Be clear about your own degree of certainty. Use expressions such as "possible" or "consistent with" when there is any uncertainty whatsoever. Return to these notes when you review the case to confirm that you have followed through on all aspects of the initial examination.

Transfer Nonanthropological Evidence

It is not uncommon for anthropologists to receive a box of bones from a police investigation and find that it still contains evidence that falls within the expertise of a different specialist. When nonanthropological evidence is discovered, record it. Then see that it is transferred to the appropriate specialist through standard chain-of-custody procedures. Examples include bullets, hair and fibers, mummified fingers with ridge detail, insects, clothing, jewelry, and even personal papers.

Clean and Stabilize the Evidence

Clean and stabilize the evidence if necessary. The type and amount of cleaning is dependent on the condition of the evidence and future analysis or use. Avoid destructive procedures unless absolutely necessary for purposes of analysis. The objective is to be able to evaluate the evidence, not to make it more pleasant to work with.

Any specimen that is to be used for DNA analysis should be treated with special care from the point of collection. Less handling is always better. Contact the genetics laboratory for preservation and packing instructions. DNA laboratories usually prefer to send their own containers for packing and shipping.

Dry bones can usually be cleaned with soft brushes. If the dirt is overly adherent, use water but do not soak. Dry in open air and store in a breathable container such as paper or cardboard.

Marks from knife blades, embedded metal fragments, and stains are more visible after cleaning, but great care must be taken to avoid altering the marks for microscopic examination. Numerous pathological conditions are also visible after exposure of the bone surface, but such evidence may be exceedingly fragile and easily damaged.

Water-soluble glues and plastics have been suggested for extremely fragile material, but form-fitting packaging may be a better alternative. Do not use any stabilizer without thoroughly studying the effects and being certain that the process will aid, and not endanger, future analysis. Plastics can be painted on with a soft brush or sprayed on. Several thin coats, each allowed to dry, are preferable to one thick application. Note that acetone dehydration is necessary before the use of plastics.

Check all teeth for stability within the sockets and overall integrity. Single-rooted teeth tend to fall out at inopportune moments. Loss or breakage is the result. Teeth are maintained better if they are left in the alveolar bone. The alveolar bone is also less likely to chip. A tiny drop of adhesive material in the correct tooth socket works to hold the tooth in place without harming it for future study. It can be removed with an appropriate solvent. (Do not alter any teeth necessary for age-related studies or DNA analysis.)

Tooth enamel dries over time and cracks easily. Coat the teeth with a non-erosive, protective glaze if necessary. Also use care in packing and setting on tables. Skulls and teeth are less likely to sustain damage if they are placed upside down in ring-type cushions. These can be made of cork, foam, cloth, acid-free plastic wrap, or any other nonabrasive, nonreactive substance.

Cleaning procedures are very different for fleshed remains. The challenge is to remove all the soft tissue (both external and internal) and the bulk of the natural oils without damaging the bone or loosing evidence that may be present on the bone surface.

Short-term cleanup for quick examination of a bone surface can be done with warm water and soap, but long-term preservation and storage requires much more time and care. The very best results are obtained from professionals such as Skulls Unlimited International, Inc. Understandably, they charge for the service and their specific methods are proprietary. Nevertheless, they have generously shared a few recommendations (Eric Humphries, personal communication, July 6, 2011).

- Never boil human bones.
- Never use ammonia or chlorinated solutions.
- Wash in warm water, but don't soak.
- Use dermestid beetles (*Dermestes maculatus*) for defleshing.

Dermestid beetles are commonly known as skin beetles. They feed on dried skin and other (dried) tissues in the wild, and they can be utilized in the laboratory for slow, non-destructive cleaning of bone. They are not, by the way, easy to maintain. A beetle colony will fail to thrive if humidity and temperature are not controlled. They will not consume wet flesh, so bones must be macerated and somewhat dry before introducing them to the colony. The beetles will also reject overly dry tissue, so moisture sometimes needs to be added. It usually requires months to clean an entire skeleton.

Dermestids can be a serious threat to other collections such as animal skins or natural-fiber clothing. Therefore, great care must be taken to keep the colony confined within a glass or metal tank.

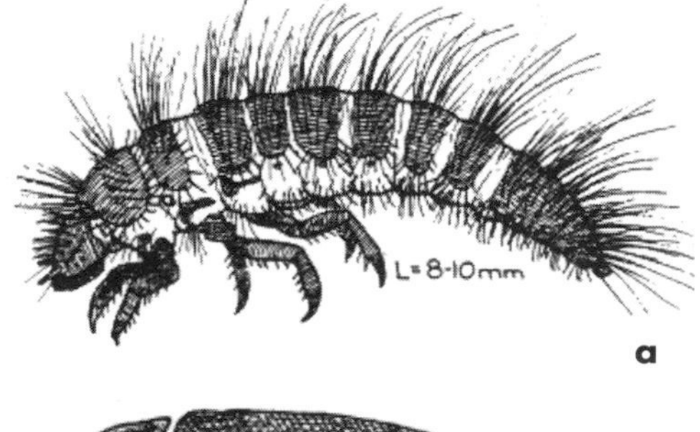

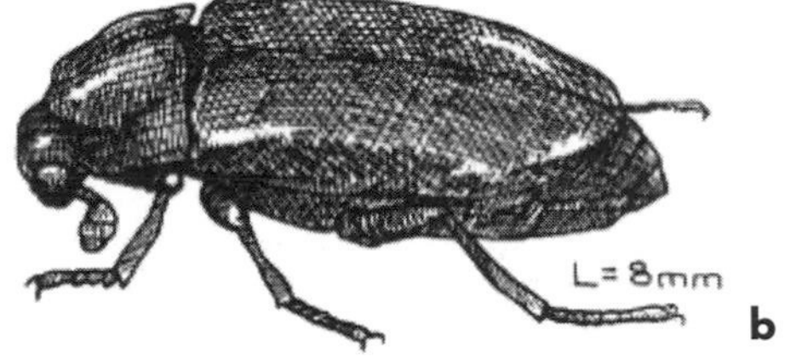

Figure 13.3
Dermestidae (Skin Beetles), Larva and Adult
Illustration by E. Paul Catts. (Catts & Haskell, 1990).

Skeletal Analysis and Description

The methods for sex and age determination from individual bones are presented in the specific bone chapters. This section provides an overview of methods and a place to discuss methods involving more than one bone, such as stature estimation.

Minimum Number of Individuals

Take time to confirm the number of individuals during the inventory. In typical single-individual cases, there will be no more than one of each skeletal element. (Supernumary teeth and sesamoid bones are exceptions.)

Many forensic cases, however, involve clandestine burials, mass graves, intrusive burials, or disturbed burials. In any of these situations, accurate assessment of the number of individuals is accomplished by searching for duplicate elements. The presence of something as simple as two right third metacarpals or two left distal ulnar fragments indicates the presence of a second individual.

The **minimum number of individuals (MNI)** is just that—a minimum. It may not be the actual number of individuals, but it is as close as one can get with certainty. The **actual number of individuals** is either the same as the MNI or more. There are statistical methods for estimating the actual number of individuals from the minimum number of individuals (Adams, 2005), but experience and common sense are useful, too. If the remains are in good condition and relatively complete, the MNI is probably the same as the actual number. If the remains are in poor condition, fragmented, or commingled, the MNI may be less than the actual number of individuals.

CASE EXAMPLES: THE MINIMUM NUMBER OF INDIVIDUALS (MNI)

Why bother to determine the minimum number of individuals (MNI)? MNI may be one of the only results possible. Under such conditions, MNI can be the one critical piece of physical evidence that supports or refutes verbal testimony.

A Mass Grave

During the Guatemalan civil war, villagers reported the location of a mass grave and requested an exhumation. Before the official exhumation could begin, someone else removed the remains in an attempt to destroy evidence of the massacre and discredit the testimony of the villagers.

We went ahead with the excavation and recovered bones from the hands and feet of the victims as well as several unfused epiphyses from a teenager. The skeletal analysis revealed an MNI of six, based solely on the left first cuneiform. None of the epiphyses were duplicated; therefore, only one of the six was confirmed to be teenaged.

The villagers had testified that five adult men and one teenaged boy disappeared just before the time that the area of recently disturbed earth was found in a nearby forest. The villagers' claims were supported by the physical evidence.

A Cemetery Relocation

A cemetery relocation firm in the United States was contracted to move a large unmarked cemetery prior to redevelopment of the site. Since the number of graves was unknown, the contractor was to be paid by the number of graves moved rather than for the job as a whole.

Previous landowners estimated that the area contained approximately two thousand separate graves. The relocation firm, however, reburied more than four thousand boxes of bones! Suspicion was finally aroused, and I was asked to find a way to examine the work of the cemetery relocation firm.

I disinterred forty of the four thousand boxes and found the MNI to be eighteen. The skeletal elements were in good condition, but there was significant postmortem breakage. It is possible that more than eighteen individuals were present, but it is highly unlikely that forty individual graves were represented. The firm was charged with fraud.

A third category is the estimate of the **probable number of individuals**. This can be based on differences in size, age, sex, or state of decomposition. For example, the presence of a left and a right humerus indicates an MNI of one, but if the humeri are of different lengths, age, or type of staining, a probable number of two can be reported as long as the reason for the opinion is clearly explained.

Age

Age-related changes fall into two categories—formative and degenerative. **Formative changes** such as dental eruption and epiphyseal union occur during growth and development. **Degenerative changes** such as dental wear and osteoarthritis result from the process of aging and generalized trauma. The body is never static. In any one area of the body, degenerative changes begin as soon as formative changes are completed. Several of the changes even overlap during the twenties—some developmental changes are just reaching completion (e.g., the clavicle) while others have already begun to show degeneration (e.g., the pubic symphysis).

There are many methods available for estimating age, and each has advantages and limitations. Keep in mind that no aging method is even close to 100 percent accurate. There are two sources of error: (1) individual variation as reported in the standard deviation of the method, and (2) differences between the sample population and the population of origin. Unfortunately, the population of origin for an unidentified body is usually unknown.

No aging method should be used alone unless there is no choice. Choice of method is, of course, limited when incomplete or fragmentary remains are the only material available.

Always provide a range when estimating age. It is far better to include a 10- to 20-year age range, especially in older individuals, and succeed in matching the missing person by other characteristics than to give a 3- to 5-year range and miss the identification entirely.

Methods for estimating age from specific bones are covered in the relevant chapters. (Chapter 4 contains methods related to the clavicles and ribs; Chapter 5, vertebral bodies; Chapter 8, the pubic symphysis; and Chapter 11, teeth.)

Sex

Sex is a little easier than age because there are supposed to be only two possibilities. In truth, the human animal is not neatly divided into female and male types. Sexual variation is better visualized as an overlapping set of normal curves. Many people fall in the area of overlap and some fall in the tails. And this is just a normal population. If you wish to investigate the abnormal, read about diseases of the endocrine system. There is more than one condition that causes masculinization of the female genotype and vice versa.

Table 13.1 summarizes basic sexual differences in the normal pelvis, skull, ribs, and sternum. Details are found in the chapters that discuss each bone.

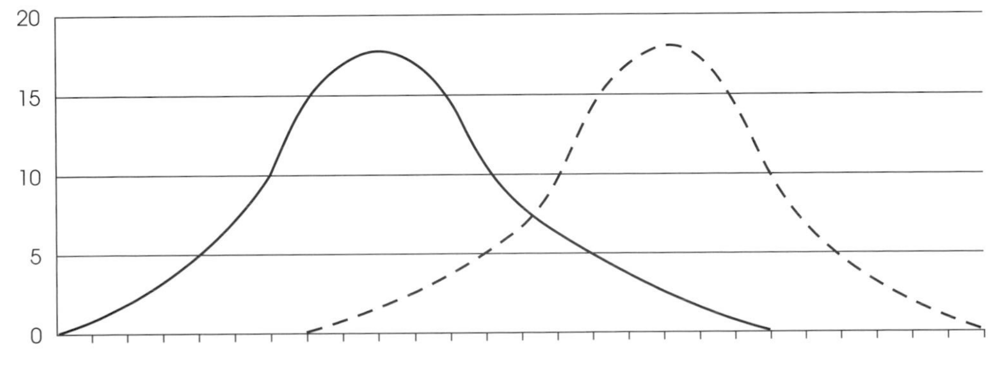

Figure 13.4 Typical Bimodal Distribution of Sexual Variables

The expression of sexual traits is highly variable, and considerable overlap is normal.

Table 13.1 Sexual Differences in the Skeleton

The Bone	The Differences	Male	Female
	overall size	larger	smaller
	muscle attachments	larger	smaller
PUBIS	pubic length	short	long
	ventral arc	absent	present
	subpubic concavity	absent	present
	subpubic angle	narrow	wide
	ischiopubic ramus	wide	narrow, "stretched"
	parturition pits	absent	sometimes present
ILIUM	preauricular sulcus	absent	often present
	sciatic notch	narrow	wide
FEMUR	femoral head diameter (Stewart, 1979)	possible: 46.5–47.5 mm probable: >47.5 mm	possible: 42.5–43.5 mm probable: <42.5 mm
FRONTAL	supraorbital ridge frontal bossing	prominent double boss	absent single central boss
TEMPORAL	mastoid process zygomatic process length	large; extends to the external auditory meatus and beyond	small; ends before the external auditory meatus
OCCIPITAL	nuchal ridges	strong muscle attachment	slight muscle attachment
MANDIBLE	ramus chin shape	wide and sharply angled square	narrow and less angled rounded or pointed
RIB	subperichondrial ossification	marginal ossification	central foci of ossification
STERNUM	sternum length	the body is more than twice the manubrium length	the body is less than twice the manubrium length

Race

Race is both a biological and a cultural concept. It is confusing because it encompasses everything from skin color to family origin, nationality, ethnicity, religion, and more. The politically charged connotations of the word *race* make racial analysis the most difficult aspect of human identification. Obviously, the analysis of skeletal remains must rely on biological information. However, the report must communicate to nonbiologists—police, attorneys, judges, and juries. The challenge is to achieve effective communication about an imprecise concept/term.

The subject of racial identification is addressed in Chapter 14.

Handedness

In a group of unidentified persons, the lone left-handed person might be more easily identified if he or she can be recognized and separated from the majority. As much as 90 percent of the human population is predominantly right-handed. Among the remaining group, a great deal of variability exists. Some people are strongly left-handed. Others are ambidextrous; they are left-handed for some activities and right-handed for others.

The hand an individual prefers is in part genetically determined, but the precise ways in which genes affect handedness are still being researched. It is not simple inheritance (i.e., two right-handed parents can have a left-handed child or vice versa).

The methods of recognizing handedness in skeletal remains are imprecise. The question is difficult to study in skeletal populations because there are seldom records of handedness as there are of stature, sex, and race. It is usually necessary to interview the family to obtain the information.

One thing is certain—the majority of skeletons are asymmetrical. The right arm is usually longer and the left leg is usually longer. It is generally accepted among anthropologists that the dominant arm tends to be the longer one. Look for any other sign of unequal use between the arms. Compare the right and left arms for inequality in major muscle attachment areas—the deltoid tuberosity of the humerus and the radial tuberosity of the radius. Examine the elbow area for differences in osteoarthritic changes that may indicate increased use of one side over the other. Also see Chapter 4 for illustrations of differences in the glenoid fossa of the scapula.

STATURE

Stature (height) is usually determined by measuring long bones and comparing the measurement with average measurements from large databases (Trotter & Gleser, 1952). Stature can also be estimated from full skeletal measurements (Fully & Pineau, 1960) or from specific segments of the vertebral column (Tibbetts, 1981; Pelin et al., 2005). The formulae vary by sex and race, so it is advisable to know the sex and race of the subject before beginning stature analysis.

Long bones are usually measured on an osteometric board. The large sliding calipers used by foresters for measuring tree diameters are also very useful. (Tree calipers are also more portable than most osteometric boards.)

MEASUREMENT SYSTEMS

It is easy to become confused when moving from one measurement system to another. People in the United States usually know just how tall a 5 foot 3 inch woman is, but they find it hard to imagine 160 centimeters. One system is adequate within any single group of people, but scientists and international workers need to be flexible.

Bone measurements are recorded in millimeters and stature estimation formulae utilize the metric system. The final results should be reported in the system or systems of common use so that they are fully available to the readers. Table 13.2 Quick Conversion Table for Stature Measurements

OSTEOMETRY

Osteometry is the measurement of bone. The process is usually called **osteometrics**, and the two words are often interchanged. Bones are measured in many different ways for a variety of purposes. Some bone measurements are obvious, such as maximum length. Other measurements require knowledge of bone anatomy and written instructions with illustrations. Complete methods for measuring human bones are given in Data Collection Procedures for Forensic Skeletal Material by Moore-Jansen et al. (1994). Illustrations and explanations are also available in the help files of the Fordisc software program.

Most long bone measurements are simple maximum lengths. This includes the measurement of the humerus, radius, ulna, femur, and fibula. The tibia is a bit more complicated. It is measured from the superior articular surface of the lateral condyle to the tip of the medial malleolus. In other words, the intercondylar eminence is not part of the measurement. Use tree calipers or an osteometric board with a hole or notch to allow for the intercondylar eminence.

The femur is sometimes measured with both condyles in contact with the osteometric board. This is called the **bicondylar length** or **oblique length** and is particularly useful because it orients the femur in anatomical position. Bicondylar length provides information about sex as well as stature. (See Q-angle in Figure 9.1c on page 126.)

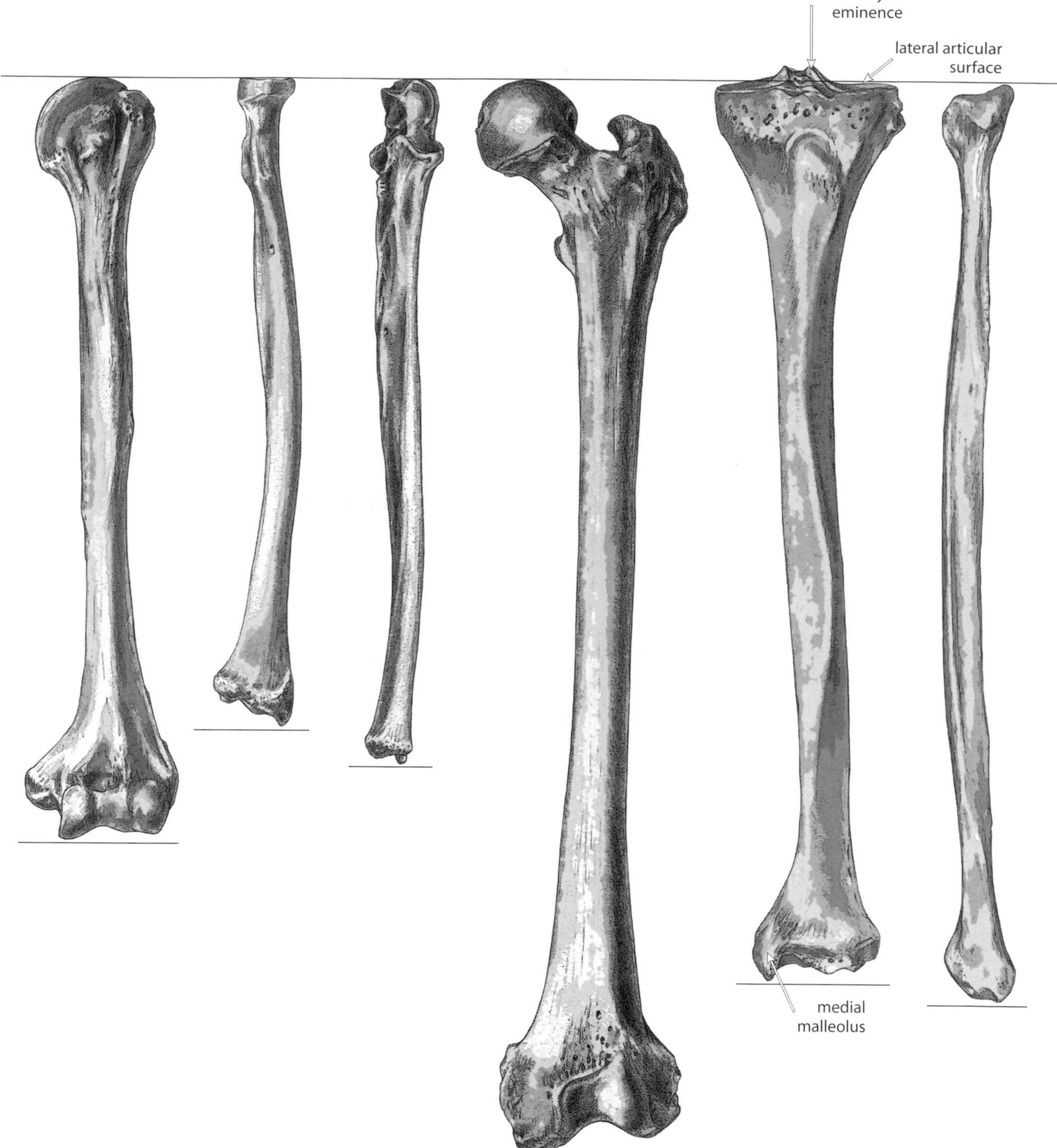

Figure 13.5
Long Bone Measurements

Maximum length is measured as illustrated for the major long bones. In all but the tibia, maximum length is the greatest possible length from the most extreme points of the bone. For the tibia, the standard length measurement is the **condylomalleolar length**. It is measured from the superior surface of the lateral condyle to the tip of the medial malleolus. The intercondylar eminence is excluded, as shown.

STATURE DETERMINATION BY FORMULAE

After measuring each bone according to instructions (see Figure 13.4), insert the measurement into the appropriate formulae (discussed next). For example, if the unidentified person is a white male and the measurement of the humerus is 32.7 centimeters, the first formula in Table 13.3 is the correct one to use:

Stature = (2.89 × 32.7) + 78.10 = 172.6 cm ± 4.57 cm standard deviation

The predicted height of the unknown person is 168.0–177.2 centimeters, 66.1–69.8 inches, or 5 feet 6 inches to 5 feet 10 inches. This may seem like a wide range (the prediction interval from the femur would be a little narrower), but think about the goal: identification. It is better to give a wide range and search a few more records for the missing person than to give too narrow a range and miss the chance at a successful identification.

STATURE ERRORS FROM SELF-REPORTING AND FAULTY MEMORY

Stature estimates are complicated by more than biological variation. The estimate may be accurate, while the records of the missing person are entirely wrong. Many records of height are self-reported verbal estimates. Self-reported height tends to be exaggerated (or sometimes diminished) according to the wishes of the individual.

Friends and family have problems remembering the height of a person they have not seen recently. Strangely enough, much-admired people tend to "grow" after death!

Table 13.2 Stature Formulae

Race/Sex	Bone	Formula (cm)	S.D.	Race/Sex	Bone	Formula (cm)	S.D.
EUROPEAN MALE	humerus	2.89 humerus + 78.10	±4.57	**AFRICAN MALE**	humerus	2.88 humerus + 75.48	±4.23
	radius	3.79 radius + 79.42	±4.66		radius	3.32 radius + 85.43	±4.57
	ulna	3.76 ulna + 75.55	±4.72		ulna	3.20 ulna + 80.77	±4.74
	femur	2.32 femur + 65.53	±3.94		femur	2.10 femur + 72.22	±3.91
	tibia	2.42 tibia + 81.93	±4.00		tibia	2.19 tibia + 85.36	±3.96
	fibula	2.60 fibula + 75.50	±3.86		fibula	2.34 fibula + 80.07	±4.02
EUROPEAN FEMALE	humerus	3.36 humerus + 57.97	±4.45	**AFRICAN FEMALE**	humerus	3.08 humerus + 64.67	±4.25
	radius	4.74 radius + 54.93	±4.24		radius	3.67 radius + 71.79	±4.59
	ulna	4.27 ulna + 57.76	±4.30		ulna	3.31 ulna + 75.38	±4.83
	femur	2.47 femur + 54.10	±3.72		femur	2.28 femur + 59.76	±3.41
	tibia	2.90 tibia + 61.53	±3.66		tibia	2.45 tibia + 72.65	±3.70
	fibula	2.93 fibula + 59.61	±3.57		fibula	2.49 fibula + 70.90	±3.80
ASIAN MALE	humerus	2.68 humerus + 83.19	±4.16	**MEXICAN MALE**	humerus	2.92 humerus + 73.94	±4.2
	radius	3.54 radius + 82.00	±4.60		radius	3.55 radius + 80.71	±4.04
	ulna	3.48 ulna + 77.45	±4.66		ulna	3.56 ulna + 74.56	±4.05
	femur	2.15 femur + 72.57	±3.80		femur	2.44 femur + 58.67	±2.99
	tibia	2.39 tibia + 81.45	±3.27		tibia	2.36 tibia + 80.62	±3.73
	fibula	2.40 fibula + 80.56	±3.24		fibula	2.50 fibula + 75.44	±3.52
				MEXICAN FEMALE	femur	2.59 femur + 49.74	±3.82
					tibia	2.72 tibia + 63.78	±3.51

Source: Trotter & Gleser, 1952, 1977; Genovés, 1967.

CHANGES IN HEIGHT WITH ADVANCING AGE

Another problem is the loss of height with age. Most people shorten with age. The intervertebral discs compress and the vertebra develop microfractures, causing the gradual loss of a few centimeters. But people seldom report themselves to be any shorter than they were at age 20.

TRAUMA

Trauma is a physical injury or wound caused by an external force or violence. The following section focuses on the two main questions about trauma in a forensic setting—"When did it happen?" and "What happened?" It includes information about the most common types of bone trauma—fractures, cutting wounds, and gunshot wounds.

WHEN DID IT HAPPEN?

Antemortem Trauma Antemortem trauma is injury that occurred before death. It shows evidence of a physiological response in the area of the injured tissue. The wound is healed, healing, or responding to some sort of infection. Bony surfaces show signs of thickening and bony proliferation. The edges are rounded, and the surfaces are characteristic of bony remodeling.

Antemortem trauma is very useful for identification purposes. Evidence of traumatic events during the life of the individual can be compared with medical records or testimony of friends and family.

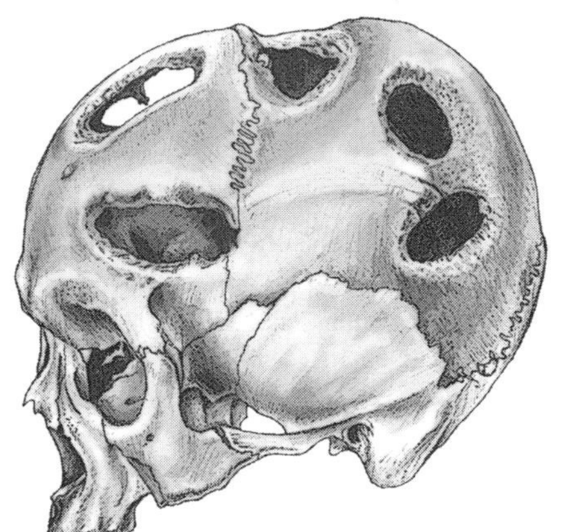

Figure 13.6
Antemortem Trephination

This amazing cranium is from an archeological site. The individual lived for many months (possibly even years) after the holes were cut into his skull. The edges of the holes are well rounded. At the time of death, lamellar bone was still continuing to develop over the exposed spongy bone. All of the holes are somewhat beveled toward the outer surface. If this were an example of modern cranial surgery, there would be small drill holes at the edges of the larger holes and bony plates would be wired back into place. (Note that the individual was edentulous. There are no alveolar sockets and little or no alveolar bone.)

Perimortem Trauma Perimortem trauma is injury that occurs around the time of death but not necessarily "at" the time of death. The trauma may have taken place immediately before, during, or after death. The edges are sharp and the wound shows no sign of healing. It should be clear that the damage occurred in fresh, not dry bone. The fracture may be incomplete or bent (greenstick fracture). Any postmortem staining or weathering should be consistent with that of the surrounding bone.

Perimortem trauma may provide valuable information about the cause and/or manner of death.

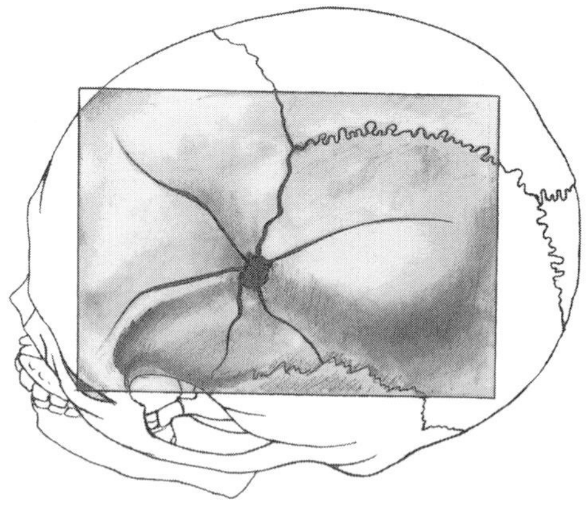

Figure 13.7
Perimortem Gunshot Wound

A projectile from a rifle pierced this skull at the coronal suture and the bone split open in a starburst pattern. The semi-elastic property of living bone allowed the bone to expand and split rather than breaking into pieces as it would have if it had been a dry skull used for target practice (postmortem damage).

Postmortem Trauma or Damage Postmortem trauma is damage that occurs long after death. The expression *postmortem trauma* has a long history of use, but postmortem *damage* is probably more accurate. Trauma is defined as serious bodily damage. This is unlikely to apply to a dry bone.

Neither perimortem trauma nor postmortem damage shows any sign of healing, but postmortem damage is recognizable because bare, dry bone breaks differently and marks differently than living bone. The edges of the break are sharp and the bone tends to break completely through rather than partially or with bent edges as in a greenstick fracture. In postmortem damage, the outer surface of bone that has been exposed to decomposition fluids, dirt, and weather is a different color from the inner surface that was, for a time at least, protected.

It is important to separate perimortem from postmortem, because perimortem events have far greater forensic implications. Perimortem trauma may have been caused by a murderer, whereas postmortem damage is more likely to have been caused by a hungry scavenger or an inattentive excavator.

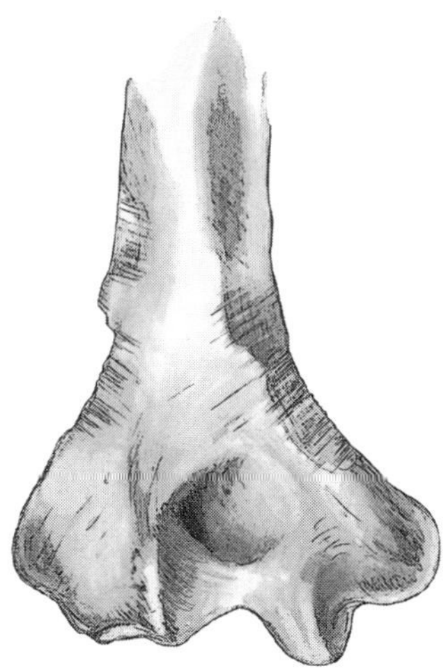

Figure 13.8
Postmortem Scavenger Activity
This humerus was gnawed on by rodents. The small parallel lines left by the incisors are plainly visible. A carnivore would have left a ragged surface with canine tooth indentations or puncture marks.

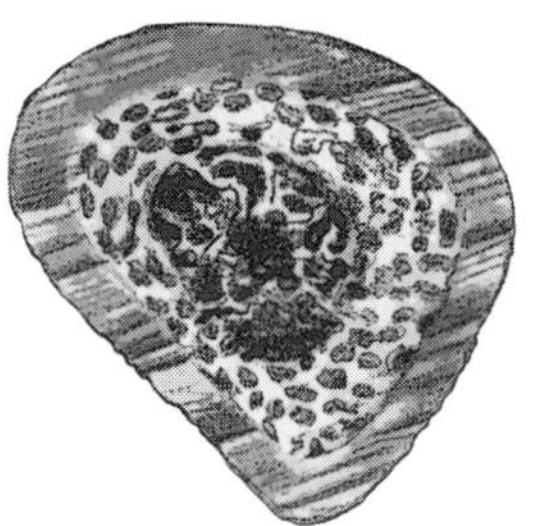

Figure 13.9
Hacksaw Marks
The repetitive, parallel marks on this femur are characteristic of a saw. The surface is flat and the edges of the bone are sharp. Compare this with the parallel lines left by a rodent in Figure 13.8.

CASE EXAMPLE: EVIDENCE OF ABUSE

Unidentified skeletal remains of a young adult female displayed multiple fractures in various stages of healing. The right ribs #7–#9 were partially healed (porous bony callus) and the left ribs #6–#7 were fully healed (thickened areas of remodeled bone). Several anterior teeth (#23–#26) were missing, and the sockets were partially healed. The left zygoma had a perimortem fracture and the right parietal displayed hairline fractures consistent with blunt force trauma. With evidence of at least three episodes of trauma in the area of the head and chest, it was suspected that the woman was the victim of an abusive relationship. The suspicions were confirmed when the woman was identified and the family testified. The boyfriend confessed to the murder.

BONE HEALING

Antemortem trauma is challenging to analyze because the wound has been altered by the healing process, but understanding the sequence and timing of healing can help to determine if several wounds happened at the same time or at different times.

There are three important factors in the bone's ability to heal—the vascularity of the particular bone or area of bone, the stability of the area, and the presence or absence of infection. The entire process of repair is sabotaged and delayed by infection. If, however, immobilization is maintained and the infection subsides, repair resumes after the fragments of dead bone are resorbed. Advanced age, poor nutrition, and systemic disease can also slow the healing process.

Bone follows a predictable six-stage process of healing—clot, vascular bridge, osteogenic cells, soft callus, bony callus, and remodeling. It is difficult to state the exact amount of time required for each stage. Under ideal conditions, osteoclastic bone resorption and subperiosteal bone apposition is visible two weeks following the fracture, and the bony callus has bridged the break by one month.

1. **Clot Formation (Time Period: Hours)** Immediately following the injury, there is an infusion of blood into the tissue surrounding the break and a clot or hematoma forms.
2. **Vascular Bridge Formation (Time Period: Days)** A vascular network is established through the clot. The vessels bridge the ends of the broken bone and provide a conduit for nutrients and cells.
3. **Infusion of Cells (Time Period: Throughout the Healing Process)** Osteogenic cells infuse the vascular bridge and differentiate into the variety of cells needed to build bone. Osteoclasts resorb bone fragments.
4. **Soft Callus Formation (Time Period: Weeks)** Osteoblasts build a soft callus. This is an organic matrix on which minerals can be deposited. The soft callus begins to buttress the damaged area.
5. **Bony Callus Formation (Time Period: 1–2 Months)** Osteoblasts continue to build by depositing minerals within the callus. The new woven bone buttresses the damaged area. At this point, a hard mass can be felt in the area of the break.
6. **Bone Remodeling (Time Period: Years)** Once the broken bone is stabilized by the bony callus, osteoclasts and osteoblasts commence to remodel the callus into lamellar bone, and osteocytes take over the long-term maintenance of the rebuilt Haversian systems. The bony callus becomes smoother and denser but remains visible in spite of remodeling. (Bones of a very young child will remodel completely.)

DELAYED UNION OR NON-UNION

Healing can be delayed if damage is severe or if bone approximation and immobilization are inadequate. Under such conditions, the body's effort to rebuild bone may finally fail. The medullary cavity is sealed off with compact bone, proliferating cells differentiate into chondroblasts which produce a hyaline-like cartilage over the ends of the fractured bones, and a **pseudoarthrosis** or false joint is formed. The scaphoid of the wrist and the femoral neck are particularly vulnerable.

AMPUTATION

The amputated end of a bone remodels in response to change or loss of function. In general, this means that the sharp edges disappear and the terminal part of the bone becomes smoothly rounded.

The femur, however, is a weight-bearing bone, and the individual represented in Figure 13.11 was a double amputee who used the stumps for modified walking. The result is function-specific remodeling. A large resorption pit is apparent at the point of compression (compression necrosis). The posterior surface of the amputated end of the femur is expanded into osteophytic growths (traction osteophytes), providing attachment for the adductor magnus muscle.

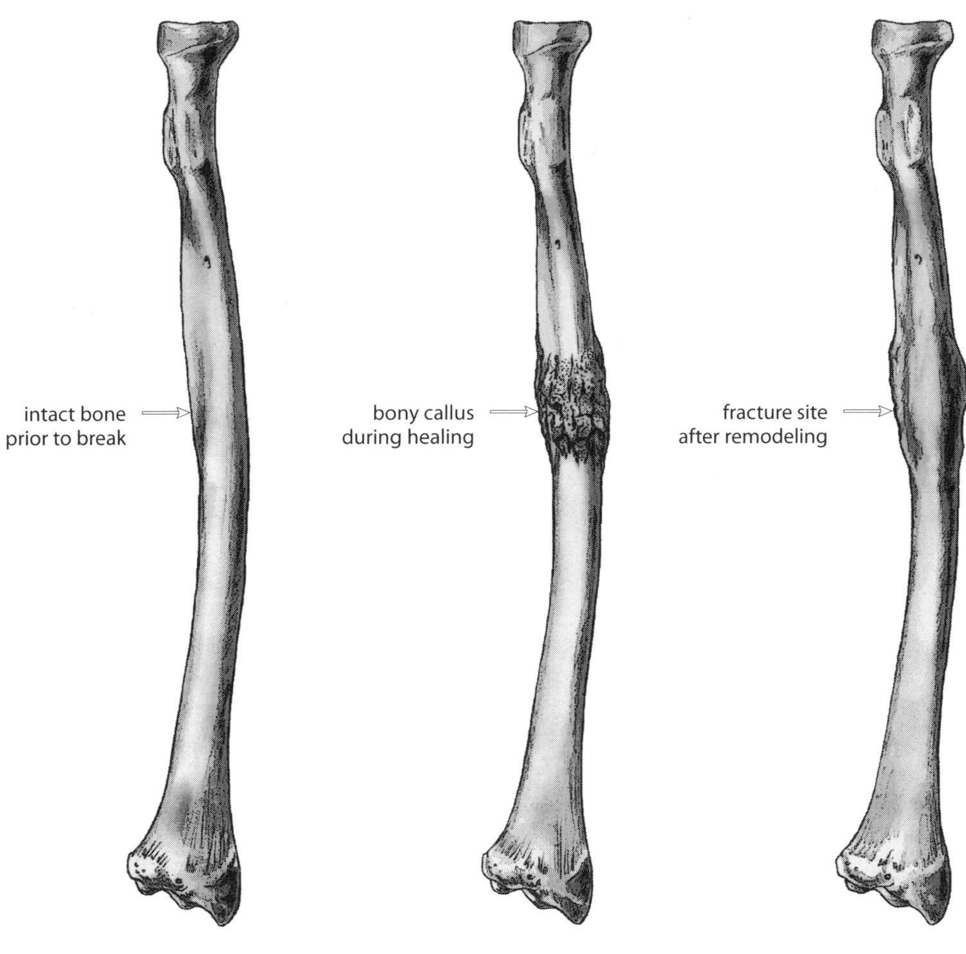

Figure 13.10
Simple Fracture of a Radius, Healing

The radius is shown first as smooth bone immediately prior to fracture, then one month later with a bony callus of porous woven bone (stage 5), and finally, two years later with dense bone covering and enlarging the fracture site (stage 6).

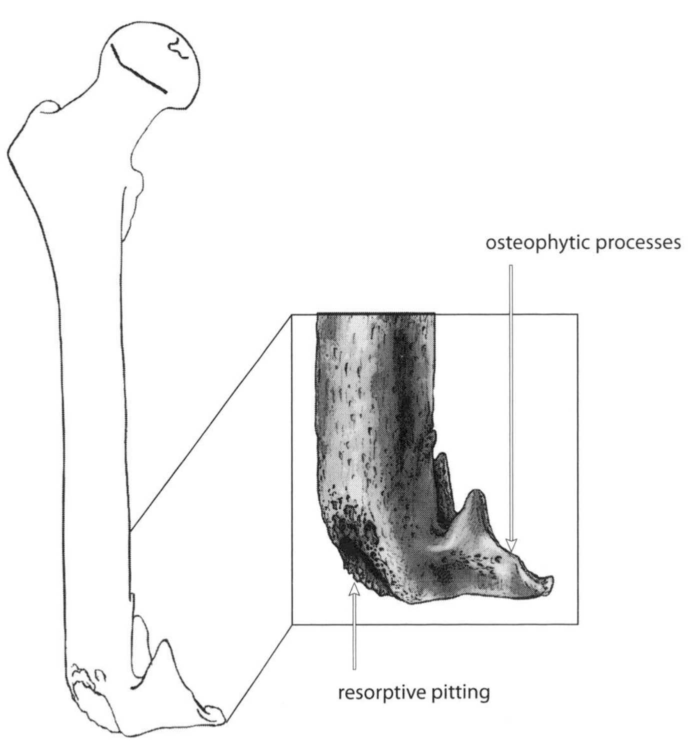

Figure 13.11
Bone Resorption and Remodeling Following Above-Knee Amputation

The healed amputated end displays traction osteophytes and evidence of compression necrosis.

CASE EXAMPLE: RECOGNIZING RAPE OR TORTURE IN GUATEMALA

Rape is usually determined by vaginal swabs and evidence of genital bruising. Of course neither is possible with skeletal remains. However, other physical evidence can be used to support verbal testimony from witnesses.

In Guatemala, an entire village (Rio Negro) of women and children were massacred during the recent civil war. One witness watched from a distance. She reported that the women were raped and beaten by the military before they were executed. The women were found with blouses still in place, but few skirts. (The blouses and skirts had been of the same fiber, so they would not have decayed at different rates.) Many of the victims exhibited perimortem fractures of zygomas, mandibles, and forearms. These fracture locations are consistent with facial beating and defense attempts. Some also had spiral fractures of the arms, typical of wrenching force. While rape could not be proven after so many years, the physical evidence clearly supported the testimony of the witness.

WHAT HAPPENED? EVIDENCE OF TRAUMA

The evidence of trauma is highly variable. It is dependent on both the instrument of trauma and the location of impact. Guns, fists, and screwdrivers all produce different effects. Skulls, ribs, and femora all respond differently to the same trauma. Some of the more obvious variables include size, shape, density, velocity, and angle of impact.

Bone Fractures A bone break of any size or shape is called a fracture. Several variables affect the occurrence and type of fracture. The quantity and direction of force and the health and robusticity of the subject are the most important. There are many different names and classifications for fractures, but the following is a list of the most common fracture types. For more information about fractures, refer to *Classification of Musculoskeletal Trauma* by P. B. Pynsent et al. (1999).

FRACTURE TYPES

- **Simple fracture:** A "clean" break with no skin penetration; including transverse and oblique fractures
- **Greenstick fracture:** An incomplete break with one side bent inward and the other side broken outward (common in children, rare in adults)
- **Spiral fracture:** A ragged break caused by excessive twisting
- **Comminuted fracture:** The bone is broken into many pieces
- **Compound fracture:** Broken ends of bone protrude through an open wound in the skin. (A compound fracture is not recognizable without soft tissues, but it is important to know the definition when reading comparative medical records.)
- **Compression fracture:** Crushed bone (common in porous bone)
- **Depressed fracture:** Broken bone is pressed inward (as in a blunt force trauma to the skull)
- **Impacted fracture:** One of the broken ends of a bone is wedged into the cancellous bone of the other end

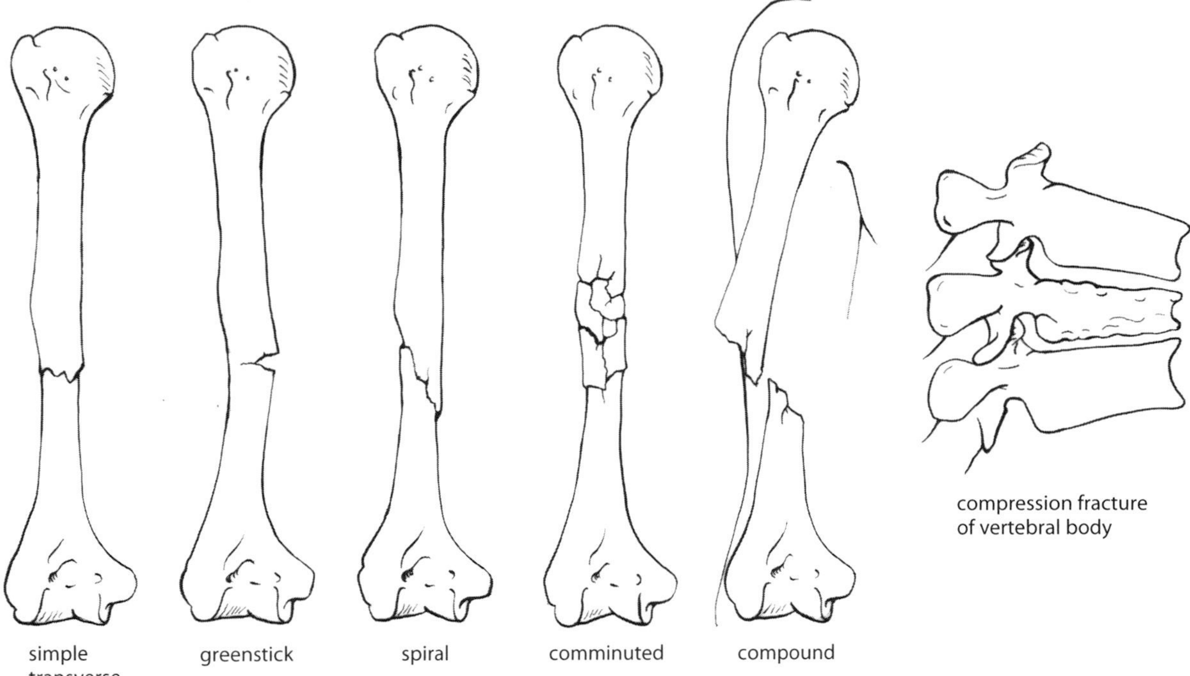

Figure 13.12
Common Fracture Types

Cutting Wounds All cutting wounds are called "tool marks." They may be caused by a knife blade or a screwdriver but they are all characterized by some sort of straight or clean-edged line. They are easy to recognize because neat, clean, lines are seldom found in nature. The fine details can be the result of difference in the type of tool or the specific tool and provide a means of specific weapon identification.

Learn more about knife and tool impressions by experimenting with fresh bones from a local butcher. Examine the marks made by every tool available. Use a low-power microscope or a magnifying glass to observe the fine patterns.

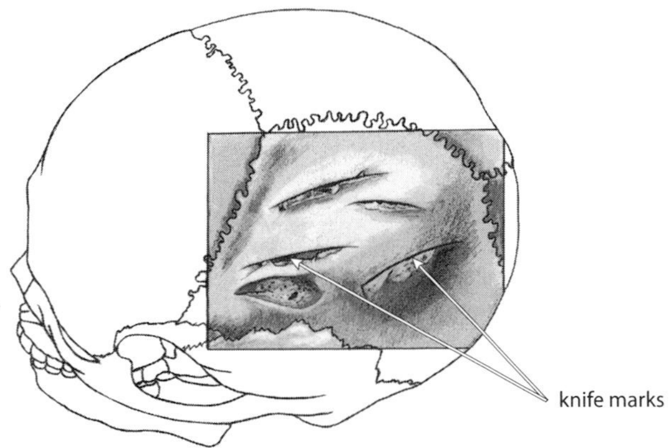

Figure 13.13
Knife Wounds from Scalping
The marks on this skull were left by a butcher knife in an attempted scalping. At least one edge is sharp on each cut mark, and the cut marks penetrate only the outer table of bone.

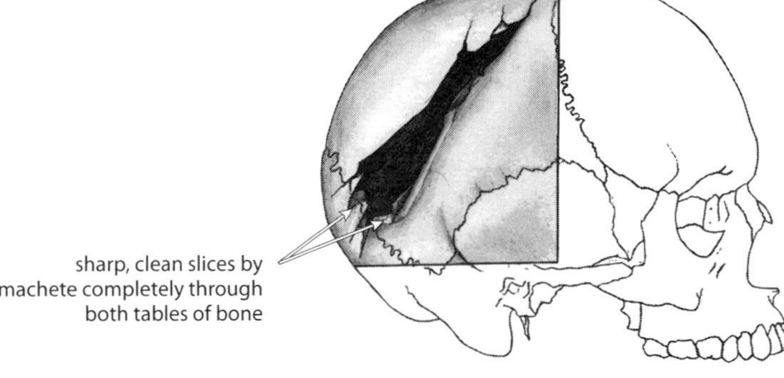

Figure 13.14
Machete Wounds from Death Blows
The deep penetrating wounds on this skull were left by a machete. All of the edges are sharp, long, and deep. A machete can decapitate and disarticulate a body with efficiency.

Gunshot Wounds The type of weapon, type of projectile, range, and trajectory all have an effect on the resulting gunshot wound. Thorough analysis of gunshot wounds is best accomplished by experts with the most experience. (Big city medical examiners are usually a good choice.) It is, however, possible for even the novice to separate out the major characteristics of gunshot wounds and report them without overstepping their expertise.

Separate the obviously high-power wounds from the low-power wounds by classifying the damage surrounding the point of penetration. Low-power weapons such as small pistols release less energy than high-power weapons. The resulting wound can be a simple hole, beveled so that the hole grows larger as it penetrates. If the projectile exits the body, the exit wound is larger than the entrance.

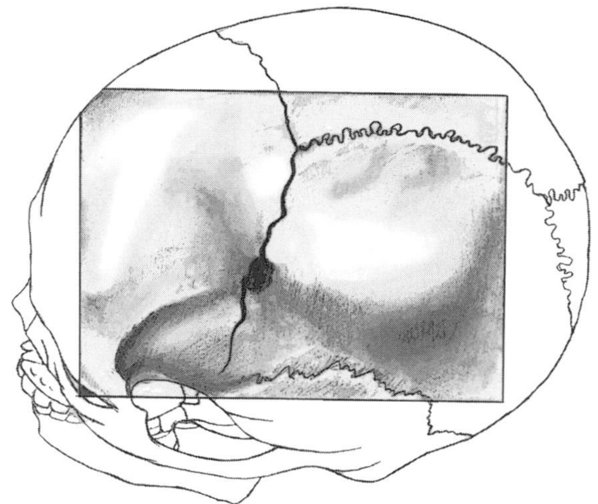

Figure 13.15
Low Power GSW (Handgun)
Low-energy gunshot wound. There is less expansion and fewer cracks. In this particular case, the energy was also partially absorbed by the cranial suture.

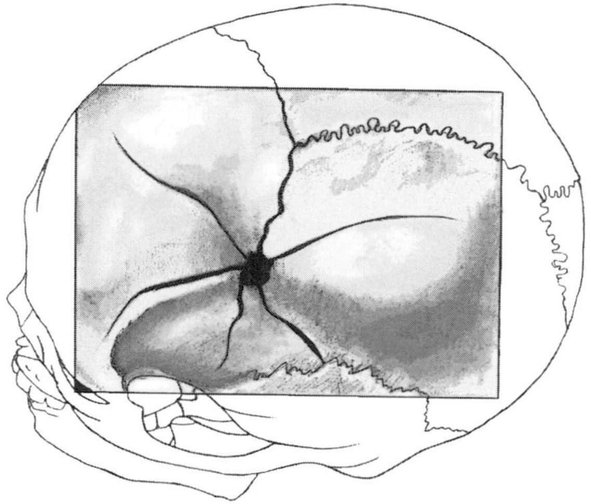

Figure 13.16
Higher Power GSW (Rifle)
Higher-energy gunshot wound. There is "starburst" pattern of cracks. This is the result of rapidly expanding gases within the cranial vault.

High-power weapons such as rifles and machine guns release large amounts of energy. As the projectile enters the body, there is a sudden expansion or bursting effect. (In soft tissue this is called **temporary cavitation**.) If the bone is not totally shattered, the wound in bone may take on a "starburst" pattern with cracks radiating out from the entrance hole.

Projectile Type The wide assortment of projectiles can be described by several primary characteristics: caliber (diameter of the bullet or shot), composition (usually lead, but sometimes plastic or rubber), shape (with or without a hollow point), and jacket (with or without, partial or full). The combination produces different effects when striking living tissue. Full metal jacket rifle bullets frequently exit the body. Partial jacket, hollow point bullets expand and often do not exit.

Bone does not accurately maintain the caliber of the projectile. The diameter of the wound may be larger because of the angle of entry, distortion of the projectile by intermediary targets, chipping of bone edges, and many other factors. The diameter of the wound may even be slightly smaller because of shrinkage of the bone during drying.

The bullet wound depicted in Figure 13.16 resulted from a direct or "straight on" hit. If the bullet had struck the bone at a tangential angle, a **keyhole fracture** could have resulted. The primary edge of entry would be rounded and beveled inward as expected, but the secondary edge of entry would

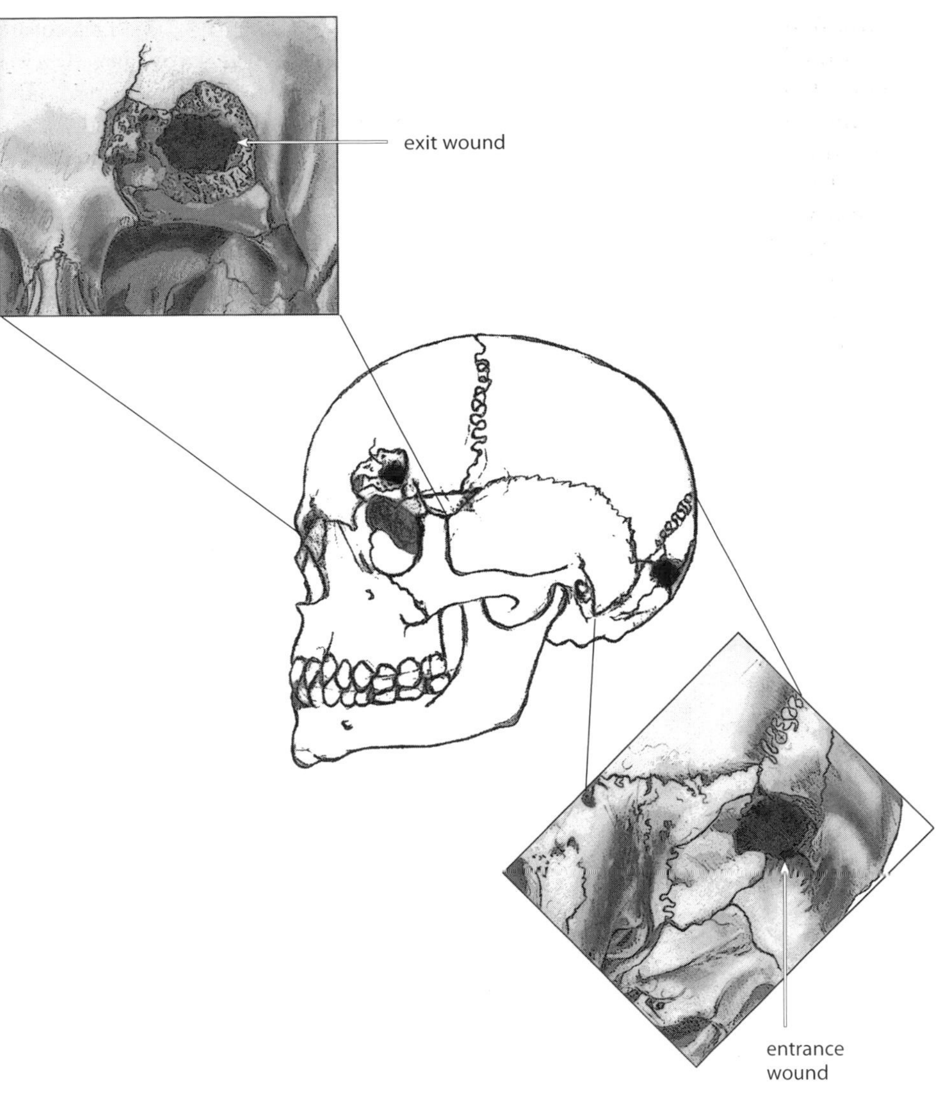

Figure 13.17
Entrance and Exit Characteristics
The wound in the back of the skull is a typical entrance wound. It is smaller than the exit wound and beveled inward. The bevel is visible from the inside of the skull. The wound above the eye orbit is a typical exit wound. It is larger than the entrance wound and beveled outward. (This entrance–exit pattern is typical of a close-range execution-style killing.)

be less uniform in shape and beveled outward. The entering projectile "levers" the secondary edge upward as it passes underneath. Keyhole fractures are ovoid or keyhole-like in shape.

Shotgun Wounds Shotguns produce entirely different types of wounds. The size of the pellets and the range between muzzle and target affect the size and shape of the wound and the degree of injury.

Figure 13.18
Shotgun Wounds
This skull was penetrated by two rounds from a .410 shotgun fired at close range. Note the scalloped margins and the small "starburst" cracks. Lead scrapings and imbedded pellets are common in this type of wound. There is only slight inward beveling of the entrance wounds and no exit wounds. (The .410 is a low-power shotgun, but even high-power shotgun pellets seldom exit the body.) If the range had been greater, the pellets would have scattered more, creating a larger pattern.

Blunt Force Trauma Blunt force trauma is caused by all sorts of "blunt" instruments—baseball bats, 2 × 4s, hammers, and so on. The force of impact is far less than in gunshot wounds and the wound edges are not so clearly defined as in cutting wounds. With less force and no cutting edge, the elastic properties of bone can be seen. Greenstick-type, concentric breaks occur around the point of impact. Other fractures may occur also, but the concentric fractures are characteristic.

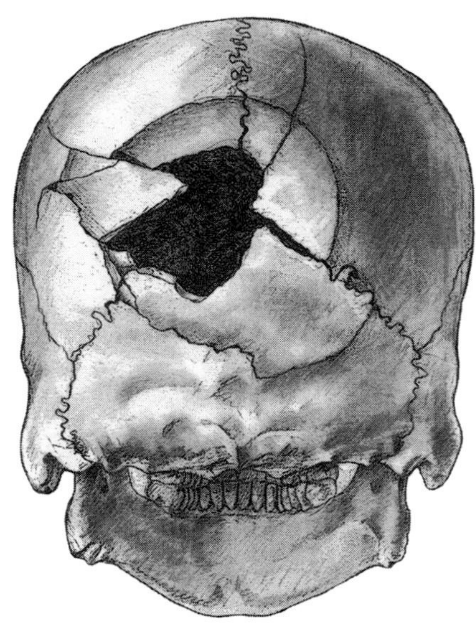

Figure 13.19
Blunt Force Skull Fracture
This skull was penetrated by a carpenter's hammer. Note the presence of concentric cracks in addition to the occasional "starburst" crack. Fragments of bone are bent inward and the outer table is broken in places where the inner table is only bent (greenstick effect).

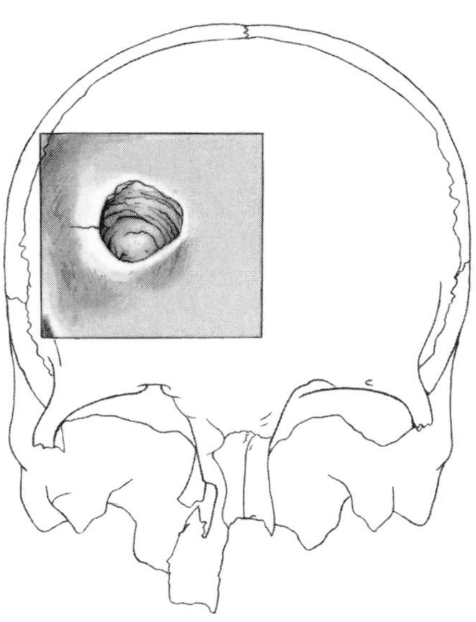

Figure 13.20
Depressed Skull Fracture
This wound was caused by the same type of instrument as in the last illustration, but with less force. Only the outer table of the skull is penetrated and fragments are depressed into the wound. The concentric fractures are close together creating an imprint of the hammer head.

Dislocation A dislocation is the temporary displacement of a bone from its normal position in the joint. If the damage to surrounding ligaments is minimal and the bone is repositioned and stabilized so the joint can heal, there may be no bony sign of the dislocation. But if full healing does not take place and the bones of the joint move abnormally against each other (chronic dislocation), the joint surfaces remodel according to use. The edges of the original joint become ill defined and a joint-like surface may develop in an abnormal location.

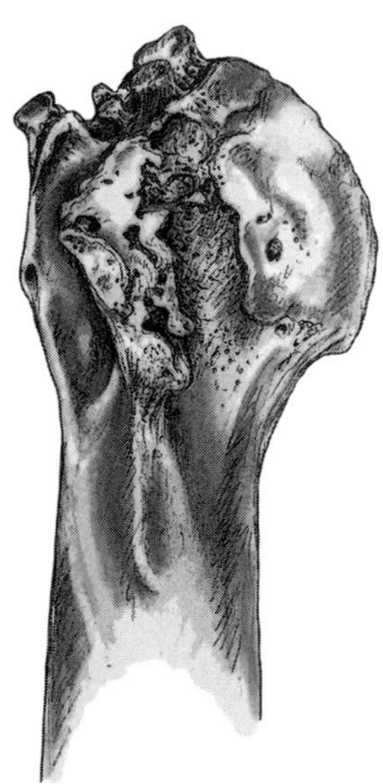

Figure 13.21
Chronic Shoulder Dislocation
The shape of this humeral head is the result of chronic dislocation. The head is flatter than normal and osteoarthritic. The articular surface is dense, smooth, and shiny (eburnated), a condition associated with loss of articular cartilage. (The adjoining scapula had developed a secondary articular fossa anteromedial to the glenoid fossa.)

Disease and Pathology

Pathology is the study of disease, its causes, processes, development, and consequences. A disease is a pathological condition, but it is not "a pathology" any more than a human is "an anthropology"—at least, not until recently. However, language evolves and changes with usage, and when the expression *pathology and trauma* appeared in the literature, it quickly gained popularity. It may have been just a shortened version of *pathological conditions and trauma*, but it opened the word *pathology* to new usage. The word *disease* is now being replaced by *pathology*, and the plural *pathologies* has followed.

Analysis of disease from bone alone is challenging and sometimes impossible. First, the effects of trauma and disease can be interrelated and confused. For instance, the primary cause of a bacterial infection may be the trauma of a compound fracture.

Even without trauma, disease analysis is complicated. Single disease agents can produce a variety of effects, and different disease agents can produce what appears to be the same effect. The expression of any disease may be influenced by advancing age, inadequate nutrition, metabolic deficiencies, infection, or neoplasm.

It is advisable to use as many descriptive terms as possible before suggesting the cause or diagnosing a disease. Begin with terms like **osteogenic** (producing bone) and **osteolytic** (dissolving bone). Report the obvious effects before suggesting possible causes. For example, report that the child had bowed legs before suggesting that the child may have suffered from rickets due to vitamin D deficiency.

A few of the most common diseases affecting the skeleton are listed here. They are divided into groups related to age, nutrition and metabolic deficiencies, infections, and neoplasms. For an in-depth study of disease effects, refer to *Identification of Pathological Conditions in Human Skeletal Remains* by D. J. Ortner (2003).

Age- and Hormone-Related Conditions

Osteoarthritis Osteoarthritis refers to a group of degenerative joint diseases. The most common is caused by progressive wear and tear on joints with age. The articular cartilage thins, bony projections proliferate at the edge of the articular surface, and in later stages, striations appear on the face of the articular surface. Osteoarthritis can be accelerated by inflammation caused by trauma or infection. Generalized osteoarthritis is more likely to be age related. Osteoarthritis caused by disease is more likely to be localized. See Figure 5.11b, An elderly or "hard-working" back.

Diffuse idiopathic skeletal hyperostosis (DISH) DISH is considered a form of degenerative arthritis and is characterized by "flowing" calcification along the sides of the vertebrae, most frequently on the right side. It is commonly associated with inflammation of the tendons (tendinitis) and calcification of tendons at their attachments points to bone. Heel spurs are a common nonvertebral expression of DISH.

Hyperostosis frontalis interna (internal frontal hyperostosis) Hyperostosis frontalis interna is characterized by irregular, ridged, thickening on the endocranial surface of the frontal bone. It is usually bilateral and symmetrical. It looks somewhat like Paget's disease on first glance, but it is usually confined to the anterior part of the cranium, and it doesn't extend to other parts of the body. It has been reported in high frequency among postmenopausal elderly women and is considered to be a benign condition.

Osteomalacia Osteomalacia refers to a number of disorders in adults in which bones are inadequately mineralized. The lower limbs tend to develop mediolateral bowing because they are not strong enough to support body weight.

Osteoporosis A group of diseases in which bone resorption outpaces bone deposition is referred to as osteoporosis. Bone becomes porous and light and fractures increase, particularly in the spine, wrist, and hip. It is a common condition of postmenopausal women but is not exclusive to women. Osteoporosis is the underlying cause of the typical "dowager's hump" as well as Colles fractures of the wrist and femoral neck fractures. Such fractures are slow to heal and often leave misshapen bones in spite of medical care. The anterior part of the vertebral discs compresses more than the posterior part, causing greater curvature of the spine and permanent loss of height.

Paget's disease Paget's disease is characterized by excessive rates of bone deposition and reabsorption. The newly formed bone has an abnormally high amount of immature woven bone and little mature compact bone. It is also less mineralized than normal bone; thus it is soft and weak. It is a disease of the elderly, progresses slowly, and is seldom life threatening. Paget's disease may affect only one bone, even a single vertebra. If the tibia is involved, it becomes "saber shaped." The legs may bow.

NUTRITION- AND METABOLISM-RELATED CONDITIONS

Cribra orbitalia Cribra orbitalia is bilateral pitting of the orbital roofs of the frontal bone. It is produced by simultaneous bone lysis (pitting) and new bone formation (thickening). Like porotic hyperostosis, cribra orbitalia is related to anemia.

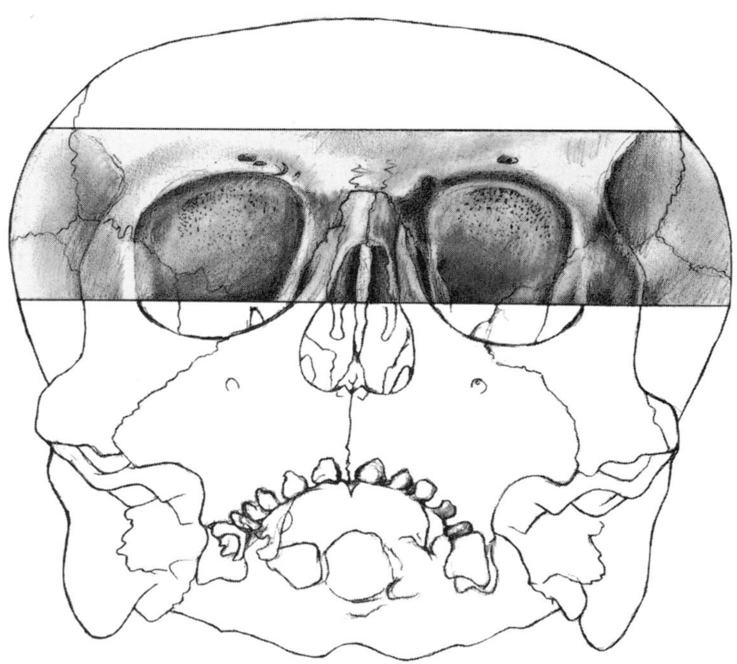

Figure 13.22 Cribra Orbitalia—A Peruvian Man

Pitting in the superior orbital wall is a typical response to anemia. In this person, anemia may have been altitude-related.

Enamel hypoplasia Enamel hypoplasia is seen as horizontal striations in tooth enamel. It results from inconsistent nutrition during formative years. Seasonal swings in food supply may cause regular enamel lines. Serious childhood illnesses may result in irregularly spaced lines.

Porotic or spongy hyperostosis Porotoc or spongy hyperostosis appears as lesions on the surface of the cranial vault and a "hair-on-end" trabecular pattern within the diploë of the cranial vault. It can be caused by anemia—usually iron deficiency anemia, or one of the congenital hemolytic anemias (e.g., thalassemia and sickle cell disease).

Rickets Rickets in children is analogous to osteomalacia in adults. The bones are inadequately mineralized and the limbs tend to bow. It is caused by inadequate amounts of vitamin D. Narrow tibia ("saber shins") can also be the result of rickets.

BACTERIAL INFECTIONS

Osteomyelitis A general term given to a bacterial infection of bone and bone marrow is osteomyelitis. It can enter from infections in surrounding tissues or through the blood stream. It can also follow a compound fracture.

Periostitis Periostitis (or periosteitis) is a general term for a bone infection with involvement of the periosteum. The periosteum is the membrane enveloping the bone.

Syphilis Syphilis is an infection caused by the bacterium *Treponema pallidum*. The effects vary depending upon the age of acquisition. If the infection is established in the fetus, it is "congenital syphilis." The skull, radius, ulna, and tibia are usually involved. Saber tibia is one of the resulting deformations.

Sexually transmitted syphilis is "acquired syphilis." Skeletal effects include gummata of the medullary cavity or the periosteum. Primary sites include the frontal bone and the proximal ends of the tibia and humerus.

Syphilis should not be dismissed as a disease of the past. According to scientists at the Centers for Disease Control and Prevention (CDC) in Atlanta, syphilis is still present in the world (including the United States). There is a new outbreak every seven to ten years. Syphilis responds well to antibiotic treatment, but there is no vaccine. Unfortunately, cultural inhibitions result in reluctance to seek immediate treatment (St. Louis & Wasserheit, 1998).

Skeletal tuberculosis Skeletal tuberculosis is caused by the bacterium *Mycobacterium tuberculosis*. Lesions caused by *M. tuberculosis* are most often found in the vertebral column (T6 to L3), the hip, and the knee.

Leprosy Leprosy is caused by *Mycobacterium leprae*, a member of the same bacterial family as tuberculosis, *Mycobacteriaceae*. The bones of the hands and feet are most affected in leprosy. The phalanges first appear to sharpen, then resorb into distorted stumps.

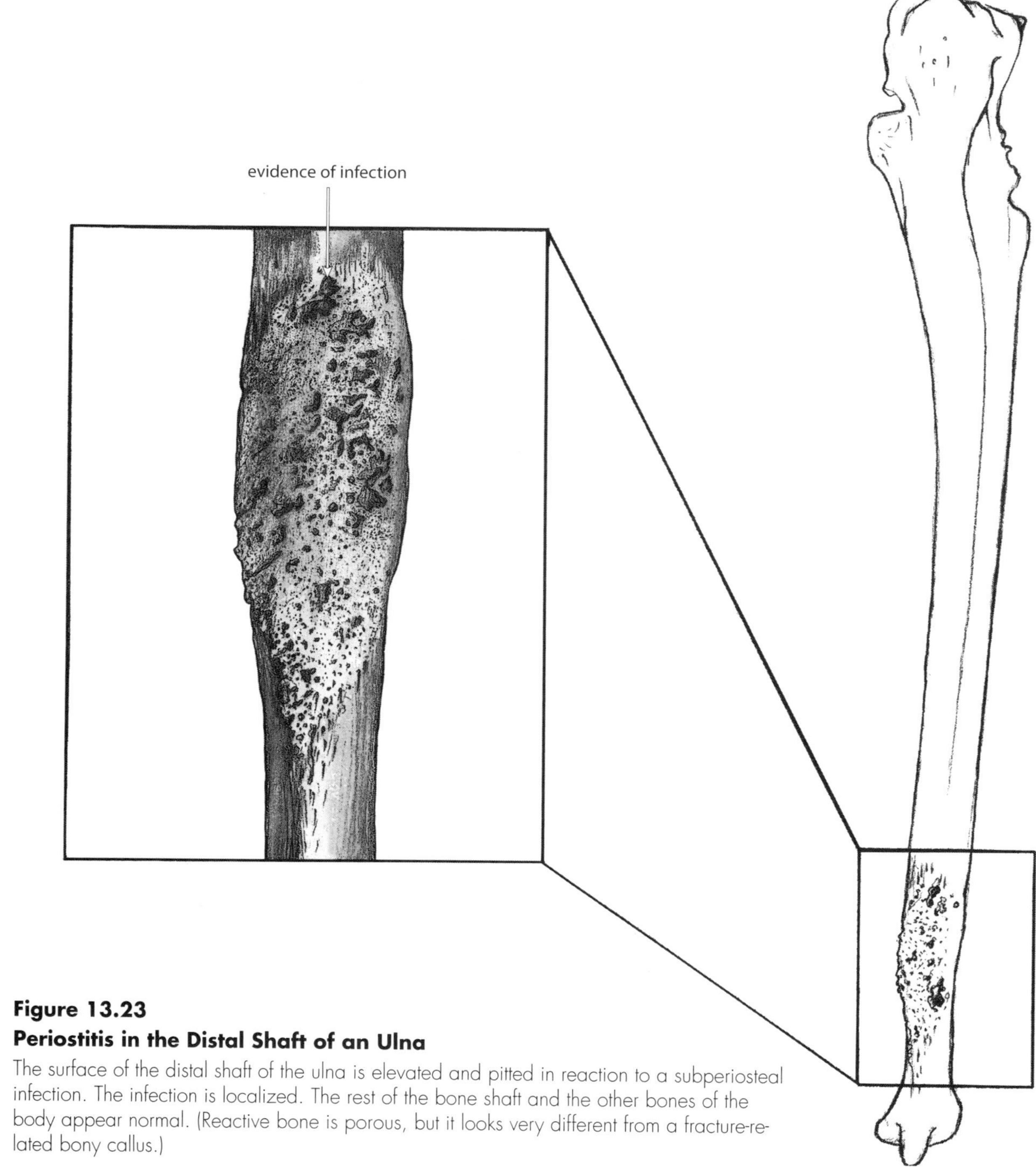

Figure 13.23
Periostitis in the Distal Shaft of an Ulna
The surface of the distal shaft of the ulna is elevated and pitted in reaction to a subperiosteal infection. The infection is localized. The rest of the bone shaft and the other bones of the body appear normal. (Reactive bone is porous, but it looks very different from a fracture-related bony callus.)

NEOPLASMS

Osteoma An Osteoma is a benign bone tumor. Osteomas are common, and many classification systems exist. Basically, they are dense, circumscribed, nonproliferating, and symptomless. Osteomas may be caused by trauma and/or excess callus formation. Most osteomas occur on the inner and outer surfaces of the cranium and mandible, but some are found in the postcranial skeleton, particularly in areas prone to injury.

Osteosarcoma An osteosarcoma (osteoid sarcoma) is a highly malignant tumor containing bony tissue. It is formed by proliferation of mesodermal cells and is more commonly known as bone cancer. Osteosarcomas primarily affect young people between 10 and 25 years of age.

Quality Check for Skeletal Analysis

Before moving from analysis to identification, go over every detail to be sure that all possible information has been considered. Use this checklist as a guide.

Age Changes

✓ Were *developmental* changes ongoing at the time of death? Give details.

✓ Were *degenerative* changes apparent at the time of death? Give details.

Sexual Variation

✓ Consider the pelvis: Is it wide or narrow? Specify areas.

- Pubis elongation
- Subpubic angle
- Ventral arc
- Sciatic notch
- Preauricular groove

✓ Consider the skull: Is it rugged or gracile? Specify areas.

- Mastoids and nuchal area—male–female comparison
- Supraorbital ridge and frontal—male–female comparison
- Mandible—male–female comparison

Racial Variation (See Chapter 14)

✓ Consider the skull: What is the most prominent feature of the face—the mouth, the nose, or the cheeks? What details correspond to known racial characteristics?

- Nasal aperture—width in relation to length
- Nasal spine—present or absent, size
- Nasal guttering—present or absent, degree
- Degree of maxillary prognathicism
- Zygomatic position in relation to the maxilla—on the same plane or posterior to that plane
- Zygomatic suture form—S-shaped, Z-shaped, or straight
- Dental arch shape—rounded or V-shaped

✓ Consider the teeth: Are there any obvious racial characteristics? (See Chapter 11)

- Shovel-shaped incisors—the maxillary centrals and laterals
- Carabelli's cusp—on the maxillary first molars

Stature Estimation

✓ Look over the entire skeleton for consistency: Are the limbs of the same general length? Is the bone density consistent throughout the skeleton? Is there evidence of scoliosis or anything else that would create inconsistency between long bone measurement and actual height?

- Measure the long bones
- Use the most recent formulae or computer analysis
- Account for incongruities when possible

Trauma

✓ Have you examined every bone for evidence of traumatic incidents?

✓ Can you explain anomalies in terms of the bone dynamics?

✓ Will radiographs be useful?

Disease

✓ Is there any evidence of systemic disease, infection, or poor nutrition?

✓ Will radiographs or other analysis such as microscopy be useful?

Human Identification (ID)

Skeletal Identification: The Challenge

Frequently, skeletonized remains are not identified. They are labeled "John or Jane Doe," boxed, buried, or cremated, and written off as "unidentifiable." The families of the missing live out their lives in limbo between hope and grief, and the murderers go undetected and unpunished. The whole problem is compounded by silence—the unidentified body doesn't complain, the family doesn't know where to complain, the public is indifferent unless a serial killer is involved, and the murderer certainly stays silent.

Nancy Ritter of the National Institute of Justice reports that missing persons and unidentified human remains constitute our nation's "silent mass disaster." Tens of thousands of persons disappear under suspicious circumstances each year, and there are as many as 100,000 active missing persons cases on any given day (Ritter, 2007).

The challenge is identification of the "unidentifiable." The solution is good analysis and description of the remains, good comparative information about the missing, and ways to efficiently store and retrieve the information.

Over the last twenty-five years, death investigators have become more willing to devote time to searching for comparative information from long-term missing persons. Success has led to more success and many medical examiner's offices now work closely with anthropologists. The result is better descriptions of skeletal cases and more access to identifications.

Identification Levels

Usually, the process of identification (ID) proceeds through a sequence of levels—tentative, presumptive, and positive—and may not ever reach the highest level. Each level says something about the reliability of the ID, but the actual numerical probability is a function of the specific method used (e.g., fingerprints or DNA). Table 13.3 provides examples of identification levels and the possible types of evidence for each.

The distinction between one level of identification and the next tends to be blurred, and the final decision regarding a contested identification is left to the courts.

Tentative ID

Tentative identification comes first. Any available clue whatsoever can provide a tentative ID—clothing, jewelry, pocket contents, body location, and so on. Tentative identification is important because it allows the investigator to focus the search for more information. If the tentative ID turns out to be wrong, another direction can always be taken.

Presumptive ID

Presumptive identification is the next level. It is also called "possible" or "probable" identification. Presumptive ID is achieved in two different ways—by excluding all other possibilities or by piling up a lot of unrelated evidence in favor of the same identification. The first is called "identification by exclusion," and the second, "identification by preponderance of evidence." Neither is the same as a positive identification, but either can be presented and decided upon in a court of law.

Positive ID

Positive identification is supposed to be faultless. Ideally, it results from information that is exclusive to one and only one individual such as fingerprints and radiographs, dental or skeletal. These are both developmentally determined and the randomness of development assures variation, even between identical twins.

Table 13.3 Levels of Certainty in Identification

Level of ID	Basis for ID
TENTATIVE IDENTIFICATION	clothing
	possessions
	location of body
	verbal testimony
	ABO blood type
PRESUMPTIVE IDENTIFICATION BY PREPONDERANCE OF EVIDENCE	multiple factors, none of which could stand alone skeletal anomalies (known, but unrecorded) photo superimposition
PRESUMPTIVE IDENTIFICATION BY EXCLUSION	everybody else is identified (and no evidence contradicts the identification)
POSITIVE IDENTIFICATION	dental identification
	radiographic identification
	mummified fingerprints
	prosthetic identification (with serial number)
	DNA analysis
	unique skeletal anomalies (with written records)

Even DNA, based on genetic rather than developmental differences, can't provide the ultimate level of certainty, but most IDs are accepted as positive on the basis of statistics. A positive DNA identification may be based on the fact that the haplotype of the unidentified individual occurs in only 1 in 400 persons within a specific population. That information, together with correct sex, stature, age, and race, makes an excellent positive identification (but not perfect).

Methods of Identification

There are many useful identification methods, and the best method for any specific case depends on the condition of the remains and the availability of comparative information. Many methods are in general use by forensic laboratories, and others are only available through specialized laboratories with state-of-the-art equipment. A growing number of nongovernmental laboratories are equipped for specialized high-tech analyses.

The following is a partial list of methods used in identification. Each is a study in and of itself.

- Blood typing (ABO system together with Rh factor)
- DNA analysis (nuclear or mitochondrial)
- Radiographic analysis (antemortem/postmortem comparison, dental, or other)
- Elemental analysis (information about nutrition, disease, or origin)
- Isotope analysis (information about year of death based on "bomb-spike" data)
- Microstructural analysis of bone or teeth (information about age at death)
- Hair analysis (race, age, and toxicological analysis)
- Fingerprint (antemortem/postmortem comparison)
- Photo superimposition (antemortem/postmortem comparison)
- Prostheses, surgical hardware (serial number identification)

More types of analyses are also possible, and each is useful in its own way. The requirements of the specific case dictate the route to follow and the experts to seek.

RADIOGRAPHIC IDENTIFICATION

First, note the difference between an x-ray and a radiograph. An x-ray is electromagnetic radiation of very short wavelength and very high energy. X-rays can penetrate soft tissues, but not bony tissue. A radiograph is a permanent image, on photographic film or as a digital image, produced by x-rays. Physicists study x-rays; osteologists study radiographs.

Almost any radiograph—dental, cranial, or postcranial—can be useful for positive identification if it shows bony detail. In societies with advanced health care, dental radiographs are common. Dental restorations are clearly visible and usually well documented. Even without restorations, dental radiographs provide individual detail of root morphology, alveolar bone configuration, vascular channels, and sinuses.

The chief impediments to radiographic identification are major bony changes over time and inaccurate angulation of the postmortem comparison radiographs. Angulation is simply a matter of orienting a three-dimensional item so that it can be represented in two dimensions. The slightest change in angle can change the two-dimensional picture. Usually several comparison radiographs are preferred.

PHOTO SUPERIMPOSITION

Photo superimposition, also known as video superimposition, can be a convincing method for presumptive identification when all else is lacking. It is accomplished by photographically superimposing a carefully positioned skull on a facial photograph. Angulation is a challenge here just as it is with radiographic comparisons.

Photo superimposition is most easily done with the use of two video cameras, but it can also be accomplished with as little as one camera, a piece of glass in a vertical stand, and two separate light sources.

Numerous points of reference should be visible on both the photograph and the skull. For example, it should be possible to match the following points and curvatures:

- Bridge of nose
- Length of nose
- Width of nose
- Distance between eyes
- Lip line
- Any visible teeth
- Chin—lowest point
- Chin—most forward point
- Angle of jaw
- Ear canal

Photo superimposition has been shown to be most successful if two photographs are used (Austin-Smith & Maples, 1994). The photos should show the individual from different perspectives such as frontal and profile. A physical anomaly such as a broken nose is very useful if it is apparent in the photograph.

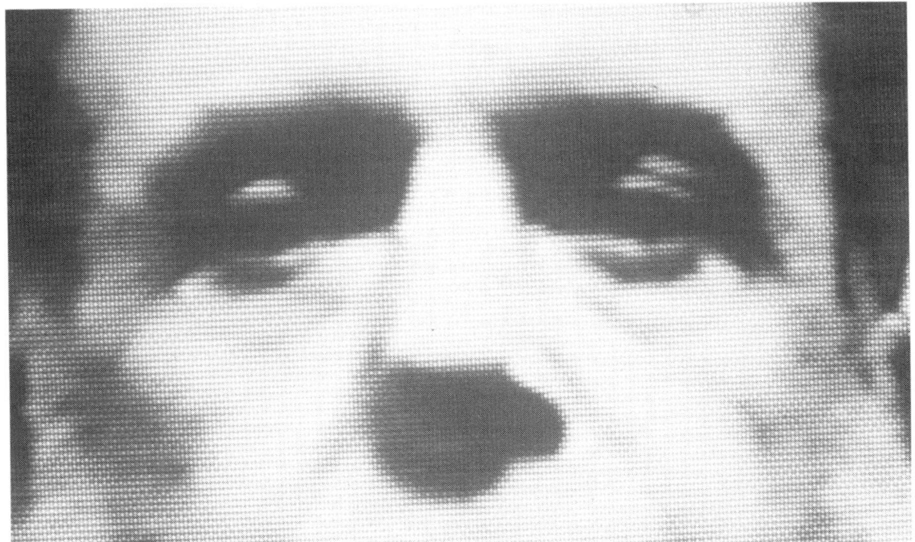

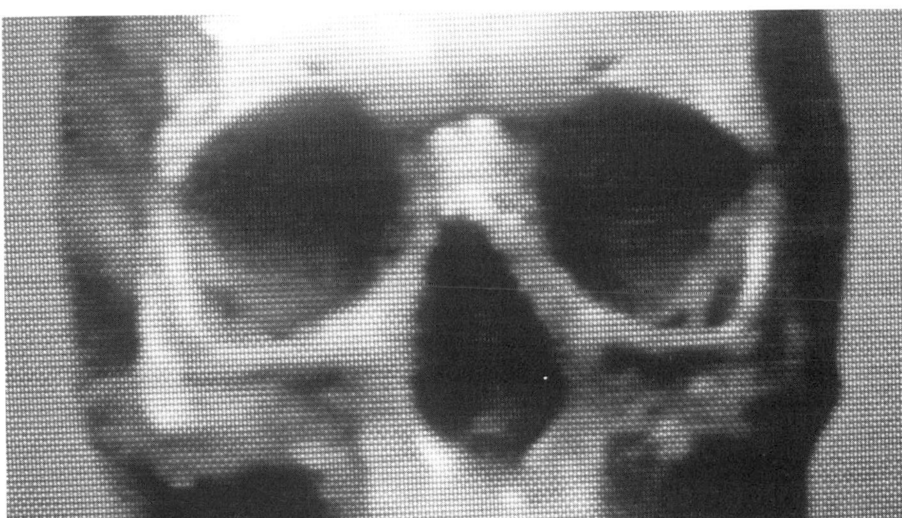

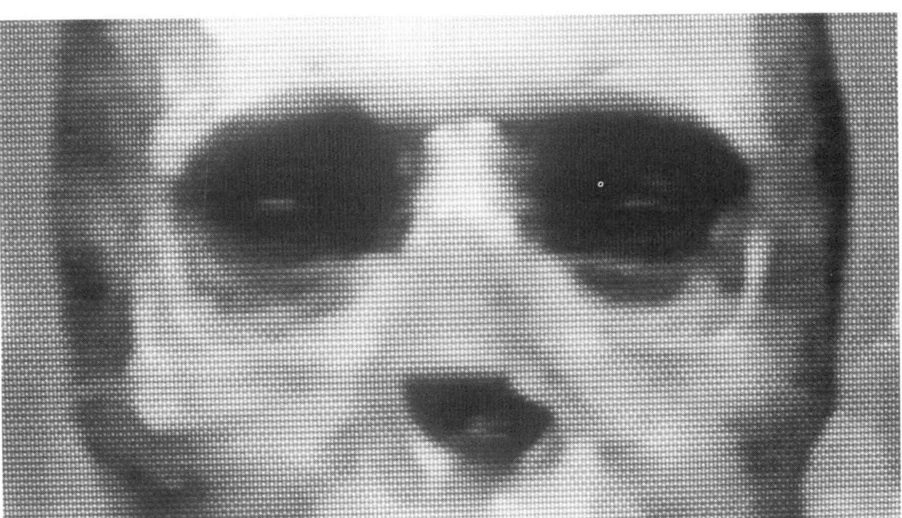

Figure 13.24
Photo Superimposition

In this case, the missing individual had a long, narrow face, and his nose was broken and healed with a decided deviation to the right side of the face. The photograph is superimposed over the image of the skull with all reference points in agreement, including the bridge of the nose. This does not stand alone as a positive identification, but it supports other information to increase the probability of the identification.

CASE EXAMPLE: "POSITIVE IDENTIFICATION" IS NOT ALWAYS ENOUGH

Convincing yourself and the investigator is not always enough. The jury and the family must also be convinced. Jurors may lack the education or experience to easily grasp the methodology used for identification. This can usually be overcome by introducing good teaching techniques in the courtroom.

The family is another problem entirely. In my experience, most families want answers. They want an end to the nightmare of not knowing what has happened to their loved one. But there are times when members of the deceased's family simply do not want to believe the evidence. They choose to turn their backs on the evidence and go on hoping that the loved one is still alive.

One family in Georgia was notified of the identification of its missing grandfather. The identification was made by radiographic records, but the family refused to accept the remains. One family member said, "We won't bury some stranger!"

The missing man had been found almost completely skeletonized, and the family didn't believe that he could have decomposed so quickly. (In fact, a body can be reduced to a skeletal state within two weeks in a hot Georgia summer. A few days are adequate if animals have access to the body.)

In an effort to provide the family members with information that they would be willing to accept, I filmed a superimposition of the skull with two separate photos of the missing man (frontal and lateral views). The family was invited to a private viewing of the video in the medical examiner's office. Afterward, the family quietly accepted the remains for burial and the case was closed.

DNA IDENTIFICATION

DNA technology is advancing rapidly and becoming increasingly more practical for human identifications. It is possible to extract and amplify DNA from ever smaller, older, and more degraded samples. In the 1990s, mitochondrial DNA was all that could be expected from old bone samples. Now, nuclear DNA is frequently extracted and utilized.

Research in **DNA phenotyping** is also advancing. It is predicted that the time will come when a full physical description of an individual can be generated with the use of a few skin cells. Eye color is already fairly well deciphered through the IrisPlex System (Walsh et al., 2011). And hair color discrimination will soon be available (Branicki et al., 2011). There is no doubt that other physical descriptors will also be deciphered within the genetic code.

A few years ago, DNA technology, although theoretically promising, was criticized for being inaccessible, ineffective, cumbersome to use, and costly—both in price and time. All of these problems have since been addressed. There are new laboratories dedicated to human identification, e.g., the Center for Human Identification at the University of North Texas; major DNA databases are available, e.g., **the National DNA Index System** (NDIS)**;** and effective tools exist for assembling and comparing data, e.g., the **Combined DNA Index System for Missing Persons** (CODIS(mp)).

In the past, attempts at DNA comparisons were not initiated until an unidentified body was found. Now, missing person protocols recommend that a DNA sample be obtained if the missing person is not found within thirty days. The sample can be from a personal item such as a toothbrush belonging to the missing person or from a close relative. (Non-invasive cheek swabs are simple to obtain.) Even cost is decreasing as robotics have been introduced in DNA analysis. The FBI's nuclear DNA lab at Quantico, Virginia, uses robots to analyze more than 500 samples per day.

With all the progress in DNA identification, the frequently asked question is, "Why bother with other methods? Why not just use DNA?" The answer is not complicated. Even if the system is working well, the match is not always there. The only way the system can positively identify every unidentified person is to database DNA samples from every person alive, but right now, even the collection of samples for reported missing persons is a goal, not a reality.

There is one other aspect of human identification that people don't often think about. The nonscientific community is not always convinced by scientific findings. Frequently, there is the need to convince families and persuade courts by multiple means.

CASE EXAMPLE: A DNA IDENTIFICATION IN HAITI

A clandestine grave on a beach in Haiti revealed the skeletonized remains of a young man. Reports suggested that he was one of many killed while trying to escape to boats during a massacre of civilians. The identification might have been easy if his relatives had reported him missing and were willing to provide samples for DNA testing. But there was no report and no samples. The political situation was such that the local people were afraid to be associated with the victim, regardless of their desire for truth or justice.

In the end, the whole identification hinged on the fact that the dead man had a badly rusted key in his pants pocket. When news of the key became generally known, a survivor came forward to say that he had loaned a key to his shore-side shack to a man who disappeared at the time of the massacre. The cleaned-up key fit the door of the shack, and a **tentative identification** resulted. The tentative identification led to friends who were willing to provide a description of the victim, including visible dental characteristics. The description provided a **presumptive identification** that supported the decision to go ahead with DNA extraction in case a relative could be found. Once the presumptive identification was generally known in the village, a local priest finally persuaded the family to come forward, and a **positive identification** was made by DNA comparison. In this supposedly easy identification, years passed between the death, the exhumation, and each level of identification. The science was available, but extensive investigation, patience, and persuasion were required before the science could be useful.

CHAPTER 14

Race and Cranial Measurements

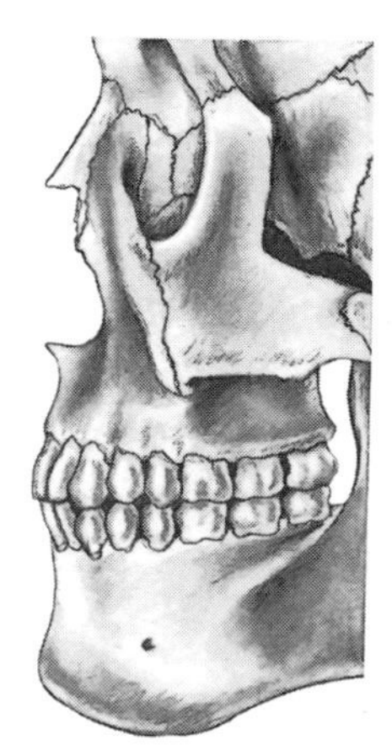

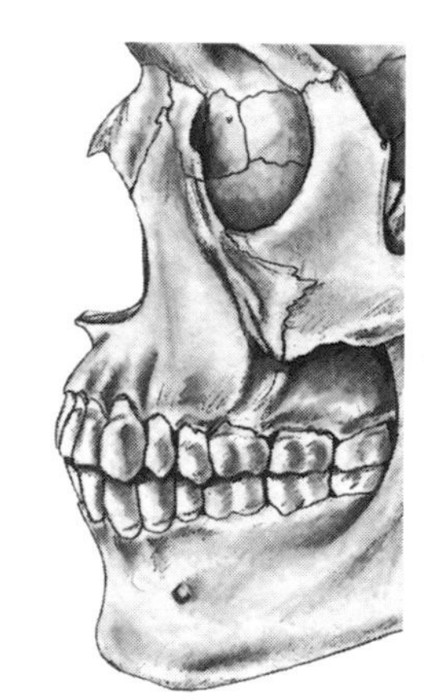

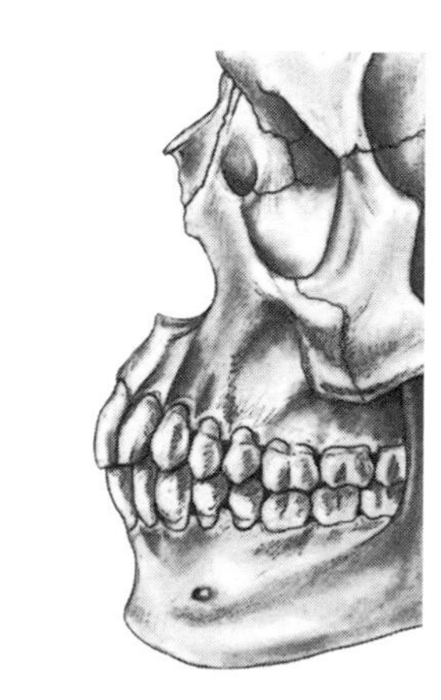

CHAPTER OUTLINE

Introduction

This chapter is separate from the skull chapter and the laboratory analysis chapter (Chapters 3 and 13) because the subject—race—is both complicated and controversial, even when the evidence is nothing but bare bones. This is a presentation of the effort to extract racial information from human remains through general morphological observations and metric methods, as well as a short discussion of possibilities for the future.

Race—Biology and Culture

Anthropologists have long worked to organize, describe, and explain variation in humankind. They have explored the globe, recorded differences in language, religion, ethnicity, and physical forms. They have also tried to explain physical differences between one group and the next by the phenomenon of genetic change through both time and space. The passage of time allows for genetic drift through mutation and natural selection, and the wandering of humankind across continents increases the intermixing of genes. Geographic (or cultural) isolation promotes the formation of racial types by separating populations, and migration dissolves the divisions by combining populations.

Just as with sexual characteristics, racial traits are continuous, not discrete. Sex, however, has only one dividing line—the one between male and female. It is admittedly a blurry line, but, at least, it is biologically based on the presence or absence of a Y chromosome. Race is not so simple. The dividing lines are many, and the definitions are varied. Many so-called "races" are not even based on biology. Studies of the human genome demonstrate clearly that racial categories do not accurately represent genetic truth. Rosenberg et al., (2002) report that within-population differences among individuals account for 93 to 95 percent of genetic variation whereas differences among major groups constitute only 3 to 5 percent. Region-specific alleles are rare. The observed differences between populations are the result of differences in the frequencies of shared alleles.

The words we use to distinguish races are culturally, not biologically, constructed. Each society creates its own ethnocentric definitions for the "others" of the world. These racial profiles help the people within a single culture to communicate mental images of human phenotypes, but they do not work well between disparate cultures. Native Africans see mixed race people as "whites"; Americans and Europeans see them as "light-skinned blacks."

In spite of all the confusion regarding race, basic racial traits provide a means to describe people during the process of identification. Groups of physical traits differ in frequency from one major region of the world to another and help to determine ancestry. For this purpose, the Fordisc program (Ousley & Jantz, 1993, 1996, 2005) is one of the more useful tools, and it may possibly become even more useful as the database increases in size and additional populations are included. (See the section on discriminant function analysis.)

For purposes of more accurate physical description, this section focuses on characteristics that appear to have existed on each of the major continents prior to the Age of (European) Discovery and subsequent extensive migration. Familiarize yourself with the traditional racial types and use the knowledge of individual traits to move toward a physical description of the persons during life. Only three groups are discussed: Asian, European, and African. (More precisely, they are East Asian, Northern European, and Central or Western African.) Native Americans are most similar to the Asian group.

The Future of Race Determination

Identification through analysis of DNA has become almost standard procedure, but until recently, DNA technology did not provide a way to describe an unidentified person. DNA was only useful if a tentative identification was established and a comparative sample was available. Without that comparative sample, the DNA could only be catalogued and stored. The first advances in decoding the human genome were monopolized by the medical sciences in the effort to locate genes correlated with various disease conditions. The genes contributing to simple descriptors like eye and hair color did not merit research funds. However, we know the potential is there.

In the future, the emerging science of DNA phenotyping will probably be able to provide enough physical descriptors to describe how a person actually looked (the phenotype). A good description should make racial identification or, at least, racial approximation, possible. Right now, eye color is the first of the standard physical descriptors to be deciphered. The researchers and developers of the IrisPlex system claim to be able to distinguish brown from blue eyes from minute DNA samples with over 90 percent precision (Walsh, 2011a,b). Hair color is predicted to be the next descriptor to be deciphered. After that, there will be more—possibly even height and facial morphology—but years of research will be required before the goal is reached (Kayser 2011).

Nonmetric Variation in Skull Morphology

Facial Traits

The following set of illustrations shows the classical morphological traits attributed to skulls from major geographical regions. All of these features can be assessed rapidly, without measurements. As a group, these traits focus attention on differences in facial features and provide a broad view of the most obvious differences between the extremes of racial types. None of these traits can be relied on to correlate perfectly with self-reported race or the race as perceived by outside observers. It is a good idea to list morphological traits and then follow up with measurements and discriminant function analysis.

When comparing skulls, begin by evaluating the extent of the projection of the maxilla and mandible in relation to the nose. A more forward-projecting mouth is called **prognathic**; a non-projecting mouth is **orthognathic**. Then compare the width of the nasal aperture and form of the nasal sill. Finally, evaluate the projection of the zygomas in relation to the nose and the mouth regions. Note that the African group can be recognized by the prominence of the mouth in relation to the rest of the face (prognathism). The European group can be distinguished by the prominence of the nose. It is often narrow and projects more than Asian or African noses. The Asian group can be distinguished by the prominence of the cheeks. They are more anteriorly placed, giving the Asian face a broader, flatter appearance. Each prominent feature affects the rest of the face. For instance, prognathism results in a change in the shape of the nasal sill.

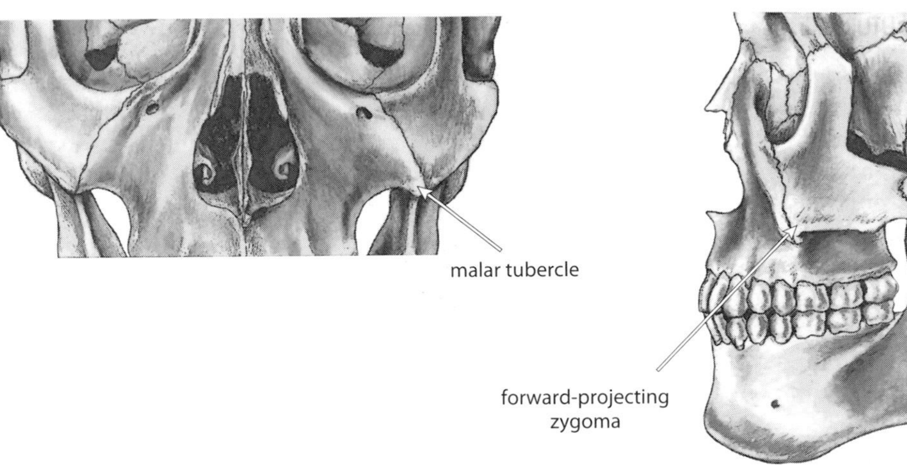

Asian (and Native American) Origin

- orthognathic profile
- moderate nasal spine
- forward-projecting zygoma
- tubercle on inferior zygomatic margin
- sometimes edge-to-edge occlusion

Figure 14.1a and 14.1b
Frontal and Lateral Views of Asian Skull

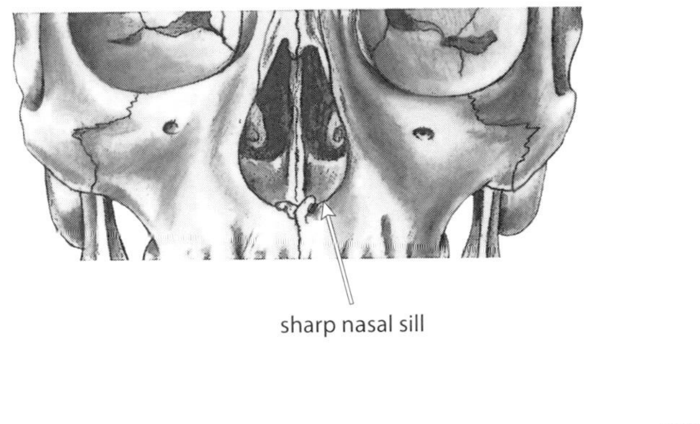

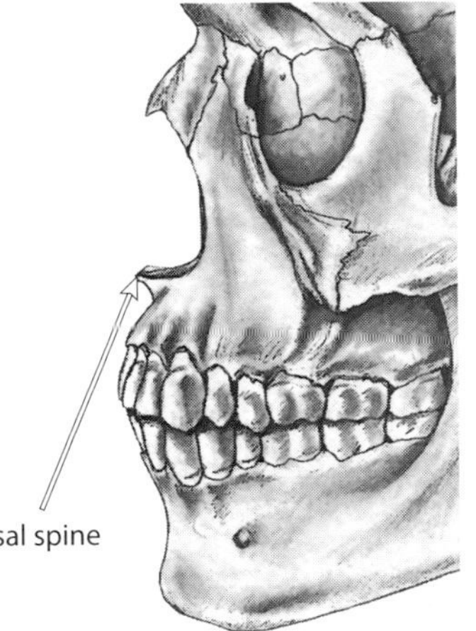

European Origin

- orthognathic profile
- prominent nasal spine
- narrow nasal aperture
- single, sharp inferior nasal margin
- more overbite
- more crowded dentition

Figure 14.2a and 14.2b
Frontal and Lateral Views of European Skull

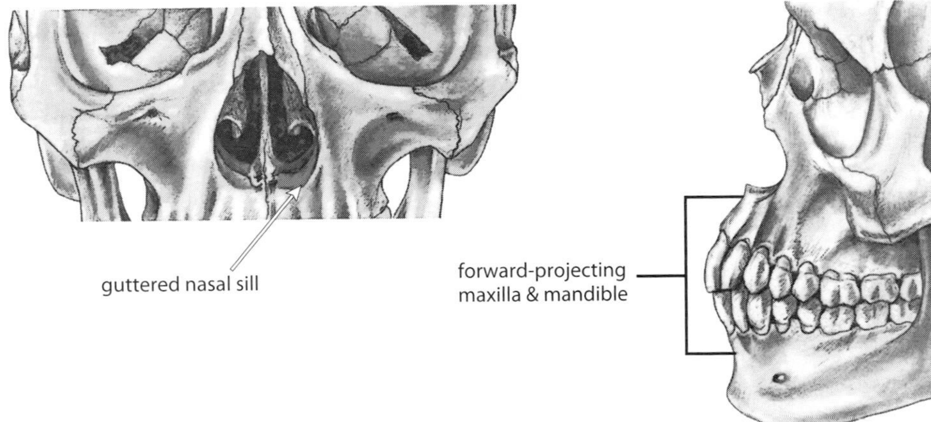

African Origin

- prognathic profile
- little or no nasal spine
- wide nasal aperture
- double (guttered) inferior nasal margin
- dentition not crowded

Figure 14.3a and 14.3b
Frontal and Lateral View of African Skull

Palatal Traits

The following set of illustrations shows the classical morphological traits attributed to skulls from major geographical regions. As with the facial traits, these features can be assessed rapidly, without measurements. The palatal traits reflect the differences in the face. A wider face of Asian origin results in a broad dental row with little, if any, overbite whereas the narrower European face displays parabolic dental row with greater tendency toward dental crowding and overbite. It is useful to record palatal traits, consider them in relation to other information from the skeleton, and follow up with measurements and discriminant function analysis.

Asian Origin

- wide palate
- simple elliptical curve of dental row
- shovel-shaped incisors
- straight palatal suture

(The reduced third molars are not a racial trait.)

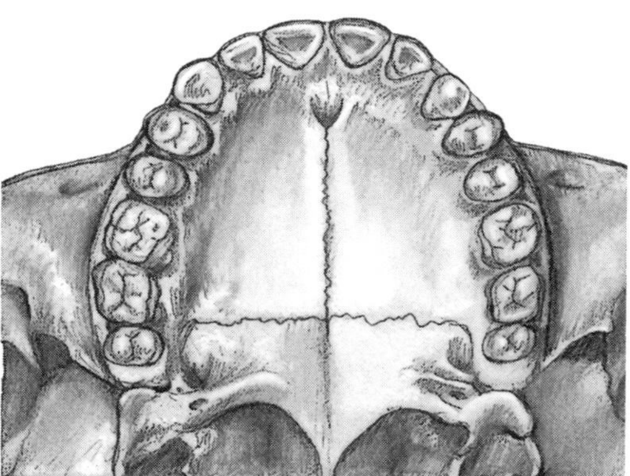

Figure 14.4
Palatal View of Asian Cranium

European Origin

- narrower palate
- parabolic curve of dental row
- no shovel-shaped incisors
- palatine suture is arched or jagged, but not straight

(This individual is missing third molars, a more common occurrence among Europeans.)

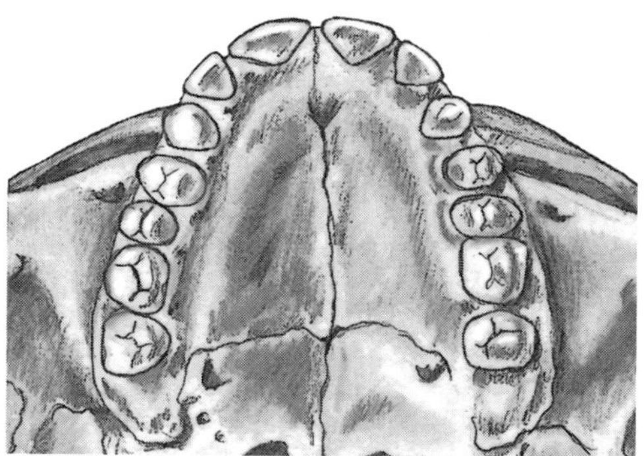

Figure 14.5
Palatal View of European Cranium

African Origin

- intermediate palatal width
- hyperbolic dental row, more U-shaped than the other two forms
- no shovel-shaped incisors
- palatine suture is not straight

(This individual is also missing third molars, an unusual occurrence among Africans.)

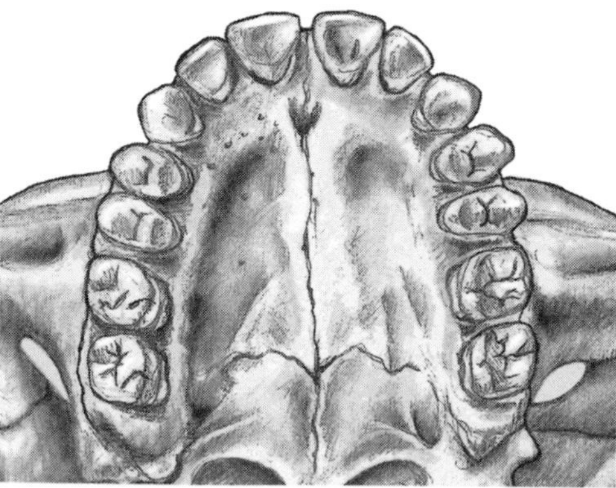

Figure 14.6
Palatal View of African Cranium

Sutural Bones

Individual variation can be seen in extra bones and/or sutures. **Sutural bones** (also called **Wormian bones** or ossicles) develop from separate centers of ossification isolated within skull sutures. They are most common in the lamdoid suture and occur also in areas where more than one suture meets, such as pterion and bregma. A large sutural bone at lambda is called an **Inca bone**. It is sometimes found in Native American skulls along with posterior cranial deformation (flattening of the back of the skull).

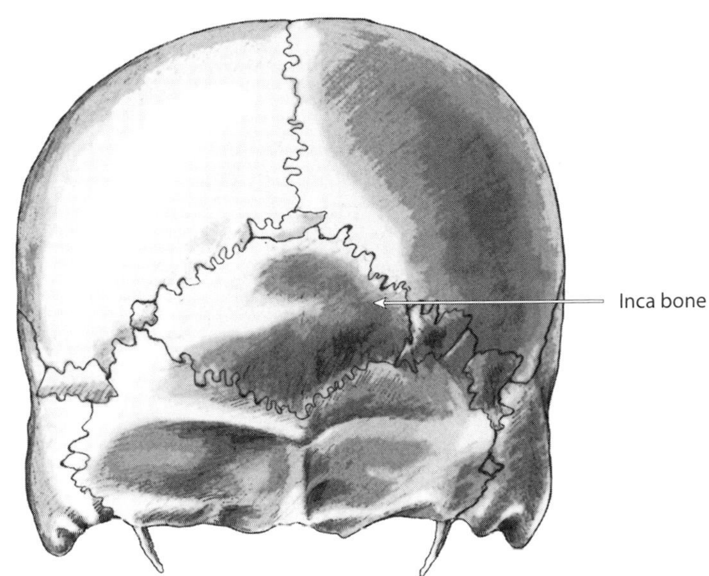

Figure 14.7
Posterior View of Skull with Sutural Bones
An Inca bone, a complicated lambdoid suture, and posterior cranial deformation (flattening) are characteristic of American Indian remains.

Table 14.1 Nonmetric Racial Cranial Traits

Elements of Difference	Asian Origin	European Origin	African Origin
MAXILLARY INCISORS	shovel-shaped	blade-shaped	blade-shaped
MAXILLARY MOLARS	simple, 4 cusps	Carabelli's cusp	simple, 4 cusps
DENTITION	not crowded	crowded with frequently impacted third molars	not crowded
ZYGOMATIC (MALAR)	robust and flaring, with malar tubercle	small, retreating	small, retreating
OS JAPONICUM	2- or 3-part zygoma (extra bone(s))	single zygoma	single zygoma
PROFILE	moderate alveolar prognathism	orthognathic	prognathic
PALATAL SHAPE	elliptic (rounded)	parabolic	U-shaped
PALATAL SUTURE	straight	not straight	not straight
CRANIAL SUTURES	complex and/or with sutural bones	simple	simple
NASAL APERTURE	medium	narrow	wide
NASAL SPINE	medium, tilted	large, long	little or none
NASAL SILL	single, sharp	single, sharp	double, guttered
CHIN	blunt chin	square, projecting	retreating
CRANIUM	low, sloping	high	low, with post-bregmatic depression
HAIR FORM	straight round cross section	wavy oval cross section	curly or kinky flat cross section

Adapted from Gill, 1995.

CRANIOMETRY

No matter what we look at, we see the grand picture before we see the details. When the grand picture is familiar, we unconsciously begin sorting through minutiae. When it is unfamiliar, we never even start sorting. Details of the faces that we see every day are so well known that the briefest glance is sufficient for recognition, but the details of unfamiliar races tend to be overlooked with the comment, "They all look the same to me."

The process of seeing and interpreting details takes time and effort. With skeletal material, instrumentation can speed up the process and help the observer to focus on significant differences. Exact measurements can also serve to support or refute hunches, suspicions, or intuitions about differences.

Anthropometry or **anthropometrics** is a broad term for the physical measurement of humankind. It includes several subsets of measurements. When the body is alive or still fleshed, measurements of the body are called somatometrics, and measurements of the head and face are cephalometrics. When only the skeleton is measured, the term is **osteometrics**, and, if only the skull is measured, the term is **craniometrics**.

General osteometrics are used most frequently to quantify sexual dimorphism and estimate stature. A few measurements, such as anterior curvature of the femur (Stewart, 1962; Trudell, 1999) have been used in racial determination. Craniometrics are used for sex determination, and they are employed more effectively than any other group of measurements for estimation of racial affinity. This could be because facial morphology is the main *skeletally-based* criteria used by groups of people to recognize and categorize other groups or races.

CRANIOMETRIC POINTS OR LANDMARKS

Craniometric points are well-defined, named, landmarks on the skull. Some are single points on the midsagittal plane of the skull, and others are bilaterally paired points. Sets of points are used for precise, reproducible measurements. For example, the measurement from basion to bregma is the *maximum cranial height*.

Craniometric points are also used as a way to identify specific areas of the skull. For example, the gonial angle of the mandible is the general area that contains the point, gonion, at the outer corner of the angle of the mandible.

Each of the commonly used points can be found in the accompanying illustrations, and all are listed in the table of major cranial measurements (Table 14.2). Definitions are in the glossary. It is easiest to learn the points by using them.

Table 14.2 Measurements for the Cranium and Mandible

The names and abbreviations are from FORDISC 2.0 and 3.0 (Ousley & Jantz, 1996 and 2005). If no points are given, the measurement can be made from the description alone.

	Abbreviation	Measurement Name	From This Point	To This Point
1	**GOL**	maximum cranial length	glabella (g)	opisthocranion (op)
2	**XCB**	maximum cranial breadth	euryon (eu)	euryon (eu)
3	**ZYB**	bizygomatic breadth	zygion (zy)	zygion (zy)
4	**BBH**	maximum cranial height (basion-bregma height)	basion (ba)	bregma (b)
5	**BNL**	cranial base length	basion (ba)	nasion (n)
6	**BPL**	basion-prosthion length	basion (ba)	prosthion (pr)
7	**MAB**	maxillo-alveolar breadth	ectomolare (ecm)	ectomolare (ecm)
8	**MAL**	maxillo-alveolar length	prosthion (pr)	alveolon (al)
9	**AUB**	biauricular breadth	root of zygomatic process	root of zygomatic process
10	**UFHT**	upper facial height	nasion (n)	prosthion (pr)
11	**WFB**	minimum frontal breadth	frontotemporale (ft)	frontotemporale (ft)
12	**UFBR**	upper facial breadth	fronto-zygomatic suture	fronto-zygomatic suture
13	**NLH**	nasal height	nasion (n)	nasospinale (ns)
14	**NLB**	nasal breadth	alare (al)	alare (al)
15	**OBB**	orbital breadth	dacryon (d)	ectoconchion (ec)
16	**OBH**	orbital height	superior margin	inferior margin
17	**EKB**	biorbital breadth	ectoconchion (ec)	ectoconchion (ec)
18	**DKB**	interorbital breadth	dacryon (d)	dacryon (d)
19	**FRC**	frontal chord	nasion (n)	bregma (b)
20	**PAC**	parietal chord	bregma (b)	lambda (l)
21	**OCC**	occipital chord	lambda (l)	opisthion (o)
22	**FOL**	foramen magnum length	opisthion (o)	basion (ba)
23	**FOB**	foramen magnum breadth	most lateral point of foramen magnum	most lateral point of foramen magnum
24	**MDH**	mastoid length	porion	mastoidale
25	**ASB**	biasterion breadth	asterion	asterion
26	**ZMB**	zygomaxillary breadth		
27	**MOW**	midorbital width		
28	**gn-id**	chin height	gnathion	infradentale
29		body height at mental foramen		
30		body thickness at mental foramen		
31	**cdl-cdl**	bicondylar breadth	condylion	condylion
32	**go-go**	bigonial breadth	gonion	gonion
33		minimum ramus breadth		
34		maximum ramus height*	gonion	superior condylar surface
35		mandible length*		
36		mandible angle*		

*Use a mandibulometer for these measurements.

Instructions For Accurate Measurements

Begin by considering the measurement name. It usually tells the general location of the measurement, its direction, and its purpose. Height is measured in a superior-inferior direction. Breadth is measured in a lateral-medial direction. Thickness is measured as defined for the specific bone.

Next, consider whether the measurement points are easy to locate by anatomical landmarks or if they can only be found with the use of a measuring device. For example, bregma is at the intersection of two easy-to-locate sutures—the coronal and the sagittal. It is therefore **anatomically determined**. Euryon, however, can only be located by a careful search with spreading calipers. It is the most lateral point on the neurocranium and can be found either on the parietal or on temporal bone. It is therefore **instrumentally determined**.

Reliable measurements take practice. The goal is consistent results that can be duplicated by others (interobserver reliability) and by yourself at different times (intraobserver reliability). It is important to use the best instrument for the measurement, and determine the most effective way to hold both the instrument and the item to be measured. It is easiest to learn with an experienced person. Test yourself by comparing your results with the results recorded by others. When the measurements differ by more than a millimeter or two, find out why.

Skull Measurements

Most skull measurements are self-explanatory, but the exact locations of the measurement points may be confusing. (See Table 14.2 for measurement names and points.) The illustrations are most effective when they are used together with the written definitions in the glossary.

The following are guidelines for dealing with common problems:

- Points that lie at the intersection of sutures should be measured from the external surface of the bone, not from the groove within the suture. This may require moving the point to the closest surface available, e.g., the anteromedial corner of the parietal for bregma.
- Lambda can be difficult to locate if the lambdoid suture is extremely convoluted or further complicated by sutural bones. In such a case, use your best judgment. Ideally, lambda should be on the midline at the most superior extent of the occipital.
- Any point that requires a decision should be marked with pencil so that the same point can be relocated for use with multiple measurements.

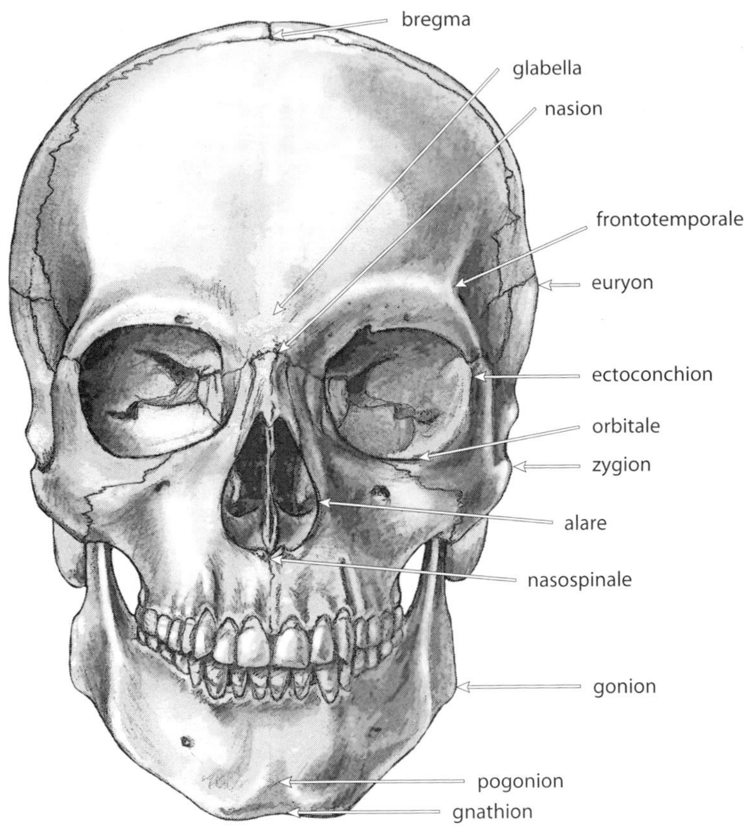

Figure 14.8
Craniometric Points, Frontal View

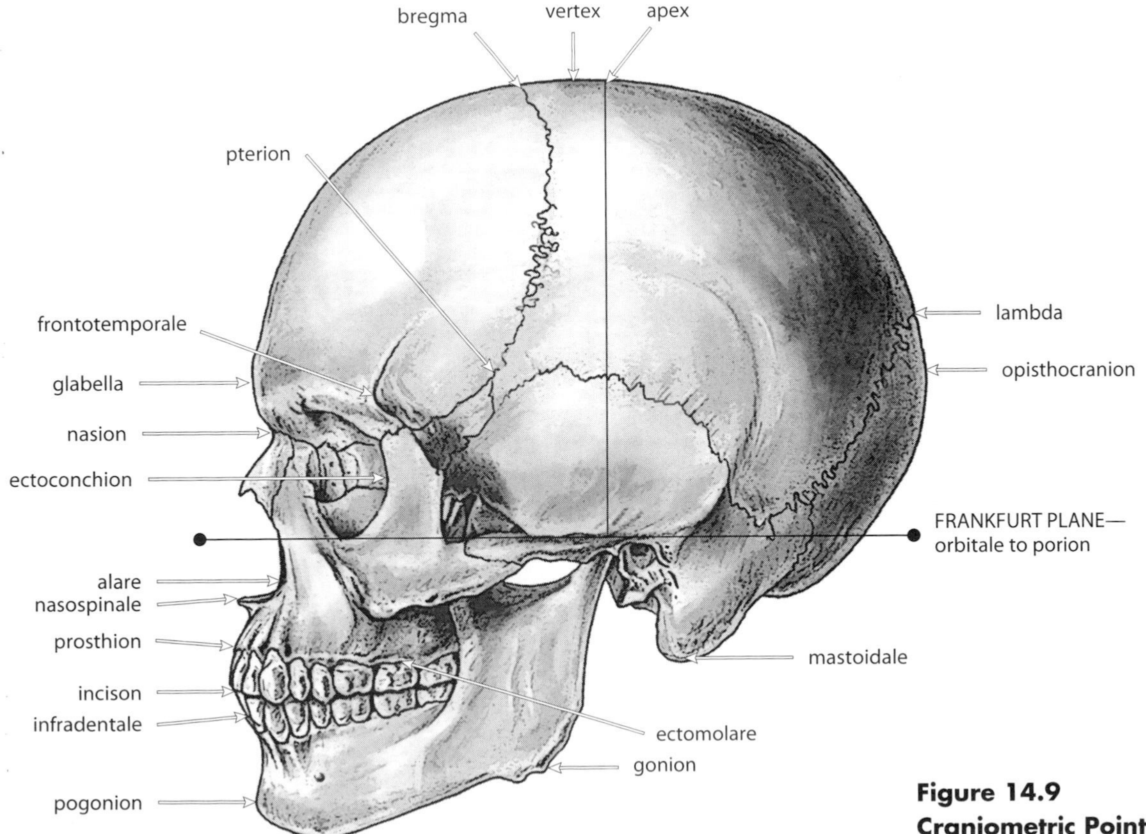

Figure 14.9
Craniometric Points, Lateral View

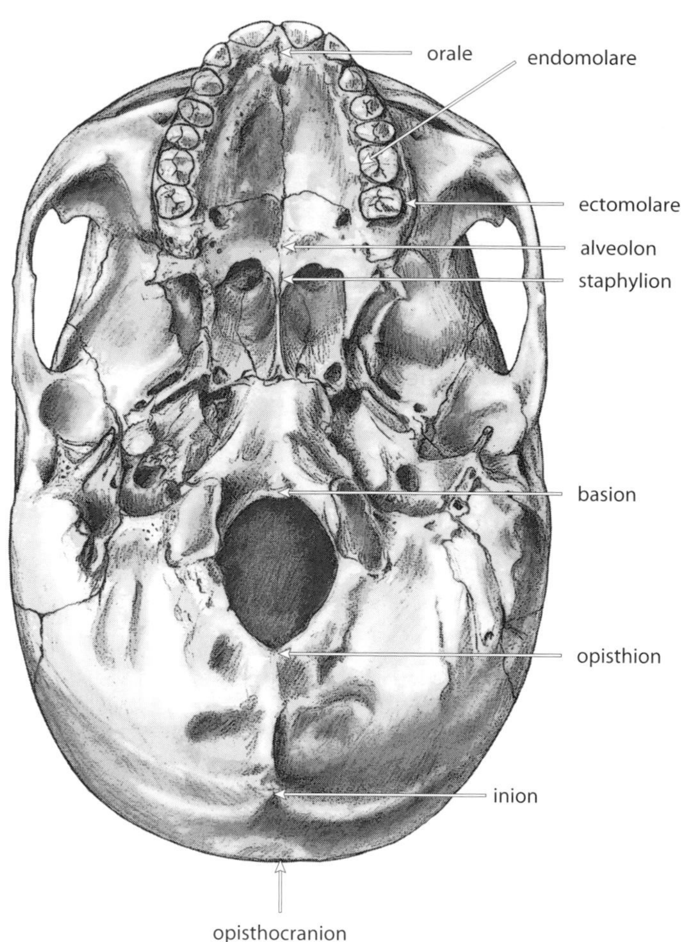

Figure 14.10
Craniometric Points, Basilar View

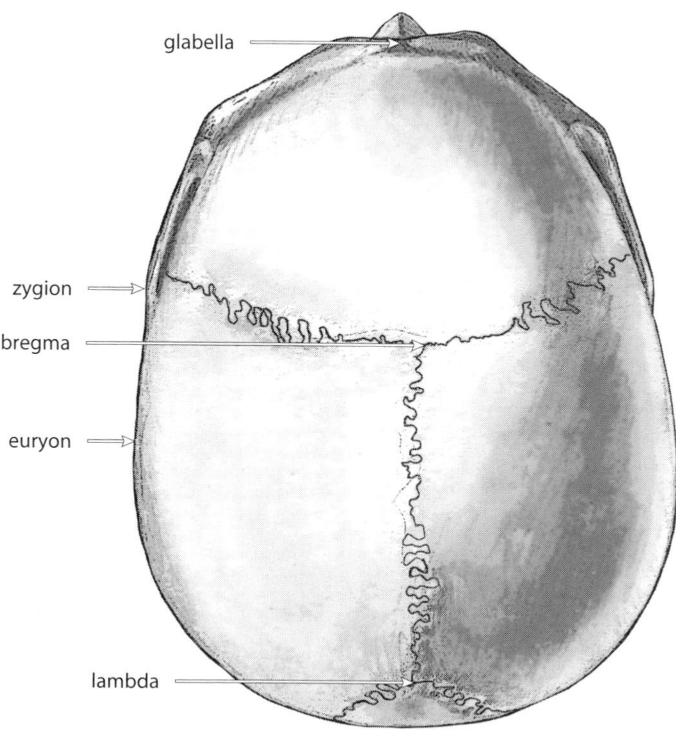

Figure 14.11
Craniometric Points, Coronal View

Orbital Measurements

It is difficult to see the exact measurement points for the orbit on a full-skull diagram, so they are enlarged here. Use extremely great care with calipers on the thin bone of the orbits. Be gentle.
The following measurements are applicable to the orbital area:

- Orbital height: Orbitale to the superior orbital border while perpendicular to the natural horizontal axis of the orbit. Some orbits are naturally oriented on a horizontal plane, but most are angled with the lateral border inferior to the medial border.
- Orbital breadth: Dacryon to ectoconchion—the greatest width of the orbit.
- Biorbital breadth: Ectoconchion to ectoconchion—the distance across both orbits.
- Interorbital breadth: Dacryon to dacryon—the distance between the eye orbits.

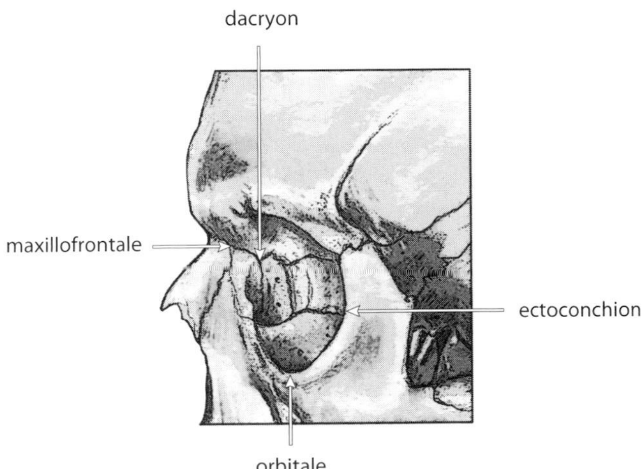

Figure 14.12
Craniometric Points, Medial Orbital Wall

Frankfurt Plane

Consider the orientation of the skull. When a bare skull is placed on a flat surface, it appears to be looking upward. If the mandible is absent, the upward angle is even greater. But the skull was in a very different position in the living person. Most people carry their heads with the chin below the base of the skull. A line drawn through the ear openings is about the same distance from the floor as a line drawn between the shadows under each eye. If you connect the ear line with the under-eye line, a plane is formed that is parallel to the floor.

In the bare skull, the anatomically correct position is defined by three cranial points—the left and right porion and the left orbitale. (These points are explained in the next section.) Thus, the external ear openings and the lower edge of the left eye orbit provide a standardized plane for a "normal" skull position. This is called the **Frankfurt Plane**, **Frankfort Horizontal**, or **auriculo-orbital plane**. It is a worldwide standard in physical anthropology, first accepted in 1877 by the International Congress of Anthropologists in Frankfurt, Germany. (See Figures 14.8 and 14.10.)

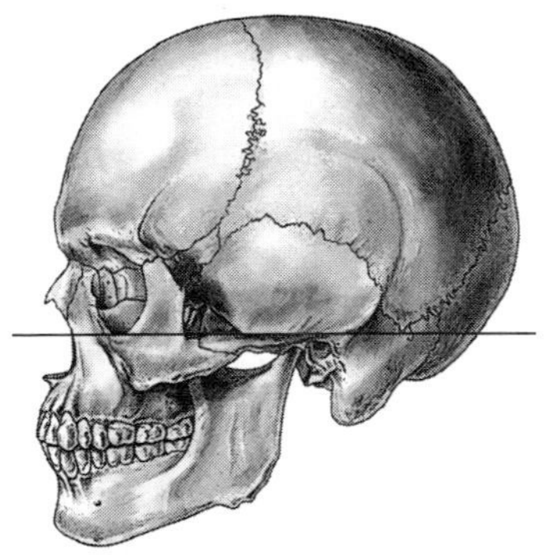

Figure 14.13
Frankfurt Plane

Palatal Measurements

The difficult part about measuring the palate is finding the three transverse lines. They can usually be visualized by sighting down on the two arms of the sliding caliper. For the post-alveolar line, a rubber band can be stretched around the alveolar ridge. It should form a straight line behind the two distal extents of the alveolar ridge. The measurement can be taken from the anterior edge of the rubber band where it crosses the medial palatal suture.
The following measurements are applicable to the palate:

- Maximum alveolar length: Prosthion to alveolon—from the most anterior point of the alveolar ridge to the intersection of the midline and a line drawn behind the alveolar ridge (regardless of the presence of absence of teeth)
- Maximum alveolar breadth: Ectomolare to ectomolare—the greatest width of the alveolar ridge, measured at the second molar
- Palatal length: Orale to staphylion
- Palatal breadth: Endomolare to endomolare

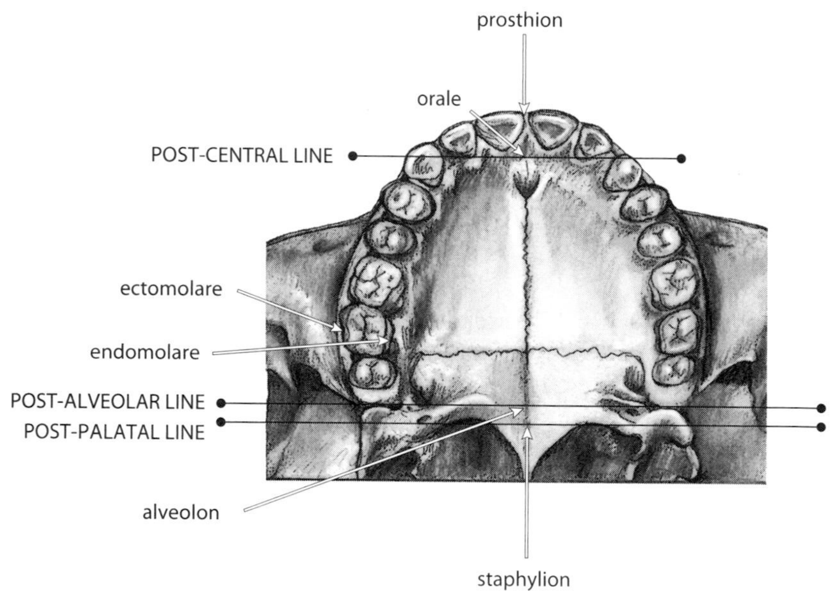

Figure 14.14
Craniometric Points, Palate

Chord Measurements

The chord is a standardized method for obtaining a straight-line measurement from a curved surface. The curvature is not important, only the direct distance from beginning point to end point. There are three common chord measurements:

- Frontal chord (frontal bone): Nasion to bregma (illustrated)
- Parietal chord (parietal bone): Bregma to lambda (illustrated)
- Occipital chord (occipital bone): Lambda to opisthion

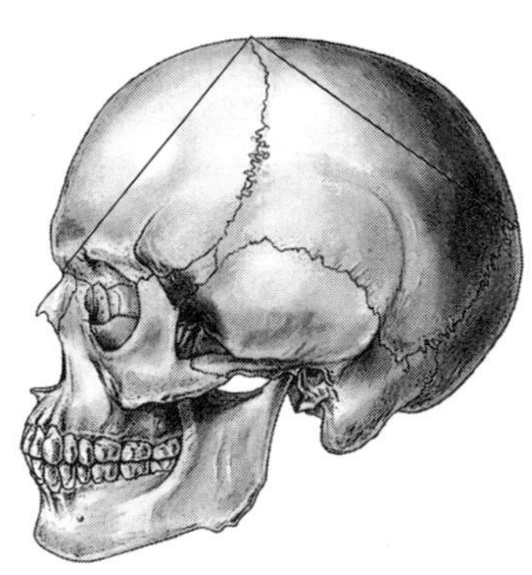

Figure 14.15
Frontal and Parietal Chord Measurements

MANDIBULAR MEASUREMENTS

There are only nine useful measurements for the mandible, and three of them require an extra piece of equipment—a mandibulometer. It is designed to measure the angle of the ramus to the body of the mandible and is also used to obtain reliable measurements of the height of the ramus and the length of the body.

The following measurements can be made without a mandibulometer.

- Bicondylar width: Condylion to condylion—the greatest width of the mandible
- Bigonial width: Gonion to gonion—the width from one angle to the other
- Mandibular symphysis height: Gnathion to infradentale
- Body height at mental foramen
- Body thickness at mental foramen

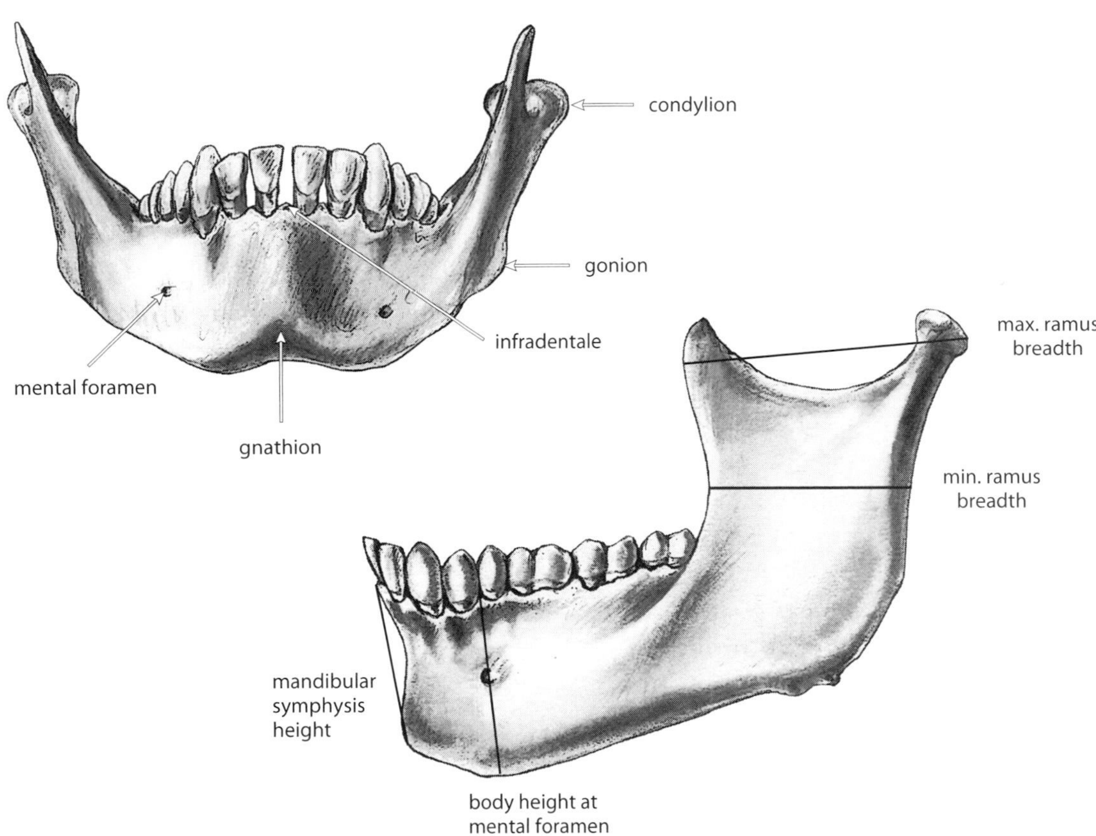

Figure 14.16
Craniometric Points, Mandible

Metric Variation in Skull Morphology

A person with a long, narrow head looks quite different from a person with a wide, round head, and populations tend to share the same general head shape. For this reason, early physical anthropologists tried many methods to describe heads by measuring skulls. They puzzled over the relevance of each measurement result in relation to topics such as sex, race, intelligence, and evolution.

Cephalic Index

Statistical approaches to the problem were advanced in the nineteenth century. A French anthropologist, Paul Topinard, recommended the use of the **cephalic index**—a simple ratio of cranial measurements—to describe the general shape of a skull and the general appearance of the face in life.

Cranial Index Formula: maximum cranial breadth/maximum cranial length x 100

- 74.99 or less is a long, narrow head (dolichocranic)
- 75.00 to 79.99 is an average head (mesocranic)
- 80.00 to 84.00 is a broad, round head (brachycranic)
- 85.00 or more is a very broad, round head (hyperbrachycranic)

Early Discriminant Function Analysis

In the twentieth century, more complex statistical approaches were tried out, and more individual measurements were utilized. By the 1950s and 1960s, discriminant function analysis had become popular. This is a statistical method for distinguishing (discriminating) one naturally occurring group from another (e.g., males and females). Discriminant function analysis starts with an assortment of variables, selects the best predictors for the specific group, and weighs the variables according to importance. In skeletal analysis, the variables are sets of well-defined measurements.

Discriminant function analysis has been used to evaluate crania, mandibulae, and long bones. The best known "pioneering" studies are those of Eugene Giles and Orville Elliot. They compared cranial measurements with race (1962) and sex (1963) and stressed the utility of their work for forensic applications. Discriminant function analysis provides not only answers, but also a measure of the reliability of those answers. Both are essential in forensic work.

Fordisc

The advent of accessible computers revolutionized skeletal analysis along with everything else. Computerized analyses provide much more flexibility and greater precision. Databases are available to a wider group of scientists and can be regularly augmented. Programs are modified and updated to reflect ongoing research and improved statistical procedures. When used according to the directions and recommendations of the authors, computer analysis is far more effective than the standardized formulae of the past. Skeletal analysis has grown more complex, but more effective, or so it would seem.

Fordisc is a Windows-based software program designed by Stephen Ousley and Richard Jantz (1993, 1996, 2005). It has become a standard tool for race assessment as well as sex and stature estimation. It is more effective than earlier methods because the analysis is multivariate, and the sample population is diverse and dynamic. Fordisc utilizes discriminant function analysis developed from a large database of skeletal measurements. Much of the sample is from the Forensic Data Bank at University of Tennessee, but other institutions and individuals have contributed (and continue to contribute). The program is interactive and user friendly. The measurements are described and illustrated within the Help files.

Fordisc 3.1 is available at the time of this printing. The reference group sample size is larger than in earlier versions of Fordisc. More measurements are used and more statistical methods are available. It is also capable of incorporating other data sets (Ousley & Jantz 2005).

One final word of caution: Don't rely on the predictions of any method, computerized or other, without considering and reporting the statistical reliability of the results. In the pursuit of a "perfect" physical description, don't lose track of the fact that race is not even definable in living persons. The goal is to produce a better, more thorough description of an unidentified person. If that means showing possible affinity to a well-described racial group, then it may be useful. If it overly narrows a description to exclude the person, it is counterproductive.

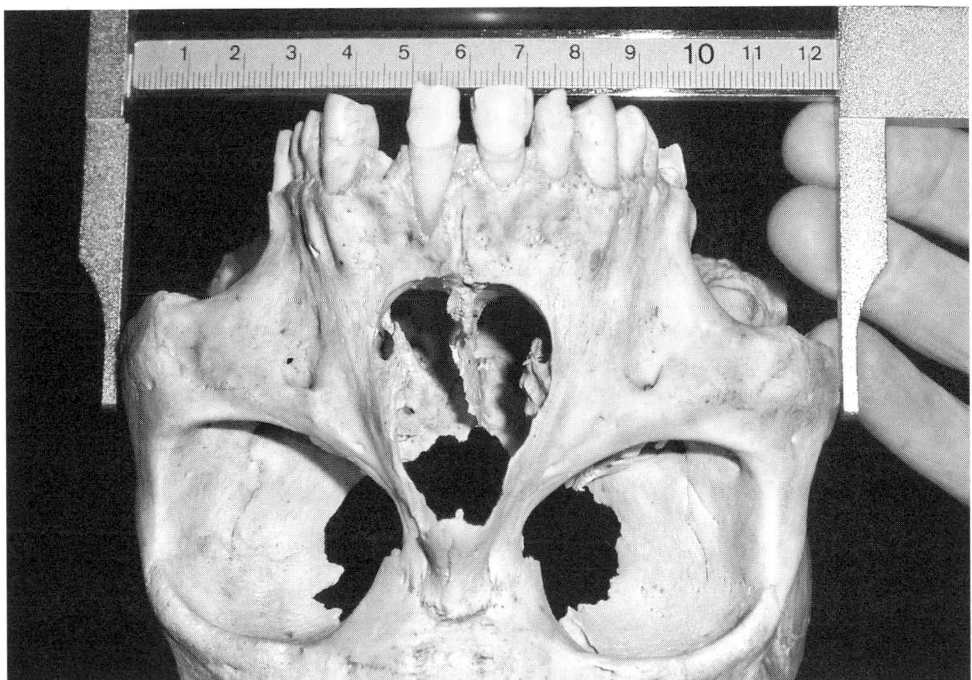

Figure 14.17
Measurement of Bizygomatic Breadth
Interobserver errors are reduced when images are used together with measurement descriptions. This photograph is an example of the type of images available in the Fordisc Program help files.

Postcranial Traits

Most postcranial research has focused on the femur. Persuasive traits include anterior curvature of the femoral shaft (Stewart, 1962; Trudell, 1999), shape of the proximal diaphysis (Gilbert & Gill, 1990), and the depth of the intercondylar notch (Baker et al., 1990). Refer to the original papers for methological details and values.

Table 14.3 Racial Differences in the Femur

	Asian Origin (incl. Native Am)	European Origin	African Origin
Anterior Curvature	straighter	more curved	straighter
Proximal Diaphysis Shape	anteroposterior flattening	rounder	rounder
Intercondylar Notch Depth	undetermined	shallower	deeper

Another method uses postcranial osteometrics related to overall body shape. The hypothesis follows the observations of Bergmann (1847) and Allen (1877) regarding body shape and environment. Bergmann's Rule states that body mass increases in inhabitants of colder climates. They tend to have short, wide bodies and short limbs. Allen's rule states that extremities increase in length in warmer climates. The people tend to have long, narrow bodies and long limbs. Holliday and Falsetti (1999) published discriminant function coefficients for seven postcranial measurements distinguishing African American males and females from European American males and females. 82 percent of a male independent test population was correctly classified. Only 57 percent of a female test population was correctly classified, but the sample may have been too small for adequate evaluation. This work should be further tested. It provides a way to assess body form, if not actual race.

Duray and colleagues (1999) reported that the C3–C6 spinous processes show a higher frequency of bifidity in whites than in blacks. It's one more thing to consider.

Chapter 15

Field Methods

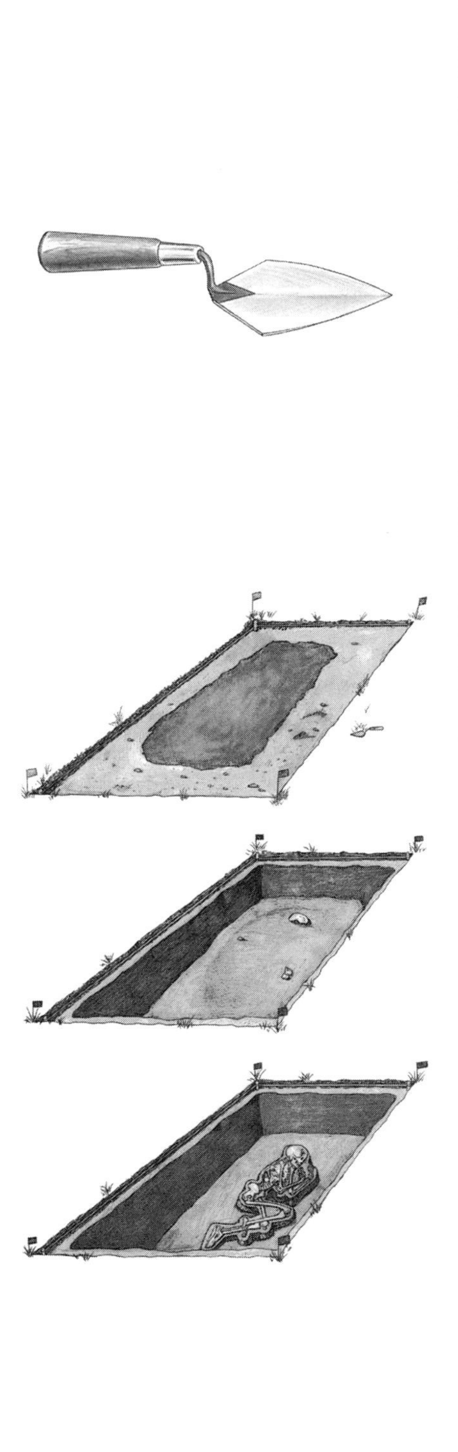

CHAPTER OUTLINE

Introduction

Traditional anthropologists, both physical anthropologists and archaeologists, analyse and study the remains of ancient humans and the sites of ancient and historic occupation. Their methods have proved to be ideal for use in modern crime scenes as well, such as clandestine burials, mass graves, and disaster sites. The archaeologist is usually responsible for excavation and mapping, and the physical anthropologist/human osteologist is responsible for collection and analysis of the human remains.

Field work is any investigation that takes place outside or away from the home laboratory or office. The purpose of field work is retrieval of information by whatever means are allowed. Archaeological field work involves activities like surveying, mapping, and excavating. Sociocultural field work involves interviews, written questionnaires, and cultural research. The usefulness of the information is decided later, during the analysis phase.

In forensic anthropology, field work takes many forms. A shallow one-body grave in Iowa is quite different from a mass disaster in New York City or a plane wreck in the Andes. There is no way to cover it all within the scope of this book. This chapter simply provides an overview of the concerns and the work that goes into planning and carrying out field investigations. I have included basic methods for interviewing survivors to obtain antemortem information and excavating human graves for physical evidence.

Preplanning for Field Work

> Success depends on serious preparation and on-the-spot ingenuity.

The unexpected is normal in field work. It can take the form of unusual weather, equipment breakdown, shortage of supplies, injury, illness, theft, and more. If the work site is close to a modern city, it is possible to send for help. However, most field work is conducted far from supply sources, and most budgets have to be planned far in advance of the actual work. Thorough preparation offers few thrills and little sense of adventure, but it is essential. The time spent in preparation is well rewarded in productivity.

Objectives

Begin by considering the objectives of the field work. Usually, there are two major objectives: recovery of all physical evidence, including human remains, and identification of the dead. There are situations in which one or the other objective will take precedence. In a situation such as an unmarked graveyard in the middle of a construction project, identification is unlikely. The primary objective is respectful recovery and reburial of the remains. In a situation such as a war-related mass grave, the circumstances of death are well known. The primary objective is identification.

Legal Permission

Legal requirements vary from state to state and country to country. It is imperative that persons planning to recover or excavate a human body be aware of the governing law and adhere to the appropriate legal procedures.

For example, in the United States, initial custody of human remains is with the responding police officer, who has the duty to notify the appropriate authority. Depending on the jurisdiction, the coroner's office or the medical examiner's office takes custody from the police officer, investigates the case further, and orders any necessary procedures. The coroner may send the body for autopsy whereas the medical examiner has both legal and medical responsibility within the same office. The coroner or medical examiner issues a death certificate and releases the body for disposition—usually to a funeral home. Later, if a disinterment is requested, the order must be issued by the appropriate office within that jurisdiction.

Legal permission for disinterment includes specific requirements, such as who must be present at the exhumation and how the body is to be reintered. The coroner or medical examiner is usually required to be present. Police officers may also be required. If the grave is in a cemetery, the cemetery regulations may specify that a cemetery official be present. Funeral directors and religious personnel may also be necessary, if not legally required.

FUNDING

Funding is not usually a problem for full-time employees of governmental law enforcement agencies in the United States. However, private consultants and contractors need to budget carefully and request adequate funds to ensure completion of a thorough job. All costs must be researched and budgeted, from the planning stage through the final report preparation. Time in the field is only part of the whole cost. Analysis may or may not be budgeted separately.

The source of funds is just as important as the quantity. If the excavation is part of an investigation that reflects on a political entity, the political motivation of the funding source will affect the general reception of the report and the results of any subsequent legal proceedings. This is particularly important in international human rights work. Private or international funds backed by general human rights interests are to be preferred over single-government funds.

INSURANCE

Make sure that both the workers and the equipment are adequately insured against risk of injury and property loss.

SECURITY AND STORAGE

Security is always an issue for the site, the evidence, and the workers. The site itself should be treated as a crime scene from the very beginning. A perimeter should be established before any work begins. Circumstances determine the size of the perimeter. A crime scene with scattered remains may cover an entire hillside in the country or a complete vacant lot in a city. A cemetery disinterment requires only the area of the grave and whatever more is necessary for restriction of onlookers and media. A person should be assigned to maintain a record of everyone allowed within the perimeter. If the excavation process takes more than one day, even in a rural setting, a night guard is essential.

The excavation record should be able to contradict claims of unauthorized disturbances. Photography provides a simple method for documenting disturbances. Establish and mark a specific point or several points from which the entire site can be observed. Take a photograph from the point(s) at the beginning and end of each work day (as well as significant times during the day). Use a tripod (or at least a photographer of the same height) to ensure that angulation is identical from one photograph to the next.

Plan to store all evidence—both human remains and other physical evidence—in a dry, secure area during all phases of the work. Refrigeration may be necessary if decomposition is a problem. Never leave evidence unguarded or unlocked—even for lunch or coffee break. Lack of security damages the chain of custody, and thereby, the legitimacy of the evidence.

In the not-so-distant past, anthropological work took place years after the critical event. At that time, it was necessary to guard the evidence, but the safety of the workers was not an issue. Today, forensic anthropologists are working in active war zones and worker safety is a vital issue.

Antemortem Information

Exhumations and disinterments can take place without antemortem information, but if identification is a primary goal, it is a good idea to have as much information as possible before beginning. We all like to think that our excavation techniques are flawless, but we will never know what we missed. If, for example, workers know they are looking for a pregnant female in a mass grave, they are more likely to locate and recover the fragile fetal remains.

There are two phases in the collection of antemortem information. The first phase precedes the field work. It consists of gathering information from personal interviews, medical records, and government records. The goal is a full description of the missing person(s), including details that may survive interment.

The second phase follows the field and laboratory work. It consists of follow-up interviews and renewed searches. The goal is to fill in missing information and resolve any discrepancies between the descriptions of the missing persons and the descriptions of the unidentified remains.

The Interview

There are circumstances under which the personal interview is the sole means of obtaining crucial information about the deceased. Plan ahead for optimal communication; I have found it helpful to have a trusted person such as a priest or other community figure present during the interview. In international settings, local translators are essential. They are more likely to understand nuances in communication. Also, be prepared with interview tools such as the following:

Questionnaires

Use standardized questionnaires that can be adapted to computerized database programs whenever possible. Programs for matching missing and unidentified persons are available in the United States from several organizations, including the National Disaster Medical System and the National Crime Information Center. A sample questionnaire is included in the Appendix. It is designed for use by families and friends of victims.

Visual Aids

Use visual aids wherever possible. Memory is enhanced with the use of pictures, and fewer left–right errors and translation errors occur when the interviewee can communicate without ambiguity by pointing or drawing.

If scars or amputations are mentioned, provide diagrams of faces or full-body diagrams. The location of the identifying characteristic can be drawn on the diagram and included with the file. When teeth are discussed, use full-mouth dental casts or drawings of teeth. It is easier to point to the location of the missing or broken tooth than to try to describe it.

If clothing is described, offer color charts and record the number of the color for each article of clothing. Color is notoriously difficult to communicate, even between people of the same culture and language group. Cloth samples can also be useful. (Samples can be collected from a local tailor or dressmaker's shop.) The samples should be representative of the types of cloth used in the area (e.g., several different weights and textures of cotton or wool).

Examples of Useful Medical Records

- dental radiographs
- cranial radiographs showing frontal sinuses
- radiographs of broken or healed bones
- radiographs of arthritic joints
- any radiograph that demonstrates the trabecular pattern in calcified tissue
- information about prostheses and implants
- written descriptions of physical problems

Medical Records

Almost any medical records can be useful, but radiographs are preferred for identification of skeletal remains. Positive identifications can be made from comparisons of antemortem and postmortem radiographs of almost any type.

Antemortem Photographs

A clear photograph can help to define distinctive traits of the missing individual, but photographs must be used with analytical skill and common sense. A *smiling* photo is particularly useful because the dentition can be observed directly in the skull. Anterior teeth may be missing, chipped, or out of alignment (crooked). A *profile* photo reveals the curvature of the forehead, brow, and upper part of the nose. The same curvatures can be observed on the frontal bones, the supraorbital ridge, and the nasal bones. A three-quarter view portrait photo or a photo with *side lighting* may reveal a trait such as a broken nose, a deeply cleft chin, or large frontal bossing. Most photos without unusual dental traits provide tentative, not positive, identification.

Preparation for Excavation and Disinterment

Numbering System

Plan a numbering system to use for all the evidence. An effective long-term numbering system incorporates useful information from the following categories:

Agency or Consultant

The name or abbreviation of the agency or institution responsible for recovery of the evidence is usually placed at the beginning. Initials or a specific code for the individual responsible for the recovery can also be incorporated here.

Date

The date of recovery or the date of accessioning should be included in the number. It is necessary to decide how much of the date is required—just the year, the year and the month, or the entire date (yyyy-mm-dd). In some cases, time of day is also important.

Site or Location

Include the site name or an abbreviation of the site name. The abbreviations employed by the law enforcement or military in a particular area may be useful because of the need to communicate with other organizations. If no other system is in effect in a particular area, grid coordinates can be used.

Specific Unit Number

The identification code must include a unique number for each set of individual remains and each piece of evidence. Ideally, the numbers are assigned in sequence of recovery. If, however, there are no numbers assigned at recovery, numbers are assigned in order of receipt in the laboratory. (See "Evidence Management" in Chapter 13 for more information on numbering systems.)

Data Record Forms

Forms are provided in the Appendix for specific categories of tasks. Use them as they are or use them as a starting point from which to develop new forms to fit the specific project needs. The major categories of field forms include burial site information forms, skeletal diagrams, skull diagrams, and dental diagrams.

Equipment and Supplies

As mentioned before, every project is different. There is no such thing as the "perfect field kit" for every situation. However, that is no reason to be unprepared. Gather as much site information as possible and think through what may or may not be needed. This section provides a guide based on experience.

Some items are essential and some are optional but nice to have on hand. Sometimes the optional items prove to be essential. Each year brings new experiences and new ideas. Begin your own lists and use your own creativity.

A T-shaped metal probe, sometimes called a tile probe, is commonly used to locate solid surfaces, such as pipes underground, but the probe serves just as well to perceive differences in soil density associated with ground disturbances such as graves. The point of the probe is closed, not hollow.

Leaf rakes are useful for removing debris from the soil surface. However, if you choose to rake the area, watch the ground carefully while raking. Hair and other small, light evidence is easily caught up and removed within the leafy debris. If evidence is anticipated on the surface rather than in a burial, it may be necessary to go through the leaf litter by hand.

Shovels are essential, but not just any shovel will do. A standard rounded point shovel is easy to find in a hardware store, but it is no good for an

Table 15.1 Equipment and Supplies for Work in the Field

	Equipment	Supplies
ESSENTIAL	compass	wooden stakes
	measuring tape	string
	probe	paper bags
	flat, square shovels	cardboard boxes
	metal file for tool sharpening	indelible ink pens
	trowels	pencils
	saw and/or root clippers	waterproof paper for mapping
	paint brushes—large and small	notebook
	whisk broom	clipboard
	plastic tools for close work	insect repellant
	buckets	photographic film or digital storage
	screens—0.5, 0.25, 0.125 in. mesh	gloves—cloth and plastic
	camera—with zoom and macro lenses	body bags and protective clothing if decomposing remains are expected
	gauge for photographs	
	calipers—small and large	
	canvas or heavy plastic sheets	
	container for drinking water	
OPTIONAL	metal detector	flags for marking
	leaf rake	spray paint for gridding
	small blackboard (for ID numbers in photos)	4 × 6 cards for tags
	colanders	background cloth for photos
	water sprayer (typical garden use)	protective clothing
	notebook computer	plastic bags for temporary storage
	tripod for camera	
	folding tables, or saw horses and plywood	
	tents	

Figure 15.1
Tile Probe
Nupla Corporation

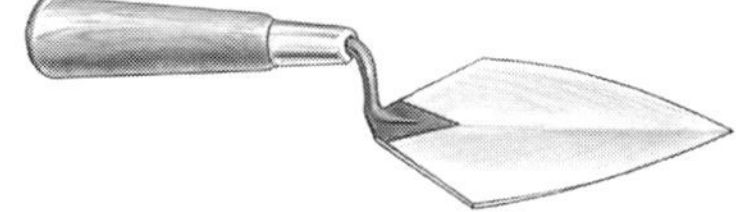

Figure 15.2
Marshalltown Trowel

archaeologically sound excavation. The objective of a forensic excavation is not only to dig a hole, but to locate and maximize information. A sharp, **square point shovel** can shave the dirt horizontally and make stains, outlines, and interrelationships of features visible.

The basic hand tool is the trowel. It must be small enough to be manipulated easily and it must be pointed with straight sides and a sharp edge. (The Marshalltown Company makes the traditional "archaeology trowel.") Brushes are useful if the soil is dry. Dental tools and thin plastic scrapers are better if the soil is damp and sticking to the brushes. Dental tools can also used (with great care) when the earth around the remains is extremely hard (e.g., sun-baked clay).

Burial Location and Scene Investigation

The process of locating human remains, buried or scattered, is both a crime scene investigation and an archaeological site survey at the same time. The entire site should be searched in the process of locating a grave. Any evidence or suspected evidence should be flagged and left in situ until after photographs and maps can be completed.

Verbal testimony may help but details can be easily distorted. The movements of earth, wind, and water are enough to befuddle the clearest of memories. Add in the action of plants and animals, or the work of devious (or well-meaning) persons, and the picture keeps changing.

Remote Sensing

Remote sensing is the preferred method for investigation under many circumstances. Ideally, search areas can be focused and hidden evidence can be located, all while maintaining the integrity of the site. Remote sensing can lead to increased productivity in the field, particularly in remote areas where field work may be expensive and security is a problem. Data from remote sensing can provide the proof necessary to obtain legal permissions and funds to continue, or it can provide the reason to discontinue and move to another location.

Ground-penetrating radar and metal detectors are commonly used for small areas. They are a practical alternative to excavation when ground disturbance is inadvisable or forbidden. For large-area searches, aerial photography and satellite remote imaging is effective. They can show change over time and reveal patterns that are not apparent without sufficient perspective. Computer-enhanced satellite images can reveal the presence of features that seem totally invisible during ground searches.

Archaeologists are using satellite **prospection** to locate ancient archaeological sites and identify archaic land-use patterns. The same methods are being

CASE EXAMPLE: LOCATING A DISTURBED GRAVE

I once worked a scene that had been fully described and mapped for the police by an informant. The map included the location (and species) of trees in relation to a dirt road and a fence. It should have been easy to find the grave, but I arrived to discover that the entire area had been bulldozed flat—no road, no trees, no fence. The grave was finally found by a systematic survey. The entire area was gridded into 3-meter squares; each square was probed for differences in soil density; and suspect areas were carefully scraped with a flat-edged shovel. The soil was dry and no color differences were apparent, but misting each area with a water sprayer revealed slight color differences in the area where topsoil had been mixed with subsoil.

used to find inconsistent or inappropriate land-use patterns associated with crimes against humanity (Madden & Ross, 2009). Satellite images (and aerial photographs) of an area can be compared over a period of years, and suspect areas of land can be identified and circumscribed. These methods are being used to investigate the evidence of genocide in the Darfur area of Sudan. For more information, explore The American Association for the Advancement of Science (AAAS) and Human Rights Program's Geospatial Technologies and Human Rights Project.

What to Look for before Disturbing the Surface

Surface Irregularities

There are numerous methods of locating graves. The appropriate method depends on the age and type of the grave and the environmental conditions. It may be possible to locate a grave visually. A person accustomed to the landscape can recognize irregularities in both the vegetation and the ground surface.

Vegetation Changes

The plants over a burial are often out of synchronization with surrounding plants. This is due to disruption in the natural succession of plant species, changes in soil nutrients, or the introduction of foreign elements. Increased nutrients from a decomposing body and increased moisture from a burial depression result in more lush vegetation. In one rather unusual case, the murderer sowed the clandestine grave of his victim with grass seed—a strange sight in the middle of a brushy thicket!

Sometimes the plants over a burial are stunted or dying. This may be the result of decreased access to nutrients caused by impermeable synthetic materials within the grave. It may also be caused by harmful chemicals introduced to the soil at the time of burial.

Changes in Soil Density

After completing a thorough visual search of the suspected area, a test of soil density provides additional information. This is accomplished with a simple metal probe (a tile probe).

The fill dirt within a grave is more loosely compacted than surrounding soil. It is easy to feel in an otherwise undisturbed area. It is more difficult to differentiate in a disturbed area such as a plowed field, a construction site, or a dump site. Probing should be carried out in a regular pattern. When the edge of a grave fill is found, search for the outline of the disturbance and avoid probing through the middle of the pit. It is not good to find probe holes in essential pieces of evidence when the excavation begins.

Anything Else: Search the Entire Area

Even if the location of the grave is known, a search of the entire area is necessary before beginning the excavation. Evidence on the ground surface is often destroyed or distorted by human activity after the excavation begins. Look for any inconsistencies on the ground—footprints, tire tracks, damaged vegetation, spent cartridges, garbage, or etc.

Look above and within the ground surface. Rodents, carnivores, and birds are known to carry off both food items and nesting materials. Check animal burrows (carefully) and nests. Fibers or hairs become entangled on branches or tree bark. Stray bullets embed in tree trunks, embankments, and buildings.

CASE EXAMPLE: AN UNUSUAL CRIME SCENE SEARCH

I have participated in many large-area searches for scattered remains. One that stands out was conducted on a forested slope. The skull and a few other major skeletal elements were recovered. The skull would probably provide a positive identification, but no trauma was apparent on any of the bones, so we lacked clues about the events around the time of death. If we could find the original site of deposition and decomposition, we might have more information, but the steep terrain and heavy leaf litter made the search difficult. The light was fading before we gave up and sat down to consider our options. It was then that I finally looked up. A nearby tree had blue wool fibers stuck in the bark of one side. The missing woman had been wearing a blue sweater when last seen. Her earrings and miscellaneous small bones were found at the base of the tree along with rope fragments. The soil was filled with insect puparia (Order Diptera) characteristic of a decomposition site. It appeared that the woman had been alive when she was tied to the tree and slid down the side of the tree during decomposition. We found the site and the information by looking up, not down.

Burial Classification

When the burial is found, begin the record of the grave by describing and classifying the type of grave. The burial classification is part of the complete description of the grave. It is useful in communicating the reasons for the methods used and the type of results expected.

Surface Burial or Below-Surface Burial

Surface burial sounds like a contradiction or an oxymoron, but it is, in fact, common usage. A surface burial is a "non-interment." The remains are left to decompose on the surface of the ground. It is not uncommon for surface burials to be disturbed or destroyed by carnivores and scavengers. Usually the degree of disturbance is directly related to the size of the animals.

- Insects feed on soft tissues and cause little or no positional disturbance.
- Small animals such as rodents feed on both soft and hard tissues. They sometimes carry away the small bones of fingers and toes. Shiny items such as rings may be found in rodent nests.
- Scavenger birds feed on soft tissues in situ. They may also carry off smaller parts to perches. The bones may then be dropped from the perch. Birds are known to collect hair to use for nesting material.
- Large mammals such as dogs and pigs carry sections of bodies for long distances. They also do the most destructive damage to larger bones.
- Exception: I once watched an entire quarter of a lamb (including long bones) completely disappear through the persistent efforts of coconut crabs in their hermit stage, each no more than four inches long, including the "borrowed" shell!

The word **burial**, by itself, usually refers to a standard below-ground interment. The depth is of no importance in the classification. The body can be with or without clothing, shroud, coffin, casket, or vault. Burials also include above-ground interments. These are crypts built on, instead of in, the ground. Above-ground interments are more consistent with below-ground interments than with surface burials. They are found mainly in coastal or lowland areas where the water table is high and water erosion is common. The body is enclosed in a vault of brick, stone, or concrete. Decomposition takes place under protected conditions and the condition of the remains is likely to be quite good.

Individual or Commingled Burial

An **individual burial** is the burial of a single person in a single location, above or below the surface of the ground.

A **commingled burial** contains more than one person buried in the same location. It can be two persons, such as mother and child buried in a single grave, or it can be a mass grave created by a bulldozer and containing thousands of intermingled bodies. The commingled remains may have been buried at the same time or at different times. A burial in the site of another burial is called an **intrusive burial**.

Isolated or Adjacent Burial

Isolated burials share no walls with other graves. **Adjacent burials** share at least one wall with another grave.

This classification is important when choosing an appropriate excavation method. Isolated graves can be excavated without concern about encroaching upon other graves, but adjacent graves such as those within crowded cemeteries require special excavation techniques. Since the wall of an adjacent grave is shared, disturbance of the wall disturbs the other grave as well. (Adjacent burials can be quite challenging.)

Primary or Secondary Burial

The **primary burial** is the initial resting place of the remains. The **secondary burial** is *any* subsequent burial. The remains may be disinterred many times, but each new burial is called a secondary burial.

Disturbed or Undisturbed Burial

An **undisturbed burial** is unchanged (except by natural processes) since the time of primary burial.

A **disturbed burial** is one that has been altered by man or animals sometime after the time of burial. The disturbance may be accidental or intentional. Sometimes the remains are not moved to a new place, but they are not in the original burial position, either. Disturbances may be caused by burrowing animals, grave diggers in the process of digging other graves, looters searching for bones or grave goods, or any number of other incidents. Land clearing and development are a major source of grave disturbance. All secondary burials are, by definition, disturbed burials.

The Excavation/Exhumation

A successful excavation is the result of teamwork, planning, and good field methods. One person needs to take responsibility for the overall operation and everyone should be clear about who that person is. The field director need not be dictatorial but does need to be capable of making and communicating decisions.

Duty Assignments

Before a single shovel is lifted, the field director assigns auxiliary duties. The entire team is usually involved in the excavation process, but several of the more reliable team members also have extra duties and responsibilities. The work flows more smoothly and the results are more complete when duties are assigned in the planning session and not after the work is in progress.

RECORDER(S)

The recorder maintains a chronological written record of the progress of the excavation. Depending on the size of the excavation, it may be necessary to have more than one recorder and further divide the duties according to records: (1) the participant log—focus on the perimeter and keep track of all participants, including visitors and press; (2) the excavation log—focus on the work itself and keep track of workers and the sequence of recoveries; and (3) the evidence log—assign numbers, record, pack, and store evidence. If evidence for DNA analysis is anticipated, one team member should be assigned exclusively to its collection. That person is responsible for keeping DNA collection kits on hand and following prescribed collection protocols, including maintaining sterile procedures. This person can be working on other tasks until called to the primary duty.

I like to maintain two types of records: (1) a simple daily log consisting of the date, starting and stopping times, persons present, burial numbers, and evidence numbers; and (2) a detailed account of each and every phase of the work, including field description of burials and evidence. This record can be compiled every night from the daily log together with the individual logs or reports filled out by all workers.

MAPPER

The mapper plans and maintains both two-dimensional and three-dimensional maps of the excavation as it progresses. First the site is measured and a grid system is planned. The entire system is reduced and drawn. Any permanent features of the landscape are recorded. Natural features such as rivers, streams, large rocks and boulders, and large trees should be included along with man-made features such as roads, walls, water towers, power lines, and buildings. Include as many things as possible for reference points.

Figure 15.3
An Excavation Ready for Mapping
The area around the suspected grave site is cordoned off with crime scene tape, allowing space for the work to take place. Vegetation was removed from the excavation area and the ground was leveled to reveal the grave outline. The excavation area is staked and delineated by string.
Source: EQUITAS, Bogota, Colombia.

Use GPS (Global Positioning System) if possible, but be aware that GPS coordinates may not be as accurate as expected. Read the equipment specifications carefully and test for accuracy. Take measurements at known points, check for repeatability at a specific point, and compare measurements with other GPS users. A local fixed base station may be necessary.

The mapper also maintains a record of each feature or piece of evidence as it is found. Cooperation is necessary. The workers stop whenever the mapper requests and provide measurements on all coordinates.

PHOTOGRAPHER

The photographer has the task of maintaining a photographic record of the site and the evidence. If it is not possible to hire a professional, one person should be assigned the task of maintaining a photographic record above all other tasks. This includes photographing the site, the evidence, and the work in progress, as well as maintaining a log of date, time, and subject for each photo.

Other workers should be able to concentrate on their specific tasks and rely on the photographer to be ready when needed. In this way, neither the work nor the photographic record is compromised. The photographer may need an assistant to maintain the photographic log.

EVERYONE ELSE

The rest of the excavation team handles the shovels, trowels, brushes, buckets, and screens. Students or large groups of workers benefit from oversight and assigned and/or rotating duties, but relatively small, well-established teams tends to sort themselves out without interference. Good team members settle into the jobs they are most suited for and take responsibility for the work and the well-being of their teammates.

Excavation Methods

There are several effective excavation methods. The best method for the job depends on the *type* of burial (e.g., below-surface, individual, isolated, primary, undisturbed), the *location* of the burial (e.g., forest, cemetery, house floor), the *condition of the soil* (e.g., loose or well packed, wet or dry), and the *depth* of the burial. Assess the conditions, establish priorities, and determine to be practical and flexible.

Figure 15.4

An Exhumation in Progress Near Chajul, El Quiche, Guatemala

The forensic anthropologists of the Guatemalan Archbishop's Human Rights Office (ODHAG) Exhumation Project demonstrate teamwork as they complete the exhumation, record and photograph all evidence, and collect the remains for laboratory analysis. They also spend time with the families of the victims, discussing items of clothing and any items not covered in the pre-exhumation interviews. In addition to doing the exhumation work, the team members are continuously respectful of religious rituals and expressions of grief. (Lancerio López)

A model excavation is presented on the following pages (Figures 15.5a–g). It is a single individual grave in a remote setting. The general location of the grave was provided by an informant, and the exact location was determined by changes in soil density and vegetation. The area around the grave is undisturbed; the soil is firm and dry; and the depth of the burial is approximately one meter.

The entire area of this model excavation was mapped by GPS. Markers (stakes) were placed in the ground to enable the excavation mapper to detail the position of the grave and its contents with the use of fixed points. Directional coordinates and major points of reference (e.g., large trees, buildings, and fences) were included in the map.

In this type of excavation, the excavation walls are placed outside the walls of the original grave pit. (Some excavation methods require that excavation follow the walls of the original grave pit.) The surface area of the excavation is delineated with string and stakes, and the stakes are positioned outside (not on) the corners of the excavation wall, two per corner. The string is stretched as close to the ground as possible along the edge of the proposed excavation. (The string should aid the mapper without tripping the excavators.)

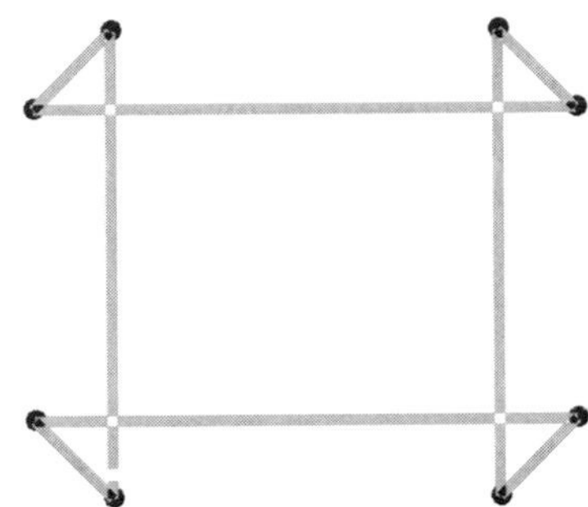

Documentation is critical at every step of an excavation. It is stressed here because it is too frequently omitted in the intensity of the moment. To document means to stop work, photograph, map, and make a written record. Experienced archaeologists and crime scene investigators know when to stop moving forward and document what has been accomplished before the information is contaminated, lost, or forgotten. Each break for documentation provides an opportunity to step back from the present task, assess the overall progress of the work, and notice what might have been overlooked. It is essential time.

A Model Excavation

The following six diagrams represent a model excavation of a single, isolated grave. The objective is to demonstrate a standard method for revealing the contents of the grave in situ, without disturbing or destroying evidence.

The perspective is a vertical cross section of the grave (a cut from the left wall to the right wall) at the level of the skull. The uppermost layer represents topsoil; the gray area is undisturbed subsoil; and the cross hatching is the grave fill dirt. The stippling beneath the skull is the organic stain resulting from seepage of decompositional fluids into the grave floor.

Figure 15.5a–g
Model Excavation of an Isolated Individual Grave

1. Remove the litter and vegetation.

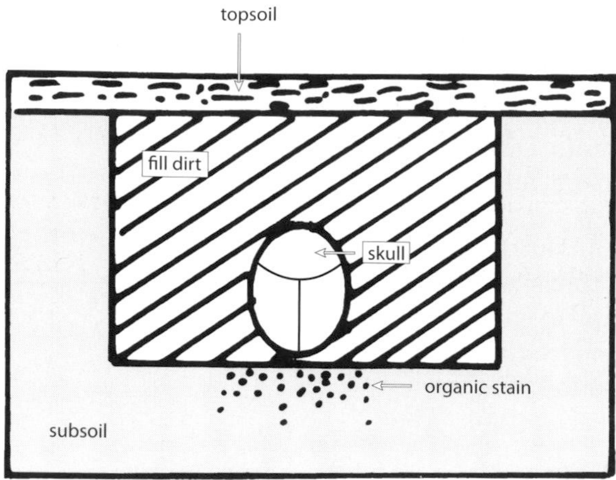

- Begin by carefully removing the leaf litter and the surface vegetation. Watch for hair, clothing, or any items that may indicate the human activity in the area.
- Probe to locate and delineate the grave walls.
- Flag the approximate location of the grave and any surface evidence.

2. Remove the topsoil and locate the grave outline.

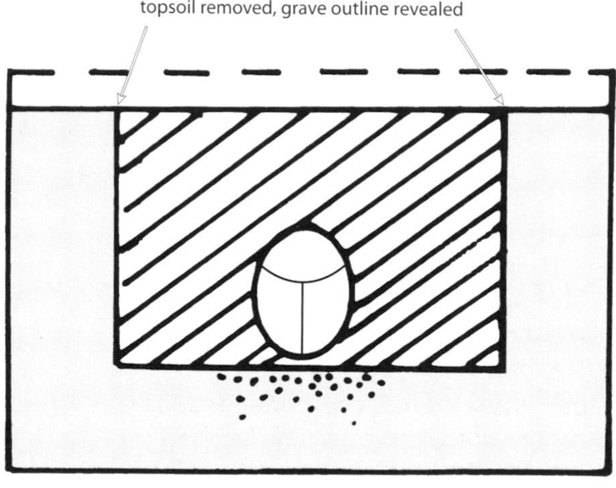

- Scrape the soil surface horizontally with a flat shovel until the topsoil is removed.
- Examine the soil for changes in coloration that can be the result of mixed topsoil and subsoil. If color differences are slight, spray lightly with water to darken organic matter and intensify color differences.
- When the grave outline is fully visible, measure, photograph, and map it.
- Examine the outline for information about the size and shape of the original digging tools (e.g., shovels, pick axes, power machinery).

3. Remove the overburden.

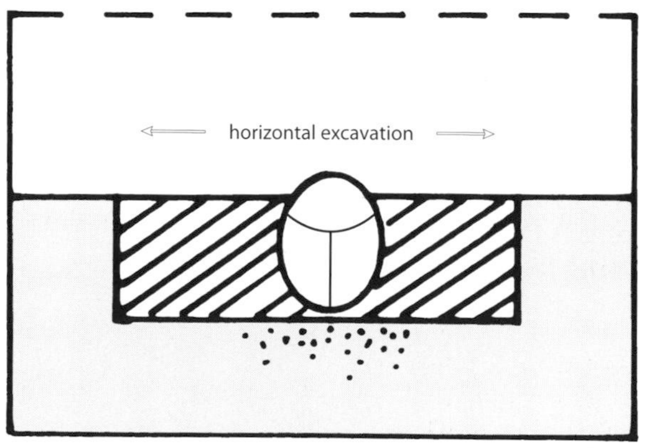

- Continue to remove the overburden of earth, including the grave fill.
- Work horizontally, peeling off thin layers of dirt and maintaining a flat working surface.
- Work with care to avoid dislodging and damaging underlying evidence.
- If you notice changes in the density, color, or texture of the soil, change from a shovel to a trowel for finer control. If an object appears, change to a brush to avoid tool marks.
- Sift the soil, level by level in sequence. Evidence can be found in the grave fill dirt. (e.g., cigarette butts, trash, projectiles, cartridges, ropes, hair).

4. Pedestal each feature.

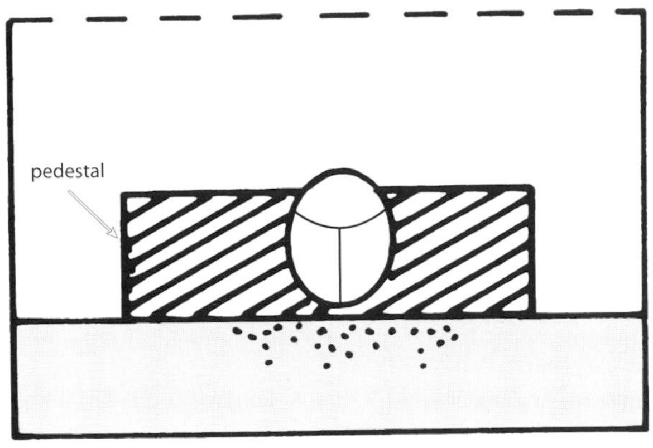

- Circumscribe the body by digging on all sides to the lowest level of the body (approximately 30 cm). This is similar to digging a ditch around the body. The result takes the form of a **pedestal**. The common archaeological term for this method is "pedestaling." The objective is to see what is going on before disturbing anything *and* to make room to work carefully. Pedestal artifacts in the same way.
- If there is no room to dig around the body, do the best you can. It may be necessary to extend (sacrifice) one wall of the excavation to make extra room to maneuver on the excavation floor.

5. Expose everything without disturbing the evidence.

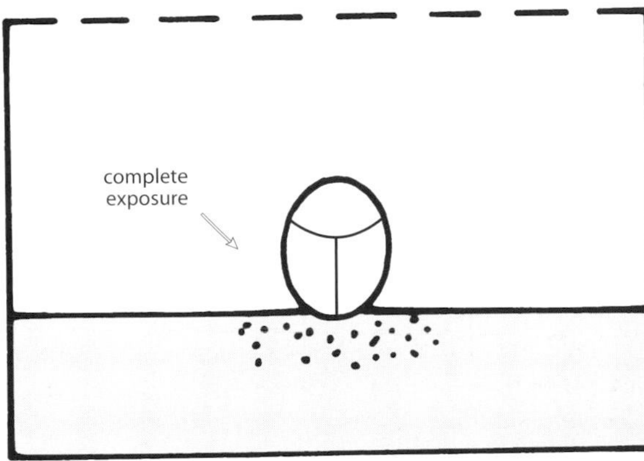

- Expose the remains and associated evidence by moving in laterally, using a soft brush and small tools. Do not use a brush on fabric, as it may destroy fiber evidence.
- Examine the soil around the skull for hair. Place this soil in a bag for laboratory study.
- If the remains are from an adult female, be alert to the possibility of associated fetal remains.
- Patience is essential. The remains may be fragile, and the interrelationships of elements may be easily disrupted.

6. Disinter the remains and all associated evidence.

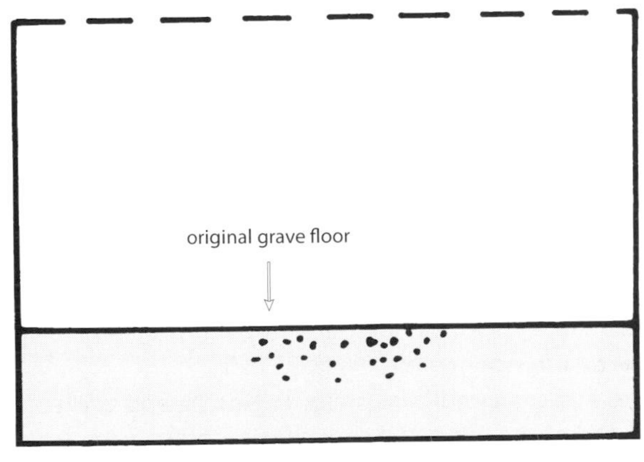

- If there is any chance that the bones will break upon removal, measure the remains while in the ground. The measurements should be appropriate for estimation of stature.
- Remove the remains carefully and do a basic inventory of everything. Note the condition of the remains. Bag each hand and each foot separately. Include fingernails if they are found. Take extreme care with facial bones. Check to see if teeth are loose and be sure none are lost.
- Remove and record all evidence associated with the remains. This includes such items as clothing, buttons, ornaments, weapons, bullets, hair pins, and eyeglasses. Some of the evidence may help identify the victim or the perpetrator, and some may help to reveal perimortem events.

7. Continue until "sterile" soil is reached.

- Do not stop until "sterile" soil is reached. In other words, continue excavating the grave floor until unstained and undisturbed soil is reached.
- Screen everything. Watch for additional evidence that has shifted downward with the tunneling activity of invertebrate necrophages (**necrophytes**). Hair, buttons, projectiles, loose teeth, tooth restorations, coins, and jewelry are just a few of the items that may be recovered.

8. **Pack carefully.**
   - Use paper bags and cardboard boxes to facilitate drying. Plastic bags encourage mold growth, causing further organic destruction.
   - Mark evidence numbers clearly on all containers with indelible ink. Include the name of the site and the date if they are not part of the evidence numbers.
9. **Finish the job.**
   - Backfill the excavation pit and clean up the site. Consider the local conditions and terrain then burn, bury, or carry out all trash. You will leave the area, but the residents of the area will remember you by what you leave behind.
10. **Document the completed project.**
    - Photograph the area upon departure. The final photographs are the evidence of completion of a professional job. They also serve to protect the team from culpability for any subsequent vandalism.

Figure 15.6
Trace Evidence
This excavation was completed with a minimum of equipment, using the original excavation walls as a guide instead of a squared-off excavation pit. The pointed handle of the brush was used to indicate north for photos. The paper label contained the date, location, and burial number. No clothing is apparent on the body, but careful excavation revealed synthetic threads from seams still in place along each leg.

CASE EXAMPLE: TRACE EVIDENCE IN IRAQ

When the remains of a human body are found, frenzy usually follows. The body may have been quietly interred for decades, but suddenly something has to be done and it has to be *now*. Questions come tumbling out. The first is, "Who is it?" Then later, "What happened? How did this person die?" Unfortunately, the physical evidence doesn't cooperate by presenting itself in the same sequence.

If the remains are ripped out of the ground and sent to the lab for immediate identification, contextual information is lost and the value of associated evidence is diminished. All evidence—the body and associated evidence—must be treated with the same care. The associated evidence may be all we have to answer the question, "What happened?"

In Iraqi Kurdistan, a skeleton was exposed in an unmarked grave on a military base. It was necessary to know if the grave preceded the military base or if it contained one of the many "disappeared" of the war.

The burial itself contained the answer to the question. Muslim burials are conducted by the family. The women wash the body and wrap it in a simple shroud without clothing. The men bury the body on its side facing Mecca. A body found buried on its back or with clothing would not have been buried by the family.

The skeleton in question had been buried on its side facing Mecca. No clothing was apparent. However, careful examination revealed a double thread on both sides of both legs. The fabric of the pants, probably wool, had decomposed with the soft tissues of the body. But the cotton-polyester thread of the pants seams remained in place. The victim was not buried by his family; hence he was most probably one of the Kurds executed on the military base. (The top of the skull contained a bullet entry wound.)

The information provided by simple dirt-stained threads proved invaluable.

Postmortem Interval (Time since Death) and Forensic Taphonomy

When a body is found in unexpected circumstances, one of the first questions is, "How long has this person been dead?" This is called the **postmortem interval** (PMI) or the time that has passed between death and the attempt to determine the time of death. The information is important to both the identification process and the death investigation itself. The PMI helps the investigator to differentiate forensic from historic or ancient cases. It can also be used to search missing persons reports for likely matches, and it can help link suspects to a particular time and place. Unfortunately, this essential information is somewhat elusive. Research has helped to define the parameters, but there are no easy answers.

Forensic taphonomy is the multidisciplinary study of the postmortem interval. By definition, **taphonomy** is the study of the fate of the remains of organisms after they die. Until recently, the word *taphonomy* was used almost exclusively by paleontologists studying the fossilization process. Forensic scientists now use the term for the earlier part of the process—decomposition. Taphonomic research for forensic purposes was first based on case studies and comparative animal studies—many using pigs as models for human decomposition. Then, in 1972, William Bass established the Anthropological Research Facility at the University of Tennessee and began accepting body donations for research purposes. After the initial shock of seeing human bodies laid out to decompose for science, the forensic community recognized the significance of the research. By the 1980s, research articles were appearing regularly in scientific publications.

Forensic taphonomy is now a standard subject in the forensic sciences, and, like everything else forensic, research and application benefit from a multidisciplinary approach. Specialists include anthropologists, entomologists, botanists, and a variety of other experts, including soil scientists and preservation specialists. The following section explores what this group of scientists has learned about the process of decomposition and lists the factors—both environmental and cultural—that affect the rate of decomposition and hence, the estimation of time since death.

Immediate Postmortem Changes

Most bodies are processed within the first few hours of death, and forensic medical investigators are all very familiar with the first postmortem changes—algor mortis, livor mortis, and rigor mortis. **Algor mortis** is simply the cooling of the body. It begins immediately upon death. **Livor mortis** is the purple coloration that develops in the skin of the underside of the body (except in compressed areas). It results from the gravitational movement of blood and appears within one and a half to two hours of death. **Rigor mortis** is muscular stiffening caused by chemical changes in the tissue. It begins in the small muscles as early as ten minutes after death and progresses throughout the body. Rigor mortis is complete by twelve to twenty-four hours and then slowly disappears (beginning again with the small muscles) over the next one to two days as decomposition begins. More precise estimates can be made if ambient temperature and muscle mass are known.

The Process of Decomposition

Decomposition begins with **autolysis**, or "self-digestion." The enzymes produced within the cells destroy the cells. The cellular structure of the tissue breaks down and the tissues soften. Putrefaction follows. As the cell membranes are destroyed, tissues that provide barriers within the body are breached.

Microorganisms that serve the digestive process spill out into the body cavity, where they feed on the organic matter, especially protein, of the body. Metabolic gases are soon trapped within the body, producing a foul odor and causing the body, mainly the abdomen, to bloat.

A long sequence of events follows the beginning of putrefaction. The most visible of the early changes include skin slippage, hair loss, and skin discoloration. Skin slippage is caused by fluid building up under the outer layer of skin and causing it to separate, almost like blistering after a bad sunburn. The skin sloughs off in the direction of gravity. It can look like a loose glove or stretched-out stockings. The hair falls out easily, usually with skin attached. The skin turns a greenish to blackish color. (Green is one of the color changes that red blood goes through as it breaks down.)

During this time, bloating continues and fluids drain from the body. When the gases are released, the body deflates and the skin tends to drape over the skeleton. Some of the bones are exposed. Ligaments, cartilage, and dried (mummified) skin are the last of the soft tissues to survive.

When bone is first exposed, it is yellow and greasy. The bone continues to change long after exposure. The oils leach out slowly, and the bones bleach white in sunlight or stain the color of the substrate. In time, the bony cortex cracks, flakes, and exfoliates, exposing the inner cancellous bone. In an acidic substrate, the bone slowly decalcifies and is destroyed. In high-mineral conditions, the natural bone minerals may be replaced in the very slow process leading to fossilization.

Environmental Factors (Climate)

Moisture and oxygen are fundamental to decomposition because they are essential for life. After the chemical process of autolysis, all of the rest of decomposition depends on the digestive processes of one life form or another. The temperature range has to be conducive to life (not burning or freezing). Within that range, more heat speeds up digestion and less heat slows it down.

> "Immediate postmortem change may be viewed essentially as a competition between decomposition (decay and putrefaction) and desiccation."
> M. Micozzi, 1986

With those simple facts in mind, it is easy to see why warm, humid climates are good for decomposition, and cool, dry climates are good for preservation. The next step is to notice that neither warmth nor moisture is good enough alone. Warm, dry conditions (deserts, dry-heated rooms) bring about desiccation and mummification. The organisms that digest the body run out of moisture before they run out of nutrients, so they don't finish the job.

Cool, wet conditions (rivers, water-filled coffins) result in the production of **adipocere**. Adipocere (grave wax) is composed of insoluble fatty acids resulting from the slow hydrolysis of the body's fats in water (Mellen et al., 1993; Hobischak, 2002). Certain bacteria consume adipocere, but slowly.

Some wet conditions (peat bogs, silted-over deep river bottoms) may bring about preservation. The missing ingredient here is oxygen. The bacteria responsible for most of the decomposition can't survive without oxygen. If the temperature is low enough, even the anaerobic microbes within the body don't succeed. In such conditions, even extremely fragile soft tissue may survive. Brain tissue was found preserved in skulls of the crew of the *H. L. Hunley*, a Civil War submarine (press release by Dr. Robert Neyland, Project Director, Hunley Commission, May 10, 2001). The oxygen had been used up by the crew and their death was followed by complete silting-in of the submarine compartment on the cool ocean floor.

Several studies have been carried out on decomposition rates in different climates and seasons, including moist, warm conditions (Bass, 1997); hot, arid conditions (Galloway et al., 1989); and "cold," dry conditions (Komar, 1998; Weitzel, 2005). (The cold conditions are from Canadian summer, not winter; therefore, the temperatures are moderate.) Unfortunately, the studies are difficult to compare because decomposition is multifactorial and continuous, grave types differ, and investigators tend to define and delineate the stages of decomposition slightly differently. (Weitzel uses Galloway's standards.) Rather than present all of the studies, I use Dr. Bass's Tennessee summer decomposition information as a model and describe the deviations to expect under different environmental conditions. It is best to read the studies in their entirety and relate them to local environmental conditions and grave type.

In Knoxville, Tennessee, mid-summer average temperatures range from 68 to 87 degrees Fahrenheit (F) (20 to 31 degrees Celsius). Mid-winter average temperatures range from 30 to 47 degrees F (–1 to 8 degrees C). The average annual precipitation is about 50 inches (127 cm). (Information provided by the National Weather Service.)

As long as moisture and temperature are constant, the decomposition rate can be relatively constant. In a dead body, with a cellular water content of 70 to 85 percent, it is a lot easier to maintain moisture than it is to maintain heat. For that reason, the early decomposition of a body in a warm, arid environment is about the same as that of a body in a warm, moist environment. Inside of the body, the conditions are the same. The differences show up when the body begins to desiccate. Rapid desiccation results in mummification. Slow desiccation results in more thorough decomposition.

Table 15.2 is based on surface burials and naked bodies—in other words, complete exposure. Add shade, clothing, protective covering, or burial and the rate of decomposition changes. Lowering the amount of exposure can either decrease or increase decomposition, depending on moisture, temperature, and one more thing—access of scavengers to the body.

Shean et al., (1993) demonstrated that exposed remains decompose faster than shaded remains. Temperature differential was the primary factor. Maggots are more active in warmer places. They slow down in the shade. Be careful applying this premise to just any shaded area. The inside of a car, for instance, may be shaded, but it can also be much warmer.

Clothing and other coverings can provide protection for the body itself—or protection for the animals feeding on the body. A completely impermeable covering can exclude insects and other carrion feeders, leaving the rate of decomposition to be determined by the bacteria alone. But if the insects can enter the

Table 15.2 Decay Rates in a Warm, Moist Environment

Large mammals and birds are excluded; major differences in wet and dry environments are added in parentheses.

Time Period and Defining Characteristics	Animals	Skin and Hair	Gas and Fluids	Molds and Plants	Bones
First 24 hours; egg masses	fly egg masses appear like fine white sawdust	blue or dark green veins	fluids seep from openings		
2–7 days; maggots and bloating	maggots hatch and feed; beetles first appear	skin slips; hair falls out; skin darkens	abdomen bloats; fluids drain from openings	molds begin to appear; volatile fatty acids kill surrounding vegetation	facial bones are exposed
2–4 weeks; beetles and decaying	less maggots; more beetles	skin drapes and becomes leathery; (adipocere develops in wet environments)	bloating passes; fluids cease; body begins to dry	molds spread over everything; plants can't grow	other bones are exposed, yellow, and oily
2–12 months; drying and full skeleton	rodents gnaw bone; small animals nest in cavities	skin disappears (skin may mummify in dry environments, hot or "cold")	drying completes	moss and green algae appear; plants begin	oils leach; bones bleach in sunlight, stain in the ground, and/or turn green with algae in shade
2–10 years; bone breakdown	further gnawing			roots and plants invade the now nutrient-rich soil	bone surfaces begin to crack and exfoliate

Source: Based on information from Bass, 1997.

covering long enough to lay eggs, the maggots have even better conditions for feeding because of the shelter, heat, and moisture. The covering takes the place of the skin, so maggots eat the skin that they would have avoided if exposed. Bone is exposed much more quickly under these conditions.

The type of fabric influences the extent of protection. Natural fibers offer very little protection because they are digestible and inviting when soaked with organic fluids. They are also permeable and allow moisture to evaporate. Artificial fibers are less permeable, mostly indigestible, and decay more slowly.

Even greater protection is provided by burial. Rodriguez and Bass (1985) buried six unembalmed cadavers at depths of 1, 2, and 4 feet. The cadavers were exhumed and examined at intervals up to one year. It was demonstrated that the rate of decomposition is much slower in buried remains. The main factors are lack (or reduction) of carrion-eating insects and lower temperatures. Deeper burials resulted in greater preservation.

Carrion Feeders

Flies and beetles are the major carrion feeders, but there are many more also. Other arthropods are attracted to carrion because of the opportunity to prey on the carrion feeders. Spiders, mites, scorpions, and centipedes are just a few examples (Catts & Haskell, 1990). Some of the best information about the postmortem interval comes from studies of arthropod life cycles. A forensic entomologist is the best person to collect and analyze the information, but if none is available, collect samples from the body, beneath the body, and in the surrounding ground. Study a field guide for proper collection procedures (Catts & Haskell, 1990; Haskell et al., 1997).

Postmortem interval is just part of the information available from carrion-feeding insects. Some have been used successfully to test for drugs and poisons ingested with the tissues of the dead body (Gunatilake & Goff, 1989; Bourel et al., 1999).

Following the flies and beetles, there is a wide assortment of larger carrion feeders. Some are specialists, such as vultures; others, like raccoons, are opportunists. In North America, remains are usually scavenged by crows, vultures, canids, and rodents. In coastal areas, crabs can be voracious carrion eaters. Where present, pigs may compete with canids. I have worked cases consumed and scattered by wild pigs in both Haiti and Fiji. Any of the larger scavengers can disrupt a carefully researched decomposition timetable.

Bird scavengers usually do little to damage bone. Small mammals, such as rodents, gnaw on them long after the flesh is gone. Larger mammals, such as dogs, disarticulate the body, carry parts to different locations, and break or pulverize the bones. Each animal leaves evidence of its presence—tooth marks are the most obvious. Large scavengers can reduce a body to fragments in a very short time and play havoc with postmortem interval estimates. Several years ago in the state of Florida, a woman died in an apartment also occupied by four large pet dogs. Only fragments of her skeleton were found just one week later.

Associated Plants

In the initial stages of decomposition, surrounding plants are destroyed by the volatile fatty acids released by the body. When the acids dissipate, the plants return. They then make use of the natural fertilizer provided by the body, and exuberant growth may follow. It is easier for most of us to use this plant growth to locate a grave than to estimate postmortem interval. Professional forensic botanists may be needed to extract additional information.

David Hall, a forensic botanist, writes, "Any plant part touching or buried with human remains can be valuable" (1997). He recommends photographing the plants in the vicinity of the grave and collecting the evidence for future analysis. Control samples should be collected from the surrounding area, and evidence samples from the area around the body—including above and below ground. The samples should include stems, branches, leaves, roots, and flowers (including pollen). Study a field guide for proper collection procedures (Hall, 1997; Coyle, 2005).

If a perennial plant such as a tree is found growing through the remains or in the grave fill, annual rings from the stem or roots can provide information about the minimum (not actual) number of years since the deposition of the body. The plant parts must be demonstrably associated with the remains (Willey & Heilman, 1987). Roots or stems can be growing through the clothing, into bony foramina, or clearly disturbed by the excavation or the placement of the body.

Roots are common in graves, and root clippers are a standard excavation tool. But sometimes roots completely consume the body, and their existence may be the only evidence remaining. I once excavated a grave of a young child in a crushed coral substrate. A few scrubby bushes existed in the area, but nothing over the grave. Only small root fragments were observed during the four-foot-deep excavation. However, the burial itself consisted of a nearly solid coffin-shaped mass of small roots. Time since death was already known, but I wonder what more a forensic botanist might have determined from the compact evidence.

Pollen analysis shows promise for determining the season (not the year) of burial. Pollen lasts for hundreds of thousands of years, and its use is already well-established in palaeogeographical research, but there are few reported forensic cases. One example is reported by Szibor and colleagues (1998). A mass grave found in Magdeburg, Germany, could have resulted from one of two known massacres—one in early spring and another in mid-summer. Pollen was filtered from the nasal passages of the skulls. The analysis showed it to be from plants that bloom in summer, not spring. (It may be good practice to routinely save a sample of dirt from nasal passages, just in case it is needed.)

Funerary Practices

The rate of decomposition can be slowed or nearly halted by various funerary practices. Preservation of the dead has been carried out in various ways since ancient times, but present-day embalming methods were devised during the seventeenth century for the purpose of preserving anatomical specimens for study. The practice of embalming human bodies destined for burial is a modern phenomenon, gaining popularity in the United States around the time of the Civil War, when bodies of soldiers were shipped home for burial (Johnson et al., 2000). Embalming is practiced in other parts of the world, but the United States is probably the only country that routinely embalms corpses for immediate burial.

Embalming fluid is an antibacterial agent. It is injected into the body through the vascular system as the blood is drained out. It is also injected directly into organs and pumped into the body cavity. This is especially important for effective preservation when the vascular system is compromised. The main ingredient of embalming fluid is formalin, an aqueous solution of the gas formaldehyde. Other ingredients may include alcohol, silicone, lanolin, coloring, fragrances, and more. The formulae vary in composition depending on the manufacturer, the date manufactured, and the length of time since manufacture. In addition, different components decay at different rates, changing the composition of the residual. Embalming is easy to recognize in a fleshed body, but the residual is difficult to identify in skeletal remains unless it contains a detectable ingredient such as a heavy metal.

Heavy metals such as arsenic, lead, and mercury have excellent antibacterial properties and were used in embalming fluids during the late nineteenth and early twentieth centuries. The results are amazing. (See the story of Elmer McCurdy in the accompanying box.) Unfortunately, a good preservative works on living tissues as well as dead ones. Heavy metals are poisonous to living

CASE EXAMPLE: ELMER MCCURDY, AN AMERICAN OUTLAW

(This is a story you should read in the original. I can give you the facts, but the culture and humor of the story is pure Clyde Snow.)

In 1977, an arm fell off a hanging dummy in a southern California house of horrors. This would have been no big deal, but a human bone jutted out. As Dr. Snow put it, the "dummy was, in fact, a mummy"! The shock of the discovery resulted in a police investigation that spanned sixty-six years and half the continent. The trail ended in Oklahoma, where the body of Elmer McCurdy had been embalmed in 1911. Elmer was a train robber who had been killed in a gun battle with law enforcement and deposited at the nearest funeral home. When the proprietor discovered that Elmer had no next of kin, he saw a profitable opportunity. He embalmed Elmer "heavily" with arsenic and put him on display in the back room. The curious could come in and view a "real outlaw" for just a nickel. A carnival operator got the body next, and Elmer toured the west before ending up as just another dummy in the Laugh in the Dark Funhouse.

I'm not sure which is more amazing—the tale of Elmer's life after death or the embalming that made it possible. On autopsy, it was discovered that the tissue preservation was excellent. Cells and fibers appeared normal. Blood cells were intact. Sections of the brain revealed recognizable neurons. Only the lung tissue was damaged, and that may have been due to antemortem circumstances.

Source: Summarized from Snow and Reyman, 1984.

things, even at very low concentrations, and they tend to accumulate in the food chain. For this reason, they are now regulated by agencies of the federal government and they are not legal for embalming purposes.

Embalming is just the beginning of the funerary practices used to preserve human remains. The encasement of the body is next. The ancient burial shroud was replaced by a wooden coffin. A coffin is easier to handle than a body in a shroud, but not too much different for long-term preservation. The wood decays and the body is surrounded by earth, just a little later than it would be without a coffin. Then metal caskets were introduced. They last for years, depending on the construction. Concrete burial vaults and grave liners were added to protect the caskets and keep the surface of the ground from sinking in over a grave.

The embalmed remains I have seen from casket/vault graves are usually damp and thick with mold decades after death. One exception in my experience was the remains of a young woman buried in the late nineteenth century in a bullet-shaped lead coffin. Her skin was essentially unchanged in color and texture and there was no mold visible. (The lead coffin provided very effective preservation.)

Other Preservation Factors

Aside from embalming, there are many nontoxic ways of preserving bodies. In fact, everything used to preserve food can be used for bodies also—drying, freezing, salting, and smoking. The results are not as cosmetically acceptable, but that's not so important in most forensic settings.

I'm sure you have heard of well-preserved frozen bodies, but few know that many of the victims of the World Trade Center disaster were somewhat preserved by smoke. Fires burned deep beneath the World Trade Center wreckage for three months after the events of 9/11. Smoke filtered up through the rubble just as it would in a smoke house, providing an antimicrobial atmosphere. The bits and pieces of bodies that arrived at the processing site were often well preserved months after the disaster. There was little odor of decomposition and friction ridge patterns were clearly visible on the hands.

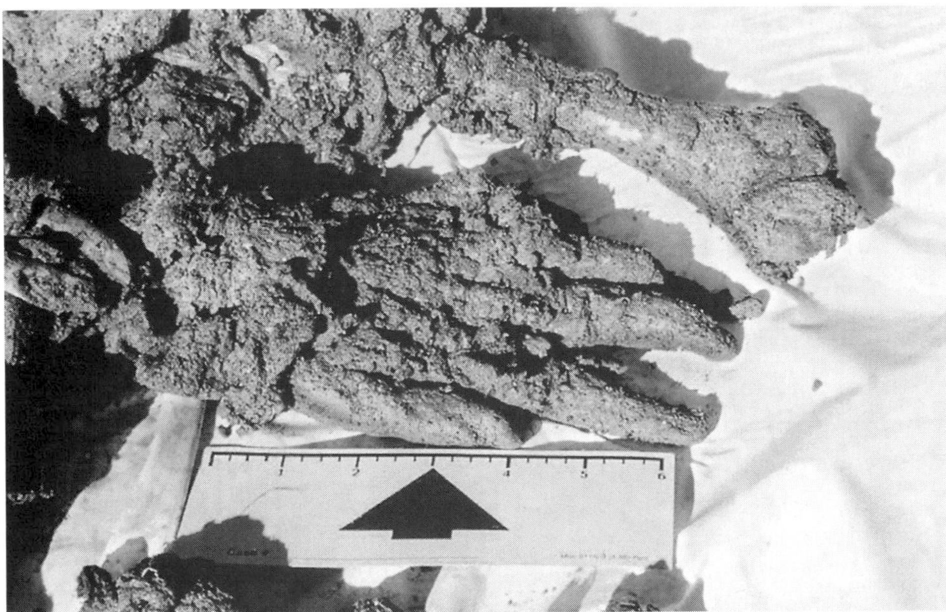

Figure 15.7
A Printable Hand from a Disaster Site

Other Evidence of Funerary Practices

Even without soft tissue preservation, evidence of the embalmer's work is often present. Plastic eye caps are used to keep the eyelids from sinking, plastic inserts keep the mouth shaped without teeth in place, and close fitting plastic garments are used to prevent seepage under the clothing. Small metal nails are inserted into the maxilla and mandible to attach wires and hold the mouth closed, lips are sewn or glued together, incisions are plugged with plastic trochar "buttons," and so on. Wax and clay may also be found with the remains. Anyone who needs to be able to sort criminal from noncriminal burials should familiarize themselves with the assortment of funerary items seldom seen by the public. For more information, see the publications by Berryman and colleagues (1991 and 1997).

Quality Check for Field Work

Has the Entire Scene Been Searched and Sampled?

- ✔ Artifacts collected from the surface and within the burial
- ✔ Insect samples collected from the surrounding soil
- ✔ Nests and burrows searched
- ✔ Plant samples taken from the grave surface, grave fill, and surrounding area

Figure 15.8
Perspective Drawings of a Grave

Are All Human Remains Recognized and Recovered?

- ✔ All fifty-four hand bones, left and right separated
- ✔ All fifty-two foot bones, left and right separated
- ✔ The hyoid, all three parts
- ✔ The coccyx
- ✔ All teeth, including single-rooted teeth
- ✔ Infant or fetal skeletons
- ✔ Epiphyses of sub-adults
- ✔ Broken bone fragments
- ✔ Hair, fibers, fingernails, and artifacts

Is the Written Documentation Complete?

- ✔ Write notes in narrative style.
- ✔ Include dates and times.
- ✔ List all participants.
- ✔ Number features consecutively.
- ✔ Map location of features, include scale.
- ✔ Sketch positions of features.
- ✔ Inventory and measure features.
- ✔ Include source material where necessary.
- ✔ Sign and date report.

Can the Scene and Sequence of Recovery Be Reconstructed from the Photographic Documentation?

- ✔ Maintain a photographic log.
- ✔ Vary lighting, flash, and lens settings.
- ✔ Photograph items in situ and in the lab.
- ✔ Include scale and identification in photo.
- ✔ Include an arrow (or trowel) indicating north.
- ✔ Photograph the entire scene with visible points of reference.
- ✔ For context and orientation of each feature, use a zoom lens to "move in" on the subject with several photos in sequence from the same position.
- ✔ For security, photograph the scene from the same position at the beginning and end of each work day.

CHAPTER 16

Professional Results

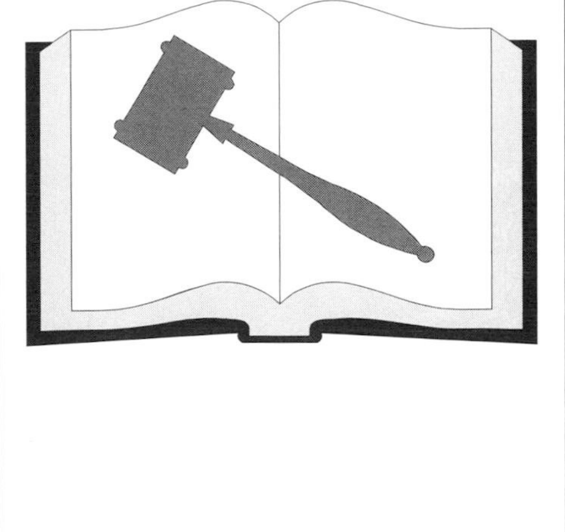

CHAPTER OUTLINE

Introduction

Professionalism is about expectations—high expectations concerning methods, standards, and character. A "professional" is a person who adheres to professional standards and produces high-quality results. A professional accepts responsibility for his or her own work and the work of subordinates.

Professional methods for forensic anthropology have been introduced in the chapters on laboratory analysis and field methods (Chapters 13 and 15, respectively). This chapter is a view of the final product—the culmination of osteological study, field work, and laboratory analysis. It is all brought together with a review of the records, a well-written final report, expert witness consultations, courtroom testimony, and a reexamination of ethics.

Record Keeping

There can be no professional report without accurate notes and records, and usually there is only one opportunity to record information before it is altered, destroyed, or forgotten. Record everything as it happens and maintain the records as if your professional reputation depends on them—as indeed it does.

Begin planning the final report at the initiation of the case. When the report is due, review everything to be sure that reliable records exist for each of the following categories.

Background Information

- Name of the person responsible for the report
- Title, address, telephone number
- Name of the agency or party to receive the report

Significant Dates

- Date of initial contact
- Date(s) of recovery
- Date(s) of entry into official records for each piece of evidence
- Date(s) of examination
- Date of report

Chain of Custody

- Who gave the evidence to you? When and where?
- Did you sign for it? Do you have the record?
- To whom did you release it? When and where?
- Did the recipient sign for it? Do you have the record?

Notes

Always err on the side of inclusiveness. Keep notes of everything—events, people, evidence recovered or received, evidence analyzed, results of analysis, disposition. Do not try to decide what is important during the work itself. Wait until later to decide what belongs in the final report and what may be extraneous observations.

Keep notes written in pen in bound notebooks with plenty of margin. Do not erase anything. Simply add in changes and corrections (with date and initials) so that you can see the evolution of your thought and the history of methods.

Report Writing

Write the final report as if amnesia were a foregone conclusion. Months or years may pass before the case goes to court or is reopened for further investigation. Many other cases will have come and gone by then, but you will be expected to remember the details of this case as if you had done the work today.

The case report becomes the permanent record of the investigator's work. It should reflect overall knowledge about the case, specific findings, well-supported conclusions, and recommendations. It must be clear, accurate, and complete. Be careful to use standard English. This is especially important in international, multicultural cases.

Note that the case report is not the same as an academic paper. Academic papers are usually written for professional peers—people with the same specialized knowledge and vocabulary. The forensic report is written for investigators, attorneys, judges, and other nonscientific specialists. Use language that communicates with the intended audience. If technical vocabulary and jargon are necessary, explain the terms.

Agencies usually have standard report formats for their employees, but independent consultants tend to develop formats to suit their own practice. Regardless of the format, typical forensic reports include the following categories of information: case background, description of the evidence upon receipt, inventory, anthropological description, conclusions, recommendations, disposition of the evidence, and an appendix of maps or photos, if useful for accurate communication. Forensic reports are always signed and dated.

Cover Page

The cover page should include the case number (and name of the case, if appropriate); the date; the name, title and address of the recipient; and all contact information for the expert (the person signing the report).

Case Background

In narrative form, give a brief history of the case as you understand it. Include names, dates, places, and events. Be very careful to differentiate between first-hand and second-hand information. First-hand information is based on your own experience and observations. Second-hand information is **hearsay**—include the source.

Condition of the Evidence (Pre-Processing Appearance)

In narrative form, describe the condition of the evidence when it comes into your custody. Include packaging, identification labels, and so on. The evidence includes all human remains as well as any associated physical evidence. This is all first impression information, not the careful inventory. For example, describe bony evidence by answering the following questions:

- Is it intact, broken, fragmented, or ... ?
- Is it wet, dry, greasy, or ... ? What does it smell like?
- Is it well-calcified and strong, demineralized and friable, or ... ?
- Is it sun-bleached, stained, or a combination of both?
- Is it clean or dirty? What kind of dirt?

Append any forms or photographs that will help convey information about the original condition of the evidence.

Inventory

Use forms and diagrams to inventory the remains and all other associated physical evidence. This is a careful description of the elements. Include any changes from the original condition. It may have been necessary to clean the evidence in order to inventory it. The inventory typically includes the following:

- Human remains (usually bones) together with basic descriptive information; use skeletal diagrams to show pertinent areas
- Teeth with basic descriptive information; use dental charts or diagrams
- All other items received (e.g., hair, nails, clothing, shoes, bullets, casings, plant life, insects, etc.)

Anthropological Description

The anthropological description is the result of the skeletal analysis. It is the description of the unidentified individual(s). Support the description with specific evidence. Include the methods used and the reliability of each method. Include references.

- Sex—based on traits such as pelvic or skull morphology, size, or muscularity
- Race—based on traits such as skull morphology, hair, or dental traits
- Age at death—based on evidence such as epiphyses, pubic symphysis, rib morphology, or osteoarthritis
- Stature—based on bone measurements (state which bones)
- Handedness—based on evidence such as glenoid beveling, arm length, or muscle attachment sites

Other Observations

- Evidence of antemortem disease and injury. Describe the evidence both verbally and graphically. Use diagrams to indicate the location of the evidence and photograph the evidence.
- Evidence of perimortem trauma. Describe the evidence verbally and graphically. Use diagrams to indicate the location of the evidence and photograph the evidence.
- Evidence of postmortem damage. Describe the effects of burial, reburial, disinterment, carnivore activity, and anything else that may have happened to the remains after death. As much as possible, differentiate postmortem effects from antemortem or perimortem effects.

Conclusions

In clear, easy-to-read narrative form, summarize the description of the individual, the possible time of death, and any other significant findings. Do not say anything you cannot defend with data unless it is qualified as an opinion. Keep in mind that cause of death is a medical determination and manner of death is a legal determination. The anthropologist has the responsibility to state all findings, but does not have the authority to state cause and manner of death.

Recommendations

If it is advisable to perform tests beyond the scope of your laboratory, state your recommendations clearly. Add any information that may be useful to the final resolution of the case.

Disposition of the Remains

State where the remains have been deposited, with whom, and when.

Signature and Date

Sign and date the report, and initial each page if requested. (If you send a report electronically, convert files into a non-editable format.)

Appendix

Clearly number and initial all diagrams, drawings, maps, and photographs that are referenced in the report. Include them at the point of reference or append them to the end of the report. Include bibliographic references.

The Foundation

The final report may be well written and full of information, but it has little value if it cannot be admitted as evidence in a court of law. To achieve a judgment on admissibility, the attorney must lay a foundation for the court by showing the qualifications of the expert witness and the relevance and authenticity of the physical evidence. This part is relatively straightforward. The real complications set in when the court must rule on the admissibility of the science behind the testimony.

Qualification of the Expert

An **expert witness** is a person qualified to testify in a specific legal proceeding because of special knowledge acquired through education, training, or experience. An expert witness may be called upon to give testimony in relation to scientific, technical, or professional matters.

After swearing to tell the truth, the whole truth, and nothing but the truth, the expert is seated and questioned about his or her qualifications. The court has to be convinced that the expert has the knowledge, skills, and experience to analyze the physical evidence correctly and provide testimony accurately. The basic questions are standard. It is much like reciting your resume to a room full of strangers. This is a time to be thorough and accurate while avoiding sounding pompous. Try not to understate or overstate qualifications.

The witness should be prepared to answer questions about each of the following topics:

1. Academic background: schools, degrees, major areas of study
2. Awards and/or scholarships
3. Specific training and continuing education
4. Certification by professional organizations and peers
5. Employment: title and grade, length of employment, duties, supervision
6. Professional activities: memberships, participation, presentations
7. Relevant publications
8. Relevant teaching experience
9. Previous testimony as an expert witness
10. Amount of experience relevant to the present case

When the attorney feels that a sufficient foundation is laid, he or she will offer the witness as an expert. The opposing attorney may object or ask more foundational questions. Testimony about the evidence doesn't begin until the judge rules that the expert is "qualified." This may take hours, or it may be over in a few minutes. (Once, a prosecuting attorney was in the middle of establishing my qualifications when an impatient judge peered down over his glasses at the attorney and said, "She's obviously an expert in something. Let her talk!" The qualifying was over.)

Authenticity of the Physical Evidence

The attorney lays a foundation for the physical evidence through the testimony of each person in custody of the evidence. He or she must establish that the evidence was collected properly and has been in safe and continuous custody ever since. The chain of custody must be documented in writing, with signatures and dates at each transferal. Any break in the chain, including faulty security while in the custody of a single person in the chain, results in inadmissible evidence. If the physical evidence is not admitted, no further testimony about the evidence is allowed.

EXPERT WITNESS TESTIMONY (SOMETHING TO THINK ABOUT)

People may lie or prevaricate, but the physical evidence is expected to tell the truth. It should need nothing more than an honest translator—the expert witness. But experts don't always agree. If facts are facts, someone must be wrong, but who? And sometimes experts *do* agree, but then change their testimony two years later. If facts are facts, why are they changing? Is the expert wrong or are the scientific methods wrong? What is the court supposed to believe and why?

Admissibility of Expert Witness Testimony

Before 1923, the general rule for expert witness testimony was simple. If the question before the court was not within the range of common knowledge or experience, a witness with special knowledge or skills was required. The witness had only to satisfy the court that he or she possessed the necessary knowledge or experience and the testimony was admissible.

As scientific knowledge and methods increased in complexity, courts were faced with conflicts in the acceptance of "scientific evidence." The foundations laid for the expert and the physical evidence are not enough to allow for novel or highly technical testimony. The most recent tests for expert testimony have rested on decisions from two significant trials. The first was *Frye v. the United States* (1923), and the second, *Daubert v. Merrell Dow Pharmaceuticals, Inc.* (1993).

Frye v. the United States

The ***Frye* test** was the main standard for admissibility of expert witness testimony from 1923 to 1993. The decision came from the Court of Appeals of the District of Columbia. It rejected admissibility of a new systolic blood pressure deception test (a forerunner of the polygraph test) and set a standard for accepting expert witness testimony.

The *Frye* decision states, "Just when a scientific principle or discovery crosses the line between the experimental and demonstrable stages is difficult to define. Somewhere in this twilight zone the evidential force of the principle must be recognized, and while courts will go a long way in admitting expert testimony deduced from a well-recognized scientific principle or discovery, the thing from which the deduction is made must be sufficiently established to have gained general acceptance in the particular field in which it belongs" (*Frye v. the United States*, 54 App. D. C. 46, 293 F. 1013 No. 3968, 1923).

The *Frye* test of "general acceptance" was the standard for seventy years in spite of three basic problems: (1) How do we know when "the thing from which the deduction is made" is "sufficiently established"? (2) Who decides when "general acceptance" is reached? and (3) What is the proper definition of "the particular field in which it belongs"?

Federal Rules of Evidence

The **Federal Rules of Evidence** (FRE) are a set of admissibility standards for federal courts first published in 1937. The FRE was updated in 1975, and federal judges were given more discretion in making admissibility determinations for all kinds of evidence. Rule 702, known as the "gatekeeper rule," requires the judge to determine if testimony will actually assist the court to understand the evidence or come to a conclusion. If so, a witness qualified as an expert may testify, but there are qualifications on the testimony: (1) It must be based upon sufficient facts or data; (2) it must be a product of reliable principles and methods; and (3) the witness must have applied the principles and methods reliably to the facts of the case (Article VII: Opinions and Expert Testimony, Rule 702).

Between 1975 and 1993, the Federal Rules of Evidence were not generally recognized by state courts. The Frye test persisted as the standard until after the *Daubert* decision.

Daubert v. Merrell Dow Pharmaceuticals

The 1993 ***Daubert* decision** was a result of a product liability case. The plaintiff claimed that prenatal use of a drug manufactured by Dow Pharmaceuticals caused serious birth defects. Dow offered several scientific studies showing the absence of relationship between its drug and the birth defects. The plaintiff tried to counter with its own experts, but the judge refused to accept the plaintiff's witnesses' expertise.

The case was eventually heard by the Supreme Court. The primary legal issue was whether the Federal Rules of Evidence (specifically FRE 702) replaced, or supplemented, previous rules—in particular, the *Frye* test. In other words, did the judge have the right to refuse the testimony of the plaintiff's expert witnesses?

The Justices ruled that the FRE replaces previous rules. They essentially redefined the use of science in court in the effort to separate legitimate science from "junk" science. The fact that a scientific principle is new or novel is no longer an issue. "General acceptance" is of little consequence under *Daubert*. All scientific evidence must be weighed the same, whether it is based on a new or an established principle.

Trial judges now have the task of assessing the scientific nature of proposed testimony. They must make a preliminary assessment of whether the testimony's underlying reasoning and/or methodology is scientifically valid and properly applied to the facts at issue. The Supreme Court suggested the following questions:

1. Has the theory or technique been tested?
2. Has it been subjected to peer review or publication?
3. What is its known or potential accuracy limitation or error rate?
4. Do standards exist for the technique or operation?
5. Has the theory or technique acquired widespread acceptance within a relevant scientific community? (This is carried over from the *Frye* test.)

The Court also allowed that other factors not listed by them might be considered in the future. The Court encouraged judges to watch for more ways to test the validity of expert witness testimony. The evolution of the *Daubert* decision has become a study in and of itself.

Daubert has had an enormous impact on expert witnesses. Under *Frye*, the witness had only to show that he or she applied the generally accepted methods. Under *Daubert*, the expert witness must be prepared to provide validation for any and all methods used.

Depositions and Demonstrative Evidence

Courtroom testimony is just part of the role of an expert witness. He or she is also expected to provide relevant information to the attorney during preparation of the case. The attorney may need an introduction to the science behind the testimony or an assessment of the technical strengths and weaknesses of the case. The attorney may also need help preparing for effective cross examination of the opposing expert witnesses. This can include reviewing the opposing expert's report and deposition.

Deposition

The **deposition** is a pre-trial opportunity for an attorney to ask questions of the opposing counsel's witnesses. The expert must be prepared to present all evidence at that time, and there should be no change in testimony without notification between the time of the deposition and the trial. The deposition often takes place in an attorney's office or conference room. It is given under oath with a court reporter and both attorneys present. The opposing attorney may use the deposition as an opportunity to assess the strengths and weakness of the opposing expert. (The expert also learns what to expect from the attorney.)

Demonstrative Evidence

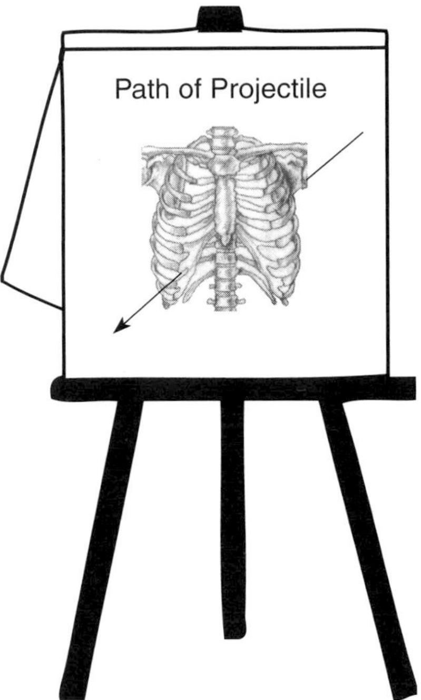

It is the responsibility of the expert witness, not the attorney, to present the evidence so that it can be fully understood by the fact-finder. Information can be communicated verbally or through demonstrative evidence. **Demonstrative evidence** is any tangible object used to illustrate, explain, or emphasize specific aspects of physical evidence.

The use of demonstrative evidence in a courtroom is very much like teaching aids in a classroom. Good visual images attract attention and get the point across. Some people tend to remember more of what they see, and others, what they hear. By engaging more than one of the senses, more information can be communicated to more people. Some jurors also benefit from actually handling demonstrative evidence. People tend to remember more with combined sensory input than with visual or auditory stimuli alone. Expert witnesses use maps, charts, graphs, diagrams, models, mock-ups, photographs, and anything else appropriate for the material at hand. I have used slide shows, large sketch pads, and even tables of bones as demonstrative evidence.

There are several foundational requirements for demonstrative evidence in a court of law. As with all evidence, it must be relevant and it must be a fair and accurate depiction of what it purports to show. It must not conflict with the rules of evidence or create unfair prejudice.

There are also several practical requirements. Demonstrative evidence is effective only if it is error-free, clearly visible, attractive, and professional-looking. It should be planned well in advance of trial, and the courtroom should be checked for compatibility and auxiliary equipment. (I once had all the equipment ready for a slide show, only to discover that there was no way to darken the room.)

Basic Ethics

In the context of professional life, **ethics** is the body of rules related to moral principles, duty, and obligation. Ethics define and determine standards of conduct. It is standard practice for each professional organization to provide a code of ethics for its members. (The Code of Ethics and Conduct of the American Academy of Forensic Sciences can be found in the back section of the annual Membership Directory. It is Article II of the Bylaws.)

Professional codes of ethics are usually based on three fundamental requirements—respect, honesty, and confidentiality. Many ethical problems result from disregard for one or more of these fundamentals.

Respect

Any work in the forensic sciences requires respect for one's fellow human and the rule of law. The work of forensic anthropologists involves human remains; it therefore tends to tread on personal, emotional, and religious aspects of life. It cannot be approached callously.

Honesty

Honesty is basic to any type of scientific endeavor. It is also the foundation of the application of forensic science to human rights. There are plenty of situations that call for silence, but there is never a time to lie.

Honesty includes the willingness to readily admit ignorance, mistakes, or failures. It is counterproductive to yield to shame or to fabricate excuses.

Confidentiality

Confidentiality is essential. This means not talking about cases until the legal process is complete and general permission is given. Silence applies not only to news media but also to close friends and relatives.

People never fail to be amazed when they hear their own words come back to them distorted. If you wish to maintain integrity, don't talk about a case prior to the formal release of the report or the completion of the judicial process. Let the written report, released by the authority in charge of the case, do the talking for you.

Hierarchy of Obligations

Obligations sometimes get in the way of the best ethical intentions. Without even thinking about it, most of us struggle from day to day with the conflict between our obligations to others and our commitments to ourselves. The courtroom magnifies the struggle. The system is designed to reveal and support the truth, but the court wants the truth in black and white. Each attorney wants the truth to advocate for his or her own client, and the expert witness wants the truth to confirm him or her as an "expert."

A forensic psychologist, Stanley Brodsky (1999), proposes an effective way to deal with the conflict by defining a four-level hierarchy of obligations. The highest level is the ethical responsibility to the evidence itself. The whole truth of the findings, as you, the witness, understand them, is foremost. (Note that the obligation to the evidence preempts obligations to the hiring attorney.)

The second level is your codified obligations to the court. The court demands that the witness conform to a specific structure of inquiry and behavior, and the court decides which evidence is admissible and which is prohibited.

The third level is your responsibility to the defendant and to both sets of attorneys. The witness is obligated to be honest and forthcoming about the quality and limits of the scientific results. The expert witness does not "win" or "lose" a case and must maintain a psychological distance from the outcome.

The fourth level is your obligation to yourself and your profession. There is a natural tendency to want to look good. You are qualified as an expert and want to live up to expectations. The pitfall is to overstate your knowledge.

Final Preparation and Courtroom Testimony

There are many books written on the subject of appropriate courtroom testimony (e.g., McKasson & Richards, 1998; Brodsky, 1999; Matson, 2004). Basically, the experts advise that you be well prepared and ethical. The following is a short exposition condensed from the advice of the experts.

Be Well Prepared

- Know your own credentials. You must be "qualified" as an expert witness before there is any chance for your testimony to be heard.
- Discuss all issues with the attorney prior to the hearing of the case—including possible weak points.
- Review the details of your findings and reports.
- If you must use notes, ask permission and expect them to be entered into evidence.
- Review the scientific background for any and all methods (see *Daubert* requirements).
- Have visual aids (demonstrative evidence) prepared and tested.

Demonstrate Honesty

- Report findings accurately. Never go beyond the limits of the evidence or your experience. If you do not know an answer, say so. Do not guess.
- Keep in mind the hierarchy of obligations. The expert witness represents the physical evidence first and foremost.

Show Respect

- Dress appropriately. If there is some question about what is appropriate, ask the attorney for instructions.
- Use proper language. Courtrooms are usually conducted in a formal manner. Any informality whatsoever is seen as disrespect. Never joke.
- Listen carefully to the question and think before responding. Refuse to be misled by leading questions or cross examination. Give the attorney time to object.
- Speak to the person or persons with decision-making authority. If a jury is present, address the answers to the jury, not to the attorney who asked the question. If the decisions are to be made by the judge, speak to the judge.
- Request permission of the judge to elaborate on or clarify a point if it is necessary for accurate communication. The testimony may have been curtailed prematurely or led off track, but the expert witness still has the responsibility to convey information accurately and completely. (Permission may be denied.)
- Request permission of the judge to step down from the witness chair, even if leaving the chair is required for the presentation of testimony.

Professional Associations

Professional associations exist to further the interests of a particular profession. Most are nonprofit organizations. They provide educational and professional enhancement opportunities through publications, meetings, and workshops. They establish and promote ethical standards for members, offer public information about the profession, and many serve as a source for information on job opportunities.

The principal professional organization for forensic anthropologists is the **American Academy of Forensic Sciences** (AAFS). It is composed of ten sections representing a wide variety of forensic specialties, including physical anthropology. The following is the statement of purpose from the American Academy of Forensic Sciences,

> "As a professional society dedicated to the application of science to the law, the AAFS is committed to the promotion of education and the elevation of accuracy, precision, and specificity in the forensic sciences. It does so via the *Journal of Forensic Sciences* (its internationally recognized scientific journal), newsletters, its annual scientific meeting, the conduct of seminars and meetings, and the initiation of actions and reactions to various issues of concern. As the world's most prestigious forensic science organization, the AAFS represents its members to the public and serves as the focal point for public information concerning the forensic science profession." (AAFS Directory of Members and Affiliates)

Other major organizations including forensic anthropologists in their membership are the **International Association for Identification** (IAI), the **American Association of Physical Anthropologists**, and the **American Anthropological Association**. There are also several area-specific groups in the United States, including the southeast Mountain, Swamp and Beach Forensic Anthropologists; the Midwest Bioarchaeology and Forensic Anthropology Association; and the southwest Mountain, Desert, and Coastal Forensic Anthropologists.

Latin Americans formed the **Latin American Forensic Anthropology Association** (ALAF) in 2003. It has quickly become a very active association with members from Argentina, Chile, Colombia, Guatemala, Mexico, Peru, and Venezuela. In addition to the standard objectives of a professional organization, ALAF promotes the protection of its members and their families from the added risks of working in some of the Latin American countries.

Table 16.1 Basic Expert Witness Vocabulary

TERM	DEFINITION
ADVOCATE	Attorney, lawyer, solicitor, legal representative. The term is a reminder that the legal system acknowledges differing points of view, each requiring an argument and someone to present that argument.
ARGUMENT	Assertion accompanied by logical reasoning.
CIRCUMSTANTIAL EVIDENCE	Proves something by inference, conclusion, or deduction (compare with *direct evidence*).
CROSS EXAMINATION	The formal questioning of a witness by the party opposed to the party that called the witness to testify (see *direct examination*).
DAUBERT	*Daubert v. Merrell Dow Pharmaceuticals, Inc.* (1993). A product liability case that resulted in a Supreme Court decision in which the Federal Rules of Evidence (specifically FRE 702) replaced the *Frye* test. Trial judges were assigned the task of assessing the scientific nature of proposed testimony.
DEPOSITION	Testimony under oath taken before trial. A person "gives a deposition" when he or she, accompanied by an attorney, answers questions put by the other side's attorney regarding the facts of a case. Depositions generally take place in an attorney's office. A court reporter is present and everything that is said is recorded and can be used during the trial.
DIRECT EVIDENCE	Proves something on its own. It is obvious to the observer (compare with *circumstantial evidence*).
DIRECT EXAMINATION	Questioning of a witness in a trial or other legal proceeding, conducted by the party who called the witness to testify (compare with *cross examination*).
DISCOVERY	The process of gathering information in preparation for trial.
EVIDENCE	Something that tends to establish or disprove a fact. Types of evidence are physical (real), verbal (testimonial), and demonstrative (used only to teach or explain). Physical and verbal evidence can be direct or circumstantial.
EXPERT TESTIMONY	Statements made in judicial proceedings by a person who is qualified to render an opinion on the issue under consideration.
EXPERT WITNESS	A person who, because of his or her knowledge, experience, and expertise, is qualified to render an opinion on the issue under consideration in a judicial proceeding.
FOUNDATION	As in "to lay a foundation"—to provide to the judge the qualifications of the witness (particularly an expert witness) or the authenticity of a piece of evidence.
***FRYE* TEST**	*Frye v. The United States* (1923). A case involving the acceptance of new or novel scientific principles. The admissibility of expert witness testimony is based on the test of "general acceptance" within the relevant scientific community.
GOOD FAITH	The intention to honestly meet an obligation.
IMPEACH	With respect to an expert witness, a process to challenge the truthfulness or bias of a witness while giving testimony under oath.
OATH	A verbal obligation to tell the truth in a judicial proceeding.
PROOF	Confirmation of a fact by evidence. Proof is sufficient evidence to satisfy the trier of fact (jury or judge). In criminal prosecution, the standard of proof is "beyond a reasonable doubt." In civil cases, the standard of proof is "a preponderance of the evidence."
QUALIFY	To make or consider eligible or fit. "His training and experience *qualified* him as an expert witness."
REPLICABILITY	In science, the concept that the outcome of a particular study will occur again if the study is repeated by another investigator. A scientific finding that cannot be replicated is easily discredited.
TESTIMONY	A statement or statements made by a witness under oath in a legal proceeding.
TRIER OF FACT	The authority at a trial who decides what the truth is. If there is a jury, it is the trier of fact. If there is no jury, the judge is the trier of fact.

CHAPTER 17

Large-Scale Applications

CHAPTER OUTLINE

Introduction

The previous chapters have been based on the "typical" forensic case in the United States—a single set of bones in a cardboard box or an isolated grave. The single-body case is usually handled by a lone forensic anthropologist working for a medical examiner's office or hired on a case-by-case basis. Large-scale operations involving mass fatalities are very different. They require more personnel, more teamwork, a command structure, and a larger infrastructure. In addition, large-scale operations are rarely local. They usually involve travel and a wide assortment of living and working conditions.

In individual, case-by-case work, the quality of the work and the final report reflects on the individual. Poor work may be damaging, but the effect is localized. In large-scale operations, the organization itself publishes the report and bears the primary responsibility for the quality of the work. Poor work reflects on the entire organization and may affect whole communities and nations. Therefore, large-scale operations typically publish standards for work and safety. Acceptance of and adherence to the standards are part of the contractual obligations of the employee-scientist.

Anthropologists tend to divide large-scale operations into disaster work, human rights work, and POW/MIA identification. This is artificial because all human death is a human rights concern, and all cases of mass mortality are disasters. The lines are drawn as they are because of other factors, such as hiring agencies, venue, and degree of urgency. Hiring agencies can be either governmental or nongovernmental, national or international. The venue can be within the United States or abroad, close to cultural amenities or remote. The degree of urgency is an awkward factor because it remains the same for most families of missing and unidentified persons. The response by the agencies tasked with the work is, however, largely dependent on time, money, and legal consequence. **Disaster work** is the most urgent of all the large-scale operations. In the United States, the national government hires forensic anthropologists to work as part of regionally-administered federal disaster teams. These teams respond to any disaster—natural or man-made—involving large numbers of casualties (mass fatality incidents). The work is episodic and intense. It may be conflict related, as it was with the 9/11 events, but the response is carried out in the same way as it is for floods and earthquakes.

Human rights work focuses on civilian casualties of recent conflicts. The funding is either multinational or nongovernmental. The degree of urgency is less than with disaster work only because human rights abuses are committed by governments or would-be governments. Recovery efforts are necessarily delayed until there is a change in or recovery of political control. If the work is called "human rights work," it is usually conducted on non-U.S. soil and involves multicultural challenges. (This is just a convention; it does not mean that the United States has never experienced human rights abuse.)

POW/MIA identification is the long postwar recovery and repatriation of remains of soldiers missing in action and buried on foreign soil (some of whom were also prisoners of war). It is funded by the U.S. military. The venue is multinational, but the effort does not involve the same type of multicultural challenges presented by human rights work. The sense of urgency is the lowest of the three types of large-scale applications. It is lessened by the passage of time and the unlikelihood of legal consequence.

Disasters and Mass Fatality Incidents

A **disaster** is a sudden, extraordinary event that involves substantial loss of life and/or property. Disasters involving large numbers of casualties are called **mass fatality incidents (MFIs)** simply because the focus is on the number of deaths. Loss of property may or may not accompany the loss of life. Disasters are broadly categorized as natural or man-made. Natural disasters include hurricanes, tornados, floods, earthquakes, volcanoes, and tsunamis. (Fires may be either natural or man-made.) Man-made disasters include major transportation accidents, technological disasters, criminal acts, and acts of terrorism, including weapons of mass destruction events. Unexpected acts of war (e.g., Pearl Harbor), and mass suicides (e.g., Jonestown) are also included. There are a few disastrous events, such as cemetery floods and the Tri-State Crematory incident, that do not quite fit the standard definition of MFIs because there are no fatalities—the bodies were dead before the incident began. They are nonetheless handled as MFIs.

THE FORENSIC ANTHROPOLOGIST'S ROLE IN DISASTERS

"A forensic anthropologist has specialized training, education, and experience in the recovery, sorting, and analysis of human and nonhuman remains, especially those that are burned, commingled, and traumatically fragmented." *Mass Fatality Incidents: A Guide for Human Forensic Identification,* National Institute of Justice Special Report, NCJ 199758, June 2005.

MFI Response within U.S. Government Jurisdiction

If the local government is overwhelmed by the number of casualties, federal assistance may be requested. The exact number of casualties is not the issue. The important question is whether or not the local government can handle the work alone. The rural township of Bourbonnais, Illinois, was not prepared to handle eleven casualties from the 1998 Amtrak crash. New York City would have had no trouble handling the eleven casualties, but it was not ready for 2792 casualties from the 2001 World Trade Center incident. Both incidents required federal assistance.

In the United States, mass fatality incident response is handled through the offices of the **National Disaster Medical System (NDMS)** which is administered by the **Department of Health & Human Services**, Assistant Secretary for Preparedness and Response. NDMS manages and coordinates medical-related responses to major emergencies and federally declared disasters.

Many well-known nongovernmental groups, including the American Red Cross and the Salvation Army, also respond to disasters. They help to support the federal teams as well as the survivors and their communities.

DMORT

Disaster Mortuary Operational Response Teams (DMORTs) are one part of the overall NDMS operation. Most of the NDMS provides medical aid to the living, but DMORT is assigned the task of recovering, identifying, and processing the dead. DMORT grew out of the work of a nonprofit group of volunteers from the National Funeral Directors Association in the 1980s. The funeral directors recognized the need for efficient processing of bodies following mass fatality incidents. They conceived the idea of a portable morgue and put the first one into operation. In time, they saw that a multidisciplinary approach would work even better by facilitating identification as part of the postmortem processing of "unidentifiable" remains. Recovery of the dead was also improved.

In the early 1990s DMORT was incorporated into the federal government and ten regional teams were formed, each with a regional coordinator.

CASE EXAMPLE: TRI-STATE CREMATORY DISASTER

Tri-State Crematory was a small-town crematory in North Georgia. Over a period of several years, the owner, Ray Brent Marsh, accepted over 300 bodies from funeral homes in Georgia, Tennessee, and Alabama and dumped them on his own property instead of cremating them. He returned boxes of concrete mix to funeral homes rather than cremains. When the crime was uncovered in 2002, help was requested from the federal government, and DMORT helped the Georgia Bureau of Investigation to recover and identify the corpses. Marsh was charged with theft by deception, abusing a corpse, burial service–related fraud, and giving false statements. He is serving twelve years in prison. (Marsh had no morbid interest in the bodies, and he made no serious effort to hide the bodies. This appears to be an ultimate example of falling behind in work.)

DMORT teams include forensic anthropologists, pathologists, odontologists, fingerprint specialists, radiologists, and computer specialists in addition to funeral directors, morticians, family assistance personnel, and a large group of support personnel.

When a request for emergency aid is accepted by the U.S. government, a response operation is immediately set in motion. DMORT personnel are selected and notified on the basis of team membership and specialty area. Local area team members are asked to respond first. All team members are required to be packed and ready to go before the call is issued. A standard deployment is two weeks with no time off. Teams work seven days a week in twelve-hour shifts. Most morgues operate only one shift per day, but some operations, such as the World Trade Center processing at Fresh Kills Landfill, ran nonstop, two shifts per day until the work was declared done.

Figure 17.1
Part of a Portable Morgue Stored on Pallets
DMORT maintains two complete portable morgue units, ready to be transported rapidly to any disaster site.

At the disaster site, local law enforcement has control of the scene and the local coroner or medical examiner is in charge of the dead. When DMORT administrators arrive, they work with the local officials to find locations for a temporary morgue and a family assistance center. Electricity and running water are essential for the morgue. A large, adaptable structure (such as an airplane hanger) is preferred, but the entire morgue can be constructed of tents if no suitable building is available. Large trailers can be used for office space. Refrigeration trucks are used to store the remains before and after processing. Flexibility and on-the-spot creativity are important in the initial setup process.

DMORT maintains two **portable morgue units**. They are warehoused in Maryland and California when not in use. The entire contents of a morgue, including partitions, furniture, equipment, and supplies, are strapped to pallets and can be transported efficiently by truck or air. Even reference materials—specific to each specialty—are packed in trunks and labeled by section. It is like having an entire laboratory ready to be up and running within hours in a remote location.

The morgue is organized with separate areas for each of the major operations—admittance, photography, radiology, pathology, forensic anthropology, odontology, fingerprints, and casketing. Partitions are set up between the areas with a wide central hallway for rolling gurneys between stations.

The Role of the Forensic Anthropologist in Disaster Operations

Forensic anthropologists work in both field recovery and morgue operations. Recovery is a special challenge in disaster situations because of the instability of the disaster site and the extreme commingling and/or disarticulation and fragmentation of the remains. Ideally, each body would be placed in a body bag in the field, transported to the morgue, and processed as a single unit. In reality, each body bag may contain fragments of one body, a part of a body, several bodies, or entirely nonhuman remains. (At the World Trade Center, many of the bones were from restaurants, not victims. Other "bones" were assorted man-made items such as toys and plastic pipes.) Forensic anthropologists are capable of making many decisions in the field to help eliminate problems later in the morgue. It is easier to reassociate bodies in context and more efficient to separate out nonhuman material in the field.

In the morgue, the work of the forensic anthropologist is standard laboratory analysis. The following is a list of duties summarized from the National Institute of Justice's special report on mass fatality incidents (June 2005). The forensic anthropologist is expected to:

- Evaluate and document the condition of the remains.
- Separate obviously commingled remains; calculate the minimum number of individuals.
- Analyze the remains to determine sex, age at death, race, stature, trauma, and disease conditions.
- Determine the need for additional analysis by other disciplines (e.g., radiology, odontology).
- Maintain a log of incomplete remains to facilitate reassociation.
- Document, remove, and save nonhuman and/or nonbiological materials for proper disposal.
- Obtain DNA samples.
- Interpret radiographs.
- Compare antemortem and postmortem records.
- Maintain communication with the other identification specialists.

In this list, the only duty that may seem out of the ordinary is the log of incomplete remains. This log is not mandatory in the typical archaeological lab, where everything is laid out on a series of tables for repeated viewing. But it is essential in the disaster scene, where there is one, and possibly only one, opportunity to view and analyze each component before it is packaged and stored. Reassociation is a serious challenge.

DMORT Processing and Temporary Morgue Stations

Each body bag that enters the temporary morgue is processed in sequence. The processing always begins at Admitting and ends at what is called Casketing. The intermediate steps depend on the setup of the morgue and the requirements of the individual case. A body may be returned to radiology for additional radiographs or sent among the pathologists, anthropologists, and dentists for consultation on shared concerns such as disassociated parts, broken bones, and exfoliated teeth.

The following is the general sequence of stations for a single gurney and escort.

1. *Admitting:* The admitting section is responsible for the chain of custody of the remains and all associated materials. Each case is entered into the DMORT computer program and assigned mortuary reference numbers for all individual items. A microchip may be inserted into the body at this time. The admitting station also assigns an escort and generates a **victim identification packet (VIP)**. The packet contains a tracking form and special forms for each of the morgue stations, including Anthropology. One escort accompanies the contents of a single body bag throughout the entire process of analysis and maintains control of the victim identification packet. The escort system is excellent because it ensures continuity, increases efficiency, and lessens the likelihood of errors.

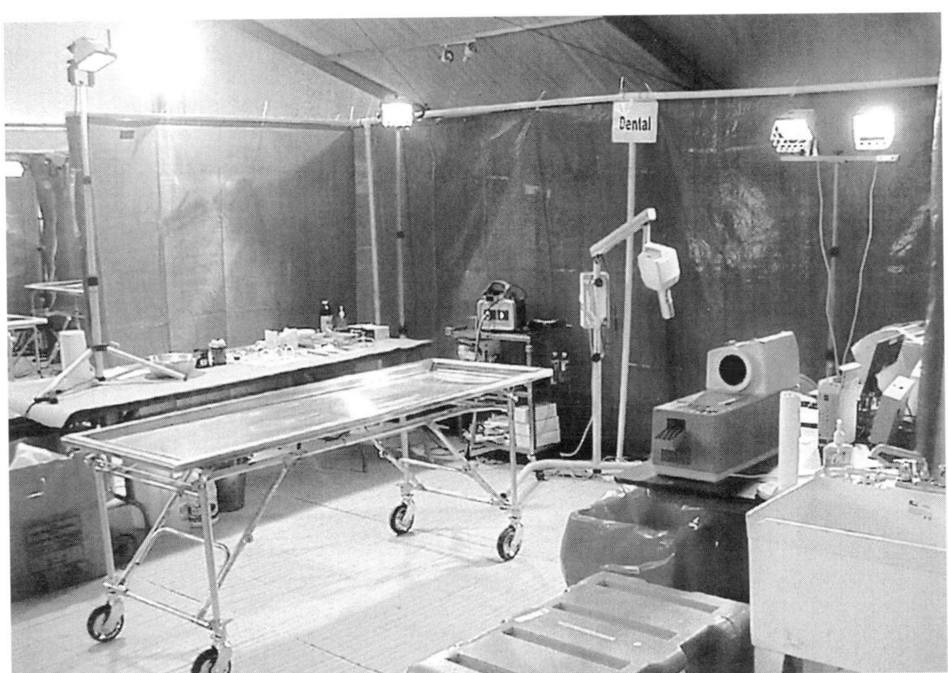

Figure 17.2
Portable Morgue Ready for Processing Bodies
DMORT uses a system of partitioned space for each identification specialty, all within the same large structure or tent. The DNA area is pictured.

2. *Photography and Personal Effects:* This is essentially part of the admitting process. The contents of the body bag are photographed and all personal effects are removed, documented, and stored. The role of the photographer may change from one deployment to another. I have served in DMORT operations where the photographer is available to all sections for photographs related to the analysis, and in others where the photographer is restricted to nonbiological evidence.
3. *Radiology:* The whole body bag is radiographed. Sometimes this is the first real view of the remains. Mud, charred flesh, or other debris may have obscured the full contents until this point. Radiographs can reveal projectiles, shrapnel, and other foreign objects as well as bony parts and prosthetics.
4. *Pathology:* Forensic pathologists autopsy the remains and try to determine cause and manner of death. Saul and Saul (2003) point out that cause of death may not be obvious, even in an airline crash. A homicide may have preceded the crash and, in fact, the death may have been the cause of the crash rather than its result. As with all forensic work, assumptions should be avoided.
5. *Anthropology:* (The role of the anthropologist is described previously.) The VIP Anthropology Examination Form is not a full analysis form; it is designed only for computer entry and comparison with antemortem information to establish a tentative identification. If time allows, the full anthropological analysis is written up separately and attached to the anthropology form. In a disaster situation, this usually means that the remains are re-examined after a tentative identification is generated.
6. *Odontology (dental unit):* Forensic odontologists radiograph all dental structures and chart the teeth. If teeth are not present, other oral structures, anomalies, and evidence of disease can be just as useful for identification. Dental teams use a specialized computer program called WinID to match a missing person to unidentified remains through dental comparisons. The program was developed to run on Windows systems and store data in a Microsoft Access Database. Like the other specialized forensic programs (e.g., AFIS, CODIS, IBIS), it increases the efficiency of forensic dentists by sorting large databases of records and locating the most likely matches for direct comparison based on basic dental and anthropometric characteristics.
7. *Fingerprinting:* Fingerprint experts obtain prints from the remains for comparison with reference prints from the files of law enforcement agencies and employers. Comparison prints can also be obtained from personal items. The DMORT fingerprint experts use a variety of special techniques to obtain fingerprints from burned and decomposing remains. They also use the Automated Fingerprint Identification System (AFIS), to store, locate, and match digital images of fingerprints.
8. *DNA:* The Armed Forces DNA Identification Laboratory (AFDIL), part of the Armed Forces Institute of Pathology in Rockville, Maryland, processes DNA samples for DMORT. AFDIL sometimes responds to mass fatality incidents alongside DMORT. If not, it relies on the DMORT DNA core group, represented by pathology, anthropology, and odontology, to collect samples. The DNA samples are stored for later use if identification cannot be obtained by conventional means. DNA is also used to to help reassociate parts of bodies. The Combined DNA Index System (CODIS) is used for sharing and comparing DNA information with other agencies.
9. *Embalming and casketing:* Morticians handle all of the preparations for storage and/or release of the remains. The morticians are fully prepared to embalm and prepare a body for a standard funeral, but in mass fatality incidents this is frequently not possible. Stabilization and storage are more important than viewing when remains are in poor condition and unidentified.

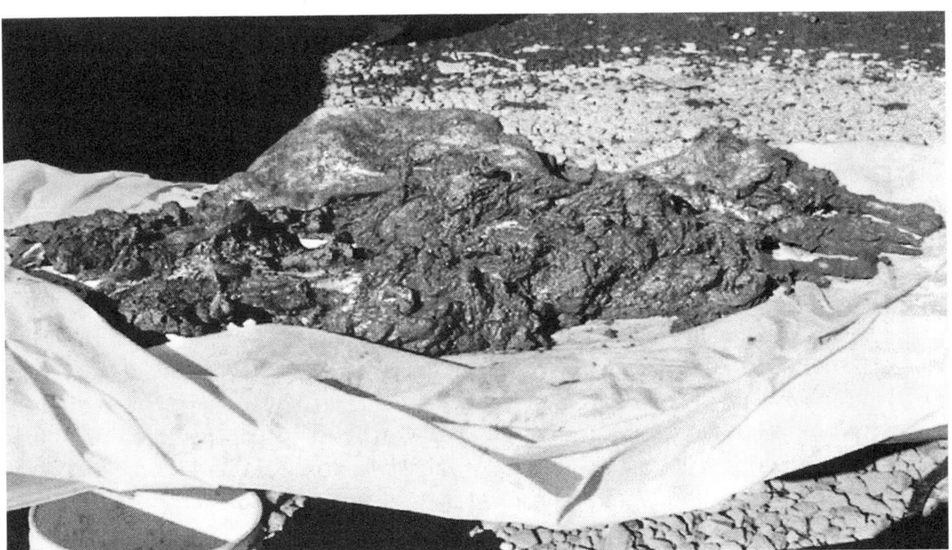

Figure 17.3
Unrecognizable Human Remains from a Disaster Site
This is one of the more complete bodies recovered at the processing site for the World Trade Center disaster. The flesh is partially preserved by smoke and contents of pockets are still present.

10. *Information Resource Center (IRC):* The whole operation is brought together by the DMORT team members at the IRC. Data from the victim identification packets are entered into the DMORT VIP computer program together with antemortem information collected from the families at the family assistance center. The system is designed to match postmortem records generated from the morgue with antemortem records. Tentative identifications can then be selected for further comparison and (hopefully) final identification.

The release of the remains to the family-designated funeral home can be complicated by missing and disassociated parts. Some families want to be informed every time a portion of a fragmented body is identified. Others want to be able to have a single memorial service and move on without further notification. The alternatives must be clearly communicated and the wishes left in writing. Some identification processes, such as the World Trade Center effort, continue for years.

Discussion

Disasters present enormous challenges. Resources are strained beyond their limits and general panic leads to unwarranted conflict and irrational decisions. The only way to keep a bad situation from getting worse is by thorough advance planning and preparation. It's not easy to prepare for the unknown, and it is hard to find the incentive when no obvious threat is present. But experience is worth listening to. The U.S. national disaster plans work fairly well. Professionals are hired and trained before they are needed; a good communication network is in place; disaster teams and their entire infrastructure are ready for deployment at all times; the employers and families of team members are prepared; and the whole system is maintained and strengthened through annual meetings, continuing education, and regular newsletters.

When we make the effort to be prepared for the expected, we have a better chance of withstanding the unexpected. But events the enormity of Hurricane Katrina will always push the limits. (And in spite of the general confusion, DMORT performed very well in both Louisiana and Mississippi.)

Human Rights Work

Introduction: The Scope of the Problem

Think back over international events of the past decade. Is there any question about the widespread disregard for human rights? Thanks to twenty-four hour cable news and the Internet, reports of violent death and human displacement come to us every minute of the day. In all of these conflicts, armed groups disregard human rights in the pursuit of political, economic, religious, and/or ethnic goals. The result is large numbers of civilian deaths through political mass murder and genocide.

In 2001, the Center for International Development and Conflict Management at the University of Maryland began publishing a series of reports called Peace and Conflict. The reports provide statistics and commentary on major trends in armed conflict, self-determination movements, and democracy. They also evaluate each country's capacity for peace-building and risk for conflict.

The first report documented a global decline in armed conflict during the latter part of the 1990s. This was attributed to the growing number of democratic regimes and the success of international efforts at containing conflicts and negotiating settlements (Gurr et al., 2001). In the 2005 report, they continued to be optimistic and attributed gains in peace to the "persistent and coordinated efforts at peace-building by civil society organizations, national leaders, nongovernmental organizations, and international bodies" (Marshall & Gurr, 2005).

However, by 2008, they reported a reverse in the trend and pointed out that thirty-one of the thirty-nine different conflicts erupting in the previous ten years had been recurrences of old conflicts. Interestingly, they placed the blame on a "conflict syndrome" of instability and state failure instead of the organizations credited with supporting peace. War leaves countries in a weakened condition. When suffering is not alleviated, more violence erupts and the cycle continues (Hewitt, 2010).

The size of the problem is hard to imagine. It is difficult to obtain accurate death counts, partially because combat-related deaths are only part of the statistic. Many die because of war-related displacement or economic disruption, resulting in starvation and disease. Large numbers of dead are simply never accounted for. They are the war-time "disappeared." It is obvious that the peacebuilding organizations need to continue working in the face of rising violence. Humanitarian work is as important as economic and political action in the effort to heal the cycle of recurring conflict. I'm grateful that many anthropologists are playing a role in the peace-building process by applying their knowledge and skills to international human rights work.

THE DISAPPEARED

The verb *to disappear* can be used to mean to arrest, imprison, or kill someone secretly. Missing and unidentified persons that result from internal conflicts such as the dirty wars of Argentina and Guatemala are known as "the disappeared." They are also called "disappeared persons" or "forced disappearances."

When viewed from the perspective of international humanitarian law, disappearance involves the commission of acts defined as war crimes. These include unlawful confinement, failure to allow due process, and failure to allow communication between the arrested person and the outside world. Disappearance may also involve torture and cruel and inhuman treatment as well as murder (Based on Gutman & Rieff, 1999).

GENOCIDE

"In 1994, Rwanda, a country of just 8 million, experienced the numerical equivalent of more than two World Trade Center attacks every single day for 100 days. On an American scale this would mean 23 million people murdered in three months. When, on September 12, 2001, the United States turned for help to its friends around the world, Americans were gratified by the overwhelming response. When the Tutsi cried out, by contrast, every country in the world turned away" (Samantha Power, 2002). (Estimates of the number of dead in Rwanda range from 500,000 to 1 million.)

Human Rights and the Law

Human rights are the rights individuals have simply by virtue of being human. Such rights are considered to be universal and nonconditional. States, governments, and private actors are expected to respect these rights, but few people can actually define them. They are nonetheless available for all to read in the **Universal Declaration of Human Rights** (1948).

After the horrors of World War II, the international community was ready to develop international standards. It hoped to find ways to prevent further gross violations of human rights. The United Nations (UN) was formed, and in drafting the UN Charter, some states wanted members to be required to safeguard and protect human rights. (Instead, today, they are only required to "promote" human rights.) In response to this request, the UN Human Rights Commission was created. The Commission crafted the Universal Declaration of Human Rights, which stands as a shining example of how things ought to be. It was adopted by the UN General Assembly in 1948 with forty-eight votes in favor and eight abstentions from the communist bloc, South Africa, and Saudi Arabia.

There are thirty articles in the Declaration. Briefly stated, they establish rights to a fair and public hearing, presumption of innocence until proven guilty,

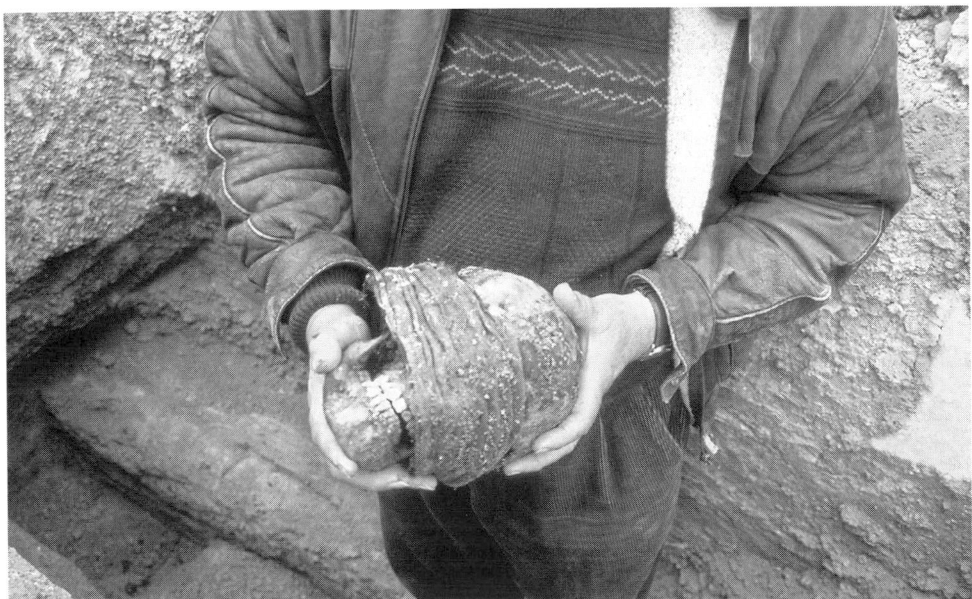

Figure 17.4
Blindfolded Skull
The blindfold is still in place on the skull of a teenaged boy who was executed with many of his friends in the city of Erbil, Iraq. The boys' only crime was that they were Kurds. The city's leader executed the boys as a show of force in order to gain greater control over the local population.

privacy, freedom of movement, nationality, family, the right to own property, freedom of thought, religion, opinion, expression, association, assembly, work, rest, health, education, and culture. The Articles also include freedom from discrimination, slavery, torture, arbitrary arrest, detention, or exile.

All this being said, the Universal Declaration of Human Rights is not law. In the six decades since the end of World War II, the international community has struggled with the question of how to make the realization of human rights a global reality. The United Nations can adopt and promote standards for the world, nations can sanction other nations by refusing trade or economic aid, but in the end, the national governments establish their own law. Even within nations, secular and religious views of human rights are often divided and religious law may conflict with state law.

Crimes of War (Gutman & Rieff, 1999) and the website of the Crimes of War Project (http://www.crimesofwar.org) are sources for information on major international humanitarian law, including conventions, declarations, protocols, resolutions, and statues.

The Role of the Scientist

Investigations into major human rights abuses usually take place following large governmental upheavals. The size and scope of the investigation depends on the authority of the investigatory body—nongovernmental, national, or international. Sometimes information from short-term, limited investigations by nongovernmental agencies, such as Human Rights Watch or Amnesty International, can lead to the establishment of truth commissions and commissions of inquiry with broader powers to investigate. (See the section titled "Critical Organizers, Funders, and Participants.")

Scientists are hired by most of the various investigative bodies to provide technical expertise. They are employed to collect evidence for war crimes investigations, recover and identify victims, provide education and training for local citizens, and offer expert witness testimony.

Physical Evidence

When war is involved, careful scene investigation and analysis is usually not an option, at least not near to the time of the event. If there are human rights violations, evidence may come solely from the verbal testimony of victims or witnesses. There is no doubt about the importance of verbal testimony, but it is far more effective if it is corroborated by physical evidence.

Physical evidence is even more important if testimonies conflict or if no verbal evidence is forthcoming. When there is conflicting testimony, the physical evidence can be used to support or contradict the witness. When the events were not witnessed by a living person or the witnesses are too fearful come forward (as is often the case in human rights abuses), the physical evidence may be the only path to truth. It may also provide the psychological support needed to bring a witness into the open.

Forensic science brings valuable objectivity to an investigation. Through their work, forensic scientists become advocates for the evidence. Even in the worst of conditions, a well-trained forensic scientist is at least able to collect and preserve evidence so that it can be useful in the future.

Professional Associations and Committees

For many scientists, involvement in human rights issues begins with participation in professional organizations. In the United States, numerous organizations have formed committees to investigate human rights issues related to specific disciplines. Physicians, lawyers, psychiatrists, psychologists, political scientists, and linguists are among the scientists who have formally committed to aiding human rights causes. These committees analyze data, review and

Figure 17.5
Secondary Burials
Prior to the arrival of the anthropologists, the Kurds of Erbil, Iraq, had dug up unidentified remains, removed the clothing, reburied the remains, and anchored the clothing to the graves with rocks. Families visited the grave sites to view the clothing in hopes of recognizing something belonging to a lost loved one. The graves were now secondary burials and less likely to yield full sets of remains.

write reports, and testify in courts of law or before commissions of inquiry. Some participate in letter-writing campaigns to encourage governments to intercede on behalf of colleagues in other countries.

The Minnesota Lawyers International Human Rights Committee recognized a major need for information in international death investigation. It organized a group of forensic scientists in 1986 to write the document now known as the Minnesota Protocol, which was designed to serve as an aid to death investigation throughout the world. The Minnesota Protocol was adopted by the United Nations in 1991 and was republished in numerous languages under the title *Manual on the Effective Prevention and Investigation of Extra-Legal, Arbitrary and Summary Executions*. It was a good start toward worldwide use of the forensic sciences in human rights cases.

Another example is the Science and Human Rights Program (SHR) of the American Association for the Advancement of Science (AAAS). The SHR was established in 1977. Its mission is to assist in protecting the human rights of scientists around the world and to make the tools and knowledge of science available to benefit the field of human rights. Among its many projects are the AAAS Human Rights Action Network and the Science and Human Rights Coalition. The Human Rights Data Analysis Group (HRDAG), initiated by AAAS, has moved to Benetech, a nonprofit organization that provides technical support to large-scale human rights data projects. Benetech maintains backup and security for sensitive human rights databases and handles advanced statistical analysis of mass atrocities. (For more on Benetech, see Ball, 1996; Ball & colleagues, 1997; Ball & colleagues, 2000.)

Contributions of Forensic Anthropologists

Forensic anthropologists (both physical anthropologists and archaeologists) join with physicians, odontologists, radiologists, criminalists, and other forensic scientists in revealing evidence of mass murder, genocide, torture, summary execution, and political "disappearances." Anthropologists are best utilized in cases requiring disinterment, personal identification, and trauma analysis. No other forensic specialist is trained to carry out careful archaeological excavation and osteological analysis. There is, however, a cultural component of the work where human rights workers and forensic anthropologists overlap.

The very nature of human rights work requires sensitivity and flexibility in the face of cultural and linguistic differences. Anthropologists are ideally suited for this work. For example, it is necessary to be able to recognize normal burial customs before it is possible to assess what may be abnormal or criminal. In the United States, we bury our dead in full clothing lying face up in coffins or caskets. If a body were found buried on its side without clothing or coffin, criminal activity would be suspected. In Islamic countries, however, the custom is to bury the dead on the right side, facing Mecca, wrapped only in a cotton shroud that quickly deteriorates. Under such cultural conditions, criminal activity is suspected if the body is found clothed or facing in a direction other than toward Mecca.

Anthropological training is also useful in conducting interviews to obtain antemortem information. Most anthropologists recognize the pitfalls associated with cross-cultural communication and search for ways to learn and adjust for more effective communication. Many things do not translate, no matter how expert the translator. Color is one example. It is far better to use a color chart, point to the color, and record it by number than to try to translate it from one language to

Figure 17.6
Kurdish Burial

Knowledge of local burial practices is essential to accurate interpretation of exhumation data. Muslims are usually buried on the right side, wrapped in a shroud, and facing toward Mecca.

With his famous facility for sizing up a problem, Clyde C. Snow exposed one of the major differences between forensic work in the United States and international human rights work. Dr. Snow was in Bolivia to analyze skeletal remains from the cemetery of a work camp. The dead were all street kids, petty thieves, and vagrants. They had never been formally charged, tried, or sentenced, but they had been imprisoned and forced to work until they died. After examining the remains, Snow commented, "Back in 1979, I was pulled into a case where I had to identify a bunch of boys killed by a psychopath in Chicago. I never imagined that ten years later I'd be down here doing pretty much the same thing. But there's a big difference in this case. Camacho [the camp commander] and his men murdered those kids with the power of the state behind them. Now for me, that's the worst crime of all" (Joyce & Stover, 1991).

another. The use of left and right in relation to the body can also be difficult. Pictures and diagrams serve to facilitate orientation to parts of the body.

Anthropologists should be able and willing to accommodate local customs and laws. These can be disconcerting to anyone solely accustomed to police procedures within the United States. In some countries, the judge assigned to the case must be present at all times during an investigation. In many places, the full community insists on being involved in the work of the exhumation, and it is normal to have whole families in attendance and grieving loudly. In Latin American countries it is not unusual for religious ceremonies to be conducted alongside a disinterment in progress.

History: The Mission in Argentina and the EAAF

The first well-publicized use of forensic anthropology in a human rights mission occurred in 1984. A group of scientists from the United States were asked to evaluate the possibility of identifying victims of the Argentine "Dirty War" (1974–1983). Clyde Snow was the forensic anthropologist who traveled to Argentina as a consultant.

The request for help was initiated by *Las Abuelas de la Plaza de Mayo*. The Abuelas are a group of grandmothers of the disappeared. For more than twenty-five years, they marched once a week on the Plaza de Mayo in Buenos Aires, wearing white kerchiefs on their heads and carrying signs about their missing loved ones. In their quiet way, they have been a powerful force. They will not let their country forget its digression from sanity and morality. (Over the years, more than one such group appeared with the same mission, including *Las Madres* [mothers] *de la Plaza de Mayo*.)

The mission to Argentina was organized by Eric Stover, who was at that time the Director of the Science and Human Rights Program of the American Association for the Advancement of Science. When the Argentine mission was initiated, Snow and Stover could not have known what far-reaching effects their work would achieve.

THE ARGENTINE FORENSIC ANTHROPOLOGY TEAM

"When we initially started our work twenty-one years ago, we needed to distance ourselves from legal-medical systems and other governmental institutions that had reportedly committed crimes and/or had lost credibility during lengthy periods of human rights violations. We worked outside these organizations, incorporating new scientific tools for human rights investigations. In order to have a long-term effect, and taking advantage of increased interest in international criminal law and domestic incorporation of it, we are now working toward incorporating international protocols for human rights work into domestic criminal procedures. In a way, then, in the past two decades we have come full circle."—EAAF Annual Report, 2005, page 13.

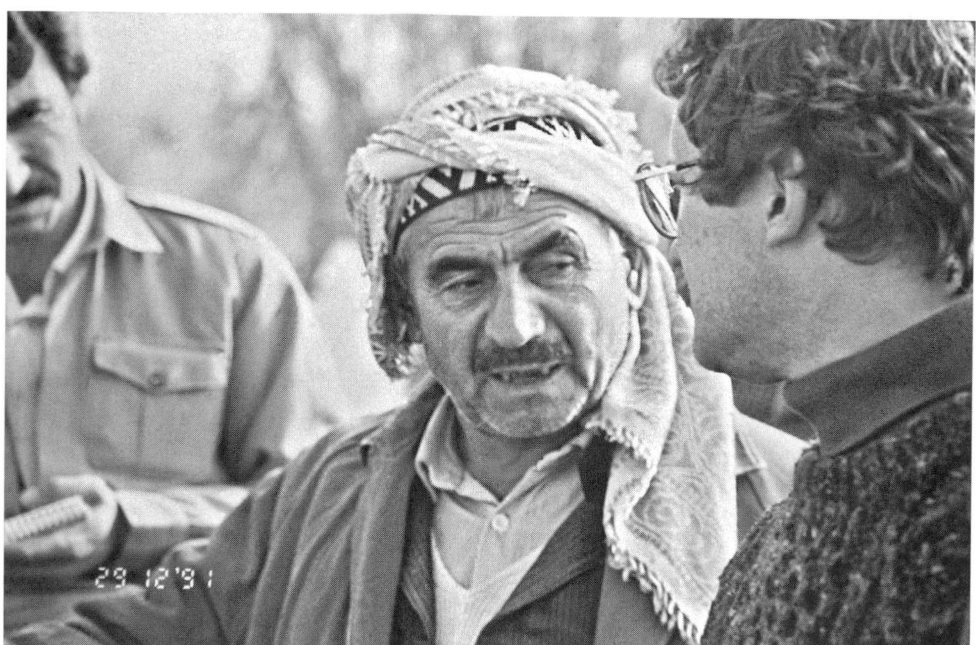

Figure 17.7
Eric Stover Interviews a Kurdish Survivor
Interviews provide essential background information and antemortem descriptions of victims.

Many Argentine victims were identified, and a team of Argentines, the *Equipo Argentino de Antropologia Forense* (EAAF), was formed in the process. Snow returned to Argentina many times during the excavations and training. He supervised the excavations, trained the team, and testified as an expert witness in Argentine courts of law. He went on to provide technical support and encouragement to the EAAF for many years.

The EAAF established its own precedents by reaching out to provide technical aid to numerous other countries from Latin America to Africa and Asia. One of its many successes was the excavation at El Masote in El Salvador. The El Masote evidence was utilized by the Salvadorean Truth Commission, and the work received international publicity (Doretti & Snow, 2003). The Argentine team is now in demand throughout the world because of its knowledge, experience, and professionalism.

OTHER NATIONAL AND INTERNATIONAL FORENSIC ANTHROPOLOGY TEAMS

In Guatemala, three independent forensic anthropology teams formed during the 1990s—the Guatemalan Forensic Anthropology Foundation (FAFG), the Center of Forensic Analysis and Applied Sciences (CAFCA), and the forensic anthropology team of the Archbishop's Human Rights Office of Guatemala (ODHAG). All were developed more or less on the model of the Argentine team and maintain nonprofit, nongovernmental status. The Guatemalan teams are primarily occupied with exhumation of and identification of Mayan peasants massacred during the government's "scorched earth policy" of the 1980s. Several of the members of the Guatemalan teams have also devoted their time and expertise to international efforts.

Independent teams have formed in a few other countries, including Peru and Chile, but, overall, the role of the independent team is changing. Whereas these teams used to provide the only available experts within their countries, more and more governmental agencies now hire their own specialists in forensic anthropology. In this light, independent teams such as EQUITAS, the Colombian Interdisciplinary Team for Forensic Work and Psychosocial Assistance, are expanding into new roles by assuming functions similar to forensic science consultants and human rights activists in the United States. Because of their nonprofit, nongovernmental status, they are able to bring balance, accountability, and transparency to governmental investigations by acting as observers during field investigations, reviewing governmental reports, and providing alternative, independent expert advice and testimony. They also have the capacity to explore new technologies not yet in use by governmental agencies. And, probably most important from a human rights standpoint, they are available to work on (and to bring attention to) cases that fall outside the interest of governmental agencies, particularly those of marginal populations.

International Human Rights Work and Domestic Forensic Work Compared

For the professional forensic scientist, the basic work on human rights cases appears to be very much the same as everyday work. Crimes have been committed; there are bodies to be identified and events to be reconstructed. The technical methods are the same. But virtually everything else is different. Unlike common crimes, human rights crimes are committed by people in authority—police, military, elected officials—or groups with concentrated power—guerrilla and paramilitary organizations. Our cultural assumptions

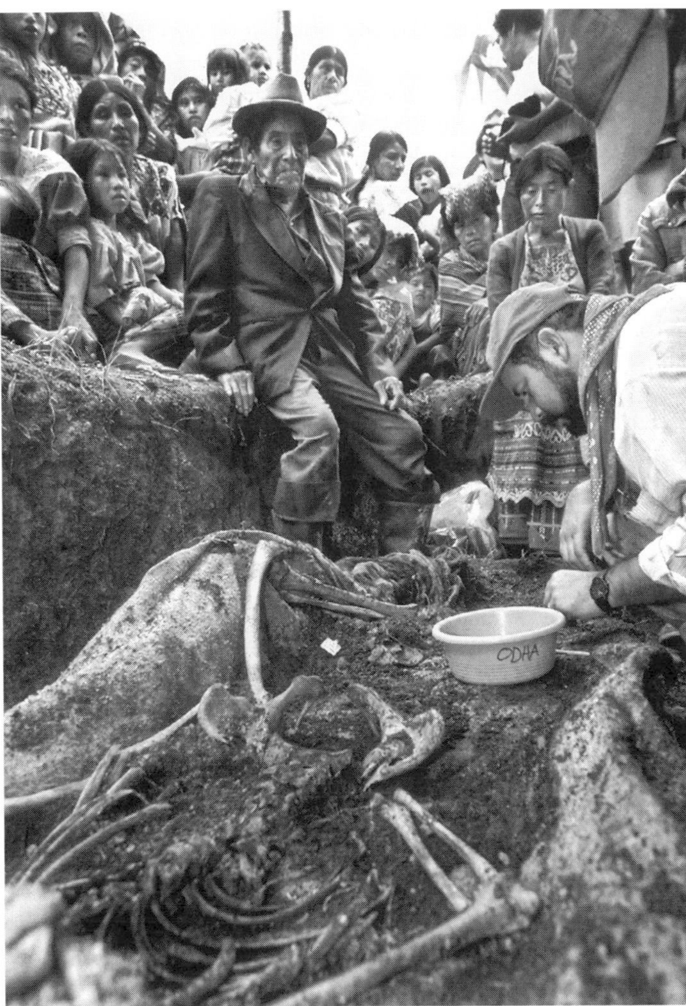

Figure 17.8
Exhumation in Progress near Chajul, El Quiche, Guatemala
In human rights cases, priorities may be different. Here, the exhumations are usually carried out in the presence of the victims' families. Sometimes local people provide physical labor. This is quite different from medical-legal procedures in the United States. (Lancerio López)

about criminals don't apply, and the scale of the forensic work is far greater. Another major difference is the lack of support disciplines. Most forensic scientists take the availability of resources and other scientists for granted. But human rights investigations often take place far from crime laboratories and other technical help.

Within the United States and most other industrialized countries, the Universal Declaration of Human Rights is largely upheld by domestic law. Therefore, on home soil, human rights tend to be identified with law enforcement and forensic investigation. In many parts of the world, however, human rights per se are not a part of civil or criminal law. The only recourse for action is through the application of international or "universal" human rights covenants. Under such conditions, the only people available to enforce human rights covenants are the people employed by private and international human rights organizations. Security takes on new meaning in such environments. In some cases, communities of families come together to provide security and protect their own interests. In other cases, private security guards must be hired.

In human rights work, forensic scientists usually experience far greater involvement in the case. In the United States, I feel comfortable describing my work as disinterment and analysis of human remains. I give recommendations to investigating officers, and I occasionally meet with families to explain the physical evidence and the reasons for establishing identification. But I do not interview people to obtain antemortem information. When I began to work on human rights missions, I discovered that there was seldom anyone trained to do the other half of the job. There was no way to succeed in identifications, especially in the absence of medical records, without taking part in the collection of verbal antemortem evidence from families and friends. (This is changing as more large investigations are able to hire psychosocial professionals as part of the team.)

Critical Organizers, Funders, and Participants

Forensic anthropologists receive a lot of publicity for their work, but recovery and identification of the missing is only one part of one type of human rights mission, and anthropologists are just one small part of the machinery. If a mission is to progress all the way from initial need to final resolution, it requires organizers, funders, and a wide assortment of participants. This section is an introduction to the larger picture.

Nongovernmental Family-Support Organizations

Human rights missions often begin with demands and requests from families of the dead and disappeared. The families have the most immediate interest in the problem, and they are usually in a good position to judge the political climate of the country. The families are most effective in their quest when they join or form support/activist groups. Examples are the *Abuelas de la Plaza de Mayo* in Argentina and ASFADES, the *Asociación de Familiares de Desaparecidos* in Colombia. These types of groups can grow to include not only the relatives, but whole communities and their legal representatives.

Truth Commissions, Commissions of Inquiry, and War Crimes Tribunals

Truth commissions, commissions of inquiry, and war crimes tribunals are established by governments for limited periods of time. They all have stated tasks and limited authority. **Truth commissions** have the power to investigate past wrongdoings of a specific government. Commissions gather information, publish reports, and make recommendations for appropriate action such as justice, amnesty, or protection. They usually have the authority to hire scientists and other investigators to aid with the collection of physical evidence.

The **South African Commission for Truth and Reconciliation** is considered to be a model for others. Truth commissions are becoming increasingly useful during times of governmental transition because of their effectiveness in slowing or ending the cycle of violence (Hayner, 1994).

Commissions of inquiry are closely related to truth commissions, but the mandate is usually more limited, such as an inquiry into specific events or the activities of certain people or groups of people during a specific time period.

International war crimes tribunals are courts of law formed to try individuals accused of war crimes and crimes against humanity in relation to a specific conflicts. Famous war crimes tribunals were held in Nuremberg and Tokyo following World War II. The **International Criminal Tribunal for the former Yugoslavia (ICTY),** established in 1993, is still active today.

INTERGOVERNMENTAL AND INTERNATIONAL INSTITUTIONS AND COURTS

Intergovernmental and international institutions have much broader powers than truth commissions and are not limited by time and task. Intergovernmental examples include the **Organization of American States, Inter-American Commission of Human Rights; the Organization of African Unity, African Commission** (the monitoring body for the African Charter on Human and People's Rights); and the **Council of Europe, European Court of Human Rights.**

On an international level, the Office of the **United Nations High Commissioner for Human Rights** is the foremost example. It was established in 1993 and serves to promote and protect worldwide human rights through direct contact with individual governments and provision of technical assistance where appropriate.

The **International Criminal Court (ICC)** was activated in 2002. It follows from the Rome Statute of the International Criminal Court, established July 17, 1998. The court is complementary to the criminal jurisdictions of national governments. Unlike criminal tribunals, it is a permanent body, treaty based, and established to promote the rule of law and ensure that the gravest international crimes do not go unpunished. At the end of 2011, 120 states were parties to the Statute of the Court. These include all of South America, most of Europe, and about half of African countries. (The United States has not ratified the Rome Statute.)

SCIENCE AND HUMAN RIGHTS GROUPS

International human rights groups usually maintain a low profile, but they play a vital role in the actualization and facilitation of human rights missions. As a group, they monitor human rights issues, review requests for aid, and compile databases (see Ball & colleagues, 2000).

Beginning in the early 1990s, a few nongovernmental organizations (NGOs) and intergovernmental groups began assembling teams of forensic scientists. The nonprofit organization **Physicians for Human Rights (PHR)** was one of the leaders. It sent forensic scientists to conduct war crimes investigations, and it advanced missions to recover and identify remains from mass graves. PHR rapidly extended its work to include the war-torn regions of El Salvador, Guatemala, Bosnia, Rwanda, Iraq, Chechnya, Kosovo, and others. Its work for the ICTY has been an enormous multinational effort, utilizing forensic anthropologists from the world over.

Other essential organizations include **Amnesty International**, London, U.K.; the **American Association for the Advancement of Science, Science and Human Rights Program**, Washington, D.C. (discussed previously); **Human Rights Watch**, New York; and **the International Committee for the Red Cross**, Geneva, Switzerland. The reports of these and other such organizations are available online. (An excellent example is *The Missing: ICRC Progress Report*, 2006.)

PHILANTHROPIC AGENCIES AND INTERNATIONAL FUNDING AGENCIES

Many private organizations, as well as national and multinational agencies, grant funding to nonprofit human rights organizations. Each funding agency has its own stated mission, and there are far too many to cite here, but extensive information can be obtained through the Human Rights Internet and **The International Centre for Human Rights and Democratic Development in Canada**, among others. (See "Human Rights Internet" in the Bibliography.)

INDIVIDUAL PARTICIPANTS

The composition of a proper investigative team depends on the country and the type of investigation. In lesser-developed countries, victims may have few or no records of any type. The comparative identification methods employed by radiologists, dentists, and fingerprint experts are of limited use. It is more important to be able to describe and document individual anomalies and effects of antemortem trauma. This requires lengthy interviews with survivors rather than record searches.

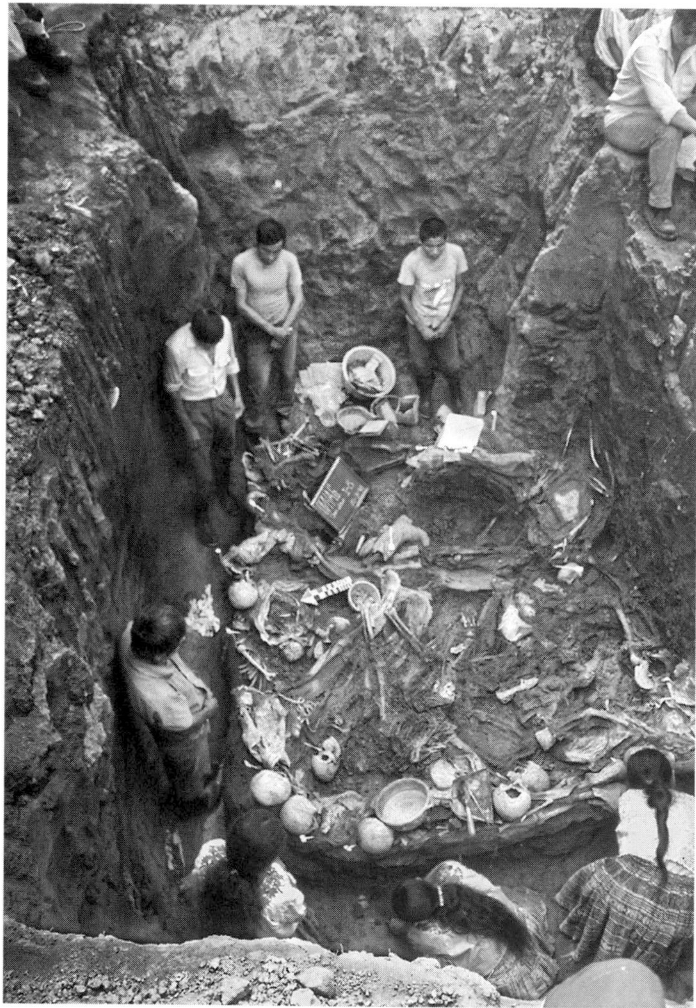

Figure 17.9
Mass Grave near San Jose Rio Negro, Alta Verapaz, Guatemala
Most clandestine graves are found near the surface because they were dug with hand shovels, and speed was the main objective. However, military operations often have heavy equipment at their disposal. Graves such as this one were dug by a bulldozer and are much deeper and larger than hand-dug graves. Bodies are more likely to be heaped haphazardly. (Lancerio López)

Basic multidisciplinary groups include human osteologists, archaeologists, pathologists, odontologists, criminalists, photographers, and skilled interviewers. Specialists may be added to or subtracted from the team according to the requirements of the case. Teaching and writing skills are necessary in addition to technical skills.

Types of Missions Related to Forensic Anthropology

There are many types of human rights missions, but those involving forensic anthropologists usually take the form of exploratory missions, major excavation and analysis missions, education and training missions, and follow-up missions for ongoing support and/or expert witness testimony.

Exploratory missions are designed to gather information and develop a work plan. They are a time to meet the people face to face and discuss their needs and wishes. During this time, the preliminary team visits and evaluates sites and locates working and living facilities. (It is possible to work under a wide variety of conditions so long as there is light, water, a surface to work on, and security for both evidence and workers.)

Major excavation missions are designed for extensive data collection—data from antemortem records and data from the excavation itself. Evidence analysis may take place during the excavation if the facilities allow, but usually analysis is carried out later in a more secure location. Local training is sometimes initiated during major excavations.

Training missions consist of general lectures and/or professional training. A training mission may be useful at any point in the overall operation. Programs can be planned for local officials as well as for the families, attorneys, judges, and

Figure 17.10
Forensic Anthropology Class in Guatemala
This class was one of many funded by human rights organizations in the 1990s. It provided an opportunity for Central Americans to study the details of human identification from war-related skeletal material. Most of the registrants were upper-level university students in anthropology and archaeology, but the classes also included practicing pathologists, lawyers, and other professionals intent on increasing their qualifications in the area of forensic science.

support groups. Most forensic anthropology teams provide this type of presentation on a regular basis. Professional training takes the form of workshops combined with field and laboratory experience. In the first Guatemalan excavations, advanced osteology classes were carried out along with and immediately following major excavations. These classes provided an opportunity to improve the analytical results while learning. Training missions are particularly important because they provide long-term results by enabling the local people to continue on their own without foreign assistance.

Conclusion

The use of the forensic sciences has far-reaching effects in human rights work. When the physical truth is revealed about genocide, politicide, and other crimes of war, the perpetrators are disenfranchised and the community of survivors is empowered. The courts increase their effectiveness in promoting justice, and, most important of all, the families of the dead gain access to the psychological closure that comes from knowing the fate of loved ones and being able to mourn according to custom.

The Universal Declaration of Human Rights was written more than a half century ago, but the world is still a long way from embracing these essential freedoms. Nevertheless, hard-won successes are making it increasingly difficult for governments to commit atrocities without international notice and censure. Hope exists as long as there are people willing to devote time, energy, and knowledge to the struggle for human rights.

POW/MIA Repatriation

Much of the information in this section is derived from Mann and colleagues, 2003; Bunch and Shine, 2003; and the information booklet of the Joint POW/MIA Accounting Command (JPAC) available for download at the JPAC website: http://www.jpac.pacom.mil/Downloads/JPAC_brochure_2011.pdf, accessed November 2011.

The Missing Americans

In the United States, we have a special set of missing persons. They are the soldiers who never returned from war. Some died as prisoners of war, some were declared missing in action, but none were mourned and buried by their families according to American customs. As with the missing the world over, their families are doomed to suffer. They are afraid to move to another house or dispose of the missing person's possessions. If they try to think of the missing person as dead, they feel guilty for losing hope. Many families belong to support groups who advocate the return of missing service persons. Several websites are devoted to reports of "sightings" of missing soldiers in foreign lands, supporting the enduring hope that the lost will someday return. James K. Boehnlein, a American psychiatrist, reports a parent saying that giving up on a lost loved one is "like killing him or her" (Boehnlein, 1987).

The U.S. Department of Defense maintains a summary of POW/MIA statistics on the Defense Prisoner of War/Missing Personnel Office (DPMO) website, http://www.dtic.mil/dpmo/summary_statistics/, accessed November, 2011. At present, more than 83,000 persons are listed as missing as a result of World War II, Korean War, Cold War, Vietnam War, and Gulf War. (More than 73,000 remain missing from WWII alone.) The U.S. Joint POW/MIA Accounting Command estimates that approximately 35,000 are actually recoverable. Most of these are located in clandestine graves and aircraft crash sites in Korea, Southeast Asia, and the Pacific Islands. The others were lost at sea and are not considered recoverable. (Those who were officially buried at sea are not included in the estimate.)

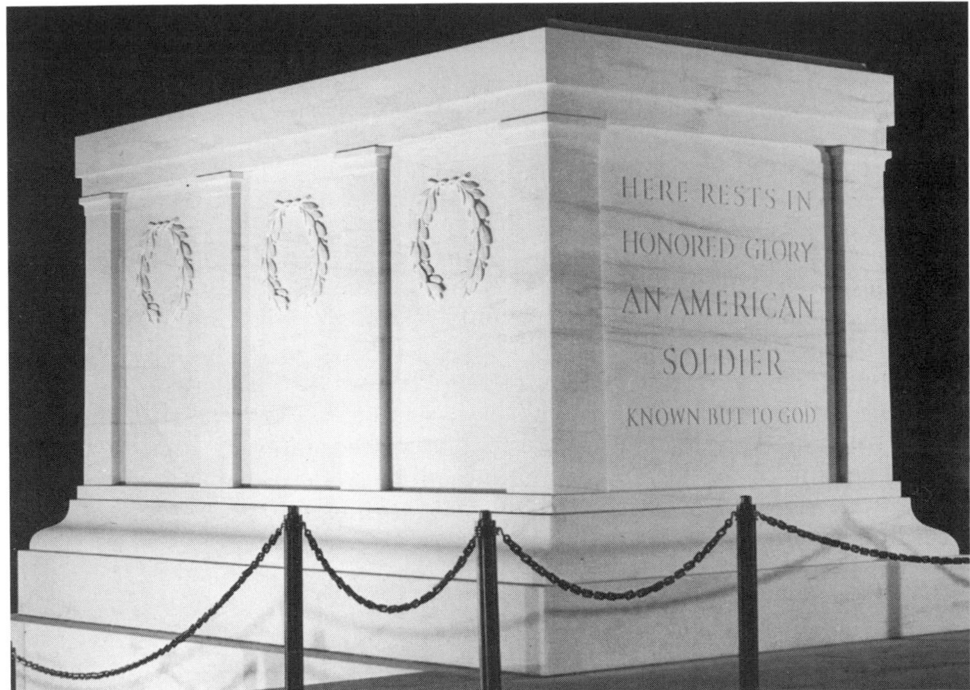

Figure 17.11
Tomb of the Unknown Soldier in Washington, D.C.
Many thousands of U.S. Military personnel remain missing from the last century of wars. The Joint POW/MIA Accounting Command (JPAC) is the U.S. Government agency tasked with their recovery and identification. SuperStock/Alamy.

U.S. Army Central Identification Laboratory in Hawaii

Repatriation of the missing is accomplished through the work of the U.S. Army Central Identification Laboratory in Hawaii (JPAC-CIL, formerly CILHI). The laboratory was established in the 1970s and merged with the Joint Task Force—Full Accounting in 2003 to become the Joint POW/MIA Accounting Command (JPAC). The combined JPAC mission is to achieve the fullest possible accounting of all Americans missing as a result of previous conflicts.

The main task of the Central Identification Laboratory (CIL) is to search for and recover the remains of American military personnel, as well as military-associated civilians. But the scientific staff also contributes expertise to related tasks, including standard crime scene investigations involving buried bodies, and disaster work. CIL's anthropologists are full-time government employees and, therefore, the most likely to be called upon in disasters involving U.S. government facilities such as the Pentagon after the 9/11 terrorist attack. They can also be deployed for mass fatality incidents involving U.S. citizens abroad. (Some of the CIL scientists are also DMORT team members.)

CIL is the best-funded and best-equipped human identification laboratory in the world. It employs more forensic anthropologists than any other organization in the United States, and the scientific staff has more advanced degrees than any similar group. At present, CIL employs approximately thirty forensic anthropologists and three dentists. CIL runs a state-of-the-art laboratory devoted to application of the best archaeological, anthropological, and odontological techniques available. Its work is large scale, but usually without the extreme urgency associated with disaster work. CIL scientists identify about one person every four days. They have identified more than 560 persons between 2003 and 2011, and more than 1800 since the effort began in the 1970s. The costs associated with maintaining and staffing such an institution would be prohibitive in most parts of the world.

Field Methods

Given information about the possible location of crash sites and burials, CIL fields twelve-member search and recovery (SAR) teams. The work of a SAR team requires international travel and sometimes includes marginal living and working conditions. Each team is made up of more than one forensic archaeologist/anthropologist, a linguist to communicate with and interview local people, an Army officer to deal with the international complications of legal repatriation, a communications specialist to handle high-frequency radio communication in remote areas, an explosive ordnance disposal technician to locate and disable live ordnance in the excavation area, a mortuary affairs specialist, and various other technicians.

In the field, the SAR team members interview local people for additional information about the incident as well as associated events during the intervening years. Often, sites have been salvaged for useful materials, and sometimes human remains and identification tags are removed for possible sale. The SAR team uses a crime scene approach to the overall site and standard archaeological techniques in the excavation.

Laboratory Methods

When the remains are received at CIL, all associated information is removed so that the analysis can be carried out "blind." The forensic anthropologist assigned to prepare a physical description is not the same person who recovered the remains in the field. In other words, the analyst has no access to information about the suspected identity of the remains. He or she is given only those details required for selection of appropriate scientific techniques (e.g., the approximate time since death). The blind analysis is an effort to avoid subconscious bias from influencing the analysis. This is a scientific advantage that most forensic anthropologists working solo do not have.

Following the physical description, the identification phase of the analysis is standard. American military personnel usually have medical/dental records or comparative DNA readily available for positive identification.

Conclusion

The work of the JPAC Central Identification Lab can be categorized as government-funded national human rights work. The experience is very different from international human rights work because the families of the dead are far removed in time and space. The local people may have a financial or humanitarian interest in the U.S. recovery operation, but no emotional investment in the outcome.

CIL helps to alleviate the long-term suffering of American families and clarify the historical record. Through the CIL work, the United States has had the opportunity to develop a world-class identification laboratory. The scientists have had the time, personnel, monetary resources, and governmental incentives to develop a laboratory manual of standard operating procedures, a quality assurance manual, and a model training program. All this has enabled CIL scientists to be the first forensic anthropology laboratory to obtain accreditation by the Society of Crime Laboratory Directors, Laboratory Accreditation Board (ASCLD/LAB).

APPENDIX

Forms and Diagrams

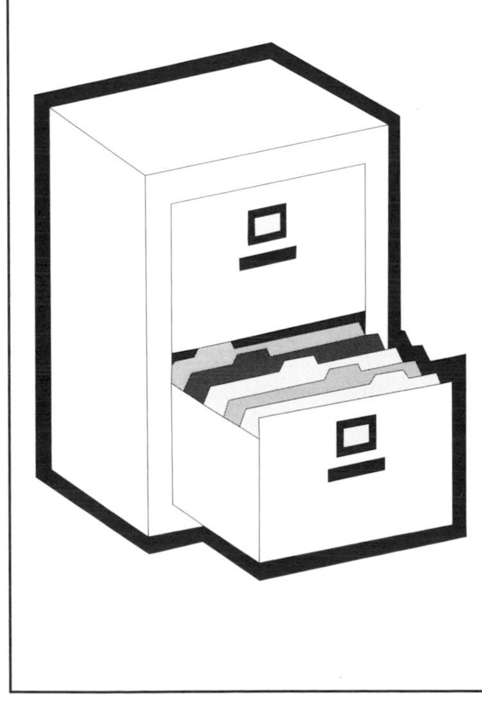

APPENDIX OUTLINE

Sources for Bones, Casts, Instruments, and Tools

Ben Meadows Company (tile probes, tree calipers)
PO Box 5277
Janesville, Wisconsin 53547-5277
http://www.benmeadows.com/

Bone Clones, Inc. (casts of human bone and teeth, including examples of trauma and pathology)
21416 Chase Street #1
Canoga Park, California 91304
http://www.boneclones.com/

Focus Design (modern, lightweight sifting screens for field work)
2354 Santa Ana Ave. Suite 14
Costa Mesa, California 92627
http://focusdesign.org/

France Casting (casts of human bone, including aging sequences of pubes and ribs)
1713 Willox Court, Unit A
Fort Collins, Colorado 80524
http://www.francecasts.com/

Go Measure 3D (Microscribe 3D digitizer)
524 Sunset Drive
Amherst, VA 24521
Phone: 434-946-9125 x 7003
http://www.gomeasure3d.com

Marshalltown Company (archaeology trowel)
104 South 8th Avenue
Marshalltown, Iowa 50158
http://www.marshalltown.com/

Paleo-Tech Concepts, Inc. (mandibulometer, spreading calipers, osteometric board)
PO Box 2337
Crystal Lake, IL 60039-2337
http://www.paleo-tech.com/

Skulls Unlimited International, Inc. (real bone skulls and skeletons, bone cleaning services)
10313 South Sunnylane
Oklahoma City OK 73160
http://skullsunlimited.com/

Dial calipers and digital calipers are used by many industries and are sold widely.

Interview Questionnaire for Families of the Missing—Page 1

Provide all information possible. Fill in the blank or check the correct box where applicable.

Information about the Disappearance

Fill in the blanks with the appropriate information.

1. How long has this person been missing? ______
2. Did you see the body? ______
3. Did someone else report the death to you? ______

Information about Circumstances of Death

Witness should answer Yes or No and describe the type of weapon and location of wounds.

Type of Injury	Yes	No	Type of Weapon	Location of Wounds
4. Gunshot			*(e.g., handgun, AK47)*	
5. Garrote			*(e.g., rope, wire)*	
6. Stabbing			*(e.g., stiletto, machete)*	
7. Beating			*(e.g., baton, fists)*	
8. Other				

Clothing When Last Seen

When colors are part of the description, the interviewer should use a color chart. Let the witness point to the correct color, and then record the color number.

Description and Color

9. Shirt or blouse ______
10. Pants or skirt ______
11. Type of shoes ______
12. Jewelry or ornaments ______

Basic Physical Description

Fill in the blanks with the appropriate description.

13. Age (*If age is unknown, list as elderly, adult, adolescent, child, or infant.*) ______
14. Sex (*male or female*) ______
15. If female, did she bear children? (*yes, no, or unknown*) ______
16. Race/Color/Ethnicity ______
17. Possible mixed race? (*yes, no, or unknown*) ______
18. Height (*If height is unknown, interviewer should ask for a comparison with a living person and record the results accordingly—e.g., if the missing person is said to be "just a little taller" than his 170 cm. cousin, list height as "slightly greater than 170 cm."*)

    ______
19. Musculature (*strong, average, or frail*) ______
20. Habitual posture (*erect, hunched, or favoring one side*) ______

Interview Questionnaire for Families of the Missing—Page 2

Dental Description

Interviewer should use a dental chart or dental casts and let the witness point to the correct tooth.

21. Were any teeth missing or extracted? (*yes, no, or unknown*) ______
22. If teeth were missing, which ones? (*Interviewer should use a dental chart and list the tooth numbers.*) ______
23. Were the teeth stained? (*yes, no, or unknown*) ______
24. Did the person smoke or chew tobacco? (*yes, no, or unknown*) ______
25. Did a dentist repair any teeth? (*yes + which ones, no, or unknown*) ______
26. Did the person wear dentures? (*yes, no, or unknown*) ______
27. Did the person complain of dental pain? (*yes, no, or unknown*) ______
28. Did the person have bad breath? (*yes, no, or unknown*) ______

Description of Antemortem Trauma

Interviewer should use an anatomical chart so that the witness can point at the body rather than trying to recall right or left. Record the information directly on the chart.

29. Did the person break any bones during life? (*yes + at what age, no, or unknown*)

    ______

30. If so, did he or she receive medical care? (*yes + at what age, no, or unknown*)

    ______

31. Did the person walk with a limp? (*yes or no*) ______
32. Can anyone remember a fall, an accident, or any unusual event? (*yes + nature of accident and at what age, no, or unknown*)

    ______

33. If there was an injury, what was the medical treatment? (*e.g., radiograph, sling, orthopaedic brace, plaster cast, surgical pin or wire, bone graft*)

    ______

34. Did the person complain of pain in a specific part of the body? (*yes + which body part [e.g., ear, jaw, shoulder, back, elbow, wrist, fingers, knees] or no*)

    ______

Records of Victim

The interviewer should collect medical records and photographs. Remember that more than one photographic view is recommended and a smiling image is preferred.

Record Type	Records Provided by (Name, Address, Phone Number)
35. Dental	
36. Medical	
37. Radiographs	
38. Photographs	

Bone Inventory Form

Use this form as a checklist or to record postcranial measurements and observations.

SINGULAR BONES		PAIRED BONES	R	L	PAIRED BONES	R	L
cranium		clavicle			hamate		
mandible		scapula			scaphoid		
manubrium		humerus			capitate		
sternum		radius			triquetral		
atlas		ulna			gr. multangular		
axis					ls. multangular		
C3		innominate			lunate		
C4		sciatic notch			pisiform		
C5		iliac crest			metacarpal 1		
C6		pubis shape			metacarpal 2		
C7		symp. phase			metacarpal 3		
T1		femur			metacarpal 4		
T2		femur head			metacarpal 5		
T3		patella			# of phalanges		
T4		tibia					
T5		fibula			talus		
T6					calcaneus		
T7		rib 1			navicular		
T8		rib 2			cuneiform 1		
T9		rib 3			cuneiform 2		
T10		rib 4			cuneiform 3		
T11		rib phase			cuboid		
T12		rib 5			metatarsal 1		
L1		rib 6			metatarsal 2		
L2		rib 7			metatarsal 3		
L3		rib 8			metatarsal 4		
L4		rib 9			metatarsal 5		
L5		rib 10			# of phalanges		
sacrum		rib 11					
coccyx		rib 12					

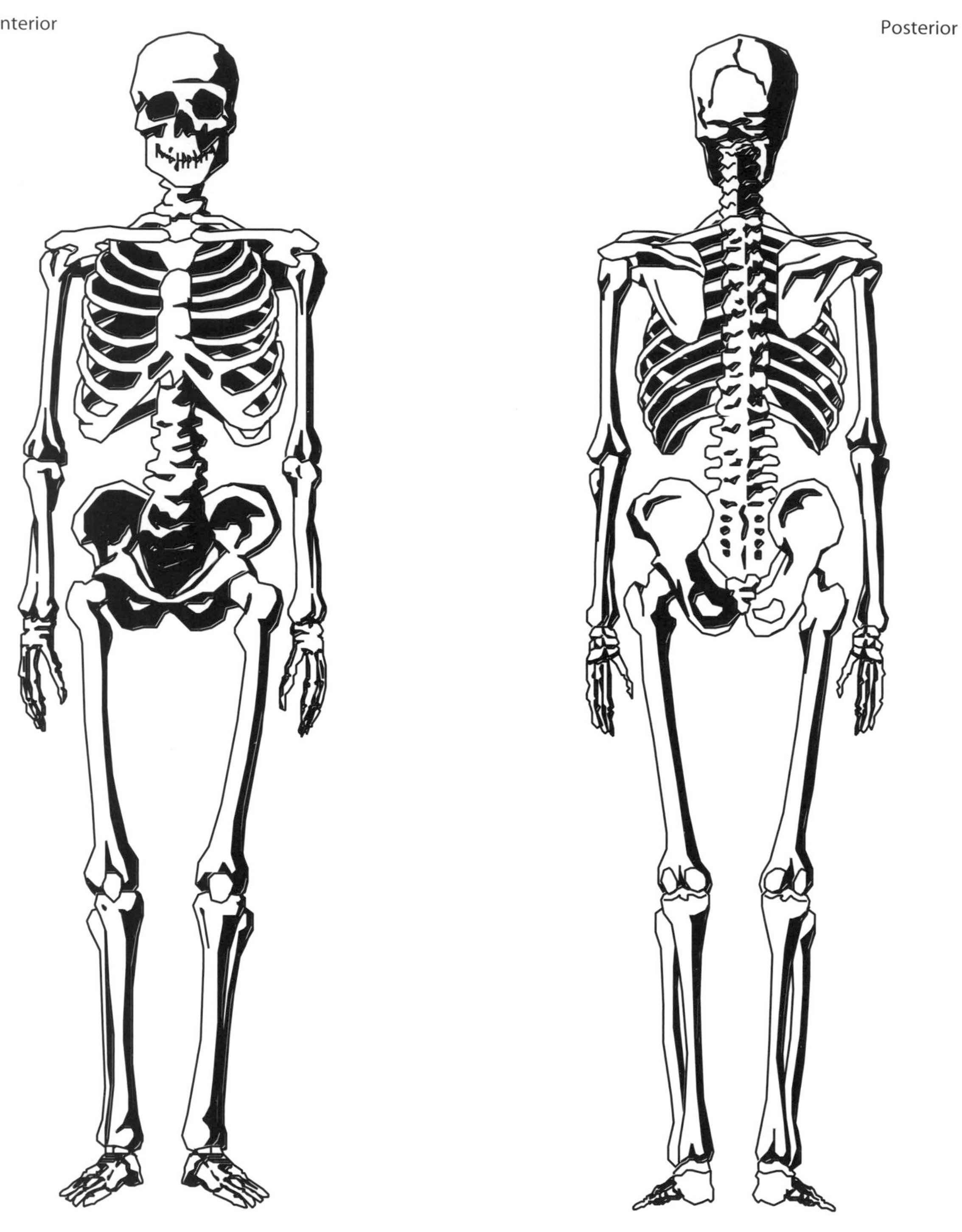

Figure AP.1
Full AP Skeleton Diagrams

Right

Left

Figure AP.2
Full Lateral Skeleton Diagrams

Cranial Measurement Form (Consistent with Fordisc System)

	abbr.	*measurement name*	*from this point*	*to this point*	*mm.*
1	GOL	maximum cranial length	glabella (g)	opisthocranion (op)	
2	XCB	maximum cranial breadth	euryon (eu)	euryon (eu)	
3	ZYB	bizygomatic breadth	zygion (zy)	zygion (zy)	
4	BBH	maximum cranial height	basion (ba)	bregma (b)	
5	BNL	cranial base length	basion (ba)	nasion (n)	
6	BPL	basion-prosthion length	basion (ba)	prosthion (pr)	
7	MAB	maxillo-alveolar breadth	ectomolare (ecm)	ectomolare (ecm)	
8	MAL	maxillo-alveolar length	prosthion (pr)	alveolon (al)	
9	AUB	biauricular breadth	root of zygomatic process	root of zygomatic process	
10	UFHT	upper facial height	nasion (n)	prosthion (pr)	
11	WFB	minimum frontal breadth	frontotemporale (ft)	frontotemporale (ft)	
12	UFBR	upper facial breadth	fronto-zygomatic suture	fronto-zygomatic suture	
13	NLH	nasal height	nasion (n)	nasospinale (ns)	
14	NLB	nasal breadth	alare (al)	alare (al)	
15	OBB	orbital breadth	dacryon (d)	ectoconchion (ec)	
16	OBH	orbital height	superior margin	inferior margin	
17	EKB	biorbital breadth	ectoconchion (ec)	ectoconchion (ec)	
18	DKB	interorbital breadth	dacryon (d)	dacryon (d)	
19	FRC	frontal chord	nasion (n)	bregma (b)	
20	PAC	parietal chord	bregma (b)	lambda (l)	
21	OCC	occipital chord	lambda (l)	opisthion (o)	
22	FOL	foramen magnum length	opisthion (o)	basion (ba)	
23	FOB	foramen magnum breadth	most lateral point of foramen magnum	most lateral point of foramen magnum	
24	MDH	mastoid length	porion	mastoidale	

Mandibular Measurement Form (Consistent with Fordisc System)

	abbr.	*measurement name*	*from this point*	*to this point*	*mm.*
25	GNI	chin height	gnathion	infradentale	
26	HMF	body height at mental foramen	alveolar ridge superior to the foramen	jaw line inferior to the foramen	
27	TMF	body thickness at mental foramen	outer surface of the mandibular body	inner surface of the mandibular body	
28	GOG	bigonial diameter	gonion	gonion	
29	CDB	bicondylar breadth	condylion laterale	condylion laterale	
30	WRB	minimum ramus breadth	anterior edge	posterior edge	
31	XRB	maximum ramus breadth	anterior edge of coronoid process	inner surface of the mandibular condyle	
32	XRH	maximum ramus height*			
33	MLN	mandular length*			
34	MAN	mandibular angle*			

*Use a mandibulometer for these measurements. They are defined by the instrument.

Simplified Postcranial Measurement Form (Consistent with Fordisc System)

	bone	*measurement*	*left*	*right*
35	**clavicle**	maximum length		
36		sagittal diameter at midshaft		
37		transverse diameter at midshaft		
38	**scapula**	height		
39		breadth		
40	**humerus**	maximum length		
41		epicondylar breadth		
42		maximum vertical diameter of head		
43		maximum diameter at midshaft		
44		minimum diameter at midshaft		
45	**radius**	maximum length		
46		sagittal diameter at midshaft		
47		transverse diameter at midshaft		
48	**ulna**	maximum length		
49		dorso-volar diameter		
50		transverse diameter		
51		physiological length		
52		minimum circumference		
53	**sacrum**	anterior height		
54		anterior surface breadth		
55		maximum breadth of S1		
56	**innominate**	height		
57		iliac breadth		
58		pubis length		
59		ischium length		
60	**femur**	maximum length		
61		bicondylar length		
62		epicondylar breadth		
63		maximum diameter of head		
64		A-P subtrochanteric diameter		
65		transverse subtrochanteric diameter		
66		A-P diameter at midshaft		
67		transverse diameter at midshaft		
68		circumference at midshaft		
69	**tibia**	condylo-malleolar length		
70		maximum proximal epiphysis breadth		
71		maximum distal epiphysis breadth		
72		maximum diameter at nutrient foramen		
73		transverse diameter at nutrient foramen		
74		circumference at nutrient foramen		
75	**fibula**	maximum length		
76		maximum diameter at midshaft		
77	**calcaneus**	maximum length		
78		middle breadth		

Anterior

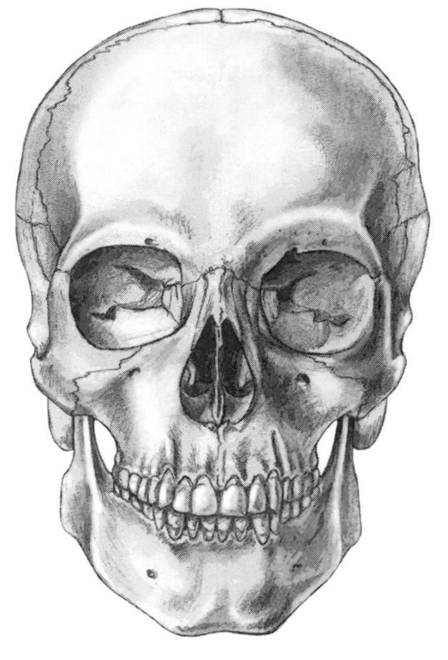

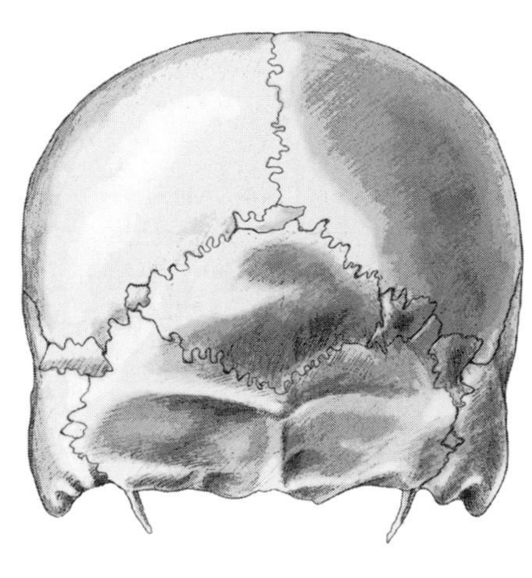

Right Lateral

Left Lateral

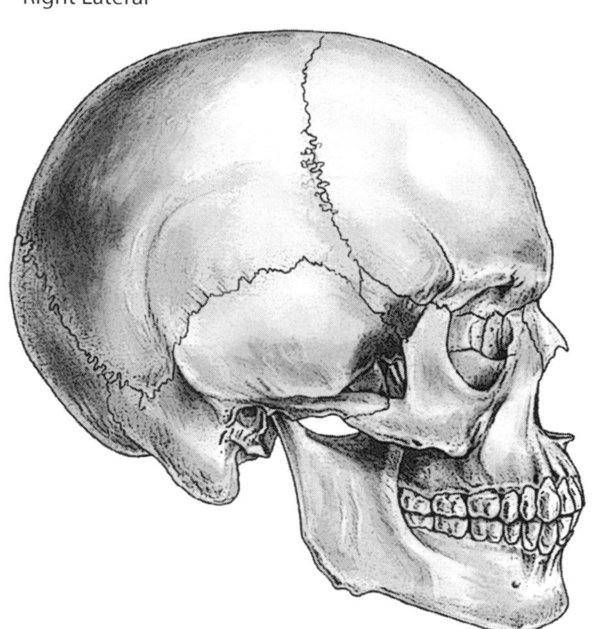

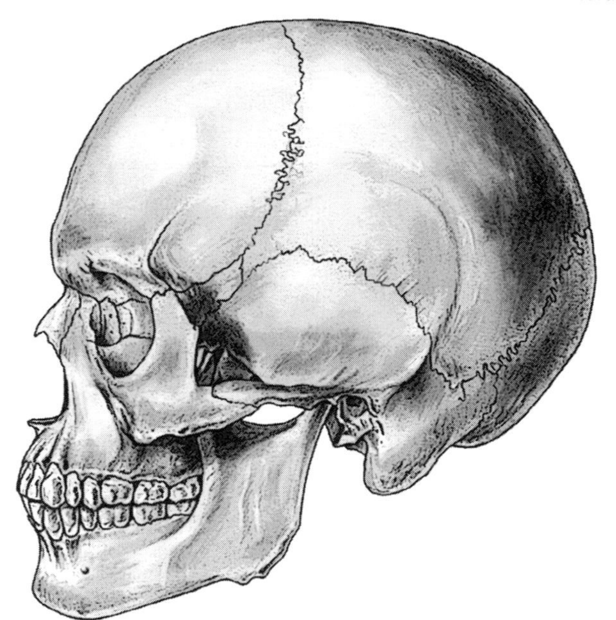

Figure AP.3
Full Skull Diagrams

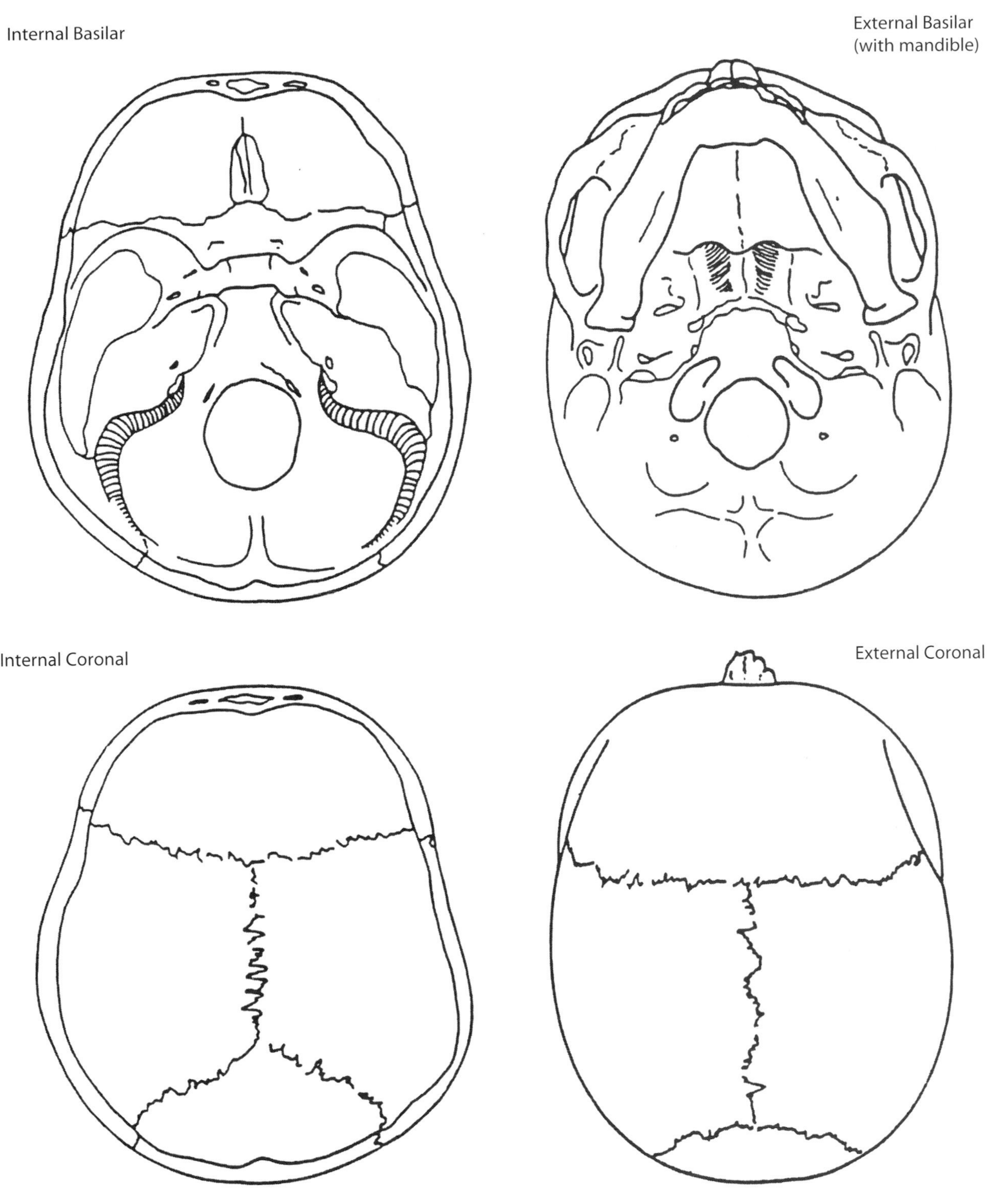

Figure AP.4
Calvarium Cut Diagrams

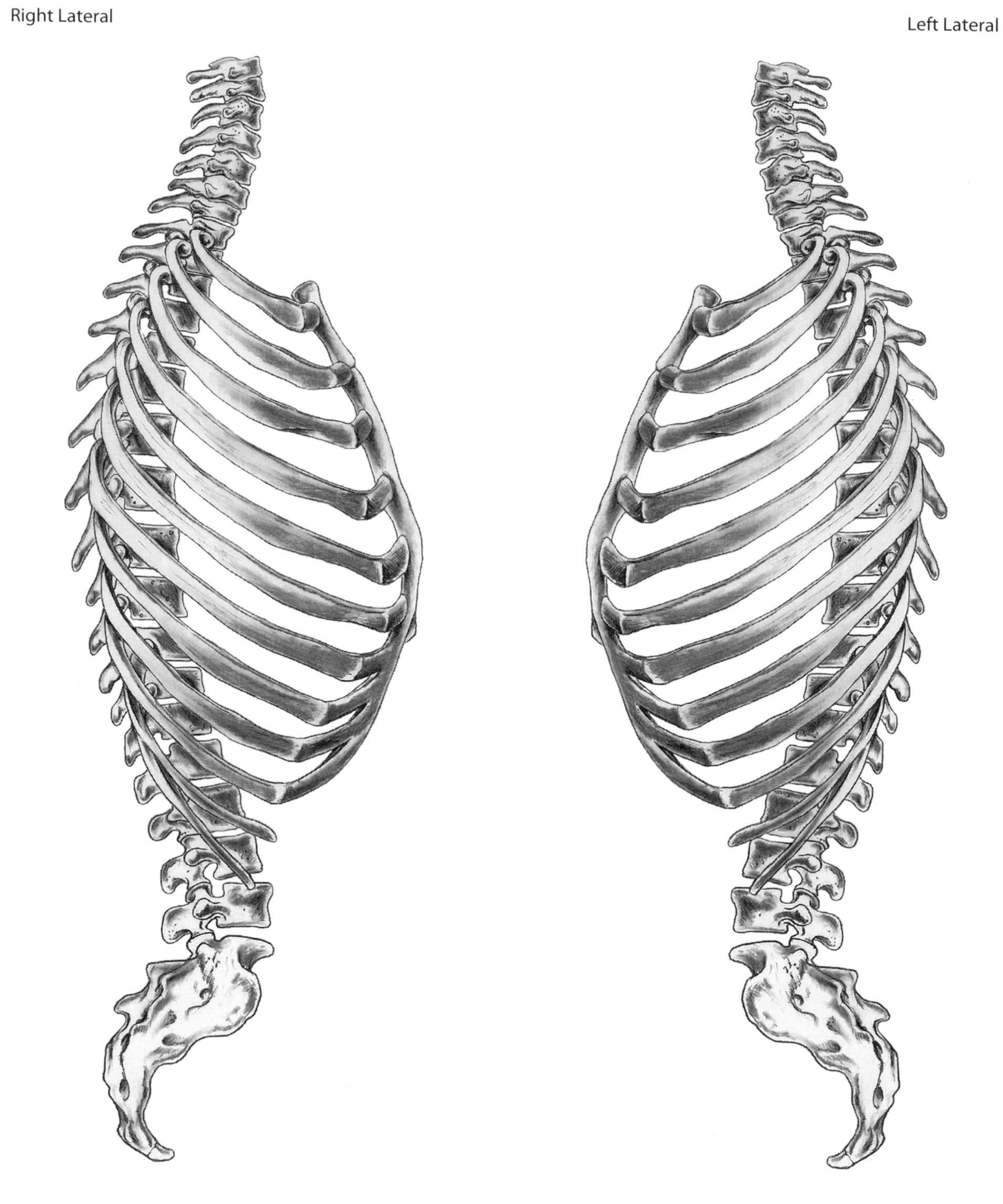

Right Lateral

Left Lateral

Figure AP.5
Axial Skeleton Diagrams

Observations:

Sciatic Notch Shape ____________

Pubis Shape ____________

Parturation "scarring" ____________

Preauricular sulcus ____________

Illiac Crest:

No Union ____________

Partial Union ____________

Complete Union ____________

Pelvic Measurements for Taylor and Dibennardo (1984) Sex Discrimination:

Notch Height (A-B) ____________

Notch Position (B-C) ____________

Acetabular Diameter (E-F) ____________

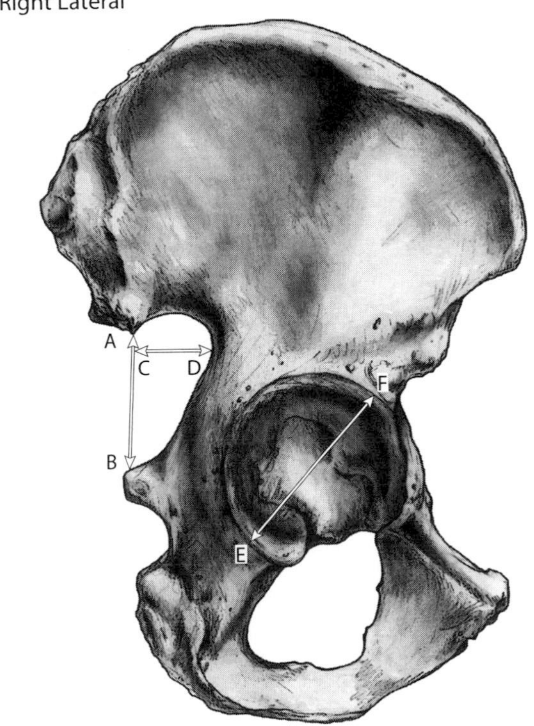

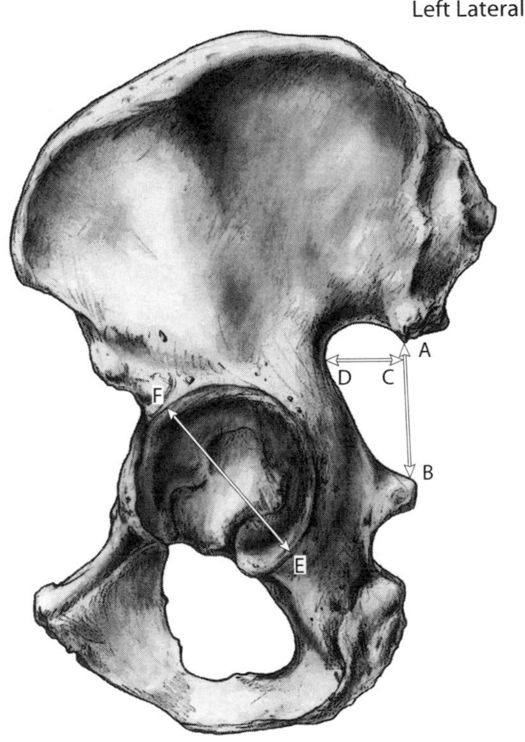

Figure AP.6
Innominate Diagrams

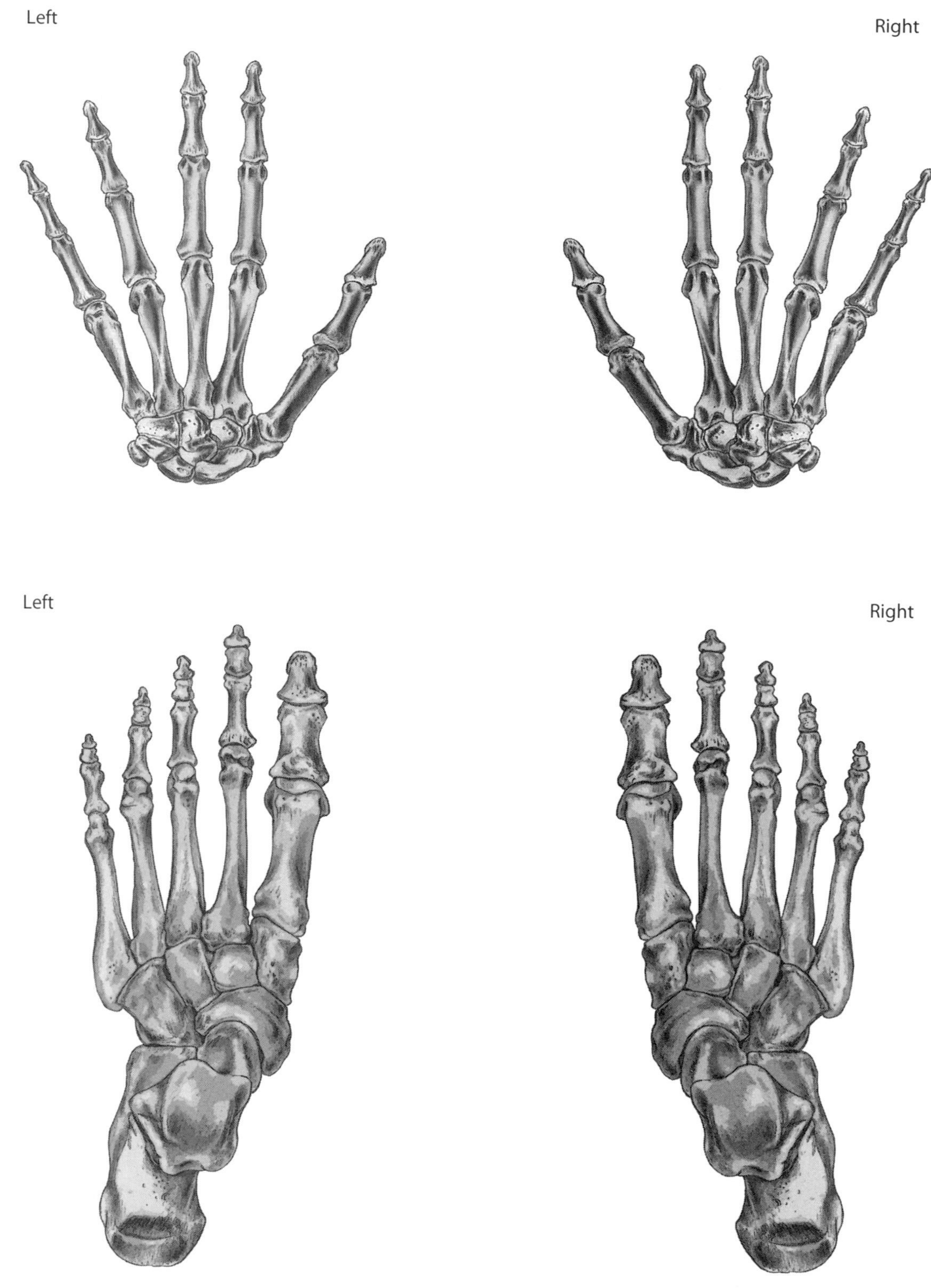

Figure AP.7
Hand and Foot Diagrams, Dorsal View

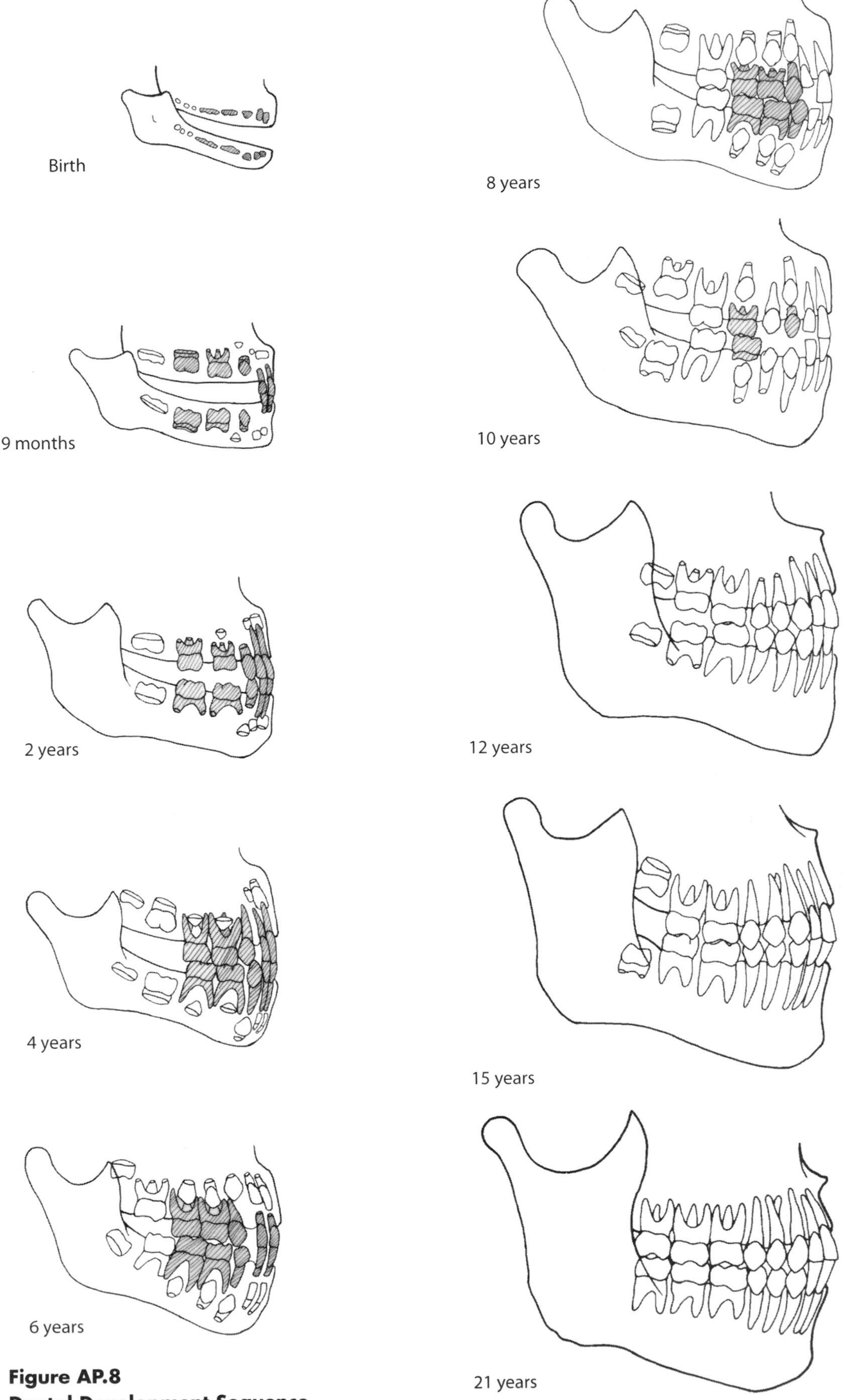

Figure AP.8
Dental Development Sequence

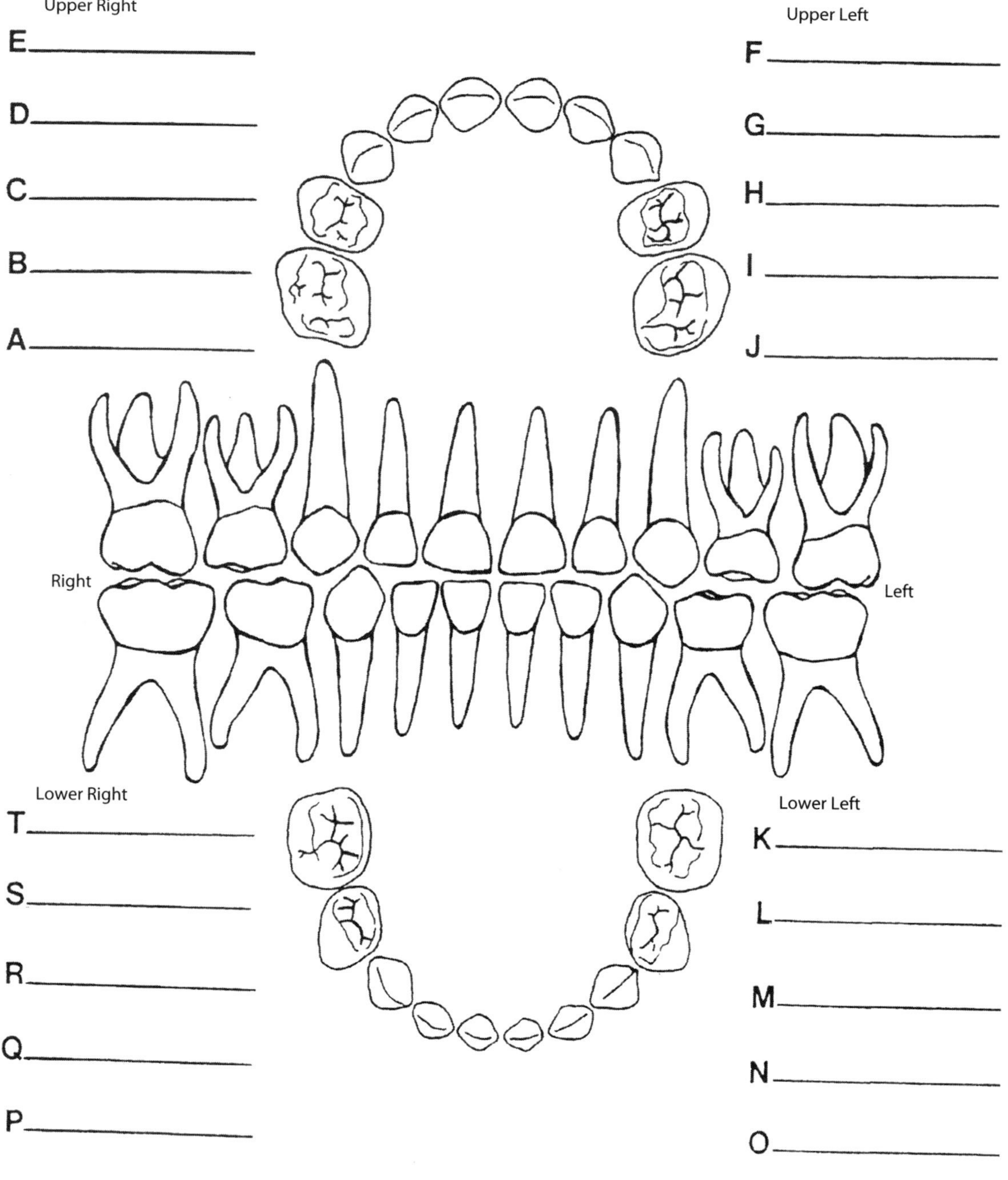

Figure AP.9
Dental Chart, Deciduous Dentition

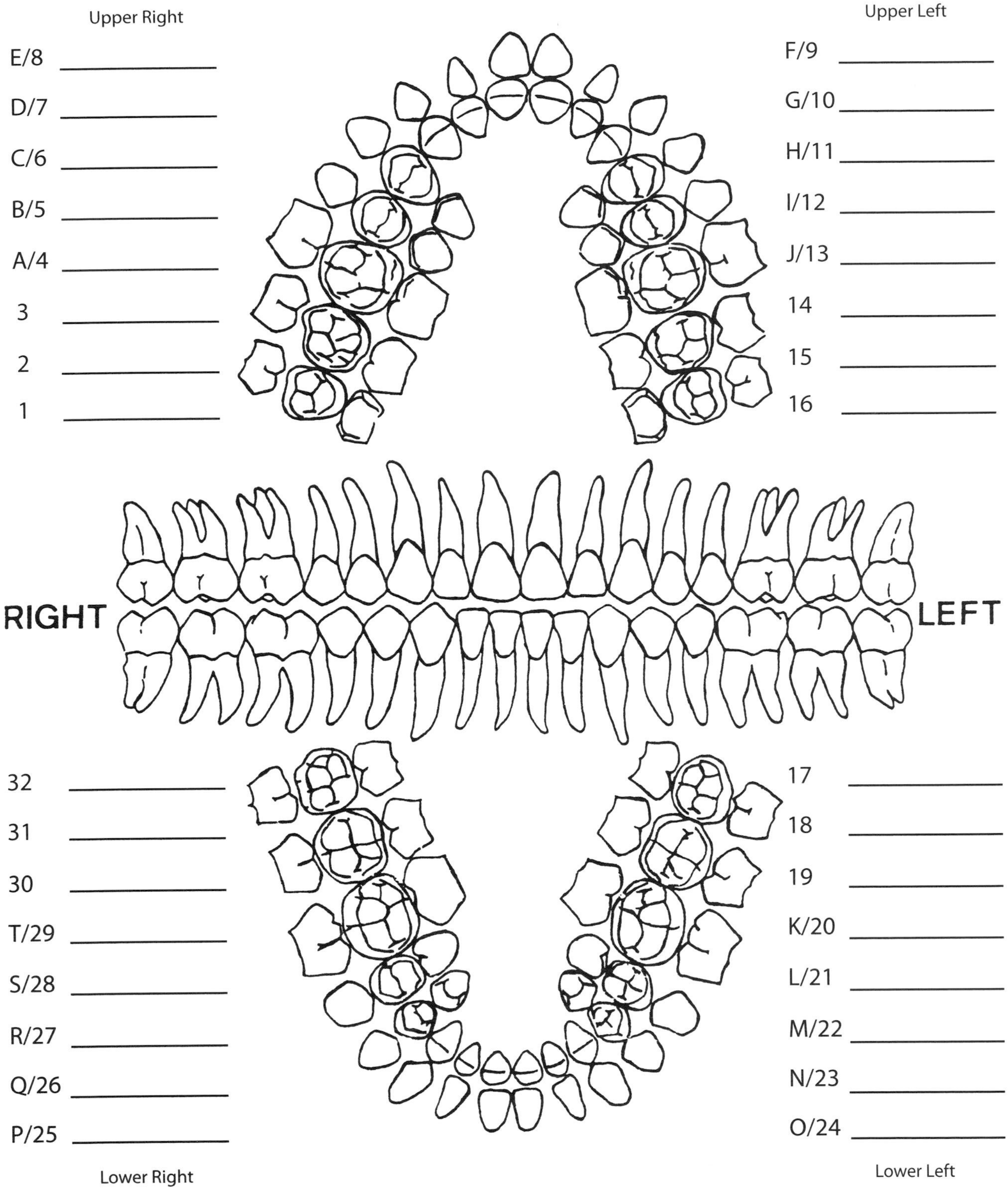

Upper Right

E/8 ______
D/7 ______
C/6 ______
B/5 ______
A/4 ______
3 ______
2 ______
1 ______

Upper Left

F/9 ______
G/10 ______
H/11 ______
I/12 ______
J/13 ______
14 ______
15 ______
16 ______

RIGHT

LEFT

32 ______
31 ______
30 ______
T/29 ______
S/28 ______
R/27 ______
Q/26 ______
P/25 ______

Lower Right

17 ______
18 ______
19 ______
K/20 ______
L/21 ______
M/22 ______
N/23 ______
O/24 ______

Lower Left

Figure AP.10
Dental Chart, Mixed Dentition

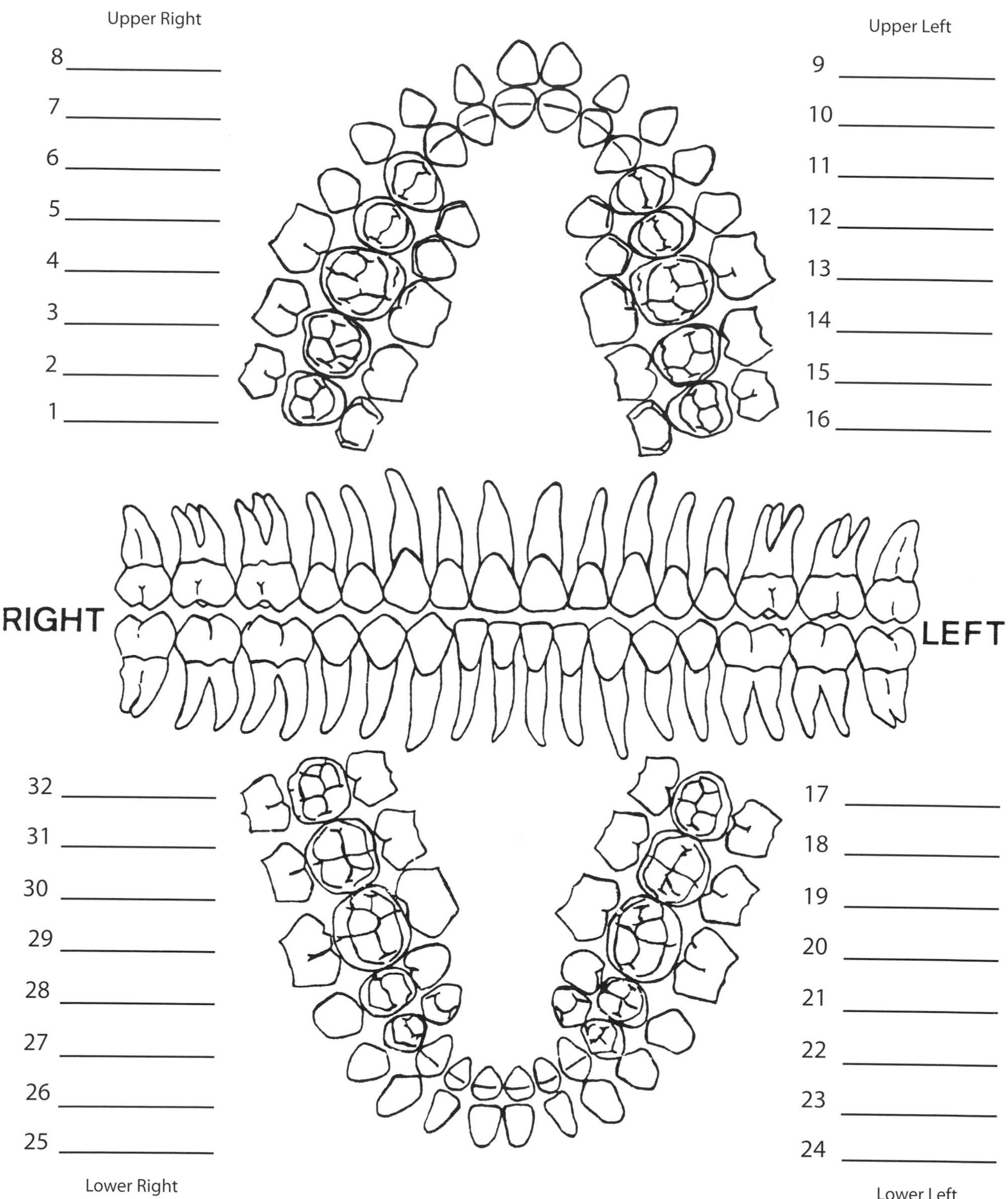

Figure AP.11
Dental Chart, Permanent Dentition

Glossary of Terms

abscess An accumulation of pus in a part of the body, formed by tissue disintegration and surrounded by an inflamed area (e.g., an apical abscess at the tip of the tooth root). An abscess on bone will cause localized bony resorption.

acetabular fossa The central, non-articular surface deep within the acetabulum of the innominate.

acetabulum The articular surface of the innominate for the rotation of the head of the femur; the place of fusion for the three pelvic bones.

acoustic meatus The internal or external opening of the ear canal within the temporal bone (also called the auditory meatus).

acromion process The larger, more posterior of the two scapular processes. The acromion process articulates with the clavicle.

adipocere A product of decomposition in water. Adipocere is composed of insoluble fatty acids resulting from the slow hydrolysis of the body's fats in water. It first resembles rancid butter, then hardens to a waxy texture (grave wax).

advocate Attorney, lawyer, solicitor, legal representative. The term is a reminder that the legal system acknowledges differing points of view, each requiring an argument and someone to present that argument.

agenesis Congenital absence or lack of development of a body part (e.g., agenesis of third molars in modern populations).

ala A wing-like structure (e.g., ala of sphenoid or sacrum).

alare The paired point at the widest place on the margin of the nasal aperture. Instrumentally determined, it is used to measure nasal width.

alveolare The lowest single point on the bony septum between the upper central incisors. This can be confused with infradentale, which is the comparable point between the *lower* central incisors. Alveolare is used to measure upper facial height.

alveolon The single point at the intersection of sagittal suture of the hard palate and a line drawn from the posterior point of the right alveolar process to the posterior point of the left alveolar process. This point can be determined with sliding calipers or with a rubber band stretched around the entire alveolar process. It is used to measure maxilloalveolar length.

alveolar process The ridge of the maxilla or mandible that supports the teeth.

alveolus dentalis The tooth socket in which teeth are attached by a periodontal ligament.

amalgam A solid metal or an alloy in a mercury solution. A dental restoration made of mercury, silver, and small amounts of tin, copper, and zinc for stability.

anatomic crown The portion of a natural tooth that extends from the cementoenamel junction to the occlusal surface or incisal edge. (*See also* clinical crown.)

anlage The primordium or initial clustering of embryonic cells that serve as a foundation or model for an organ or structure (e.g. a cartilaginous anlage for a forming bone).

antemortem Significantly prior to death; antemortem trauma demonstrates some evidence of healing.

ankylosis The stiffening and immobility of a joint; abnormal bone fusion.

anterior crest The shin; the long, anterior-projecting ridge of the tibia.

anterior inferior iliac spine The small projection between the anterior superior iliac spine and the acetabulum.

anterior superior iliac spine The larger, more anterior, projection of the ilium.

apex The highest single point on the frontal section of the cranium defined by left and right porion with the skull oriented to the Frankfort Plane. The apex is posterior to bregma.

appendicular skeleton Bones of the limbs, including the scapula, clavicle, and innominates. (Compare with axial skeleton.)

arch Any vaulted or arch-like structure (e.g., palatal arch, dental arch, vertebral arch).

argument An assertion accompanied by logical reasoning.

arthritis Inflammation of a joint. Arthritis has many causes and various forms.

arthrosis A joint; an articulation between bones.

articular disk A pad of fibrocartilage which separates synovial cavities and provides greater stability within the joint. An articular disk is present in the medial side of the wrist. A meniscus is a specific type of articular disk.

articular facet Any bony surface that articulates with another bony surface (e.g., superior articular facet of the vertebra).

articular process Any projection which serves to articulate.

asterion A craniometric point at the junction of the lambdoid, occipitomastoid, and parietomastoid sutures.

atavistic epiphysis A bone that is independent phylogenetically but now fuses with another bone. An example is the coracoid process of the scapula.

auditory canal The ear canal, extending from the external acoustic meatus to the internal acoustic meatus through the petrous portion of the temporal bone.

auditory meatus The internal or external opening of the ear canal (also called the acoustic meatus).

auditory ossicles The bones of the middle ear that serve to transmit sound. There are three in each ear canal—the stapes, malleus, and incus. They are the smallest bones in the body and are identifiable by side.

auricular surface The ear-shaped roughened surface for the sacroiliac joint. The ilium and the sacrum both have auricular surfaces.

Automated Fingerprint Identification System (AFIS) A computer program used to store, locate, and match digital images of fingerprints. AFIS was originally produced for the FBI by Lockheed Martin in 1999.

axial skeleton Bones of the skull and trunk, including the ribs, sternum, and complete vertebral column. (Compare with appendicular skeleton.)

axillary border The lateral border of the scapula; the border closest to the axilla (armpit).

basion The single point on the inner border of the anterior margin of the foramen magnum. It is used to measure maximum cranial height.

body of rib The main part of the rib.

body of scapula The main part of the scapula (a thin triangular plate of bone).

body of sternum The main part of the sternum, the corpus sterni, fused from the four central centers of ossification; the sternum without the manubrium or the xiphoid process.

boss A rounded eminence or tuberosity (e.g., a frontal boss).

bregma The single point at the intersection of the sagittal and coronal sutures. It is used to measure maximum cranial height.

bridge, dental A fixed or removable replacement for missing teeth, attached to natural teeth by wires or crowns; a pontic.

calcination Disintegration by heat. Calcination of bone results from thorough burning. The organic component is lost and only the mineral component, hydroxyapatite, remains. Calcined bone is grayish-white and friable. Cremation or extremely long cooking is required for calcination.

callus The woven bone that forms around a fracture during healing. The callus is normally remodeled over time.

calvaria, pl. calvarias Skullcap; the upper, dome-like portion of the skull; the cranium without the facial bones. (Calvarium is an incorrect, but frequently used, term for calvaria.)

capitulum The articular surface for the head of the radius on the distal end of the humerus.

Carabelli's cusp An extra cuspid on the mesiolingual surface of upper molars; more common in people of European origin.

caries, dental A localized, progressively destructive disease beginning at the external surface with dissolution of inorganic components by organic acids produced by microorganisms. Also called a carious lesion.

cause of death The specific disease or injury responsible for the lethal sequence of events. It is necessary to differentiate between *underlying* (proximate) and *immediate* cause of death. The underlying cause may be a gunshot wound with perforation of the colon, whereas the immediate cause may be generalized peritonitis and septicemia.

cementodentinal junction (CDJ) The surface at which cementum and dentin meet.

cementoenamel junction (CEJ) The line around the neck of the tooth at which cementum and enamel meet.

cementum A porous layer of calcification covering the tooth root; the cementum provides a surface for periodontal fibers to anchor.

centrum The center of ossification for the body of the vertebra, specifically the body without epiphyseal rings.

cervix (neck) The slightly constricted part of the tooth between the crown and the root.

character In biology, a distinguishing feature or attribute, as of an individual, group, or category. Key characters define the group; individual characters distinguish the individual.

circum-mortem *See* perimortem.

circumstantial evidence Evidence that proves something by inference, conclusion, or deduction. (Compare with direct evidence.)

clavicular notch The articular facet for the clavicle, located on either side of the jugular notch of the manubrium.

clinical crown The portion of the tooth visible in the oral cavity. (Compare with anatomic crown.)

composite, dental A plastic resin restoration that mimics the appearance of enamel.

condyle A rounded articular surface at the end of a long bone.

condylion laterale A paired point at the most lateral edge of the mandibular condyle. It is used to measure bicondylar width.

condyloid process The posterior process of the mandibular ramus. The condyloid process supports the mandibular condyle.

connective tissue One of the four basic tissue types. Connective tissue consists of more or less numerous cells surrounded by an extracellular matrix of fibrous and ground substances. Examples: bone, cartilage, fat, ligaments, fascia, and blood.

conoid tubercle The bump on the posterior superior edge of the lateral end of the clavicle.

coracoid process The smaller, more anterior of the two scapular processes.

coronoid fossa The hollow on the anterior surface of the distal end of the humerus, just above the trochlea, in which the coronoid process of the ulna rests when the arm is flexed. (Compare with olecranon fossa.)

coronoid process The smaller of the two processes on the anterior side of the proximal end of the ulna; the anterior process of the mandibular ramus.

costal Pertaining to the ribs; adjacent to the ribs (e.g., costal surface of scapula).

costal notch The seven pairs of notches for joining of the costal cartilage with the sternum.

costal pit Articular surface for rib on the thoracic vertebral body and transverse processes; rib facet.

cranium The skull without the mandible; the fused bones of the skull. Note that definitions vary. The cranium is variously defined as the skull, the part of the skull that contains the brain, the skull without the face, and the skull without the jaws (mandible *and* maxillae). *See also* calvaria, neurocranium, splanchnocranium, and viscerocranium.

cremains A shortened, elided version of "cremated remains."

cribriform plate The superior surface (horizontal lamina) of the ethmoid, located in the ethmoid notch of the frontal bone. It is perforated by foramina for the passage of the olfactory nerves. The crista galli rises through the cribriform plate.

crista galli The most superior part of the ethmoid. A trapezoidal process projecting through the anterior midline of the cribriform plate. It serves for attachment of the falx cerebri and is named for its resemblance to a rooster's comb.

cross examination The formal questioning of a witness by the party opposed to the party that called the witness to testify. (*See* direct examination.)

crown The enamel-capped portion of the tooth that normally projects beyond the gum line; a permanent replacement for a natural crown, made of porcelain fused to metal, ceramic, or metal alone. *See* clinical crown and anatomical crown.

cusp A conical elevation arising on the surface of a tooth from an independent calcification center.

cusp pattern The recognizable alignment of cusps on a particular tooth type.

dacryon A paired point on the medial wall of the orbit where the lacrimomaxillary suture meets the frontal bone. It is between maxillofrontale and lacrimale and is used to measure orbital width and interorbital width.

Daubert *Daubert v. Merrell Dow Pharmaceuticals, Inc.* (1993); a product liability case that resulted in a Supreme Court decision in which the Federal Rules of Evidence (specifically FRE 702) replaced the *Frye* test. Trial judges were assigned the task of assessing the scientific nature of proposed testimony.

deltoid tuberosity The attachment area for the deltoid on the anterior surface of the humerus.

dens A tooth-like projection, an abbreviated name for the *dens epistropheus,* also called the odontoid process of the axis.

dental prosthesis Fixed or removable replacement of one or more teeth and/or associated oral structures; denture, bridgework, or oral appliance.

dentin The main mass of the tooth, structured of parallel tubules; about 20 percent is organic matrix, mostly collagen with some elastin and a small amount of mucopolysaccharide; about 80 percent is inorganic, mainly hydroxyapatite with some carbonate, magnesium, and fluoride.

dentinal tubule The tubules extending from the pulp to the dentinoenamel junction; odontoblastic processes extend into the tubules from the pulp surface.

dentinoenamel junction (DEJ) The surface at which the dentin and enamel meet. The interface between dentin and enamel.

denture A complete or full denture replaces all of the natural dentition of the maxilla or mandible; a partial denture replaces one or more teeth and is retained by natural teeth at one or both ends.

deposition Testimony under oath taken before trial. A person "gives a deposition" when he or she, accompanied by an attorney, answers questions by the other side's attorney regarding the facts of a case.

dermestid beetle A member of the Coleoptera family, Dermestidae (skin beetles). Most are scavengers that feed on dry animal or plant material. The species, *Dermestes maculatus* (hide beetles) is particularly useful in forensic entomology investigations. Laboratory colonies of dermestids are used for cleaning dry soft tissue from bones.

diaphysis, pl. diaphyses The shaft of a long bone. More accurately, the portion of the long bone formed from the primary center of ossification; the part that grows between the metaphyses.

diffuse idiopathic skeletal hyperostosis (DISH) A form of degenerative arthritis characterized by flowing calcification along the sides of the vertebrae of the spine, mainly on the right side. It is commonly associated with inflammation and calcification of tendons at their attachments points to bone, leading to the formation of bone spurs.

diploë In the neurocranium, the layer of spongy bone sandwiched between the two tables (layers) of dense bone.

direct evidence Evidence that proves something on its own. Evidence that makes the facts obvious to the observer. (Compare with circumstantial evidence.)

direct examination Questioning of a witness in a trial or other legal proceeding, conducted by the party who called the witness to testify. (Compare with cross examination.)

discovery The process of gathering information in preparation for trial.

dorsal plateau The convex inner surface at the dorsal margin of the pubic symphysis; one of the first areas of modification in the aging pubic symphysis.

dorsal surface The posterior surface; the back.

dorsal tubercles The bumps on the dorsal surface of the distal end of the radius. The grooves between the dorsal tubercles allow for passage of forearm tendons.

ectoconchion A paired point at the outer edge of the eye orbit. Instrumentally determined, this is the point at which a line extending from dacryon reaches the lateral orbital rim and divides the orbit horizontally into equal halves. It is used to measure orbital width.

ectomolare A paired point on the lateral (buccal) surface of the maxillary alveolar process. Instrumentally determined, it is usually located at the upper second molar. It is used to measure maximum alveolar width.

edentulous Toothless; a mouth without teeth.

enamel The dense mineralized outer covering of the tooth crown; composed of 99.5 percent inorganic hydroxyapatite with small amounts of carbonate, magnesium, and fluoride, and 0.5 percent organic matrix; structured of oriented rods consisting of rodlets encased in an organic prism sheath.

endobasion The single point at the posterior margin of the anterior border of the foramen magnum. It is usually internal to basion. It is used for facial measurements, not cranial height.

endomolare A paired point on the lingual surface of the alveolar process at the location of the second molar. It is used to measure palatal width.

endosteum Dense connective tissue that covers the inner surfaces of compact bone. Endosteum is thinner than periosteum.

enthesis, pl. entheses A bony attachment site. The defined area on bone for insertion of a ligament or tendon. Entheses are roughened and sometimes bulbous areas on bone.

epicondyle A bulbous projection from a long bone near or adjacent to the articular condyle (e.g., medial and lateral epicondyle of the humerus). The epicondyle provides attachment for ligaments and tendons.

epiphyseal ring The secondary centers of ossification that fuse to the superior and inferior surfaces of the vertebral centrum.

epiphysis, pl. epiphyses A secondary center of ossification that fuses to the primary center when bone growth is complete.

euryon A paired point used to measure maximum cranial width. Instrumentally determined, it is located on the parietal or temporal.

extensor carpi ulnaris groove The groove lateral to the styloid process of the ulna. The tendon of the *extensor carpi ulnaris muscle* lies within it, providing adduction and dorsiflexion of the hand.

evidence Anything that tends to establish or disprove a fact.

expert testimony Statements made in judicial proceedings by a person who is qualified to render an opinion on the issue under consideration.

expert witness A person who, because of his knowledge, experience, and expertise, is qualified to render an opinion on the issue under consideration in a judicial proceeding.

false rib Ribs #8, #9, and #10 which do not join directly to the sternum. They are attached to the sternum via the seventh rib cartilage.

fascia Dense connective tissue that encases muscles, groups of muscles, and large vessels and nerves.

FBI Laboratory's Combined DNA Index System (CODIS) a computer program that facilitates the exchange of DNA profiles between crime laboratories. It stores, sorts, and compares DNA profiles for identification purposes. (Developed under the DNA Identification Act of 1994, Public Law 103 322.)

femoral head The ball-shaped upper extremity of the femur; the femoral head articulates within the acetabulum of the innominate; the proximal epiphysis of the femur.

femur, pl. femora The thigh bone.

fibula, pl. fibulae The smaller of the two bones of the lower leg, lateral to the tibia.

fibular head The knob-like portion of the proximal end of the fibula.

floating rib Ribs #11 and #12, which do not attach to the sternum or to any other rib.

foramen, pl. foramina A round or oval aperture in bone or a membranous structure for the passage or anchorage of other tissue; any aperture or perforation through bone or membranous structure (e.g., occipital foramen).

forensic science Any systematic form of knowledge applied to legal issues; science and technology used to investigate and establish facts in criminal or civil courts of law.

forensics The art or study of formal debate; argumentation. More recently, science and technology used to investigate and establish facts in criminal or civil courts of law.

foundation (as in, "to lay a foundation") To provide information for the judge regarding the qualifications of the witness, particularly an expert witness, or the authenticity of a piece of evidence.

fovea capitis The pit in the femoral head providing attachment for the *ligamentum teres.*

frontomalare temporale The most laterally positioned point on the frontomalar suture (between frontal and zygoma), used to measure upper facial breadth.

frontotemporale A paired point on the curve of the temporal line. Instrumentally determined, it is the point on the frontal bone that gives the smallest measurement from the left to the right temporal line. It is used to measure minimum frontal width.

Frye test *Frye v. The United States* (1923); a case involving the acceptance of new or novel scientific principles. The admissibility of expert witness testimony is based on the test of "general acceptance" within the relevant scientific community.

gingiva The "gums"; the dense fibrous tissue covered by mucous membrane that envelops the alveolar processes of the upper and lower jaws and surrounds the necks of the teeth.

glabella The most anterior single point in the midsagittal section of the frontal bone at the level of the supraorbital ridges. It is above nasion and is used to measure maximum cranial length.

glenoid cavity or fossa The articular surface on the scapula for the head of the humerus.

gnathion The lowest point on the midsagittal plane of the mandible; the bottom of the chin. It is used to measure total facial height and mandibular symphysis height.

gomphosis The joint between a tooth and its bony socket; joined by a periodontal ligament.

gonion A paired point at the outer corner of the angle of the mandible. It is the junction of the body and ramus of the mandible and is used to measure bigonial width and ascending ramus height.

good faith The intention to honestly meet an obligation.

granular pits Depressions on the inner surface of the skull along the course of the sagittal suture. During life, they lodge arachnoid granulations, which tend to calcify with advanced age (also called pacchionian depressions).

greater sciatic notch The large indentation on the posterior border of the innominate; the superior border is formed by the ilium, and the inferior border is formed by the ischium.

greater trochanter The larger and more superior of the two protuberances between the neck and the shaft of the femur.

greater tubercle The larger of the two tubercles on the proximal end of the humerus. The greater tubercle is lateral to the lesser tubercle.

greenstick fracture An incomplete fracture involving only the convex side of the bent bone. Greenstick fractures occur only in fresh bone and therefore suggest perimortem injury.

groove, costal The groove on the inferior edge of the inner surface of the rib.

humeral head The proximal articular surface of the humerus; it is half ball-shaped (hemispherical) and has no fovea.

humerus, pl. humeri The bone of the upper arm.

iliac fossa The smooth, depressed (concave) inner surface of the ilium.

iliac tuberosity The posterior, inner thickening of the ilium, superior to the auricular surface; the attachment site of the posterior sacroiliac ligament.

impeach With respect to an expert witness, a process to challenge the truthfulness or bias of a witness while giving testimony under oath.

Inca bone A large sutural bone at lambda, usually triangular or trapezoidal in shape, and dividing the superior part of the squamous portion of the occipital. The Inca bone is most common in Native Americans.

incison The single medial point at the incisal level of the upper central incisors; the lower edge of the upper central incisors.

individual characters Traits that distinguish the individual from others within the same group. (Compare with key characters.)

inferior articular process One of the two processes on a single vertebra that articulate with the superior articular processes of the adjacent inferior vertebra.

infradentale The highest single point on the bony septum between the lower central incisors. This can be confused with alveolare which is the comparable point between the *upper* central incisors. Infradentale is used to measure mandibular symphysis height.

Inion A single point at the intersection of the left and right superior nuchal lines. It is at the base of the external occipital protuberance, and there may be a slight projection of bone at this point.

inlay A prefabricated dental restoration (usually gold or porcelain) sealed in a dental cavity with cement.

innominate The hip bone; one side of the pelvis; a composite of three bones that fuse at puberty: the ilium, ischium, and pubis. The innominates meet at the pubic symphysis anteriorly and join the sacrum posteriorly.

Integrated Ballistics Identification System (IBIS) It is used to store, locate and correlate digital images of ballistics evidence.

intercondylar eminence The bony projection between the two condylar platforms of the tibia.

intercondylar fossa The depression between the two condyles on the posterior surface of the femur.

interosseous crest The somewhat sharp edge on a bone shaft directed toward an adjacent bone and serving for attachment of an interosseous ligament. This occurs on the radius, ulna, tibia, and fibula.

intertubercular groove The groove between the greater and lesser tubercles of the humerus. The tendon of the long head of the biceps extends through the intertubercular groove.

involucrum A layer of new bone outside of existing bone. It occurs in pyogenic osteomyelitis and is the result of separation of the periosteum from the existing bone by the accumulation of pus within the bone. The new bone grows from the separated periosteum and the existing bone becomes a sequestrum (dead bone).

ischial tuberosity The large, roughened eminence inferior to the acetabulum; the major weight-bearing bone in the sitting position; the site of origin for the hamstring muscles.

ischial spine The process on the posterior border of the ischium bounded by the greater and lesser sciatic notches.

ischiopubic ramus The bridge between the ischium and the pubis.

jugular notch The medial, superior notch on the manubrium. Also called the suprasternal notch.

key characters Traits that can be readily recognized, formally analyzed, and used as a basis for generalization. Key characters define a group.

kyphosis Abnormal outward curvature of the upper thoracic spine resulting in a hunchback appearance. Also called a dowagers hump in postmenopausal females.

lacrimale A paired point on the medial wall of the orbit at the intersection of the posterior lacrimal crest and the frontolacrimal suture. It is posterior to dacryon and maxillofrontale.

lambda The single point at the intersection of the sagittal suture and the lambdoidal suture. If lambda is obscured by fusion, a complicated suture or sutural bones, estimate the point by drawing lines along the general direction of the two branches of the lambdoid suture and finding the point of intersection with the sagittal suture.

lateral malleolus The laterally rounded portion of the distal end of the fibula; the outer "ankle bone."

lesser sciatic notch The indentation on the posterior border of the ischium bounded by the ischial spine and the ischial tuberosity.

lesser trochanter The smaller and more inferior of the two protuberances between the anatomical neck and the shaft of the femur.

lesser tubercle The smaller of the two tubercles on the proximal end of the humerus.

ligament Dense connective tissue connecting bone to bone or cartilage at a joint or supporting an organ; bands or sheets of fibrous tissue.

line A thin mark distinguished by texture or elevation—often the outer edge of a muscle or ligament attachment (e.g., the temporal line on the frontal and parietal bones).

linea aspera The slightly rough, two-edged, muscle attachment line on the posterior surface of the femoral shaft.

Locard's Exchange Principle A theory first proposed by the French scientist, Edmond Locard, in the early twentieth century. It states that all contact results in exchange of information and serves as the basis for collection and examination of trace evidence.

lordosis Excessive inward curvature of the lumbar spine resulting in a swayback appearance.

malleolar fossa The hollow on the posterior surface of the distal end of the fibula.

mandible The lower jaw; a nonpaired bone in adults.

manner of death How death happened. Manner of death is usually classified as natural, accidental, homicide, suicide, or undetermined. (Compare with cause of death.)

manubrium The superior-most section of the sternum.

margin An edge or a border. A bone margin is the peripheral edge or the area immediately adjacent to it. If the bone articulates with another bone, the margin takes the name of that bone (e.g. frontal margin of the parietal bone).

mastoidale A paired point at the inferior tip of the mastoid process. It is used to measure mastoid length.

material evidence Any evidence (verbal or physical) that is likely to affect the determination of a matter or issue. (Material evidence is not the same as physical evidence.)

maxilla The upper jaw; a paired bone.

maxillofrontale A paired point at the intersection of the anterior lacrimal crest (on the frontal process of the maxilla) and the frontomaxillary suture. It is on the medial margin of the orbit and can be used to measure orbital width.

meatus A natural opening or passage (e.g. external auditory meatus, nasal meatus).

medial malleolus The medially rounded projection on the distomedial end of the tibia; the inner "ankle bone."

meniscus, pl. menisci A crescent-shaped ridge or collar of fibrocartilage found in certain synovial joint capsules. It provides greater stability and durability to the joint. Examples are the knee, acromioclavicular, sterno-clavicular and temporomandibular joints. A type of articular disk.

metaphysis, pl. metaphyses Growth plate. The area of hyaline cartilage located between diaphysis and epiphysis of growing bone. The metaphysis allows for growth in length through the process of endochondral ossification.

metopic suture A midline suture of the frontal bone. The result of nonunion of left and right centers of ossification.

nasal concha, pl. conchae Turbinates. Thin, curled, mucus membrane–covered bones within the nasal cavity. The superior and middle nasal conchae are part of the ethmoid. The inferior nasal conchae are separate bones attached to the medial wall of the maxilla. (Concha is derived from the Greek word for shell.)

nasion The single point at the intersection of the nasofrontal suture and the internasal suture. It is used to measure total facial height and upper facial height.

nasospinale The single point on the intermaxillary suture at the base of the nasal aperture. It is used to measure nasal height.

neck The area immediately adjacent to the head of a bone (e.g., neck of the radius, humerus, femur, or rib).

nutrient foramen A major vascular opening between the exterior of a bone and the medulla. Notable nutrient foramina are on appendicular bones, the mandible, and parietals.

oath With respect to judicial proceedings, a verbal obligation to tell the truth.

obturator foramen The large opening bordered by the pubis, the ischium, and the ischiopubic ramus.

odontoid process The dens, a superior projection from the body of the axis, articulating at the anterior margin of the vertebral foramen of the atlas, tooth-like in form.

olecranon foramen (septal aperture) A hole in the septum between the olecranon fossa and the coronoid fossa of the distal humerus. It is more common in females than males.

olecranon fossa The large hollow on the posterior surface of the distal humerus in which the olecranon process of the ulna rests when the arm is extended.

olecranon process The large process on the posterior side of the proximal end of the ulna; the bony projection of the elbow.

opisthion The single point at the posterior margin of the foramen magnum.

opisthocranion The most posterior single point on the skull, but not on the occipital protuberance. Instrumentally determined, it is used to measure maximum cranial length.

orale The most anterior single point on the hard palate where a line drawn lingual to the central incisors intersects the palatal suture. It is used to measure palatal length.

orbitale A paired point at the lowest part of the orbital margin. It is used to define the Frankfort Plane and to measure orbital height.

orthopedics The branch of medicine concerned with the musculoskeletal system, including bones, joints, ligaments, tendons, muscles, and nerves.

os japonicum An extra bone in a bipartite or tripartite zygoma. It is rare but found with greater frequency in Asian populations.

ossicle A tiny bone; any one of the three middle ear bones. Auditory ossicle.

osteoarthritis A group of degenerative joint diseases characterized by worn articular surfaces and osteophytic growth at the articular margins. Osteoarthritis is progressive and associated with age. It can be accelerated by inflammation due to trauma or infection.

osteology The study of bones; the science that explores the development, structure, function, and variation of bones.

osteomalacia A number of disorders in adults in which bones are inadequately mineralized. The lower limbs tend to develop mediolateral bowing.

osteomyelitis Infection of the bone and bone marrow. Direct infection occurs through open fractures or penetrating wounds. Indirect infection reaches the bone via the bloodstream. Osteomyelitis is characterized by formation of an abscess at the site of infection, resulting in bone destruction.

osteopathy or osteopathic medicine A form of western medicine based on the belief that structure and function are interrelated and most diseases are the result of problems in the musculoskeletal system.

osteoporosis A group of diseases in which bone reabsorption out-paces bone deposition. Bone becomes porous and light. Fractures increase, particularly in the spine, wrist, and hip. It is a common condition of postmenopausal women, but is not exclusive to women.

pacchionian depression *See* granular pit.

pars An archaic term used to mean a part or a portion of a bone (e.g. *pars lateralis* of the occipital bone or *pars orbitalis* of the frontal bone).

parturition pits Fossae on the inner surface of the female pubic bone, possibly associated with childbearing.

pathology The study of disease. The branch of medicine that deals with study and diagnosis of disease.

pelvis, pl. pelves or pelvises The bony, bowl-shaped structure that provides articulation for the legs and support for the organs of the lower trunk; formed from two innominate bones and a sacrum. The pelvic girdle.

periapical Around the tip of the tooth root.

perimortem Around the time of death; immediately prior to death, at the time of death, or immediately after death; synonymous with circummortem; distinguished from antemortem and postmortem.

periodontal disease Inflammation of the tissues surrounding the teeth, resulting in resorption of supporting structures and tooth loss.

periodontal ligament The fibrous tissue anchoring the tooth by surrounding the root and attaching to the alveolus.

periodontosis Lowering of the attachment level of the periodontal ligament (associated with periodontal disease or general aging).

periosteum Dense connective tissue that encases (covers) the outer surfaces of compact bone.

phalanx, pl. phalanges A bone of the finger, either proximal, intermediate (medial or middle), or terminal (distal). There are fourteen phalanges in each hand.

physical evidence Evidence apparent to the senses. Tangible evidence.

pits and fissures The depressed points and lines between cusps of premolar and molar teeth.

platymeric Having a broad femur (flattened in cross section).

pogonion The most anterior single point on the midsagittal plane of the mandible; the front of the chin.

popliteal Pertaining to the area behind the knee; structures posterior to the femorotibial joint.

popliteal line On the posterior surface of the proximal tibia, a curved roughened attachment surface.

porion A paired point at the most lateral part of the superior margin of the external auditory meatus. It is used to define the Frankfort Plane and to measure mastoid length.

posterior inferior iliac spine The more inferior projection of the ilium adjacent to and superior to the greater sciatic notch.

posterior superior iliac spine The more superior of the posterior projections of the ilium.

postmortem After death; anything occurring after death (e.g., postmortem trauma). "Postmortem" is also a synonym for "autopsy."

postmortem interval Time between death and the attempt to determine time of death; sometimes used as the time between death and recovery.

preauricular sulcus A groove adjacent to the auricular surface of the ilium. Found most frequently in adult females, possibly related to the trauma of childbearing.

primary dentin The dentin that forms as the root is completed in the growing tooth; tubular dentin.

process Any bony projection.

process, spinous The vertebral process that projects posteriorly, toward the dorsal surface of the back.

process, transverse Paired vertebral processes that project laterally, some of which articulate with ribs.

promontory A raised place; the most ventral prominent median point of the lumbosacral symphysis; the most anterosuperior point on the sacrum.

pronation The act of turning the palm or palmar surface of the hand downward. Rotation of the foot so that the inner edge of the sole bears weight (flat feet). The opposite of supination.

proof Confirmation of a fact by evidence. In law, proof is the evidence that satisfies a judge or jury that an assertion is true.

prosthion The most anterior single point on the upper alveolar process. It is superior to alveolare and is used to measure maxilloalveolar length.

provenience The origin or source of an object: the geographic location where the object was found; the three-dimensional location of a feature within an excavation, measured by two horizontal dimensions and a vertical elevation (an archaeological term now applied to all types of evidence).

pterion A paired point on the upper end of the greater wing of the sphenoid. This is more often a region than a point.

pterion bone A sutural bone at pterion, the area where the sphenoid, parietal, frontal, and temporal bones approach or articulate.

pubic ramus The bridge of bone between the acetabulum and the pubic symphysis; the superior border of the obturator foramen.

pubic symphysis The medial surface of the pubic bone where the two innominates are joined together by fibrocartilage.

pubic tubercle A small projection at the anterior extremity of the crest of the pubis about 1 cm lateral to the symphysis.

pulp (of tooth) The soft tissue in the central chamber of the tooth, consisting of connective tissue containing nerves, blood vessels, lymphatics, and, at the periphery, odontoblasts capable of dentinal repair.

pulp chamber The central cavity of the tooth surrounded by dentin and extending from the crown to the root apex.

pulpectomy Removal of the entire pulp, including the root; commonly known as a "root canal"; without the pulp, the tooth is no longer living.

Q-angle (quadriceps angle) An angle formed in the frontal plane by the intersection of two lines, one drawn from the from tibial tubercle to the middle of the patella, and the other, from the middle of the patella to the anterior superior iliac spine. The angle is greater in females than males.

qualify With regard to expert witness testimony: to make or consider eligible or fit (e.g., "His training and experience *qualified* him as an expert witness").

radial nerve groove The diagonal groove on the posterior surface of the shaft of the humerus.

radial notch The concavity for the radius on the lateral side of the proximal end of the ulna.

radial tuberosity The rounded elevation distal to the neck of the radius; one of the two insertions of the biceps muscle.

radiograph An image produced on a radiosensitive surface, such as a photographic film, by radiation other than visible light (usually x-rays) passed through an object.

radiograph, apical A film produced by exposure of vertically-oriented intraoral film; the x-ray beam is angled from above maxillary teeth or below mandibular teeth to capture the complete tooth, including the apex.

radiograph, bite-wing A film of posterior teeth produced by exposure of laterally-oriented intraoral film; the x-ray beam is angled between the teeth; the crowns are the main focus of the films.

radiograph, Panorex A film of the entire oral cavity produced by immobilizing the head and moving the x-ray beam behind the head while film is exposed in synchrony in front of the face.

radius, pl. radii One of the two bones of the forearm. The radius is lateral to the ulna.

ramus A part of an irregularly-shaped bone (less slender than a process) that forms an angle with the main body (e.g., mandibular ramus, ischiopubic ramus).

remains A collective term for dead organic tissues. In forensic anthropology, remains are typically human skeletal and/or dental but may also include other tissues such as ligaments, tendons, hair, blood, and fingernails or toenails.

reparative dentin Calcification (sclerosis) of dentinal tubules immediately beneath a carious lesion, abrasion, or injury.

replicability In science, the concept that the outcome of a particular study will occur again if the study is repeated by another investigator. A scientific finding that cannot be replicated is easily discredited.

restoration, dental Any inlay, crown, bridge, partial denture, or complete denture that restores or replaces lost tooth structure, teeth, or oral tissues.

rib head The vertebral end of the rib.

rib neck The constricted part between the rib head and tubercle on upper ribs (not obvious on lower ribs).

rib, sternal end The open end of the rib that connects to the sternal cartilage; useful for skeletal aging.

rib tubercle The center of ossification below the neck; part of the tubercle articulates with the vertebral transverse process.

ridge A long narrow elevation; a linear elevation; a crest.

root (of tooth) The cementum covered portion of the tooth, usually below the gum line but increasingly exposed with age or advanced periodontal disease.

root, anatomic The portion of the root extending from the cementoenamel junction to the apex or root tip.

root, clinical The imbedded portion of the root; the part not visible in the oral cavity.

scapular notch The indentation on the superior border of the scapula.

Schmorl's node A large pit or concavity in the superior or inferior surface of a vertebral body caused by intrusion of the intervertebral cartilage into the surface of the bone. A result of aging or trauma. May be completely asymptomatic.

sclerotic dentin Generalized calcification of dentinal tubules as a result of aging.

scoliosis Abnormal lateral deviation of the spine. Curvature of the spine.

secondary dentin Not actually dentin, it is a non-tubular calcification of the pulp chamber which forms after the tooth has erupted as a response to irritation from caries, abrasion, injury, or simply age.

sella turcica A saddle-shaped depression in the sphenoid bone, also called the *hypophyseal fossa*. It holds the pituitary gland.

semilunar notch The proximal articular surface of the ulna, bounded by the olecranon and coronoid processes. The semilunar notch articulates with the trochlea of the humerus.

septal aperture *See* olecranon foramen.

sequestrum A piece of dead bone surrounded by normal living bone. A sequella to osteomyelitis, sometimes surrounded by an involucrum.

shaft The elongated cylindrical structure that is the main body of a long bone, specifically the humerus, radius, ulna, femur, tibia, and fibula; in immature bones, the diaphysis

shoulder girdle The clavicles, scapulae, and manubrium of the sternum; the bony ring (incomplete posteriorly) that provides attachment for the arms. (The manubrium is also part of the thorax.)

shovel-shaped incisors Central incisors formed with lateral margins bent lingually, resembling the form of a coal shovel; common in populations of Asian origin, including Native Americans.

skull All the bones of the head as a unit, including the mandible.

splanchnocranium The bones of the face including the mandible. Also called viscerocranium.

spondylolysis A fracture in the lamina of the vertebral arch immediately posterior to the articular surface(s). The major portion of the lamina and spinous process are free-floating. It usually occurs in the fifth lumbar vertebra and may result from hyperextension, particularly in sports such as gymnastics, weight lifting, and football. It may cause backache or be asymptomatic.

spine, scapular The long thin elevation on the dorsal surface of the scapula that ends laterally as the acromion process.

staphylion The single point on the posterior hard palate where the palatal suture is crossed by a line drawn tangent to the curves of the posterior margin of the palatal bones. It is used to measure palatal length.

sternal foramen An anomalous perforation in the sternal body.

sternal-end ossification Osteophytic growth from the rib end into the sternal cartilage; cartilaginous calcification; it increases with age and varies with sex.

styloid process A pointed process of bone; styloid processes are found on the radius, ulna, fibula, third metacarpal, and the temporal bone of the skull.

subpubic angle The inferior angle formed when the two pubic bones are approximated; the angle is larger in females.

subpubic concavity A depression on the inferior border of the female pubic bone; a structural byproduct of elongation of the female pubis.

superior articular process On the vertebra, the two processes that articulate with the superior vertebra.

supination The act of turning the hand so that the palm faces upward. Rotation of the foot so that the outer edge of the sole bears the weight of the body. The opposite of pronation.

supramastoid Above or superior to the mastoid process of the temporal.

suprameatal Above or superior to the external auditory meatus, the outer opening to the ear canal.

suture The fibrous joint between bones of the skull (basilar, coronal, lambdoidal, sagittal, and squamosal sutures).

symphysial rim The margin of the pubic symphysis; the edge of the symphysial face; one of the later areas of modification in the pubic symphysis.

symphysis, pl. symphyses An articulation in which bones are united by cartilage without a synovial membrane (e.g., the pubic symphysis). Also a growing together of bones originally separate (e.g., the two halves of the lower jawbone).

synchondrosis, pl. synchondroses A form of articulation in which the bones are rigidly fused by cartilage (e.g., the articulation between ribs and sternum).

syndesmosis, pl. syndesmoses An articulation in which the bones are joined by a ligament (e.g., the interosseous ligament between radius and ulna).

synovial joint Complex, freely movable articulations, classified according to their range of motion. The bone surfaces are covered with hyaline cartilage. The joint may contain menisci of fibrocartilage as well as bursae, enclosed sacs made of synovial membranes and containing synovial fluid.

taphonomy The processes of decay associated with death and decomposition. Taphonomic changes take place from death to complete disintegration or fossilization.

tendon Dense connective tissue attaching muscle to bone. Tendons tend to be narrower and more cord-like than ligaments.

testimony A statement or statements made by a witness under oath in a legal proceeding.

thorax The ribs, sternum, costal cartilage, and associated soft tissues; the rib cage; part of the axial skeleton.

tibia, pl. tibias The major bone of the lower leg, medial to the fibula; the shin bone.

trace evidence Physical evidence that transfers in small quantities and usually requires advanced technical equipment of analysis (e.g. dust, pollen, hair, fibers, gunshot residue, paint chips).

tramatology The branch of medicine that deals with the treatment of serious wounds, injuries, and disabilities.

transverse foramen The aperture in the transverse process of the cervical vertebrae.

transverse line of fusion In the sacrum, the furrow or ridge that remains between individual vertebral bodies after fusion of the sacral elements has taken place. The remnant of the cartilaginous joint between sacral vertebral bodies, especially S1–S2.

trier of fact The authority at a trial who decides what the truth is. If there is a jury, it is the trier of fact. If there is no jury, the judge is the trier of fact.

trochanter One of the bony prominences developed from independent centers of ossification near the upper extremity of the femur. *See* greater and lesser trochanter.

trochlea A spool-shaped structure. The articular surface for the ulna on the distal end of the humerus or the articular surface for the patella on the anterior surface of the distal femur. A trochlea allows for bidirectional movement.

true rib Ribs #1–#7; the ribs that attach directly to the sternum via cartilage.

tubercle A slight elevation from the surface of a bone giving attachment to a muscle or ligament (e.g., dorsal tubercles of radius, greater and lesser tubercles of the humerus).

tuberosity A large tubercle or rounded elevation from the surface of a bone (e.g., ischial tuberosity, tibial tuberosity).

ulna, pl. ulnae One of the two bones of the forearm. The ulna is medial to the radius.

ulnar notch The facet for the ulna on the medial side of the distal end of the radius.

ventral arc A slightly elevated ridge of bone that crosses the ventral surface of the female pubis at an angle to the inferior corner.

ventral rampart The concave outer surface of the margin of the pubic symphysis; this part develops a steep bevel in the middle phases of Todd's aging sequence.

verbal evidence or testimonial evidence Oral or written evidence. (This is the only evidence protected by the Fifth Ammendment to the U.S. Constitution.)

vertebra, pl. vertebrae A single segment of the spinal column. There are seven cervical vertebrae, twelve thoracic vertebrae, five lumbar, five sacral (fused to form the sacrum) and four coccygeal (often fused to form the coccyx and sometimes fused to the sacrum).

vertebral body The centrum and its epiphyseal rings; the vertebral body fuses with the vertebral arch at 3–7 years of age.

vertebral border The medial border of the scapula.

vertebral canal The channel formed by all the vertebrae encircling the spinal cord.

vertebral foramen The aperture between the vertebral arch and the vertebral body encircling the spinal cord.

vertex The highest single point on the midsagittal section of the skull when positioned in the Frankfort Plane.

viscerocranium The bones of the face including the mandible. Also called splanchnocranium.

WinID A computer program designed to match a missing person to unidentified remains through dental comparisons. The program was developed to run on Windows systems and store data in a Microsoft Access Database.

xiphoid process The inferior projection of the sternum. Xiphoid comes from the Greek word for sword and means "sword-shaped."

zygion A paired point at the most lateral edge of the zygomatic arch. It is used to measure bizygomatic width (mid-facial width). Some sources define this point on the zygoma, but it is usually on the zygomatic process of the temporal bone.

zygomatic arch The arch resulting from meeting of processes from the zygomatic and temporal bones.

zygomatic process The part of the maxilla and the part of the temporal extending toward and meeting the zygomatic bone.

Bibliography

Adams BJ, and Konigsberg LW (2005) Quantification of commingled human skeletal remains: Determining the most likely number of individuals (MLNI). Proceedings of the American Academy of Forensic Sciences *11:*309–310.

Aglietti P, Insall J, Cerulli G (1983) Patellar pain and incongruence: Part I. Clin Orthop *176:*217–224.

Ahlquist J, and Damsten O (1969) A modification of Kerley's method for the microscopic determination of age in human bone. Journal of Forensic Sciences *14:*205–212.

Albert AM, and Maples WR (1995) Stages of epiphyseal union for thoracic and lumbar vertebral centra as a method of age determination for teenage and young adult skeletons. Journal of Forensic Sciences *40:*623–633.

Allen JA (1877) The influence of physical conditions in the genesis of species. Radical Review *1:*108–140.

Amnesty International (1993) Getting Away with Murder: Political Killings and "Disappearances" in the 1990s. London, UK: Amnesty International Publications.

Amnesty International Dutch Section (1994) "Disappearances" and Political Killings: A Manual for Action. Amsterdam: Amnesty International.

Aulderheide AC, and Rodríguez-Martín C (1998) The Cambridge Encyclopedia of Human Paleopathology, UK: Cambridge University Press.

Austin-Smith D, and Maples WR (1994) The reliability of skull/photograph superimposition in individual identification. Journal of Forensic Sciences *39:*446–455.

Averill DC, ed. (1997) ASFO Manual of Forensic Odontology. Colorado Springs, CO: American Academy of Forensic Sciences.

Baccino E, Ubelaker DH, Hayek LAC, and Zerilli A (1999) Evaluation of seven methods of estimating age at death from mature human skeletal remains. Journal of Forensic Sciences *44:*931–936.

Baker SJ, Gill GW, and Kieffer DA (1990) Race and sex determination from the intercondylar notch of the distal femur. In GW Gill and S Rhine (eds.): Skeletal Attribution of Race. Albuquerque, NM: University of New Mexico, Maxwell Museum of Anthropology.

Ball P (1996) Who Did What to Whom? Planning and Implementing a Large Scale Human Rights Data Project. Washington, D.C.: American Association for the Advancement of Science.

Ball P, Girouard M, and Chapman AR (1997) Information technology, information management, and human rights: A response to Metzl. Human Rights Quarterly *19:*836–859.

Ball P, Spirer HF, and Spirer L (2000) Making the case: Investigating large-scale human rights violations using information systems and data analysis. Washington, D.C.: American Association for the Advancement of Science.

Ballard MB (1999) Anterior femoral curvature revisited: Race assessment from the femur. Journal of Forensic Sciences *44:*700–707.

Bang G, and Ramm E (1970) Determination of age in humans from root dentin transparency. Acta Odontologica Scandinavia *28:*3–35.

Barnes, E (1994) Developmental Defects of the Axial Skeleton in Paleopathology. Niwot, CO: University Press of Colorado.

Bass WM (1971) Human Osteology: A Laboratory and Field Manual. Columbia, MO: Missouri Archaeological Society. (5th edition, 2005)

Bass WM, III (1997) Outdoor decomposition rates in Tennessee. In WD Haglund and MH Sorg (eds.): Forensic Taphonomy: The Postmortem Fate of Human Remains. Boca Raton, FL: CRC Press, pp. 181–186.

Bass WM, and Birkby WH (1978) Exhumation: The method could make the difference. FBI Law Enforcement Bulletin *47(7):*6–11.

Bedford ME, Russell KF, and Lovejoy CO (1989) The auricular surface aging technique: 16 color photographs with descriptions. Kent, OH: Kent State University.

Bedford ME, Russell KF, Lovejoy CO, Meindl R, Simpson S, and Stuart-Macadam P (1993) Test of the multifactorial aging method using skeletons with known ages-at-death from the Grant collection. American Journal of Physical Anthropology *91(3):*287–297.

Benedetti F (1996) Haiti's Truth and Justice Commission. Human Rights Brief *3:*4–5.

Bennett JL, and Rockhold LA (1999) Use of alternate light source for tattoo recognition in the extended postmortem interval Journal of Forensic Sciences *44:*182–184.

Bergmann C (1847) Über die Verhältnisse der wärmeökonomie der Thiere zu ihrer Grösse. Göttinger Studien, Göttingen *3:*595–708.

Beristaín C (1999) *Reconstruir el tejido social: Un enfoque crítico de la ayuda humanitaria.* Barcelona: Icaria Editorial.

Berrizbeitia EL (1989) Sex determination with the head of the radius. Journal of Forensic Sciences *34:*1207–1213.

Berryman HE, Bass WM, Symes SA, and Smith OC (1991) Recognition of cemetery remains in the forensic setting. Journal of Forensic Sciences *36:*230–237.

Berryman HE, Bass WM, Symes SA, and Smith OC (1997) Recognition of cemetery remains in the forensic setting. In W Haglund and M Sorg (eds.): Forensic Taphonomy: The Postmortem Fate of Human Remains. Boca Raton, FL: CRC Press, pp. 165–170.

Besana JL, Rogers TL (2010) Personal identification using the frontal sinus. Journal of Forensic Sciences *55(3):*584–589.

Bevan BW (1991) The search for graves. Geophysics *56:*1310–1319.

Black J, and Mattson RU (1982) Relationship between porosity and mineralization in the Haversian osteon. Calcified Tissue International *34:*332–336.

Blanton P, and Biggs NL (1968) Density of fresh and embalmed human compact and cancellous bone. American Journal of Physical Anthropology *29:*39–44.

Bogin B, Sullivan T, Hauspie R, and Macvean RB (1989) Longitudinal growth in height, weight, and bone age of Guatemalan Ladino and Indian schoolchildren. American Journal of Human Biology *1:*103–113.

Bourel B, Hedouin V, Martin-Bouyer L, Becart A, Rournel G, Deveaux M, and Gosset D (1999) Effects of morphine in decomposing bodies on the development of *Lucilia sericata* (Diptera: Calliphoridae). Journal of Forensic Sciences *44:*354–358.

Bouvier M, and Ubelaker DH (1977) A comparison of two methods for the microscopic determination of age at death. American Journal of Physical Anthropology *46:*391–394.

Boyd RM (1979) Buried body cases. FBI Law Enforcement Bulletin *48(2):*1–7.

Brodsky SL (1999) The Expert Expert Witness. Washington, D.C.: American Psychological Association.

Branicki W, Kayser M, et al. (2011) Model-based prediction of human hair color using DNA variants. Human Genetics *129(4):* 443–454.

Brogdon BG (1998) Forensic Radiology. Boca Raton, FL: CRC Press.

Brogdon BG, Vogel H, and McDowell JD (2003) A Radiologic Atlas of Abuse, Torture, Terrorism, and Inflicted Trauma. Boca Raton, FL: CRC Press.

Brooks S (1955) Skeletal age at death: The reliability of cranial and pubic age indicators. American Journal of Physical Anthropology *13:*567–597.

Brooks ST, and Suchey JM (1990) Skeletal age determination based on the os pubis: A comparison of the Ascádi-Nemerskéri and Suchey–Brooks methods. Human Evolution *5:*227–238.

Bruzek J (2002) A method for visual determination of sex, using the human hip bone. American Journal of Physical Anthropology *117:*157–168.

Buckberry J, and Chamberlain AT (2002) Age estimation from the auricular surface of the ilium: A revised method. American Journal of Physical Anthropology *119:*231–239.

Buergenthal T (1994) The United Nations Truth Commission for El Salvador. Vanderbilt Journal of Transnational Law *27:*497–544.

Buikstra JE, and Ubelaker DH (1994) Standards for data collection from human skeletal remains. Fayetteville, AR: Arkansas Archeological Survey Research Series vol 44.

Bunch AW, and Shine CC (2003) Science contextualized: The identification of a U.S. MIA of the Vietnam War from two perspectives. In DW Steadman (ed.): Hard Evidence: Case Studies in Forensic Evidence. Upper Saddle River, NJ: Prentice Hall, pp. 278–289.

Burness GP, Diamond J, and Flannery T (2001) Dinosaurs, dragons, and dwarfs: The evolution of maximal body size. PNAS *98:*14518–14523.

Burns KR (2009) The Herring case—An outlier, In Steadman DW, ed. Hard Evidence: Case Studies in Forensic Anthropology, 2nd ed. Upper Saddle River, NJ: Prentice-Hall.

Burns, KR (2008) Manual de Antropologia Forense. Barcelona, Spain, Edicions Bellaterra.

Burns KR (1998) Forensic anthropology and human rights issues. In K Reichs (ed.): Forensic Osteology: Advances in the Identification of Human Remains. Springfield, IL: Charles C. Thomas, pp. 63–85.

Burns KR (1991) Model protocol for disinterment and analysis of skeletal remains. In United Nations Office at Vienna Centre for Social Development and Humanitarian Affairs (ed.): Manual on the Effective Prevention and Investigation of Extra-Legal, Arbitrary and Summary Executions. New York, NY: United Nations, pp. 34–40.

Burns KR, and Maples WR (1976) Estimation of age from individual adult teeth. Journal of Forensic Sciences *21:*343–356.

Burris BG, and Harris EF (1998) Identification of race and sex from palate dimensions. Journal of Forensic Sciences *43:*959–963.

Burrows A, Zanella V, and Brown T (2003) Testing the validity of metacarpal use in sex assessment of human skeletal remains. Journal of Forensic Sciences *48:*17–20.

Butler JM (2005) Forensic DNA Typing: Biology, Technology, and Genetics of STR Markers. Burlington, MA: Elsevier Academic Press.

Byrd JH, and Castner JL (2000) Forensic Entomology: The Utility of Arthropods in Legal Investigations. Boca Raton, FL: CRC Press.

Carver R (1990) Called to account: How African governments investigate human rights violations. African Affairs *89:*391.

Catts EP, and Haskell NH (1990) Entomology and Death: A Procedural Guide. Clemson, SC: Joyce's Print Shop, Inc.

Chamberlain A (1994) Human Remains. Berkeley, CA: University of California Press.

Chernick MW (2003) Colombia: Does injustice cause violence? In SE Eckstein and TP Wickham-Crowley (eds.): What Justice? Whose Justice? Berkeley, CA: University of California Press, pp. 185–214.

Cho H, Stout SD, Madsen RW, and Streeter M (2002) Population-specific histological age-estimating method: A model for known African-American and European-American skeletal remains. Journal of Forensic Sciences *47:*12–18.

Christensen AM (2004) The Impact of Daubert: Implications for testimony and research in forensic anthropology (and the use of frontal sinuses in personal identification). Journal of Forensic Sciences *49:*427–430.

Christensen AM (2005) Testing the reliability of frontal sinuses in positive identification. Journal of Forensic Sciences *50:*18–22.

Clement AJ (1963) Variations in the microstructure and biochemistry of human teeth. In DR Brothwell (ed.): Dental Anthropology, Symposium of the Society for the Study of Human Biology. New York, NY: Pergamon Press, pp. 245–269.

Cobb WM (1952) Skeleton. In AI Lansing (ed.): Cowdry's Problems of Ageing: Biological and Medical Aspects. Baltimore, MD: Williams & Wilkins, pp. 791–856.

Cond HV (2004) A Handbook of International Human Rights Terminology. Lincoln, NE: University of Nebraska.

Coy A, and Ohlson JW (2000) Special case in three-dimensional bone reconstruction of the human skull. Journal of Forensic Identification *50:*549–562.

Coyle HM, ed. (2005) Forensic Botany: Principles and Applications to Criminal Casework. Boca Raton, FL: CRC Press.

Dahlberg A (1945) The changing dentition of man. Journal of the American Dental Association *32:*676–680.

Dahlberg A (1956) Materials for the establishment of standards for classification of tooth characteristics, attributes, and techniques in morphological studies of the dentition. Chicago, IL: University of Chicago Zoller Laboratory of Dental Anthropology.

Danner M (1993) The Truth of El Mozote. The New Yorker, p. 12.

Danner M (1994) The Massacre at El Mozote: A Parable of the Cold War. New York, NY: Vintage Books.

Daubert (1993) *Daubert v. Merrell Dow Pharmaceuticals* (92-102). Washington, D.C.: Supreme Court of the United States (509 U.S. 579).

Davey M (2005) Grisly Effect of One Drug: "Meth Mouth," Section A, Page 1: New York Times, June 11, 2005, Late Edition—Final. New York, NY.

Department of Public Information (2004) Basic Facts about the United Nations. New York, NY: United Nations.

Dequeker J, Remans J, Franssen R, and Waes J (1971) Aging patterns of trabecular and cortical bone and their relationship. Calcified Tissue Research *7:*23–30.

Di Maio VJM (1999) Gunshot Wounds: Practical Aspects of Firearms, Ballistics, and Forensic Techniques. Boca Raton, FL: CRC Press.

Dill K (2005) International human rights and local justice in Guatemala: The Rio Negro (Pak'oxom) and Agua Fria trials. Cultural Dynamics *17:*323–350.

Decker SJ, Davy-Jow SL, Ford JM, and Hilbelink DR (2011) Virtual determination of sex: Metric and nonmetric traits of the adult pelvis from 3D computed tomography models. Journal of Forensic Sciences *56:*1107–1114.

Demirjian A (1978) Dentition. In F Falker and JM Tanner (eds.): Human Growth. Vol 2. Postnatal Growth. New York: Plenum Press, pp. 413–444.

Doretti M, Carson L, and Kerr D (2005) Argentine Forensic Anthropology Team Annual Report. Buenos Aires, Argentina: Argentine Forensic Anthropology Team, p. 184.

Doretti M, and Snow CC (2003) Forensic anthropology and human rights: The Argentine experience. In DW Steadman (ed.): Hard Evidence: Case Studies in Forensic Anthropology. Upper Saddle River, NJ: Prentice Hall, pp. 290–310.

Dudar JC (1993) Identification of rib number and assessment of intercostal variation at the sternal rib end. Journal of Forensic Sciences *38:*788–797.

Dudar JC, Pfeiffer S, and Saunders SR (1993) Evaluation of morphological and histological adult skeletal age-at-death estimation techniques using ribs. Journal of Forensic Sciences *38:*677–685.

Duray SM, Morter HB, and Smith FJ (1999) Morphological variation in cervical spinous processes: Potential applications in the forensic identification of race from the skeleton. Journal of Forensic Sciences *44:*937–944.

Dwight T (1898) The Identification of the Human Skeleton, a Medico-Legal Study. Boston, MA: (Prize Essay) Massachusetts Medical Society.

Eckert WG (1997) Introduction to Forensic Sciences. Boca Raton, FL: CRC Press.

Eckstein SE, and Wickham-Crowley TP, eds. (2003) What Justice? Whose Justice? Fighting for Fairness in Latin America. Berkeley: University of California Press.

El Equipo de Antropología Forense de Guatemala (EAFG) (1995) Las Masacres en Rabinal: Estudio Historico-Antropologico de las Masacres de Plan de Sanchez, Chichupac y Rio Negro. Guatemala City, Guatemala: EAFG, p. 28.

Ellwood BB (1990) Electrical resistivity surveys in two historical cemeteries in northeast Texas: A method for delineating unidentified burial shafts. Historical Archaeology *24:*91–98.

El-Najjar MY, and McWilliams KR (1978) Forensic Anthropology. Springfield, IL: Charles C. Thomas.

Eugene AM (1995) Sex estimation using the first cervical vertebra. American Journal of Physical Anthropology *97:*127–133.

Falsetti AB (1995) Sex assessment from metacarpals of the human hand. Journal of Forensic Sciences *40:*774–776.

Fausto-Sterling A (2000) Sexing the Body: Gender Politics and the Construction of Sexuality. New York: Basic Books.

Fazekas G, and Kosa F (1978) Forensic Fetal Osteology. Budapest: Akademiai Kiado.

Federal Rules of Evidence (1975 to present) Federal Evidence Review. Retreived from http://federalevidence.com/rules-of-evidence.

Feik SA, Thomas CDL, Bruns R, and Clement JG (2000) Regional variations in cortical modeling in the femoral mid-shaft: Sex and age differences. American Journal of Physical Anthropology *112:*191–205.

Ferembach D, Schwidetzky I, Stloukal M (1980) Recommendations for age and sex diagnoses of skeletons. Journal of Human Evolution *9(7):*517–549.

Ferllini Timms R (1993) Principios de Arqueología Forense. San José, Costa Rica: Editorial Universidad Estatal a Distancia.

Fierro MF, ed. (1986) CAP Handbook for Postmortem Examination of Unidentified Remains. Skokie, IL: College of American Pathologists.

Finnegan M, and Schulter-Ellis FP (1978) The tympanic plate in forensic discrimination between American blacks and whites. Journal of Forensic Sciences *23:*771–777.

France DL, Griffin TJ, Swanburg JG, Lindemann JW, Davenport GC, Trammell V, Armbrust CT, Kondratieff B, Nelson A, Castellano K, and Hopkins D (1992) A multidisciplinary approach to the detection of clandestine graves. Journal of Forensic Sciences *37:*1445–1458.

Frohlich B, and Lancaster WJ (1986) Electromagnetic surveying in current Middle Eastern archaeology: Application and evaluation. Geophysics *51:*1414–1425.

Frye (1923) *Frye v. United States* (54 App. D. C. 46, 293 F. 1013, No. 3968): Court of Appeals of District of Columbia.

Fuller JL, Denehy GE, and Hall SA (2001) Concise Dental Anatomy and Morphology, 4th ed. Iowa City, IA: University of Iowa College of Dentistry.

Fully G, and Pineau H (1960) Determination de la stature au moyen du squelette. Annales de Médicine Legal *40:*145–154.

Galera V, Ubelaker DH, and Hayek LC (1998) Comparison of macroscopic cranial methods of age estimation applied to skeletons from the Terry Collection. Journal of Forensic Sciences *43:*933–939.

Galloway A, Birkby WH, Jones AM, Henry TE, and Parks BO (1989) Decay rates of human remains in an arid environment. Journal of Forensic Sciences *34:*607–616.

Geberth VJ (2006) Practical Homicide Investigation: Tactics, Procedures and Forensic Techniques. Boca Raton, FL: CRC Press.

Genovés S (1967) Proportionality of the long bones and their relation to stature among Mesoamericans. American Journal of Physical Anthropology *26:*67–77.

Gibbons A (1992) Scientists search for "the disappeared" in Guatemala. Science *257:*479.

Gilbert BM, and McKern TW (1973) A method for aging the female os pubis. American Journal of Physical Anthropology *38:*31–38.

Gilbert R, and Gill GW (1990) A metric technique for identifying American Indian femora. In GW Gill and S Rhine (eds.): Skeletal Attribution of Race. Albuquerque, NM: University of New Mexico, Maxwell Museum of Anthropology, pp. 97–99.

Giles E (1970) Discriminant function sexing of the human skeleton. In TD Stewart (ed.): Personal Identification in Mass Disasters. Washington, D.C.: National Museum of Natural History.

Giles E (1991) Corrections for age in estimating older adults' stature from long bones. Journal of Forensic Sciences *36:*898–901.

Giles E, and Elliot O (1962) Race identification from cranial measurements. Journal of Forensic Sciences *7:*147–157.

Giles E, and Elliot O (1963) Sex determination by discriminant function analysis of crania. American Journal of Physical Anthropology *21:*53–68.

Gill GW (1995) Challenge on the frontier: Discerning American Indians from whites osteologically. Journal of Forensic Sciences *40:*783–788.

Gill GW, and Rhine S, eds. (1990) Skeletal Attribution of Race. Albuquerque, NM: University of New Mexico, Maxwell Museum of Anthropology.

Grauer AL, ed. (1995) Bodies of Evidence: Reconstructing History through Skeletal Analysis. New York, NY: Wiley-Liss.

Greenberg B, and Kunich JC (2002) Entomology and the Law: Flies as Forensic Indicators. Cambridge, UK: Cambridge University Press.

Greenspan A, and Remagen W (1998) Differential Diagnosis of Tumors and Tumor-Like Lesions of Bones and Joints. Philadelphia, PA: Lippincott-Raven.

Gregory T, and Rogerson JG (1984) Metal detecting in archaeological excavation. Antiquity *58:*179–184.

Greulich WW, and Pyle SI (1959) Radiographic Atlas of Skeletal Development of the Hand and Wrist. Stanford, CA: Stanford University Press.

Gunatilake K, and Goff ML (1989) Detection of organophosphate poisoning in a putrefying body by analyzing arthropod larvae. Journal of Forensic Sciences *34:*714–716.

Gurr TR, Khosla D, Marshall MG (2001) Peace and Conflict 2001, A Global Survey of Armed Conflicts, Self-Determination Movements, and

Democracy. College Park, MD: Center for International Development & Conflict Management (CIDCM), Department of Government and Politics, University of Maryland.

Gustafson G (1950) Age determination on teeth. Journal of the American Dental Association *41:*45–54.

Gustafson G (1966) Forensic Odontology. New York, NY: American Elsevier.

Gutman R, and Rieff D, eds. (1999) Crimes of War: What the Public Should Know. New York, NY: W. W. Norton.

Haglund WD, and Fligner C (1993) Confirmation of human identification using computerized tomography (CT). Journal of Forensic Sciences *38:*708–712.

Haglund WD (1997) Dogs and coyotes: Postmortem involvement with human remains. In WD Haglund and MH Sorg (eds.): Forensic Taphonomy: The Postmortem Fate of Human Remains. Boca Raton, FL: CRC Press, pp. 367–381.

Haglund WD, and Sorg MH, eds. (1997) Forensic Taphonomy: The Postmortem Fate of Human Remains. Boca Raton, FL: CRC Press.

Haglund WD, and Sorg MH (2002) Advances in Forensic Taphonomy: Method, Theory, and Archaeological Perspectives. Boca Raton, FL: CRC Press.

Haglund WD, and Sperry K (1993) The use of hydrogen peroxide to visualize tattoos obscured by decomposition and mummification. Journal of Forensic Sciences *38:*147–150.

Hall DW (1997) Forensic Botany. In WD Haglund and MH Sorg (eds.): Forensic Taphonomy: The Postmortem Fate of Human Remains. Boca Raton, FL: CRC Press, pp. 353–363.

Hanihara K, and Suzuki T (1979) Estimation of age from the pubic symphysis by means of multiple regression analysis. American Journal of Physical Anthropology *48:*233–240.

Hannibal K (1990/1991) AAAS sponsors forensic mission to Brazil. AAAS Committee on Scientific Freedom and Responsibility: Clearinghouse Report on Science and Human Rights *XII(2).*

Hannibal K (1992) Taking Up the Challenge: The Promotion of Human Rights, A Guide for the Scientific Community. Washington, D.C.: Science and Human Rights Program, American Association for the Advancement of Science.

Haskell NH, Hall RD, Cervenka VJ, and Clark MA (1997) On the body: Insects' life stage presence and their postmortem artifacts. In WD Haglund and MH Sorg (eds.): Forensic Taphonomy: The Postmortem Fate of Human Remains. Boca Raton, FL: CRC Press, pp. 415–448.

Hayner PB (1994) Fifteen truth commissions—1974 to 1994: A comparative study. Human Rights Quarterly *16:*597–655.

Hayner PB (1999) In pursuit of justice and reconciliation: Contributions of truth telling. In CJ Arnson (ed.): Comparative Peace Processes in Latin America. Washington, D.C. and Stanford, CA: Woodrow Wilson Center and Stanford University Press, pp. 363–384.

Herman J (1992) Trauma and Recovery: The Aftermath of Violence from Domestic Abuse to Political Terror. New York, NY: Basic Books.

Hershkovitz I, Latimer B, Dutour O, Jellema LM, Wish-Baratz S, Rothschild C, and Rothschild BM (1997) Why do we fail in aging the skull from the sagittal suture? American Journal of Physical Anthropology *103:*393–399.

Hewitt J, Wilkenfeld J, and Gurr TR, (2010) Peace and Conflict 2010, Executive Summary. College Park, MD: Center for International Development & Conflict Management (CIDCM), Department of Government and Politics, University of Maryland.

Hobischak NR, and Anderson GS (2002) Time of submergence using aquatic invertebrate succession and decompositional changes. Journal of Forensic Sciences *47:*142–151.

Hoffman JM (1979) Age estimations from diaphyseal lengths: Two months to twelve years. Journal of Forensic Sciences *24:*461–469.

Holliday TW, and Falsetti AB (1999) A new method for discriminating African-American from European-American skeletons using postcranial osteometrics reflective of body shape. Journal of Forensic Sciences *44:*926–930.

Holt CA (1978) A re-examination of parturition scars on the human female pelvis, American Journal of Physical Anthropology, *49(1):*91–94.

Hoppa R, and Saunders S (1998) Two quantitative methods for rib seriation in human skeletal remains. Journal of Forensic Sciences *43:*174–177.

Horton MG, and Hall TL (1989) Quadriceps femoris muscle angle: Normal values and relationships with gender and selected skeletal measures. Physical Therapy *69:*897–901.

Hoving GL (1986) Buried body search technology: Identification News, pp. 3,15.

Howells WW (1978) Cranial Variation in Man: A Study by Multivariate Analysis of Patterns of Difference Among Recent Human Populations. Cambridge, MA: Harvard University Press.

Human Rights Internet (1999) Funding Human Rights: An International Directory of Funding Organizations and Human Rights Awards. Ottowa, Ontario: Human Rights Internet. (http://www.hri.ca/books.aspx [accessed 2011-12-09]).

Imaizumi M (1974) Locating buried bodies. FBI Law Enforcement Bulletin *43(8):*2–5.

Inman K, and Rudin N (1997) An Introduction to Forensic DNA Analysis. Boca Raton, FL: CRC Press.

International Committee of the Red Cross (2003) The Missing. Geneva, Switzerland: International Committee for the Red Cross.

Isçan MY, and Derrick K (1984) Determination of sex from the sacroiliac joint: a visual assessment technique. Florida Scientist *47:*94–98

Isçan MY, and Loth SR (1986) Determination of age from the sternal rib in white females: A test of the phase method. Journal of Forensic Sciences *31:*990–999.

Isçan MY, Loth SR, and Wright RK (1984) Age estimation from the ribs by phase analysis: White males. Journal of Forensic Sciences *29:*1094–1104.

Isçan MY, Loth SR, and Wright RK (1985) Age estimation from the rib by phase analysis: White females. Journal of Forensic Sciences *30:*853–863.

Isçan MY, and Kennedy KAR (1989) Reconstruction of Life from the Skeleton. New York, NY: Alan R. Liss.

Isçan MY, Loth SR, and Wright RK (1984) Metamorphosis at the sternal rib end: A new method to estimate age at death in white males. American Journal of Physical Anthropology *65:*147–156.

Isçan MY, and Miller-Shaivitz P (1984) Discriminant function sexing of the tibia. Journal of Forensic Sciences *29:*1087–1093.

Jantz RL (1992) Modification of the Trotter and Gleser female stature estimation formulae. Journal of Forensic Sciences *37:*1230–1235.

Jensen RA (2000) Mass Fatality and Casualty Incidents: A Field Guide. Boca Raton, FL: CRC Press.

Johanson G (1971) Age determinations from human teeth. Odontologisk Revy *22:*1–126.

Johnson EC, Johnson GR, and Williams MJ (2000) The origin and history of embalming. In RG Mayer (ed.): Embalming: History, Theory and Practice. New York, NY: McGraw-Hill.

Joint POW/MIA Accounting Command Public Affairs (2005) J.P.A.C. Command Brochure. Honolulu, HI: Defense Automated Print Service.

Jowsey J (1966) Studies of Haversian systems in man and some animals. Journal of Anatomy *100:*857–864.

Joyce C, and Stover E (1991) Witnesses from the Grave: The Stories Bones Tell. New York, NY: Ballantine.

Juhl K (2005) The Contribution by (Forensic) Archaeologists to Human Rights Investigations of Mass Graves. AmS-NETT 5, Stavanger, Norway: Museum of Archaeology. http://am.uis.no/getfile.php/Arkeologisk%20museum/publikasjoner/ams-nett/Mass_Graves2.pdf.

Kalacska ME, Bell LS, et al. (2009) The application of remote sensing for detecting mass graves: An experimental animal case study from Costa Rica, Journal of Forensic Sciences *54(1):*159–66.

Kalmey JK, Thewissen JGM, and Dluzen DE (1998) Age-related size reduction of foramina in the cribriform plate. Anatomical Record *251:* 326–329.

Katz D, and Suchey JM (1986) Age determination of the male os pubis. American Journal of Physical Anthropology *69:*427–435.

Katzenberg MA, and Saunders SR, eds. (2008) Biological Anthropology of the Human Skeleton, 2nd ed. Hoboken, NJ: John Wiley and Sons.

Kayser M (2011) The new eyewitness. Forensic Magazine *8(4):*8.

Kelley MA (1978) Phenice's visual sexing technique for the os pubis: A critique. American Journal of Physical Anthropology *48(1):* 121–122.

Kelley MA, and Larsen CS, eds. (1991) Advances in Dental Anthropology. New York, NY: Wiley-Liss.

Kennedy KAR (1995) But professor, why teach race identification if races don't exist? Journal of Forensic Sciences *40:*797–800.

Kennedy KAR (2003) Trials in court: The forensic anthropologist takes the stand. In DW Steadman (ed.): Hard Evidence: Case Studies in Forensic Anthropology. Upper Saddle River, NJ: Prentice-Hall, pp. 77–86.

Kerley ER (1965) The microscopic determination of age in human bone. American Journal of Physical Anthropology *23:*149–163.

Kerley ER (1969) Age determination of bone fragments. Journal of Forensic Sciences *14:*59–67.

Kerley ER, and Ubelaker DH (1978) Revisions in the microscopic method of estimating age at death in human cortical bone. American Journal of Physical Anthropology *49:*545–546.

Killam EW (1990) The Detection of Human Remains. Springfield, IL: Charles C. Thomas.

Kirschner RH (1994) The application of the forensic sciences to human rights investigations. International Journal of Medicine and Law *13:*451–460.

Klales AR, Vollner JM, Ousley SC (2009) A new metric procedure for the estimation of sex and ancestry from the human innominate. Proc Am Acad Forensic Sci. H23 p.311.

Klepinger LL, Katz D, Micozzi MS, and Carroll L (1992) Evaluation of cast methods for estimating age from the os pubis. Journal of Forensic Sciences *37:*763–770.

Komar DA (1998) Decay rates in a cold climate region: A review of cases involving advanced decomposition from the Medical Examiner's Office in Edmonton, Alberta. Journal of Forensic Sciences *43:*57–61.

Krogman WM (1939) A guide to the identification of human skeletal material. FBI Law Enforcement Bulletin *8(8):*3–31.

Krogman WM (1943a) Role of the physical anthropologist in the identification of human skeletal remains. FBI Law Enforcement Bulletin *12(4):*17–40.

Krogman WM (1943b) Role of the physical anthropologist in the identification of human skeletal remains. FBI Law Enforcement Bulletin *12(5):*12–28.

Krogman WM (1946) The reconstruction of the living head from the skull. FBI Law Enforcement Bulletin *15(7):*11–18.

Krogman WM (1962) The Human Skeleton in Forensic Medicine. Springfield, IL: Charles C. Thomas.

Krogman WM, and Işcan MY (1986) The Human Skeleton in Forensic Medicine. Springfield, IL: Charles C. Thomas.

Krogman WM, McGregor J, and Frost B (1948) A problem in human skeletal remains. FBI Law Enforcement Bulletin *17(6):*7–12.

Kunos CA, Simpson SW, Russell KF, and Hershkovitz I (1999) First rib metamorphosis: Its possible utility for human age-at-death estimation. American Journal of Physical Anthropology *110:*303–323.

Kvaal SI, Kollveit KM, Thompsen IO, and Solheim T (1995) Age estimation of adults from dental radiographs. Forensic Science International *74:*175–185.

Kvaal SI, and Solheim T (1994) A non-destructive dental method for age estimation. Journal of Forensic Odonto-Stomatology *12:*6–11.

Lamendin H, Baccion E, Humbert JF, Tavernier JC, Nossintchouk RM, and Zerilli A (1992) A simple technique for age estimation in adult corpses: The two criteria dental method. Journal of Forensic Sciences *37:*1373–1379.

Livingston LA (1998) The quadriceps angle: A review of the literature. J Orthop Sports Phys Ther *28(2):*105–109.

Locard E (1930) The analysis of dust traces, part I. The American Journal of Police Science *1(3):*276–298.

Locard E (1930) The analysis of dust traces, part III. The American Journal of Police Science *1(5):*496–514.

Locard E, and Larson DJ (1930) The analysis of dust traces, part II. The American Journal of Police Science *1(4):*401–418.

Lollar C (1990) Forensic scientists uncovering fate of Brazil's "disappeared" with help of AAAS. Science *250:*1750.

Love JC, and Marks MK (2003) Taphonomy and time: Estimating the postmortem interval. In DW Steadman (ed.): Hard Evidence: Case Studies in Forensic Anthropology. Upper Saddle River, NJ: Prentice Hall, pp. 160–175.

Lovejoy CO, Meindl R, Mensforth RP, and Barton T (1985) Multifactorial determination of skeletal age at death: A method and blind tests of its accuracy. American Journal of Physical Anthropology *68:*1–14.

Lovejoy CO, Meindl R, Pryzbeck TR, and Mensforth RP (1985) Chronological metamorphosis of the auricular surface of the ilium: A new method for the determination of adult skeletal age at death. American Journal of Physical Anthropology *68:*15–28.

Lovejoy CO, Meindl R, Tague RG, and Latimer B (1995) The senescent biology of the hominoid pelvis: Its bearing on the pubic symphysis and auricular surface as age-at-death indicators in the human skeleton. Rivista di Antropoligia (Roma) *73:*31–49.

MacLaughlin SM, and Bruce MF (1986) The sciatic notch/acetabular index as a discriminator of sex in European skeletal remains. Journal of Forensic Sciences *31:*1380–1390.

Madden M, and Ross A (2009) Genocide and GIScience: Integrating personal narratives and geographic information science to study human rights. The Professional Geographer *61(4):* 508–526.

Mann RW (1993) A method for siding and sequencing human ribs. Journal of Forensic Sciences *38:*151–155.

Mann RW, Anderson BE, Holland TD, Rankin DR, and Webb JE, Jr. (2003) Unusual "crime" scenes: The role of forensic anthropology in recovering and identifying American MIAs. In DW Steadman (ed.): Hard Evidence: Case Studies in Forensic Anthropology. Upper Saddle River, NJ: Prentice Hall, pp. 108–116.

Maples WR (1978) An improved technique using dental histology for estimation of adult age. Journal of Forensic Sciences *23:*764–770.

Maples WR, and Browning M (1994) Dead Men Do Tell Tales: The Strange and Fascinating Cases of a Forensic Anthropologist. New York, NY: Doubleday.

Maples WR, and Rice PM (1979) Some difficulties in the Gustafson dental age estimations. Journal of Forensic Sciences *24:*168–172.

Marieb EN, and Hoehn K (2007) Human Anatomy and Physiology. Upper Saddle River, NJ: Prentice-Hall.

Marieb EN, and Mallatt J (1992) Human Anatomy. Redwood City, CA: Benjamin/Cummings.

Marlin DC, Clark MA, and Standish SM (1991) Identification of human remains by comparison of frontal sinus radiographs: A series of four cases. Journal of Forensic Sciences *36:*1765–1772.

Marshall MG, and Gurr TR (2005) Peace and Conflict 2005: A Global Survey of Armed Conflicts, Self-Determination Movements, and Democracy. College Park, MD: Center for International Development & Conflict Management (CIDCM), Department of Government and Politics, University of Maryland.

Martin RB, Burr DB, and Sharkey NA (1998) Skeletal Tissue Mechanics. New York, NY: Springer-Verlag.

Matshes EW, Burbridge B, Sher B, Mohamed A, and Juurlink BH (2005) Human Osteology and Skeletal Radiology: An Atlas and Guide. Boca Raton, FL: CRC Press.

Matson JV, Daou SF, and Soper JG (2004) Effective Expert Witnessing: Practices for the 21st Century. Boca Raton, FL: CRC Press.

Mayer RG (2000) Embalming: History, Theory, and Practice. New York, NY: McGraw-Hill.

McCormick WF, and Stewart JH (1988) Age related changes in the human plastron: A roentgenographic and morphologic study. Journal of Forensic Sciences *33:*100–120.

McCormick WF, Stewart JH, and Langford LA (1985) Sex determination from chest plate roentgenograms. American Journal of Physical Anthropology *68:*173–195.

McEvoy K, and Conway H (2004) The dead, the law, and the politics of the past. Journal of Law and Society *31:*539–562.

McKasson SC, and Richards CA (1998) Speaking as an Expert: A Guide for the Identification Sciences from the Laboratory to the Courtroom. Springfield, IL: Charles C. Thomas.

McKern TW, and Stewart TD (1957) Skeletal age changes in young American males: Analyzed from the standpoint of age identification (Technical Report EP-45). Natick, MA: U.S. Army Quartermaster Research and Development Command.

Meindl R, Lovejoy CO, Mensforth RP, and Don Carlos L (1985) Accuracy and direction of error in the sexing of the skeleton: Implications for paleodemography. American Journal of Physical Anthropology *68:*79–85.

Meindl R, and Lovejoy CO (1989) Age changes in the pelvis: Implications for paleodemography. In MY Işcan (ed.): Age Markers in the Human Skeleton. Springfield, IL: Charles C. Thomas, pp. 137–168.

Mellen PFM, Lowry MA, and Micozzi MS (1993) Experimental observations on adipocere formation. Journal of Forensic Sciences *38:*91–93.

Melton T (2003) Mitochondrial DNA: Solving the mystery of Anna Anderson. In DW Steadman (ed.): Hard Evidence: Case Studies in Forensic Anthropology. Upper Saddle River, NJ: Prentice-Hall, pp. 205–211.

Merbs CF (1996) Spondylolysis and spondylolisthesis: A cost of being an erect biped or a clever adaptation? American Journal of Physical Anthropology *101:*201–228.

Merz WA, and Schenk RK (1970) A quantitative histological study on bone formation in human cancellous bone. Acta Anatomica *76:*1–15.

Merz WA, and Schenk RK (1970) Quantitative structural analysis of human cancellous bone. Acta Anatomica *75:*54–66.

Micozzi MS (1986) Experimental study of postmortem change under field conditions: Effects of freezing, thawing, and mechanical injury. Journal of Forensic Sciences *31:*953–961.

Moore-Jansen PM, Ousley SD, and Jantz RL (1994) Data Collection Procedures for Forensic Skeletal Material, Report of Investigations no. 48. Knoxville, TN: University of Tennessee.

Murray KA, and Murray T (1991) A test of the auricular surface aging technique. Journal of Forensic Sciences *36:*1162–1169.

Murray RO, and Jacobson HG (1977) The Radiology of Skeletal Disorders. Edinburgh, Scotland: Churchill Livingstone.

National Institute of Justice (2005) Mass Fatality Incidents: A Guide for Human Forensic Identification. Washington, D.C.: U.S. Department of Justice, Office of Justice Programs (Report NCJ 199758, available at http://www.ncjrs.gov/pdffiles1/nij/199758.pdf [accessed 2006-04-22]).

Ortner DJ (2003) Identification of Pathological Conditions in Human Skeletal Remains. San Diego, CA: Academic Press.

Osborne DL, Simmons TL, and Nawrocki SP (2004) Reconsidering the auricular surface as an indicator of age at death. Journal of Forensic Sciences *49:*905–911.

Ousley SD (1995) Should we estimate biological or forensic stature? Journal of Forensic Sciences *40:*768–773.

Ousley SD, and Jantz RL (1993, 1996) FORDISC 2.0. Knoxville, TN: University of Tennessee, Department of Anthropology, Forensic Anthropology Center.

Ousley SD, and Jantz RL (1998) The Forensic data bank: Documenting skeletal trends in the United States. In Reichs KJ (ed.): Forensic Osteology, Advances in the Identification of Human Remains. Springfield, IL: Charles C. Thomas, pp. 441–458.

Ousley SD, and Jantz RL (2005) The Next FORDISC: FORDISC 3. Proceedings of the American Academy of Forensic Sciences *11:*294–295.

Ousley S, Jantz R, and Freid D (2009) Understanding race and human variation: Why forensic anthropologists are good at identifying race. American Journal of Physical Anthropology *139:*68–76.

Owsley DW (1993) Identification of the fragmentary, burned remains of two U.S. journalists seven years after their disappearance in Guatemala. Journal of Forensic Sciences *38:*1372–1382.

Padgett T (1992) Subtle clues in shallow graves: Uncovering evidence of massacres in Guatemala. Newsweek (August 31).

Pasquier E, Pernot L, Burdin V, Mounayer C, LeRest C, Colin D, Mottier D, Rouxand C, and Baccino E (1999) Determination of age at death: Assessment of an algorithm of age prediction using numerical three-dimensional CT data from pubic bones. American Journal of Physical Anthropology *108:*261–268.

Patriquin ML, Steyn M, Loth SR (2005) Metric analysis of sex differences in South African black and white pelves. Forensic Science International *147(2–3):*119–127.

Pearson K, and Bell J (1919) A study of the long bones of the English skeleton: Part 1. The femur. Drapers' Company Research Memoirs: Biometric Series *X:*1–224.

Pelin C, Duyar I, Kayahan EM, Zagyapan R, Agildere AM, and Erar A (2005) Body height estimation based on dimensions of sacral and coccygeal vertebrae. Journal of Forensic Sciences *50:*294–297.

Pfeiffer S, Milne S, and Stevenson RM (1998) The natural decomposition of adipocere. Journal of Forensic Sciences *43:*368–370.

Phenice TW (1969) A newly developed visual method of sexing the os pubis. American Journal of Physical Anthropology *30:*297–301.

Pickering RB, and Bachman DC (1996) The Use of Forensic Anthropology. Boca Raton, FL: CRC Press.

Post RH (1969) Tear duct size differences of age, sex and race. American Journal of Physical Anthropology *30:*85–88.

Power S (2002) A Problem from Hell. New York, NY: Basic Books.

Prince DA, and Ubelaker DH (2002) Application of Lamendin's adult dental aging technique to a diverse skeletal sample. Journal of Forensic Sciences *47:*107–116.

Purkait R (2003) Sex determination from femoral head measurements: A new approach. Legal Medicine *5:*S347–S350.

Pyle SI, and Hoerr NL (1992) Radiographic Atlas of Skeletal Development of the Knee. Springfield, IL: Charles C. Thomas.

Pynsent PB, Fairbank JCT, and Carr AJ (1999) Classification of Musculoskeletal Trauma. Oxford, UK: Butterworth-Heinemann.

Quirk GJ, and Casco L (1994) Stress disorders of families of the disappeared: A controlled study in Honduras. Social Science and Medicine, *39:*1675–1679.

Rao V, and Hart R (1983) Tool mark determination in cartilage of stabbing victim. Journal of Forensic Sciences *28:*794–799.

Rathbun TA, and Buikstra JE, eds. (1984) Human Identification: Case Studies in Forensic Anthropology. Springfield, IL: Charles C. Thomas.

Raveendranath V, Nachiket S, Sujatha N, Priya R, and Rema D (2009) The quadriceps angle (Q angle) in Indian men and women. European Journal of Anatomy *13(3):*105–109.

Redsicker DR (2001) The Practical Methodology of Forensic Photography. Boca Raton, FL: CRC Press.

Reichs KJ, ed. (1986) Forensic Osteology: Advances in the Identification of Human Remains. Springfield, IL: Charles C. Thomas.

Reichs KJ, ed. (1998) Forensic Osteology: Advances in the Identification of Human Remains. Springfield, IL: Charles C. Thomas.

Reid SA, and Boyde A (1987) Changes in the mineral density distribution in human bone with age: Image analysis using backscattered electrons in the SEM. Journal of Bone and Mineral Research *2:*13–22.

Relethford J (1994) Craniometric variation among modern human populations. American Journal of Physical Anthropology *95:*53–62.

Ritter N (2007) Missing persons and unidentified remains: The nation's silent mass disaster. NIJ Journal *256(1)*. http://www.nij.gov/journals/256/missing-persons.html.

Robertson B, and Vignaux GA (1995) Interpreting Evidence: Evaluating Forensic Science in the Courtroom. New York, NY: John Wiley and Sons.

Rodriguez WC, and Bass WM (1985) Decomposition of buried bodies and methods that may aid in their location. Journal of Forensic Sciences *30:*836–852.

Rogers NL, Flournoy LE, and McCormick WF (2000) The rhomboid fossa of the clavicle as a sex and age estimator. Journal of Forensic Sciences *45:*61–67.

Rogers TL (2005) Determining the sex of human remains through cranial morphology. Journal of Forensic Sciences *50:*1–8.

Rome Statute of the International Criminal Court (1998) Text of the Rome Statute circulated as document A/CONF.183/9 of 17 July 1998 and corrected by procès-verbaux of 10 November 1998, 12 July 1999, 30 November 1999, 8 May 2000, 17 January 2001, and 16 January 2002. The Statute entered into force on 1 July 2002. (http://untreaty.un.org/cod/icc/statute/99_corr/cstatute.htm [accessed 2011-12-09]). New York, NY: United Nations.

Rosen CJ, Glowacki J, Bilezikian JP, eds. (1999) The Aging Skeleton. London: Academic Press.

Rosenberg NA, Pritchard JK, Weber JL, Cann HM, Kidd KK, Zhivotovsky LA, and Feldman MW (2002) Genetic Structure of Human Populations. Science *298:*2381–2385.

Saferstein R (2004) Criminalistics: An Introduction to Forensic Science. Upper Saddle River, NJ: Prentice-Hall.

Salcedo D (1993) Forensic anthropology in Guatemala: A project report. AAAS Committee on Scientific Freedom and Responsibility: Clearinghouse Report on Science and Human Rights *XIV.*

Sarajlić N, Cihlarž Z, Klonowski EE, and Drukier P (2005) The application of the Lamendin and Prince dental aging methods to a Bosnian population: Formulas for each tooth group challenging one formula for all teeth. Proceedings of the American Academy of Forensic Sciences *11:*324.

Sauer NJ, and Simson LR (1984) Clarifying the role of forensic anthropologists in death investigations. Journal of Forensic Sciences *29:*1081–1086.

Sauer NJ (1992) Forensic anthropology and the concept of race: If races don't exist, why are forensic anthropologists so good at identifying them? Social Science and Medicine *34:*107–111.

Saul FP, and Saul JM (2003) Planes, trains, and fireworks: The evolving role of the forensic anthropologist in mass fatality incidents. In DW Steadman (ed.): Hard Evidence: Case Studies in Forensic Anthropology. Upper Saddle River, NJ: Prentice Hall, pp. 266–277.

Schaefer M, Black S, Scheuer L (2009) Juvenile Osteology, A Laboratory and Field Manual, San Diego, CA: Elsevier Academic Press.

Scheuer JL, and Elkington NM (1993) Sex determination from metacarpals and the first proximal phalanx. Journal of Forensic Sciences *38:*769–778.

Scheuer L, and Black S (2000) Developmental Juvenile Osteology. London: Academic Press.

Scheuer L, and Black S (2005) The Juvenile Skeleton. San Diego, CA: Elsevier Academic Press.

Schmitt S (2002) Mass graves and the collection of forensic evidence: Genocide, war crimes, and crimes against humanity. In WD Haglund and MH Sorg (eds.): Advances in Forensic Taphonomy: Methods, Theory, and Archaeological Perspectives. Boca Raton, FL: CRC Press, pp. 277–292.

Schulter-Ellis FP, and Hayek LC (1988) Sexing North American Eskimo and Indian innominate bones with the acetabulum/pubis index. Journal of Forensic Sciences *33:*697–708.

Schulter-Ellis FP, Hayek LC, and Schmidt DJ (1985) Determination of sex with a discriminant analysis of new pelvic bone measurements: Part II. Journal of Forensic Sciences *30:*178–185.

Schulter-Ellis FP, Schmidt DJ, Hayek LC, and Craig J (1983) Determination of sex with a discriminant analysis of new pelvic bone measurements: Part I. Journal of Forensic Sciences *28:*169–180.

Scott GR, and Turner CG, II (1997) The Anthropology of Modern Human Teeth: Dental Morphology and Its Variation in Recent Human Populations. Cambridge, UK: Cambridge University Press.

Sellier KG, and Kneubuchl BP (1994) Wound Ballistics and the Scientific Background. Amsterdam, the Netherlands: Elsevier.

Shean BS, Messinger L, and Papworth M (1993) Observations of differential decomposition on sun exposed v. shaded pig carrion in coastal Washington State. Journal of Forensic Sciences *38:*938–949.

Shipman P, Walker A, and Bichell D (1986) The Human Skeleton. Cambridge, MA: Harvard University Press.

Skinner M, and Lazenby RA (1983) Found! Human Remains: A Field Manual for the Recovery of the Recent Human Skeleton. Burnaby, BC: Archeology Press, Simon Fraser University.

Skolnick AA (1992) Game's afoot in many lands for forensic scientists investigating most-extreme human rights abuses. Journal of the American Medical Association *268:*579–580, 583.

Šlaus M, Strinovic D, Škavic J, and Petrovecki V (2003) Discriminant function sexing of fragmentary and complete femora: Standards for contemporary Croatia. Journal of Forensic Sciences *48:*509–512.

Sledzik PS, and Willcox AW (2003) Corpi aquaticus: The Hardin cemetery flood of 1993. In D Steadman (ed.): Hard Evidence: Case Studies in Forensic Anthropology. Upper Saddle River, NJ: Prentice Hall, pp. 256–265.

Smay D, and Armelagos GJ (2000) Galileo wept: A critical assessment of the use of race in forensic anthropology. Transforming Anthropology *9:*19–40.

Smekalova TN (1996) The use of magnetic prospecting in archaeology. St. Petersburg, Russia: Radiophysics Department, Physical Institute, St. Petersburg University, pp. 1–43 (53 figures).

Snodgrass JJ (2004) Sex differences and aging of the vertebral column. Journal of Forensic Sciences *49:*458–463.

Snow CC, Levine L, Lukash L, Tedeschi LG, Orrego C, and Stover E (1984) The investigation of the human remains of the “disappeared” in Argentina. American Journal of Physical Anthropology *5:*297–299.

Snow CC (1982) Forensic anthropology. Annual Review of Anthropology *11:*97–131.

Snow CC (1983) Equations for estimating age at death from the pubic symphysis: A modification of the McKern-Stewart method. Journal of Forensic Sciences *28:*864–870.

Snow CC, and Bihurriet MJ (1992) An epidemiology of *ningún nombre* burials in the Province of Buenos Aires from 1970 to 1984. In TB Jabine and RP Claude (eds.): Human Rights and Statistics: Getting the Record Straight. Philadelphia, PA: University of Pennsylvania Press, pp. 328–363.

Snow CC, and Reyman TA (1984) The life and after life of Elmer J. McCurdy: A melodrama in two acts. In TA Rathbun and JE Buikstra (eds.): Human Identification. Springfield, IL: Charles C. Thomas, pp. 371–379.

Snow CC, Stover E, and Hannibal K (1989) Scientists as detectives: Investigating human rights. Technology Review *February/March:*43–51.

Solheim T (1988) Dental attrition as an indicator of age. Gerodontics *4:*299–304.

Solheim T (1988) Dental color as an indicator of age. Gerodontics *4:*114–118.

Solheim T (1989) Dental root translucency as an indicator of age. Scandinavian Journal of Dental Research *97:*189–197.

Solheim T (1990) Dental cementum apposition as an indicator of age. Scandinavian Journal of Dental Research *98:*510–519.

Solheim T (1992) Amount of secondary dentin as an indicator of age. Scandinavian Journal of Dental Research *100:*193–199.

Solheim T (1992) Recession of periodontal ligament as an indicator of age. Journal of Forensic Odonto-Stomatology *10:*32–42.

Solheim T (1993) Dental age-related regressive changes and a new dental method for calculating the age of an individual. Oslo, Norway: University of Oslo.

Solheim T (1993) A new method for dental age estimation in adults. Forensic Science International *59:*137–147.

Solheim T, and Kvaal S (1993) Dental root surface structure as an indicator of age. Journal of Forensic Odonto-Stomatology *11:*9–21.

Solheim T, and Sundnes PK (1980) Dental age estimation of Norwegian adults—a comparison of different methods. Forensic Science International *16:*7–17.

Soomer H, Ranta H, Lincoln MJ, Penttila A, and Leibur E (2003) Reliability and validity of eight dental age estimation methods for adults. Journal of Forensic Sciences *48:*149–152.

Spirer H, and Spirer L (1994) Data Analysis for Monitoring Human Rights. Washington, D.C.: American Association for the Advancement of Science.

Spitz WU, ed. (2006) Spitz and Fisher's Medicolegal Investigation of Death: Guidelines for the Application of Pathology to Crime Investigation. Springfield, IL: Charles C. Thomas.

St. Louis ME, and Wasserheit JN (1998) Elimination of syphilis in the United States. Science *281:*353–354.

Steadman DW, ed. (2003) Hard Evidence: Case Studies in Forensic Anthropology. Upper Saddle River, NJ: Prentice-Hall.

Steadman DW, and Haglund WD (2005) The scope of anthropological contributions to human rights investigations. Journal of Forensic Sciences *50:*23–30.

Steele, DG, and Bramblett CA (1988) The Anatomy and Biology of the Human Skeleton. College Station, TX: Texas A&M University Press.

Stewart JH, and McCormick WF (1984) A sex- and age-limited ossification pattern in human costal cartilages. American Journal of Clinical Pathology *81:*765–769.

Stewart TD (1958) The rate of development of vertebral osteoarthritis in American whites and its significance in skeletal age identification. The Leech *28:*144–151.

Stewart TD (1962) Anterior femoral curvature: Its utility for race identification. Human Biology *34:*49–62.

Stewart TD, ed. (1970) Personal Identification in Mass Disasters. Washington, D.C.: Smithsonian Institution.

Stewart TD (1979) Essentials of Forensic Anthropology. Springfield, IL: Charles C. Thomas.

Steyna M and İşcan MY (2008) Metric sex determination from the pelvis in modern Greeks. Forensic Science International *179(1):*86.e1–86.e6.

Stimson PG, and Mertz CA, eds. (1997) Forensic Dentistry. Boca Raton, FL: CRC Press.

Stojanowski CM (1999) Sexing potential of fragmentary and pathological metacarpals. American Journal of Physical Anthropology *109:*245–252.

Stout SD (1986) The use of bone histomorphometry in skeletal identification: The case of Francisco Pizarro. Journal of Forensic Sciences *31:*296–300.

Stout SD (1978) Histological structure and its preservation in ancient bone. Current Anthropology *19:*601–604.

Stout SD, and Gehlert SJ (1980) The relative accuracy and reliability of histological aging methods. Forensic Science International *15:*181–190.

Stout SD, and Simmons DJ (1979) Use of histology in ancient bone research. Yearbook of Physical Anthropology *22:*228–249.

Stout SD, and Teitelbaum SL (1976) Histological analysis of undecalcified thin sections of archeological bone. American Journal of Physical Anthropology *44:*263–270.

Stover E (1981) New responses to attacks on human rights of scientists in Latin America called for. Science *211:*134–135.

Stover E (1985) Scientists aid search for Argentina's "desaparecidos." Science *230:*56–57.

Stover E (1985) Scientists search for Argentina's missing. AAAS Committee on Scientific Freedom and Responsibility: Clearinghouse Report on Science and Human Rights *VII:*1–3.

Stover E (1992) Unquiet Graves: The Search for the Disappeared in Iraqi Kurdistan. New York, NY: Middle East Watch and Physicians for Human Rights.

Stover E, and Eisner T (1982) Human rights abuses and the role of scientists. BioScience *32:*871–875.

Stover E, Haglund WD, and Samuels M (2003) Exhumation of mass graves in Iraq: Considerations for forensic investigations, humanitarian needs, and the demands of justice. Journal of the American Medical Association *290:*663–666.

Stover E, and Shigekane R (2002) The missing in the aftermath of war: When do the needs of victims' families and international war crimes tribunals clash? International Review of the Red Cross *848:*845–866.

Strongman KB (1987) Forensic applications of ground penetrating radar. Edmonton, Alberta, Canada: Royal Canadian Mounted Police, "K" Division, pp. 1–27.

Suchey JM (1979) Problems in the aging of females using the os pubis. American Journal of Physical Anthropology *51:*467–470.

Suchey JM, and Katz D (1998) Applications of pubic age determination in a forensic setting. In KJ Reichs (ed.): Forensic Osteology: Advances in the Identification of Human Remains. Springfield, IL: Charles C. Thomas, pp. 204–236.

Suchey JM, Wiseley DV, and Katz D (1986) Evaluation of the Todd and McKern-Stewart methods for aging the male os pubis. In KJ Reichs (ed.): Forensic Osteology: Advances in the Identification of Human Remains. Springfield. IL: Charles C. Thomas, pp. 33–67.

Sutherland LD, and Suchey JM (1991) Use of the ventral arc in pubic sex determination. Journal of Forensic Sciences *36(2):*501–511.

Szibor R, Schubert C, Schoning R, Krause D, and Wendt U (1998) Pollen analysis reveals murder season. Nature *395:*449.

Thieme FP (1957) Sex in Negro skeletons. Journal of Forensic Medicine *4:*72–81.

Thompson DD (1980) Age changes in bone mineralization, cortical thickness, and Haversian canal area. Calcified Tissue International *31:*5–11.

Thompson DD (1981) Microscopic determination of age at death in an autopsy series. Journal of Forensic Sciences *26:*470–475.

Thomsen JL, Gruschow J, and Stover E (1989) Medicolegal investigation of political killings in El Salvador. Lancet *Jun 17;1(8651):*1377–1379.

Tibbetts GL (1981) Estimation of stature from the vertebral column in American blacks. Journal of Forensic Sciences *26:*715–723.

Todd TW (1920) Age changes in the pubic bone. I. The male white pubis. American Journal of Physical Anthropology *3:*285–334.

Todd TW (1921) Age changes in the pubic bone. II: The pubis of the male Negro-white hybrid; III: The pubis of the white female; IV: The pubis of the female white-Negro hybrid. American Journal of Physical Anthropology *4:*1–70.

Todd TW (1930) Age changes in the pubic bone. VIII. Roentgenographic differentiation. American Journal of Physical Anthropology *14:*255–271.

Todd TW, and Lyon DW, Jr. (1924) Endocranial suture closure. Its progress and age relationship. Part I.—Adult males of white stock. American Journal of Physical Anthropology *7:*325–384.

Todd TW, and Lyon DW, Jr. (1925) Cranial suture closure. Its progress and age relationship. Part II.—Ectocranial closure in adult males of White stock. American Journal of Physical Anthropology *8:*23–45.

Todd TW, and Lyon DW, Jr. (1925) Cranial suture closure. Its progress and age relationship. Part III.—Endocranial closure in adult males of Negro stock. American Journal of Physical Anthropology *8:*47–71.

Todd TW, and Lyon DW, Jr. (1925) Suture closure—its progress and age relationship. Part IV—Ectocranial closure in adult males of Negro stock. American Journal of Physical Anthropology *8:*149–168.

Topinard P (1885) Elements d'Anthropologie Générale. Paris, France: A. Delahaye et É. Lecrosnier.

Trotter M (1970) Estimation of stature from intact long limb bones. In TD Stewart (ed.): Personal Identification in Mass Disasters. Washington, D.C.: Smithsonian Institution, pp. 71–83.

Trotter M, and Gleser G (1958) A re-evaluation of estimation of stature based on measurements taken during life and of long bones after death. American Journal of Physical Anthropology *16:*79–123.

Trotter M, and Gleser GC (1952) Estimation of stature from long bones of American Whites and Negroes. American Journal of Physical Anthropology *10:*463–514.

Trotter M, and Gleser GC (1977) Corrigenda to "estimation of stature from long limb bones of American Whites and Negroes," American Journal Physical Anthropology (1952). American Journal of Physical Anthropology *47:*355–356.

Trotter M, and Gleser G (1951) The effect of aging on stature. American Journal of Physical Anthropology *9:*311–324.

Trudell MB [corrected at JFS 44:1108 to indicate ME Ballard as author] (1999) Anterior femoral curvature revisited: Race assessment from the femur. Journal of Forensic Sciences *44:*700–707.

Turner CG, II, Nichol CR, and Scott GR (1991) Scoring procedures for key morphological traits of the permanent dentition: The Arizona State University dental anthropology system. In M Kelley and C Larsen (eds.): Advances in Dental Anthropology. New York, NY: Wiley-Liss, pp. 13–31.

Ubelaker DH (1999) Human Skeletal Remains: Excavation, Analysis, Interpretation. 3rd ed. Washington, D.C.: Taraxacum.

Ubelaker DH, and Adams B (1995) Differentiation of perimortem and postmortem trauma using taphonomic indicators. Journal of Forensic Sciences *40:*509–512.

Ubelaker DH, and Buikstra J (1994) Standards for Data Collection from Human Skeletal Remains. Fayetteville, AR: Arkansas Archeological Survey.

Ubelaker DH (1987) Estimating age at death from immature human skeletons: An overview. Journal of Forensic Sciences *32:*1254–1263.

Ubelaker DH, and Scammell H (1992) Bones: A Forensic Detective's Casebook. New York, NY: M. Evans and Company.

Ubelaker DH, and Smialek JE (2003) The interface of forensic anthropology and forensic pathology in trauma interpretation. In DW Steadman (ed.): Hard Evidence: Case Studies in Forensic Anthropology. Upper Saddle River, NJ: Prentice Hall, pp. 155–159.

Ubelaker DH, and Volk CG (2002) A test of the Phenice method for the estimation of sex. Journal of Forensic Sciences *47:*19–24.

United Nations Department of Public Information (2004) Basic Facts about the United Nations. New York, NY: United Nations. (Also available at http://www.un.org/aboutun/basicfacts/ [accessed 2006-04-26]).

United Nations General Assembly (1948) Universal Declaration of Human Rights: Adopted and proclaimed by UN General Assembly resolution 217 A (III) of 10 December 1948 (http://www.un.org/Overview/rights.html [accessed 2006-04-23]).

United Nations Office at Vienna Centre for Social Development and Humanitarian Affairs, ed. (1991) Manual on the Effective Prevention and Investigation of Extra-Legal, Arbitrary and Summary Executions. New York, NY: United Nations.

Vystrèilová M, and Novotný V (2000) Estimation of age at death using teeth. Variability and Evolution *8:*39–49.

Waldron T (2009) Palaeopathology. UK: Cambridge University Press.

Walsh S, Lindenbergh A, Zuniga SB, Sijen T, de Knijff P, Kayser M, and Ballantyne KN. (2011b) Developmental validation of the IrisPlex system: Determination of blue and brown iris colour for forensic intelligence. Forensic Science International: Genetics *5(5):*464–71.

Walsh S, Liu F, Ballantyne KN, van Oven M, Lao O, and Kayser M (2011a) IrisPlex: A sensitive DNA tool for accurate prediction of blue and brown eye colour in the absence of ancestry information. Forensic Science International: Genetics *5(3):*170–180.

Washburn, SL (1948) Sex differences in the pubic bone. American Journal of Physical Anthropology *6:*199–207.

Watts A, and Addy M (2001) Tooth discolouration and staining: A review of the literature. British Dental Journal *190:*309–316.

Webb PAO, and Suchey JM (1985) Epiphyseal union of the anterior iliac crest and medial clavicle in a modern multiracial sample of American males and females. American Journal of Physical Anthropology *52:*191–195.

Weissbrodt D, and Fraser PW (1992) Report of the Chilean National Commission on Truth and Reconciliation. Human Rights Quarterly *14:*601–622.

Weitzel MA (2005) A report of decomposition rates for a special burial type in Edmonton, Alberta from an experimental field study. Journal of Forensic Sciences *50:*641–647.

White TD, and Folkens PA (2005) The Human Bone Manual. Burlington, MA: Elsevier Academic Press.

White TD, Black, MT, and Folkens, PA (2012) Human Osteology, 3rd ed. San Diego, CA: Academic Press.

Willems G (2001) A review of commonly used dental age estimation techniques. Journal of Forensic Odonto-Stomatology *19:*9–17.

Willey P, and Heilman A (1987) Estimating time since death using plant roots and stems. Journal of Forensic Sciences *32:*1264–1270.

Williams FLE, Belcher RL, and Armelagos GJ (2005) Forensic misclassification of ancient Nubian crania: Implications for assumptions about human variation. Current Anthropology *46:*340–346.

Wiredu E, Kumoji R, Seshadri R, and Biritwum R (1999) Osteometric analysis of sexual dimorphism in the sternal end of the rib in a West African population. Journal of Forensic Sciences *44:*921–925.

Yoder C, Ubelaker DH, and Powell JF (2001) Examination of variation in sternal rib end morphology relevant to age assessment. Journal of Forensic Sciences *46:*223–227.

Index